CHRIST PROCLAIMED

Theological Inquiries

*Studies in Contemporary
Biblical and Theological Problems*

General Editor
Lawrence Boadt, C. S. P.

PAULIST PRESS
New York • Ramsey • Toronto

Christ Proclaimed

Christology as Rhetoric

Frans Jozef van Beeck, S.J.

Paulist Press
New York • Ramsey • Toronto
1979

Acknowledgements

Thanks are due to the following for the use of copyright sources:

William Collins Sons & Co. Ltd., London, and Harper & Row, Inc., New York: Dietrich Bonhoeffer, *Act and Being, Christ the Center,* and *No Rusty Swords* (translations frequently revised)

Chr. Kaiser Verlag, Munich: Dietrich Bonhoeffer, *Akt und Sein* and *Gesammelte Schriften* (E. Bethge, ed.), Vol. III

Faber and Faber, Ltd., London: T. S. Eliot, *Murder in the Cathedral* and *Collected Poems, 1909-1962*

Harcourt Brace Jovanovich, Inc., New York: T. S. Eliot, *The Collected Poems and Plays*

New Directions Publishing Company, New York: Lawrence Ferlinghetti, *A Coney Island of the Mind;* copyright 1955 by Lawrence Ferlinghetti

Uitgeverij Ambo, Bilthoven: Han Fortmann, *Heel de mens*

Uitgeverij G. F. Callenbach, N.V., Nijkerk: J. H. van den Berg, *Het menselijk lichaam*

Van Gorcum & Comp., N.V., Assen: J. W. M. Verhaar, S.J., *Some Relations Between Perception, Speech and Thought*

Yale University Press, New Haven: Hans W. Frei, *The Eclipse of Biblical Narrative;* copyright 1974 by Yale University

Imprimi potest:
Richard T. Cleary, S.J.
Provincial, New England Province,
June 30, 1978

Library of Congress
Catalog Card Number: 79-66459

ISBN: 0-8091-2208-1

Published by Paulist Press
Editorial Office: 1865 Broadway, New York, N. Y. 10023
Business Office: 545 Island Road, Ramsey, N. J. 07446

Printed and bound in the
United States of America

Contents

v

INTERLUDE

PART III

TOWARDS AN OPEN-ENDED SYNTHESIS

PREFACE

This is not the book I think needed to be written—the book I wish I could write. When I think of books that needed to be written I tend to think of Augustine's *Confessions*, of Thomas à Kempis' *The Imitation of Christ*, of Bunyan's *The Pilgrim's Progress*, of Francis de Sales' *Introduction to the Devout Life*, of Schleiermacher's *Speeches on Religion, Addressed to the Cultured Among Its Despisers*, of Cardinal Newman's *Apologia pro Vita Sua*, and of Bonhoeffer's *The Cost of Discipleship*. All of these writings, and many others like them, have grown out of the Word sown in the soil of very different sensibilities; in this way, they set an agenda for theological reflection. What is needed, now as always, are books that speak *out of* God; the present book merely intends to speak *about* God, as theological works tend to do. A steady supply of the former is essential if the faith is to be handed on alive; the latter may come and go.

What I *can* affirm, however, is that this is the book which *I* needed to write, to answer to myself—and, I hope, to others—for the *call to freedom* which I have come to associate with the Christian faith, a freedom, not only of self-awareness and action, but also of thought.

Freedom of thought is not easily achieved; in fact, it comes at a fairly high price, to be paid in the coinage of anxiety. Freedom of theological thought is especially problematic; hence, as I have discovered, most theologians have a good deal of anxiety in their systems. Most of it is caused by the sheer weight of the doctrinal tradition. The Creeds, the various confessional writings, Denzinger's *Enchiridion*, and the history of doctrine, not to mention Scripture, set formidable standards. Yet, as if these curbs on freedom were not enough, there are the theologians' own pastoral desires not to disturb

1

the faithful unnecessarily (yes, most theologians care, despite the repeated suggestions to the contrary!), and the pressures that come from those who are, for better, for worse, in a position of teaching authority in the churches.

There is a fourth source of theologians' anxiety; it is no less demanding than the ones mentioned, though it is more congenial, and in the long run, I think, no less reliable than the latter two just mentioned. I am thinking of the pressure to achieve what the tradition calls the *consensus theologorum*—the product of the ongoing, painstaking, patient, demanding discussion among professional men and women unable to resist the stern attractions of the *fides quaerens intellectum*.

Given these four sets of pressures, there is cause for some surprise that new insights develop at all in theology. But apparently, this is the lot of the palm-tree: to grow with a weight bearing down on its crown; *palma sub pondere crescit*; slow growth insures full foliage. Paul had to explain to his Corinthians why their fine sense of freedom needed to be chastened by a rather more prosaic dedication to affectionate concern for others; analogously, theologians must let their urge to enjoy theological freedom of speech—*parrhēsia!*—be tempered by "the jading and jar of the cart, Time's tasking" (Gerard Manley Hopkins). Theological reflection thus mirrors the Church's slow and somewhat bumbling course in this world, along roads never quite clearly indicated by the directions set by past decisions.

If freedom and temperance must go into the making of theology, the right balance is hard to achieve. My own road has led me from excessive temperance to freedom-cum-temperance; I started, rather lopsidedly, with more anxiety than *parrhēsia*. The attractiveness as well as the authority of the doctrinal tradition on the one hand, and, on the other, the intractability of "modern life" long conspired to make me—a congenital conservative in matters of faith—reluctant to raise the central concern of the Christian faith as a theological issue. This book, first envisaged as a possibility in late 1968, then actually started in early 1973, and finally completed in mid-1978, reflects my slow trek from an excessive concern with normative, conciliar christology, through the healthy ambiguities of biblical christologies and secularization theology, to a new organization of christology in an open-ended system. If this book proves stodgy in places, this is nothing but the reflection of my struggle with the old doctrinal establishment which I refused to either canonize or reject; instead, I came to wrestle with it, unwilling to let go until I had wrung a blessing from it. And this blessing came in the form of the discovery that the doctrinal tradition in christology is itself the product of freedom, not anxiety. Classical christology turned out to be the fruit of the freedom of the Christian, moving about, with critical empathy, among the manifold concerns of human life— concerns which must have seemed as intractable in the past as modern concerns do today. I came to see that the christological tradition has everything to do, not with anxious worry, but with *parrhēsia*, and that, therefore, freedom of christological speech and thought in close touch with modern life is entirely warranted.

As I said before, I wish I could have written such a free-speaking book. Instead, somewhat comically, I came to produce a weighty tome to argue the need for free speech. Sometimes I sound to myself like a tone-deaf musicologist arguing that Bach is great. Writing long pages of rigorous analysis and argument in order to show the need for freedom in faith-expression is indeed a slightly incongruous pursuit, were it not for the realization that it might be profitable for others to witness my struggle to wiggle out of the paralysis brought on by excessive concern with orthodoxy. Those others may be men and women like myself, looking for a way out of a doctrinal ghetto, but also—paradoxically—folks tempted to produce modern christology at cut rates, dodging the dues owed to the great tradition.

Where did I find the tools of discovery? Obviously, they awaited me outside the camp of theological conceptuality. There was the study of English and Italian literature at the University of Amsterdam in the fifties, which, in the course of my training as a Jesuit, followed upon the heels of three years of philosophy study, the third of which was marked, for me, by my first acquaintance with phenomenology, with Max Scheler and Maurice Blondel and John Henry Newman's *Grammar of Assent*. Then there were the excitements of studying theology in the early sixties, in the honeymoon atmosphere of the Second Vatican Council, and with an inspiring trip to Oxford for an ecumenical encounter at Cuddesdon College. This was followed by the painful polarization of the late sixties and early seventies, when it became clear to me that there must be other factors besides doctrine that determine theological options. In those years, I learned a lot from two groups of people. First, there were my students at Boston College, most of whom are undergraduates; not being interested for the most part in becoming professional theologians, they tend to ask questions that require—at least at first—imaginative and sympathetic answers rather than conceptually compelling ones. The second group were the many men and women I met in the context of sensitivity-training and related forms of experience-based education, mainly between 1968 and 1972; I have greatly profited, both personally and intellectually, from the practice of personalness and undefended openness of expression, and from the temporary suspense of intellectual and judgmental language in the interest of discovering the influence of interpersonal and situational dynamics upon the life of the mind. Another piece of needed education came from my involvement in ecumenical situations. Ecumenism is such an excellent school for the appreciation of non-conceptual, personal, situational factors in theology, and the perennial challenge is for free Christian people to seek and find new formulas that will place seemingly irreconcilable past statements in a comprehensive perspective which unites them and which will last. Finally, I have drawn upon the resources of the religious communities I have been associated with: the charismatic group at Boston College, various communities of religious women, and, most of all, a number of Jesuit communities. In all of them I learned to understand the truth of what Cardinal Newman wrote on the title-page of his *Grammar of Assent*, namely, that it has pleased God not to save his people by means of logic and dialectic—no matter how authoritative.

In this way, the theme of personal, unpremeditated, concrete, and imaginative speech in concrete, practical, interpersonal situations became, for me, a central concern, to be brought into christology. The result was, to start with, the introduction and the first two chapters, together entitled "Three Conversions." They represent a scarcely veiled autobiographical account of my turning away from ecclesiology, intellectual discussion of the God-problem in a secularized world, and an excessive reliance on conceptual statements of doctrine, authoritatively proposed as rules of faith. I realize, of course, that, from an objective point of view, the issues discussed and the positions taken in the introduction and the first two chapters admit of different points of view. Thus I suspect that I am a little less sanguine about *The Resilient Church* than Avery Dulles. I am fairly skeptical about the usefulness of modern notions of "God" when it comes to making the central Christian affirmation that in Jesus Christ we meet the living God in person. Finally, I admit that I have become extremely sensitive to the limitations of the use of terminological language, especially in theology; hence, I admit to a slight allergy to methodology.

All this, I hope, will help to account for the words "proclaimed" and "rhetoric" in the title of this book. Not teaching, but proclamation is the primary mode in which the Christian faith comes to this world's attention; rhetoric is not incidental to Christian doctrine. It is part of the aim of this book to investigate the abiding consequences of the fact that the Christian faith has its roots in free speech. I realize that the word "rhetoric" has its dubious overtones, but I think it can be rescued, as Mr. Amos Wilder obviously does, too, witness his *Early Christian Rhetoric*. One consequence of my decision to adopt the word as well as the idea has been, however, that I have had to practice at times what I am preaching. Hence, I must ask my readers to respond to large parts of this book as if they were listening to a speaker; a willing suspension of disbelief and a preparedness to be charmed into insight rather than taught by recourse to authority and reason—these are some of the ingredients, I think, which could profitably go into the reader's attitude.

Let me add a few more random reflections on some of the intentions implicit in this book, before I declare some of my manifold indebtednesses. First, it has been my concern to help break an increasingly meaningless *impasse*—I mean the orthodoxy-piety syndrome. Where the former is proposed as paramount, for example by means of a wholly inappropriate appeal to the "no other Gospel" of Galatians 1, 6-9, the latter tends to pale into blind (and often self-righteous) conformity with authoritative teaching; this tends to turn the assurance of God's presence in Jesus Christ alive in the Holy Spirit into a faceless ideology. Where the latter—piety—becomes the norm of faith, orthodoxy tends to pale into insignificance and total relativity, often under the aegis of the (usually self-righteous) slogan that the Lord is more important than the doctrine; this tends to set up the human religious *a priori* as the final tribunal to determine what it means to believe in God. It is essential to recover a stance in which *spirituality* becomes, once again, a live possibility. The Christian confession that God can be (and has been, and is being) encountered personally, in the Holy Spirit, in the person of Jesus Christ, must once again become a focal point in christology. If this does not come about, we will continue to act as if we were really living in an experiential vacuum, dependent either on total objectivity or total subjectivity, never to be in any way personally assured of the truth that "I will be with you" (Exodus 3, 12; Matthew 28, 20).

A second remark concerns other authors. The last two decades have witnessed an unprecedented activity in christology. We have seen the New Testament christologies of men like Günther Bornkamm, Eduard Schweizer, Rudolf Bultmann, Ernst Käsemann, Oscar Cullmann, and Ferdinand Hahn, and, in this country, Reginald Fuller, Norman Perrin, and Bruce Vawter, to mention but a few. There have been a good number of important historical studies such as those by Aloys Grillmeier (the patristic period, with the promise of more to come), Walter Principe and Philipp Kaiser (the Middle Ages), Ian D. K. Siggins (Luther), E. C. Willis (Calvin), Hans Küng (Hegel), again to mention only a few. New speculative attempts include those by A. Hulsbosch and Piet Schoonenberg, and by Wolfhart Pannenberg. While this book was being written Walter Kasper's *Jesus der Christus*, Edward Schillebeeckx' *Jezus—het verhaal van een levende*, and Hans Küng's *Christ sein* appeared. Many of the books just mentioned, and especially the last three, deserve fuller treatment than they receive in this book, but they have been recognized in passing. I managed to miss some important books altogether; chief among these, it seems to me, is Peter C. Hodgson's *Jesus—Word and Presence*, many of whose ideas and concerns are strikingly like my own.

Thirdly, let me raise a rather more neuralgic issue. I have made serious, though limited, efforts to avoid the language of male dominance. Though I must disagree with the many theories that argue that the very grammatical and syntactic structures of the English language reflect the impact of male dominance, I do realize that certain turns of English grammar and syntax are sufficiently irritating to many women (and men) to warrant their avoidance. Many times, however, in the interest of clarity, and in order not to divert the reader's attention from the main point being made, I decided to use "he," "him," and "his," and even "man," as common-gender words (which, incidentally, by the standards of descriptive grammar, they have always been). I hope that some of the substantive theological points I make with regard to the concerns of feminism will somewhat alleviate the irritation caused by traditional English usage in this regard. In any case, I wholeheartedly agree that christology in particular must make every effort to make it clear that humanity, not masculinity, is glorified in the person of Jesus Christ.

I am indebted to many institutions and people. Among the former I must first mention Regis College, Toronto (formerly Willowdale), which allowed me to get the book underway in the spring semester of 1973, by inviting me as a visiting lecturer in christology with no further obligations. Three places provided me with stimulating company during a sabbatical year that saw the production of almost half of this book: Westcott House, Cambridge, England (with its marvelous staff, Mark Santer and Raymond Pelly with their families, and John Armson), Kolese Santo Ignatius, Yogyakarta, Indonesia, and the "Docentenhuis" Jesuit community of Amsterdam, The Netherlands. Finally, I owe a lot to the climate of the Theology Department at Boston College, and especially to Robert J. Daly, S.J., and Thomas J. Fitzpatrick, S.J., both experts at vigorous and fraternal encouragement.

Among the persons who deserve mention are numerous students, mainly undergraduates, who participated in the regular christology seminars over the years; they taught me mainly by their questions, forcing me to learn. The members of the Boston Theological Society, who read and discussed several of this book's chapters deserve credit for their competence and frankness. One of the Society's membership deserves special mention, namely, Gabriel Fackre, whose *The Christian Story* I was privileged to read in manuscript (and who takes a far more positive, visionary, and action-oriented view of visual categories than I do in Chapter Seven!). Susan Seifert and Brenda Andrews Natchek were of considerable assistance in typing the rough copy. Most of the editorial credit, however, must go to two persons. The first is my fellow Jesuit Michael Czerny, from Toronto. He volunteered to read my rough copy, and to offer what reflections occurred to him. The result of this generous gesture was an extraordinary expenditure of time and energy, and a wealth of stylistic and substantive suggestions, both of them hard to do justice to, except by saying that they improved the quality of the first nine chapters by a quantum leap. Michael's was the kind of help that makes one appreciate the Society of Jesus. The other person is Virginia M. Ryan. Upon her graduation from seminary, Ginny spent an entire summer with me as a research assistant and typist. Without her intelligent and careful help it would have taken me years to finish this book. She also deserves most of the credit for the subject index, which she carried into the penultimate stage of preparation.

In the original version of this preface, I paid a special tribute to one of my ecclesiastical censors, who (I wrote), "in keeping with long-standing tradition, shall remain unnamed." He had deplored the fact that all the footnotes, which he thought were "generally quite relevant, and really should be on the same page," would be placed at the end of the book. Unlike my saner censor, I had long reconciled myself to this seemingly unavoidable prospect, given the likelihood of a prohibitive price, should my censor's wishes be granted. Hence, I wrote a little homily into the preface, exhorting my readers to refer to the notes frequently, in a spirit of thankfulness for the low price of the book. But when the page proofs arrived, there they were, at the bottom of the page: real, old-fashioned *foot*notes! This is reason, not only for thankfulness, but also for positive exultation, especially given the fact that the book's price is still surprisingly low. Incidentally, the next to total omission of Scripture references in the body of the text was intentional from the start. I grant that the references at the bottom of the page do not facilitate the quick identification of texts, but is this not a small price to pay for the avoidance of this traditional disfigurement of the main text? Should the reader not be able to walk along the road unhindered, without having to negotiate all kinds of hurdles?

The last stages of the preparation of this book were marked by the kindness of Jan C. Boyce, chief reference librarian at Boston College, who cleaned up the bibliography and the original index of proper names, by the friendliness of Lawrence Boadt, C.S.P., who represented the Paulist Press to me, and by the cooperation of two Boston College honors program undergraduates, John L. Mahoney and Elizabeth J. Travers, who helped me read the page proofs and prepare the first two indexes. Still, my chief memory of the home stretch concerns the excitement supplied by a remarkable group of students. Thomas Artz, C.Ss.R., Michael Durrer, James Nickoloff, S.J., Barbara Ann Radtke, Thomas Savage, S.J., David Thorp, and Kenneth Williams constituted, along with myself, the membership of the graduate christology seminar during the spring semester of 1978. They not only identified a good many errors and unhappy turns of phrase, but also provided an atmosphere of intellectual adventure which it was a true privilege to be a part of.

And thus this long preface comes to an end. But ends are always provisional, and this particular ending at once opens the door to this book, just as the end of the book, for me, opened the door to further reading, and the first book to come my way was Sebastian Moore's profound *The Crucified Jesus Is No Stranger*. It reminded me that the completion of this book could not possibly mean that this was, for me, the end of christological reflection.

On the very day this book is scheduled to go to press I am forced to change its dedication. I had dedicated it to three Dutch Jesuits to whom I owe much of what faith-cum-intellectual-integrity I can call my own, and that dedication still stands: this book is offered to Felix Malmberg, Piet Schoonenberg, and Pieter Smulders. What unites me with Fathers Schoonenberg and Smulders, both former teachers, is that Malmberg taught all three of us. I must now add that he did not live to see in print what for years he encouraged me to write: he died on June 19, 1979. A fine theologian who lived for years in the toughness as well as the serenity of the tradition, he had both the courage and the humility to let himself be taught by the uncertainties of Catholic life in Holland and in the United States, where he taught for six years after his retirement at 68. He enjoyed being right, and was converted to a willingness to be proven wrong at times, and to be called wrong many times more often. He knew something about the living God. He never lost faith. He encouraged many. *Vivat in pace.*

Boston College, Spring 1979　　　　　　*Frans Jozef van Beeck, S.J.*

PART I

Three Conversions

I shall take refuge in the *Phaedrus*. You remember at the end Socrates tells Phaedrus that words can't be removed from place to place and retain their meaning. Truth is communicated from a particular speaker to a particular listener.

Iris Murdoch

INTRODUCTION

From Ecclesiological Fatigue to Christian Identity

In one body are found   both prayer and faith;
one hidden, one visible   for the hidden and the visible.
The hidden prayer   for the hidden Ear,
and faith for the ear   outwardly seen.

Ephrem the Syrian

For he is our peace, who has made us both one, and has broken down the dividing wall of hostility, by abolishing in his flesh the law of commandments and ordinances, that he might create in himself one new man in place of the two, so making peace, and might reconcile us both to God in one body through the cross, thereby bringing the hostility to an end. And he came and preached peace to you who were far off and peace to those who were near; for through him we both have access in one Spirit to the Father. So then you are no longer strangers and sojourners, but you are fellow citizens with the saints and members of the household of God, built upon the foundation of the apostles and prophets, Christ Jesus himself being the cornerstone, in whom the whole structure is joined together and grows into a holy temple in the Lord; in whom you also are built into it for a dwelling place of God in the Spirit.

The Letter of Paul to the Ephesians

Ecclesiological fatigue
    In 1964 Hans Küng opened his comprehensive study of the Church with the statement: "The problem of God is more important

than the problem of the Church, but the latter often stands in the way of the former. This ought not to be the case."[1] Ten years ago, in the afterglow of the Second Vatican Council, which had shaken both Catholics and non-Catholics out of so many prejudices, this statement could still function as an introduction to an ecclesiology aimed at renewal. Focus on the Church, its nature and its mission was widely thought to be capable of paving the way for a renewed sense of God.

Of late, however, ecclesiological ardor has waned considerably. Many causes, no doubt, lie at the basis of this apparent loss of interest; many reasons could be enumerated to explain the ecclesiological fatigue. Sometimes it is difficult to tell causes from symptoms; often it is even harder to tell whether we are dealing with influences that come from nowhere and everywhere or influences clearly attributable to identifiable culprits.

Let us mention a few things that have contributed to, or are symptoms of, this decline in ecclesiological enthusiasm.

—The updated liturgy has failed to live up to the high—and in retrospect unrealistic—hopes of the Second Vatican Council's first session.

—The task of developing realistic consultation procedures at the parochial, diocesan, national and global levels has proved to be tedious and beset with passive resistance.

—The revision of the Code of Canon Law seems to be beset with problems, judging from the pale, unpromising, and spotty news releases emerging occasionally out of a dense fog that bodes ill.

—In many places, the bishops have disappeared as a significant spiritual influence at the local level, in complete contrast to their apparently confident corporate leadership during the Council. But in as many places they have returned to the disciplinary, centralist, and secretive style of pre-Vatican days and made themselves into the all-engrossing focus of attention.

—The fervor of ecumenism has declined; the ecumenical enterprise suffers from increasing clericalization owing to the increasing importance of necessary committee-work aimed at achieving harmony of creeds and church orders.

---

[1] *The Church*, New York, Sheed & Ward, 1967, p. xiii.

—Many of the Church's more notable ways of exercising authority and showing muscle have disappeared. This seems to have created a vacuum which favors (or exposes) apathy as well as quasi-democratic fast talk rather than creating room for initiative.[2]

—Many Christians in many places are disappointed at the Church's social and political role. Many are turning away to "secular" involvement on ideological or pragmatic rather than theological terms—often very uncritically.

—A staggering number of men and women have left the ministry and the religious life. This has made it more difficult for Catholics to see how explicit identification with the Church can be relevant to "real life."

—Many Christians are fleeing into neo-spiritualism, conservatism and restorationism; many of them were committed to renewal at one time, but they either ran out of energy, or felt threatened by the conservative and liberal backlashes set off by their efforts. Analogously, there is a flight into a pale sort of liberalism and theological skepticism on the part of many others. It is often difficult to give reasons why some should have moved to conservatism, others to liberalism, and this lack of clarity adds to the general sense of uncertainty with regard to the Church.

—Lastly, ever so many Christians realize that the Church is not everything. Many are coming to the hard realization that those who totally identify their faith and personal vocation with ecclesiastical concerns are in deadly danger of selling their souls.[3]

These factors, and doubtlessly many others, have contributed to disenchantment with the Church, and thus to lowered expectations from ecclesiology.

---

[2]Joseph Ratzinger, in the context of a treatment of the limited competence of the Church's ministry, points to the possibility of a "wide area for free, democratic initiatives," for instance, in the "possibility, and—in certain circumstances—even the duty to engage in voluntary association for the actualization of the faith-message in certain particular situations"; he then argues that free association on this basis remains a possibility in the hierarchical Church. Cf. Joseph Ratzinger—Hans Maier, *Demokratie in der Kirche—Möglichkeiten, Grenzen, Gefahren*, Limburg, Lahn-Verlag, 1970, p. 37.

[3]Cf. W. J. Berger, "Die Seele verkauft und zurückgewonnen?" *Orientierung* 40 (1976) 241–245.

Church in diaspora as a call to Christian identity

Besides the many particular reasons that may be given, there is one comprehensive reason that explains present-day ecclesiological fatigue. Lively interest in the Church, or the churches, was a ready possibility as long as churches were still readily identifiable as institutions. With the disappearance of the last remnants of the medieval and baroque establishments, however, the clear demarcation-lines between the Church and "the world" are finally disappearing; the world is now found inside the Church, not outside it. The course taken by the Second Vatican Council is a telling demonstration of this trend. The dogmatic constitution *Lumen Gentium*—a task undertaken early on—was still mainly an *ad intra* document, defining and describing the Church in terms of her intrinsic nature and constitution; the pastoral constitution on the Church in the modern world *Gaudium et Spes*—a task undertaken much later—made it a point to present the nature of Church in terms of her mission *ad extra*. From being the ensign raised for the nations and the mystical Body of Christ, the Church came to see herself more and more as the people of God on the way and finally even as the servant of the world.

The first response to this situation was, quite naturally, a review of ecclesiology and ecclesiastical practice in an ecumenical perspective; the agenda for this review was boldly set in the middle stages of the Second Vatican Council. But, as Karl Rahner had already pointed out in a prophetic little tract in 1953, the Church needed to prepare, not only for a review of her structures and her style, but also, and more basically, for a renewal of her faith.[4] A predominantly ecclesiastical approach to the contemporary situation is too narrow a basis to establish *the credibility of the faith*; this applies not only to the world, but also to the Church membership itself. The Church is no longer a closed system creating a Christian environment. What Christian environment still remains is overwhelmed by the "secular

---

[4]"The Prospect for Christianity," in: *Free Speech in the Church*, New York, Sheed & Ward, 1959, pp. 51–112; for example: "If anyone begins to protest at this point that he himself is a thoroughly convinced Christian, he had better be careful. For he might get asked the question whether his own actual words and behaviour are as attractive and compelling to others as they should be, if his claim to be full of courageous orthodoxy is to ring true" (pp. 55–56).

city." In such an open Church, religious habit training and rote catechetical instruction are methods far too ecclesiastical and external for the handing on of the faith; they are certainly no match for the forces of socialization wielded by the culture at large. Only a living, rather highly personalized faith can deal with a diaspora-situation. The naked question of the Christian faith having thus been raised, no mere ecclesiology will serve anymore.

Jürgen Moltmann's *Theology of Hope* of 1965 shared many of the high hopes so evident in the ecclesiological renewal of Vatican II. In his subsequent book, *The Crucified God*, Moltmann sounds less sanguine. He argues that attempts to make ecclesiastical structures relevant to social realities, and activities undertaken to change social structures in accordance with the Church's mission to the world have led to an identity crisis. The failure to find Christian identity in the Church and in secular involvement drives the Christian back to the primal question.

> Where does the identity of Christian faith lie? Its outward mark is church membership. This, however, takes us no further, but merely moves the problem on. For the Christian identity of the Church is itself questionable, when the form it takes is affected by so many interests. One can point to the creed. But to repeat the formula of the Apostles' Creed is no guarantee of Christian identity, but simply of loyalty to the fathers and to tradition. One can point to particular experiences of vocation, conversion and grace in one's own life. But even they do not guarantee one's identity as a Christian; at best, they point to what one has begun to believe in such experiences. Ultimately, one's belief is not in one's own faith; within one's experiences in faith and one's decisions, one believes in someone else who is more than one's own faith. Christian identity can be understood only as an act of identification with the crucified Christ, to the extent to which one has accepted the proclamation that in him God has identified himself with the godless and the godforsaken—to whom one belongs oneself.[5]

The issue of Christian identity imposes itself inescapably on the life of reflection as well as on the lived life. Many Christians have already felt the challenge and responded in some way. The formation of numerous charismatic groups bears this out, much to the perplex-

---

[5]New York–Evanston–San Francisco–London, Harper & Row, 1974, pp. 18–19 (slightly corrected).

ity of conservatives and liberals alike. Charismatics sound too non-ecclesiastical to the former and too spiritual to the latter. And so the identity questions are there: Who is God? Who is Jesus Christ? Who am I? Who are we? Who are we called to be? Where does our calling, in the Lord, lead us?

The dynamics of resignation

In such a situation human beings tend to run for cover. It is not surprising that we can see some of this happening. The combination of ecclesiological fatigue and lack of officially shared answers to central questions tends to drive people in various directions in search for shelter. Some do not want to be bothered any more by an institutional church that so seldom seems to come up with an appropriate response to the world, and which treats the faithful in patronizing ways where the world treats them as responsible citizens.[6] The irritations—not to mention the boredom—frequently connected with ecclesiology-in-practice often exceed their tolerance. Thus they give up hope; the Church will never be able, they tend to feel, to make the central issues of the faith meaningful to them. Some turn to prayer, mysticism, *communautés de base* and charismatic communities to avoid institutional involvement and gain a sense of freedom; in this way they can remain members of the Church despite their disappointments.

Another option is to join the increasing ranks of "third men" in the Church[7]—Christians who are neither the full-committed church members of yore nor the classical lapsed Christian, but persons who are no longer interested in theological discussions and in the structures of the Church. They are irritated by the institution but live with it because they do not find it important enough to get very excited about. They quietly stay in the Church largely on their own terms, in order to be inspired by the Gospel and to celebrate the sacraments.

Others have quietly dropped out of the Church and become Christians entirely on their own terms. They acknowledge the Christian tradition as theirs to the extent that they feel it illuminates their

---

[6]Cf. Frans Jozef van Beeck, S.J., "Sacraments, Church Order, and Secular Responsibility," *Theological Studies* 30 (1969) 613–634, esp. 613–614, 623–634.

[7]Cf. François Roustang, "Le troisième homme," *Christus* 13 (1966) 561–567.

lives and provides general guidance in life-decisions.

All these Christians have this in common—that they have resigned themselves to what they perceive as the Church's essential inability to provide more than *a framework* for faith. At one end of the range, this amounts to the substitution of attitude for ecclesial faith. Two of the most dubious characteristics of conventional Christianity were its tendency to keep the faithful more concerned about their own salvation than about their mission, and its emphasis on conformity rather than strong personal conviction. Many of those resigning themselves to the Church's inability to inspire them show that they are heirs to this tradition—they are disappointed at a Church that does not do enough *for them*, and their personal faith amounts to little more than a rather vague attitude in life.

At the opposite end of the range there are highly motivated Christians who tolerate the large-scale institutional Church rather than loving it, let alone depending on it. But there is one feeling across this entire pluralistic range, namely, that the Church as such is not likely to inspire. This has consequences for theology; it means that many no longer look upon ecclesiology as theology's most promising part.

The dynamics of anxiety

Pluralism and the lack of shared answers to central questions are driving others to a very different shelter. Neo-orthodoxy, with all the characteristics of revelational positivism or conciliar positivism, is trying to call the Church to order. Its advocates are renewing their attempts to enshrine the faith once again in the authorized formulas hallowed by tradition. Made nervous by the real or apparent liberalism of many clergy and countless faithful, they demand that orthodoxy be restored. A faith that is firmly objective and an orthodoxy firmly enforced by external means is preferable, they say, to the formless pluralism brought about by too much trust in personal faith.

This typically Roman Catholic counterpart of free-church fundamentalism is only apparently concerned with faith; in fact, it is almost entirely concerned with church order and authoritative faith-expression. Its very vehemence testifies to the underlying ecclesiological fatigue; authority is prescribed as a last-resort measure—the tonic to restore the languid Church's failing muscle-tone.

It must be feared, however, that such a call to order without sufficient diagnosing of the problem will only do harm; it tends to take far too external a view of faith. A forced return to the mansions of the past will never make Christians feel at home. Wholesale efforts at restoration overrate the significance of established doctrine. Even Karl Barth, for many the father of Protestant neo-orthodoxy, cautioned against overrating doctrine:

> 'Orthodoxy' means agreement with the Fathers and the Councils. As that it can never be an end in itself. Repristination is nonsense.[8]

The function of all "utterance of knowledge" is always the building-up of the Church in the Spirit, not the forced restoration of the admirable cathedrals of past centuries of belief, in which people of today cannot be expected to believe and pray—at least not habitually or by way of obligation. A militant drive in favor of orthodoxy, no matter how well argued the tenets and no matter how lucidly set forth the arguments, would alienate and not liberate understanding; hence, it would not build the Christian Church. Fear and anxiety are poor guides, especially if they masquerade as authority. Only faith freely professed will produce a community of faith.

We have reason to suspect that under cover of the defense of the faith, the hidden agenda of the neo-orthodox drive is a refusal to deal not only with the need for reform at the heart of the Church, but also, and principally, with the world. The eminent Dutch religious psychologist Han Fortmann has mainly (though not exclusively!) the Catholic Church in mind when he writes:

> I have been wondering for a long time if anxiety is still not too much the overriding factor in the Catholic community, despite all the efforts to re-engage in a dialogue, all too long died down, with this modern world. Then it becomes impossible to see today's world with the objectivity of love, to fathom it down to its deepest intentions. It takes the courage of love to let the many new things that emerge from this restless world—restless and confused like a brilliant but schizoid boy in adolescence—come to oneself calmly, to take them seriously, and really to understand them. Without this, the thread of dialogue is irrevocably

---

[8] *Credo*, New York, Charles Scribner's Sons, 1962, p. 182.

broken. Thus it may happen that one is sometimes already on the defensive before one understands what is the matter. Anxiety has prevented the person from seeing it. The Church can count on her militant sons, but she cannot always be sure that they will not strike out at a friend instead of an enemy. For whoever is anxious does not always know any longer where he lands his blows. The anxious person is a menace to his environment.[9]

This does not mean that all emphasis on church order and doctrine is inspired by fear and anxiety. There is no doubt some legitimacy to demands for clarity and for common answers and stances. Still, all forms of neo-orthodoxy must continually ask themselves the question if and to what extent their insistence is based on reluctance to deal with the world; and they must continually realize that the price of uniformity is always to some extent a lack of personal conviction.

Those resigned to an irrelevant Church and those anxious to tighten up the institutional Church both treat the Church's diaspora situation *in a purely ecclesiastical-political fashion.* The latter fail to recognize the fact of the Church's *diaspora*, and want to have a Church that is visibly and tangibly unified against the forces of dispersal. The former fail to recognize that it is the *Church* in diaspora, and want to live as Christians in the world without having to be concerned with the unity of the Church. As a consequence, both fail to treat the diaspora of the Church as a *theological situation*—a situation not to be solved by means of a political compromise on a purely ecclesiological basis, but only by the kind of radical renewal of faith that renews the Church from inside.

The need for such a radical renewal means, for the theologian, that he must be unworried about where his efforts are going to lead him, and that he must steadily refuse to let himself "be annexed either by progressives or by conservatives,"[10] trusting that Jesus Christ, and any serious theological attention paid to him, will undercut the debilitating penchant for polarization inherent in purely

---

[9] *Heel de mens*, Bilthoven, Uitgeverij Ambo, 1972, p. 26.
[10] Piet Schoonenberg, *The Christ*, New York, Herder & Herder, 1971, p. 8—This book, which did not get the translators it deserves, has been one of the most inspiring writings behind my own struggle with christology. It will be discussed several times in this book; cf. below, pp. 168–173, 254, 385–396.

ecclesiological positions and oppositions.

New theological ventures are needed. Such new efforts will have to do justice both to the central core of the faith—God in Jesus Christ alive in the Spirit—and to what is called, with convenient vagueness, the modern world.

New sensibilities

Each culture produces a steady stream of new sensibilities in the process of its historical growth. Theology, therefore, can express the Christian identity only in an ongoing encounter with a plurality of cultural sensibilities, in the course of history as well as across the world at any given period. "A new question needs a new answer," as Cardinal Newman said; and Paul Tillich was aiming at the same when he proposed his method of correlation whereby "philosophy formulates the answers implied in human existence, and theology formulates the answers implied in divine self-manifestation under the guidance of the questions implied in human existence."[11] The tradition answered concrete questions and met concrete cultural attitudes; today's questions and attitudes may not be fobbed off with fair words, no matter how hallowed they are. They must be faced with the same confidence and integrity that inspired the solution of traditional problems when *they* were contemporary. Theologies which present themselves—along with verbal orthodoxy—as somehow above the cultural shifts of history betray themselves by that very fact as very much historically determined.[12]

A refusal to take the culture seriously is not only an injustice done to it; it is also a false form of self-denial. We Christians must develop the integrity to acknowledge present-day cultural traits

---

[11]Paul Tillich, *Systematic Theology*, Vols. I–III, Chicago, University of Chicago Press, 1967, Vol. I, p. 61.

[12]An example of the point of view rejected here: "Those concepts have the same property as all the others which the Church uses to propose the dogmas of the faith. They express concepts that owe no debt to a particular form of human culture, to particular progress in science or scholarship, or to particular models of theology. Rather, they express what the human mind, in virtue of universal and necessary experience, perceives about reality and then expresses in appropriate and sure words, be they derived from ordinary or cultured speech. This is why they meet the needs of all people regardless of differences of time and place"—Encyclical *Mysterium Fidei*, *Acta Apostolicae Sedis*, 57 (1965) 753ff.; quotation p. 758.

frankly as our own, too. Religion does not make anybody into a citizen of a separate world. Wherever Christians pretend to be separate or force themselves to be separate, the result will be what Fortmann calls "ecclesiogenic neurosis"—church-engendered neurosis.[13] Evangelical self-denial, which is at the heart of Christian identity, is a call to self-forgetfulness out of love for the other. But in order for the Church to be able to forget about herself, there must be a self to forget—a self which acknowledges, lovingly and empathetically, the special temper of the culture as part of her own makeup.

Love and empathy—these two are by no means incidental to the enterprise. Uncaring accommodation between faith and culture runs the risk, not only of losing the identity of the Christian faith in total relativity under the banner of quick relevance, but also of treating the culture as cheap and superficial. The confrontation between Christian identity and worldly culture must be one of patient and respectful dialogue, not of quick doctrinal bargains struck at cut rates.

Meeting the culture is not for the naive either; no Christian should live in the illusion that adopting cultural stances is easy. Conceptions derived from the culture, as Barth never ceased to warn, already have a definite content that cannot be escaped, and this content, be it ever so residual, may in some cases so decisively color the theology expressed in them that the purity of the faith is compromised.[14]

Hence, it is imperative that any accommodation with the culture should be a welcome extended to the culture *out of freedom*, not because the Church wants the culture's approval in order to be acknowledged as "contemporary" or "relevant." When he was reminded that he had used "a strange incrustation of Kantian-Platonic terms" in his exposition of Romans, Karl Barth replied: "I was *at liberty* then to use these conceptions, but if I were to be told to-day that I *had* to use them, I should say with decision, No." This is so because "the rule for the theologian is: All things are lawful for me. For example, it is lawful for me—I am answering a question—to

---

[13]Han Fortmann, *Heel de mens*, p. 69.
[14]Cf. Karl Barth, *Credo*, pp. 183–184.

speak of 'noetic' and 'ontic.' All things are lawful for me, but nothing shall take me captive."[15]

Barth's undying merit is to have reminded the Church that, as Church, she had no business founding herself on anything but the Word of God in Jesus Christ, crucified and risen, scandalous or foolish as such foundation may be. On the basis of that foothold the Church can feel *free* to speak out in such a way that all can hear her speaking "in their own languages."[16] Dogmatic theology must justify itself, not before the tribunal of present sensibilities and concerns, but

> only before God in Jesus Christ; concretely before Holy Scripture within the Church. Certainly it has also the responsibility of speaking so that it can be *understood*, but there is not the slightest chance that any philosophy could here step in as norm.[17]

The task of doing justice to new sensibilities, then, is grounded in a double recognition. New questions need new answers today just as much as yesterday; new questions are not foreign to the Church, and therefore need to be taken seriously in the interest of the Church's integrity. The task is delicate because the Church would be disrespectful to the culture if she gave quick, cheap answers, and because the Church would be naive if she thought that accommodating the culture is free from the risk of theological distortion. Only if the Church turns herself inside out and involves herself with the culture freely—that is out of the confidence derived from Christian identity—will concern with new cultural sensibilities build a truly Christian Church—one that does not generate feelings of fatigue and resignation.

Interpreting the tradition

It takes free people, Christians with a sense of identity—not merely Christians who depend upon the Church—to take on the

---

[15] *Ibid.*, pp. 185, 183. Cf. Dietrich Bonhoeffer, *Letters and Papers from Prison*, New York, The Macmillan Company, [2]1967, p. 170, for a reference to Barth's "neo-Kantian egg-shells."

[16] Acts 2, 11.

[17] Karl Barth, *Credo*, pp. 185–186.

culture. Such people will rise to the occasion every time a new idea arises. Frederick Crowe, in a very elegant article, has pointed out that

> the widest range of possibilities obtains at the level of ideas, and unlimited freedom reigns. How can you prohibit the occurrence of an idea? If it occurs, it occurs, and there is nothing pope or council can do about it.[18]

The realization that issues and questions crop up forever will help Christians not to absolutize either the old or the new, and to entertain the new wherever it appears.

It takes people equally free, Christians with no less a sense of Christian identity, and with as healthy a realization of their freedom in the Church, to take on the tradition. Frederick Crowe stresses that doctrinal statements, including statements found in Scripture, do not exhaust the Son's unfathomable riches, nor do they do justice to God's unsearchable judgments governing the course of salvation-history.[19] This realization will keep Christians from mistaking definitions for definitive statements; it will remind them of the depths below the surface of the traditional formulas. What is needed is not an authoritarian call to order, but a delicate interpretation of the tradition in the light of its own historical assumptions and intentions, and against the background of the need for a *living* understanding of the tradition today.

The need for such an interpretative approach to tradition is already obvious at the purely linguistic level. Though the Church used the language of the past to formulate the faith of which she is the teacher and guardian, she is not the teacher or the guardian of that language. That language remains a sliding structure of interrelated functions, in which no single elements can be nailed down to last for centuries with certain abiding meanings. The words—and, for that matter, the syntax, the idioms, the standard patterns of

---

[18]Frederick Crowe, S.J., "Development of Doctrine: Aid or Barrier to Christian Unity?" in: *Proceedings of the Twenty-First Annual Convention of the Catholic Theological Society of America*, Yonkers, N.Y., St. Joseph's Seminary, 1967, pp. 1–20; quotation p. 10.

[19] *Ibid.*, pp. 2–8.

rhetoric, in short, all the elements of language—are in a process of continuous flux. That flux may often seem very illogical and erratic, but it is never without inner coherence; language-elements adapt to changes that occur in the system to safeguard and even enhance the language's potential for expression. The standardization which is the result of the art of printing, and the tightening-up of language-conventions which is one of the fruits of widespread literacy, may have slowed down the flux, but they have not stopped it. Hence, the very formulations of dogma may become obstacles to faith; the ancient words and terms, when repeated too obstinately, become part of the problem instead of a solution to it. Obviously, the meaning of past statements always remains to a large extent retrievable; but past statements must be truly understood before they yield their meaning. And understanding them requires a great deal of interpretative effort, which can be expected only from experts, and not even from them all the time. Taking linguistic developments seriously, therefore, is indirectly an act of faith, in that it recognizes that the formulas of the past may not be capable of permanently re-evoking the living faith of which the historical formulas were both the expression and the safeguard.

The need for an interpretative approach to the ancient formulas, however, is not just a result of linguistic developments. There are many more reasons—too many to mention here—why established dogma should not be credited with absolute authority in matters of faith. We can think of the fact that people's *intentions* in making statements—the *points* they are trying to make—cannot be grasped from the statements taken at face value; the interpretation of dogma will have to ask not only the question what that means, but also the question what *they* meant. We can also think of the ineffability of God's mystery, which implies that whatever formulations are authoritatively adopted will still have an aura of the mysterious. They can be expected to be less than entirely accurate or decisive when it comes to telling the true from the false, let alone the true from the false brethren.

It stands to reason, therefore, that *faith itself*—not just linguistic developments and the relative inadequacy of dogmatic pronouncements—will call for new doctrinal developments. Developments of this kind will be really new, even though they will have to be in some way compatible with the doctrinal deliverances of the past. But mere compatibility with past doctrine is not new formulation, but mere restatement. Even the most syllogistic doctrinal developments can be startling, as the seventeenth-century Spanish scholastics discovered. Neither the doctrines nor their developments are easy to understand; faith-interpretation is an essential part of understanding them.[20]

Interpreting dogmatic formulations is also psychologically risky. It must therefore be undertaken with delicacy and gentleness. Carl Gustav Jung states that dogma has the ability to evoke *and* shackle religious experience; it both expresses and safeguards faith.[21] From a psychological point of view there is a *formal* similarity between adherence to dogma (and ritual) and the compulsive neurotic compromise. For this reason interpreting dogma rather than swallowing it whole will always have a component of guilt-feeling for a good many people; undertaking it feels like breaking a taboo. This feeling is often enhanced by the external enforcement of traditional dogma, by ecclesiastical authorities, the weight of tradition, and local conservatism.

Added to this is an extrinsic factor of great power. Many confirmed unbelievers will object—sometimes openly, but more often covertly—when Christians take an intelligently interpretative approach to their faith, and especially when they start to restate their faith in accordance with the sensibilities of the culture. Having once decided that Christianity equals obscurantism, they want Christians to stay in the dark corner where they belong; at the very least they want them to remain the way they always were. And so we sometimes witness the edifying spectacle of professed unbelievers exhort-

---

[20]The suggestion that development by means of greater explicitness is sufficient to deal with new cultural situations and new questions is of doubtful validity. The suggestion is implied when it is stated that the Church "reverently preserved the mystery of the Son of God made man, and 'in the course of the ages and the centuries' has proposed it to be believed in an ever more explicit way"; cf. the "Declaratio ad Fidem Tuendam in Mysteria Incarnationis et Sanctissimae Trinitatis a Quibusdam Recentibus Erroribus," *Acta Apostolicae Sedis* 64 (1972) 237–241; ET in: *Origins* 1 (1972) 666–668; quotation 237 (*Origins* 666). We will have occasion to come back to this document.

[21]Cf. Carl Gustav Jung, *Psychology and Religion*, New Haven, Yale University Press (1960), pp. 51–58, 62–63. Cf. also pp. 26–38, 50 for Jung's insight that religion is inappropriately used if it is used to drive a wedge between the conscious self and the *anima*.

ing Christians to orthodoxy in the interest of well-worn clarity. Certain types of political leaders, too, have always appreciated the loyalties of religious groups clinging to a conventional creed that avoids the confrontation with the culture; conventional Christians relying on authoritarian dogmatic assurance are liable to be politically dependent on authority, too.

The task of doing justice to the faith of our fathers, then, is one of interpretation, not repetition. Various reasons support the need for interpretation; we have mentioned the recognition that subsequent linguistic shifts make past doctrine hard to understand, the realization that the intentions of the Church in defining past doctrine cannot be directly grasped from the doctrinal statements taken by themselves, and the mysterious character of the truth intended by any doctrinal statements. Only on the strength of a comfortable sense of Christian identity will such an interpretative stance be possible; without it the faithful believer is likely to be moved by anxiety rather than the assurance that comes from conviction enjoyed in freedom. The anxiety will express itself in the form of advocacy of authoritative exclusion of all dissent and freedom *in* the Church, and in the form of casting those outside the Church in the role of adversaries.

Prospect

Frederick Crowe mentions a third reason for doctrinal development, namely, that the Holy Spirit is active in the work of the Christian.[22] Reliance on this assurance must always encourage Christians to engage in being Christians without worrying too much about the Church; the ambiguities attendant upon ecclesiology today make this reliance even more urgent. This book will therefore concentrate on Christian identity, in the hope that this will produce the outlines of an ecclesiology capable of intergrating both the tradition and the modern world.

We will take the view that an attempt at a *direct* reconciliation between traditional Christian doctrine and "the world" runs a serious risk of being too narrow or too shallow. We have already pointed out that Christian doctrine must be interpreted on the basis of

---

[22]Cf. Frederick Crowe, "Development of Doctrine," pp. 11–14.

Christian identity; and this Christian identity is not primarily a theoretical pursuit, but *an act of faith identical with a way of life.* In the same way, concern with the world is not primarily a theoretical pursuit, but a participation in a process; integrating the world into the theology of the future, therefore, is achieved by *an active participation in the world on the part of Christians* who live their faith before they express it, and express it directly before they reflect upon it. This means that Christianity must be understood in terms of action before it can be understood as an intellectually coherent view of the world. In this book, the concern with *Christian faith as action and event* which is never quite reducible to insights and statements will take many forms. It will lead to an emphasis on a variety of themes: rhetoric, interpersonalness, the role of the Holy Spirit, the importance of human concerns for christology, the possibility for a universal inclusion of all that is human, the need for obedience and conversion, the offer of unlimited hope, the crucial significance of the Resurrection for christology, witness, the experience of grace, the primacy of eschatology, worship and witness, the mystery of the life of the historical Jesus, the ongoing integration of humanity into Christ, the relationship of Jesus with the Father, compassion and pathos as divine attributes, martyrdom, doctrinal development, and the *imitatio Christi* as a task of theology. This list is bound to bewilder the reader at this point; it is the task of this entire book to explain that there is an inner coherence in this vast array of issues.

Retrospect and outlook

This introduction has argued that a consideration of Christian identity rather than a theology of the Church is indicated if the resolution of important pending theological questions is to amount to more than a church-political compromise. The next two chapters will treat two additional changes of focus. It will be argued that we must concentrate on Jesus Christ rather than on God, and that we must understand language in terms of interaction rather than knowledge. Once the three conversions, away from concern with ecclesiology, God-talk, and logic and toward Christian identity, christology, and rhetoric, have been discussed, the road will be open for a first analysis of the dynamics of christology, which will be the task of the second part of this book.

CHAPTER 1

From God-Talk to Christology

The Bible does not support the view that God is God in the same way at all times.

Karl Barth

                    Words strain,
Crack and sometimes break, under the burden,
Under the tension, slip, slide, perish,
Decay with imprecision, will not stay in place,
Will not stay still. Shrieking voices
Scolding, mocking, or merely chattering,
Always assail them. The Word in the desert
Is most attacked by voices of temptation.

T. S. Eliot

No one has ever seen God. The only-begotten God who is in the bosom of the Father—he has been our guide.

The Gospel of John

An opening thesis
      Someone uses the predicate "God" about Jesus, but only half-heartedly or with hesitation, or omits it altogether. Someone denies "the divinity of Jesus" outright, setting aside the conciliar tradition

and certain New Testament texts.[1] The serious Christian responds with horror, or suspicion—but *this is not the only possible or even the most appropriate reaction.* Why not?

LINGUISTIC INSTABILITY AND CULTURAL SHIFTS

Words as such are not reliable, even when defined
The *words* "God" and "divinity" do not in and of themselves, as *words*, guarantee shared meaning. It must be noted immediately that the only kind of meaning that makes sense is *shared* meaning, that is, the kind of meaning in virtue of which people build a community and are built into a community, while using a "common language." If abiding and clear and indisputable meaning were connected to certain words as such, there would be no need for a science of semantics, and people would not, at times, have to come to the conclusion, after a heated debate, that they had once again been engaged in a fight about semantics. In fact, the very realization of the possibility of mutual misunderstanding in spite of a shared vocabulary is very often precisely the cause of the fighting. If words as such guaranteed meaning, James Barr's brilliant book *The Semantics of Biblical Language*[2] could have remained unwritten, because the words by themselves would have insured certain or, in our case, orthodox understanding.

A variant of the mistaken assumption that words as such guarantee shared meaning is often couched in the misleading phrase: "What this expression, or word, *really means* is this: ..."[3] The problem here is: What does "really" mean? Surely it cannot be supposed to refer to an innate property of a certain word? The medieval adage that words are "artificial signs" refers precisely to

[1]The New Testament reserves *ho theos*—the Greek word for "God," with the definite article—for the Father, and in six places (Rom 9, 5; Jn 1, 1.18; 20, 28; 1 Jn 5, 20; Tit 2, 13) applies the word—either without article or with the article *and* a qualifying epithet—to Jesus Christ. Cf. Raymond E. Brown, *Jesus God and Man*, Milwaukee, Bruce, 1967, pp. 1–38; also, Karl Rahner, "Theos in the New Testament," in: *Theological Investigations*, Vol. I, Baltimore, Helicon Press, 1961, pp. 79–148.
[2]London, Oxford University Press, 1961.
[3]For the philosophical and educational assumptions behind the thesis that a word or a literary work "really means" something, cf. Walter J. Ong, S.J., *Rhetoric, Romance, and Technology*, Ithaca–London, Cornell University Press, 1971, esp. pp. 160–164.

the experienced reality of their inability to confine the jinnee "meaning" to the well-sealed bottle of a group of sounds. The medieval nominalists, with their passionate, if overdrawn, interest in precision and consistency, were driven to the discouraging conclusion that words are *flatus vocis* on the basis of the same experience. Taken in isolation, words do tend to turn into meaningless mumbo-jumbo. When repeated aloud and out of context a number of times, a word tends to draw more and more attention to its sound and to retain less and less of its meaning.

In certain situations, however, it is indeed possible to lay down what a word "really means." For example, the shared interest in terminological consistency may lead a community of scholars to attribute clear, unambiguous meanings to certain words. Such terminological fixations carry the promise of perfect stability of discourse, afford the necessary distance from the unorganized reality and relative confusion of everyday speech, and create a kind of quasi-pictorial clarity that supports the quest for scholarly accuracy.[4] In such milieus it is even possible to coin new words, or neologisms—a procedure designed to capture thought with less risk of ambiguity than recourse to an already existing word. Even in this case, however, the consensus of the community of discourse is the necessary prerequisite for terminologically constant meaning. In effect, the situation is this: a word "really means this or that" because there is a "they" or "we" who "really mean this or that" whenever the word occurs in the course of speaking the particular language that is appropriate to the shared concerns of the group.

The majority of situations, however, are not concerned with terminology. Hence, in most situations the meaning of words is ascertained with reference, not to an act of definition, but to much wider and less easily determinable frameworks of contexts, uses, and cultural sensibilities. In ordinary language, moreover, evocative, con-

---

[4]The *Decree on the Most Holy Eucharist*, promulgated by the Council of Trent in 1551, shows an awareness of what we are discussing here by affirming the appropriateness, the purposefulness, and the aptness of the term transubstantiation, without going into the question what the term really means. Cf. H. Denzinger and A. Schönmetzer S.I., *Enchiridion Symbolorum Definitionum et Declarationum de Rebus Fidei et Morum*, Barcinone-Friburgi Brisgoviae-Romae-Neo-Eboraci, Herder, [12]1963 (henceforth DS), nn. 1642, 1652.

notative, emotional, rhetorical, and metaphorical elements are part of the web that determines the meanings of words. The abstract terminology used by experts for "free thought" is, in fact, not the original and most typical form of language. Ultimately, it is dependent, for its very existence, on the abiding availability of those wider frameworks, whence it is drawn by way of simplification, clarification, rationalization, categorization, and definition—all procedures to reduce the wider frameworks to a minimum, in the interest of maximal denotative power.[5]

But it may be asked: Is not the meaning of "God" and "divinity" in christological statements clear at least within the wider framework of the *Church*? Don't *Christians* agree on what they really mean by these words? If the answer to this question were an unqualified "yes," then a Christian's reluctance, failure, or refusal to use the words "God" and "divinity" would be proof of heterodoxy, disobedience, ignorance, or a combination of all three. In fact, when certain ecclesiastical authorities or certain conservative organizations of Christians, both in the Roman Catholic Church and in other Christian churches, decry the collapse of orthodoxy these days, they often seem to put it down to heterodoxy, disobedience, and ignorance. Yet we do have sound reasons to question the assumption that the meaning of "God" and "divinity" is clear in the Christian Church. There *are* grounds for holding that the predicates "God" and "divinity" are not as uncomplicatedly viable as they are claimed to be. A conservative who denies that "God" and "divinity" in christological statements are ambiguous may indeed be expressing a strong conviction, but the very fact that the claim needs to be made so emphatically suggests that the *linguistic* situation is more complex than it is alleged to be. Adding that at least "all true Catholics" find no ambiguities here—apart from begging the question—does not

---

[5]Cf. J. W. M. Verhaar, S.J., *Some Relations Between Perception, Speech, and Thought*, Assen, Van Gorcum, 1963, esp. pp. 57–64; and Ian T. Ramsey, *Models and Mystery*, London, Oxford University Press, 1964, *passim.*—The book by Verhaar, a linguist and philosopher who is no stranger to theology, is one of the books to which the present approach to christology is indebted to a far greater extent than the footnotes suggest. It has the advantage of presenting a coherent theory in continuous dialogue with the great language-theorists from von Humboldt and de Saussure on.

sound too ecumenical, nor does the suspiciousness it creates help the unity of the Catholic Church.

It is inappropriate and humiliating, however, to appeal to the *mystery* conveyed by the words "God" and "divinity" in order to defend their ambiguity against conservative clarity. Christians for whom "God" is a viable predicate ought not to be accused of having a simplistic, infantile, magical, mystery-less notion of God. Many of them may have such a notion, but, then, this is not their exclusive prerogative; images, concepts, and mind-sets which, if proposed as doctrine, would turn out to be fledgling and even full-fledged her-esies are part and parcel of the Christian struggle for expression; and respect for the conciliar tradition need not be a sign of anxious dependence on authority as a substitute for the personal surrender to the mystery of God. The line between dogma as catalyst of religious experience and dogma as straitjacket is hard to draw.[6]

Whatever one's position on the conservative-liberal range, we must maintain that the meaning of the word "God" in christological statements is not in and of itself a known quantity, nor has the Church ever claimed that the word "God" has an obvious, indisput-able meaning based on unequivocal definition. The traditional proofs for the existence of God and the traditional discussion of the "divine attributes" were never intended to form the basis of Christian faith. Yet when Bishop Robinson wrote in *Honest to God*, "Traditional Christian theology has been based upon the proofs for the existence of God,"[7] much as he may have stated—historically speaking—a howler, he expressed—and rejected—something that is a feature of much conventional Christianity, namely the tacit assumption that, of course, we all somehow know what "God" really means. But if Christians are to maintain that "no one has ever seen God," that no one knows the Father except through Jesus Christ, that God is known in the darkness of faith, they may certainly never succumb to the temptation to claim an obvious meaning for the word "God." Conventional Christianity has, in this regard, everything to learn from Karl Barth's refusal to tie the living God to the rickety or, in any case, shifting answers of "natural theology."

---

[6]Cf. Carl Gustav Jung, *Psychology and Religion*, esp. pp. 52ff.

[7]John A. T. Robinson, *Honest to God*, London, SCM Press, 1963, p. 29.

The same point can be made in yet another way. "Jesus is God" is not an identifying statement, in which an already known predicate is applied to a subject, as, for example, in the sentence, "That wall is green." Once you have an approximate consensus as to what is meant by "green," the sentence about the wall is capable of conveying shared meaning. But it must not be assumed that "God" is that kind of predicate—which assumption often underlies the refusal to discuss the meaning of statements attributing divinity to Jesus.

Our discussion so far is obviously far from adequate. Later on in this book we *will* argue that the Christian assurance in using "God" and "divinity" is fully warranted. But we will also argue that this very assurance does not make of God a known quantity, and in addition we will show that the Christian assurance must manifest itself in patient understanding.[8] It is in this latter attitude that we must continue our present discussion of the ambiguities in christology today.

Traditional Christian understanding no longer effectual

But the question remains, as a theological, not a linguistic issue: Don't Christians understand one another when they use the word "God" in connection with Jesus Christ? Of course they do—*if* we were to maintain that such shared understanding is available to Christians provided they adhere to the great conciliar and theological traditions, authoritatively interpreted—in the case of the Roman Catholic Church by the *magisterium.* Such an answer, however, would confuse a historical judgment with a contemporary question. The historical judgment is: The settlements of the Councils of Nicaea (325 A.D.) and Chalcedon (451 A.D.) presented a very consistent and impressive statement of the Church's faith in the mystery of God made man, and thus of the Christian meaning of "God"—a statement both in tune with, and a critique of, the human conception of God in the fourth and fifth centuries. The contemporary question is: Does the statement still have the same vigor and elucidating power that it had for the early Church and for many centuries afterward?

The first judgment need not be contested. In the Bampton Lectures for 1966, David Jenkins has shown that the Nicaean and

---

[8]Below, p. 479.

Chalcedonian settlements provided the Church with a comprehensive statement about the coherence of the worlds of persons and of things, of history and of materiality, all within the encompassing grasp of God's personal plan as decisively evidenced in the life, death and Resurrection of Jesus. Jenkins goes on to argue that the basic concerns of Nicaea and Chalcedon are still with us, and that modern man must not dismiss as "unthinkable" statements which, in themselves, were just as unthinkable sixteen centuries ago, but which the Church made nevertheless.[9] To despise such statements would be short-sighted and narrow-minded: they were "not only used, but also sanctioned by the Ecumenical Councils," and to declare that these words and notions have no true certainty about them would take the nerve out of all speculative theology, and wreak havoc by disturbing the mandatory pattern of ecclesiastical "rules of speech."[10] So far so good.

However, the coherence of the statements made by Nicaea and Chalcedon does not decide the question of contemporary meaningfulness at all. When it is said that certain expressions were "not only used but also sanctioned," it must be asked: What did such sanctioning aim at? What was its intended result? The Council of Chalcedon, for instance, declared that its text was intended to prevent heretics from engaging in any machination against the truth, to teach the original *kerygma* without wavering, and, above all, to uphold the faith of the 318 Holy Fathers of Nicaea.[11] The intention of ecclesiastical pronouncements is not to prescribe language-habits *as such*, and even less to predict that the "rules of speech" laid down will keep their ability to counter heresy and hand on the faith into the indefinite future. Whether or not a particular piece of conciliar language is still *capable* of doing that has to be determined *a posteriori*. As we have pointed out, the Church is not the teacher or

---

[9]David E. Jenkins, *The Glory of Man*, New York, Charles Scribner's Sons, 1967, esp. pp. 15, 37–65.

[10]Cf. DS 3883—although the passage's conclusion (that departure from established terminology leads to dogmatic relativism) does not follow. For the expression "rules of speech" (*Sprachregelung*), cf. Karl Rahner, "What Is a Dogmatic Statement?" in: *Theological Investigations*, Vol. V, Baltimore/London, Helicon Press/ Darton, Longman & Todd, 1966, pp. 42–66, esp. 51–58.

[11]DS 300.

the guardian of language as such; linguistic development is relatively autonomous, and new sensibilities may bring up new questions, to which the "rules of speech" laid down in the past may not be an *effectual* answer forever, given the cultural shifts that occur in the course of history. The *truth* of conciliar statements is not at stake here; of that the First Vatican Council stated: "The meaning of the sacred dogmas, too, must be retained forever; this meaning has been once and for all laid down by Holy Mother Church."[12] But this does not in any way mean that dogmas of the past can *function* in the same way as they certainly did when first laid down.

Two principal factors must be mentioned as having contributed to this loss of effectual meaning: the demise of the medieval-baroque Christian establishment, and the declericalization of theology.

First, the Church no longer functions as the closed language-community she claimed to be. When Karl Rahner described "The Prospect for Christianity," what he was describing was the end of the medieval Church:

> The medieval form of the Church's public prestige in society, state, and civilization cannot by any means be regarded as something essentially demanded by the nature of the Church, if it is her destiny to be the Church that is a sign of contradiction and at the same time must become a truly universal Church: that form was only possible as long as the Church was the Church of a more or less restricted culture. The moment the West became an unenclosed part of world-history, such a form was impossible. Now contradiction has to exist everywhere or nowhere. But because it has to exist, it has to exist everywhere.[13]

But being a Church *in diaspora* means feeling the impact of the language—and the concerns—of the civilization at large. Can the Church demand that people speak two languages, one of the civiliza-tion—in which, for example, the word "God" evokes such a train of associations that talking about the "divinity" of Jesus often becomes very confusing and sometimes downright misleading—and one of the ecclesiastical tradition? Under the present circumstances it will not do to stress the need for study and careful interpretation of dogmatic

---

[12]DS 3020.
[13]"The Prospect of Christianity," pp. 83–84 (translation slightly corrected after the German original).

formulas in order to regain the "real meaning"; neither will a mere process of explanation and explicitation salvage the *effectualness* of the proposition explained and explicitated; nothing short of a new language is called for—not to discredit dogma already laid down, but to do what dogmatic theology of old always meant to do, namely, to help preach the Gospel to humankind, to use the language of the culture in the service of the preaching of the freedom of the Gospel in the teeth of "the powers that be." Hence the program becomes to speak the language of dogma with the language of the world; to make use of the sensibilities of the culture in order to speak to the culture with the confidence and freedom of the Gospel.[14]

It is, of course, *possible* to decry the fact that culture and faith have come to represent two near-incompatible languages, and to go on to exhort the faithful to adhere to the conceptions which the Church, rather than the culture, associates with "God." But this is tantamount to an implicit denial of the role Christianity itself played in the development of the language of our culture. David Jenkins rightly points out that the Church's failure to be actively concerned with the liberation and development of the natural powers in the universe is largely to blame for the disastrous and fundamentally un-Christian manner of co-existence between the Church's clumsy approach to the material universe and her traditional attitude of appreciation when human issues are concerned—as if humanity were not homogeneous with the rest of the universe.[15]

This brings us to the second factor, namely, the declericalization of the theological enterprise in all its ramifications. The education explosion, the presence of thinking Christians outside the circles of those who have been technically trained to interpret Church doctrine, and, even more widely, the average citizen's increased consciousness of his right to have his opinions regarded with respect if not understanding—all these factors have challenged the tradition of Christian theology in an unheard-of way. Added to this is the cultural awakening of the nations which two generations ago still considered the Western civilization as the only one, but which are now cultivating their national sensibilities and even witnessing an

---

[14]Cf. below, chapter 13, p. 519ff.
[15]Cf. David E. Jenkins, *The Glory of Man*, pp. 59–65.

increasing—if sometimes dubious—popularity of their wisdom in Western countries. In such a domestic and international climate the patterns of theological thought and language can simply no longer be dictated by traditional technical expertise. Total dependence on the clergy and the professional theologians is no longer appropriate. This means, of course, that the authority of clergy and professional theologians to lay down the "real meaning" of certain words and phrases is no longer a significant source of theological usage.

Two remarks are appropriate at this point. A claim is often made that the "majority of good Catholics and Protestants" still believe what the Church teaches them about the divinity of Jesus Christ. This relegates a supposed "minority" to the outer darkness just because one specific formula of orthodoxy has ceased to have effectual power of illumination for them. This is unjustified and unwarranted. Second, the exclusive use of what amounts to *one* christological model—no matter how authoritatively defined and developed—has resulted in "cryptogamous heresies"[16] whose potential for damage must not be underestimated. Theological and dogmatic statements are first and foremost statements of *faith*; they may never be allowed to become the object of faith in themselves, for we believe in God, not in faith. When dogmatic statements "freeze," they start doing an injustice to the riches of God because they start acting as inauthentic substitutes for faith, and thus they prevent the believer from engaging in the authentic surrender of faith. Alternative christologies, not *immediately* reducible to statements about "the divinity of Christ," may yield a sense of mystery far above and beyond the security of the hallowed formula, which sometimes cloaks conceptions and practices that border on covert heresy. These are some of the reasons why "God" and "divinity" must not be used to enforce orthodoxy, squelch doubts, or alienate those who search for their Christian identity. In fact, it seems preferable to follow the advice of Karl Rahner, who wrote in 1973:

> In this enterprise it must not be thought that the word "God" should occur at the beginning. In a situation in which religious language does

---

[16]Cf. Karl Rahner, "What Is Heresy?" in: *Theological Investigations*, Vol. V, Baltimore/London, Helicon Press/Darton, Longman & Todd, 1966, pp. 468–512, esp. 498–512.

not hold undisputed pride of place in society any more, it occurs, rather, at the end. But in this way it is also possible to shape a conception of God that will not later on cause most dangerous crises in man's religious consciousness on account of its infantile nature.[17]

CULTURAL OVERTONES OF "GOD" AND "DIVINITY"

Secularization

What are some of the problems inherent in the use of "God" and "divinity" in connection with Jesus Christ? What is the meaning of the word "God" as it emerges from its use in the language? What company does the word "God" preferably keep? Why do "God" and "divinity" frustrate rather than elicit the faith-response of many Christians?

During the last few years before his death at the age of 39 in 1662, Blaise Pascal was afflicted by fears that his disease might cause the loss of his memory. He jotted down in his *Pensées:*

I cannot pardon Descartes; in his entire philosophy he would have liked to do without God; but he was forced to have him flick his finger in order to put the world in motion; after that he had no use for him any more.[18]

And almost three centuries later, Dietrich Bonhoeffer, who was to die at the same age on April 8, 1945, wrote in his prison journal: "The beyond is not what is infinitely remote, but what is nearest at hand." Then, with a clear allusion to Pascal, he concluded: "Please excuse these rather pretentious *pensées.*"[19]

Two protests—both by men at death's door—against a far-away God, three hundred years apart, two landmarks in the process that

---

[17]Karl Rahner, "Kirchliche und ausserkirchliche Religiosität," *Stimmen der Zeit* 191 (1973) 3—13, quotation II. Cf. also the beautiful *Meditation über das Wort "Gott"* in Rahner's *Grundkurs des Glaubens,* Einführung in den Begriff des Christentums, Freiburg–Basel–Wien, Herder, 1976, pp. 54–61, where the occurrence of the word "God" in the language is primarily interpreted as a challenge, not an affirmation (ET, pp. 44–51).

[18]Blaise Pascal, *Pensées,* Léon Brunschvicg (ed.), Paris, Editions de Cluny, 1934, n. 77; cf. 242, 243 for expressions of Pascal's skepticism with regard to a belief in God on the basis of nature.

[19]Dietrich Bonhoeffer, *Letters and Papers from Prison,* pp. 199, 200.

has been called "secularization." Many books have been written on the subject, and many appraisals have been proposed, from total rejection—as in many orthodox and fundamentalist groups—to cordial welcome—Bonhoeffer in his *Letters and Papers from Prison* being among the warmest. Whatever the appraisal however, the process of secularization has given rise to a conception of "God" that is marked by one or more of the following characteristics.

"God" as a function of human limits

First, "God" is referred to only to account for those areas of inquiry into, and manipulation of, the world, where human knowledge and endeavor reach their limits.

Vesalius, the author of the first "modern" anatomical atlas, *De Humani Corporis Fabrica* (1543), describes how he had been unable to find any openings between the left ventricle and the right ventricle of the heart—openings which, according to traditional anatomy going back to Galen, should have been there. And he goes on:

> Therefore we are forced to praise the ingenuity of the Maker of all things, which causes the blood to sweat from the right ventricle to the left, through openings invisible to the human eye.[20]

But William Harvey's discovery of the circulation of the blood, published in 1628, was to cut out this piece of worship. There are no openings, the blood does not miraculously pass through a closed interventricular wall, and if there is an opening there is little reason to praise the ingenuity of God for a congenital heart defect.[21] In the same way, all the moving outcries by the seventeenth- and eighteenth-century naturalists about the ingenuity of the Creator[22] were

---

[20]Quoted from the first edition of Vesalius' work in: J. H. van den Berg, *Het menselijk lichaam*, Vol. I, p. 41, n. 12.—The illustrations from Vesalius' atlas are available in an American edition: J. B. deC. Saunders and Charles D. O'Malley, *The Illustrations from the Works of Andreas Vesalius of Brussels*, New York, Dover Publications, 1973.—Cf. also below, pp. 525–530.

[21]J. H. van den Berg, *Het menselijk lichaam*, Vol. I, pp. 49–52. My indebtedness to this and other works by this author, and to the method of interpretation developed by him far exceeds the indebtedness suggested by the occasional footnotes in this book.—Cf. also below, p. 531.

[22]Cf. W. H. van de Pol, *The End of Conventional Christianity*, New York, Newman Press, 1968, pp. 134–135.

to be silenced by the interest in scientific observation and experimentation, leaving, in the end, only a very pale, distant, transcendent watchmaker *à la* Paley, as the ultimate working hypothesis to account for the clockwork of the universe. Adam Smith's "Invisible Hand" is hardly "God." And as progress occurs, "God" is pushed toward the outer reaches of the knowable and manipulable universe.

On the historical side: There is one great development that leads to the world's autonomy. In theology one sees it first in Lord Herbert of Cherbury, who maintains that reason is sufficient for religious knowledge. In ethics it appears in Montaigne and Bodin with their substitution of rules of life for the commandments. In politics Machiavelli detaches politics from morality in general and founds the doctrine of "reasons of State." Later, and very differently from Machiavelli, but tending like him towards the autonomy of human society comes Grotius, setting up his natural law as international law, which is valid *etsi deus non daretur*, "even if there were no God." The philosophers provide the finishing touches; on the one hand we have the deism of Descartes, who holds that the world is a mechanism, running by itself with no interference from God; and on the other hand the pantheism of Spinoza, who says that God is nature. In the last resort, Kant is a deist, and Fichte and Hegel are pantheists. Everywhere the thinking is directed towards the autonomy of man and the world.

(It seems that in the natural sciences the process begins with Nicolas of Cusa and Giordano Bruno and their "heretical" doctrine of the infinity of the universe. The classical cosmos was finite, like the created world of the Middle Ages. An infinite universe, however it may be conceived, is self-subsisting, *etsi deus non daretur*. It is true that modern physics is not as sure as it was about the infinity of the universe, but it has not gone back to the earlier conceptions of its finitude.)

God as a working hypothesis in morals, politics, or science, has been surmounted and abolished; and the same thing has happened in philosophy and religion (Feuerbach!). For the sake of intellectual honesty, that working hypothesis should be dropped, or as far as possible eliminated. A scientist or physician who sets out to edify is a hybrid.[23]

So it may be asked: Are not the blank spots on the map of human knowledge and the untapped resources of the universe precisely that—blank spots and untapped resources—and not "God"?

---

[23]Dietrich Bonhoeffer, *Letters and Papers from Prison*, pp. 186–187.

The equation between the "yet unknown" and the ultimately mysterious is unconvincing; and it remains always questionable whether in thus locating "God" at the edges of the known, humanity is really in touch with the living God and not just with its own (provisional) limits.

> In arguments for the existence of God the world is given and God is sought. Some characteristics of the world make the conclusion "God" necessary. God is derived from the world. This does not mean that God is dependent on the world. Thomas Aquinas is correct when he rejects such an interpretation and asserts that what is first in itself may be last for our knowledge. But, if we derive God from the world, he cannot be that which transcends the world infinitely. He is the "missing link," discovered by correct conclusions. He is the uniting force between the *res cogitans* and the *res extensa* (Descartes), or the end of the causal regression in answer to the question, "Where from?" (Thomas Aquinas), or the teleological intelligence directing the meaningful processes of reality—if not identical with these processes (Whitehead). In each of these cases God is "world," a missing part of that from which he is derived in terms of conclusions. This contradicts the idea of God [. . .].[24]

"God" as the source of human diminishment

If "God" is postulated as the working-hypothesis that accounts for the coherence of the universe beyond the availability of human explanation and manipulation, a second characteristic of "God" becomes obvious. God reminds man of his limits, of the weakness of his knowing and his activity. He starts, so to speak, where man runs out.[25] But this conception carries with it a most dangerous association: "God" seems to be the enemy of man's full development; he may even appear as the source of human diminishment,[26] a God who

---

[24]Paul Tillich, *Systematic Theology*, I, p. 205. We need not at this point elaborate the thesis that to characterize the Thomist *quinque viae* as demonstrations of God's existence *based on a deficiency in the world* is a misunderstanding of Aquinas.—Cf. also Dietrich Bonhoeffer, *Letters and Papers from Prison*, pp. 168–169, 176.

[25]Cf. Dietrich Bonhoeffer, *Letters and Papers from Prison*, p. 142.

[26]Hence F. Malmberg's resolute rejection of the christological constructs of Capreolus, Cajetan, and Billot, who were prepared to sacrifice a human "act of existence" in Christ to the divine *Logos*: Felix Malmberg, *Ueber den Gottmenschen*, Basel–Freiburg–Wien, Herder (*Quaestiones Disputatae*, 9), 1960, pp. 28–30.—Cf. also Piet Schoonenberg, *The Christ*, pp. 13–49, and Karl Rahner, "The Eternal Significance of the Humanity of Jesus for Our Relationship to God," in: *Theological Investigations*, Vol. III, Baltimore, Helicon Press, pp. 35–46, esp. p. 40.

puts man in his place and who keeps him under tutelage. The exercise of man's ability to know and act may then eventually appear as a promethean struggle against "God." But at the same time this God is weak, as human knowledge and activity edge him out of the world and conquer the world for man; the "working-hypothesis" is proved superfluous, and Feuerbach's plea to invest the energy spent on "God" in service to neighbors is the obvious next step.

In this set of associations and assumptions "God" often appears as the power that keeps man moral, as the judge who will control man by means of the enticements of after-life or the prospect of judgment, as the super-power who will put human *hybris* to shame. "It is better to be simple," and other *Ressentiment*-responses (Nietzsche!) come to symbolize man's craving for security and his reluctance to be independent and courageous.

But it may again be asked: Is not this "God," who is the projection of human weakness, just that—the projection of human weakness? Schleiermacher saw that very clearly: "Piety cannot be an instinct craving for a mess of metaphysical and ethical crumbs."[27] Under this assumption, religion becomes "the sigh of the oppressed creature, the heart of a disheartened world, just as it is the spirit of spiritless situations," as the young Marx wrote.[28] And believing in this "God," people open themselves to the tutelage of the forces of exploitation ("Opium of the people, for the people")[29] and to the cheap grace connected with dependence on clerical reassurance.[30]

"God" as a function of "pure interiority"

A third set of associations which the word "God" tends to keep seems at first blush to present a complete contrast to the two just mentioned, namely, "pure interiority."[31] Yet the contrast is only

---

[27]Friedrich Schleiermacher, *On Religion, Speeches to Its Cultured Despisers*, New York, Harper & Row, 1958, p. 31.

[28]Quoted in: Jürgen Moltmann, *The Crucified God*, p. 48 (revised).

[29]*Ibid.*

[30]Cf. Dietrich Bonhoeffer, *The Cost of Discipleship*, New York, The Macmillan Company, [2]1959, pp. 45–60.

[31]An impressive protest against this association of interiority with God, denounced as a hidden feature of all occidental philosophy in: Emmanuel Levinas, *Totality and Infinity: An Essay on Exteriority*, Pittsburgh, Duquesne University Press, 1969. A good collection of scattered essays by Levinas, not available in French: *Het menselijk gelaat*, Essays van Emmanuel Levinas, Ad Peperzak (ed.), Utrecht, Ambo, 1969 (comprehensive bibliography).

superficial. A conception of God beyond the limits of the (known) world evokes, spontaneously, a conception of God at the depth of the soul; where reason runs out the heart takes over; where *l'esprit de géometrie*—that ideal of all worldly knowledge for so many centuries—leaves off, *l'esprit de finesse* proves itself an alternative with inexhaustible promise.

When Vesalius discovered that the human brain, size apart, was almost entirely identical with the brains of animals, he taunted the "crowd of philosophers and theologians" who

> ridiculously discredit the divine and most admirable machinery of the human brain by foolishly and without regard for truth dreaming up, as if they were as many Prometheuses, I-don't-know-what sort of structures of the brain, thus impiously insulting the creator of the human anatomy [...].[32]

But Vesalius did more than ridicule philosophers and theologians; he also sang the praises of God—in gratitude for the soul which is totally beyond the body—the body which the anatomical knife had reduced to a pure *bête-machine*:

> Let us therefore sing hymns and give thanks to God, the maker of all things, for having granted us a rational soul, which we [...] have in common with the angels, and by means of which, if there is only faith, we will enjoy eternal happiness; then it will no longer be necessary to inquire into the seat of the soul and its substance by means of an autopsy or by means of our reason, now impeded by the shackles of our bodies.[33]

This association of the soul—Vesalius expressly mentions Plato—with "God" antedates by almost 250 years Schleiermacher's famous phrase: "Religion resigns at once all claims to science and morality,"[34] and by more than four centuries Tillich's "depth of being" and Bultmann's "authentic existence." The difficulty of associating "God" with the world-out-there, illustrated by Vesalius and made almost axiomatic since Schleiermacher, has led to a near-identification, in our day, of "God" with interiority.

---

[32]Quoted in: J. H. van den Berg, *Het menselijk lichaam*, Vol. II, p. 220, n. 1.
[33]*Ibid.*, p. 221, n. 5.
[34]Cf. Friedrich Schleiermacher, *On Religion*, p. 35.

[. . .] in the area of religion the category of "exteriority" has become useless to us. If traditional religious conceptions meet with opposition, both among scholars and in the sensibility of many of the faithful, they do so because they are too "externalistic." We do not refer to ordeals and oracles any more, because we do not believe that God, as a foreign, extrinsic power, offers any solutions. The cloud of the Ascension, the high wind of Pentecost, and the angels' song of the nativity have become, for the exegetes, the props of a literary convention, just as much as, obviously, the sign of the Son of Man on the last day, and the last day itself, too. People have trouble with vicarious satisfaction or with the ransom of mankind by Christ, if one is to imagine this in terms of a transaction between Jesus and the Father à la Anselm's *Cur Deus Homo* or of a struggle between the Redeemer and the Evil One, in other words: as something accomplished above our heads and outside us. The doctrine about the efficacy of the sacraments *ex opere operato* meets with resistance, because this effect is a stranger to ourselves. And there is an inability to view the transubstantiation of the bread as an event unrelated to the faithful *for whom* the bread has become a sign. The ideas behind the theologians' laborious attempts to loosen up obsolete conceptions have long been at work in the sensibility of the people in the form of malaise and feelings of estrangement. The type of preaching that talks about the sacred and the Divine as realities outside man has less and less impact.[35]

This association of "God" with interiority has many possibilities, but the question may be asked: Is "pure interiority" not just that—"pure interiority"? Is it not just the irretrievable *a priori* form of all human reasoning and activity? And is the identification of the inward feeling of dependence on "the Whole that stands over against man,"[36] or of the "ultimate concern about the ground and meaning of our being,"[37] with "God" not all too easily unmasked as, for instance, the remnant of the oedipal situation, so that "God" becomes a crutch for the immature person who needs an ultimate source of courage and assurance to depend on? Is "God" in this assumption not just a projection of the needs that lurk beneath the ego?[38] And is the association of "God" with "pure interiority," the *salto mortale* of the soul to the God beyond all limits, not an act of

---

[35] Han Fortmann, *Heel de mens*, p. 212.
[36] Friedrich Schleiermacher, *On Religion*, p. 37.
[37] Paul Tillich, *Systematic Theology*, I, p. 42.
[38] The reader will recall Sigmund Freud's *The Future of an Illusion* and *Civilization and Its Discontents*.

contemplation that is nothing but riskless, false assurance, and therefore the final act of irresponsibility, avoiding the hardships involved in life in the world? And does this not, as Bonhoeffer remarked, represent an effort on the part of "modern pastoral workers," resembling "the dirtiest gutter journalists," to make godliness out of weakness—a procedure "far too unaristocratic for the word of God to ally itself with them"?[39] And if "authentic existence" and "freedom" are made to carry the entire burden of faith in God, what distinguishes "God" from a confusing linguistic device to denote "human authenticity" in the most noble existentialist sense?[40]

"God" as a linguistic conundrum

Fourth, "God" and "divinity" are often found associated with discussions about the meaning and workings of religious language. This is, perhaps, the most significant symptom of the semantic crisis "God" and "divinity" are in, with the result that to use "God" and "divinity" as predicates of Jesus leads to problematic, ambiguous responses.

In many cases the solution to this semantic crisis has been sought in terms of the three sets of associations mentioned above. For example, Paul van Buren at one time came up with the "pure interiority" notion of the "freedom of Jesus" as viable "God-talk" in the name of modern man's inability to appreciate any language-use other than statements; more recently he has moved to a plea in favor of associating it with the edges (= the limits?) of language.[41] In Tillich we find the advocacy of pure interiority ("ground and meaning of being") combined with expressions associated with weakness ("the courage to accept acceptance") and pure transcendence ("God above God").[42] Karl Barth's appeal to the "Wholly Other" repre-

---

[39]Cf. Dietrich Bonhoeffer, *Letters and Papers from Prison*, pp. 181, 184.

[40]For a good discussion and analysis of the debate about God explored so far in this chapter, cf. David Jenkins, *Guide to the Debate About God*, London, Lutterworth Press, 1968.

[41]Paul M. van Buren, *The Secular Meaning of the Gospel*, New York/London, The Macmillan Company/Collier-Macmillan, [2]1968, esp. pp. 121ff.; *The Edges of Language*, New York, The Macmillan Company, 1972.

[42]Paul Tillich, *The Shaking of the Foundations*, Harmondsworth, Penguin Books, [2]1962, pp. 59–70; *Systematic Theology*, I, pp. 116–117, 155–159; *The Courage To Be*, London and Glasgow, Collins, [2]1962, pp. 159ff., 176ff.

sents an attempt to secure for the living God a place removed far above every human need and every natural theology based on human need; in this way God-talk is predicated on man's absolute limits—no matter how much Barth goes on to assert, convincingly, that in faith all human and worldly reality comes into its own. Langdon Gilkey's analyses seem to be the product of a careful and guarded return to the *humanum* after the strictures of neo-orthodoxy; he employs the notion of "dimension or context of ultimacy" as a basis for meaningful talk about God,[43] thus aligning himself with the ideas proposed by Tillich and with Macquarrie's existential-ontological approach;[44] but an awareness of a "dimension" or "context" is not yet the affirmation of a *reality* and certainly does not warrant the use of "God" as an incontrovertible predicate.

Underlying these discussions is the assumption that "God-talk" does not have the status of a statement about "the real world." And even if it is admitted that the highest use one can put language to is not a "mere statement" that can be verified or at least falsified, still religious language, and especially its key word "God," is acknowledged to have such an "odd logical status"[45] that to use it tends to raise semantic and logical discussions. Yet the key question is not whether coherent meaning can be discovered in religious language; Eliade, Hart, Ramsey, Evans, Gilkey, and ever so many others have shown that religious language, and "God" in particular, are calculated to have meaning in terms of symbolic evocation, imagination, religious disclosure, commitment and discernment, self-involving logic, and the dimension of ultimacy.[46] Nor is the question whether it

---

[43] Langdon Gilkey, *Naming the Whirlwind*, Indianapolis and New York, The Bobbs-Merrill Company, 1969, esp. pp. 247–413.

[44] John Macquarrie, *God-Talk*, London, SCM Press, 1967.

[45] Ian T. Ramsey, *Religious Language*, London, SCM Press, ²1967, pp. 37ff.

[46] For instance, Mircea Eliade, *Images and Symbols*, New York, Sheed and Ward, ²1969; *id.*, *Myth and Reality*, New York, Harper & Row, ²1968; Ray L. Hart, *Unfinished Man and the Imagination*, New York, Herder and Herder, 1968; Ian T. Ramsey, *Religious Language*; id., *Models and Mystery*; Langdon Gilkey, *Naming the Whirlwind*; W. Luijpen, "*De erwtensoep is klaar!*" Bilthoven, Ambo, 1970; Thomas Fawcett, *The Symbolic Language of Religion*, Minneapolis, Augsburg Publishing House, 1971; Gerhard Ebeling, *Introduction to a Theological Theory of Language*, Philadelphia, Fortress Press, 1973; Kenneth Burke, *The Rhetoric of Religion*, Studies in Logology, Berkeley and Los Angeles, University of California Press, 1970; James I. Campbell, *The Language of Religion*, New York/London, The Bruce Publishing Company/Collier Macmillan Ltd., 1971; Donald D. Evans, *The Logic of Self-Involve-*

can be shown that religious language "*is able* to deal with reality, and more importantly, with reality as it transcends the empirical world," no matter how important it is to do justice to the assertiveness of religious language, as Dupré does.[47] The question for christology is whether the association of "God" and "divinity" with Jesus Christ is *actually* capable of conveying the meaning it is traditionally supposed to convey, given the welter of ambiguous associations connected with the words "God" and "divinity."

"God": a symbol for injustice done to the humanum?

"God" associated with the "beyond" beyond all limits, with human weakness, with interiority, and with the limits of language— this "God" is characterized by opposition to "the world and to man as he is continuous with the world."[48] This opposition, however, between God on the one hand and man and world on the other, tenuously and inexplicably bridged by the immortal "soul,"[49] does make it possible to uphold the Chalcedonian emphasis on the difference between divinity and humanity; at the same time this difference finds itself hardened into the kind of mutual incompatibility that can never again be united.

In "The Triumphalist Tendency in Exegetical History" Walter Brueggeman supports Jenkins' contention that the Church is largely to blame for this pernicious split between "God" and "the world and man insofar as he is continuous with the world." Brueggeman reviews some of the results of the selective reading of the Scriptures that characterizes the Protestant tradition, and then suggests:

> Through a long historical process, we have become alienated from precisely those parts of Scripture that provide the most likely points of

---

ment, New York, Herder and Herder, 1963; Helmut Fischer (ed.), *Sprachwissen für Theologen*, Hamburg, Furche-Verlag, 1974. Cf. also J. Verhaar, S.J., "Language and Theological Method," *Continuum* 7 (1969) 3–29; also in *Bijdragen* 30 (1969) 39–65.

[47]Louis Dupré, *The Other Dimension*, Garden City, New York, Doubleday, 1972, p. 208.

[48]The expression is used by David E. Jenkins, *The Glory of Man*, for instance on p. 55.

[49]Other tacit admissions of the total separation of divinity from humanity and world are, of course, Malebranche's occasionalism and Leibniz' concept of *harmonia praestabilita*. The Council of Chalcedon worked with a paradox on this point; not only did it state that Christ had to be acknowledged in two natures "without confusion, without change" (namely of the natures), but also "without division, without separation": DS 302.

contact with the dilemmas of contemporary culture. The canon within the canon [an allusion to the primacy of Romans and Galatians] has largely stressed the *helplessness of man* and the *grace of God.* This is easily and consistently translated into *social irresponsibility* because man is helpless, and into the *centrality of Church authority* because it dispenses the grace needed by helpless man and granted by a gracious God. [. . .] Much exegesis has been informed by a decision about Christ and culture which resolved the question into a relation of *againstness*.[50]

He then proposes that the *distinctiveness* of Christian faith is not to be necessarily understood as *againstness*, and points to the royal traditions of the Old Testament with their exaltation of human power, the creation theology with its strong stress on human responsibility, and the wisdom traditions with their emphasis on human wisdom. Gregory Baum has shown that the tradition of Roman Catholic apologetics put similar emphases on "againstness" by means of an "extrinsecist" overemphasis on the authority of the Church and the divine authorship of revelation as evidenced by the historical reliability of the biblical books and the miraculous character of the Church's historical existence.[51] Faith, in this context, appears as the obedient acceptance of a heavenly message, independently of its *experienced* meaning for man and its *felt* effect on human life.

THREE CONSEQUENCES FOR CHRISTOLOGY

In Christology, the dissociation of "God" from the "matters pertaining to this life"[52] has appeared in various forms. Altizer's recent substitution of Jesus for a God who is dead[53] and van Buren's "contagious freedom of Jesus" in a world without transcendence are merely the (provisional?) extremes of a centuries-long process during which God and man were allowed to turn into competitors in church theology. A few examples of this trend will suffice.

---

[50]*Journal of the American Academy of Religion* 38 (1970) 367–380; quotation 368–369.

[51]Cf. Gregory Baum, *Man Becoming*, New York, Herder and Herder, 1970, pp. 3–8.

[52]I Cor 6, 3.

[53]Thomas J. J. Altizer, *The Gospel of Christian Atheism*, Philadelphia, The Westminster Press, 1966; Paul M. van Buren, *The Secular Meaning of the Gospel*, pp. 121ff.

Divinity and humanity not synthesized

First, there is the tendency of scholastic theology, especially of Thomist thought since Capreolus (d. 1444) and Cajetan (d. 1534), whose ideas were revived by Billot (d. 1931), to deny a formally human "act of existence" to the person of Jesus Christ.[54] A. Grillmeier, the great historian of Chalcedon, has shown more than once that Chalcedon, understood on its own terms, did not intend to construct a "Hellenistic" conception of Christ based on a "symbiosis" of two separate natures, but committed itself to the "un-Hellenistic" recognition of God's power to create for himself a truly human existence in this world, and thus, remaining fully transcendent, to be in our midst.[55] To reduce the humanity of Christ, therefore, to a mere anhypostatic human nature goes against the intentions of Chalcedon, which never meant to indulge in an effort to "salvage" Christ's divinity by reducing his humanity to a pure "nature."[56]

It is true that the theologians of the Franciscan school, Durandus de Sancto Porciano and the "modalist" school, and Suarez and his followers, so ably summarized by Philipp Kaiser, tend to do more justice to the completeness of Christ's humanity than the Thomists.[57] Yet, in their very efforts to think the unity of Christ's person they feel they must construe various types of *relationes* or *modi essendi* between divinity and humanity, all bearing witness to the assumption that "divinity" somehow needs to be harmonized with "humanity" by means of various logical mediating devices. If all these theologians can be said to have done justice to Chalcedon's "without confusion, without change," they never matched the council's boldness in juxtaposing to these adverbs two

---

[54]Felix Malmberg, *Ueber den Gottmenschen*, pp. 28–30.

[55]For example, *Christ in Christian Tradition*, Atlanta, John Knox Press, ²1975, pp. 107, 272–273, 426–428, 477–478, 555–557. Cf. also the very important study "Die altkirchliche Christologie und die moderne Hermeneutik," in: Joseph Pfammatter— Franz Furger (eds.), *Theologische Berichte I*, Zürich–Einsiedeln–Köln, Benziger Verlag, pp. 69–169, esp. 114–131.

[56]For a good explanation of *anhypostasia* and its background, cf. John McIntyre, *The Shape of Christology*, Philadelphia, The Westminster Press, 1966, pp. 86–106.

[57]Philipp Kaiser, *Die gott-menschliche Einigung in Christus als Problem der spekulativen Theologie seit der Scholastik*, München, Max Hueber Verlag (*Münchener theologische Studien*, II. Systematische Abt., Bd. 36), 1968, pp. 11–39, 80–91, 94–156.

others: "without division, without separation";[58] in the very act of inserting their *relationes* and *modi* they betray their lurking despair of ever attaining to Ignatius of Antioch's majestic synthesis:

One is the physician,
of the flesh	and	of the spirit
begotten	and	unbegotten
in man		God,
in death		the true life,
as well from Mary		as from God,
first passible		then impassible,

Jesus Christ our Lord.[59]

The earthly life of Christ de-emphasized

Second, in the very construction of traditional speculative christologies there are signs that they take the absolute transcendence of "God" for their starting point and then painfully proceed to account for the unity of Christ by either diminishing his full humanity or by inserting mediating devices to salvage the unity of Christ's person. This tendency is even more evident in their inability to do full justice to the earthly life of Jesus.[60] Kaiser concludes at the end of his survey of speculative christology since the rise of scholasticism:

> The mystery of the incarnation presents itself to this kind of theological speculation primarily in its objectivity [*An-sich-sein*], with reference to its intrinsic metaphysical constitution, and without any intrinsic constitutive connection with the data and the demands of salvation history and the messianic mission of Christ.[61]

Thus the meaning of the earthly life of Christ, both in his own life and in the earthly history of the Church, is lost sight of because there is no room for it. A fairly recent *Declaratio* of the Roman Congregation for the Doctrine of Faith bears witness to this inability to do justice to the *divine* significance of the *worldly* life of Jesus, when it says:

---

[58]DS 302.

[59]Eph 7, 2; quoted in P. Smulders, *The Fathers on Christology*, De Pere, Wisc., St. Norbert Abbey Press, 1968, p. 9, with a good discussion.

[60]Cf. Piet Schoonenberg, *The Christ*, pp. 91–175 as a significant attempt to correct this flaw in the tradition.

[61]Philipp Kaiser, *Die gott-menschliche Einigung*, p. 319.

Jesus Christ, while dwelling on this earth, manifested in various ways, by word and by deed, the adorable mystery of his person. *After* being made "obedient unto death" he was divinely exalted in his glorious resurrection, *as was fitting* for the Son "through whom all things" were made by the Father.[62]

This formula conspicuously fails to do justice to the *humanum*; it establishes a *temporal* rather than *causal* connection between Jesus' obedience in life and death and his glorification, while giving *meaning* ("fitting") to the connection between glorification and pre-existence. Paul's letter to the Philippians (". . . obedient unto death, even death on a cross. *Therefore* God has highly exalted him . . ."[63]) is toned down by omission in the interest of salvaging divine pre-existence. But is this not a sign that the Congregation's text labors under the common assumption of the culture that "God" can only be properly "God" when posited in a beyond beyond all limits, and beyond the contingencies of time and place? And is this not a sign of the *Declaratio*'s inability to transcend the limitations of the culturally conditioned conception of God?

The excessively notional character of christology
The tendency of traditional christology to let "God" and the world and man insofar as he is continuous with the world turn into competitors can yet be shown in a third way, namely, by pointing to the excessively notional character of traditional christology, a fact which a reading of Kaiser's book will abundantly establish. If the "medium is the message," then logical analysis, when excessively relied on, tends to get transferred to reality by the uncritical mind if it fails to remember what the Buddhist sage, pointing to the moon, said to his disciple: "Look at the moon.—Fool, look at the moon, don't look at my finger!" The predominantly notional approach, in other words, suggests, by its Cartesian clarity, in which the *res cogitans* is somehow associated with "God," that the *central object* of christology is unclouded serenity, divinity entirely above the vicissitudes of history. The central truth about Jesus Christ is then easily felt to be incompatible with sublunary reality, and Lessing's "acci-

---

[62]*Declaratio, AAS* 64 (1972) 237; *Origins* 1 (1972) 666.
[63]Phil 2, 8–9.

dental truths of history can never become the proof of necessary truths of reason"[64] lurks just around the corner. An excessively notional christology leads to consequences with which the cultural history of the West has been all too familiar since the mid-eighteenth century. These consequences can be best summed up by T. S. Eliot's phrase "dissociation of sensibility."

> Tennyson and Browning are poets, and they think; but they do not feel their thought as immediately as the odour of a rose. A thought to Donne was an experience; it modified his sensibility. When a poet's mind is perfectly equipped for its work, it is constantly amalgamating disparate experience; the ordinary man's experience is chaotic, irregular, fragmentary. [. . .] In the seventeenth century a dissociation of sensibility set in, from which we have never recovered; [. . .] The sentimental age began early in the eighteenth century and continued. The poets revolted against the ratiocinative, the descriptive; they thought and felt by fits, unbalanced; they reflected.[65]

The ratiocinative, the descriptive: these are precisely the two elements into which reality had been dissolved: the clear head full of clear ideas, but detached from the real world, and the world full of facts to be observed. This is the beginning of the late eighteenth-century declaration of Lessing and Reimarus that the truth of Christianity is the truth of reason, independent of history, and that the factual story of Jesus may be no more than a hoax. This dilemma—the option is between reason or fact—is matched, in the secular realm, by the clean, rational philosophy of the deists and the nature theologians on the one hand and, on the other, Linnaeus' classification-by-description of the animal and vegetable realms, the rational, purely functional division of labor in Adam Smith's pin-factory, and Rousseau's purely rational social contract.

But where is a person to go if the world has been divided up into the realm of pure reason and the realm of pure fact? What is one to do if reasoning and objective description seem to be one's only options? So when in 1763 J. G. Sulzer writes that feeling is "an

---

[64][H. S. Reimarus], *Reimarus: Fragments*, Charles H. Talbert (ed.), Philadelphia, Fortress Press, 1970, p. 31.

[65]T. S. Eliot, "The Metaphysical Poets," in: *Selected Essays*, New York, Harcourt, Brace & World, ³1950, pp. 241–250; quotation pp. 247–248.

activity of the soul, which has nothing to do with the object that causes or occasions it,"[66] he is merely stating in secular fashion what the pietists had been saying all along: that (purely immanent) feeling was the only way to Jesus. And so we get, caught in the middle, *in meines Herzens Grunde*, all the dislocated feelings of Cowper's *Olney Hymns*, of the new *Empfindsamer Stil* in symphonic music with its deliberate crescendos and decrescendos, *The Sentimental Journey*, and, last but not least, the precursors of so many twentieth-century people—the neurotics of George Cheyne's *The English Malady* (1735).

Thus Cartesian clarity left the Christian with only two options. On the one hand he could cast his religion in the mold of worldly, observable story; on the other hand he could associate himself with the *homo religiosus* of Schleiermacher. In terms of Christian theology: an excessively rational, notional christology with a great deal of emphasis on pre-existence thinking is liable to leave only two alternatives to modern man. For if "God" is too rational then the only remaining options are: the Jesus of the heart, that last refuge of identity, or the "merely human" Jesus, the ethical teacher, the revolutionary, the healer, the social worker in a wasteland world debunked by detached observation; Jesus freed from Catholic dogma, "the reflection of a Liberal Protestant face, seen at the bottom of a deep well."[67]

Solution: the conception of "God" as immanent?

It is not surprising, therefore, that there have been consistent attempts to put God back into the world again. All these attempts can be roughly characterized as consisting in an association of "God" with "the process of life" itself. Yet the type includes many variants that cannot be easily reconciled with each other. There is a great difference between the undergraduate who claims that "God" is the name for the struggle for justice or for love, and the process thinker for whom God is present in the process of "Man Becoming";[68] and the identification of "God" with the process of creative

---

[66]Quoted in: J. H. van den Berg, *Het menselijk lichaam*, Vol. II, pp. 181–182.

[67]George Tyrrell's famous phrase, quoted in: D. M. Baillie, *God Was in Christ*, New York, Charles Scribner's Sons, ²(1955), p. 40.

[68]Title of Gregory Baum's book; cf. esp. pp. 162ff.

evolution is something else again. But the protest against "extrinsecism," the refusal to locate "God" beyond some ultimate borderline, as a heavenly power or an absolute lawgiver, is something all these sets of associations have in common, while at the same time refusing to place "God" in pure interiority or subjectivity.

There is, no doubt, a great deal to be said for this approach, quite apart from its excellent credentials in the history of Christian thought. Thus, for instance, Felix Malmberg, in his difficult but very enlightening *Ueber den Gottmenschen*, has appealed to Augustine's "God has nothing for his opposite"[69] in order to elaborate a christology along Thomistic lines that does justice to the full humanity of Christ on the basis of God's involvement with the world. In a related but much more radical way Piet Schoonenberg, in *The Christ*, prefaces his christology with a long opening chapter designed to show that "God or Man" is "a false dilemma."[70]

Yet it must be said that conceptions that stress divine immanence do not very often succeed in re-establishing "God" as a viable predicate in christology. If we prescind for a moment from the extraordinary range of interpretations connected with the notion of divine immanence—a range wide enough to give this "God" a dubious significance at best—we can point to two sets of reasons.

First, the assertion that "God" is present to all human growth and reconciliation may too easily *function* as a false reassurance—a possibility that must not be underrated, if "the meaning of a word is determined by its use in the language." People for whom the stopgap, working-hypothesis God has become a symbol for their own super-ego or for the compulsions and restrictions of organized religion are liable to seek for the assurance that they "need not be so worried about God." The assurance that God is present in all human growth and reconciliation may indeed free a person from undue and unchristian anxiety, and bring a person—often for the first time—to

---

[69]Felix Malmberg, *Ueber den Gottmenschen*, p. 48.

[70]Cf. Piet Schoonenberg, *The Christ*, pp. 13ff. Mention must also be made, in this context, of Blondel's shift to the "method of immanence" to show that "God is present in the growth and reconciliation of Man" and that "there is no human standpoint from which God is simply Man's over-against" (Gregory Baum, *Man Becoming*, pp. 36, 170). Process-thinkers like Pittenger and Hartshorne, and, of course, Pierre Teilhard de Chardin must be mentioned, too, as having made significant moves away from an extrinsecist notion of God.

the kind of trust and openness that is so necessary for true faith to develop. But it may also lead to a peculiar type of laziness and unconcern, a sort of theological *accidie*, which would lead a person to say: "God is present in everything *anyway*." The doubts and worries of the troubled believer must not be cheaply assuaged, as Bonhoeffer warns in a similar context.[71]

More speculatively and theologically, to say that God is present in all human growth and reconciliation (and in all the processes of the world) is an expression of a mystery, and not a facile, reductionist sort of objectifying statement. It is "salvational knowledge," just as the acknowledgement of divine transcendence is "a salvational process by which a person is ready again and again to detect the absolutizing trend in himself and in his culture, and is willing, by a painful step, to abandon his idolatry." But if it is true that "divine transcendence cannot be accepted by a man once and for all," neither can divine immanence; and if it is true that divine transcendence is "not an idea which [a man] acquires and carries around with him,"[72] neither is divine immanence. "God is involved in history and materiality"[73] can be a statement of idolatry or of all-prevading faith, depending on the way it is used; used in the interest of a facile identification of God with "process," it turns into an automatic religious patina for everything. "I find God in everything" can be the abandonment of all faith as well as its consummation.[74]

"GOD" AND CHRISTOLOGY

A transcendental approach: Tillich and Rahner

Paul Tillich has pointed out that it is impossible to make statements about God that are not symbolic, once the most abstract and completely non-symbolic statement has been made: that God is not God if he is not being-itself. But he adds:

> Of course, religious assertions do not require such a foundation for what they say about God. *Theologians* must make explicit what is

---

[71]Dietrich Bonhoeffer, *The Cost of Discipleship*, pp. 59–60.

[72]Gregory Baum, *Man Becoming*, pp. 236–237.

[73]One of the key phrases in David E. Jenkins' *The Glory of Man*.

[74]We will come back to the conditions on which human immanence can be associated with God in chapter eleven; below, pp. 450–451.

implicit in religious thought and expression; and, in order to do this, they must begin with the most abstract and completely unsymbolic statement which is possible, namely, that God is being-itself or the absolute.[75]

It is obvious that Tillich is here making an option in favor of a particular type of theology, the type that departs from the question of God and then moves into other questions. This is a thoroughly responsible procedure, as long as it is not claimed that *the Christian faith* must also move in this way—a claim which Tillich obviously does not make. In this respect Tillich is completely within the great tradition of systematic theology. Perhaps the most monumental example of this tradition is Aquinas' *Summa*, starting, as it does, with the question of God.

Karl Rahner's theology finds itself in this tradition, too. Although he has not set it forth in a systematic way,[76] the core of his theology is his conception of the *potentia obedientialis*, the radical openness of the creature to God as constitutive of the creature as such. Rahner has systematically explicated this in a "transcendental christology" by elaborating the conception of man as that being which, in every contingent act and in every contingent object, cannot but be aware of, and choose, the incomprehensible mystery which illumines and grounds both act and object and is called God. Hence, the transcendent appears in the contingent and the historical, and man yearns for the transcendent in the contingent and the historical—that is to say, he yearns for the "absolute bringer of salvation."[77] True, the facticity of this "absolute bringer of salvation" can only be established in historical experience, and cannot be derived from transcendental christology; but a transcendental christology

---

[75]Paul Tillich, *Systematic Theology*, I, pp. 238–239 (italics added).

[76]But notice that the second article in the first volume of the *Theological Investigations* (Baltimore, Helicon Press, 1961, pp. 20–37), entitled "A Scheme for a Treatise of Dogmatic Theology," and a complete survey of the topics of Catholic theology, opens with the theme of the fundamental relationship between God and creature. Interestingly, Rahner's *Grundkurs des Glaubens* opens with an existential anthropology (*Der Hörer der Botschaft*: pp. 35–53), and only then proceeds to a discussion of "God." Cf. ET, pp. 24–43.

[77]Karl Rahner—Wilhelm Thüsing, *Christologie—systematisch und exegetisch*, Freiburg–Basel–Wien, Herder (*Quaestiones disputatae*, 55), 1972, pp. 21ff.; *Grundkurs des Glaubens*, pp. 206–211; ET, pp. 206–212.

can achieve a reflective and articulate hope for salvation, which enables the Christian to see, and, in seeking, understand, what he has already, and from the beginning, found in Jesus of Nazareth.[78]

Both Tillich and Rahner take their point of departure from man's search for God, yet for both, in the end, it is the *harmony* between the yearning of man and the fulfillment in Jesus Christ that produces the Christian notion of God[79]—albeit with distinctive differences, which can be traced back to Tillich's Protestant fear of natural theology and Rahner's Roman Catholic confidence in the hidden resources of the *natura lapsa*. They both allow for a creative interplay between the search for God and the experience of Jesus Christ.

Models, not concepts

However, this creative interplay can only take place if the *cultural* associations with "God" and "divinity" are not allowed to turn into fixations. In other words, "God" can only reliably be used if the word is used in the service of that "odd logic" which is the specific property of religious utterances. God beyond the known, God the powerful one against weak and sinful man, God in the depth of self-awareness, God the ineffable, God within the process—these are viable as symbols, as models, not as hard and frozen premises. Hence, it is dangerous to expect too much of them by making them bear the semblance of unequivocal predicates.[80] Christian theology has always been careful to avoid the trap of treating the statement "Jesus is God" as a synthetic judgment, in which a known quantity is predicated of Jesus of Nazareth. In fact, only in a culture that is (rightly or wrongly) experienced as thoroughly and unproblematically Christian can it be maintained that the human

---

[78]*Ibid.*, p. 24 (14. *Lehrsatz*).

[79]Cf. also D. M. Baillie, *God Was in Christ*, pp. 63–71.

[80]Problems analogous to the ones hinted at in these paragraphs are, of course, the subject-matter of Martin Buber's *Eclipse of God* (New York, Harper & Row, [2]1957), whose central thesis is that every religious utterance of a philosophical, literary-imaginative or psychological kind is a vain attempt at capturing the meaning attained in the encounter with God, and that efforts to construct an idea of "religion" or "God" on the basis of such utterances *divorced* from their original contexts fail to do justice to the nature of the religious act.

mind can "acquire certain knowledge of the one and true God, our creator and Lord, by way of the things that are made, with the help of natural human reason."[81] As Thüsing remarks:

> Rahner's transcendental point of departure is admittedly determined by the already given, a posteriori conception of Christology; hence it is also determined in advance by the aim that is implicitly, and legitimately so, intended.[82]

Tillich has articulated this interplay in terms of his method of correlation, which closes the "theological circle."[83] Yet, serious questions can be raised with respect to this transcendental approach, so that caution is in order. Tillich's analysis of Jesus Christ as "the New Being" has, for instance, met with the serious objection that a person cannot be reduced to a *neutrum*.

Thüsing grants Rahner that it is possible to find a basis for a transcendental approach to christology in the biblical notions of creation/salvation and history of humanity/history of election, in the notion of *pneuma* in the Bible and especially in Paul, and in the gnoseology of 1 John, in which the all-determining knowledge that God is love is inextricably tied to the fulfillment of God's self-communication in the surrender-to-death of his Son, in the gift of the Spirit, and in the love of the brethren.[84] But after this concession Thüsing enumerates a number of questions which suggest the insufficiency of the transcendental approach when compared with the data of Scripture. Does the Old Testament not hold out *more* promises than are fulfilled in Christ, the "absolute bringer of salvation"? Does the transcendental approach do justice to the dialogical relationship between God and Israel, in which the messianic promises are only dim and ambiguous when compared with the power of the conception of God as "the God of hope"? Is not the claim that "God's irreversible gift of himself can only be a human person" contingent upon an *a posteriori* christological model? Does not this claim limit

[81]DS 3026.

[82]Karl Rahner—Wilhelm Thüsing, *Christologie—systematisch und exegetisch*, p. 110.

[83]*Systematic Theology*, I, pp. 8–11, 30–31, 59–66.

[84]Karl Rahner—Wilhelm Thüsing, *Christologie—systematisch und exegetisch*, pp. 98–103.

the absolute freedom of God? Does this transcendental approach do justice to the *central* place which the scandal of Jesus' cross has in the New Testament message?[85]

Some conclusions

   If the Christian notion of God is the result of an interplay between a transcendental analysis of "The Eternal in Man"[86] and the *a posteriori* data that are constituted by "the things concerning Jesus," then there is room for *judgment.* In other words: if Christianity is more than an inquiry into the nature of God, more than a way of life to promote contact with the transcendent, and if this "more" has something to do with the factual appearance of the historical Jesus and the continued appeal to him in the history of the historical Church, then the Christian notion of God is not just made up of *theōria,* but has a *practical* component. This practical component must be allowed to have full scope if some very serious consequences are to be avoided.

   First, dogma will suffer from an over-concentration on the truth-aspects of the faith, with undesirable overtones of immutability, verbal orthodoxy, and irrelevance in the face of cultural shifts. One of the criteria of good theology is *helpfulness,* just as the solution of the problem raised by the availability of meat offered to idols was solved by Paul, not just by a "transcendental" appeal to the fact that "we *know* that 'an idol has no real existence,' and that 'there is no God but one,' "[87] but also by means of an appeal to *agapē.* If this procedure might seem to put Christian theology on a lower level of excellence than many of the more "ideological" philosophies (*perennis* or otherwise) and human sciences, it might be good to remember that Christian theology can hardly hope, even in its method, to have the dubious privilege of avoiding confrontation with the scandal of the Incarnation. This kind of humility of Christian theology may, incidentally, prove to have a strong appeal to the modern scientist, who has developed a strong taste for modesty in

---

[85]*Ibid.*, pp. 104–111. For Rahner and Tillich, cf. below, pp. 217–226.
   [86]With a bow to Max Scheler's *Vom Ewigen im Menschen* (*Gesammelte Werke,* Bern und München, Francke Verlag, Bd. 5).
   [87]1 Cor 8, 4.

the fact of the data, and who is less liable to ideologize than were his nineteenth-century predecessors.

Second, the under-emphasis on the historical Jesus and the concreteness of salvation enacted in the "matters pertaining to this life,"[88] which is the most notable limitation of christology in the Chalcedonian tradition, may be rectified.

Third, for all the emphasis on the mystery of God, the cultural debate about God has tended to present God in a variety of "frozen" forms, in a variety of particular "places." If these approaches to God are to be unfrozen so that they can become symbols again and, consequently, gain relevance to real life, the services of christology are indispensable. This is especially true in view of the fact that the cultural overtones of the conceptions of God exhibit features that make "God" and "world and man insofar as he is continuous with the world" mutually exclusive.

Fourth, the fact that the question of God has increasingly become a *debate* about God makes the concentration of the theological effort on a theology of Jesus Christ imperative. Debates tend to harden positions instead of reconciling them, while at the same time the dubiousness of the positions taken tends to go unnoticed. The "conservative" over-concern with the explicit affirmation of Jesus Christ's "divinity" and the "liberal" over-concern with christology without explicit mention of God are both in need of healing.

Fifth, a salutary warning comes to us from Karl Rahner. He has insisted on the need for a transcendental reflection on the human predicament, in order to show that the traditional statements of christological doctrine are graciously consonant with the deepest aspirations of human nature, and not just historical judgments enhanced by means of vulgar mythologizing.[89] In this way, christological statements can be understood as true statements of *faith* and be told

---

[88] 1 Cor 6, 3.

[89] Karl Rahner—Wilhelm Thüsing, *Christologie—systematisch und exegetisch*, p. 20 (9. *Lehrsatz*): "[The absence of transcendental christology] in traditional theology creates the danger that the statements of traditional christology are taken to be no more than mythological (in the vulgar sense of the word) involutions (*Ueberhöhungen*) of historical events, or, as the case may be, [it creates the danger] that there will be no available criterion to tell the difference, in traditional christology, between true faith-reality and the kind of interpretation which is no longer capable, today, of conveying the meaning of the faith."

apart from time-determined faith-interpretations. In this book we propose, at first, to be a little bit more hesitant in making christological statements than the great tradition has been, confident that the use of "God" and "divinity" are not the sole warrants for orthodoxy. In fact, we will argue, in the next chapter, that the *style* of a renewed christology will have to be practical, i.e., it will have to pay attention to christological rhetoric and rely less on notional adequacy. But this exposes us to the risk signaled by Rahner. Suggestive understatements about Jesus may sound very relevant, and so they may be more eagerly taken for granted as conclusive, according as their incompleteness is less easily detected. "Jesus-theology," in other words, may turn into just another form of vulgar mythologizing; it may amount to little more than our cultural judgments writ large.

Still, the risks of provisionality must be taken. Hence, this book is predicated on the *judgment* that in the present situation we have, practically speaking, more to expect from christology in order to gain a Christian conception of God, than from "God-talk" in order to gain a notion of who Jesus Christ is.

CHAPTER 2

From Logic to Rhetoric

They say the Spiritual is best conceived
in abstract terms
          and then too
walking around in museums always makes me
          want to
                    'sit down'
          I always feel so
                              constipated
     in those
               high altitudes

Lawrence Ferlinghetti

come, poor Jackself, I do advise
You, jaded, let be; call off thoughts awhile
Elsewhere; leave comfort root-room; let joy size

At God knows when to God knows what; whose smile
's not wrung, see you

Gerard Manley Hopkins

Everything that is said is said for a reason, and so the meaning of what
is said must be determined with reference to the speaker's intentions.

Hilary of Tours

Dialogue is what people do to each other.

Virginia Woolf

Some fundamental assumptions about language

The first chapter was not a plea in favor of dropping the predicates "God" and "divinity" altogether in christology. A ban on these words would be as foolish as it would be to insist that *only* "God" and "divinity" are capable of signifying the truth. More importantly, however, both would amount to usurping lordship over language—a futile enterprise at best. But the first chapter did recommend that we stop expecting "God" and "divinity" in christology to have infallible illuminating force, and therefore that we stop treating "God" and "divinity" as the shibboleths of orthodoxy.

Underlying this thesis are some fundamental assumptions whose consequences will be explored and applied in this chapter. They are the following. First, truth is not tied down to *concepts*, but can be—and mostly is—found in *meanings*. Second, meaning is a function, not primarily of terms, but of *words*. Third, the meaning (or "point") of a *sentence as spoken* exceeds the meanings of the words.[1] It will be the task of this chapter to elaborate, in a variety of ways, the reasons for these assumptions as well as their consequences, and thus pave the way for a less notional approach to christology.

We will tackle this task in two rounds. The first round will consist of the first two sections of this chapter. They will describe, in a general way, what happens when the meanings of words or statements become the focal point of attention and discussion, at the expense of their non-cognitive aspects. The description will largely rely on a review of some authors; we will make some tentative suggestions about the applicability of their insights to christology. The second round will consist in a more thorough exploration of the

---

[1] Cf. Georges Gusdorf, *Speaking* ["*La parole*"], Paul T. Brockelman (trans. and intro.), [Chicago], Northwestern University Press, 1965, pp. 85–86: "Thus a sound exegesis must not be content to consider a man's every word, to somehow reduce his words to a single plane. One must carry out a kind of study in relief. It must be a study in which the statement each time takes on form and life according to the degree of personal commitment of the man who is speaking, according to the reciprocity of the encounter and according to the meaning of the moment. The apparent meaning of the speech gives way to its personal value. Besides, such an evaluation can only be carried out by those in whom the very sense of the situation is in some way restored. The extreme speech of a crisis only takes on its full meaning in a compl[e]mentary critical situation. All true understanding is itself an accomplishment. The hero speaks to heroes, the poet to poets, and the appeal of the saint is only effective if it releases in us a dormant possibility of saintliness."

limitations of conceptualization, followed by a reasoned plea in favor of a return to a less narrow view of the language-range. The chapter will close with an affirmation of the priority of language as activity, intersubjectivity and rhetoric over language as cognition, objectification, and logic.

It may be useful to place a caution at the beginning of this chapter. It may seem, at times, that this chapter is a statement of a complete theory of language, though in an extremely narrow compass. This is not so. It is a presentation of a select number of coherent arguments aimed at clarifying the main point, which is the affirmation mentioned in the previous paragraph. This affirmation will find a variety of applications in the course of the book, and must therefore be properly understood. It is true, however, that the arguments proposed *are* borrowed from, and consistent with, a far more comprehensive theory of language which must remain unstated; the footnotes refer the interested reader to the sources of this theory. In view of all this, it is suggested that the reader should focus on the particular arguments rather than try to guess the system out of which the arguments flow; in this way he will be best prepared to follow the remainder of the book.

THE CONCEPTUAL IMPASSE

Walter Ong on conceptualization

Walter Ong has identified and analyzed, in a variety of publications, an important shift to logic, analysis, and concepts in the mid-sixteenth century's conception of the nature of knowledge. Now the middle of the sixteenth century was also when Vesalius' dissecting knife produced a totally new brand of professional, visualized anatomy, and the analogy between what happened in the *theatrum autopsiae* and the classroom is striking.[2] Until then, rhetoric had

---

[2] It is tempting here to elaborate the thesis that the mid-sixteenth century shows a variety of moves in the direction of visualization and objectification. J. H. van den Berg's *Metabletica van de materie*, Vol. I, Meetkundige beschouwingen, Nijkerk, G. F. Callenbach. N.V., 1969, pp. 303–319, mentions the following: the increasing popularity of the rules of perspective in pictorial art, illustrated by Albrecht Dürer's *Unterweisung der Messung*, and by Giorgio Vasari's enthusiasm, in his *Vite*, for the optical illusions created by it, and the theories of perception of Melanchton and Juan

reigned supreme; the active knowledgeable discussion of important topics was carried on with the help of collections of authoritative *sententiae.* Now, beginning with Petrus Ramus, rhetoric is replaced by *analysis* as a device for finding "matter" for discourse; the spoken dialogue is replaced by silent reading of printed texts; curricula and systems replace the ongoing process of learning; knowledge becomes what is "contained" in the mind as it is "contained" in books, rather than the intelligent traffic of ideas (not necessarily concepts!) among persons; the classroom ("formal education"!) becomes the focus of learning; hearing is replaced by seeing; finally, concentration on words becomes the substitute for concentration on meaning by a process of "reification of the word for intellectual purposes."[3]

Ong compares the intellectual process to which language was subjected to the phenomenon of the mass-production of books made possible by the printing-press. The merchants made verbal expression into a commodity—an object that could be handled, bought and sold; the logicians wanted "to hypostatize expression so as to subject it to formal analysis." In this way, words and statements born out of intelligent human communication are frozen and thus made into objects for the purposes of logical analysis; this in turn leads to the situation in which words are no longer considered as words, that is, as "functional units used in such and such a way in the linguistic system of such a time,"[4] but as concepts to be studied in and by themselves. Hypostatizing and the reduction of words to concepts— these are the phenomena James Barr has criticized.

James Barr on hypostatization

Barr objects to what may be called false hypostatization. This

---

Luis Vives, who teach that the senses, and ultimately the mind, are nothing but receptacles of objective reality. To this it would be possible to add Cajetan's "naturalization of the soul, or the human being"—de Lubac's characterization of the purely objectivist application of the Aristotelian notion of nature to human reality; as a result human nature is declared a closed system, in the interest of circumscriptive definition: Henri de Lubac, *The Mystery of the Supernatural,* New York, Herder and Herder, 1967, *passim,* but esp. pp. 32–33, 36–39, 86–87, 122–123, 181–216.

[3]Cf. Walter J. Ong, *Rhetoric, Romance and Technology,* pp. 142–189, esp. pp. 160–164, 174–175, 182–183. The chapter on Swift (pp. 190–212) is a brilliant exploration of the consequences of the mechanization of understanding. Cf. also Walter J. Ong, S.J., *The Barbarian Within,* New York, The Macmillan Company, 1962, pp. 69–77.

[4]James Barr, *Biblical Words for Time,* London, SCM Press, 1962, p. 58.

consists in ascribing to a *word* characteristics that cause it to bear the semblance of something real in its own right—which is inconsistent with its actual linguistic function in contexts.[5] Often this process starts with a thoroughly legitimate hypostatization, for example, when a theologian talks about "the word *hayah*" in order to describe its semantic range. But when he then goes on to say things like: "It is God's *hayah* to come forward and act as God,"[6] or to speak of "the dynamic aspect of *qahal*," or "the eschatological aspect of *ekklēsia*," he is smuggling in the assumption that the *word* as such, the lexical element, contains, in a mysterious yet thoroughly objective way, the "true" or "real" *theological* meaning of *hayah*, *qahal*, and *ekklēsia*— a meaning which "to be," "assembly," and "church" cannot hope to contain. The latter part of this sentence is obviously true; the problem is that *hayah* as a word has no more ability than "to be" to contain the "real meaning," since that real meaning is conveyed in sentences addressed by persons to other persons, and not contained in words acting like capsules full of meaning to be stored in "the mind."

In Barr's thought, false hypostatization is very often the result of what he calls the "concept method" in theology,[7] which consists in "the habit of saying 'concept' for the reality we would normally call a 'word,' "[8] which in turn leads to "mishandling of linguistic facts," as when "the words and sentences of the New Testament" are said (by Kittel) to "*cease to exist for themselves* and become, as it were, vessels of transparent crystal which have one sole purpose, that of making their *contents* visible"[9]—as if it were the natural thing for a word or a sentence to exist for itself, and as if words—or even sentences—essentially *contain* meaning!

Barr's analyses are confirmed and put in a wider perspective by the linguist J. Verhaar. After endorsing Barr's complaint that "even prominent Scripture scholars will treat biblical semantics as if there we are concerned with *terms*, or *concepts*, instead of with *words*, and

---

[5] Cf. James Barr, "Hypostatization of Linguistic Phenomena," *Journal of Semitic Studies* 7 (1962) 85–94.

[6] James Barr, *The Semantics of Biblical Language*, p. 71.

[7] *Id.*, *Biblical Words for Time*, pp. 50–58.

[8] *Ibid.*, p. 51.

[9] *Id.*, *The Semantics of Biblical Language*, p. 212 (italics added).

their *meanings,*" he goes on to point to the same problem in theology.

> In the Western sense of concepts as hypostatized meanings, the Bible has no concepts. [. . .] If this is already [insufficiently realized] among exegetes, what about those going in for "systematic theology"? Occasionally one wonders how many of their ideas are, in discouraging anachronism, and unbeknownst to those proclaiming them, still the "ideas" of Plato, pseudo-realities‚ of crypto-sacred status to which reality as we know it is supposed to submit in humble participation.[10]

False hypostatization and the concept method, therefore, lead to the kind of dominance of established concepts that diminishes the user's ability to take a fresh look at reality and to deal with others in a meaningful fashion. This bears closer analysis.

J. Verhaar on derealization

Toward the end of his book *Some Relations Between Perception, Speech, and Thought,* Verhaar gives a penetrating analysis of what happens when the process of conceptualization, which normally serves to stabilize perception, speech, and especially thought in the interest of rational discourse, is pushed to its extreme. Verhaar describes the result as "derealization,"[11] a process bearing an astonishing resemblance to the christological discussions that make the words "God" and "divinity" into shibboleths of orthodoxy.

Language *is* capable of rationality; words *are* vehicles of thought. But this very capability of language harbors in itself the risk of disintegration—a risk that increases according as language is further removed from everyday speech. Verhaar points out that terms are especially prone to this; they are in continuous danger of "isolation," i.e., lack of contact with the world in which our experience evolves. This isolation occurs when the word—or, rather, the word used as term—is allowed to demand so much attention for itself that "overhypostatization" occurs. This in turn causes the term to atrophy into an obstacle to living thought in close touch with

---

[10]J. Verhaar, "Language and Theological Method," pp. 28–29; cf. pp. 25–26; *Bijdragen,* pp. 65, 61–62.

[11]J. Verhaar, *Some Relations,* pp. 148–154; cf. pp. 30–33.

reality and with others. Thus, language runs in and of itself "the quite positive risk of falling back on its own words."[12]

> Language suffers from overhypostatization [. . .]. The word objectifies and it can only be looked upon as doing this to a too large extent if and when the word is too much considered (rather: experienced) in its own right.[13]

Following Brice Parain, Verhaar puts language thus experienced in the context of *freedom*; language so run to seed becomes *un personnage gênant*, breathing down our necks, in our contact with the world. It causes me to be part of the whole of being and yet divorces me from it. The word/idea in this experience possesses, deceptively, the limpid transparency of an idea and yet it has the impenetrability of the thing; meant to serve the dynamism of our thought, it takes revenge on us by behaving with the inertia of things. We are responsible for our words, since we speak; yet we are wholly innocent because we do not know what we are saying.[14]

Overhypostatization of words leads to incapacity to think; words degenerate into sounds and labels, and they are no longer capable of handling perception, which disintegrates into a stream of impressions. What was meant to be a tool of rational discourse with some measured distance from the flux of reality perceived and named and articulated at close quarters becomes a meaningless set of isolated *flatus vocis* that have lost connection not only with thought and with the speech-making community of shared meaning, but also with mundane reality.

Some applications to christology

It is probably an overstatement to say that such is the situation today in the discussions of classical christology, and especially in the discussions about Christ's "divine nature." Still there is enough analogy to warrant a few comparisons. There is, for example, the one-sided emphasis on the authority of the traditional christology,

---

[12]*Ibid.*, pp. 63–64, 148–149.

[13]*Ibid.*, p. 153. "Overhypostatization" is very close to Barr's "false hypostatization."

[14]*Ibid.*, pp. 149–150, 154.

which serves to enhance the sense of futility which many Christians—including theologians—experience when trying to extricate themselves from the compulsive preoccupation with speculations about the hypostatic union of the two natures in the one person of Jesus Christ. There is, in many quarters, a clear lack of *experienced freedom* of thought when it comes to framing alternative articulations of christology that are more in touch with the world in which our experience evolves[15]—the world in which the life and death of Jesus as well as the lives and deaths of Christians are enacted. The hypostatized use of "nature," "humanity," and "divinity" tends to draw all attention to these terms, so that the *realities* of "divine nature" and "human nature," once *conceptually* isolated, can never be thought together again except in very notional ways, which do not cease to act as neuralgic irritants, even when the mind manages to satisfy itself that it grasps the solution to the problem. One wonders, for example, if A. Hulsbosch's attempts to revise the diphysitic structure of christology, for all their nobility of purpose, do not remain secretly haunted by the same concept of "nature" that haunts the staunch defenders of neo-Chalcedonian diphysitism.[16]

Elsewhere, it is the hypostatized use of "person" that is striking. Schoonenberg firmly opts for the modern *usage*, well aware of the different pre-scholastic and scholastic traditions in this regard;[17] he is equally aware that his proposal not to use "person" for the pre-existent Word and for the *Dynamis* which is the Holy Spirit goes against the *terminology* of most of the tradition, but substantively speaking has excellent credentials from Justin Martyr on. Yet, typically, one rejection of his proposal takes the form of yet another explanation of what *person* "really means," namely, "*être relationnel*."[18] On top of that, a doctrinal declaration from Rome

---

[15]Cf. J. Galot, *La personne du Christ*, Gembloux–Paris, Duculot–Lethellieux, 1969, which opens with the thesis that Chalcedon is not an obstacle to freedom, but a basic point of departure, and then goes on to tie truth down to the terms allegedly necessitated by Chalcedon.

[16]A. Hulsbosch, "Jezus Christus, gekend als mens, beleden als Zoon Gods," *Tijdschrift voor theologie* 6 (1966) 250–273. Cf. Robert North, *In Search of the Human Jesus*, New York–Cleveland, Corpus Books, 1970.

[17]Piet Schoonenberg, *The Christ*, pp. 66–75. Cf. D. M. Baillie, *God Was in Christ*, p. 91, for a proposal to use "person" and *persona* side by side, with different meanings.

[18]J. Galot, *La personne du Christ*—a clear case of a book soundly arguing that

states that Schoonenberg cannot possibly *mean*—because he has changed *terms*—what the New Testament and the Fathers of Chalcedon meant.[19]

And so we have the Laputan spectacle of theologians engaging in debates which they claim are about the true faith, but which in reality are about the meaning of *terms*, because the participants are insufficiently aware of how language actually functions. And the question arises: What is "contained" in these terms that so debilitatingly assert themselves? If it cannot be the truth that is contained, it must be the participants in the debate themselves who, in the eyes of many puzzled Christians, have become the prisoners of their concepts. The language of christology has become *un personnage gênant.*

This diagnosis may sound excessively pessimistic and anti-intellectual. But Hulsbosch, Schillebeeckx, and Schoonenberg have at least clearly recognized the urgent pastoral necessity of a restatement of christology.[20] That the need is real is, perhaps, most poignantly borne out by the fact that the two-nature doctrine strikes many Christians as an improbable rational construction, and so they simplify it into the kind of cryptogamous monophysitism that makes Jesus Christ into a less than completely human individual, or into the kind of monophysitism that makes him "purely human." It is, incidentally, striking that this latter expression would never be used with regard to any man or woman alive; "purely human" owes its existence to a christological, dogmatic concern—a need to insist on Christ's humanity. This is done by means of an implicit rejection of his "divinity"; but the question is: What kind of divinity is rejected? And is that rejected divinity a known quantity? It is certainly good Christian doctrine to reject the kind of "divinity" in Jesus Christ that would be an *additional* quality, over and above his humanity, or a "divinity" that would diminish his full humanity. Or if (often the same) people say that Jesus Christ "was divine" (note the past

---

"relational being" is at the heart of human existence, but wrongly tying this conception down to "person." Cf. also *id., Vers une nouvelle christologie,* Gembloux–Paris, Duculot–Lethellieux, 1971, p. 109, where Chalcedon and the Johannine "I am" are alleged to reject the definition of "person" by means of consciousness and freedom.

[19] *Declaratio, AAS* 64 (1972) 237–241; *Origins* 1 (1972) 666–668, section 3.

[20] A. Hulsbosch, E. Schillebeeckx, P. Schoonenberg, "Gods heilspresentie in de mens Jezus Christus," *Tijdschrift voor theologie* 6 (1966) 249–306. Cf. Robert North, *In Search of the Human Jesus.*

tense!), they will add, in explanation, that he was divine in virtue of God's indwelling in his soul, just as God is present in each person. One could go on like this, the debate would again be endless, the hypostatic union and the "Christian concept of God" would once again be explained, and "christological derealization" would once again lurk around the corner.

The fallacy at the root of this problem is that the real meaning of a statement is assumed to be directly dependent on the definable meaning of *terms*. But if "real meaning" is only attributed to terms/concepts (e.g., "man," "God"), then it is implied that language does not come into its own until it has been made univocal, unambiguous, and as totally denotative as possible. This implied thesis can be expressed in a different way: language becomes more geared to the *truth* according as the elements of dialogue and persuasion (the old *dialectica* and *rhetorica*) recede into the furthest possible background.

In theology this thesis leads to the impasse of "fideistic orthodoxy": the orthodoxy is in the clear-cut dogmatic statements (which in reality are devoid of living meaning), and the act of faith becomes increasingly an irrational, fideistic *sacrificium intellectus* allegedly demanded by the "divine" authority of, say, the officially interpreted conciliar tradition or of Scripture literally understood. Without denying that there is a *sacrificium intellectus* in faith, one should deny that *sacrificium intellectus* obliges the mind to stretch itself out on a conceptual bed of nails. Thought and meaning do occur outside the realm of strict conceptual, terminological rationality.

THE NON-COGNITIVE ELEMENTS

The need for useful, salvational knowledge

The first chapter made a case for the discretionary judgment that in the present situation God-talk has more to expect from christology than christology has from a further exploration of the meaning of "God" and "divinity." The case was mainly based on the observation that the cultural meaning of "God" and "divinity" is predicated on the next to total separation of "God" and the world and man insofar as he is homogeneous with the world, which circumstance robs "God" and "divinity" of their effective illuminating force when used in christology.

The first section of this chapter has added another consideration: the *style of thought* which both christology and God-talk have been associated with is so strongly characterized by conceptualism that both in the interest of pastoral concerns and for the sake of all-round theological method, a christology must be attempted that is less dependent on the diphysitic model with its tendency to be understood in terms of the two mutually exclusive *concepts* of "God" and "man and world." Again, it must be emphasized that, for all its *truth*, the tradition of two-nature christology owes its inability to account for the full significance of the *humanum* in Jesus Christ as well as its inability to function as a message of salvation, to the conceptualism of its *vehicle*; the medium—with all its terminological associations—conveys a message that is at odds with the message it purports to convey. The same can be said for the debate about God; it, too, owes far too great a debt to the rational style of inquiry that precipitated it. Both classical christology in its scholastic and neo-scholastic forms and the debate about God have come to be carried on in the atmosphere of the Cartesian split, in which procrustean terminological rigor *more mathematico* has been mistaken for thought, and in which there is no room for the kind of knowledge which Eliade called "useful," and Baum "salvational"—the kind of knowledge in virtue of which a person's life "becomes, and remains, a fully human, responsible, and significant life."[21]

At this point it is imperative to realize an important point. We often hear the claim made that "we just want to know what those words mean," the implication being that the entire meaning of the statement can be discovered by a thorough consideration of it. This claim is false. The entire meaning was given in the direct lingual experience of making the statement. When we stop the flow of events and then look at what was said and consider its meaning, the statement becomes an object—it gets hypostatized.[22] If this consideration of meaning gets pushed far enough (let us say, to the point where *logical* analysis is presumed to be the only tool that will yield insight into meaning) the ordinary statement is hypostatized to the

---

[21]Mircea Eliade, *Myth and Reality*, p. 125; Gregory Baum, *Man Becoming*, p. 237.

[22]Cf. J. Verhaar, "Language and Theological Method," p. 15; *Bijdragen*, p. 51.

point where it turns into a linguistic entity that has all the character-istics of the term/concept; in the transition from direct experience to consideration of meaning the total meaning of the "statement"—even of the "ordinary statement"—has been lost sight of in the interest of detached, purely denotative, factual "meaning," here viewed as "contained in" the statement, and not co-dependent on the actual use in the situation and the speaker's intentions.

It is clear that the impasses produced by terminological myopia and by the purely logical-analytic approach to "ordinary language" just discussed imply the same hypothesis, namely, that purely deno-tative language-use is the comprehensive and normative model of all language-use. Terminological language is *designed* to be as exclu-sively denotative as possible; "ordinary language" is *reduced* to purely denotative language by the logical-analytic approach.

If it is further realized that religious language can never be reduced to pure denotation, it becomes intelligible that J. Verhaar should have argued that there is a disguised metaphysic in logical empiricism, namely, that the non-religious statement is the compre-hensive model of all meaningful discourse.[23] For this reason we must make efforts to explore the non-cognitive elements in language; only in this way will we be able to carry out our task of setting up a christology that is less notional. A brief characterization of the works of Ian Ramsey and Donald Evans will serve as an introduction.

Ian Ramsey on disclosure and models

For Ian T. Ramsey religious statements are only then ade-quately understood when they are seen as statements that are signifi-cant in terms of "disclosure."[24] In this regard religious statements are not unique; there are many non-religious assertions whose meaning is only realized in a disclosure, when "the penny drops," "the ice breaks," "the light dawns." From the outset, religious statements are expressive of commitment as well as discernment:[25] they mean to

---

[23] *Ibid.*

[24] Ian Ramsey, *Religious Language*, esp. pp. 11–48.

[25] Ramsey's recognition of discernment is the critical point of improvement over R. M. Hare's purely subjective *blik*; cf. Antony Flew, R. M. Hare, Basil Mitchell, "Theology and Falsification," in: Antony Flew, Alasdair MacIntyre (eds.), *New Essays in Philosophical Theology*, New York, The Macmillan Company, [2]1964, pp. 96–108.

convey a total commitment as well as a particular, fuller interpretation of reality. Hence, religious language must exhibit a "suitably odd" logic, if it is to evoke the appropriate kind of situation; it must be "object language and more."[26]

This means that in the religious situation the language associated with objects is used for the purposes of disclosure; the object is used as a model (for example, "cause," "goodness"), whose function it is *at once* to found the theological story in empirical fact *and* to carry the hearer beyond empirical fact. In many cases the latter function of the model is enhanced by a "qualifier" (for example, "first," "infinite"), which develops the theological story to the point where the typically religious situation is evoked. In the discernment/commitment prompted by that religious disclosure, the qualified model is placed in a position of pre-eminence; it comes to preside over a whole universe of discourse.[27]

In *Models and Mystery*, Ramsey explores two kinds of models. The "picturing model" is used as if it were a pictorial representation of reality; the "disclosure model" relates two different contexts in virtue of their structural analogy, which evokes the insight proper to the disclosure situation. Ramsey shows that picturing models have only limited use in theology as well as in science, mainly on account of the distortion caused by the change of scale inherent in picturing models. Disclosure models are the main expedient of clarification, for they have the advantage of not claiming that our knowledge of a reality is an absolutely true and congruent picture of that reality in our minds, let alone in the words we use.

Ramsey's analyses suggest that, whatever conceptualizations theology may use, they must never be allowed to turn into hard and fast containers of "the truth." Unless they are used as *models* whose capacity for disclosure and insight resides primarily in their ability to "echo and chime in with" the phenomena,[28] they easily lend themselves

---

[26]Ian Ramsey, *Religious Language*, p. 38.

[27]*Ibid.*, pp. 49–89, esp. 66–71.

[28]Notice that these expressions, used frequently by Ramsey to characterize the consonance (!) between model and reality—the quality that makes the model tick (!)—are acoustical, not visual images; cf., e.g., *Models and Mystery*, p. 12. For the connections between knowing and seeing, and between trusting and hearing, cf. chapter seven; below, pp. 274–286.

to misunderstanding. Such misunderstanding occurs when conclusions are drawn from a model without somehow keeping in mind that it is a model. This means that we cannot "read off discourse from it without let or hindrance," since it always remains to be seen "*which* development inferences are *reliable.*"[29] Hence, only through a variety of disclosure models is reality done justice to; this implies that different communities (including different communities of Christians) may have different *key* concepts, different *dominant* models. "What we have to learn is that there is no single inward track to mystery, and no single outward road from the infinite."[30]

Ramsey's theories are important for the present discussion in more than one respect. First, christological terminology remains healthy if it is remembered that its basic function is not to present a pictorially adequate representation of the truth, but, in a systematized way, to help evoke the religious disclosure. "No model will ever 'explain' or 'describe' that which its use evokes"[31]—that is to say, no model is denotatively adequate.

Second, *every* model, including the Chalcedonian one, and, we will argue, especially the neo-Chalcedonian one, has limited effective illuminating force. If this is not realized, the "passionate desire to understand" can turn into a compulsive preoccupation with one model,[32] in which the user of the model turns into its slave. Then it is time to turn to other models, which will make up for the inadequacy of the first. What keeps models from becoming opaque is *our experience* of their ability to disclose the mystery.

Third, and most importantly, it is *not just the concept* that does justice to reality, but also *the dynamic process of disclosure* in the service of which the concept is *used.* Hence, the adequacy of the concept must be determined, not only by testing its "internal reference,"[33] but also by testing its ability to help its user relate to reality. Hence, "extra-conceptual" elements, such as a model's *de facto* ability to precipitate the disclosure, enter into the determination of the concept's ability to further understanding.

---

[29]Ian Ramsey, *Models and Mystery*, p. 59.
[30]*Ibid.*, p. 65.
[31]*Id.*, *Religious Language*, p. 168.
[32]Cf. *ibid.*, p. 170.
[33]Cf. J. Verhaar, "Language and Theological Method," p. 22; *Bijdragen*, p. 58.

Donald Evans on self-involvement

Ramsey's analyses concentrate mainly on those characteristics of religious language which, by their "suitably odd logic," serve to bridge the logical gap between a model and the mysterious reality it points to, thus establishing the disclosure situation with its attendant discernment and commitment. Although not neglected by Ramsey, the characteristics of "self-involvement" on the part of the *speaker* have been analyzed in great and somewhat laborious detail by Evans. His *Logic of Self-Involvement*, born out of concerns similar to those that gave rise to Ramsey's writings, offers the rudiments of a logic that would enable us "to classify with precision the various ways in which language may involve a speaker in something more than a bare assent to facts."[34]

To achieve this, Evans takes J. L. Austin's analysis of "performative" language for his point of departure:[35] there are expressions in which "in saying what I do I *perform* a speech-act of a certain kind."[36] This performative element is often explicit, as in: "I promise to do it." It may, however, be left unexpressed; yet the fact that it is unexpressed in so many words does not mean that it is absent. Thus Evans explains:

> Older logics deal with propositions (statements, assertions); that is, they deal with relations between terms of propositions. Modern biblical theology, however, emphasizes non-propositional language, both in its account of divine revelation (God's "word" to man) and in its account of human religious language (man's word to God). In each case the language or "word" is not (or is not merely) propositional; it is primarily a self-involving activity, divine or human. God does not (or does not merely) provide supernatural information concerning Himself, expressed in flat statements of fact; He "addresses" man in an "event" or "deed" which commits Him to man and which expresses His inner Self. Similarly man does not (or does not merely) assert certain facts about God; he addresses God in the activity of worship, committing himself to God and expressing his attitude to God. In so far as God's self-revelation is a self-involving activity ("His Word is claim and

---

[34]Donald D. Evans, *The Logic of Self-Involvement*, p. 14.

[35]J. A. Appleyard, S.J. has successfully applied Austin's theory to sacramental theology: "How Does a Sacrament 'Cause by Signifying'?" *Science et Esprit* 23 (1971) 167–200.

[36]Donald D. Evans, *The Logic of Self-Involvement*, p. 28.

promise, gift and demand") and man's religious language is also a self-involving verbal activity ("obedient, thankful confession and prayer"), theology needs an outline of the various ways in which language is self-involving—and, more generally, an outline of the various ways in which language is an activity.[37]

The entire first part of Evans' book is devoted to an analysis of expressions of activity, commitment, feeling and attitude. Under the rubric of attitude he treats "onlooks," by which he means all statements that can be reduced to the scheme: "to look on x as y."[38] We will have occasion to make special use of Evans' valuable analyses and conclusions in the area of onlooks.

SOME LIMITATIONS OF CONCEPTUALIZATION

The considerable acumen involved in the analyses of Ong, Barr, Verhaar, Ramsey and Evans raises the question of why such a monumental clyster was needed to relieve the notionalist's constipation. Several points are needed here to clarify the issue as well as to lend background to the humbling realization that considerable intelligence was needed to prove and authenticate the obvious, namely that language is more than terms, and christology more than terminologically coherent orthodoxy. Once we have explored this, the way will be open to a definition of what we call rhetoric.

Implicit assumptions the cause of the ambiguity of terms
    To start with an observation of Verhaar's, conceptualized thinking is self-supporting; definition takes place increasingly by *internal reference*, as objectifying systematization and the degree of reflexivization grow. But this only appears so. In fact, the ambiguity and vagueness of natural language "now comes in through the back door, dragging along a number of implicit assumptions not always easily detected."[39] The disclosure-evoking and self-involving elements, which are so prominent in natural language, can never be

---

[37]*Ibid.*, pp. 14–15.
[38]*Ibid.*, pp. 124–141.
[39]Cf. again J. Verhaar, "Language and Theological Method," p. 22; *Bijdragen.* p. 58.

completely excluded, no matter how overriding the interest in stable rationality. Thus, the *illusion* that terminology is completely rational allows the non-conceptual elements to reassert themselves in uncontrolled ways, which makes it hard to identify and accept them. A case in point is the highly technical and terminological statement about nutritional value on the breakfast cereal package and about engine cleaning and performance ingredients in gasoline at the filling station; the information may be factually true, but the way the statement *functions* has more to do with incantation than with technical information. The irrational gnostic myth ("Science and expertise know what is good for you!") is hard to unmask in the teeth of such clean and rational statements of the "truth."

The crypto-sacred status of terminology

Hidden persuasion is not the only hazard. A second persistent temptation, hidden in the process of reflexivization, is the tendency to attribute to second-order reflection a special "crypto-religious" status.[40] Religion and conceptualization start as friends, until conceptualization advances claims that make the partnership superfluous. Verhaar arrives at the same conclusion after a brief survey of the pedigree of second-order reflection, in which he states that it was the (largely implicit) identification of the soul, the intellectual, and the divine that caused some superior status to be claimed on behalf of the process of conceptualization itself. The preoccupation with systematization, moreover, lent to "reduplicative thinking" certain totalitarian features. Thus, the *philosophia perennis* was to be all-encompassing, and valid for all people of all cultures.

But the assumption that somehow associates reflection, purification of the soul, and enlightenment tends to *function* as a gnostic myth, which attributes a pseudo-sacred status to conceptualization in and of itself. Under such a set of assumptions, the extra-conceptual elements become things that thought has to be purified of in the name of superior wisdom. Faith, historical probability, persuasion, personal commitment and so many other elements of life are now liable to find themselves dragged before the Sacred Tribunal of Reason and found guilty.

---

[40]*Ibid.*, pp. 9–12; *Bijdragen*, pp. 45–48.

Precision not always helpful

But even if such obvious crypto-religious bedevilments are absent, a certain value assumption often gets overlooked. Thus, for example, while his application of Ramsey's conception of models to christology yielded some interesting insights, John McIntyre can still write with considerable ambiguity:

> [. . .] the phenomena which constituted the events of the life, death and resurrection of Jesus Christ were so complex and involved, and the minds of Christ's followers were still so far removed from precise theological definition, that models were called in to give immediate interpretation to the phenomena. They provide a basis for conversation concerning the phenomena and for the further proclamation of them without anticipating the precision of later dogmatic formulae.[41]

This paragraph is meaningful only if it is assumed that, owing to the *complexity of reality*, models are somehow a provisional and inferior substitute for precise dogmatic formulae—which implies that models somehow have the same function as dogmatic formulae, namely precise theological definition. But even "precise theological definition" is a misleading phrase, for precision in dogma is never an art for its own sake. Rather, the meaning is determined by its *use*—for example, to tell the true from the false brethren in a situation in which the Church finds itself in a "state of confession." In other words, it takes a particular situation to impel the Church to reflect on what is meant and to arrive at a definition. McIntyre seems to relegate to second rank the ability to evoke the religious disclosure and the self-involving elements of models *as they actually function*, while comprehension (and, of course, only *comprehension* does justice to reality, complex and involved as it is!) takes pride of place.[42]

---

[41]John McIntyre, *The Shape of Christology*, p. 57.

[42]Similar, though more serious criticisms could be leveled at E. L. Mascall, whose deep insight into "the fundamental dependence of analogical predication upon the metaphysical analogy of being" is quite unnecessarily coupled with a depreciation of metaphor as a "spurious use of analogy." If analogy-in-action (which is what metaphor is!) is to be called spurious, are we to conclude that closeness to life and encounters and situations are nothing but an undesirable smudge on the metaphysical purity of being? Cf. E. L. Mascall, *Existence and Analogy*, London, Longmans, Green and Co., 1949, for instance, p. 120.—Cf. also McIntyre's characterization of models as "rough approximations" which compare unfavorably with "immediately descriptive terms" applied to Christ, such as (Tillich's) "Being Itself," and "life," "truth,"

Example: the impasse of christology versus soteriology

Another irritating problem must be mentioned in this connection—the separation between (ontological) christology and (functional) soteriology, and thus between Christ's "person" and his "work." Western thought, with its apparently ineradicable tendency to moor everything that lives and moves to an anchor at the level of substance, is responsible for this rather than the Christ-event itself. The problem here is one of perceived priorities. If it is assumed that soteriology is vacuous unless (two-nature) christology is safely asserted as its foundation, let it be admitted then that this assumption is a *philosophical* one, predicated on some form of an *agere-sequitur-esse* postulate and contingent on the *non-religious* acceptance of the excellence of the process of conceptualization. For Melanchton as for Oscar Cullmann there was no way out of the dilemma involving the relative priorities of christology and soteriology any more than for the late medieval Schoolmen. The Schoolmen opted for the priority of christology—to speculate about Christ's natures and the modes of incarnation (*eius naturas modos incarnationis contueri*), as Melanchton put it. For him, the only available alternative was to know Christ by knowing his benefits (*beneficia eius cognoscere*).[43] Cullmann is caught on the horns of the same dilemma when he advocates a functional interpretation of New Testament christology, based on the observation:

> We shall see of course that these various titles implicitly raise also the question concerning the relationship between God and the person and the origin of Christ. But the problem is not really a "problem of natures" even here.[44]

"*logos*," etc.; how McIntyre can lump the latter four together remains a riddle until it is realized that he secretly considers direct predication the only reliable one (cf. *The Shape of Christology*, p. 69).

[43]Melanchton's famous expression quoted in: Dietrich Bonhoeffer, *Christ the Center*, New York, Harper & Row, 1966, p. 37. All quotations from this translation have been checked (and often corrected) by comparison with the German original: "Christologie," in: Dietrich Bonhoeffer, *Gesammelte Schriften*, Eberhard Bethge (ed.), Dritter Bd., München, Chr. Kaiser Verlag, 1966, pp. 166–242 (henceforth GS), quotation p. 176.

[44]Oscar Cullmann, *The Christology of the New Testament*, Philadelphia, The Westminster Press, ²1963, p. 4. In this context, another expression in Cullmann's book is not without interest, on account of its strongly conceptual language: "The Christology of the New Testament was *conceived* (*konzipiert*) on the basis of these

This kind of alternative, however, is not a theological alternative at all. The theological question is: Can christology make sense of the work of Jesus Christ without a pre-eminent concern with the *person* of Christ?

In reply, Bonhoeffer posits, as the fundamental question of christology, "Who are you?"[45]—a question that voices the longing for disclosure and expresses self-involvement. In this way, Bonhoeffer undercuts the debilitating alternative between a merely notional christology and a merely functional soteriology—in which dilemma the latter tends to come out as second-rate and less accessible to rational discourse, given the assumed conceptual pre-eminence of the former. It is interesting and instructive, then, to understand why Bonhoeffer should insist so strongly, not only on the impossibility of divorcing Jesus Christ from his work, but also on the fact that christology deals with "the personal structure of being of the whole, *historical* Jesus Christ."[46] Christology, in other words, is not a purely conceptual affair for Bonhoeffer.

The cultural impasse: rationality and reality

The difficulty of doing justice to the "extra-conceptual" elements in rational discourse is also the product of a cultural impasse felt in theology as well as in other areas of culture.

When in 1874 the first exhibition of impressionistic paintings by Monet, Renoir, Sisley, Cézanne, Pissarro, and Degas was held, people were bewildered—the world does not really look like that, does it? So caught up was the earlier nineteenth-century artistic perception in its conviction that its visual art was "realistic" that people did not recognize worldly reality when it was painted for them in the raw.

The same year saw the publication of Franz von Brentano's *Psychology from an Empirical Point of View*, in which for the first

---

events [. . .]. The way in which the first Christians *worked out* (*erarbeitet haben*) the various Christological *concepts* (*Begriffe*) [. . .]": p. 317. On the same page the English words "understanding," "perception," and "concepts" are renderings of the one German word "*Erkenntnis(se)*." Cf. *Die Christologie des Neuen Testaments*, Tübingen, J. C. B. Mohr (Paul Siebeck), ⁴1966, p. 327.

[45]Dietrich Bonhoeffer, *Christ the Center*, pp. 30ff. (GS pp. 170ff.).
[46]*Ibid.*, p. 40 (GS p. 178—italics added).

time since Sulzer, a hundred years earlier, psychical phenomena were characterized by their *intentionality*. The impressionists went out and looked at the *things* rather than going by established *taste*; in parallel fashion Brentano claims that what happens in the "mind" happens because we are in touch with something out-there[47]—a move that Husserl was to complete around 1900 with his "Back to the things!" (although he soon withdrew again into an idealistic castle; had the world become too cold to feel comfortable in?). The outside world had become so totally determined by detached observation and purely rational functionalization, and the inside world had become so much a world unto itself, that it was—and for many still is—hard to believe that the things in themselves are not purely *ignotum X* and the mind not purely a knower of its own ideas. It is hard to heal such a thorough-going dissociation of sensibility, which has led not only to the dissociation of feeling from thought, but also to the mutual estrangement between idealist rationalism and objective observation.[48]

In theology, therefore, we must strive for integration. The categories and tools which dogma and systematic theology use to clarify faith must be the result of *dealing with* reality, and may never be allowed to lose touch with their *use*. Just as the hand's grasp kills unless it is sensitive enough to grope, so concepts kill unless they betray that originally they are conceptions born out of intercourse with reality. The difference between scientism and dogmatism on the one hand, and knowledge and dogma on the other, is nothing but the difference between ruthless orthodoxy (and eventually derealization) and relatedness to reality. No one can safely know unless he consciously adopts the stance of a relative; reality is his kith and kin, and justice is only done to it in partiality.

The road toward the integration of thought, in, with, and under the reality of the world, is, given the cultural tradition, extremely narrow and difficult. David Jenkins is right when he says that one of the basic meanings of christology lies precisely in this integration.[49] This is true at the level of content as well as at the level of process.

---

[47]Cf. J. H. van den Berg, *Het menselijk lichaam*, Vol. II, pp. 257–266.

[48]J. H. van den Berg points out the irony of the fact that Descartes puts the connection between the (separated!) mind and world in an organ—the pineal gland—whose function is unknown! *Ibid.*, pp. 222–227.

[49]Cf. *The Glory of Man*, esp. pp. 37ff., 97ff.

Theology stands to gain from christology when it comes to developing a renewed conception of God (as we argued in our first chapter). The *style of thought*, too, stands to gain from christology, in that the latter must concern itself with history and thus may free theology from the age-old dilemma between the "truth of reason" and the "truth of history and facticity."

Closely related to these methodological concerns is Ewert Cousins' suggestion to underpin the various "expressive models," which deal with "religious experience in words, concepts, and symbols," with "experiential models," by which he means "the structures or forms of religious experience, the term 'experiential' implying the subjective element and the term 'model' implying the varieties of religious experience." It would indeed seem that such an approach would serve the purposes of "break[ing] the illusion that we are encompassing the infinite within our finite structures of language,"[50] by opening up theological expression to doctrinal pluralism as well as to the variety of experience.

Cousins' suggestion has the clear advantages of making room for variety on the one hand, and of distinguishing between modes of theological expression on the other. If followed, it may be expected to yield some badly needed categories to order a vast array of experience and expression. Yet it is doubtful whether the suggestion will alleviate the estrangement between experience and expression, of subject and object of feeling and thought. Is it legitimate to lump together words, concepts, symbols, biblical imagery, Christian creeds and theological systems, all under the heading of expressive models? If all these are "expressive models," what would "experiential" models cover? Hence, this book will attempt to set up a scheme of reference that is less liable to build on such dissociations and clusterings. The following analysis of the range of language-use will serve to illustrate this.

THE FULL RANGE OF LANGUAGE-USE

From displaced terminology to natural language

So far this chapter has been excessively critical of terminology

---

[50]Ewert Cousins, "Models and the Future of Theology," *Continuum* 7 (1969) 78–92, quotation 78.

and conceptualization. The reason for this is that the theology of Jesus Christ needs renewal, away from classical, diphysitic christology. This type of christology has too long enjoyed an ascendency at the expense of effective enlightenment. Owing to a great deal of emphasis on christological orthodoxy, especially in religious instruction, two-nature christology has come to have the semblance of natural language—everybody learned it. But this means that the *instrumental function* of the christological terminology has largely been *mistaken for thought itself*, owing to our tendency to treat *terms* as if they were *words*.[51] An analogous point can be made with regard to the debate about God and religion. Owing to its strong philosophical origins, it has yielded formulas and terms for "concepts of God," some of which we discussed in the first chapter. Some of these terms, too, have come to be misused as counters in natural language.

The conclusion is that both popular God-talk and "popular" christology—whether of the "orthodox" variety or of the kind that refuses or hesitates to attribute "divinity" to Jesus Christ—have suffered from what may be called "displaced terminology." Verhaar describes this as follows.

> Good examples of this phenomenon are sometimes furnished by vulgarizations of scientific terms. Thus the psychological term "inferiority complex" is at once pregnant in meaning and strictly delimited; but since everyone has laid his hands on this term, or rather this word—for that is what, as a consequence, it has become—it apparently stands for the most amazing variety of emotional qualms. It has lost its terminological exactitude. We should not be surprised if this also has its drawbacks for the use of the term among psychologists.[52]

The process takes place as follows. A term, instead of being carefully used, as a tool, in the service of understanding *something else*, comes to be *identified with* understanding. Then it gets popularized, so that it looks like a (very prestigious) household word. But because of its ambiguity to non-initiates, it becomes the carrier of very ambivalent meanings. Such words are then often used in the service of concerns, which, as terms, they were never meant to

---

[51]Cf. J. Verhaar, *Some Relations*, p. 133.
[52]*Ibid.*, pp. 140–141.

promote. While the word was used as a *term*, the lack of contact with natural language was compensated for by terminological exactitude and professional usage; reinserted into daily speech the term-become-word gets used as a flag to cover very dubious cargoes. When people discover the uncertain quality of the cargoes, the flag gets discredited. However, flags are sacred, especially if they are hallowed by tradition and sanctioned by authority, and a debilitating, nervous flight about the flag ensues. Put less figuratively: derealization occurs in the use of classical terminology; the terminology is experienced as an alienating irritant; and conflicts occur that are merely semantic.[53] All three steps have been taken in the case of diphysitic christology.

It has already been argued in the first chapter that christology stands to gain from more attention paid to the historical life of Jesus. This chapter is concerned with *the style of christological thought*, and it advocates a return to natural language-use in christology. Hence, our task is to investigate not only how thought is available in non-terminological, non-conceptual language-use, but also what other aspects besides thought can be discovered in language, and how the use of language refers to transcendence. We will do so in reverse, so to speak. Starting from an exploration into the conditions for the possibility of terminology, we will trace our way back to where new perspectives for christological language open up.

Terminological language based on the representative nature of words
    What is the linguistic point of anchorage that renders a *word* capable of being used as a *term*? What in the word enables us to enlist it in the service of "free thought," conceptualization, second-order reflection, terminologically coherent rational discourse?

The answer is: the ability of the word to *reify*. As Verhaar puts it: "It is essential to any word to exceed the purely "egological' in man, that is, to be *essentially bound up with objectivity*."[54] Words even present as "things" what we know are not "things": heat, splendor, immensity. They even make "things" out of the so-called "syncategorematics": realities designated by adverbs, prepositions,

---

[53]One is reminded of Goethe's *Faust*, first part, lines 1995–1996: *Denn eben wo Begriffe fehlen,/da stellt ein Wort zur rechten Zeit sich ein* ("It is where meanings fail that a word will eventually come in").

[54]J. Verhaar, *Some Relations*, p. 65.

conjunctions—we can say: "That is a big if," or "You have to go into the why of things."[55]

This is connected with another property of the word, namely that it is *representative*. We can properly know a "thing," integrate it into our cognitive experience, and give it a place in our frame of reference, without the thing itself being part of our concrete situation; thus, the word allows us to deal with something and at the same time to be at one remove from the immediacy of concrete situations.

This in turn is connected with the fact that words are *non-situational*. In Verhaar's words:

> Representation, as the relation between a lingual sign and the "things"-spoken-about, is not a *function of* this lingual sign, it is *identical with* this sign; this is the same as to say that the meaning of every word is independent of communicative and situational factors.[56]

In virtue of these three properties we really *think in words*, no matter how many other elements of meaning (connotative, "con-experiential", etc.) may be involved in our actual use of words in a particular situation.

Thus, words have the ability to "place" things, to "reify," to denote, to represent, to create distance between ourselves and the flux and the involvement inherent in the concrete situation, to objectify, to visualize, to clarify. They enable us to think and, in doing so, to transcend situations. We rise above the situation, which in virtue of our words we command "spiritually."

The representative nature of words is that property of words which enables us to take them out of context—without total loss of meaning. This means: it enables us to move from direct language experience to *consideration of meaning*. Whenever we do so we start the process that leads to increasing reflection, conceptualization, "free thought," and terminologizing. Thus terminology is based on the representative nature of words.

In words we also deal with reality—naming

However, we can also move the opposite way, away from

---

[55]Cf. James Barr, "Hypostatization of Linguistic Phenomena," p. 85.
[56]J. Verhaar, *Some Relations*, pp. 67–68.

consideration of meaning, away from the word's cognitive side. It remains true that consideration of meaning and reflective systematization are real signs of human transcendence over situations. They show that we not only *know* in words, but also that we know that we know. Whatever we will have to say from now on is not meant to annul or cast doubt on the excellence of the word as a launching-pad for cognitive transcendence.

The knowledge given in the words in which we think has strong and lasting roots in perception. Now perception occurs in *Gestalts.* In our perceptions, we not only passively take in units of perception; we also *constitute* them and thus make them *nameable.* This means that perception is already a prelude to cognition, in that the lending of sense, as we perceive and name things as units of perception, already foreshadows thought. Perceiving in *Gestalts* is the "prelude to cognition."

Now it is at this point that a new perspective opens up. The "prelude to cognition" is only one aspect of the total experience of dealing with reality in language. For in "naming" things we do more than "place" them in the "light" of thought. Words have indeed a clarity, but this clarity "is relevant to thought rather than to the things thought about."[57] A word is not merely clear, not merely representative, not merely reifying, not merely a distance feature, but also a gesture of outreach in response to a presence. Verhaar explains:

> In calling a cow, table, chair or porridge "cow," "table," etc., it is not as if these objects remained strange to us, inaccessible to our thought and action, and only classifiable by means of arbitrary words as their "labels"; *we use these words as names.* And in direct experience these names affect us as belonging to the things rather than to ourselves. All that pertains to the things with regard to our experience with them, to what they "mean" to us, is expressed in the name. The sense thus lent to the things could not even be theirs without the name. Just as in perception the unity of the objects that we perceive strikes us as inherent in the things themselves, likewise in denomination we get hold of what is essential in these objects. [. . .] By means of a name we do not simply "label" a thing, we always somehow say something about *what* the thing *is.* With words we draw the objects designated within our

---

[57]*Ibid.*, pp. 124–125.

own sphere, but naming involves an approach to the thing as something in its own right. While a word expresses what *we mean*, a name tells us what a certain thing *is*, quite independently of what anyone might choose to think of it. A name has, of itself, some claim to "truth."[58]

Accordingly, if we view language *merely* as a cognitive mode of behavior, we neglect the fact that in language we *deal with* reality. In words, things are marshaled in a certain order by our own activity; in names *we* are influenced by things.

This has consequences for our idea of cognitive meaning. If we are justified in expecting real cognitive meaning in language, we must also realize that putting our experience in words always involves us in a process of negotiation—we have to settle for elements of obscurity. As we perceive in *Gestalts*, as we name things and lend sense, and as we speak words in which we think, we do indeed involve ourselves in a process of increasing rationalization of our lived experience. We can only do this, however, to the extent that we "free ourselves from what, in our lived experience, somehow affects us as refusing integration" into our cognitive construct.[59]

Not everything we experience can be called to order. Comprehension and grasp are highly provisional victories, for what eludes our grasp or resists verbalization remains present to remind us that we are *dealing with* (in the sense of negotiating with) a reality that confronts us as "other," as "strange." There is a presence out there that we cannot control, so we control it cognitively and verbally only as much as we can, or want to. In the very act of doing so we must be selective. We place and stabilize and get a clear picture, but we also have to let be, let go, and not despise what escapes our grasp.

Metaphoric language-use is primarily naming

To name, as we have said, means to respond to a presence. This means: naming is an act of acknowledgement of encounter. True, the meaning of the word by itself is constant on account of its reifying,

---

[58]*Ibid.*, pp. 82–83.

[59]Cf. *ibid.*, p. 125. The cognitive construct is both more and less than the primary experience: cf. Karl Rahner, "The Development of Dogma," in: *Theological Investigations*, Vol. I, Baltimore, Helicon Press, 1961, pp. 39–77, esp. pp. 63ff.

representative, non-situational nature; yet *in actual use* this bearer of constant meaning functions as a gesture of outreach and response. In naming, we treat others as persons, and other things as quasi-personal—personification is but an intentional, heightened form of the naming which goes on in everyday speech.

The word: response to a presence and unit of constant meaning—particular gesture in a particular situation and meaning that transcends all situations: How are the two elements related? To clarify this we must analyze the working of the *metaphor*.

In order to do this, let us take the example, as Verhaar does, of a biologist conversing with his six-year-old son about a cow. By our definition, "cow," being reifying, representative, and non-situational, has a unitary, constant meaning; yet we also know that the biologist and his son "mean different things" when they are talking. Verhaar explains:

> In our example, the biologist and his son do not have the same interpretation; each of them "selects" different elements from the meaning. But they both "select" their elements from the *one* meaning-unit, which, as a unit, always remains intact. From this curious fact that there are distinct elements within one and the same meaning we infer—to use Reichling's term—that these distinct elements are only *disjunctively relevant to the constancy of the meaning as a unit*. It is the constancy of the whole meaning as a unit that makes it possible to converse with someone else without (too great) misunderstandings, even if—as is mostly the case—the conversation-partners "select" different "meanings"; this may be all right as far as the saying goes, but systematically we would have to say that each of them selects different disjunctively relevant elements from *all* the elements relevant to the meaning-unit; that is, they are relevant so far as they—and not other elements—can be selected, but they always take along with them the *whole* meaning in its unbreakable constancy.[60]

Now, when by "cow" I designate a "real" cow, we have what Verhaar calls *denomination proper*, which is characterized by the fact that *all* the meaning-elements in the word are applied *conjunctively*. But when I call a man a "bulldog," I *disjunctively apply* some meaning-elements (e.g., that the person is thick-necked, always on

---

[60]J. Verhaar, *Some Relations*, pp. 85–86.—The reference in the quotation is to A. Reichling's *Het woord*, Nijmegen, Berkhout, 1935, pp. 321–322.

the alert, or aggressive), while merely *actuating*—or "taking along"—the other meaning-elements.[61]

Now we are in a position to sum up how a metaphor works. On the *cognitive side*, meaning is negotiated—selectively as always—by the disjunctive application of a select number of meaning-elements. The basis for the selection is the likeness between the man and the bulldog. As we have pointed out, the meaning thus achieved leaves part of the reality intended outside the cognitive construct. Metaphors, therefore, in their very attempt to express *meaning*, also express, and testify to, the strangeness, the otherness of the object, and to the essential limitations of our cognitive power.

What, then, makes the metaphor viable, if it leaves—cognitively speaking—a gap to be bridged? To answer this question, let us take our analysis so far one step further.

In the concrete situation, we have argued, only so much is amenable to cognitive grasp; the lived experience of the situation must partly remain outside any cognitive construct. When I respond to a concrete situation by the use of a metaphor, I must expect the metaphor to reflect both the situation's intelligibility *and* its strangeness. The latter is conveyed in that I *name* the situation *metaphorically*, and in so naming it I testify to my presence to it and its presence to me. The former is conveyed in that I structure and illuminate the situation, causing the isomorphism between the situation and the metaphoric name (seen as word) to function as a clarifying agent by means of the disjunctive application of those meaning-elements in the metaphor that are relevant to the situation. To put it simply, metaphors are indeed ways to structure a situation cognitively, but only in the context of my immediate encounter with the situation as it confronts me in its irreducible strangeness. Metaphor is primarily: addressing oneself to reality, and it is in that context of address that the metaphor also illuminates.

Naming is handling reality

What is very prominent in metaphors, namely their ability to handle situations on account of the speaker's immediate presence to (his immanence, or involvement in) situations, is given in *the name*

---

[61]*Ibid.*, p. 86.

aspect of every word. The name is the symbol of the thing itself, and in using its name we are "handling" it. The non-cognitive aspect of the metaphor, therefore, is a striking example of what obtains in *every* word; in the word, we do not only think, we also deal with "strange" things as they meet us. Put otherwise: what in the *consideration of language* we call a *word* with a *meaning,* in *direct experience* functions as the *name* of a *thing.* In naming, especially in actual speech (and hearing of speech) we experience our immanence in, and proximity to, our world, as we stretch ourselves out to it.[62]

ACTIVITY, INTERSUBJECTIVITY, RHETORIC

We are now ready to develop a survey of the "other side" of language, its non-cognitive and in that sense a-rational aspects. We will do so by elaborating three characteristics of language, namely that it is an activity, that it is interpersonal, and that it is rhetorical. All three have this in common that they are concerned with the setting in which words make sense. This setting is: the fact that language occurs in situations and that it occurs among people immanent in situations, for from these the cognitive ascent from involvement to thought takes place.

Language is not only cognition, but also activity
    First of all, no matter how independent of situations the *meaning* of *words* is, language, especially in its original form, which is speech, only occurs as a specific mode of *behavior in* particular situations. This means that, no matter how objective the meaning of the *words* spoken may be, they are embedded in what *I mean* when saying what I say. The *meanings* of *words* are integrated into the *points* made by *people.* The words spoken are not *things* with a life of their own (although when considered in themselves they prove to be sound-complexes with a constant meaning), but they are ingredients

---

[62]In this connection it is relevant to point out that Rita Vuyk has shown that "pointing" coincides with the first successful attempts at speaking and understanding. Pointing and, *a fortiori,* handling/taking (rather than "holding on to") is considered the first expression of "language function" by G. Révèsz. We "say something" with our gestures. Cf. F. J. J. Buytendijk, *Algemene theorie der menselijke houding en beweging,* Utrecht–Antwerpen, Uitgeverij Het Spectrum, ⁷1974, pp. 318–319.

for *activity,* for expression of personal self, and for personal response to situations experienced in their "otherness."

This quality of active personal involvement in and response to situations as it is reflected in language we call the language's "egological" feature. It is to be expected that this egological feature will be most prominent in speech, since speech is language in its original form.

The egological nature of speech is most clearly borne out by the importance of the acoustical elements (hearing is the sense of "nearness" and "time").[63]

By contrast, more cognitive language-use, in words, and especially reflective language-use, in terms, tends to reduce those egological elements, owing to the fact that more concentration is brought to bear on the meanings of words, or terms, with proportionate loss of the direct experience of speech. Accordingly, silent reading of terminological language—a *visual* approach to *spatialized* language (Verhaar refers to "the cognitive primacy of visual categories"[64])—is much more productive and appropriate than listening. Terminology is the result of *reflection* on meanings given in words, so that many of the connotative, con-experiential, mostly acoustically conveyed meanings of speech must be excluded to do justice to terminology. This may also partly account for the difficulty of relating technical language to "real life," and thus harbors the possibility of derealization.

Language is not only objectifying but also intersubjective

It would obviously be a simplification to assume that the non-cognitive, egological elements in speech are always merely personal or individual. A *group* of people may respond to a situation in one, corporate involvement, and in this involvement view and interpret and structure it in the same way.[65] This leads to a second important conclusion to be drawn from the fact that in speech we not only structure a situation cognitively, but also deal with it.

---

[63]We will come back to this in the seventh chapter; below, pp. 281–286.

[64]J. Verhaar, *Some Relations,* p. 38.

[65]Cf. Donald D. Evans' comments on "institutional-relation words": *The Logic of Self-Involvement,* pp. 66–68.

Language is not only activity in a situation; it is also interaction between persons in a situation. In language we *communicate with others*.[66] This dimension of *intersubjectivity* becomes more prominent as language moves more in the direction of personal, egological speech-activity and the use of the word as a name, and decreases as language moves more toward the cognitive. In the latter case, however, *communication-with* is never quite absent; the writer of a very abstract, theoretical monograph wants most of his readers' attention to go to *what* he has to *communicate to* them, but in order to achieve this goal he implicitly assumes that his readership shares his concerns and interests.

In the case of actual speech, the opposite may be true. Especially in cases where the main emphasis of the speaker is not on *what* he has to *communicate to* others, but on his *communication with* others itself—we can think of the delightful foolishness exchanged between lovers as well as of a politician's grandstanding—then is it clear that, given the dominance of intersubjectivity, the actual quality of speech also becomes more important.

The range of interaction, of communication-with is very wide. First, it exceeds the cognitive realm of language, the meaning of the words and statements. Verhaar demonstrates this in a telling example.

> Suppose I am stopped in the street by a man I do not know at all, saying to me: "If I catch the two o'clock train, I shall have plenty of time." Whatever judgement my amazement will allow me to make, perhaps that the man is mad, or that he is mistaking me for someone else, at any rate there is no denying that I perfectly understand what he is saying. The trouble is not that; the trouble is that there is no communication-situation at all, within which alone the speech-occurrence makes sense. The man's words make no sense to me, I do not know what he is driving at though I do know what he means. The riddle is not what he is saying, but why he is saying it, or what comes to the same thing, why he is saying it to me.[67]

But not only does communication between persons exceed the cognitive aspects of speech; *it also exceeds speech itself.* To demon-

---

[66]Cf. J. Verhaar, *Some Relations*, pp. 93ff.
[67]*Ibid.*, p. 102.

strate this, let us take two examples.

Of a certain couple, people say: "They don't speak the same language." Usually this does not refer to the fact that the two belong to different language-groups such as French, English, or Swahili, and so we are not talking about an external circumstance leading to lack of communication. Rather, we refer to a lack of communication that is already there before either one starts to speak, and that remains untouched by the meaning of the words *and by the act of speaking*.[68]

Similarly, when a speech-situation really comes off, when we experience mutual understanding, when "we really speak the same language"—what is happening is not just cognitive fit (or mutual information without distortion), nor even just a communion in experience and expression (or fit at the level of lingual interaction); rather, we experience intersubjective interaction *tout court*, beyond the meaning of words and beyond speech itself. We experience that irreducible transcendence which Martin Buber has called "Spirit," given in the I—Thou encounter.[69]

This can give us insight into the meaning of the *proper name*. Even if most proper names have the kind of meaning that can be etymologically established, that is not their real meaning. Michael does not really mean "who is like God?" nor does Agatha really mean "good girl" or Francis "Frenchie" *when used as proper names*. The cognitive element is absent in proper names. That means, the proper name, symbol of the person and his or her presence, is the *name par excellence*,[70] not the word that also functions as the name of a thing. We handle things by naming them; we address persons—and address ourselves to persons—by calling them by their names—names emerging out of that "full" silence which is the wordless communication of mutual presence.[71]

---

[68] Cf. *ibid.*, pp. 109–113.

[69] Cf. Martin Buber, *Ich und Du*, Köln, Verlag Jakob Hegner, ²1966, pp. 49ff.; ET *I and Thou*, Walter Kaufmann (trans.), New York, Charles Scribner's Sons, 1970, pp. 89ff.; cf. also J. Verhaar, *Some Relations*, pp. 109–113.

[70] Cf. J. Verhaar, *Some Relations*, p. 83. Notice how Ian Ramsey attributes high disclosure-value to proper names: *Religious Language*, pp. 19–20, 26–27.

[71] For naming things and calling on persons, cf. Martin Buber, *Ich und Du*, pp. 12ff.; *I and Thou*, pp. 56ff. For the connection between address, metaphor, personification, and doxology, cf. Wolfhart Pannenberg, "Analogy and Doxology," in: *Basic Questions in Theology*, Vol. I, Philadelphia, Fortress Press, 1970, pp. 212–238.

Language is not only logical, but also rhetorical

The intersubjective aspect of speech can be further developed by an analysis of the judgment, the statement. *Cognitively* speaking, the subject of a judgment *stat pro ignoto—within the confines of the statement* the subject is unknown and undefined, and about to be illuminated by the predicate. When I say: "That wall is green," I make use of the non-situational, constant meaning of the *word* "green" and predicate the "greenness" of the wall, thus conveying cognitive information about it. The efficacy of the predication will depend on the predicate's constancy of meaning; if I were to say: "That wall is grewgious,"[72] there would be a lack of cognitive efficacy owing to the lack of such meaning. Similarly, if I say: "Jesus is God," appropriate cognition is contingent on the viability of the predicate at the cognitive level—which, as was shown in the first chapter, suffers a wide margin of doubt in this case.

But we must approach the statement also from another angle. In terms of *communication*, the subject of the statement is not an *ignotum*. *Supponit pro re*—it represents the thing itself—as some Thomistic textbooks were wont to say. It is a *name*. This means that I reach out, gesturally, to that strange given, which is the "thing"— in this case the wall—and "handle" it in speech. But in doing so, I assume that my hearer has an interest in the thing; otherwise he would be like the man accosted by the stranger in Verhaar's example cited above. If I say: "That wall is green," my *intersubjective* assumption is that I am in communication with my hearer, and that the wall—which in the confines of the statement taken by itself is logically, or cognitively, vacuous—is the thoroughly familiar meeting-place of interests for me and the person I am talking to. Hence, the subject of the sentence, whose presence I invoke by naming it, is the symbol of intersubjective communication, the place where I render myself present to the person who is listening to me, and where I find that person present to me.

This implies an experience of transcendence. How?

It is, obviously, a different kind of transcendence from the cognitive experience of transcendence that moves from patterned perception through meaningful words to the free thought where, in a

---

[72]With a bow to that master of the suggestive proper name, Charles Dickens (in *The Mystery of Edwin Drood*).

final perspective, "ultimate meaning" is sought after. In the cognitive transcendence-experience the situation is first gradually purified of its unmanageable elements by means of the selective, objectifying capacity of words; then the situation is abandoned, so that the universal *eidos* is finally set free in an ultimate consideration of meaning. In the intersubjective transcendence-experience the *situation itself* becomes transparent, in that the "I—It" relationship expressed in the statement becomes the medium for the "I—Thou" encounter.

Speech is thus halfway between two transcendences. Making sense in speech demands sometimes that we move more in the direction of objectivation, distance, abstraction and conceptual clarity; concepts like "being-itself" are liable to be found at the summit of such an ascent. But the ascent to the idea is not without risks; it is likely to be safe only if the cultural situation in which it takes place is one of felt integration and coherence. In such a situation cognitive flights tend to stay in touch with real life.

But at other times the movement in the opposite direction will be indicated. In such situations, real understanding will be dependent on handling reality, proximity, and concretion. Rhetoric and dialectic, the cultivation of *loci communes*—meeting-places for persons!—and dialogue will then be the road to transcendence in the experience of the "We."

Heribert Mühlen on "Thou-lessness"

In a small book, entitled *Die abendländische Seinsfrage als der Tod Gottes und der Aufgang einer neuen Gotteserfahrung*,[73] Heribert Mühlen, the author of a monumental study on the Holy Spirit, has identified the "Thou-lessness" of the Occidental question of being as the tragic assumption leading to the death of God. Our discussion so far has tended to show that there is a strong linguistic component in this, namely the almost exclusive concentration on the meaning-aspect of speech at the expense of the "handling"-aspect. The Occidental concept of God, according to Mühlen, is nothing but the

---

[73]Paderborn, Ferdinand Schöningh, 1968. Cf. also *id.*, "Das unbegrenzte Du—Auf dem Wege zu einer Personologie," in: *Wahrheit und Verkündigung* (Festschrift M. Schmaus), München–Paderborn–Wien, F. Schöningh, 1967, pp. 1259–1285.

absolute objectification of what technical reason perceives as "thing," or of technical reason itself. And it is true that, starting from reification, there is no road but that which leads to a God beyond the limits of what is knowable and manipulable. Mühlen finds this God, identical with an impersonal power of being, in the theology of Paul Tillich who, perhaps more than any other great theologian in this century, had a developed sensitivity vis-à-vis the broken symbols and the broken myths lying about in a secularized world. Hence his effort to "transcend both mysticism and the person-to-person encounter" in an act of "absolute faith" in "the God above the God of theism," a God who cannot be realistically said to "exist" anymore and who is, as a most intimate power of being in the depth of reality, beyond all language and all encounter. But in the light of our present discussion it must be asked whether Tillich, for all his great sensitivity to the futility of attempting to revive a god that would be merely a pious *mythologoumenon*, has not fallen a victim to the Gnostic myth, for example when he postulates that symbolic assertions about God can be made theologically only on the basis of the non-symbolic statement that God is being-itself.[74] In calling symbolic statements "assertions," he completely ignores the fact that, linguistically speaking, they are close to names, and, hence, not just words-with-meaning or terms representing concepts, but means of *encountering* reality, and, above all, other persons.

The return to human dynamics

The concerns expressed in this analysis bear a close resemblance to the insights developed in the field of applied behavioral science over the last twenty or thirty years.[75] Social scientists no longer look

---

[74]Cf. Paul Tillich, *The Courage To Be*, pp. 173, 176, 180; *Systematic Theology*, I, pp. 236, 238–239.

[75]Cf., for instance, Warren G. Bennis, Kenneth D. Benne, Robert Chin (eds.), *The Planning of Change*, New York, Holt, Rinehart and Winston, 2 1969; Leland P. Bradford, Jack R. Gibb, Kenneth D. Benne (eds.), *T-Group Theory and Laboratory Method*, New York–London–Sydney, John Wiley & Sons, 1964; Dorwin Cartwright, Alvin Zander (eds.), *Group Dynamics*, New York, Harper & Row, 3 1968; Gerard Egan, *Encounter: Group Process for Interpersonal Growth*, Belmont, Brooks/Cole Publishing Company, 1970; Joseph Luft, *Group Processes*, An Introduction to Group Dynamics, Palo Alto, National Press Books, 2 1970; Douglas McGregor, *The Human Side of the Enterprise*, New York–Toronto–London, McGraw-Hill Book Company, 1960; Cyril R. Mill (ed.), *Selections from Human Relations Training News*, Washing-

upon a human organization as a "machine of great beauty"[76] in which the dynamics of the process are assumed to occur in strict accordance with the rational goals and procedures formulated at the top. Human communication is no longer presumed to reach its highest peak when purely objective information is faultlessly passed on, nor are feelings, attitudes, interests, inclinations, and even personal conflicts any longer considered as entirely undesirable components in what could ideally be a perfectly operating rational institution. Human weakness is no longer exclusively seen as technical failure, but as a source of discovery, fulfillment, and creativity, even at the technical level. Collaboration and consensus at all levels in an *organic* way rather than behavior-prescription from the top, quality of communication rather than mere information storage and retrieval, have become the hallmarks of the truly humanistic organization. The same applies to the revival of interest in community organization by consensus-seeking, and even to the training provided in countless encounter groups, to help people find meaning in social life. Sensitivity to others, freedom of expression, appropriate personal depth, coping with interaction, trust-formation, creative handling of tension between provisional situations and overall goals—all these concerns show that the human sciences have developed ways to abandon the compulsive concern with total objectivity and discovered means to deal with personalness and concreteness as original, irreducible values. No wonder, then, that sensitivity-training, human relations laboratories, transactional analysis seminars, personal growth workshops and the like have provided many people, including Christians, with settings in which they have had religious experiences—something, they say, the rational formulas of their catechisms and the prescriptive practices of their churches had never been able to provide. The same can be said for the charismatic

---

ton, D.C., NTL Institute for Applied Behavioral Science, 1969; Carl R. Rogers, *On Becoming a Person*, Boston, Houghton Mifflin Company, 1961; William C. Schutz, *The Interpersonal Underworld*, Palo Alto, Science & Behavior Books, ²1966; Clovis R. Shepherd, *Small Groups*, Some Sociological Perspectives, San Francisco, Chandler Publishing Company, 1964; Philip E. Slater, *Microcosm*, New York–London–Sydney, John Wiley & Sons, 1966.

[76]Herbert A. Shepard, "Changing Interpersonal and Intergroup Relationships in Organizations," in: James G. March (ed.), *Handbook of Organizations*, Chicago, Rand McNally & Company, 1965, pp. 1115–1143; quotation p. 1115.

movement, the revival of group prayer and communal discernment, the Cursillo movement, and many other strongly personalized ways of sharing the life of the Gospel.

The charge of emotionalism should not be brought lightly here, even though objectively speaking there may be a goodly admixture of anti-intellectualism present. Resisting these developments, in things human as well as in things specifically Christian, is all too often based on an anxious dependence on conceptual orthodoxy (whether of the Christian or the organizational kind); defensiveness, here as elsewhere, is ultimately a self-defeating attitude. It is in response to the *caro Christi* that the Father's presence is revealed, just as it is in commitment to the visible world that the visible Church is called to discern the Father. Transposed into linguistic terms, it is in rhetoric and dialogue that christo*logy* makes sense.

Rhetoric and dialogue

We are now in a position to attempt a first definition of rhetoric as it will be used in this book. Rhetoric is the sum of all those elements and aspects of language which show that language is primarily an activity in situations and only on that basis a cognitive act; it is language insofar as it is evidence of, and incentive to, persons' active communication with one another in particular situations; it is language insofar as it bears the traces of worldly situations being places for personal encounter and interaction, in which the experience of the "other" also becomes an experience of transcendence; it is language insofar as it is marked by the process of change brought about by interpersonal encounter and orientation to transcendence; it is language insofar as it evinces the *process* of intelligent articulation of these experiences of situation, encounter, transcendence, and change.

At this point let us limit our comments on this definition to five remarks. First, the definition is extremely condensed and abstract; the next chapter, and indeed the rest of the book, will be devoted to elaboration and concretization.

Second, as Amos Wilder concedes, "the term rhetoric has unfortunate connotations,"[77] associated as it is with manipulation and

---

[77]Amos Wilder, *Early Christian Rhetoric*, New York, Harper & Row, 1964, p. 10.

deceit. We will come back to this; for the time being suffice it to say that the definitions given above prescind from the issue as to whether rhetoric is rightly or wrongly used.

Third, the definition differs considerably from the definitions usually given in manuals of rhetoric, where the emphasis is customarily on the whole array of *stylistic devices* (*loci, figurae,* etc.) that have proved to have persuasive power; in this book, the focus will be on the *fact* that christology is the precipitate of *acts* of faith and faith-interpretation rather than on the stylistic *means by which* these acts are conveyed.

Fourth, the definition is not meant as a programmatic manifesto for the development of a new christology; rather, it is meant as a hermeneutic tool. This means that this book will make a consistent effort to place the statements of *traditional* christology against the background of the question: What is the rhetorical setting in which these statements made logical sense?—a question, in other words, aimed at retrieving the *acts* of faith-commitment and faith-discernment that gave rise to the statements made.

Fifth, this entails that this book will consider christological statements primarily as expressions of dialogue among persons in dialectical response both to the living Lord and to the concerns of their culture,[78] and only secondarily as parts of an intellectually coherent system of thought.

Summary and outlook

The first chapter ended with the judgment that, given the ambiguity and the defective illuminating force of "God" and "divinity," theology has more to expect from christology than christology from theology.[79] This chapter ends with the parallel judgment that, in christology, given the ambiguity and the defective illuminating force of concepts, logic has more to expect from rhetoric than rhetoric from logic. Diphysitic christology has largely lost its interpretative force and tends to lead Christians into derealization, owing to its lack of contact with the actual situations in which communication occurs. A fatal distance has developed between the terms of

---

[78]For dialogue with all its implications, cf. *ibid.*, pp. 48–62.
[79]Above, pp. 61–63.

diphysitic christology and the words exchanged among Christians as they live and die, the words in which the apostolic community expressed its life as well as the life and death of the historical Jesus.

The inability of classical christology to do full justice to the significance of the life and death of Jesus is, therefore, partly due to a linguistic assumption, namely, the identification of "real meaning" with "concepts" that recognize very little, if any, debt to any actual situation. This linguistic assumption, however, betrays an allegiance to the gnostic myth, which strips language of its vigorous closeness to life.

But classical christology also fails to do full justice to the significance of the life and death of Christians today. To the extent that it is still adhered to, it leads to many illegitimate development inferences and cryptogamous heresies, in the same way as the *term* "inferiority complex" lost its useful meaning and became downright dangerous when it became popularized. To the extent that, under the pressure of the authority of the tradition or the *magisterium*, classical christology continues to be dutifully debated, it acts as a neuralgic irritant, preventing Christians from the kind of discernment and commitment that would enable them to see, and live by, the uniqueness of Jesus Christ. To the extent that it is rejected in favor of a "purely human" Jesus, it blinds people from seeing the mystery of the Christ in the earthly Jesus and in the Church.

Hence, the next chapter proposes to go back to the New Testament, to explore some of the *rhetorical* aspects of New Testament christology. It is obvious that this point of departure will be characterized by two basic ideas. The first is that all christology is uttered in the Spirit. "No one can say 'Jesus is Lord' except by the Holy Spirit,"[80] who, in Mühlen's phrase, is "the precondition of all well-ordered personal encounter."[81] The second is that in the language of Spirited encounter, in performative language, in worship, proclamation, admonition, preaching, and witness, the *situation itself* is interpreted by discernment and changed by commitment.

This in turn leads to two consequences. First, the immanence of

---

[80]1 Cor 12, 3.

[81]Heribert Mühlen, *Die abendländische Seinsfrage*, p. 56; cf. *id.*, "Die epochale Notwendigkeit eines pneumatologischen Ansatzes der Gotteslehre," *Wort und Wahrheit* 4 (1973) 275–287.

God in the world that is borne out by the Christian rhetoric is not a bland "datum of nature"; it is in a *particular* kind of commitment/ discernment that God's immanence, and who he is, is discovered.[82] Second, the christological rhetoric will be characterized by *patience*—situations are partial and even fragmentary, and illuminating them is always provisional. But it is precisely in this variety of settings, creatively handled, that the Spirit leads into the full truth.

---

[82]Again, the conditions on which immanence is a useful category in theological discourse will be further explored in chapter eleven; below, pp. 450–451.

PART II

Back to the Source

The faith is to be weighed by the sentence, not by the word; hence the real consensus, coupled with occasional verbal battles, among the Orthodox Fathers when it came to the defense of the one hypostasis and the two natures in Christ. [. . .] We must take our stance in the time of the Church in which we happen to live, and be of service there. [. . .] If we go by individual words, the Holy Fathers departed not a little from our present way of speaking. Actually, they themselves had great differences among themselves; words frequently used by some were rejected by others, who ordered them exiled from the speech of the faithful. We, therefore, must count on the benefit of humane and open-minded judges—it is hardly possible for us to bring back to light the teachings of the Fathers (and that only in a selective fashion) without running the risk of inflicting pain on the ears and the stomachs of other theologians, even contemporary ones. Now the Fathers' common eagerness to agree on one faith is matched by their intolerance of verbal discord. Present-day theology in its turn, so young an heir to so great a tradition, more than agrees with them, except that its unimpaired awareness of the unity of the faith causes it to regard verbal differences as relatively unimportant.

Thomassin

CHAPTER 3

The Rhetoric of Christology

Laeti bibamus sobriam ebrietatem Spiritus. *

Ambrose of Milan

There is, indeed, such a thing as a rhetoric of faith, the language of the Spirit; one can recognize that the early Christians were endowed with new tongues; but all such heavenly discourse remains rooted in the secular media of ordinary speech. Pentecost, indeed, we may take as a dramatization of the fact that there is no peculiar Christian tongue.

Amos Wilder

The truth brought forth names in the world for our sakes, since it is not possible to learn it without names.

The Gospel of Philip

The word or dogma that claims sovereignty over the whole of the image, and does not often and humbly present itself before the image for renewal, in the end imprisons us.

Laurens van der Post

I will pray with the spirit and I will pray with the mind also; I will sing with the spirit and I will sing with the mind also.

The First Letter of Paul to the Corinthians

---

*Let us joyfully drink the sober intoxication of the Spirit.

Retrospect and outlook

The introduction and the first two chapters provided us with the outlines of a program. We are to concentrate on Christian identity, we are to seek the renewal of God-language by recourse to christology, and we are to liberate christology from its notional shackles. In the next four chapters we will analyze the underlying dynamics of christology. The goal of our analysis will be to lay bare the *acts* of "confidence in speaking"—Paul's *parrhēsia!*[1]—that animate and give meaning to the statements made. In doing this we will discover a threefold dynamic, or, as we will call it, a *triple rhetoric*. In all its statements christology wants to make three points, namely that in Jesus Christ there is the offer of absolute hope, the call to total obedience, and the possibility for universal inclusiveness. Hope, obedience and inclusion, we will argue, are the dynamics that lead to the formulation of articulate christological statements. Chapters four and five will be devoted to this.

Before we will argue this case, however, we must lay bare the fact that christology in the New Testament is primarily action, and only secondarily cognition, and explore the relationships between this action—to be characterized as total surrender—and the cognitive articulations that it produces—to be characterized as discernments taken from human concerns. This is the task of the present chapter.

Finally, the sixth chapter will ask the question about the origin of the triple rhetoric.

From Reflective Christology to Response to Christ

In this first section we will apply some of the findings of the previous chapter to christology by slowly working our way to the thesis that there is an original non-cognitive element in christology, namely, the response to the person of Jesus Christ. We will do so by starting with the most terminological shape of christology.

---

[1]*Parrhēsia* means confident outspokenness before people, as in 2 Cor 3, 12 and Eph 6, 19, and confidence in addressing oneself to God, as in Eph 3, 12 and 1 Tim 3, 13.

THE RHETORIC OF CHRISTOLOGY   109

The use of terminological christology

Second-order reflection, "free thought," and an increasing use of terminology in the service of conceptualization are, as we have seen, the result of reflection on the *meaning of words*, with proportionate de-emphasizing of their *use* and of those aspects of language-use we have called activity, naming, "situationalness," and intersubjectivity. This reflection is based on the relatively constant extrasituational meaning of words; its tools are conceptualization, definition and analysis, and its goal is stabilization of discourse.

Terminology's almost exclusive focus on coherent and rigorous meaning, however, may easily obscure the fact that rigorous and stable discourse has a use of its own. Terminological, conceptual language-use remains, for all its non-situational characteristics, a linguistic *activity*, deemed appropriate and productive in particular situations, even though, when considered in relation to ordinary language, it appears to be non-situational. Taking an example from christology, the Chalcedonian settlement, with its strongly terminological bent, was meant to be *useful*. It was aimed at preserving the unity of the Church by means of a "rule of speech"[2] in the face of heretical and ambiguous talk, and at safeguarding the Church's continuity with the Councils of Nicaea and Constantinople.[3] Even the most formal language has a point, although this does not always readily appear; activity-aspects (the "use") of terminological, conceptual language, though not immediately visible, are part of its total reality.

To quote another example, even a cursory reading of the portions in Grillmeier's book that treat Nestorius and Cyril[4] makes it clear that the problem with Nestorius was not the legitimacy of his concerns over the inappropriate understanding of the *communicatio idiomatum*[5] or his inability (in Grillmeier's view) to come up with a

[2]Cf. above, p. 36 and note 10.
[3]Cf. DS 300.
[4]Aloys Grillmeier, S.J., *Christ in Christian Tradition*, New York, Sheed and Ward, [1]1965, pp. 363–419.
[5]*Communicatio idiomatum*—"sharing of characteristics"—refers to the thesis that both divine and human attributes are attributable to Christ in virtue of the hypostatic union of the two natures in the one person. This in turn makes it legitimate

satisfactory metaphysical tool-kit to articulate both the unity and the duality in the person of Christ. Nestorius' basic problem was that his anti-Arian and anti-Apollinarian concerns led him to formulations which, *concretely* speaking, jeopardized not only the truth (every formulation does that!), but also the Church's *unity in understanding* the truth.

In the same way, the Church could prefer "Cyril's christological *idea* to his *formulation* of it."[6] The Cyril of the very confusing *Anathematisms*[7] was obviously animated by the same concerns as the Cyril of the beautiful Second Letter to Nestorius;[8] the formulas of the latter became authoritative, those of the former were rejected, or at least de-emphasized. Again, the formulation adopted was judged, ultimately, in the light of its *factual ability* to speak coherently to the culture as well as to safeguard the unity of the Church around the integrity of the faith.

We conclude that there is an a-rational element even in terminological language as it is concretely used, namely, the situation in which it is used. The situation co-determines the meaning of the terminology, at least in the sense that terminology may fail to provide the clarification wanted on account of situational lack of consensus about the meaning or appropriateness of the terms. Put concretely, both Nestorius' title "Christ-bearer" for the Blessed Virgin and Cyril's phrase *henōsis physikē* (physical union) to convey the oneness of Christ's person failed to make sense because they failed to make consensus.

This leads to a conclusion: it is wrong to belittle the significance of situations when it comes to making christological statements.

The significance of the christological situation

In the previous chapter we explained that situationalness harbors the possibility of transcendence-experience as we encounter

---

to couple divine and human attributes, as in the expressions "God suffered and died" and "The man Jesus Christ is one of the Trinity."

[6]Aloys Grillmeier, *Christ in Christian Tradition*, [1]1965, p. 409.

[7]DS 252–263, esp. 254.

[8]DS 250–251.

other persons, but also other things in their very otherness.[9] Situations, therefore, are not mere settings, extrinsic sets of circumstances ("things standing around"), accidental stages on which "real meaning" is somehow enacted.[10] In the previous chapter a distinction was made between the cognitive elements and the interaction elements in speech, the former associated with the name as *word*, the latter associated with the word as *name*. What from a *cognitive* point of view presents itself as *accidental* is, in fact, the sum of those elements in lived experience which somehow present themselves to us as not amenable to our cognitive structuring activity. But what is thus left "meaningless" is *not pointless*. Lived experience is never entirely reducible to rational meaning; hence, cognition would overstep the boundaries of its competence if it were to conclude that what is meaningless, and in that sense a-rational, has no point. "Handling" may, in and of itself, be a-rational, but that does not justify the conclusion that it is purely incidental to "the real thing."

If we apply this to christology we must conclude that the situation in which christological statements are made is not irrelevant to the meaning of the statements. Rather, the statements will only yield their full meaning if they are appreciated as situationally conditioned. We will have to ask, therefore, in what way the christological situation is reflected in the christological statements made.

As we saw in the previous chapter, language is not only a form of knowing, but also, and primarily, a form of acting; in language, we *handle* a situation. We do so by naming, and naming, we saw, often takes the form of metaphor. If, then, we are to ask the question about the nature of the christological situation we must expect to find names and metaphors used in that situation.

In dealing with the christological situation as it is expressed in language, we must also be willing to be modest. As we have argued, the naming element in language reminds us of those elements in our

---

[9]Above, pp. 97–98.

[10]This insight has occasioned Piet Schoonenberg to develop a concept of original sin that is less individualistic and more social; cf. *Man and Sin*, Notre Dame, University of Notre Dame Press, 1965, esp. pp. 98–123, 177–191.

lived experience which are not amenable to integration into our cognitive construct. If, then, we are to explore the christological situation, we must be open to description rather than argument. Cognitive structures can be argued; situational elements, activity elements, names, metaphors—in short, the rhetorical elements— must be accepted, taken for granted in the literal sense of that expression. Only after they are accepted will they begin to make sense.

The names and titles of Jesus

In the previous chapter we argued that the point of a metaphor is not exhaustively determined by its cognitive, structuring ability. A metaphor, we said, was primarily a way of addressing oneself to an encountered reality outside oneself. Let us apply this to a concrete example of a christological metaphor.

It is quite customary to hear the liturgy or a preacher refer to Jesus, or to address him in prayer, as "Son of Man," often in a stylistically effective juxtaposition with "Son of God." Whatever the answer may be to the much-debated question as to what the prophetic, apocalyptic, rabbinical, etc., meanings of this expression once were, it is clear that in our context "Son of Man" expresses, in an imaginative way and by means of what was originally a Semitic turn of phrase,[11] what the Christian tradition has always meant by *homoousios hēmin*—Jesus' consubstantiality with us in human nature. Between the New Testament and our situation, however, an important shift of meaning has occurred.[12] An expression which used to carry, say, mainly apocalyptic overtones and associations, and which was in no way calculated to deal with the paradox of the Incarnation, is now used to do precisely the latter. A tolerant Scripture scholar may point out here that the title has changed meaning at the hands of modern users; an intolerant one may point

---

[11]The past tense here is intentional. The meaning of a word is established synchronically (i.e., with reference to present usage), not diachronically (i.e., with reference to etymology or semantic development).

[12]The shift is at least as old as Irenaeus, *Adv. Haer.* III, 17. 19; cf. B. Xiberta, *Enchiridion de Verbo Incarnato*, Matriti, Consejo Superior de Investigaciones Cientificas, 1957, pp. 37, 38. Cf. also the passage in Novatian's *De Trinitate*, n. 23; *ibid.*, p. 78. Further quotations from Apollinarius and Athanasius are on pp. 110, 190.

out that the stylistic juxtaposition of "Son of God" and "Son of Man" uses the latter phrase *wrongly*, because the expression in the New Testament carries a different set of meaning-elements.

The expression "Son of Man" is not the only expression whose original New Testament meaning has changed. It is well known that the Greek word for "Anointed One"—*Christos*—became a proper name very early; "the Lord," "the Messiah," "the Savior" have become standardized designations that are so close to the status of the proper name that the original meaning of these metaphors is virtually lost in present-day usage.[13]

The significance of this process of change can be analyzed more technically. The use of "Son of Man" in the earliest tradition (going back to the period before the redaction of the Synoptic Gospels) can be described in terms of metaphoric language-use. Out of all the meaning-elements of "Son of Man"[14] a certain number were applied to Jesus, on the strength of the disjunctive applicability of meaning-elements in the metaphor. Now it must be remembered that the cognitive, clarifying function of the metaphor is only part of its total function. One use of "Son of Man" was doubtless to enable its users to be articulate, but that does not exhaust the total response on the part of the believer. The total response was first and foremost, to *name* Jesus, and in naming we are more affected by the thing or the person named than vice versa. The quality of response is the fundamental element in a name; it is all-encompassing (*das Umgreifende*); the cognitive *structuring* that evolves *in* the metaphoric designation is always secondary and partial.

We have seen that an expression like "Son of Man" has changed its meaning. The question is now what the significance of this change is. What took place was a change, or even a loss, of cognitive structuring, of articulation; but the *basic function* of the expression— the one that is irreducible to cognition—was preserved, namely, the *response* to the person of Jesus. It is obvious that this harbors the risk of irrationality and fundamentalism, but one isolated responsive

---

[13]Except, of course, in *discussions* about "Savior-myths" and "Christ-figures."

[14]For the purposes of our present discussion it is unnecessary to determine what the precise meanings of "Son of Man" were in the beginning of the first century A.D.—"heavenly," "coming," "working," etc.

phrase need not, in and by itself, be depreciated for not having much structuring power,[15] no more than a person's proper name is to be considered pointless because it is meaning-less.

The Christian response to Christ surpasses knowledge

We conclude that the fundamental significance of all christological names is found in the irreducible fact—to be accepted as such—that the Christian responds to the person of Jesus Christ. This may seem to be too obvious a truth to be worth insisting on, yet the implications of this fact have been often neglected. Whenever this happened, the *conceptual content* of christology was presented as a *premise*, leading to conclusions about *the kinds of response* the Christian owes to Christ. For example, the definition of Christ's divinity led to the conclusion that he must be worshiped. The true order of priorities, however, is the reverse; the fundamental fact is the response to the person of Jesus Christ. The divinity of Christ was defined precisely because Christians worshiped Christ. How can we find this quality of response to Christ? It is reflected in the language of christology, in the christological names and metaphors, whose rhetorical element—their use as address to Christ—is far more constant than their cognitive significance. "Son of Man" has survived centuries of use as *address*, although its *meaning* has undergone significant change. This is very important, for in a metaphor, we said, the cognitive structuring elements never exhaust the lived experience. This means that the lived experience of encounter with Christ in the title "Son of Man" has survived the shifts of meaning.

In the previous chapter we quoted Verhaar to the effect that "naming involves an approach to the thing in its own right."[16] When we use a name we testify to the fact that we are influenced by things. It is true that *I* do the naming, *I reach out*, by means of the metaphoric title, to the reality encountered, but at the same time I feel somehow *inspired*, or *compelled*, by the reality encountered to approach it with this metaphor. This is what we have previously

---

[15]An eloquent example of the primacy of address over cognitive structuring is afforded by Rev 5, 5—"the Root of David"—and Rev 22, 16—"the Root and Offspring of David." These are, of course, scrambled references to Isaiah 11, 1. 10, where *Jesse* is called "root" and "stump."

[16]Above, p. 90.

called the interaction-element in all language, which becomes particularly prominent in the metaphor. This interaction-element in language is irreducible to cognition, for it issues out of the creative, responsive freedom involved in the person's encounter with reality. This is—again—the reason why a metaphor must be *taken for granted*—it is an irreducible given. Rhetoric, therefore, must be *described* rather than made the subject of an investigation that tries to find the sources of its intellectual cogency; cogency, coherence and structure evolve *within*, not prior to, the activity by which persons deal with reality.

Personal response to Christ is the setting of all cognitive christological statements. This personal response is conveyed by the rhetorical elements in christology. Let us turn, then, to a consideration of rhetoric in christology.

RHETORIC AND THE SPIRIT

Dangers of irrationality?

Rhetoric has always been the target of suspicion. The reason for this is clear. Rhetoric represents the unstructured and unstructurable element in language; what are the norms that govern its use? Rhetoric can control people; but how can rhetoric be controlled? If we base all christological statements on rhetoric, are we going to end up with anything more solid than a merely fideistic sort of piety?

In Plato's *Gorgias* we find rhetoric defined as "craft of persuasion."[17] Arguments can be specious, promises can be empty, rogues can pretend they are virtuous; rhetoric is meant to persuade, and therefore it can mislead the uneducated and the inexperienced by means of a semblance of, for example, compelling argument. Rhetoric is thus associated with unwarrantable influencing of the gullible, with manipulation of the unaware.

Yet the fact remains that people will affect each other one way or another when they speak and listen to each other. Rhetoric is unavoidable. Sometimes its persuasiveness is warranted, at other times it is not. In the latter case it is often possible to unmask the faulty persuasiveness, for example, by pointing out that the cognitive

---

[17]Cf. 453a; *peithous dēmiourgos hē rhētorikē.*

structures implied in the rhetoric are not compelling and even contradictory, thus exposing the rhetorician as at best a misguided enthusiast, at worst a person inspired by envy, by rivalry, partisanship, and the like, so that he becomes insincere, spiteful, deceitful, etc. Still, the possibility of abuse *does not discredit rhetoric as such*, inasmuch as it may also be inspired by good will and truthfulness.

It is even possible to see some good hidden in the evil of the abuse of rhetoric. Paul was able to resign himself to the fact that the proclamation of Christ was colored by false and even immoral *motives*; but at least it was a response to Christ and it brought him to others' attention.[18] In the same way we might say that, even though the *contents* of a christological statement may be incomplete or even downright untrue, this does not detract from the fact that the mere act of speaking about him makes a difference; heresy *about* Christ can exist only by the grace of a response *to* Christ.

Language-as-activity, or rhetoric, is an original given; as such, it is not discredited, in advance, by the possibility of immorality or untruthfulness on the part of its users. In the same way the rhetoric of christology, being the Christian's lingual way of responding to the reality of Jesus Christ, is an original given; it may be perverted or distorted, but never quite ruled out of order. It represents the given response to the givenness of Jesus Christ, and as such it undercuts the distinctions between good and evil, and between truth and falsehood.

Fideism must be rejected because of its *exclusive* reliance on irrationality. But it would be wrong to reject fideism to get rid of all a-rationality—in order to reduce the faith to a morally good response to Christ based on insight into christological truth; that would amount to making doctrine the premise for the surrender of faith. Cognitive structuring and moral integrity evolve *within* the setting of the act of encounter, not prior to it.

This is the reason why we must first consider the nature of the Christian "situation" and of the active, responsive encounter(s) that evolve(s) in it. After that we must face the issue of the structuring of this situation.

---

[18]Cf. Phil 1, 15–18.

The Christian situation: the Spirit

In his analysis of the primal relationship involved in the active, responsive encounter of the I with a Thou, Martin Buber uses the crucial word "Spirit."[19] The New Testament uses the same word to characterize what we have called the irreducible element of responsive interaction in christological language. Whatever Christians do stands under the sign of the Spirit.

The Spirit of God is both the source from which, and the environment in which, all Christian activity evolves, as well as the quality, the "charge" that accounts for the effectualness of all Christian activity. When Christians go astray they "extinguish," "lie against," or "grieve" the Spirit. When the members of the Sanhedrin confront Stephen, the man who spoke so irresistibly on the strength of the Spirit, they find themselves characterized as obstacles to the Spirit. To call the Spirit that moves Jesus an "unclean spirit" is unforgivable blasphemy against the Holy Spirit; conversely, no one can call Jesus "Lord" except in the Holy Spirit.[20]

The Spirit in and of himself, has no "program": in the Spirit Christians (and even unbaptized believers) can speak ecstatic gibberish, and sing "spiritual" songs-without-words. You have to trust that the Spirit will lead you into all truth, and that he will prompt you to speak without your being worried about what to say. The Spirit prays in the Christian even if he does not know what to say, and the Spirit's prayer is a prayer of groans beyond words. But this does not mean that the human spirit is rendered inactive, for the witness of the Spirit is a witness in unison with the witness of our own spirit.[21]

The Spirit is not only the Christian's inner motive force; he is also outside him. He is like a wind with no perceptible direction, no ascertainable origin. The experienced unity of the Church in love is the experience of the Spirit as a climate of inspiration; the Church is built up into a temple in the constructive atmosphere of the Spirit. He is the air of freedom where people can breathe and so become free

---

[19]Martin Buber, *Ich und Du*, pp. 49ff.; *I and Thou*, pp. 89ff.

[20]Cf. 1 Thess 5, 19; Eph 4, 30; Acts 5, 3; 6, 10; 7, 51; Mk 3, 29–30; 1 Cor 12, 3.

[21]Cf. Acts 10, 44–45; Eph 5, 19; Col 3, 16 (spiritual songs as against psalms and hymns); Lk 12, 11–12; Rom 8, 26–27; 1 Cor 2, 10–13.

to love others. The Spirit is the invitation to respond, the urge to respond, and the response itself. It is expressed, most mysteriously, in Paul's first letter to the Corinthians. Only the Spirit fathoms the depths of God; we have actually received that Spirit; and when you hear God's mystery conveyed in spiritual words, you can actually understand it in virtue of the Spirit.[22]

The Spirit is given, and, as such, pure grace, pure faith, to be accepted as gift and to be "taken for granted." It is God's presence experienced in the present moment[23]—a presence that owes nothing to the past by way of causality and contains no definite, particular assurances with respect to the future; it is peace the world can neither give nor take away; it is the forgiveness of all sins. The Spirit causes Christians to be fearless in the face of death and joyful in the face of suffering. In the Spirit, they are unworried about their own righteousness because they have, in faith, committed their cause to God and no longer sit in judgment on themselves in the name of "Law." They have received the Spirit of liberty, of sonship, which enables them to be at home with God in the familiarity of the "Abba" and the love of the brethren, and even of their enemies. Paul gives a list of all the attitudes that result from the dynamic presence of the Spirit: love, joy, peace, patience, kindness, goodness, faithfulness, gentleness, self-control—just as he enumerates all the functions in the Church that, instead of competing with each other, contribute, in the Spirit, to the building-up of one body: utterance of wisdom, utterance of knowledge, faith, healing, miracle-working, prophecy, discernment of spirits, gifts of tongues, administration, apostleship.[24]

The presence of God in the Spirit is also particularly felt in the qualities of confidence and freedom, both with regard to God and with regard to others. At home with God, Christians need not ensconce themselves in a defensive fortress of their own or in their own powers. Even the consciousness of their own sins is not a captivating concern for them. They are not dependent on others'

---

[22]Cf. Jn 3, 8; 1 Cor 12, 1–13; Eph 2, 22; 2 Cor 3, 17; Gal 5, 13. 25; 1 Cor 2, 10–13.

[23]The tradition has preserved this in such notions as Ignatius of Loyola's consolation without preceding cause (*Spiritual Exercises,* n. 330), and in the tradition of "spiritual reading," which consists in the reading of old texts in the light of the *present* experience of the Spirit.

[24]Cf. Acts 5, 41; Mk 13, 11; Gal 4, 4–11; 5, 22; 1 Cor 12, 8–10.

approval or sanction; they confess their faith and live their life. Their prayer is marked by God's presence in the Spirit. Their worship is not limited to words and ritual, but extends to their whole being—Christians *are* a spiritual sacrifice of praise and thanksgiving.[25] The presence of the Spirit also animates and informs Christians' response to the world and their fellow men: they live in freedom and confidence for all to see, and so they become witnesses in word as well as in deed, in the surrender of love to the brethren and in the witness to Jesus Christ.

The theme of the presence of God in the Holy Spirit is an all-pervasive element in Acts and in the Pauline writings, in which it appears very explicitly; it is easily recognizable in the rest of the New Testament. Writing, for example, to the Thessalonians, Paul makes a point of reminding them that it is not just confident, powerful, and convincing *preaching* that warrants their faith; he disowns any human effectualness, both to them and to others, especially the Corinthians. They themselves experienced power in the *accepting* of the Gospel "with joy inspired by the Holy Spirit"; they can go back to their own experience of the Spirit and are no longer dependent on Paul's assurance or authority. This experience of God's presence in the Spirit is more basic than the authoritative apostolic preaching, no matter how strongly aware Paul is of the fact that it was *he* that brought them the Gospel; whatever authority was his in preaching has *its* roots, too, in the Holy Spirit.[26] And so we could go on; words would convey the Spirit's reality, and yet always fall short of doing justice to it. If we must sum up what we have said, let us say that the Spirit is the presence that creates the Christian situation.

Christ-talk is talk in the Spirit

In this Spirit, in the real presence of God's love setting his chosen free to love others, Christians surrender and address themselves to, and act and speak in the name of, Jesus Christ. The main characteristic of the Christian's commitment to Jesus Christ, as it emerges from the New Testament viewed as the earliest expression of the Church's dealing with reality, is that it is an *active* commitment.

---

[25]Cf. 1 Cor 6, 20; Eph 1, 12; Phil 1, 11.
[26]Cf. 1 Thess 1, 2–10; 1 Cor 2, 1–5; Phil 2, 12–18; 1 Thess 1, 9–12, 19–20; Gal 4, 19.

All christological statements, while having clear cognitive functions, are embedded in this act—an act of worship and witness—of surrender to Jesus Christ.

COMMITMENT TO CHRIST AS THE SETTING OF DISCERNMENTS

Introductory

Three characteristics of special importance will require exploration and analysis in this section. First, the commitment to Jesus Christ is as original a "given" as the awareness of the presence of God in the Spirit. Second, the concern with, and the commitment to, Jesus Christ is not one among many, not even in the sense of being the most important one, but it is the source, the medium, and the goal of all concerns and commitments. Third, all the articulations of this commitment to, and concern with, Jesus Christ in the Spirit are shaped by particular concerns brought into the act of total commitment and all-embracing concern.

Concern with Jesus Christ and awareness of the Spirit

The commitment to Jesus Christ is as original a "given" in the New Testament as the awareness of the presence of God in the Spirit. The Spirit *is* the Spirit of Jesus Christ, sent by him, breathed on to the apostles, and given up on the cross. In the Spirit, Christ is alive and at work in the Church, his Body; if the community enjoys anything in the way of identity, life, holiness, forgiveness and freedom, it does so in the name of Jesus Christ. In the Spirit, the community knows that it is at home with God, and this God is "the God and Father of our Lord Jesus Christ." The Father is present to the community in the Spirit, and he is present with Jesus Christ. The community's life comes from the Father and goes to the Father through Christ, but it is also said to be mysteriously "hidden in God with Christ." He is their life, and, in the immediacy of life-giving presence, "the Lord is the Spirit." [27]

For Paul, this naming of the life in the Spirit by the name of Jesus Christ acquires the most intimately personal, mystical dimen-

---

[27] Cf. Jn 16, 7; 20, 22; Mt 27, 50; 2 Cor 1, 3; 1 Jn 2, 23; Jn 14, 23; 1 Cor 8, 6; Col 3, 3–4; 2 Cor 3, 17.

sions, especially in his letter to Philippi. He yearns for the Philippians with the affection of Christ Jesus, for whom he is imprisoned. If such is his imprisonment, then Christ is honored in his person, for to live is Christ, and what gain there is in dying is in being with Christ. In the light of his knowledge of Christ Jesus, "my Lord," everything is garbage, worth giving up to gain him and to be found in him, "who has made me his own." And to the Galatians he can write: "I have been crucified with Christ; it is no longer I who live, but Christ who lives in me; and the life I now live in the flesh I live by faith in the Son of God, who loved me and gave himself for me."[28]

There is no attempt either in Paul, or elsewhere in the New Testament, to *prove* the central significance of Jesus in the life of the Spirit. It is not as if the community first enjoyed the Spirit as its all-encompassing religious experience, then set out to look for a striking example of this religious experience, and finally settled on Jesus as a particularly illuminating one. We do not get the picture of a spiritually enlightened community that fully understands the spiritual meaning of the promises and the prophecies, and then uses this knowledge as the touchstone to determine that Jesus is the Promised One. Not by a process of determination or choice on the part of an inspired religious community is Jesus identified as "the One," but in an act of response to his person; those who so respond know that, rather than choosing, they have been chosen, and rather than designating, they have been designated. Philip, in John's Gospel, says indeed: "We have found him of whom Moses in the Law and also the prophets wrote, Jesus of Nazareth, the son of Joseph," but this saying is only the response to what immediately precedes, viz. that Jesus "found Philip."[29] The promises and prophecies are illuminated by the present encounter with Christ. In and of themselves they fade into shadows and "types" in the light of the immediacy of the encounter (a central theme of the letter to the Hebrews[30]); the actuality of the fulfillment completely surpasses all the promises and the yearnings for the promises.

We conclude that the act of surrender to Jesus Christ, like the

---

[28]Cf. Phil 1, 8. 13. 23–24; 3, 8–9. 12; Gal 2, 20.
[29]Jn 1, 45. 43.
[30]Cf. Heb 8, 5; 10, 1 (*skia*); Heb 8, 5 (*typos*).

awareness of the Spirit's presence, precedes all insights, not only those about the fulfillment of the promises and the prophecies, the place of the Law, or the significance of the Baptist (especially in the Fourth Gospel), but also all insights about who Jesus is, and about what the Christian's relationships are with respect to God, himself, other Christians, outsiders, and indeed the world as a whole.

Commitment to Christ is pre-eminent—Spirit-christology

   What we have just said leads to a second characteristic of the Christian's act of surrender to Jesus Christ. The very givenness of the relationship to Jesus Christ causes Christians to address themselves to everything under invocation of Jesus Christ. We explained in the previous chapter how in the name, and especially in the proper name, we are influenced by reality rather than influencing it. Christians meet and deal with reality under invocation of the name of Jesus Christ; this means that Jesus Christ has become the presence that suffuses, and the light that illuminates, all of reality for them. Through him, and with him, and in him the mystery of life has been disclosed, the broken pieces have been assembled, the all has been made one.

   All kinds of metaphors are used to express this. Some are taken from the various traditions in the Jewish heritage, some borrowed from past or current Hellenistic sensibility and world-picture, some from less thematically developed "human experience." Now we must realize that the material for metaphors is taken from significant areas of human experience, from things that people find important. We will express this by the term "concern"; everything that is significant and valuable to a person or a group of persons is thus a concern.[31] If, then, we find metaphors used to express the Christian's surrender to Jesus Christ we must conclude that Christians express their surren-

---

[31]A concern, therefore, is everything that, *as a matter of actual fact*, engages my interest (our, their interest), no matter whether it is something physical, psychological, or spiritual, no matter whether it is voluntary or involuntary. In short, a concern is everything that *matters*. For an excellent statement of this, in tune with the patristic tradition as well as with modern sensibility, cf. Aelred Squire, *Asking the Fathers*, London, SPCK, 1973, pp. 51–66. Cf. *ibid.*, pp. 71ff., where Squire makes an excellent case for the thesis that *eros* and *agape* must not be separated in such a way as to make Christianity irrelevant to the "teeming life of the universe." Hence, our term "concern" can also be defined as "everything that involves *eros*."

der in this way because they experience their concerns as illuminated by Jesus Christ, and hence as usable in the process of addressing themselves to Jesus Christ. The wide range of metaphors used by the Christians of the New Testament to address themselves to Christ bears witness to the fact that concern with Jesus Christ is pre-eminent, and inclusive of all other concerns. We must conclude, therefore, that the commitment to Jesus Christ is not one among many commitments, not even in the sense of being the most important one, but it is the source and goal of all other commitments, and capable of placing all concerns.

Awareness of the powerful presence of the Spirit and all-inclusive commitment to Christ—two original, closely-connected givens of New Testament christology. No wonder, then, that the community develops a taste for an expression of Christ's significance in terms of the Spirit. The community acknowledges, in worship and in witness, that it has received the Spirit through, with and in Jesus Christ. It acknowledges the activity of the Spirit in itself. What better way to convey who Jesus is than having its own experience of the Spirit's activity chime in with and echo the Spirit as he is active in Jesus Christ? The powerful presence of the Spirit is one of the overriding *motifs*, an all-inclusive *locus communis*, for the celebration of and witness to the community's own self-awareness vis-à-vis Jesus Christ. It should come as no surprise that some of the New Testament communities will speak about Christ in terms of Spirit experience, and thus develop what may be called a pneumatological christology.[32]

It is clear that this christology must consist of *specific* pneumatological statements about Christ; in addition there was ample Old Testament precedent for such statements. But it must not be forgotten that Christ-talk about "Spirit" (and, as we will see, "power" and "*exousia*") involves more than the making of christological statements by means of apt expressions borrowed from the tradition. "Spirit" sums up the "christological situation"; it is the *linguistic commonplace* to convey the quality of the setting *in which* specific christological statements are made. Spirit-talk represents the

---

[32]Cf. P. Schoonenberg, "Spirit Christology and Logos Christology,' *Bijdragen* 38 (1977) 350–375.

Christian reality-experience in the acknowledgement of Jesus Christ. In virtue of Christians' own experience of the actuality of the Spirit they can name Jesus Christ and start to articulate his significance.

Thus, there is correspondence between the proclamation that Jesus is alive "according to the Spirit of holiness by his Resurrection from the dead" and Paul's assurance that "if the Spirit of him who raised Jesus from the dead dwells in you, he who raised Christ Jesus from the dead will give life to your mortal bodies also through his Spirit which dwells in you."

Looking back from present experience to the earthly life of Jesus, Christians see him as anointed by God with the Holy Spirit and with power. Conceived by the overshadowing of the Holy Spirit and the power of the Most High, led into the desert by the Spirit, baptized under the wings of the Spirit, preaching, exulting, and driving out demons in the Spirit, he will finally give up the Spirit in death.[33]

Similarly, "power" issues from him; his wonderful acts are referred to as *dynameis*, "powers"; people wonder about the origin of his power. But underlying all these articulations is the *community's* experience of power in the confession of Christ, "the power of God."[34]

Similarly, if the community recognizes, and is awed at, its own confidence and freedom, it cannot but recognize the *exousia* of Jesus in his earthly life.[35]

"Spirit," "power," "authoritative, confident freedom," in other words, are some of the *loci communes*[36] which enable the believers to express, in a comprehensive way, their response to each other, to non-Christians, and, indeed, to all of reality, and therefore function as the

---

[33]Rom 1, 4; 8, 11.—Cf. Acts 10, 38; Lk 1, 35; Mk 1, 12; Lk 3, 22; 4, 14–18; 10, 21; Mt 12, 28; 27, 50.

[34]Cf. Lk 6, 19; 8, 46; Mt. 11, 21. 23; 13, 54; 1 Cor 1, 24.

[35]For *exousia* ("authoritative freedom") as characterization of Jesus' behavior, especially in teaching, forgiveness of sins, the cleansing of the temple, exorcisms, and miracles, cf., for example, Mk 1, 22; 2, 10; Mt 9, 8; Mk 11, 28; 1, 27, etc.; for the disciples' *exousia* in the Synoptics, cf. Mk 6, 7; Mt 10, 1; Mk 3, 15. In 1 Cor the word (and its verbal relative *exestin*) refers to the freedom in the Spirit claimed by the Corinthians.

[36]Others are, obviously, "wisdom," "glory," "justice," and "love." Our emphasis here is not on completeness, but on the fact that we are dealing with themes, commonplaces, *loci communes*.

setting for partial christological statements. By means of these partial statements the community will articulate the *structure* of its relationship with Christ, but all partial statements make sense only within the setting of the encompassing *loci communes.* Let us illustrate this by means of two examples. Christians develop the idea of the fullness of the Spirit in Jesus Christ, whereas they themselves have the Spirit only as a pledge, or a seed. Paul develops his idea of God's power, manifest in Christ, defeating, by its very weakness, what passes for power in human eyes. In these and similar expressions, the commonplace is used to be *articulate* about the relationship between Christ and the Christians. But it remains true that such themes as "Spirit," "power," and "confident freedom" are first and foremost *loci communes,* symbolizing the quality of the Christian response to reality in their all-encompassing response to the person of Jesus Christ.

We have, as promised, characterized the commitment to Jesus Christ as original and as all-encompassing. We must now pass on to an analysis of the fact that Christian response to Jesus Christ is also *articulate.* At this point it is useful to allow ourselves an interlude in order to be taught by a great master, who has pointed out the risks we run in the transition from religious encounter to conceptual apprehension, from commitment to discernment.

Interlude: Martin Buber on response to reality

Martin Buber, in a profound study entitled *Eclipse of God,* has in his own way dealt with the problem of rhetoric vs. structure, commitment vs. discernment, responsive interaction vs. cognitive structuring, polarities which he discusses in the chapter on "Religion and Philosophy." In some periods, Buber explains,

> that which men "believe in" as something absolutely independent of themselves is a reality with which they are in a living relation, although they well know that they can form only a most inadequate representation of it.[37]

In other times, "this reality is replaced by a varying representation that men 'have' and therefore can handle"; in such times, religious people "usually fail to realize that the relation conceived of as

---

[37]Martin Buber, *Eclipse of God,* p. 13.

religious [. . .] has existence only within the mind—a mind which [. . .] contains hypostatized images, hypostatized 'ideas.' "[38] Obviously

> this does not mean that a given concept of God, a conceptual apprehension of the divine, necessarily impairs the concrete religious relationship. Yet, the more abstract the concept, the more does it need to be balanced by the evidence of living experience, with which it is intimately bound up *rather than linked in an intellectual system.*[39]

This leads Buber to the statement that religious meaning is not

> to be won and possessed through any type of analytical or synthetic investigation or through any type of reflection on the lived concrete. Meaning is to be experienced in living action and suffering itself, in the unreduced immediacy of the moment. Of course, he who aims at the experiencing of experience will necessarily miss the meaning, for he destroys the spontaneity of the mystery. Only he reaches the meaning who stands firm, without holding back or reservation, before the whole might of reality and answers it in a living way. He is ready to confirm with his life the meaning which he has attained. Every religious utterance is a vain attempt to do justice to the meaning which has been attained. All religious expression is only an intimation of its attainment. The reply of the people of Israel on Sinai, "We will do it, we will hear it," expresses the decisive with naive and unsurpassable pregnancy. The meaning is found through the engagement of one's own person; it only reveals itself as one takes part in its revelation.[40]

The placing of the discernments

The basic christological utterances we have explored so far are the expression of *personal* (and interpersonal) *response and commitment to the person of Christ.* This response and this commitment put the cognitive, structuring elements in christological language in their places. These cognitive, structuring elements, which we will also call "discernments," remain, on account of their partial and even frag-

---

[38] *Ibid.*

[39] *Ibid.*, p. 14 (italics added). The linkage in an intellectual system mentioned by Buber is what Verhaar means when he says that the meaning of terms is primarily determined by "internal reference": "Language and Theological Method," p. 22 (*Bijdragen*, p. 58).

[40] *Ibid.*, pp. 35–36.

mentary nature, secondary to the overriding and all-encompassing element of commitment and surrender. The commitment and surrender to Christ is conveyed by the *act* of speaking itself, by the christological statement viewed as rhetorical. A few pages back we referred to partial christological statements in the setting of the comprehensive commitment to Jesus Christ in the Spirit; we will argue, later on, that these partial statements are discernments of partial concerns in the light of this commitment. For the time being we must inquire into the relationship between the conveyance of total commitment and the making of partial articulations.

Let us go back to a thesis developed in the previous chapter, namely, that we think in *words* and handle reality in *names*. Now words and names mostly coincide in the concrete act of speech. Sometimes language (mostly spoken) approximates the "pure name," in which case the function of responsive activity will be most prominent. Sometimes, and certainly in terminological usage, language (very often: written language) approximates free thought, in which case the function of discernment and articulation will be most prominent. But there is never an absolute division between words-with-cognitive-meaning on the one hand, and names-with-responsive-meaningfulness on the other hand, certainly not in the middle of the range of language-use.

With regard to the metaphors used in christology an analogous observation is in order. They function as *names*—they function rhetorically—and in doing so they convey the believer's responsive act of surrender, which cannot be reduced to cognition. They also function as *words*; they have clarifying characteristics. This means that, to the extent the speaker successfully manages to negotiate cognitive meaning, metaphors serve to capture particular discernments. These particular discernments are relatively non-situational; metaphors *can* be removed from the situation and considered by themselves without complete loss of meaning.

This leads to a conclusion. Some time ago we wondered whether our stress on the primacy of rhetoric was not going to lead to a purely fideistic kind of christological piety.[41] We can now see that the very nature of the language we use prevents this from coming about.

---

[41] Above, p. 115.

The coincidence of name and word, of speech as activity and speech as structuring, of commitment and discernment, of rhetoric and logic, prevents the rhetoric of faith from lapsing into purely irrational surrender.

Still, though the word and the name coincide, they have two different functions, which cannot be reduced to each other; language-as-activity and language-as-cognition, *functionally speaking*, are not identical. This leads to a conclusion.

Ian Ramsey gives evidence of his having noticed the difference between activity and cognition when he states that the religious situation is characterized by a "fuller discernment" and a "total commitment." Discernments are always particular and partial when considered in and by themselves, and thus require the use of the comparative: a full*er* discernment. But why are discernments partial? They are partial because in the act of removing a metaphor (now reduced to a mainly cognitive structuring device to articulate a discernment) from the concrete situation something is lost, namely, the concrete speech-act in the concrete situation, in which alone the "point"—the total meaning, the "total commitment" to Christ—is realized. Hence, discernments are always open to gradation; they are rightly called approximative; they do not by themselves tell the whole story.[42] We will henceforth refer to this characteristic of discernments by saying that discernments are "placed."

A very important conclusion follows from the fact that discernments are placed. *No discernment taken by itself may be allowed to lead to conclusions which curtail or belie the commitment, nor can any discernment lay claim to being the sole bearer of the commitment.*[43]

We must sum up this section, which set out to argue the thesis that articulations of the commitment to Jesus Christ are done by means of particular concerns.

The total surrender to Jesus Christ in the Spirit is the all-encompassing "christological situation." No single statement does

---

[42]*Pace* DS 3882.

[43]This thesis has the same purpose as Bonhoeffer's critical christology: *Christ the Center*, pp. 104–106 (GS pp. 229–231). Its task is to guard against false theological content and inappropriate thought-forms in christology, by measuring them against the "fact of Jesus Christ."

justice to the full reality of the Christian community's total commitment-response; the latter is only realized in the acts of worship and witness. The total response is conveyed by such *loci communes* as "Spirit" and "power," which primarily serve as symbols of reality-experience, and sometimes also provide the material for structural discernments. Mostly, however, the material for structural discernments comes from a variety of human concerns. The meaning of all the discernments is not lost when they are removed from the christological situation, but their full meaning is only realized in the context of the total commitment-response. Discernments are, and must remain, placed, if their total meaning is to be discovered.

TERMS, DISCERNMENTS, CONCERNS

Preliminary

The first section of this chapter provided a theoretical basis for the description of New Testament christological rhetoric given in the second section. In the third section we slowly moved away from the consideration of rhetoric as the conveyor of total commitment, in the direction of discernment as the means to articulate the commitment. The present section is meant to form a theoretical introduction to the fifth and final section of this chapter. Our purpose in the rest of the chapter will be not only to clarify the relationship between commitment and discernments in christology, but also to explore the ways in which both are related to human life and the concerns involved in it.

Rhetoric is not a pastoral cosmetic

In the course of the Second Vatican Council many outcries were heard against the legalistic, intellectualistic language in which the *schemata* prepared by the many preparatory commissions were couched. Consequently, the Council Fathers demanded a more pastoral, biblical style, in keeping with the pastoral objectives Pope John XXIII had so movingly emphasized in his opening address.[44] One of the *periti* who had been very influential in the Council's preparatory stage was heard to say, in regard to this demand, that it could easily

---

[44] In: Walter M. Abbott, S.J. (ed.), *The Documents of Vatican II* [London/New York], Geoffrey Chapman/The America Press, 1966, pp. 710–719.

be satisfied by a goodly admixture of pious and profound quotations from Scripture to make the texts more acceptable. This is an extrinsecist notion of rhetoric, and some texts of Vatican II, prolix as they are, do indeed suffer from this use of rhetoric as a pastoral cosmetic. Adding rhetoric to highly legalistic and intellectualistic content never achieves more than pious verbosity around dead bones.

Chalcedon: the rhetoric of the act of faith

The text of Chalcedon is a rhetorical statement:

> Following therefore the holy Fathers, we all teach harmoniously that we should confess one and the same our Lord Jesus Christ, the same perfect in Godhead, the same perfect in manhood, truly God and truly man, the same of a reasonable soul and body; consubstantial with the Father in Godhead, and the same consubstantial with us in manhood, like us in all things except sin; begotten before the ages of the Father in Godhead, the same in the last days for us; and for our salvation [born] of Mary the virgin *theotokos* in manhood, one and the same Christ, Son, Lord, unique; acknowledged in two natures without confusion, without change, without division, without separation—the difference of the natures being by no means taken away because of the union, but rather the distinctive character of each nature being preserved, and [each] combining in one Person and hypostasis—not divided or separated into two Persons, but one and the same Son and only-begotten God, Word, Lord Jesus Christ.[45]

We have here a dogmatic passage cast in the rhetorical *figura* of the double *inclusio*: "one and the same our Lord Jesus Christ . . . one and the same Christ, Son, Lord, unique . . . one and the same Son and only-begotten God, Word, Lord Jesus Christ." The beginning of the passage is explicitly personal: "Following . . . the holy Fathers we all teach." These rhetorical traits are not cosmetics, but part of the message itself. They echo worship and witness—the sole setting in which the dogmatic statement sanctioned by the definition makes its point. The rhetorical figures of the definition remind us that we are dealing with an *act* of speech. Its authority and confidence prevent us from assuming that the full meaning of the definition can be arrived at by means of an analysis of the words and terms employed.

---

[45]DS 301–302.

The definition goes on to state: "We all teach harmoniously *that we should confess* one and the same, our Lord Jesus Christ." The object of the teaching is authoritatively to urge and endorse the worshipful *act* of the confession of Jesus Christ. It is only in this context that the discernments and the rule of speech that expresses the discernments are enforced.

The Chalcedonian "definition" is first and foremost an *act* of faith which consists in urging the faithful to engage in an *act* of faith; this is borne out by the rhetorical structure—an echo of worship and witness—and by the fact that the immediate object of the teaching is the *homologia*, the act of confessional worship of, and witness to, "one and the same, our Lord Jesus Christ." The largely terminological rule of speech is taught only secondarily.

Chalcedon: the concern behind the terminology

In the Chalcedonian statement we distinguished between those parts that embody the immediate object of the Fathers' teaching, which is the act of confessional worship of, and witness to, Christ, and those parts which mainly stress the secondary object, which is the technical, conceptual rule of speech. It was relatively easy to do this because the definition proper—the rule of speech that is enforced—is couched in such highly *terminological* language. If the definition had used natural-language *words*, it would have been much harder to separate the rhetorical parts and the cognitive, structuring parts of the definition. Names and words, evocation and articulation coincide in natural language. By contrast, terms have lost their evocative ability; they are non-situational when considered in and by themselves. This made it easy to tell the discernments apart from the rhetoric in the Chalcedonian definition. Yet, as was stated at the beginning of the present chapter, terminological language, no matter how conceptual, is by no means use-less. The only thing is that its usefulness in situations is experienced as more or less extrinsic to its validity as a vehicle of coherent rational discourse.

At this point we must recall a point made in the previous chapter. The self-involving, disclosure-evoking and community-building, that is to say, the rhetorical elements inherent in natural language—having once been excluded in the interest of stable rationality—reassert themselves in terminological language in ways that make those elements hard to identify and accept.[46] *How* terms are to be used *appropriately*—in the interest of the concerns which they were meant to serve—cannot be read off by looking at the meaning of the terms themselves.

In the cultural community that employs terms, however, there is an often tacit understanding about the appropriate use of such terms. Thus psychologists know that to call a person "neurotic" does not entail any value-judgment with regard to the person. The appropriate concern behind the use of "neurotic" is classification or diagnosis, not, for example, discrimination. In spite of the fact, then, that terms are extremely objective and remote from situations, they can doubtlessly *function* as vital words in a cultural community. This will be the case if such a community understands and endorses and shares the *concerns* that are tacitly agreed upon as being served by the terminology employed, even though the *meaning* of the terms is mainly established by internal reference.

There is a second point to be made about the use of terms. Precisely because terms are defined by a community, the natural connection between a term and its meaning is much looser than the bond between a *word* and its referent. Terms are extremely stable for those who know how to use them. For others they are very ambiguous. A fight about semantics is infinitely more liable to occur with reference to a term than to a word/name.

An alternative way of putting this is as follows: terminological language only creates the *illusion* that we can talk without *loci communes*—that we need no setting on which the terms and their meanings are dependent for their meaningfulness or relevance.

Terminology assumes rather than expresses common concerns. But this assumption—namely that we all know what we are talking about—opens terminological language to misuse on the level of "point." When we use terms we appear to be enormously articulate; but that is not necessarily so. Only those who know the meaning of the terms and the concerns behind the terminology are articulate and make the point. The others—those who miss both the meaning of the terms and the points made—are taking the first step on the road to derealization.

If we apply this to the interpretation of Chalcedon's highly

---

[46]Cf. above, pp. 79–80, 86–87.

terminological definition, we can understand two important points. First, the relatively loose connection between terms and their meanings largely accounts for not only some of the difficulties surrounding the understanding of the *communicatio idiomatum*,[47] but also, and especially, for the problem involved in settling on the concepts of *hypostasis* to convey the unity and *physis* to convey the duality in Christ. This became a matter of careful definition, and so the use of both *hypostasis* and *physis* was only safe in the hands of those who knew how to use them. In and of itself the term *physis* or nature could have been used with a different meaning,[48] and, in fact, was so used by Cyril in his second anathematism.[49] Second, there was an urgent need for the unity of the Church in faith. The Church found itself set in a particular culture. This culture expressed *its* concerns in highly formalized ways, by means of terms like *physis*, *hypostasis*, and *ousia*. The need for Church unity *in this situation* brought home the urgency of the intelligent, coherent use of these highly relevant terms if unity in faith was to be brought about. But something else happened as well when the Church made this move: in using *culturally significant terms* the Church recognized *relevant cultural concerns* and brought them to the confession of Jesus Christ as Lord. These *concerns* account for the viability of the terms; considered in and by themselves the terms had no effectual illuminating force; their cognitive structuring capacity is dependent on cultural commitments, and may disappear, or recede, when cultural concerns undergo a shift. It is *the culture's concerns*, and the enlightenment *the culture* has experienced in the use of terms that gives them their effective illuminating force in theology.[50]

---

[47]Cf. above, p. 109 and note 5.

[48]In connection with this, Bernard Lonergan has argued that terms like *hypostasis* and *physis* are purely heuristic: Bernard J. F. Lonergan, S.J., *A Second Collection*, William F. J. Ryan, S.J., and Bernard J. Tyrrell, S.J. (eds.), Philadelphia, The Westminster Press, 1974, pp. 25, 259. Cf. also below, p. 456.

[49]DS 254. This formula was considered Athanasian by Cyril; in fact it was Apollinarian, but circulated under Athanasius' name. The same must be said for Cyril's famous expression "the one enfleshed nature of the Word (of) God" (*mian physin tou theou logou sesarkōmemēn*) in *Ep.* 46.

[50]Hence, the terminological development that led to the neo-Chalcedonian notions of *enhypostasia* and *anhypostasia* must be said to have run a high risk of illegitimate conclusions; the development was made almost exclusively on the basis of Aristotle's definition of *physis*, i.e., by internal reference and in the interest of coherent

Conclusions regarding the interpretation of Chalcedon

We are trying to determine, in this section, the relationship between cognitive structuring elements (or discernments) and the total surrender (or commitment) in christology. The Chalcedonian definition is an example of a discernment couched in strongly terminological language. What can be said about the relationship between discernment and commitment in this definition?

First, the setting of all discernments is the responsive *act* of faith in Christ, fruit of the Spirit. This applies also to predominantly conceptual discernments expressed in terminology.

Second, the effective illuminating force—the experienced relevance—of terminology in matters theological is dependent on the experienced relevance of the terminology to living human and cultural concerns. In a dogmatic statement, therefore, "matters pertaining to this life"[51] are indirectly brought into the total response to Jesus Christ, in an effort to structure cognitively, and even conceptually, the all-encompassing reality of Jesus Christ.

Third, the true meaning of such strongly terminological christological statements as Chalcedon's cannot be derived from looking at the terms or asserting the perpetual validity of the concepts. Concepts are too loosely tied to terms to provide stability of meaning; moreover, the appropriate use of the concepts/terms—their use in the service of appropriate concerns—is dependent on familiarity with the concerns and a felt awareness of the terminology's relevance to, and meaning in the context of, the concerns. It follows that it is hazardous to enforce Chalcedonian christology today as *the* touchstone of orthodoxy; by itself the terminology gives no indication as to its appropriate use, and the concerns behind the terminology have shifted. In view of the cultural shifts *behind* the terms, and in view of the need for clarity about the theological use to which the terms may be put, theologians must apply the methods of hermeneutics to Chalcedon and the neo-Chalcedonian developments.

---

terminology, *not* in the interest of doing justice to the person of Jesus Christ, nor in the interest of pressing cultural concerns.—Similarly it must be feared that internal reference, not effective illuminating force, is the main point of attention for the *Declaratio* of 1972 when it says that the christological doctrine was proposed by the Church with ever increasing clarity and explicitness: *AAS* 64 (1972) 237; *Origins* 1 (1972) 666.

[51]For this phrase, rendering Gk. *biōtika*, cf. 1 Cor 6, 3.

Cognitive structuring in words, not terms

"The Bible has no concepts."[52] The "refinement of later dogmatic definition"[53] is not available in the New Testament. Obviously, there *is* cognitive structuring in the New Testament; but cognitive structuring in the New Testament takes place in *words* rather than terms. This is the real difference between statements of faith like the definition of Chalcedon (in which it is possible to tell apart, *in the text*, rhetoric and logic, commitment and discernments) and the language of the New Testament.

In New Testament christology we have that coincidence of name and word,[54] of speech as activity and speech as structuring, of commitment and discernment, or rhetoric and logic, which prevents the rhetoric of faith from becoming a merely fideistic sort of piety, but which also prevents faith from becoming primarily objectifying and cognitive. But the New Testament and Chalcedon have this in common, that all discernments are set in the context of commitment; all cognition evolves within the act of surrender; all meaning evolves within the context of "point." In both, discernments are expressive of, and thus dependent on, human concerns, which in the act of faith are brought to the reality of Jesus Christ as he meets the believer. It is to the structure of this intimate union of commitment and discernments, of ebriety and sobriety, that we must now turn our attention.

DISCERNMENTS AND CONCERNS: MATTERS PERTAINING TO THIS LIFE

Onlooks

Christians surrender themselves totally to Jesus Christ in the Spirit. But this surrender is not a blind, undiscerning act of fideism. In their very surrender to Jesus Christ, they are concerned with who and what he is. To use Evans' term, the Christian commitment to Jesus Christ expresses itself in "onlooks," whose basic structure is: "I look upon *x* as *y*."

Now an onlook "depends for its communicable meaning on the fact that there is an obviously-appropriate way of behaving or thinking in relation to *y*: the speaker commits himself [. . .] to a similar

---

[52]J. Verhaar, "Language and Theological Method," p. 29; *Bijdragen*, p. 65.
[53]John McIntyre, *The Shape of Christology*, p. 57.
[54]Cf. above, pp. 90–93.

attitude towards x." Evans adds that there is "no sharp dividing-line between onlook-comparisons and metaphors."[55]

Onlooks enable Christians to be *articulate* in their surrender to Christ by saying things about him according to the formula: "I look on Jesus Christ as . . . . " Yet the very use of onlooks presupposes something that goes beyond the mere similarity between x and y as intellectually perceived, beyond the isomorphism, which prevails between the reality and the model. There is something that exceeds the *cognitive* structuring of the intended reality, effected by the disjunctive application of relevant *meaning*-elements.[56] What, then, is this "something"? As Evans explains, the speaker who utters an onlook conveys implicitly that he has adopted a certain *attitude* with regard to y, which attitude (or at least one similar to it) he pledges to adopt with regard to x (if he has not done so already). Now since attitudes are habitual predispositions to insight as well as to action, clearly two elements are implied in the onlook. First, the speaker pledges to commit himself, or indicates that he has committed himself, to a particular personal response to x. For the onlook to be an effective communication-device, it is necessary that this response can be shared by the listener. But this requires that the speaker's attitudinal response to y represents an attitude shared by the listener, namely, an "obviously appropriate way of behaving" according to Evans. But this implies in turn that y represents a shared concern—something of significance to both speaker and listener. Second, the speaker commits himself, *with this concern*, to a particular personal response to x. Accordingly, the speaker should have been touched or moved by x to respond—first to respond at all, and then to respond in this fashion. The onlook thus has a double function. It bears *witness* to the listener that the speaker has been moved to respond by x, and it *clarifies* the speaker's response to x by means of the isomorphism between x (unknown to the listener) and y (known to him).

Prescinding momentarily from its effect on the listener, there is a double movement in the onlook. As the speaker brings *familiar common concerns* to the intended reality ("x") he achieves not only

---

[55]Donald D. Evans, *The Logic of Self-Involvement*, pp. 125, 131.
[56]Cf. above, pp. 91–92.

clarification, but also a commitment to respond to it by certain types of activity; on the other hand the intended reality moves the speaker to approach it with these concerns. This fits in with what was said earlier about the metaphor:[57] clarification is only part of its total function, which also comprises surrender; both the clarifying expedient and the surrender are somehow evoked by the experience of the encounter with the intended reality.

It is time to leave the cool cellars of abstract analysis and apply these considerations to christology. When Christians are articulate about Jesus Christ, they use statements that can be put in the form of onlooks. "I look on Jesus Christ as the Good Shepherd, the Son of David, the Man for others," etc. The onlooks function in a double way. They are metaphors used in the service of clarification and articulation, but, as metaphors, they also carry with them attitudes and obviously-appropriate ways of behaving or thinking with regard to "the Good Shepherd," "the Son of David," "the Man for others." And it is *the person of Jesus Christ* that compels Christians to approach him with such metaphors. In the metaphors the surrender to Christ becomes articulate and at the same time the concerns of human life as it is lived and shared are integrated into the act of surrender.

Surrender in worship and witness: the setting of discernments

Even if we do full justice to Evans' stress on the strong attitudinal experiences and commitments implied in an onlook we must say that onlooks are cool. There is a quality of distance and indirectness about them; their unrhetorical form is not calculated to carry conviction. When in certain situations I say: "Jesus Christ is the Good Shepherd," I do more than transfer an obviously-appropriate attitude with regard to a good shepherd to Jesus Christ; I bear witness to him *before the person I address.*

The expression "Jesus Christ is the Good Shepherd" can indeed be reformulated as an onlook: "I look on Jesus Christ as the Good Shepherd"; a further analysis, such as the one above, can then show up the attitudinal elements implied in it *for me.* But *my saying*: "Jesus Christ is the Good Shepherd," though fully implying such an

---

[57] *Ibid.*

onlook on my part, is more: it is a witness, in which I personally *commend*, in front of someone else, the kind of attitude toward Jesus Christ that would be the obviously-appropriate attitude toward a good shepherd. The statement *in actual use* has only the semblance of what Buber has called an "I—It" statement. "The good shepherd" functions not as a flat predicate to a subject, but as a *title—a name*. And *names* are signs of activity—in this case, that particular activity among people which is called witness.[58] As I witness I convey personally that I have been "touched" by Jesus Christ; I share my attitude to Christ by means of a reference to the shared attitude to the "good shepherd"; I clarify my attitude to Jesus Christ by means of a metaphor designed to convey to others who and what he is.[59]

If christological titles are to sound true to the hearer, they must be used by the speaker in worship, too. Addressing myself to another person with words of witness to Jesus the Good Shepherd makes sense only if I address myself to Jesus, at least equivalently, as the Good Shepherd. Stanley contends rightly that Paul must have prayed to Christ;[60] he must have done so in words identical with, or at least similar to, the titles he uses for him in his letters. It is hard to imagine that the Apocalypse, so full of liturgical associations, would use christological titles in the service of witness, encouragement and teaching, if many of those titles were not also used in worship to address Christ. The testimony of Pliny the Younger who refers to Christians as people "together singing hymns to Christ as to a God"[61] is amply confirmed by the New Testament, not only with

---

[58]In the final analysis, this attitude of witness, by which a person personally addresses himself to others, and thus puts them in a decision-situation, goes back to Jesus confronting others in particular situations. Cf. Joachim Jeremias, *The Parables of Jesus*, New York, Charles Scribner's Sons, ²1963, *passim*, but esp. pp. 21–22, 230.

[59]This clarification may be very elementary, and even totally implicit. As long as the metaphor makes sense, it also clarifies. There is no need for a complete explanation, after the pattern, say, of the allegorical exposition of "the Good Shepherd" in Jn 10, 11–13.

[60]Cf. David M. Stanley, S.J., *Boasting in the Lord*, New York, Paulist Press, 1973, pp. 52–60, 103–104, 151–152, 180.

[61] "And they asserted that this had been the whole of their guilt or error, that it was their custom to assemble before sunrise on a fixed day, and in antiphonal style to sing a hymn to Christ as to a god, and to bind themselves by a *sacramentum* not to any crime, but that they would not commit any fraud, theft or adultery, that they would not deceive, that they would not deny a trust when called upon to deliver it up": Pliny the Younger (*Epist.* 10, 96, 7) to the emperor Trajan, quoted in Cyprian

regard to titles used to address the historical Jesus but also, and principally, with regard to titles used in worshiping him as the Lord.

To clarify this further, let us return to the concepts of *word* and *name*. In a *word* we structure, which means that we cognitively place the referent in our own world to the extent that the referent is amenable to our cognitive structuring efforts. In a *name* we handle— we deal with reality; in naming we are more affected by reality than it is by us. These two rules also apply to metaphors used as christological titles. We clarify the person of Christ by means of the disjunctively relevant meaning-elements of the titles. But these titles are also the names of Jesus,[62] inasmuch as we experience those names as belonging, not to us, but to him as he meets us who have encountered and been touched by him. At the same time we borrow those titles—remember that they have to connote "obviously appropriate ways of behaving and thinking"—from our lived encounter with other realities—an encounter shared by others. In witnessing to Christ we call upon those realities; we name them, we evoke them, and in doing so we also evoke the experiences of others in relating to the realities from which we borrow the titles. The christological titles, therefore, represent lived and shared concerns "pertaining to this life."

Therefore, in all our christological articulations two things happen.

First, matters pertaining to this life are brought into the responsive encounter with Jesus Christ; in being articulate *about* Jesus Christ we bring ourselves to him *along with* the concerns of our lives.

Second, Christ is made to preside over these matters;[63] the titles—those representatives of our concerns—become his names. In response to him, who is present in the Spirit, we call him by the

---

Vagaggini, O.S.B., *Theological Dimensions of the Liturgy*, Collegeville, The Liturgical Press, 1976, p. 159, n. 1.

[62]On this subject, cf. Vincent Taylor, *The Names of Jesus*, New York, St. Martin's Press, 1953; Oscar Cullmann, *The Christology of the New Testament*; Ferdinand Hahn, *The Titles of Jesus in Christology*, New York–Cleveland, The World Publishing Company, 1969; Leopold Sabourin, *The Names and Titles of Jesus*, New York, The Macmillan Company, 1967; Robert Murray, *Symbols of Church and Kingdom*, [London], Cambridge University Press, 1975, pp. 293ff., 354–363.

[63]For the expression "preside over," cf. Ian Ramsey, *Religious Language*, pp. 59–60.

names of our own concerns. Thus he becomes at once the one who presides over, and does justice to, the concerns of our lives. The names of Jesus, therefore, do not represent timeless truths, but his present acceptance of the concerns of those who in response to him name him.

Now it is clear how christology is concerned with the lives and deaths of Christians in that the latter provide christology with the very stuff it is made of, namely, the names of Jesus Christ.[64]

Christology is obviously also concerned with the life and death of Jesus, because there are names of Jesus that arose out of the historical encounter between Jesus and those around him and out of the metaphors Jesus used to articulate his self-consciousness. With regard to the latter we must say—in the interest of consistency with our second point above—that he presides over, and does justice to, the concerns implied by these historical titles; what meaning can be attached to this will become clearer later on.

Most importantly, *all the titles*, those expressive of the Church's concerns in response to Jesus Christ as well as those going back to the historical Jesus and those around him, *will function properly only in the Spirit in which the Lord is present to Christians and they respond to him in total commitment.*

This thesis is not at all novel or revolutionary. With regard to the Gospels, for instance, it is no more than a restatement of the thesis that the primary concern of the Gospels is not biography, but the risen Lord present to his community in the Spirit. It is also a restatement of something discussed earlier in this chapter, namely, that the actuality of the fulfillment, in Christ, of the prophecies and the yearnings far outstrips the prophecies and the yearnings. The concerns of the primitive community and their expression were to a large extent shaped by the Old Testament; these concerns were in the surrender to Christ, brought to him for him to preside over them. The same can be said for those concerns that were not specifically Jewish, and which are, for lack of a more specific designation, usually characterized as Hellenistic; they were also brought to Christ for him to preside over them.[65]

---

[64]Cf. above, p. 71.

[65]One may think of such titles as *Kyrios* (Lord) and *Sōtēr* (Savior) as used by a Greek-speaking citizen of the Roman Empire in the first century A.D.

This leads to a conclusion. It may be possible to reconstruct the original meanings of such titles with great accuracy. Such reconstructions will yield insight into the early Church's understanding of Christ. But the *total meaning* of christological titles can only be established if it is remembered that they are addressed to Christ in the Spirit, carriers of concerns that are offered to Christ for him to preside over them—that is, *for him to determine their full meaning.*

We can now conclude our discussion of *the fact that* christological discernments are "placed." We started with the thesis at the end of the third section of this chapter that no discernment may ever belie or curtail the total commitment, nor may any discernment ever lay claim to being the sole bearer of the commitment.[66] We have since added reflections on the relationship between commitment and discernments, and on the relationship between discernments and the concerns involved in human life. Let us now conclude this chapter with two final observations designed to emphasize points already made rather than to develop new conclusions.

Discernments are doubly bound

First of all, discernments are attempts at cognitive structuring, in the interest of being articulate about who and what Jesus Christ is. They are metaphors used in their structuring capacity. The use of metaphoric onlooks, we said, implies shared concerns and attitudes. Hence, each discernment must be viewed—and this is their first characteristic limitation—in the context of such concerns and attitudes if their true meaning is to be realized. *The full meaning of a metaphor is dependent on the realization of its bond with human concerns.*

This is why the procedure of looking at a particular isolated metaphor, or even concept, in order to determine its meaning, and then transferring this meaning to Christ, runs the risk of losing sight of the human concerns of which the metaphor or "concept" is the carrier. Such a procedure can easily lead to conclusions and development inferences based only on an analysis of the metaphor without taking into account the concerns which it was meant to reflect. This in turn may lead to further insensitivity to human concerns which may prompt new metaphors.

---

[66]Above, p. 128.

Second, in metaphoric titles, we have argued, concerns and attitudes are brought to Christ for him to preside over them. This bringing to Christ is *in response* to his presence in the Spirit. Only the responsive surrender to Christ, which *is* the Holy Spirit at work, guarantees that the metaphors carrying the concerns and attitudes function properly. Hence, it is more true to say that Jesus Christ determines *their* meaning than to say that *they* determine Christ's "meaning."[67] Concretely: "Jesus Christ is the Good Shepherd" *in actual use* better conveys to me what kind of person is a good shepherd than who and what Jesus Christ is,[68] and hence what kind of person I am called to be as I call him by this name. An awareness of this will prevent discernments, along with the human concerns and attitudes that animate them, from asserting themselves as somehow independent from the act of surrender which is the fruit of the Spirit.

This applies not only to the interpretation and evaluation of past christological discernments, but also to the development of new ones on the basis of present concerns that are alive and shared by a cultural community. They are obvious material for christological titles and christological articulation, precisely because they are alive and shared. At the same time, because they are the favorite concerns of a culture, they tend to assert themselves rather vigorously in their own right, even to the point of turning into ideologies.[69] This circumstance tends to prompt some Christians to proclaim new, "relevant" christologies, which are in effect nothing but partial discernments about a present human situation applied to Christ, to "place" him in the modern world, rather than letting him preside over *them*. The conservative response to such new christologies is very often an emphatic, authoritarian return to the tradition, pro-

---

[67]Bruce Vawter (*This Man Jesus*, Garden City, Doubleday & Company, 1973, pp. 82–99, 103) also implies that it is in the appellation "Christ" used for Jesus that the full meaning gets established beyond the ken of Old Testament meanings and emphases. The same is true for the title "*Kyrios*," Lord.

[68]The primacy of the quality of address in the names of Jesus would seem to account for the fact that many titles that have lost their immediate significance for the modern city-dweller are still usable. The modern megalopolis could hardly generate such titles as "shepherd," "door of the sheepfold," "king," etc.

[69]One might think of titles like "Man for Others," "fully actualized person," "totally free person," "social revolutionary," "critic of ideologies," etc.

claiming as the only orthodox christology what is, in effect, a discernment of a cultural community of the past, based on shared concerns of the past. *Both* positions agree in making one single discernment into the sole bearer of the commitment, either on the basis of an uncritically accepted dominance of a presently alive cultural concern, or on the basis of an exclusivist understanding of one single established christology considered in isolation.

This chapter has explored *the fact that* christological discernments are placed. We have seen that the surrender to Jesus Christ is articulate, and not a blind act of fideistic surrender, and that the articulations represent human concerns. Now we must ask the question: *How* are the discernments—and the concerns they represent—placed in the act of surrender? The next two chapters will consist in an exploration of this question.

CHAPTER 4

The Human Concerns: Included and Made Obedient

For our sake thou wast named by names.

The Acts of Judas Thomas

Creature with Creator   cannot be compared
for their very names   are incommensurable
and even more than the names   are the essences different.
. . . .
The Lord, the Merciful One   when he put on our name,
humbled himself by images   even to the mustard-seed.
He gave us his names   and accepted our names from us.
His names made us great   while our names made him small.
Happy is he who has spread   your good name over his own
and has made his names   beautiful through yours!

Ephrem the Syrian

We must also understand reverently what we believe [Christ] is when he is called upon by this name. When we do understand this, we shall, as a consequence, also learn clearly what sort of persons we should be shown to be as a result of our zeal for this way of life and our use of his name as the instructor and the guide for our life.

Gregory of Nyssa

All that the Father gives me will come to me; and him who comes to
me I will not cast out. For I have come down from heaven, not to do
my own will, but the will of him who sent me; and this is the will of
him who sent me, that I should lose nothing of all that he has given me,
but raise it up at the last day.

The Gospel of John

Introduction

The opening paragraph of the third chapter stated that christology has three comprehensive points to make and that it does so by
means of a triple rhetoric. Rhetoric is the expression, in language, of
the Christian *act* of faith-surrender; any discernment-statements in
christology make their point only to the extent that they are understood as articulations of this *act* of faith.

This present chapter intends to explore two of the three points,
two of the three rhetorical intentions mentioned in the beginning of
the third chapter, namely, the possibility of total inclusiveness and
the call to total obedience. In speaking about Christ, therefore,
christology must be careful not to speak in such a way as to create
the impression that there is anything that cannot be integrated into
Christ, or that anything can be integrated into Christ without a
conversion. All christological discernments, we will argue, must fit
into these two comprehensive attitudinal faith-responses to Christ.
The next chapter will then be devoted to a third, namely the offer of
absolute hope.

The need for all discernments to fit into the comprehensive
contexts of faith-surrender, we said, is expressed by saying that
discernments are "placed."[1] In the present chapter, we will discover
that the Christian's faith-surrender is an experience of unconditional
acceptance by Christ and of conversion to Christ. The conclusion
will have to be that whatever we will say about Christ by way of
faith-discernments will have to be placed in the context of that
acceptance and conversion. Thus, the first two answers to the question as to *how* the discernments are placed will be that they are
included and that they are made obedient.

---

[1]Above, pp. 126–129.

Our analysis will take us to the New Testament and the christo-logical tradition to see if we can find examples of the ways in which discernments in christology are placed. Completeness is obviously out of the question here; what we want is telling instances of the way in which Scripture and tradition were articulate about Christ. In these articulations, we will see, close contact was maintained with the human concerns that gave rise to the use of metaphorical titles in the interest of articulation. But close contact was also maintained with the responsive act of surrender to Jesus Christ present in the Spirit.

Before we launch into our analyses, however, we must expand our discussion about the names of Jesus given in the previous chapter.[2] Hence, in the first section of this chapter we will discuss two points, the first briefly, the second rather more fully. The first point will be that christological titles arise from human concerns—"matters pertaining to this life." The second point will be that these concerns, when brought to Christ, become his names, and he thus assumes presidency over them. Not until after this introductory section will it be possible to analyze the ways in which Christ's presidency reflects back on the human concerns, namely, by includ-ing them and by calling them to obedience.

THE NAMES OF JESUS

Christological titles arise from human concerns

The dependence of New Testament christology on the living tradition of the Old Testament on the one hand and the living concerns of Hellenistic culture on the other has been well established by New Testament theology. This use of Old Testament and Helle-nistic images and metaphors in New Testament christology is a *living* use, not the notional use of available concepts or ideas. We find the primitive Church enthusiastically marshaling metaphors available in its living cultural-religious heritage for the purpose of dealing with, and articulating, the new reality of Christ. Many of these metaphors, part of Israel's rather loose religious and moral synthesis, were alive and functioning at the time as the key concepts or dominant models

---

[2]Above, pp. 139–143.

of particular groups and particular traditions—groups and traditions, incidentally, which often experienced strong mutual incompatibilities. The groups that the Synoptic Gospels, the Fourth Gospel and Acts have preserved are evidence for this: Pharisees, high priests, Sadducees, "Hellenizers," etc.; outside Scripture, we have such groups as the Qumran-sect. To mention not a group but a metaphor, we know the bewildering variety of interpretations of the "Son of Man": suffering or not, eschatological or not, one person or personification of the nation. All such strands reflect, by their very resistance to complete harmonization, the scattered concerns of varied groups and traditions, with very different axes to grind.

The same may be said for the concerns that are conveyed by images and metaphors of Hellenistic provenance, such as the virgin birth, the powers of the heavens and the spirits in the air, etc. All these vital concerns are carried along into the surrender to Christ and function in the process of articulation of meaning, as the New Testament communities engage in worship of, and witness to, the risen Lord.[3]

Leaving aside, for now, the question of Jesus' self-designations, there are titles that doubtlessly go back to the historical Jesus: son of Mary, son of Joseph,[4] prophet, teacher, master, the Son, bridegroom, rabbi. Vincent Taylor[5] has probably been a little too generous in enumerating nineteen of them in all, for we can legitimately doubt historical use of such titles as the Christ, Son of Man, Messiah, and Son of David, or, if they were so used, we cannot easily determine their original significance. The use of these titles testifies to the fact that people addressed Jesus with their concerns, and the latter were shaped by some of Israel's great national themes and their contemporary derivates. Some of these concerns are also apparent in the abuse used in relation to Jesus; abuse and invective, after all, are also titles, in which people bring their concerns or prejudices to bear on a person. Thus, such titles as "eater and wine-drinker" and "friend of sinners and tax-collectors" betray the concerns of those for whom an

---

[3]For address and clarification as the two functions of metaphor, cf. above, pp. 91–92.

[4]"Son of Mary" and "Son of Joseph," *read in context*, are not simply objective statements of fact; they carry an agenda—unbelief! Cf. Mk 6, 1–6; Lk 4, 22.

[5]In: *The Names of Jesus, passim.*

ascetical propheticism *à la* John the Baptizer or a purist attitude with regard to the Torah epitomized the resolution of all of life's most fundamental questions.[6] "King of the Jews," too, represents concerns on the part of the Jewish establishment in Jerusalem as well as the very different worries on the part of the Roman authorities.[7]

We are now ready to discuss the second point mentioned earlier, namely the naming of Christ by means of human concerns and his presidency over them. Our discussion will consist of six points. The first two will treat the naming of the historical Jesus and of the risen Lord. The next three will point to some stylistic devices. The sixth and last point will concern the changed designations of the Church as a result of Christ's presidency.

The historical Jesus eluded categorization

Since the start of the New Hermeneutic it has become abundantly clear that the historical Jesus somehow eluded all categorization, all identification with any single concern or select set of concerns. His cause somehow defied definition in terms of the concerns that he was born into and was part of—Eduard Schweizer entitled the second chapter of his book *Jesus*: "Jesus, The Man Who Fits No Formula."[8] As a prophet he was questionable, since he seemed to blaspheme or at least overindulge.[9] As a teacher he was unconvincing because he avoided casuistry (as the man discovered who approached him for a solution to an inheritance problem[10]) and clearly failed to defer to tradition. While teaching the way of God in truth, and raising people's hopes for the fulfillment of the prophecies, he refused to be called "Good Master"[11] and declined designations that could put him in a position of leadership over popular and tradition-hallowed causes.[12] His parables were a very personal way of confronting people rather than teaching them.[13]

While refusing to be associated with any particular cause, how-

---

[6]Cf. Mt 11, 19.
[7]Cf. Jn 18, 33—19, 22.
[8]Richmond, John Knox Press, 1971, pp. 13–51.
[9]Mt 11, 18–19.
[10]Lk 12, 13–14.
[11]Mk 10, 17–18.
[12]Cf. Jn 6, 15.
[13]Cf. Joachim Jeremias, *The Parables of Jesus*, pp. 21–22, 230.

ever, he did not add yet another cause, his own, to the mixture of causes already competing for ascendancy, and continually referred his listeners and followers away from himself to God and his kingdom. Ironically, this same Jesus still made himself—however implicitly or unthematically—into the pivotal figure of whatever personal decisions with regard to God, others, and self his listeners, followers and antagonists would make. He could even make a person's standing in God's judgment dependent on his response to himself[14]—a clear suggestion that he somehow regarded himself and his cause as one, not two.[15]

No wonder that the people were astonished at what they perceived as a new teaching characterized not so much by new content, but by authority.[16] No wonder also that we can surmise the unique nature of Jesus' self-consciousness as expressed in such usages as "Amen I say to you," "Abba," "I have come to . . ."[17]—locutions which the tradition would soon enough explicate into an understanding of Jesus as the Father's Word sent into the world. Jesus' refusal to identify with any single concern, therefore, is a gesture of active engagement and confrontation, in which those concerns are taken seriously and are embraced, and (as we will explain later on) assayed and put in perspective. His refusal to identify with any single con-

---

[14]Lk 12, 8.

[15]When we said (above, p. 140) that Jesus presides over and does justice to the concerns conveyed by the *historical* titles with which he was addressed, this is what we meant. If, e.g., Jesus is called "teacher," he does not derive prestige from the authority attributed to him by those who call him by that name; rather, he in his person determines what it means to teach. He "presides over the concern with teaching." This means that the teaching does not become a cause or a power-base for him. Person and cause are one in Jesus.

[16]For the words expressing the people's astonishment at Jesus' authoritative behavior, cf. Oscar Cullmann, *The Christology of the New Testament*, p. 318, n. 1 (31 items from the Synoptics).

[17]The formula "Amen I say to you" occurs forty-nine times in the Synoptics, and in various traditions; the Fourth Gospel uses it twenty-five times, with "Amen" doubled into "truly, truly." I am not convinced by E. Schillebeeckx (*Jezus, het verhaal van een levende*, Bloemendaal, H. Nelissen, ²1974, p. 80, following Klaus Berger) in his rejection of this formula as historical Jesus-usage.—For "Abba," cf. Mk 14, 36 coll. Mt 23, 9.—For "I have come," cf. Mt 10, 34 par.; Mk 2, 17 parr., Mk 10, 45 par.; Lk 12, 49; 19, 10; Mt 5, 17; Mt 11, 18–19 par.; cf. Mt 15, 24 for the far more explicitly christological "I have been sent" (secondary in Lk 4, 43 coll. Mk 1, 38), which is the standard formula of the Fourth Gospel.

cern, therefore, must not be interpreted as a gesture of withdrawal. In this way Jesus' "style" and, indeed, Jesus himself become, however unthematically, the touchstone for what it means to be true to the Law, a teacher, a son of one's mother, a prophet, a master.

The risen Christ as the focus of human concerns

What historical critical analysiꞏ discovers as unthematized intimation and ambivalent suggestion in the life of the historical Jesus becomes, after the Resurrection, explicit realization and expression in the testimony of the entire New Testament. Not only does the New Testament proclaim the Lordship of Jesus directly; it also conveys it rhetorically. We must, therefore, pay attention to the *dynamics* by which the realization and expression of Jesus' significance took place—dynamics which can be observed in the *rhetorical structure* of the New Testament witness. We just referred to embracing, assaying, and putting into perspective; we find these procedures reflected in the rhetorical structure of New Testament christology.

Radicalizing transformation[18]

First of all, there is the striking transformation of familiar Jewish titles into related abstract nouns that function as personal titles. There are numerous examples of this.

Christ, who is called "the Just One," comes to be called "our justice." He is indeed a "prophet," that is, one who speaks the word of God; but he comes to be called "the Word." He is a teacher, who "teaches the way of God in truth," but he comes to be addressed as "the truth" and "the way." He is designated as "the author of life," who has come so that others may have life, but he is also called "the life," "your life." "He is risen," yes, but he *is* the Resurrection. His characteristic way of speaking to the Father is "Amen," but that is only the introduction to the full realization that: "With him it was, and is, Yes. He is the Yes pronounced upon God's promises."[19]

---

[18]By the words "radicalizing transformation" we do not mean to characterize *an actual historical process* that can be traced by means of form-critical method. We are merely pointing to an existing pattern found in the New Testament, sometimes across various traditions.

[19]Cf. Acts 3, 14; 1 Cor 1, 30; Mt 13, 57; Jn 1, 1. 14; Mt 22, 16; Jn 14, 6; Acts 3, 15; Col 3, 4; Mt 28, 6; Jn 11, 25; 2 Cor 1, 19–20; cf. Rev 3, 14.

This radicalizing transformation bears analysis. A title that expresses a salvific *function* of Jesus Christ becomes absolutized and then *identified* with him, so that person and cause are identified. The simple titles—names of persons with certain functions—reflect the concerns of the believer; the bold metonymy (*parrhēsia* again!) makes these concerns into the very names of Christ. The change in usage reflects a change on the part of the believer; he realizes that his concerns are fully accounted for, and done justice to, in Jesus Christ. He expresses this rhetorically, by address and witness, not notionally by explanation.

Naming by way of excellence

An analogous dynamic, in which the believer finds himself prompted to call Jesus Christ by the names of his own concerns, is found in the *par excellence* usages of the New Testament. The comparison of Jesus with Moses in the Letter to the Hebrews and by implication in the Gospel of Matthew, the "more than Solomon" and "more than Jonah" in Q, and Paul's meditation on "the second Adam" sum up living concerns and place Jesus Christ squarely at the center of the community of believers, of sinners come to life, of listeners to words of wisdom, and of the human race. He is the *true* Moses, the *true* Jonah, the *true* Solomon, and the *true* Adam. In the same way he is "truly a (the?) son of God," the "good" shepherd, the (true) image of the invisible God, and truly "the Son."[20] Thus the living concerns of the believers become the names of Jesus, and he comes to preside over the concerns. This *par excellence* style of fixing human concerns on Jesus Christ produced, understandably, a number of revisions in the metaphoric self-designation of the Christian community; we will come back to this in a few moments.[21]

Key and headship images

Closely related to the titles just mentioned are designations that could be described as key-titles or headship-images. Their character-istic quality is that they explicitly place Christ in a position of pre-

---

[20]Cf. Heb 3, 1–6; Mt 12, 41–42; 1 Cor 15, 45–49; Rom 5, 14; Mk 15, 39; Jn 10, 11; Col 1, 15; Mt 11, 27.

[21]Below, pp. 152–153, 163–164.

eminence over human concerns, while the latter are sometimes explicitly stated but more often left implicit. The Fourth Gospel, with its preference for christological explicitness, refers to Jesus Christ as "the vine" and "the door" and "the shepherd," and explicitly calls Christ's followers "the branches," "the sheepfold," "the sheep."[22] All three similes, of course, are based on the concerns of people who live with the Old Testament.[23] In a metaphor which is Hellenistic rather than Judaic, and which appears to go back to a cosmological myth,[24] Paul can refer to Christ as "the head" and correlatively to Christians as "members." He also calls Christ the key-stone, and here the *prima Petri* provides the correlative: the Christians are to be "living stones."[25]

The radicalizing conversion, the *par excellence* figure, and the headship-image show that there is a *dynamic* underlying the process of articulation involved in the names of Jesus. This dynamic is the act by which the believer acknowledges Jesus Christ as presiding over all concerns. Clarification and discernment occur in the surrender to Jesus Christ conveyed by this implicit rhetoric. The means of clarification are metaphors derived from human concerns; in the metaphorical address these concerns become the names of Jesus and he is acknowledged as presiding over them.

Effects of Jesus' presidency

If Jesus comes to preside over the concerns that are brought to him in the act of articulate surrender, we can expect that his presidency will not leave those concerns unaffected. We can clarify this as follows.

Ian Ramsey has pointed out that the qualified model in religious language, *once the disclosure occurs,* starts to preside over the whole area of discourse covered by the model.[26] This means that the model

---

[22]Jn 15, 1. 5; 10, 7. 9. 11. 14. 1. 3. 8. 27.

[23]Cf. Ps 80, 8–16; Jer 23, 1–4.

[24]For Col 1, 15–20 cf. Eduard Schweizer, *Jesus*, pp. 77–86; Bruce Vawter, *This Man Jesus*, pp. 156–159, 172–173.

[25]Col 1, 18; Eph 4, 15; 5, 23; 1 Cor 12, 27; Eph 2, 20; 1 Pet 2, 5 (the image of living stones is implicit in Eph 2, 21–22).

[26]Ian Ramsey, *Religious Language*, p. 60.

starts to function in a new way, and that it becomes "object language and more," thanks to the disclosure.[27]

Now what Ramsey terms the disclosure is what we have called the realization of the presence of Jesus Christ in the Spirit. If Jesus Christ then comes to preside over a whole area of discourse, this will cause the names applied to him to become "human concerns and more." In the Spirit the "matters pertaining to this life" will become the vehicles of disclosure and the stuff of commitment. No wonder, then, that the concerns will "feel" different; this difference is expressed by changes in the metaphors.

One of the remarkable features of the picture of the historical Jesus is that his style was one of active engagement and confrontation vis-à-vis the multifarious and conflicting concerns with which people approached him. In the encounter people found themselves involved with Jesus in a way that both baffled, and did justice to, their dearest concerns and most precious causes. Thus Jesus himself became the touchstone for what it meant to be true to the law, a teacher, a son of one's mother, a prophet, a master. His very person, as we put it, embraced, assayed, and put in perspective the concerns of their very lives.[28] As a result of this, the concerns were changed; in their being related to Christ they were placed in a totally new context. Metaphoric self-correction is the expression of this change; we will treat this more fully in the beginning of the third part of this chapter.[29]

The rhetorical devices which we have briefly analyzed so far are only some patterns in what may very well prove to be, on closer study, a multitude. All such patterns, however, can be presumed to do duty in the one central task of rhetoric in christology, namely, to convey the realization that all discernments occur in the *act* of faith-surrender.

We can now turn to the first basic way in which discernments are placed in christology. We have already intimated the nature of this placing by means of the words "embrace" and "the possibility of total inclusiveness."

---

[27]Cf. *ibid.* pp. 11–48, *passim.*
[28]Above, p. 149.
[29]Below, pp. 163–164.

THE RHETORIC OF INCLUSION

Acceptance of all human concerns

What happens to the human concerns which in the act of worship and witness have been appropriated by Jesus Christ?

First of all, they are embraced and *accepted.* The human concerns of the Christian are not rejected as false or irrelevant, no more than the historical Jesus' refusal to identify with any single cause consisted in a gesture of withdrawal. The expression "to despise earthly things" is a hallowed one in Christian tradition; whatever it may mean, however, it does not mean rejecting them. The Fourth Gospel thematizes this when Jesus says: "Whatever the Father has given me will come to me, and the person that comes to me I will not cast outside."[30] Faced with ecstatic Corinthians, Paul encouraged them to do justice to the demands of marriage, to take issues between members of the community seriously and to settle them in the community, to take residual belief in idols and conscientious worries of others seriously; and he sums it up in the telling phrases that they are to order their lives according to the gift granted to them by the Lord and *in the conditions in which they were called.*[31] In the Lord, ordinary concerns are accepted.

Christ's acceptance of all concerns also means *forgiveness*—not a forgiveness that would consist in toning down or white-washing or explaining away the seriousness of evil inherent in every human concern, but an acceptance that can look it squarely in the face: "If you, then, evil as you are, can give good things to your children. . . ."[32]

The accepting and forgiving appropriation of all human concerns by Christ, implied in his names, is conveyed by a *rhetoric of inclusion.* This means that *every human concern is capable of becoming a name of Jesus.* The Fourth Gospel has Pilate point to a suffering Jesus as to a mirror of the crowd before him and say: "Look, this is Man"—the Lamb of God has indeed taken *upon himself* the human condition and the sin of the world. The rhetoric

---

[30]Jn 6, 37.
[31]1 Cor 7, 1–7; 6, 1–8; 8, 7–13; 10, 28–29; 7, 17.
[32]Lk 11, 13.

of inclusion lies at the basis of the teaching of the Sermon on the Mount, especially where it accepts the challenge to shoulder and absorb and outsuffer the impact of violence rather than counter with more of the same. Even human violence is welcome. Paul could even write that Jesus Christ was made into sin for us.[33] No doctrine of Jesus' sinlessness should, therefore, obscure this central fact: Jesus Christ appropriates *all* human concerns as his own, and does not preside over them at some safe, clinical, judgmental distance. Today, for example, the cause of women's liberation is obviously reluctant to accept Jesus, a man, as the decisive revelation of God. Mary Daly even speaks of christolatry.[34] It is contrary to the basic rhetoric of christology to say that there is no way to get around the fact that Jesus was a man, or that his maleness is part of the "scandal of particularity" essential to the Incarnation. This subterfuge is no more than a strategy to make a cause out of masculinity in order to confront the feminists with a counter-cause. It raises one particular discernment, namely, that Jesus is a man, into a cause that jeopardizes total commitment on the part of women, and it locks Jesus into the male sex in a way that he himself did not. Jesus is indeed a man, and not a woman, but his masculinity is not a cause; he presides over it. Hence, to say that a woman cannot speak and act as a sacramental representative of Christ is a betrayal of him who failed to fit the rabbinical formula because of his close association with women, who provoked his followers' amazement at being found talking to a woman, who was suspect because of his ties with prostitutes, who spoke of himself, when moved by compassion over Jerusalem, in a feminine metaphor, and whose Resurrection was announced—in his Spirit—to the apostles by women. To argue in favor of the exclusion of women from the ministry because of the maleness of Jesus is to sin against the rhetoric of inclusion.[35] There *may* be other arguments

---

[33]Jn 19, 5; Mt 5, 39–41; 2 Cor 5, 21.

[34]*Beyond God the Father,* Toward a Philosophy of Women's Liberation, Boston, Beacon Press, 1973, pp. 69ff.

[35]Cf. the Vatican Declaration "Women in the Ministerial Priesthood," *Origins* 6 (1977) 519–531; the seventh paragraph under n. 5 on p. 522 is close to heresy.—On this whole subject cf. Patricia A. Kendall (ed.), *Women and the Priesthood: A Selected and Annotated Bibliography,* [Philadelphia], The Episcopal Diocese of Pennsylvania, 1976.—In our terminology we might say: Jesus is indeed a man and not a woman, but his maleness is not a cause; he "presides over it."

favoring the exclusion of women from the ordained ministry; this one does not hold up.[36]

The fullness of humanity in Christ

Christ's acceptance of human concerns was formulated as broadly as possible in the debates preceding Chalcedon. It took the form of the universalist thesis that Jesus Christ is truly and fully human, consubstantial with us according to the humanity, *homoousios hēmin*.[37] That piece of discernment, apparently so straightforward, was later to lead to a bewildering variety of speculations about Christ's human nature, all claiming Chalcedon for their justification. If this statement had been consistently interpreted in the light of the faith-surrender to Jesus Christ its point would have been better appreciated, and many illegitimate development inferences would have been avoided. We will argue that the function of this statement is to express Jesus' *universal relatedness*, and that its rhetoric is one of *inclusion*.

Jesus Christ, so Christians bear witness, bears the names of all our concerns as his own; he accepts them and does justice to them in our surrender to him and in his presence-in-the-Spirit to us. To say that Jesus Christ is fully human, therefore, is not a truism but a significant tautology, as Ramsey calls it.[38] This significant tautology functions in the process of the surrender of faith, in which the Christian finds all his concerns appropriated by Christ.

This tautology may be terminologized for the purposes of theological meditation and reflection, by saying that human nature *as such* must be predicated of Christ, that is to say, in such a way that the individual characteristics are excluded. Schoonenberg explains this, following a long tradition.

> The only thing that is not implied in the general terms used by Chalcedon are the individual characteristics. For that reason the saying

---

[36]Cf. Frans Jozef van Beeck, S.J., *Priesthood: Ordained and/or Real?* Kansas City, The Propers, 1975 [Gm.: "Thesen zur Ordination von Frauen," *Orientierung* 39 (1975) 153–154], for a plea to view the question of women's ordination primarily in terms of real ministry.

[37]DS 301.

[38]Cf. Ian Ramsey, *Religious Language*, pp. 40–44.

"what is not assumed is not redeemed" may be understood only of the specific nature and not of these characteristics. In other words, Christ would not have to be a woman, an atomic physicist, or a Japanese in order to be redeemer for women, atomic physicists, and Japanese.[39]

Everything that goes into the making of human nature must be attributed to Christ. Nothing that is human is alien to him. But that does not mean that everything people are and do must be attributed to Christ, but only those things the denial of which would imply the denial of his humanity.

The point of the use of "human nature"

A distinct danger has arisen at this point; it is caused by the fact that we are speaking terminologically. Terminology does not show very clearly, as natural language does, the concerns in the service of which it must be employed. The use of terminology, the point made by means of terms, is experienced as more or less extrinsic to the meaning of the terms as considered by themselves; the opportunity for misunderstandings and for illegitimate applications and conclusions is just around the corner.[40]

Here we have an obvious example of such a misunderstanding. "Human nature" (clearly a term) is predicated of Christ "*without* the individual characteristics."[41] The "without" suggests a rhetoric of *exclusion*, whereas the concern that prompted the use of "human nature" in the first place was *inclusion*. In the absence of a clear reminder of this inclusive concern, theologians have been known to take "human nature" by itself, and to analyze its meaning apart from the context that made it meaningful. "Human nature" for many of them came to mean something vague and abstract, a *natura* remote from all vital human concerns, even to the point where, in the theory known as "nihilianism," it was maintained that Christ, according to his humanity, "is nothing in particular"—*non est aliquid*—and hence that he is as such not a fit subject of particular attributes.[42] At the

---

[39]Piet Schoonenberg, *The Christ*, pp. 72–73.

[40]Cf. above, pp. 79–80, 86–87.

[41]Cf. the expression *non sane in peculiaribus suis proprietatibus* in Xiberta's rendering of Gregory of Nyssa (PG 45, 1276); *Enchiridion de Verbo Incarnato*, p. 211.

[42]Piet Schoonenberg, *The Christ*, p. 59.

opposite extreme of this, the expression "fully human" came to be interpreted as referring to the "perfection of humanity." This in turn was read as an overstatement expressing the absolute individual superiority of Jesus as a human being; his obvious limitations were overlooked,[43] as it was piously ignored that Jesus is a man and not a woman, a Jew and not a Japanese, a carpenter and not a nuclear physicist.

These false conclusions have this in common: they start by overlooking the fact that "human nature" was originally used in the service of *relational concerns.*[44] Speculation thus tended to concentrate on "human nature" as such and on its place in the hypostatic union of the God-Man *taken as an individual.*[45] This, in turn, either

---

[43]Cf. John A. T. Robinson, *The Human Face of God*, Philadelphia, The Westminster Press, 1973, p. 68: "He has been set on a pedestal by himself, an immaculate paragon, of whom it was impossible to think that he should fall short in anything. And as such he quickly becomes unique not because he is normal but because he is abnormal. What we want to say of him as *the* man paradoxically undercuts his humanity. And this is a powerful factor today in making him for many an unreal figure with the static perfection of flawless porcelain, rather than a man of flesh and blood."

[44]Cf. Maxentius (sixth century): "One should not think of the reality of the nature, which is scattered over many persons and individuals, as unsubstantial and even non-existent (*non tibi insubstantialis esse videatur, ut nihil sit*)": B. Xiberta, *Enchiridion de Verbo Incarnato*, p. 548. Notice the concretion attributed to "human nature" by Gregory of Nyssa (*ibid.*, p. 211), and the emphasis on the fact that this concrete human nature is *common* and shared (Maxentius, *ibid.*, p. 548, and esp. Anastasius, who compares human nature to a lump of dough—*totam nostram massam in uno relicto nobis semine assumpsit, ibid.*, p. 575). Finally notice the telling expression "God has assumed the whole man"—*Deus totum hominem assumpsit pro nobis*—in Fulgentius (*ibid.*, p. 597), and John Damascene's highly personalized "all of him has assumed all of me, and all of him was united with all of me, so that he might bring salvation to all of me"—*totum quippe me totus assumpsit, ac totus toti unitus est, ut toti salutem afferret (ibid.*, p. 667).

[45]G. L. Prestige (*God in Patristic Thought*, London–Toronto, Heinemann, 1936, p. 272) emphasizes the shift in outlook which led to the habit of speaking of "the two ousiai of Christ, in such a way as to make the human ousia no longer mean the total physical substance of the whole race, but the metaphysical analysis of Christ's individual humanity; and to make the divine ousia similarly mean not the content of God but the metaphysical analysis of Christ in his divine aspect." He assigns Leontius of Byzantium the principal blame for this development, which led to a completely separate doctrine of atonement based not on the person, but on the "work of Christ," whose "fruits" were then to be applied to other human beings—a matter to be considered by yet another set of tracts: on grace, sacraments, and Church. The classical doctrine of *inclusio* was designed to prevent this disintegration of christology and ecclesiology; cf. Felix Malmberg, *Ein Leib—ein Geist*, Freiburg–Basel–Wien, Herder, 1960, pp. 223–273.

led to such a rarefied conception of Jesus' humanity that anhypostatic christology could develop, with leanings toward monophysitism, or it imprisoned Jesus in the particularities of his humanity, so that he could no longer be more than a teacher, an example, a prophet—an individual man, a Jew, a Palestinian, a person of the first century. In all this the basic error consisted in mistaking the instrumentality of terminological language for thought itself; thus the point of the use of "human nature" was lost sight of; conclusions were drawn from a term; the statement led to positions never intended.

An illustration from John A. T. Robinson

Let us look at an example of the correct functioning of the rhetoric of inclusion. In the first chapter of Bishop John Robinson's *The Human Face of God* we are told that christology must start with our concerns.[46] The author goes on, in the second chapter, entitled "A Man,"[47] to stress that Jesus Christ is an individual human being in exactly the same sense as any other human individual. He emphasizes that the full humanity of Jesus Christ is inconceivable without this recognition of Jesus' human individuality, and that an essential element of this recognition is that Jesus Christ is "a product of the process" like all of us.[48] Environmental conditioning and heredity must be said to have affected the very person of Jesus Christ, if he is to be human in the full meaning of that word. To put the human person Jesus at one remove from the rest of humanity, for example by postulating a timeless, unchangeable inner entity *in his humanity* that would be unaffected by the human condition (as, for example, Schleiermacher proposed), would amount to putting part of Jesus' person outside the common stock of matter and energy on which the stream of humanity moves forward.[49] This in turn would amount to presenting Jesus as the product of an act of divine intervention—a kind of "insertion" which, incidentally, is not only questionable from a scientific point of view, but would also raise very substantial theological problems from the point of view of belief in God's faithfulness to his own creation.

---

[46] Pp. 1–5.
[47] *Ibid.*, pp. 36–66.
[48] *Ibid.*, p. 42.
[49] *Ibid.*, pp. 42–47.

Robinson then asks questions about Jesus' origin and his sexuality.[50] Viewed as a biological fact the virginal conception of Jesus runs into serious problems, both genetic and theological. It is possible to read the first chapter of Matthew in such a way that Jesus was conceived outside wedlock, with Joseph subsequently condoning this—a possibility Robinson rightly describes as "the most embarrassing alternative for the Church and one that Christians would naturally have been most concerned to repudiate."[51] Similar and only slightly less embarrassing questions may be raised, and have been raised, about Jesus' own experience of his sexuality.

Robinson insists that it is impossible to give historical, factual answers to these and similar questions: "*Of course* there is no answer. The gospels are not there to answer such questions." So we will not get historical answers. But, Robinson continues, that is no problem, for "the [theological] issue is not what historical statements we can confidently make about Jesus of Nazareth." What, then, *is* the issue? Robinson answers: "What we can do is to use the questions to test *our* presumptions about what is implied by asserting of Jesus that he was completely human. Are we *free* to say certain things of him?" The question regarding Jesus' responses to sexual stimuli is "a good question to ask *ourselves*, to test our reaction."[52] What is happening in this discussion? We are bringing a central human concern to Jesus Christ. And, in virtue of the rhetoric of inclusion, we are obliged to say: Yes, that is a legitimate question to ask about Jesus, fully human as he is.

To say that such questions are totally irrelevant to Jesus' significance as Lord may sound, at first blush, like good theology. To reject even the possibility of Jesus' illegitimacy may look, at first blush, like an act of reverence due to the holiness of Jesus and his mother. But rejecting the appropriateness of these questions may be short-sighted, and even downright mistaken theologically. If sexual concerns are taken to be irrelevant to Jesus' saving significance, then Jesus becomes, *as Savior*, less than human, for to be human is to be involved with sexuality. So it is short-sighted to deny the relevance of sexual

---

[50]*Ibid.*, pp. 47–66.

[51]*Ibid.*, p. 57.

[52]*Ibid.*, pp. 64, 56.

questions to Jesus; in the end the denial produces a Savior who is not fully human, and, therefore, not significant. To make the saving significance of Jesus *dependent on* the absence of sexual intercourse, let alone extra-marital intercourse, at his origin is not only short-sighted; it is a downright theological mistake. For if the divinity of Jesus Christ is made *dependent on* the virgin birth, and if his (possible) illegitimacy—and, again, there are *no historical answers* to these questions—is taken as *proof* that he is not the Son of God, then Christian belief in the divinity of Jesus Christ has been made depen-dent on certain convictions about sexual morality. This means that those convictions have come to preside over the affirmation of Christ's divinity—Jesus Christ, *in order to be acceptable as Lord,* must pass the test of those moral convictions.

In all this, much as Robinson may be indulging in the fine art of shocking the bourgeois, he sees very well that the surrender to Jesus Christ in the Spirit is the essential context of all discernments. It is not our concerns that make Jesus acceptable as Lord; he, as Lord, makes our concerns acceptable. Jesus' "significance, even unique significance, is not *dependent upon* any particular supposition of regularity or irregularity, of mutation or intervention."[53] In the total surrender to Christ, all human concerns can become his names, including *our* worries about the regularity of his origin and the nature of his sexual feelings and activities. Christians need not defend Christ, least of all if the defenses used are in fact poorly disguised aggressive stances against vital, though embarrassing, hu-man concerns with sex and morality.

Now it must be said that Robinson rests his case a little bit too early; once he has made the point just explained, he stops. He does not inquire into the reasons why those embarrassing questions about Jesus were raised. This is naive and uncritical. Is it too far-fetched to suspect that the question about Jesus' illegitimacy has a hidden agenda? Was it perhaps asked to find a justification or a rationaliza-tion for a freer sexual morality? Is the concern behind these ques-tions perhaps a desire for reassurance on the part of new-morality Christians who want christological sanction for their ideas? If this should be the case it should be remembered that the rhetoric of

---

[53] *Ibid.*, p. 66.

inclusion deals with the *acceptance* of all human concerns, *not with condoning or permissiveness.* The picture of the historical Jesus is indeed that of a man who embraces every concern and every person he meets; he rejects nothing and no one. But embracing and accepting do not mean telling everybody that he and his wishes are as good as any. Condoning and permitting are just as judgmental as condemning; the arrogance of power lies at the root of both. If the latter must not be attributed to Jesus, neither must the former.

The only conclusion that can be drawn so far is that sexual concerns are acceptable in the Lord. No conclusions can as yet be drawn as to the effects of this acceptance on the human concerns with sexuality. The next section of this chapter will explore the dynamics of obedience that follow upon the dynamics of acceptance. Not that we will use the occasion to outline a Christian sexual morality, or to decide the historical issues of Jesus' origin and his experience of sexuality. These latter issues were merely taken as an *example* of a correct functioning of the rhetoric of inclusion in Robinson's christology, and as an illustration of the fact that the rhetoric of inclusion does not tell the whole story.

Before we make the transition to the next section, however, let us briefly restate the main point of the present one.

Summary

What happens to the human concerns which, in the act of worship and witness, have been appropriated by Jesus Christ? They are embraced and accepted. With this answer we came to a fuller understanding of the point of asserting the full humanity of Jesus Christ. The human person Jesus Christ has a universal significance; he is universally related; all human concerns are embraced by him; nothing in our lives needs to remain outside him; we are not the victims of any forces incapable of integration into the act of surrender to Christ.

The Rhetoric of Obedience

What happens to the human concerns which in the act of worship and witness have been appropriated by Jesus Christ in a gesture of total acceptance and inclusion? They find themselves tested and assayed, humbled and purified. They are called to obedience and converted to the way of Jesus. No human concern will be the same once it has become a name of Jesus. Christological statements employing human concerns will give evidence of this by means of what we will call the *rhetoric of obedience.*

Metaphoric self-correction

We have suggested twice already that the *par excellence* style of attributing titles to Jesus produced a number of revisions in the metaphoric self-designations of the Christian community.[54] The Church thought of herself as the new Israel, and hence as the vine the Lord had planted; but she was also aware that it was all owed to Jesus Christ. He, and not the Church, had to be called the Vine. By a process of "metaphoric self-correction" the Church-members then came to refer to themselves as "the branches." Christians experienced themselves as "children" or "sons" of God; the process of self-correction produced the metaphor of "adoptive sons" and of "younger brothers," to do justice to Christ's status as "the Son" and "the first-born." The Church was aware of the gift of the Spirit; but it looked upon itself as having the Spirit only as a pledge, for the fullness of the Spirit was in Christ.[55]

We must interpret such self-designations in the context of their *rhetorical structure*, in the light of their relationships to *corresponding designations* of Jesus Christ, and not by an analysis of the self-designations taken by themselves. If we analyze the corrected self-designations *by themselves*, they become disappointing put-downs; Christians are *only* branches, *only* adoptive children; the Church has the Spirit *only* by way of pledge. The joy and the confidence that come from the surrender to Christ are gone. The fact that "Vine" and "Son" are no longer simply applicable to Christians *does* imply a correction, but a correction that is gladly suffered and even embraced *in the light of total acceptance.*

"Corrected" implies judgment, a judgment in acceptance—the kind of judgment that brings with it, as part of itself, the ability to

---

[54]Above, pp. 151–152.

[55]Cf. Hos 10, 1; Is 5, 1–7; Ezek 15, 1–8; 17, 3–10; 19, 10–14; Ps 80, 8–16; Jn 15, 1–4; Rom 8, 15; Gal 4, 5; Eph 1, 5; Rom 8, 29; Col 1, 15. 18; Rev 1, 5; Heb 1, 6; 2 Cor 1, 22; 5, 5; Eph 1, 14.

accept it. It is not a judgment that comes from outside, a forensic act of correction as from a totally extrinsic tribunal. That would contradict what we have already established, namely, that human concerns find themselves accepted and appropriated by Jesus Christ *as his own.* The Son was not sent into the world to judge the world, but to save it.[56]

The acceptance that undergirds the judgment also overcomes the opposition between good and evil. The judgment is not an act of approval so that the good can now bask in its own right and righteousness; nor is the judgment an act of reproof, experienced as an act of rejection and thus a reason to despair. What is good is humbled, and what is evil is humbled, and both are freed from the concern with self. The Christian finds all his concerns done justice to in the surrender, in which they become the titles of Jesus, and not his own in isolation. He need no longer be his own judge, nor be worried about the judgment of any human court. The freedom he finds is rooted in the surrender to Christ in the Spirit: "You are no longer your own."[57] This means: You have become obedient.

The poverty of Jesus: basis for obedience

This obedience is not to a superpower but to a poor man. Jesus embraces all concerns as his own, but patiently, meekly, as a Lamb, and not as their proprietor, not seeking a foothold in them, not using them as a base of power. The historical Jesus embraced and confronted all concerns, but he refused to identify himself with any of them. He presides over them, not from above, lording it over them, but, as it were, from below, serving them. The presidency of Jesus over all concerns is not one of power, but of poverty and of the freedom that comes from poverty. No one can take anything, including his life, away from him; he has already given up everything, including his life, in advance.[58] The powers that be, seeking assurance in their causes and concerns, are threatened at once by the welcome Jesus extends to them and by his refusal to identify with them. They conspire and take his life, and thus they open the road for the Resurrection that will seal their demise.

---

[56] Jn 3, 17.
[57] 1 Cor 4, 3; 6, 19; cf. 1 Pet 1, 18–19.
[58] Cf. Jn 10, 18.

In the surrender to Jesus Christ all human concerns are stripped—or rather relieved—of their inherent power, disarmed by poverty, not put down by violence. They can afford to stop asserting themselves with force, since they have found their justification in Jesus Christ. They become capable of being given up, capable of being shared, capable of being taken away. The surrender to Christ opens the way to voluntary poverty and to voluntary suffering without the threat of ultimate loss of life. This is very dangerous ground, for religion has been invoked far too many times to depreciate human concerns, to cast doubt upon enjoyment, and to glorify suffering and sacrifice. Only concerns that are *embraced* can be given up; if this is not realized, Christian self-denial, which should be the fruit of freedom, turns into judgmental self-abasement and self-deprivation—both morbid, perverted forms of self-maintenance in isolation, a refusal to accept.

The rhetoric by which all human concerns are appropriated by Christ, so that they become his names, is, therefore, not only a rhetoric of inclusion, but also a *rhetoric of obedience.* This means that in the act of worship and witness *every human concern is corrected and converted from self-assertiveness, surrenders to Christ's presidency, and thus becomes the stuff of obedience.*

There is no concern that owes it to itself to remain something in its own right, nothing that needs to assert its independent value for fear of diminishment or annihilation, for all concerns are accepted. But every endorsement of the *humanum* in christology is only truly Christian to the extent that it is understood to model itself, in obedience, after Christ.

We will have to apply this insight to some pertinent christological problems. We will choose two. The former, to be treated briefly, is the need for the definition of Chalcedon to be complemented by the Third Council of Constantinople. The latter, to be treated at some length, is the problem created, in our own day, by the fact that traditional christology does not recognize the formula: "Jesus Christ is a human person."

The limitations of Chalcedon

The Chalcedonian settlement, as it stands, is not explicitly based on the rhetoric of obedience, but only on the rhetoric of inclusion. This means, of course, that the Chalcedonian settlement is a very limited statement. The way in which the full humanity of Jesus Christ is stated, in conceptually frozen form, and the way in which this is enhanced by "without confusion, without charge,"[59] creates the impression that we are dealing with an autonomous, well-defined human nature. This in turn tends to obscure the fact that the human nature in the hypostatic union is a human nature with a very definite stance, namely, one of obedience. The depth of this *stance*—identical with what we have previously called the style of Jesus—is not just a "moral" attitude, for the obedience of the man Jesus most deeply permeates whatever is involved in Jesus' being human.

The definition of Chalcedon, however, does not concern itself with this all-pervading quality of Jesus' humanity. In fact, the issue was clouded rather than clarified by one of the crucial documents at Chalcedon, namely, the *Tomus Leonis*, the letter sent by Leo the Great in Rome to Flavian in Constantinople as his authoritative contribution to the council.[60]

The *Tomus* defines, in a long series of contrasting phrases in Leo's best oratorical style, the reality of both the human and the divine natures in Christ, as well as their unity in the same person. It does so by pointing to the characteristics and the *operations* of each nature, and concludes that "each *forma* does the acts which belong to it, in communion with the other." Hence, the flesh really "accomplishes what is proper to the flesh," just as the "Word accomplishes what is proper to the Word."[61]

The symmetrical formulation is misleading, for it "gives the impression that the 'flesh' regulates the human activities as an *independent* subject."[62] This ambiguity was solved by the Third Council of Constantinople (680–681 A.D.), which explains:

> [. . .] his human will follows his divine and almighty will, and far from resisting it or struggling against it, it subjects itself to it. For the will of the flesh had to be moved, but it also subjected itself to the divine will.[63]

Smulders explains the significance of this formula.

---

[59]DS 302.
[60]DS 290–295.
[61]DS 294.
[62]P. Smulders, *The Fathers on Christology*, p. 143.
[63]DS 556.

THE HUMAN CONCERNS 167

Here the apparent symmetry of Leo's formula "each form accomplishes what is proper to it, in community with the other" is refined. This expression remains completely true, but this "community with the other" means something different for the divine and for the human nature. The divine in Christ is the self-giving and the re-creating, the human is the receiving and the accepting. Community with the other nature means for the divine that it empties itself and imprints itself in the form of man so that this becomes the expression of the divine Son himself. But for the human, this community means divinization, through which the human freedom is thoroughly ablaze with divine resoluteness, as we saw in Cyril. For this human freedom is truly the freedom of the Son of God himself, who expressed his absolute sanctity and love in the act of this earthly flesh.[64]

Jesus is fully and completely human; that means that every human concern can become a name of Jesus and be integrated into the surrender to him. But the result of this is communion with the divine, or free obedience to the will of the Father; hence, every human concern, in becoming a name of Jesus, must allow itself to be humbled, agree to give up its self-assertiveness, and cease to function as a power-base. Or rather, *in* the surrender to Jesus Christ every human concern discovers, to its own amazement, that it is converted from self-sufficiency and anxious self-maintenance and the need for independence, in order to follow Christ in his poverty and obedience. The formal affirmation of Chalcedon does not convey this obedience; it took another Council to stress it.

Concern with personalness

A second, present-day issue to be confronted in connection with the rhetoric of obedience is the question of Jesus' human personalness. According to Chalcedon the term "person" (*hypostasis*) could not properly be used for the human Jesus, since the two natures were united in the one person of the Word of God. In later, neo-Chalcedonian developments, this led to the development of the

---

[64]P. Smulders, *The Fathers on Christology*, p. 145.—Smulders' interpretation of Constantinople III as a belated recognition of the Antiochene concern with Christ's obedience is excellent. Cf. also *id.*, "Dogmengeschichtliche und lehramtliche Entfaltung der Christologie," in: Johannes Feiner and Magnus Löhrer (eds.), *Mysterium Salutis*, Band III/1, *Das Christusereignis*, Einsiedeln–Zürich–Köln, Benziger Verlag, 1970, pp. 389–476, esp. pp. 469–474.

thesis that the human nature in Christ is "non-personal," *anhypostatos*; a further refinement of this consisted in calling the human nature in Christ "in-personal," *enhypostatos*, to signify that it found its personalness in its existence in the person of the Word.[65] In the Chalcedonian tradition it looks as if the human nature in Christ had to pay for its assumption into the Word of God by renouncing human personalness.

Now every age has its key symbols and expressions for what it means to be truly human. One of the key expressions for full humanity in our age is "personal worth." Humanity, in our eyes, is intimately tied up with being treated as a person, personal growth, self-awareness, consciousness of self, personal freedom. It is not surprising, therefore, that David Jenkins should have taken "personalness," which strikes us as a quality of life irreducible to anything else—hence, a real key concern, expressing shared ideals— as the point of departure for his christology.[66] Similarly, Schoonenberg's decision to use "person" in the ordinary meaning of that word ("subject-center of freedom and consciousness") is clearly inspired by such shared contemporary concerns about personalness.[67] Schoonenberg's decision to speak about the human person of Jesus Christ is such an interesting instance of the use of terminology in the interest of a shared concern that it seems good to analyze and interpret his proposal for a new christology somewhat more closely. We will do so by approaching the matter in three ways. First, we will ask if a change in terminology such as proposed by Schoonenberg is linguistically justifiable at all. We will then ask the question if in this particular case the proposed change is an improvement, and why. Third, we will test Schoonenberg's proposal against the demands of the rhetoric of inclusion. Once these three moves have been made we will be in a position to discuss the question of Jesus' human personalness in terms of the rhetoric of obedience.

---

[65] A good explanation is given in John McIntyre, *The Shape of Christology*, pp. 86–99.

[66] *The Glory of Man*, pp. 1–24.

[67] Cf. Piet Schoonenberg, *The Christ*, pp. 71–74, 78–80, 87–91.

Can the term "person" be employed differently?

The first question is: From a *linguistic* point of view, may we use the *term* "person" in a different sense from that hitherto employed in christology—namely, exclusively as referring to the person or *hypostasis* of the divine Word? Schoonenberg takes "person" in its ordinary, everyday meaning as applied to human individuals, and defines it accordingly as subject-center of freedom and consciousness; as a result "person" can no longer serve to refer to the pre-existent divine Word.

Now we have previously argued that the meaning of terms is mainly dependent on internal reference, and the link between term and concept is fairly loose.[68] This means, as we have explained, that the *use* of a term is experienced as more or less extrinsic to its meaning, for in terminology the "con-experiential" elements have been largely strained out, in the interest of coherent, rigorous discourse.

This yields some interesting conclusions. On the one hand, we must say that there is no linguistic reason why Schoonenberg cannot change the meaning of the term "person" as long as he defines it properly—which he does. From the *same* linguistic point of view, however, it is possible for the teaching authorities in the Church to continue enforcing the use of the term in the traditional meaning, in the interest of coherent discourse as well as of Church unity in the profession of the faith.

To defend the latter point of view it is unnecessary and linguistically mistaken to argue that "subsistent relationship" (as predicated of the person of the Word) or "relational being" is what "person" really means, as Galot does. If Galot wants "person" to be taken as a *term*, there is no need to say that *être relationnel* is what "person" *really* means, for terms are defined rather arbitrarily, often with minimal reference to natural language.[69] If Galot means that the *word* "person" really means *être relationnel*, he must show that this is what *people* really mean when *they use* the word in ordinary

---

[68]Above, pp. 132, 134.

[69]Cf. J. Galot, *Vers une nouvelle christologie* and *La personne du Christ.*

language—which seems a difficult thing to do, no matter how much relationships are part and parcel of "persons."

We conclude that from a linguistic point of view the case cannot be settled as long as we treat "person" exclusively as a *term*.

Is Schoonenberg's revision of the terminology an improvement?

Schoonenberg's basic appeal, however, is not to terminology, but to ordinary *usage*, and it is against this background that we must consider his proposal. The question, therefore, must be whether Schoonenberg's terminological option, namely, to speak of Jesus as a human person, represents an improvement in terminology, and if so, why. We suggest that the answer must be yes.

Terminology never loses *all* connections with natural language, and "subject-center of freedom and consciousness" as a definition is infinitely closer to the meaning of "person" *as it is actually used in natural-language contexts* than is *être relationnel* or subsistent relationship. It is unwise, therefore, for the teaching authorities in the church to go on enforcing the use of "person" in the traditional meaning for the purposes of *regular confession of faith* in the church. Regular confession of faith needs to be as close to natural language as possible, since the faithful at large confess their faith, not in terms, but in words. To demand that Christians without theological sophistication make the distinction between the *term* "person" when talking about the Trinity and the Incarnation and the *word* "person" when talking about ordinary human beings is highly questionable from a pastoral point of view. The Church, after all, no longer represents the kind of closed language-community that would make it possible to enforce the use of words-with-certain-meanings without regard for different meanings which those words have in the usage of the culture at large.[70] Hence, it would be inconceivable for Christians to go on being obliged to say that "Jesus Christ is not a human person." For the person who weighs his words and reflects on their meaning this can only mean a denial of the full humanity of Christ. It can even be argued that this is precisely what many average Christians *mean*, albeit in a very implicit manner (for Jesus Christ,

---

[70]Cf. above, pp. 31–40.

after all, is God!); this cryptogamous heresy must be discouraged, not promoted.

We conclude that the need for a profession of the faith in words and terms that most people can understand constitutes a plea in favor of Schoonenberg's proposal.

The concern behind Schoonenberg's proposal

The linguistic case was inconclusive; the closeness-to-natural-language case went in favor of Schoonenberg. The third question must be: Are there *theological* grounds to refer to "the human person of Jesus Christ" in christology, as Schoonenberg proposes?

Let us start our inquiry by asking whether Schoonenberg's proposal reflects, not only a return to natural language, but also a shared *concern*. The answer again must be yes, and this can be argued as follows.

Nobody changes terminology just for the sake of change. Precisely because the link between term and concept is relatively unstable, scholars tend to be careful and conservative in preserving terminology, sometimes even at the expense of quick relevance. A change in terminology is generally warranted only in the light of new data or open conflict between terminology and common-sense language. The latter, we have argued, is the case with regard to "person."

But "person" represents more than a piece of common-sense language to be taken seriously by theology. It represents *a shared concern for freedom and self-awareness* in our culture. Books like Carl Rogers' *Client-Centered Therapy*[71] and *On Becoming a Person* are only pointers to a widespread unthematized worry about personalness. Many psychiatrists are observing that personal identity, not sex, has become the prevalent concern of their patients,[72]

---

[71]Boston, Houghton Mifflin Company, 1951.—For a treatment of personhood in a humanistic-psychological perspective sympathetic to religion, cf. Abraham H. Maslow, *Religions, Values, and Peak-Experiences*, Columbus, Ohio State University Press, 1964, and *Toward a Psychology of Being*, New York, Van Nostrand Reinhold Company, [2]1968.

[72]So, John Robinson's choice of sexuality as a concern to be faced in christology may after all be less contemporary than it looks!

owing to many persons' inability to hold on to a *lived experience of self* in the multiplicity of "parataxic" experiences of functional relationships with significant others.[73] It is safe to say that Schoonenberg's proposal for a new christological construct is part of a widespread attempt to do justice to an overriding concern with the value of human personhood; it is not based on a wanton propensity to change terminology with the aim of confusing theological usage, nor on a mistaken definition of the term or word "person," nor even merely on a desire to afford Christians an opportunity to use the word "person" in only one meaning, namely, "subject-center of freedom and consciousness."

Precisely because personalness is threatened, it becomes a great and precious good. That is why Christians *need* to be able to confess the fullness of human personalness in Jesus Christ. Any christological construct that diminishes, or seems to diminish, the fullness of Jesus' human personhood is suspect, because it fails to do justice to a crying human concern, *not* because it cannot be speculatively argued (*anhypostasia* is not nonsense!).[74] To sacrifice the full human personalness of Jesus to his divinity amounts to making God and full human personhood into competitors, and constitutes, therefore, an invitation to atheism for those whose concern is with personalness. Hence Schoonenberg's well-chosen starting-point: "God or Man—A False Dilemma."[75]

The Chalcedonian construct of two natures in the one person of Jesus Christ was meant to reconcile humanity in its fullness and divinity in its fullness. But perhaps it now only acts as a neuralgic irritant for people who are beset by half-conscious fears about "the divided self." If this is really the case, even the revival of Aquinas' attribution of an *esse secundarium*—a *relative* existential auton-

---

[73]Cf. J. H. van den Berg, *Leven in meervoud*, Nijkerk, G. J. Callenbach, ⁵1967, 205–213. The term "parataxic" is borrowed from Harry Stack Sullivan, *Conceptions of Modern Psychiatry*, Washington, D.C., The William Alanson Psychiatric Foundation, ³1947, esp. pp. 87ff., and the concluding essay by Patrick Mullahy, "A Theory of Interpersonal Relations and the Evolution of Personality," *ibid.*, pp. 119–147.

[74]D. M. Baillie, *God Was in Christ*, pp. 85–93, rejects *anhypostasia* and *enhypostasia* as *misleading* notions in christology, and proposes to use "person" for the human Jesus and *persona* for the divine Word.

[75]*The Christ*, pp. 13–49.

omy—to the humanity of Jesus,[76] for all its speculative boldness, will do little to comfort those who are preoccupied with the integrity of the human person.

Let us conclude. We must pay respect to the speculative acumen that went into the successful proof of the thesis that the denial of human personhood, far from being a denial of Jesus' full humanity, actually enhances it; Mersch's famous phrase: Jesus is "divinely human"—*divinement humain*—must be treasured, not disposed of. We will come back to the tradition's interpretation of the denial of Jesus' human personhood in a few moments. But in today's world it is good christology to attribute full human personalness to Jesus Christ, without any limitation or diminishment, and this is certainly not effectually done by saying that Jesus Christ is not a human person. The *rhetoric of inclusion* demands that "a fully human person" become a name of Jesus.

To diminish the full human personhood of Jesus on behalf of his full divinity would have two closely related ill effects. First, it would *exclude* those concerned with human personalness from him who makes all human concerns his own. Second, it would further those conceptions, discussed in the first chapter, of a God who is associated with human limits and who is experienced as the source of human diminishment.[77] Accordingly, it would promote a christology unfair to the full humanity of Jesus' life and death *and* to the lives and deaths of men and women today, in the name of a God who is known apart from, and in advance of, the event of Jesus Christ.

It is time to end our discussion of the demands which the rhetoric of inclusion places upon christology in its dealings with the present-day concern about human personalness. We must press on and treat the applicability of the rhetoric of obedience, the proper subject-matter of this section of the present chapter. We will do so by first doing justice to some important traditional insights, and then by clinching our own case.

[76]Cf. Bernard Lonergan, S.J., *De Verbo Incarnato*, Romae, Pontificia Universitas Gregoriana, 1964, pp. 265–266, and Felix Malmberg, *Ueber den Gottmenschen*, pp. 60–61, and n. 103.

[77]Cf. above, pp. 41–44.

Personalness and the rhetoric of obedience

If the rhetoric of inclusion must be applied to the epithet "a fully human person," so must the rhetoric of obedience. It is important to ask how Jesus is a fully human person, and how this affects the Christian investment in full human personalness.

In the total surrender to Jesus Christ the fullness of human personalness becomes a gift, not an achievement. Christians would only be projecting if they defined the full human personalness of Jesus in terms of what being a fully human person means to them. Christians are truly surrendering when they define full human personalness in virtue of how Jesus Christ is a human person. In the surrender, the rhetoric of inclusion permits the Christian to recognize his human concerns as accepted by Christ and thus as acceptable to himself, but the rhetoric of obedience prompts the Christian to put his concerns up for correction and judgment in the light of who Jesus Christ is. Such an openness to correction is a burden, but the burden is made light by the surrender. It involves mortification and self-denial on the part of the Christian, but he is only sharing in the humility and poverty of Christ. To be drawn into the surrender and to be shaped by Christ is a grace, not a form of self-abasement that would do dirt on being a person, a denial of the dignity of the person, or an instance of that religious submission which all the great atheists have rightly denounced.

What is Jesus' style of being a person? We have already mentioned that the historical Jesus was poor; he had nowhere to lay his head; he also avoided all reliance on a power-base in any of the standard ways of achieving authority or identifying with any of the prevalent causes. This poverty is a mystery. In the life of the historical Jesus it is couched in ambiguity; his particular historical stances and decisions were as open to misinterpretation and rejection, as they were accessible to faith and acceptance in discipleship.

But the mystery becomes, for those who believe, a powerful and Spirited realization after the Resurrection. Especially the Fourth Gospel explicates christologically what is hidden in the historical Jesus. "I do not seek my own glory." "I have not come to do my own will." "I have nothing out of myself."[78] Jesus' human personhood is

---

[78]Jn 8, 50; 5, 30.

not in self-possession, self-maintenance, or self-actualization. Others may derive ego-strength from causes; he relies on none. He does not even seek a foothold in his own self. Nothing in him resists surrender; there is no last line of defense, no ontological, inalienable personal identity to be upheld. At the core of Jesus there is a void, a negation of power, a nothing. "He emptied himself."[79]

At the same time, paradoxically, Jesus is full. The Gospels testify to the fact that he made himself into the focus of decision for all who encountered and followed him. The apostles were chosen "to be with him," and in the parables it is he himself who confronts the person. He is present and open to everything; nothing stays outside him. The Fourth Gospel explicates this christologically: "All that the Father has given me will come to me," and "The Father has put everything in my hands." There is nothing that meets him that is strange or foreign, nothing that is not, so to speak, already accounted for: "He knew what went on in their hearts," so that it was "not necessary for anyone to teach him."[80] At the core of Jesus there is everything, a fullness of presence, an authority which surpasses that of the Pharisees and scribes and which mocks the powers that be.

When, therefore, Jesus Christ gives, he does not offer *some thing*, for that would mean that as giver he would hold himself back in a position of safety, taking his refuge in self-possession. Jesus complains: "You come because you have eaten, but you have missed the true bread. I am the bread.[81] You have taken the gift, and refused the giver."

Jesus offers himself, and in doing so offers room for everything and justice done to everyone. We can say that *the giver is identical with the gift*, just as we said before that Jesus is identical with his cause. He is personally rooted not in power, but in poverty. When, in the kind of embarrassment that leads to violence, and mistaking poverty for power, authorities and powers that be take Jesus on, the hurt that they inflict on him goes to his very undefended self. The wound is not superficial, leaving an inner core of his person some-

---

[79]Phil 2, 7.

[80]Cf. Jn 6, 39; 13, 3; 3, 35; Mk 2, 8; Jn 2, 25; 16, 30 (*erōtai* in the sense of teaching-by-questioning; cf. *eperōtōnta* in Lk 2, 46).

[81]Jn 6, 26. 35.

how untouched. For his very self is gift and surrender, total openness and vulnerability. The hurt one is identical with the hurt, *the offended one is identical with the offense.* Other persons' sins taken out on him go right to the self, too; thus Jesus Christ was made into sin for us.

Since he *gave* himself willingly, the offerer is also identical with the offering; *the Priest is identical with the Victim.* The human person Jesus Christ is pure, undefended openness and self-giving.

Therefore, in the surrender of faith, if we attribute the fullness of human personhood to Jesus on the strength of the rhetoric of inclusion, we must expect, in virtue of the rhetoric of obedience, to have our concern with human personalness corrected, judged, and purified. The correction consists in this: the fullness of human personalness is not a fullness of power, of self-maintenance, of self-actualization—that preoccupation, and indeed worry, of our culture.[82] Jesus is most free, most fully his own person, precisely by doing the will of the Father.

The concern with personhood is thus both legitimized by inclusion and liberated by obedience in the Christian's surrender to Jesus Christ. The Christian accepts the concern positively; he need not shirk from it or apologize for it, for "fully human person" is now a name of Jesus Christ, who is total openness and who can embrace the Christian's concern and take it upon himself. In thus entrusting his very person to Jesus Christ and in thus knowing himself to be accepted with all his goodness and all his sin, the Christian can afford to drop the preoccupation with his own personhood, and let it be. He can stop being anxious about his own righteousness, whether he finds his conscience clean or soiled, for his own righteousness is in the care of Jesus Christ. He can also stop being worried about the question whether his own person is being done justice to. For he can cast his anxiety on the Lord, knowing that he is cared for.[83] He can

---

[82]The New Testament discourages worry and anxiety (*merimna*) in many places; e.g., Mk 4, 19; Mt 6, 25. 28. 31. 34; Phil 4, 6; 2 Cor 11, 28; 1 Cor 7, 33. 34b; but concern for others is encouraged: 1 Cor 12, 25; Phil 2, 20; 2 Cor 11, 28.

[83]"The church could not bear anything if it were not itself borne by Christ": Dietrich Bonhoeffer, *The Communion of Saints*, A Dogmatic Inquiry into the Sociology of the Church, New York and Evanston, Harper & Row, 1963, p. 129.—Cf. Bonhoeffer's thought on the unity of passivity and activity in *Act and Being*, London, Collins, 1962, pp. 130–132.

even cease to resist evil, opposing it with all the genuine and dubious resources of his person; instead, he can start absorbing the impact of evil and taking upon himself the sin of the world, for his own sufficiency, that is, his self, is in Christ. In surrendering himself to Christ a Christian both finds himself acceptable, and loses himself to become poor in the Spirit. His self-actualization is no longer self-justification, but gift.

Anhypostasia

The tradition of christology has seen the essential place of poverty and obedience in Jesus Christ, and has even tried to account for it within the limits set by the definition of Chalcedon. This was done, as we have explained, by calling Christ's human nature non-personal and in-personal—*anhypostatos* and *enhypostatos.*

We have already concluded that these expressions are open to radical misunderstanding today, and we will see that conclusion confirmed. But we have also suggested that the tradition is entitled to understanding.

Let us start with a representative of the Thomist tradition. In his *Ueber den Gottmenschen*, Felix Malmberg argues that the union with the Word does not in any way make Christ's humanity incomplete. It is a mistake to conclude that the "unmediated actuating causality" of the Word in the hypostatic union leads to a loss of personalness, integrity, and autonomy in the human nature of Christ.

In order to understand such formulas correctly we base ourselves on the following clear thesis of Saint Thomas: "The assumed nature [of Christ] does not lack a personalness of its own on account of its lacking something that pertains to the perfection of human nature, but on account of the fact that something that surpasses human nature has been added to it, namely, the union with a divine person." In our view we are really dealing with an *"assumptus homo"*; he is fully and wholly man like everyone of us, yet in an incomparably more perfect way and to an incomparably higher degree "propter unionem ad divinam personam." Christ's humanity, therefore, is not *less* "autonomous" and "sui iuris" than ours, but on the contrary, as Mersch rightly puts it, "by being *iuris verbi* it is all the more *sui iuris*, but *iure divino.*" We may and indeed we must here understand "human personalness" to be much more intensive than we understand ourselves, who are merely human persons, to have "human personalness"; and this is so, not *in spite of*, but precisely *because of* the fact that Christ's human nature is sustained by the divine person of the Word: "deificata non est perempta, salvata est autem magis."[84]

To say, therefore, that the *humanum* in Jesus Christ exists entirely in virtue of its unmediated union with the Word—in traditional terms, to call Christ's human nature anhypostatic—is to enunciate a perfection of that humanity, not a defect. Malmberg, in unison with the mainstream of the Thomist tradition, rests his case here; human nature has been done justice to.

Scotus, in keeping with the Franciscan tradition of christology, sees that there is more involved. Not only must we discuss the human nature as a static given, but also its dynamics. Now there was obviously no way in which Scotus could attribute human personalness to Jesus; the conciliar insistence on the one divine person was too strong. But Scotus did see the problem, and even was prepared to define "human person" in such a way as to solve it constructively. Kaiser explains:

> The doctrine of the two natures in the one person of the divine Word is the fundamental point of departure for the mystery of the Incarnation. If, however, Christ may not and cannot be a human person, did Christ's human nature lose a positive element when it was united with the Logos? Scotus rejects this, and, in doing so, makes a fundamental decision, which has its effects on the rest of his speculative effort. Had the human nature lost a positive element through the Incarnation, then Christ's humanity would be different from ours, and the redemption and assumption would not involve man entirely and fully. In this case part of us would be *incurabilis*.[85]

Hence, Scotus defines personhood *negatively*: a rational creature is person in virtue of its aptitudinal *and* actual *in*dependence vis-à-vis another *suppositum*. *Aptitudinal* independence means that a being, given the opportunity, would gravitate to independence, unless some other being prevented it from doing so; Scotus uses the metaphor of a stone which in and of itself would gravitate toward "the center." *Actual* independence means that the opportunity is actually given,

---

[84]Pp. 50–51.—The Latin phrase at the end of the quotation means that the human nature "was not taken away by being divinized, but better preserved."

[85]Phillip Kaiser, *Die gott-menschliche Einigung*, pp. 17–18.

and the being, so to speak, "falls into being a person." But that is an imperfection, for *independence is an imperfection.*

However, every being also has a *potentia oboedientialis* as part of its very nature, and only God in his absolute power can actuate this. In Christ, the Word actuates this *potentia* for total obedience, so that *his human nature loses the imperfection of actual independence,* though it retains, in and of itself, its aptitudinal independence.

However abstract and notional this construct may be, Scotus at least conveys his awareness that, in the eyes of a Christian, personal independence is at best a mixed perfection, not evil in itself, but always "apt" to assert itself in its own right and abandon the attitude of obedience to God. Yet, maintains Scotus, at the same time this obedience is pure grace.

We will have to go back to our discussion of *anhypostasia*, and our conclusion will turn out to be negative. Still, *anhypostasia* deserves reflection. It may be that the development of the concept owed more to the need for terminological coherence than to christological insight, as McIntyre seems to suggest.[86] In any case, the tradition used it, and often used it well; to insist that it is nonsense, as John Robinson tends to do,[87] betrays a lack of hermeneutical ability. Thomas Aquinas and John Duns Scotus were not surrounded by worries about personhood, but they knew that it was important and saw the christological problem.

The cultural and linguistic case against anhypostasia

Anhypostasia is not nonsense; it embodies a deep insight. However, as we have already pointed out, if we consider today's actual usage and appreciate today's concern with personalness, it is hardly advisable to go on saying that Jesus Christ is not a human person. Given the sensitivity of our culture to personal integrity, such a phrase gives the impression that Jesus Christ is not completely human and that Christianity cannot do justice to the person. *Anhypostasia* becomes an alienating irritant.

We must not be the slaves of terms and concepts, for they are only

---

[86]John McIntyre, *The Shape of Christology*, pp. 88–92.

[87]Cf. John A. T. Robinson, *The Human Face of God*, pp. 39–41 (confusion of *anhypostasia* with docetism), 105–109, 201 n. 89.

tools for thought and must never be mistaken for thought itself; in any case they do not in and of themselves guarantee thought. Accordingly, *the instrumentality of the neo-Chalcedonian anhypostasia-construct must not be mistaken for christology.* Dear though the theory of the *natura humana anhypostatica* may be to theologians, it does not guarantee thought, except to those who have patiently gone the way of scholarly study and meditation. Today's *living* concern is with personalness, and this concern is expressed, not only in the technical language of philosophy and humanistic psychology, but also in the everyday language of persons in search of meaning and identity. In the face of this the terminological tools of the tradition have precious little value. In addition, as we have already pointed out, the relatively loose connection between term and concept allows us, linguistically speaking, to replace one terminology by another. It would seem advisable in this case to do so.

A theological case against anhypostasia

Finally, there are theological as well as linguistic and cultural grounds for such a change. Christological discernments, as we have said, are at the service of the Christian's surrender to Jesus Christ. This surrender is conveyed by a rhetoric of inclusion and a rhetoric of obedience. We have argued above that clinging to the construct of the anhypostatic human nature in Christ offends against the rhetoric of inclusion, and thus takes away, in advance, the possibility to discover that the fullness of human personalness *for a Christian* consists in poverty and surrender. To appeal to the prestigious authority of the neo-Chalcedonian tradition is hardly a gesture of humble welcome extended to the culture, is it? Does this appeal to tradition not elevate the neo-Chalcedonian construct to the status not only of a sure-fire linguistic device and a warranty for thought, but also of a cause?

Linguistically, it is indeed legitimate and possible to enforce the Chalcedonian settlement as the one and only normative obligatory rule of speech in christology, in the interest of the unity of the Church, as we have already pointed out. By contrast as we have argued, attributing fully human personalness to Jesus Christ would move christology closer to natural language. But most importantly, given the culture's *concern with personalness,* it would be contrary to the rhetoric of inclusion to maintain the Chalcedonian and neo-Chalcedonian constructs as the central and normative christological formulas.[88]

This willingness to relativize the traditional *anhypostasia*-construct, however, would not only be a gesture of inclusion, *but also of obedience.* It would demonstrate that no discernment in christology is sovereign, and thus convey that no human concern is sovereign. It would welcome the concern with human personalness into christology, and thus welcome those concerned into the Church, in the hope that, having been thus welcomed, they will drop their anxious concern and be less worried about self-maintenance and self-justification. In this way the acceptance of "fully human person" as a title of Jesus would be a new and truly apostolic instance of that Christian freedom which extends a welcome to every human concern *and* which refuses to be dominated by any cause. It is part of the Christian's surrender to Christ to extend an unworried and humble welcome to a world involved in (and often enslaved by) the things pertaining to this life. The Church is called to the imitation of Christ in her doctrine and her theology, too.[89] Established dogma may not degenerate into a cause. If it does, no new discernments will be accepted, let alone corrected.

There is, obviously, another side to this question. Dogmatic formulas are also the symbols of *agapē*, and of ecclesiastical communion. Any change in emphasis or expression is bound to have a somewhat disturbing effect on those among the faithful who need the assurance of traditionally formulated orthodoxy. However, as we have already pointed out, the risk of cryptogamous heresy under cover of verbal orthodoxy, and the necessity of acknowledging that the Church is no longer a closed language-community, make it advisable not to treat the Chalcedonian and neo-Chalcedonian constructs as if they were the only central and normative christological formulas.

We will pursue the subjects of inclusion and obedience no further for the time being. Also, we will leave Schoonenberg's christological proposals for now, in order to come back to them in our

---

[88]Cf. above, pp. 167–173.
[89]Cf. above, p. 61; also below, pp. 510–518, 566–574.

tenth chapter. Let us, therefore, summarize our discussion so far and prepare the ground for a discussion of the third element of the triple rhetoric of christology.

Summary and outlook

Inclusion and obedience: these are the two cardinal attitudes which the Christian involvement with the *humanum* must manifest in the surrender to Jesus Christ. The picture of the historical Jesus, embracing all that is human around him, and thus making all concerns acceptable in his person, is a warrant for the inclusion. The picture of the historical Jesus, poor, undefended, seeking no foothold in anything he encounters, is an invitation to the obedience. Only if grounded in these two basic attitudes of the historical Jesus can the human concerns that make up the lives and deaths of Christians become the material for christological discernments. Only in these perspectives, inclusion and obedience, are the discernments correctly placed and understood. Surrender to Jesus Christ means acceptance and purification of all human concerns in his name.

Toward the end of the third chapter we argued that christological discernments are doubly bound.[90] On the one hand they represent shared human concerns; on the other hand they function in the act of total, responsive surrender to Christ. We also argued that it is easy to lose sight of both bonds. If we do, christological discernments are likely to start leading a very notional life of their own.

If we lose sight of the concerns' placement in the responsive *surrender* to Christ, we will mistake christological statements for "eternal truths which, once they are brought to awareness, also become theoretically understood," as Herbert Braun phrased it.[91] Christians, including theologians, tend to forget that the basic situation that gives meaning to discernments is worship and witness, not a metaphysical search for a cogent and comprehensive world-view. If we lose sight of the concerns' connection with the *culture*, we will again mistake christological statements for timeless, unhistorical

---

[90]Above, pp. 141–143.
[91]"The Meaning of New Testament Christology," in: Robert W. Funk (ed.), *God and Christ: Existence and Provi[de]nce, Journal for Theology and the Church*, 5, New York, Harper & Row, 1968, pp. 89–127; quotation p. 119.

truths, thus ignoring the need for each generation *as it is*, with its own dominant concerns, to surrender to Christ.

Keeping the awareness of the discernments' dependence on the culture alive is often a specialized task. It is largely the task of theological and historical scholarship to retrieve the original meaning of *past* christological discernments, by placing them against the background of the contemporary culture. The incorporation of *new* christological discernments will very likely prove to be the result of the spontaneous prophetic insights of Christian communities living their faith on the crossroads of Church and culture, and of the theological visionaries in the Church.

Keeping alive the awareness of the discernments' dependence on the act of surrender to Christ, however, is the task of all, for it is the soul of the act of faith itself. That act of surrender, we have argued, is one in which the human concerns are accepted and purified. The concerns' being included and made obedient is what makes them into the stuff of *christology*; we must, therefore, concentrate on the act of surrender to Jesus Christ if we want to appreciate the properly *christological* meaning of all the culturally-determined titles and predicates of Christ.

This chapter made the first two steps. It has dealt with what traditional christology means by "Incarnation": all human concerns have been assumed by the Word. It has also dealt with the christological theme of "humiliation": all human concerns have been drawn into the imitation of Jesus poor and powerless. What remains to be treated is the meaning of the Resurrection, and its effect upon christology, namely, the rhetoric of hope. We will do this in the next chapter.

CHAPTER 5

The Human Concerns:
Grounds for Hope

And time yet for a hundred indecisions,
And for a hundred visions and revisions . . .
. . . . .
Would it have been worth while,
To have bitten off the matter with a smile,
To have squeezed the universe into a ball,
To roll it towards some overwhelming question,
To say: 'I am Lazarus, come from the dead,
Come back to tell you all, I shall tell you all'—

T. S. Eliot

The secret is this: Christ in you, the hope of a glory to come.

The Letter of Paul to the Colossians

It may seem a somewhat startling leap to make, but to the great spiritual masters of the undivided Church, the revealed doctrine of man as having been made in the image of God universally inspires [a] feeling of glad recognition. They go on, in fact, to take it seriously for what it claims to be, a long lost memory of their true selves, and from that all the rest they have to say follows. Their doctrine is concerned to arouse in their disciples a sense of the implications of a memory they believe could not have been initially reawakened without a divine intervention.

Aelred Squire

Preliminary

In the third chapter we discussed the dynamic involved in the process of naming Jesus Christ, and, hence, the fact that the discernments in christology are placed. Christological discernments, we argued, represent human concerns, which are brought to Christ and become his names, so that he comes to preside over them.[1]

In the fourth chapter we argued that human concerns get accepted and humbled in this process; they are entrusted to the care of Christ for him to do justice to them *and* to purify them. Another way to express this was: Christ accepts and assays all human concerns. We argued that Christ's acceptance of all human concerns is conveyed by the rhetoric of inclusion. Christ's purifying judgment of all human concerns, we said, is conveyed by the rhetoric of obedience; all christological discernments must be understood to model themselves after Christ poor and powerless. Underlying all christological statements, therefore, is the possibility for universal inclusiveness and the call to total obedience. However, we added another expression. Christ not only accepts and purifies all human concerns, he also puts them in perspective. Underlying christological statements are not only universal inclusiveness and total obedience, but also the offer of absolute hope.[2] A treatment of the rhetoric of hope, therefore, will round off our discussion of the rhetoric of christology.

We will do this in three stages. First, we will briefly introduce the subject of this chapter by means of the metaphors of "perspective," "stance," and "horizon." We will then treat the Resurrection of Christ as the ground for absolute hope. This will raise the question how human concerns are related to their own divine fulfillment; in that context we will critically examine Paul Tillich's christology.

Prelude: things, perspective, stance and horizon[3]

Perspective both belongs and does not belong to things. On the face of it, it would seem that perspective is *not* a property of things in themselves, but something extraneous to them. Perspective, it seems,

---

[1] Cf. above, pp. 126–129, 137–143.

[2] Above, pp. 145, 149–150, 153.

[3] This section was inspired by some thoughts in J. Verhaar, *Some Relations*, pp. 26–30.

comes to things merely because they are placed in a certain relationship to the horizon, to each other, and to ourselves. Because I am where I am the horizon is where it is. It would seem therefore that *I* am responsible for the way things around me, as far as the eye can see, are "placed," not the things themselves. On the other hand, though, things are "placeable" in my world by their own nature; they "lend themselves" to perspective. Things are far from being merely inert, intractable counters, with a perspective that is purely extrinsic and in the eye of the beholder. Rather, they are related; they are positively susceptible to perspective. What I see—"what *I* make of them"!—really tells me something about *them.* They are "other," but that does not make them alien and impregnable; their "irreducible strangeness" never makes them into totally unknown quantities. If they are set in perspective, that perspective is also truly theirs.

Second, things are in perspective for me because I have a *stance.* My stance contributes essentially to things being in perspective. Now without the consciousness of my stance *as my own*, I cannot make any sense of perspective. Unless I know where I am, perspective becomes *merely* relative; in that case it only "so happens" that things look in such and such a way to me, but there is no intrinsic truth to the way I see them from my vantage-point. Perspective only acquires meaning *to the extent that I am personally committed to my stance* and experience it as meaningful. Only in that case will the perspective not only truly belong to the things as I see them but also truly belong to me as my perspective.

Third, my stance determines my horizon; if I change my stance, my horizon changes too. If, then, I must be committed to my stance to have a meaningful perspective on things, *I must be committed to my horizon, too.*

Fourth, my horizon is not only the horizon against which I see the things I choose to see or happen to see; I see *everything* in my world against my horizon. My horizon is comprehensive; it places *all* things in my world, including the things I am not aware of having a perspective on. When new things enter into my awareness, therefore, my commitment to my horizon may be tested. If my new perceptions fit into the perspective already established, my horizon proves once more meaningful, and I am confirmed in my stance. But if the newly perceived things do not lend themselves to the perspective given with my stance and my horizon, I may have to choose between my established horizon and a new one called for by my new perceptions. If I do the former I will have to revise not only all my previous perceptions, but also my entire stance, so that I get a fresh perspective and a new horizon.

Fifth, what does my horizon represent? On the one hand it is part of my world, though a very special part, namely its limit; by being the limit of my world, the horizon rounds off, places, structures and determines my world and everything in it. The horizon, however, is also where the yonder world starts. Hence it is the representative of the beyond, as part of my world. The horizon as the symbol of transcendence is conveyed most notably by the fact that it recedes as I approach it; I will never get *there*. It is the ultimate reference-point, the standard of all my perceptions; but it is a *receding standard*, to be yearned for rather than ever attained.[4] And yet, because it places everything in my world, my only choice is to be totally committed to my horizon; unless I am *totally committed* to this fugitive, receding standard of all my perceptions, none of the things in my world will have perspective. I realize, of course, that the horizon is not really the ultimate. It is simply the limit where I see the last things I can see. But that means that *total* commitment to my horizon is only available to me if I *experience* the horizon, not simply as the farthest place that I can see, but precisely as *horizon*—as the representative of something else that *is* ultimate.

There are, therefore, three ways of speaking about the horizon. The first way is to speak about it purely as the farthest-away place in my world; this, however, misses the distinctive point, namely, that the horizon is the limit of my world. The second way is to speak about the horizon as the limit of my world, and as the "objective correlative"[5] of my stance; as we speak about that interplay of stance

---

[4] I owe the idea of a receding horizon to John Henry Newman, *Fifteen Sermons* (*Oxford University Sermons*), London–New York–Bombay, Longmans, Green and Co., 1906, pp. 18–19, and to *id.*, *An Essay in Aid of a Grammar of Assent*, Westminster, Maryland, Christian Classics, 1973, pp. 101–121.

[5] I owe this term to T. S. Eliot, "Hamlet and His Problems," in: *Selected Essays*, New York, Harcourt, Brace & World, ³1950, pp. 121–126; term on pp. 124–125 (cf. F. R. Leavis, *The Great Tradition*, Garden City, Doubleday and Company, 1954, p. 213). In Eliot "objective correlatives" are items capable of objective description, but used in order to convey an unobjectifiable emotional atmosphere. Here it is used to convey the unobjectifiable ultimate limit of my world.

and horizon, we will also be able to speak about the way all the things in my world are placed in perspective. The third way is to speak about the horizon precisely as the symbol of the beyond, which therefore draws me into a stance of total commitment.

Speaking in the first way amounts to treating the horizon just like all the other things in my world taken by themselves—as a particular place, not as horizon. Speaking in the second way allows me to make sense of the perspective in which things in my world are set; only in relation to the horizon do they fall into place and add up to "my world." This second way, therefore, also allows me to speak of the horizon in an *indirect way*, namely, by discussing how the horizon reflects on the things in my world and how it lends them perspective. But most importantly, this second way allows me to discuss how the horizon *precisely as the symbol of the beyond* reflects on the things in my world, and how the things in my world figure in my *total commitment*. This indirect way of speaking about the beyond will then obviously raise the question how we can engage in the third way of speaking about the horizon, namely, *directly*, in terms of its being the symbol of the beyond.

The images of perspective, stance, and horizon may illustrate how we can speak of, and witness to, Jesus Christ in terms of particular discernments. We have already characterized the presence of Christ in the Spirit as the comprehensive christological situation which draws the Christian into total surrender.[6] It is, to use the metaphors just developed, the comprehensive horizon of the Christian world. This horizon reflects upon the things in the world in a threefold manner. First, it includes everything; all things are welcome in the world. Second, it purifies everything; all things are redirected and called to open themselves to relationships. Third, it places everything in perspective; in their being related to the horizon things become pointers to, and bearers of, total meaning. We have argued before that discernments reflect human concerns, the things pertaining to this life. If, then, the presence of Christ in the Spirit places all things in perspective, we must expect that all discernments in christology are placed, not only in a rhetoric of inclusion and obedience, but also in a rhetoric of hope. The next section will be devoted to an analysis of this rhetoric.

---

[6]Above, pp. 111, 117–119, 122–123, 128.

CHRIST'S RESURRECTION:
THE HORIZON OF ALL CONCERNS

The partiality of discernments and concerns

If christological discernments represent human concerns, what is their ultimate value? Human concerns are partial and fragmentary; they doggedly resist total integration into an all-encompassing answer to an overwhelming question. Just as the words we use to convey them "slip, slide, perish, decay with imprecision,"[7] so too the concerns *themselves* defend their particularity and resist universal synthesis. Sometimes they light up, for a moment, and show their depth; but even when they thus come off as symbols, they are never entirely compelling.

In the surrender to Christ the concerns indeed become ways towards him because he accepts and liberates them; in the surrender, they become both legitimized and transparent. Yet they remain approximations, approaches that betray that they come from a particular angle, answers that remain tied to the partiality of the questions, tools for visions that evoke the need for revisions.

For instance, when in their search for the truth Christians call Jesus Christ "teacher," they recognize that he is indeed a teacher, "for that I am," although "not like the scribes."[8] But still we ask: Is that all he is? Similarly, all the titles that the New Testament and the Christian tradition have used to address Christ add up to an impressive list of concerns accepted and purified; yet the question remains: But is that all? The rhetoric of inclusion gave the answer to the question: "Are our concerns acceptable?" and the rhetoric of obedience gave the answer to the question: "Can our concerns become the stuff of obedience and freedom?" The question remains whether our concerns, no matter how acceptable and no matter how obedient, have any standing in the universal synthesis. And if we give up our preoccupation with them, how will they be vindicated in the end?

We are faced with the tension between the partiality of the discernments in christology and the totality of the commitment

---

[7] T. S. Eliot, "Burnt Norton," V, *Collected Poems, 1909–1962*, London, Faber and Faber, 1963, p. 194 (*The Complete Poems and Plays*, Harcourt, Brace, & World, [n.d.], pp. 121–122).

[8] Cf. Jn 13, 13; Mt 7, 29.

involved in the surrender to Jesus Christ. This tension involves, first, the tension between knowledge and insight on the one hand and the act of responsive surrender on the other hand. Discernments never do justice to the act of commitment, just as the word-with-meaning never completely manages to capture the fullness of the response that is involved in the name.[9] *A fortiori*, then, discernments never add up to an act of *total* commitment, to an act of responsive surrender without any reservation.

Hence, second, underneath the tension between partial discernment and total commitment lies a deeper and much more fundamental tension. Discernments, as we saw, represent shared concerns brought to the surrender to Jesus Christ.[10] These concerns become the names of Jesus on the strength of the rhetoric of inclusion. But human concerns are potentially legion. Who will tell what *tomorrow*'s causes will be? Will they be amenable to inclusion? And, with regard to *today*'s causes and concerns, have they become the names of Jesus, and, indeed, are they capable of becoming his names? Jesus, the man of Nazareth, the first-century Jew, certainly cannot be said to be the "solution to all of today's problems"; he did not even know them. How, then, can Christians claim that he can be called by the names of all their present-day concerns? Are we even sure that *yesterday*'s concerns have been included?

> Christianity, having settled down into its medieval moulds, was largely unable to "take" the strictly neutral and secular approach to everything in the universe (including, eventually, man in so far as he is homogeneous with the rest of the universe), which is the essence of the scientific approach and which gives it its liberating and creative effect. Thus scientific developments were frequently seen, and indeed still are seen, as threats to the Christian religion. In this we have what is perhaps the most outstanding and the most disastrous example of the way in which the Christian religion—i.e. the alleged following of Jesus Christ as organized, practiced and institutionalized—again and again gets off-centre from its true and only *raison d'être*—Jesus Christ himself. [. . .] Scientists may have brought about the apparent exclusion of God, but if there is any point in allotting *blame* for this then we would probably do better to apportion it to the Church who attempted to

---

[9]Cf. above, pp. 89–90.
[10]Above, pp. 135–141.

confine the God and Father of Jesus Christ to the so-called sacred when Jesus Christ himself had already abolished the separation of sacred and secular *within* the universe.[11]

Could we not also point to the Church's partial or even total failure to "take" and appropriate the emergence of humanism, of national consciousness, of female self-consciousness, of the working-class movement? Recognition and acceptance came too late in some cases, in others never. And we have not even touched on the concerns represented by Buddhism, by Marxism, by Taoism—concerns which, even if they have managed not to set themselves up as causes, have all too often met, not Jesus Christ, but the cause that Christians made out of following him or belonging to the Church.

Thus, both the *factual* failure on the part of Christianity to meet and integrate the concerns of history and the *theoretical* realization that there is no limit to the variety of human concerns make one wonder: Do all these concerns add up to something final and comprehensive? Is there not a tension, never to be resolved, between the partiality of the concerns and the discernments derived from it, and the totality of the surrender? There is. The *total* surrender, in other words, represents *a qualitative leap when compared with the partiality of the concerns* that are brought into the surrender.

Jesus Christ is risen

This qualitative leap is what is involved in the Christian's announcement that Jesus Christ is vindicated, risen from the dead, exalted in virtue of his self-emptying unto death. This confession puts all human concerns, once included and humbled, into perspective. The inclusion of all human concerns by itself would amount to a noble, enlightened and all-encompassing humanism; their conversion to obedience would turn this humanism into an impressively compassionate moralism. But Jesus Christ is more than true man and more than the invitation to obedience. He is risen. This creates a perspective beyond all concerns. Prufrock's debilitating stalemate is broken; Christians start to speak as if they have come from the dead;

---

[11]David Jenkins, *The Glory of Man*, pp. 62–63.

they can speak and "tell you all."[12] The leap from the provisional and partial concerns to the final synthesis is justified.

The New Testament is aware of this qualitative difference between the central significance of Christ and the partiality of the human concerns in which he is involved. It stresses the particularity of Jesus. He was from Nazareth—and what good could come from there? He felt that his mission was restricted to "the lost sheep of the house of Israel," and for lack of compelling evidence it took "faith" to recognize the messianic secret. No matter how true it is that "God's wisdom is proved right by its results," yet "this generation" acts like pouting hard-to-please children: "We piped for you and you would not dance. We wept and wailed, and you would not mourn."[13] The Fourth Gospel is particularly explicit both in claiming the universal significance of Jesus "for the world" and in recognizing the futility of the attempt to express it by accumulation of narrative: "There is much else that Jesus did. If it were all to be recorded in detail, I suppose the whole world could not hold the books that would be written."[14] The unique significance of Jesus differs qualitatively from the concerns in which he is involved.

Paul van Buren and Willi Marxsen: two interpretations

In view of recent theological attempts to account for the Resurrection we must be very explicit here. The total surrender is directed *to Jesus*, "this same Jesus"[15] who shows himself alive with the marks of his *kenōsis* in his human person.[16] *He* is vindicated by the Father, present and alive, risen from the dead, exalted, in the Spirit.

Jesus Christ is alive, not just the *cause* of Jesus Christ; no cause would ever warrant the total devotion and dedication of Christians. Even the historical Jesus refused to associate himself with any cause or to set up a rival one of his own. *If* we are to identify a cause in the life of the historical Jesus, it is the kingdom of God; but this kingdom

---

[12]Allusion to "The Love Song of J. Alfred Prufrock," in: T. S. Eliot, *Collected Poems, 1909–1962*, pp. 13–17, from which the first epigraph of this chapter (above, p. 184) is taken (pp. 14, 16; *The Complete Poems and Plays*, pp. 4, 6).

[13]Cf. Mt 2, 23; 21, 11; Lk 2, 39. 51; Jn 1, 45–46; Acts 10, 38; Mt 15, 24; Lk 7, 31–32.

[14]Jn 21, 25; cf. 20, 30–31.

[15]Cf., for example, the emphatic *touton ton Iēsoun* in Acts 2, 36.

[16]Cf. Jn 20, 20.

is "not of the world."[17] It is not a cause set by Jesus against other causes (as an inappropriate exegesis of Matthew 22, 15-22 and related passages would have it). The kingdom of God accepts *and* questions *all* causes and concerns, and the embodiment of this acceptance and questioning is the person of Jesus himself as he embraces and assays the people who bring their concerns to him. And since there is no distinction between Jesus and his cause, as we saw before, he is, in Origen's eloquent phrase, "the kingdom in person" (*autobasileia*).

When van Buren calls Jesus a "remarkably free man," whose *freedom* becomes contagious in the Easter faith of his followers, he is not saying enough.[18] He *is* hitting on a key human concern, a dominant metaphor, which may open modern man's eyes to the *disclosure* of what is involved in the Resurrection. But he neglects that it is *to Jesus Christ* that Christians surrender, and in doing so, whatever freedom they acquire is *their own*, although they acquire it in their surrender to Jesus Christ—just as, incidentally, the Christian's obedience consists in carrying *his own cross*, although he does so in following Jesus Christ.[19]

If van Buren means to *replace* the confession of the living Christ by the confession of the contagious freedom of Jesus, he allows a (very contemporary) human discernment to preside over Jesus Christ. But if *only* Jesus' freedom has become contagious, or only his cause has come to life or been vindicated, then the Christians' concerns are *ultimately* left to themselves. No single discernment can lay claim to the totality involved in the commitment;[20] the point of departure, the context, and the goal of all Christian discernments about Christ (and discernments are the representatives of human concerns!) is precisely the surrender to the *person* of Jesus Christ in the Spirit. Here lies the totality of the commitment and not in any concern in and of itself, not even in the most relevant and up-to-date one.[21]

---

[17]Cf. Jn 18, 36.
[18]Cf. Paul M. van Buren, *The Secular Meaning of the Gospel*, pp. 126–134, esp. 133–134.
[19]Cf. Gal 4, 31; Mk 8, 34.
[20]Cf. above, p. 128.
[21]Cf. the cautionary words about this, above, pp. 142–143.

Hence, van Buren's analysis can be accepted only if "contagious freedom" is understood to function *symbolically*, not descriptively, as a *key metaphor* that represents the ultimate, not the known quantity in human experience as such. In van Buren's theology, human freedom acts as a model, and, it must be added, a well-chosen one, for it is liable to evoke the typical religious disclosure and to precipitate the total commitment. To the extent that it does *that*, van Buren succeeds in conveying the absolute uniqueness of Christ as manifested in the Resurrection.

The only problem *in the context of van Buren's book* is that the author claims that he wants to talk only in terms that have calculable cash value to "modern man."[22] But what makes the formula "contagious freedom" successful as a christological phrase is not its readily determinable meaning, but its capacity to precipitate the total surrender.

The phrase "contagious freedom," therefore, is unacceptable as a *substitute* for the confession of Christ alive; it subordinates Jesus to a modern cause. It is acceptable as a way to *convey* the significance of the living Christ by means of a telling metaphor.[23]

We must now discuss Willi Marxsen's proposal to look upon the Resurrection of Jesus as an *Interpretament*, that is, as an interpretation of something that remains unattainable.[24] We cannot claim to be able to say what corresponds, in reality, to what we tentatively convey by "resurrection."

Marxsen's concern is both obvious and legitimate. The Resurrection of Jesus must not be presented as a brute fact, accessible in principle to verification by some objectifying method of historical research. That sort of resurrection is nothing more than resuscitation, which flies in the face, not only of 1 Corinthians 15, but even of the most physical Easter passages in the Synoptics. But, granted this,

---

[22]Cf. Paul M. van Buren, *The Secular Meaning of the Gospel*, pp. 97–106.

[23]An excellent discussion of christology in terms of freedom in Ernest Käsemann, *Jesus Means Freedom*, Philadelphia, Fortress Press, 1972.

[24]Cf. for the following Willi Marxsen, *The Resurrection of Jesus of Nazareth*, Philadelphia, Fortress Press, 1970, esp. pp. 138–148. For an interesting example of Marxsen's ambiguity on the subject, cf. p. 126, where Marxsen stresses that it is really *he*—Jesus—who comes today, and immediately proceeds to talk about this coming in neuter terms: "what comes today," "the same thing that Jesus of Nazareth brought."

does the concept of interpretation do justice to everything involved in the Christians' witness that Christ is risen?[25]

"Resurrection from the dead" represents, not only an idea, but more basically an *aspiration* and hence a *concern* in late Judaism. In response to the person of Jesus Christ this concern is activated. In what the Gospels call "appearances," *he* compels the women and the apostles to *witness*: "He is risen."

Witnessing is more than interpreting; interpretation represents only the cognitive part of the total response, just as the clarifying force of the metaphor represents only part of its total function.[26]

The marshaling of "resurrection" to express what is involved in the presence of Jesus Christ alive must be viewed as an instance of metaphoric language-use. To the extent that "resurrection" clarifies what is involved in the presence of the living Christ it is indeed an interpretation—one based upon a pre-existing and familiar theme of yearning for immortality. But the *reality* of the Resurrection is not reducible to this yearning, for a metaphor does more than clarify; it is first and foremost an address, a response to a reality. When Christians use the word "resurrection" to convey what is involved in Jesus' living presence in the Spirit, they do more than interpret; *in actual use* the word conveys the Christians' surrender to him who presides over every concern with immortality and determines what resurrection means. *What "happened to Jesus" is adequately conveyed, not by the partiality of the concerns, but only by the totality of the surrender.*

The phrase "He is risen from the dead" represents not only an interpretation, but also and primarily an act of witness grounded in total and worshipful faith-surrender. *Within the situation of faith in Jesus Christ*, therefore, there is as much room for a Sadducean as for a Pharisean interpretation of his presence to, and impact on, the Christian.[27] This is so because the phrase "Christ is risen" conveys its real meaning much more fully when two Russian peasants greet each other with a *Khristos voskres* on Easter Sunday morning than when it

---

[25]For a sympathetic and critical discussion of Marxsen, cf. Piet Schoonenberg, *The Christ*, pp. 156–166.

[26]Cf. above, pp. 91–92, 135–137.

[27]Cf. Piet Schoonenberg, *The Christ*, p. 159.

functions as an answer to the question: "What, if anything, happened to Jesus after he died?" It is in the *rhetoric* that the real meaning of the phrase "Christ is risen" is found; that rhetoric is an act of expressed and shared total surrender to him, conveyed by the phrase "Christ is risen" *in the direct experience of speech.* Only secondarily can we consider the meaning of the statement, as in the question: "What does 'resurrection from the dead' mean?" The Fourth Gospel conveys this in its own characteristic way when it transforms the Synoptics' "He is risen" into "I am the Resurrection," thus identifying Jesus with his cause, and having Jesus *in person* preside over the human concern represented by the late-Judaic metaphor "resurrection," while conveying the claim to total surrender in the radicalizing transformation preceded by "I am."[28]

Both van Buren and Marxsen have legitimate concerns. Both want to avoid a cheap "miraculist" explanation of what is involved in the Resurrection; such an explanation is not only unbelievable to modern man, it also does violence to the New Testament. But in doing so both tend to *reduce* the Resurrection to a Christian interpretation. Van Buren appeals to modern man's need for clear understanding and thus comes close to reducing Christ's Resurrection to the Christian experience of freedom. Marxsen appeals to the essential connectedness of the living Lord and the Christian faith; as a consequence he refuses to speak about the living Lord in any "objectivist" fashion; in the end Christian speech about the Resurrection is left to itself—a mere *Interpretament.* We have argued that there is more involved in the Resurrection.

The objectivity of the Resurrection

The proclamation "Christ is risen" must have something to say about Jesus *himself;* if it did not do that it would be merely a pious *mythologoumenon,* essentially replaceable by a more "human" statement, which would make it clear that what is involved is, essentially and exhaustively, an interpretative faith-response on the part of the believer.

"The statement must have something to say about Jesus himself." We must proceed cautiously here.

---

[28]Cf. above, pp. 150–151.

Let us suppose that in saying this we were to mean: "There is something about what we call the Resurrection which is thoroughly and irreducibly Jesus' own, something that happened to him and has nothing to do with his followers—something completely objective in its own right." In saying this we would be making a claim on behalf of Jesus Christ *which he would refuse to make for himself,* namely, a quality of life strictly his own, which he does not communicate to his followers.[29] Quite apart from the epistemological problem (how would we know about a reality that remains outside our lives in virtue of its total objectivity?), the statement, by making Jesus Christ hold something of himself back for himself, is un-Christlike and goes against the whole message of the Gospel: "He gave himself."[30] Christians must not jump to the defense of Christ where he was not prepared to defend himself. To defend the reality of the Resurrection in this way against those who seem to reduce it to a "mere faith-experience" is not good christology.

How then can the statement "Christ is risen" have something to say about Christ himself? It does so because it reflects a *responsive act.* The presence of Christ in the Spirit has prompted the response. The living Lord has inspired the respondent to turn to him and to bring with him his concern with final justice and immortality—that universal human aspiration conveyed by the late-Judaic metaphor "resurrection." No wonder, then, that the speaker experiences Christ's Resurrection as primarily something that concerns *Christ:* his presence in the Spirit is what prompts him to speak in the first place. To insist, therefore, on the objectivity of the Resurrection is not to suppose a factuality accessible, in principle, to historical verification or to defend a quality of Christ that is strictly for himself and not for us, but to convey the overriding, compelling presence of Christ both as the power that releases the believer's speech and as the fulfillment of what he has to say.

This is the reason why the believer will find it hard to take part in any debate about the question what "resurrection from the dead"

---

[29]Professor Donald MacKinnon of Cambridge, in the christology seminar in the divinity school in late 1975, stressed again and again that the Resurrection of Jesus is not a power-move in the interest of self-preservation: "The Resurrection of Jesus is not the equivalent of a descent from the Cross postponed by 48 hours!"

[30]Gal 2, 20.

means or how the reality of Christ's Resurrection is verified. The Christian's surrender to Christ, conveyed *by the fact that he says what he says*, is the verification of the Resurrection of Jesus Christ. Only the totality of the surrender, conveyed by the *act* of speaking, conveys adequately what happened to Jesus. The uniqueness of Jesus Christ is not first argued (for instance, by claiming the objectivity of the Resurrection) and then acted upon; it is first conveyed by the rhetoric of christological speech, symbol of the total surrender, and then subsequently articulated in terms of human concerns. When Paul faces the Council in Acts 23 he causes some of the Pharisees to side with him on the *idea* of the resurrection, which the Sadducees— in the simplified presentation of the author of Acts—deny. But that is as far as his alliance with the Pharisees goes. No longer the metaphor for an aspiration, resurrection has become, in Christ, *a confirmed hope*, for which Paul puts *himself* on the line by his confidence in speaking. Whether his preaching of Christ risen meets with Jewish assassination plans as in Acts 23, or with Greek disdain as in Acts 17, it does not matter.

> For, as I passionately hope, I shall have no cause to be ashamed, but shall speak so boldly that now as always the greatness of Christ will shine out clearly in my person, whether through my life or through my death.[31]

Partial concerns drawn into an act of hopeful surrender

So far we have emphasized the qualitative leap represented by the Christian's total surrender to the living Lord compared to the partiality of the concerns brought into the surrender. In Christian speech this is manifested by the fact that the act of speech conveys decisively more than the discernments add up to.[32] We must now ask ourselves the question what happens to the human concerns in the act of total surrender to Christ.

Using the set of metaphors developed at the outset of this chapter we can say that thus far we have emphasized the comprehensiveness of the horizon as the ultimate perspective of all things in my world, and the stance of total commitment to the horizon. Christ's

---

[31]Phil 1, 20.
[32]Above, pp. 195–196.

presence in the Spirit places all things in perspective and it elicits the Christian's total commitment. We must now ask ourselves the question what happens to things when they are placed in perspective; in doing so we will be *indirectly* talking about the horizon—how it reflects upon things and how things come to figure in my total commitment to the horizon. How does Christ's presence in the Spirit reflect upon human concerns, and how can partial things figure in the Christian's total surrender to the living Lord?

The person of Christ himself is the warrant for the claim that partial concerns have standing in the final synthesis. All human concerns are legitimate, for Christ embraces them all. All human concerns are the stuff of obedience and poverty, for Christ refuses to seek his strength in them, not even to escape death. But there is more to Christ than human concerns accepted and abandoned: he is alive beyond all concerns and beyond obedience unto death. It is *in his life now* that he warrants for the Christian both the acceptance and the abandonment of all the concerns that make up the human condition, including the yearning for fulfillment implied, as a precondition for any desire, in all the partial concerns that men and women have. In his fulfillment, Jesus Christ also bears the names of all human aspirations; in his exaltation he presides over the longing of the human heart. The mystery is this: Christ in you, the hope of glory.[33]

The total surrender exceeds the concerns that are brought to Christ in the christological discernments; it is conveyed by the very *act of speaking* to and about Christ. The act of speaking, therefore, exceeds the discernments, and yet these same discernments are all that we, given the partiality of our concerns, can use to speak. It takes special courage in speech, *parrhēsia*,[34] to proclaim a final perspective on the strength of, *and* in spite of, very fragmentary and partial discernments. Only the presence of Christ in the Spirit enables Christians to speak so out of proportion with *what* they say. But that means that christological discernments are drawn into an act of speaking that says more. The presence of Christ elicits an affirmativeness not quite warranted by the discernments. The point of christological speaking is far more than the sum of the meanings

---

[33]Col 1, 27.

[34]For *parrhēsia*, cf. above, p. 108 and note 1.

of the statements made; here more than anywhere else Christian language is object-language and more.

Let us here recall that the discernments represent human concerns. This obliges us to say that not only are the discernments drawn into an act of speaking, but also the human concerns they represent are drawn into an act of responsive surrender. In the surrender to Christ the human concerns, so partial and so provisional, *become the stuff of confident hope.* Thus the Christian act of speaking also represents the Christian's hope in and beyond any and all concerns accepted and purified. Those very concerns become the bearers of an unsuspected perspective.

The surrender to Jesus Christ is an *act of response* to his presence in the Spirit. That means: *in the act of surrender to Christ the human concerns drawn into it are revealed as having a capacity for response-in-total-surrender to Jesus Christ.*

Human concerns and their fulfillment

We started by pointing out the *tension* between the partiality of the human concerns and the total commitment. We went on to argue that these very partial concerns were nonetheless drawn into the surrender, where they proved to have a capacity for response-in-total-surrender to Jesus Christ. This capacity comes from outside, and yet it is the actuation of the concern's own potentiality, just as perspective comes to things from their relationship to the horizon and from their own susceptibility to perspective. This raises the issue of tension again, only this time in relation to the human concerns themselves; far from being completely foreign to them, orientation to Christ, so Christians claim, is part of every concern's very nature.

So on the one hand we must maintain that the human concerns' orientation to Christ comes from outside—it is totally gratuitous. This gratuitousness can be argued in more than one way.

As we have seen, the concerns assert their partiality and resist total integration. Integration into an act of total surrender is therefore what scholastic theology aptly described as surpassing the powers and the exigencies of created nature; any actual integration into a total synthesis is an unowed gift of perspective and *élan.* What at the level of language, considered as carrier of meaning, shows itself as object language and more, shows itself in *the act of surrender* conveyed by the rhetoric as "concerns and more."

The gratuitousness is also manifested by the fact that the concern functions in an act of response to Jesus Christ present in the Spirit. Encountering another person already exceeds what is strictly due to any person. Encountering the person Jesus Christ present in the Spirit totally exceeds all powers and exigencies of any person, along with all his concerns. In the Christian's witness "Christ is risen" humanity and its concerns do indeed profess their own firm hope for the ultimate; but this assurance comes from "the power which is at work among us," and which enables us to do "immeasurably more than all we can ask or conceive."[35]

On the other hand we must say that human concerns lend themselves by nature to incorporation into the total surrender. *From within* this act of surrender, and in that sense only by hindsight, Christian reflection pronounces itself on what, in virtue of Christ's Resurrection, it now joyfully recognizes as the deepest potentiality and yearning of humanity itself, of all human concerns, and indeed of the whole world. They are all made in the image of God.

> For I reckon that the sufferings we now endure bear no comparison with the splendor, as yet unrevealed, which is in store for us. For the created universe waits with eager expectation for God's sons to be revealed. It was made the victim of frustration, not by its own choice, but because of him who made it so; yet always there was hope, because the universe itself is to be freed from the shackles of mortality and enter upon the liberty and splendor of the children of God. Up to the present, we know, the whole created universe groans in all its parts as if in the pangs of childbirth. Not only so, but even we, to whom the Spirit is given as firstfruits of the harvest to come, are groaning inwardly while we wait for God to make us his sons and set our whole body free. For we have been saved, though only in hope. Now to see is no longer to hope: why should a man endure and wait for what he already sees? But if we hope for something we do not yet see, then, in waiting for it, we show our endurance.[36]

In committing himself totally to Jesus Christ the Christian professes that this deepest potentiality of humanity, of all human concerns, and indeed of the whole world, is actualized. Any theological reflection on the relationship between the human concerns and their fulfillment in Christ, therefore, must not only pass the tests of

---

[35]Eph 3, 20.
[36]Rom 8, 18–25.

the rhetoric of inclusion and the rhetoric of obedience, but also the test of the rhetoric of hope, if it is to make sense of the Resurrection of Christ as the horizon that lends perspective to everything in the world.

This rhetoric of hope involves the conviction that no human concerns will be ultimately cancelled, superseded or lost, but rather that they will find themselves abundantly justified in the surrender to Christ. This raises the issue of the relationship between the human stiuation and its fulfillment in Christ. Paul Tillich has chosen this relationship as the fulcrum of his theological method. We can therefore expect to gain further insight into the connection between the human situation and its fulfillment if we ponder and test some of Paul Tillich's basic theological and christological positions. We will do this in the next section.

HUMAN CONCERNS:
BASIS FOR HOPE—
PAUL TILLICH'S THEOLOGY

Introduction

In the act of total surrender to Jesus Christ actual human concerns, humanity itself (as the sum of all actual and possible human concerns), and thus the whole world are drawn into a total meaning and fulfillment that are truly their own, and yet beyond their power and beyond what is due to them.[37] Both must be kept in mind. The whole world *itself* is drawn into fulfillment, and yet the fulfillment is beyond the reach of the whole world. Losing sight of the former leads to what Paul Tillich calls the first inadequate method of "relating the contents of the Christian faith to man's existence"; this method would imply that man would have to "become something else than human in order to receive divinity." Losing sight of the latter leads to the second inadquate method; "the contents of the Christian faith [are] explained as creations of man's religious self-realization in the progressive process of religious history"—in other words, divinity is human growth and nothing else.[38]

---

[37]Readers familiar with the scholastic tradition will recognize in this formula the traditional definition of grace: *quod excedit vires et exigentias naturae creatae.*

[38]Paul Tillich, *Systematic Theology*, I, pp. 64–65.

Tillich then mentions a third, "dualistic" method. Without naming names he clearly means the traditions that regard grace as the fulfillment of nature, and revelation as the confirmation and expansion of the findings of natural theology. Tillich commends this method for its awareness of the need for a positive relation between man's spirit and God's Spirit; what he finds unacceptable in it is its tendency to "derive an answer from the form of the question," chiefly by "positing a body of theological truth which man can reach through his own efforts or, in terms of a self-contradictory expression, through 'natural revelation.' "[39]

Tillich's own method is the "method of correlation." In this method we have a division of functions between philosophy and theology, which, as we will see, corresponds to the mutual relationship between human existence and divine self-manifestation. Tillich writes:

> Philosophy formulates the answers implied in human existence, and theology formulates the answers implied in divine self-manifestation under the guidance of the questions implied in human existence.[40]

Tillich's method of correlation provides us with an interesting test case for what has been said so far, and it lends itself well to being used as a negative illustration of what this chapter means to say.

The question of God and the quest for courage

It is unwarrantable to try to build any theology upon the *rational* judgment that man is capable of attaining God—*capax divini*. "Reason" means either technical reason (the human ability to reason) or ontological reason (the mind's ability to grasp and transform reality).[41] Technical reason can only arrive at God as the term of a means-end relationship, and therefore it cannot attain the living God; ontological reason, although its essence, the "universal *logos* of being," is "identical with the content of revelation,"[42] is caught in the conditions of existence, which incapacitate it, so that it cannot reach

---

[39] *Ibid.*
[40] *Ibid.*, I, p. 61. Cf. also above, p. 22 and note 11.
[41] *Ibid.*, I, pp. 71–75.
[42] *Ibid.*, I, p. 74.

God. There are, of course, realities and dimensions in human and other finite beings that seem to point to God's existence or appear to contain elements of positive knowledge of his properties; but the value of these realities and dimensions is merely symbolic. And a symbol only points, it does not affirm. It does not lead to a knowledge of God that can be cast in the form of a concept, a category, or a universal essence.[43] God is indeed

> the substance underlying the whole process of becoming. But this "underlying" does not have the character of a substance which underlies its accidents and which is completely expressed by them. It is an underlying in which substance and accidents preserve their freedom. In other words, it is substance not as a category but as a symbol. And, if taken symbolically, there is no difference between *prima causa* and *ultima substantia*. Both mean, what can be called in a more directly symbolic term, "the creative and abysmal ground of being."[44]

The "ground of being" is also the reality intended by the mythological *tohu-va-bohu*, Böhme's *Urgrund*, Schopenhauer's will, Nietzsche's will to power, Hartmann's and Freud's unconscious, Bergson's *élan vital*, and Scheler's and Jung's strife. "None of these concepts is to be taken conceptually. Each of them points symbolically to that which cannot be named."[45] "Neither experience nor language allows us to say more about it," although it remains true, paradoxically, that "man is never cut off from the ground of being."[46] Man's own essential being, too, is merely potential, no matter how good it is in its essential character.[47] We cannot even say that creation is good, for created goodness is not a matter of existential experience; there is no point in time and space at which created goodness was or will be actualized, for man is irretrievably caught in the conditions of alienation. Making the distinction between created goodness and estranged existence is not a matter of human experience, but a purely logical move, designed to prevent the Fall from

---

[43]Cf. *ibid.*, I, pp. 209, 236, 238.

[44]*Ibid.*, I, p. 238.

[45]Cf. *ibid.*, I, p. 179.

[46]*Ibid.*, II, p. 78, where the context is God's creativeness even in the act of destruction—eternal punishment.

[47]Cf. *ibid.*, II, p. 44.

becoming an ontological, structural necessity.[48] With regard to "created goodness," to "essential being," Tillich wishes to remain agnostic. No wonder that no theological assent to God's existence and his attributes is possible on the basis of a creation whose very nature is so unfathomable and so inaccessible to the human mind.

How can this apparent antinomy between a knowledge of God and the existential situation of humanity in the world become a *positive* relationship between the finite and the infinite? Tillich's answer is the method of correlation, in which natural theology becomes the analysis of existence in terms of the questions involved in it, while supernatural theology becomes the statement of the answers given to the questions implied in existence.

For Tillich, in other words, human existence merely raises the *question* of God, and no answer can be framed on the basis of the question. The answer is revelation. There is indeed "universal revelation," but it provides no more than the categories and forms to receive the "final" revelation. Universal revelation is no more than asking the question; final revelation is the answer.[49]

The concept of "question" provides Tillich with an opportunity to reduce the positive element in created nature to an absolute, ineffable minimum. The question of God does not come out of a positive experience of creation; that would amount to reducing God to a function of human self-realization and introducing the specter of analogy with the attendant danger of naturalism.[50] The human question about God comes out of a negative experience; it comes out of the threat of loneliness, rigidity, or determinism on the one hand and collectivization, chaos, and arbitrariness on the other.[51] The question of God arises out of the anxious awareness of the threat of non-being in all its forms—meaninglessness, despair, and guilt. "Ultimate concern" is really ultimate: God is only encountered when all else has run out. All that the human concerns have to contribute to the universal synthesis is a question born from anxiety. And if there is an underlying "substance" that is *positively* related to the universal

[48]*Ibid.*
[49]Cf. *ibid.*, I, p. 139.
[50]*Ibid.*, II, pp. 59–78.
[51]Cf. *ibid.*, I, pp. 174–186, 198–201.

synthesis (characteristically termed by Tillich "the *New* Being")[52] it is a reality "which cannot be named," only pointed to symbolically.

Tillich is most consistent in adhering to this fundamental thesis of his theological system. Thus he can write about the sanctified life: "The infinite distance between God and man is never bridged; *it is identical with man's finitude.* Therefore creative courage is an element of faith even in the state of perfection."[53]

The creative courage to be, needed to affirm existence rather than non-existence and meaning rather than meaninglessness, is not just needed as an initial means to overcome existential estrangement; the latter is an abiding condition, and so the courage to be remains necessary. This courage to be comes from the ultimate ground and power and source of being; it is unattainable by any natural efforts; it has to come as an absolute gift. A person with the courage to be never becomes autonomous; his courage remains "based upon participation in the ultimate power of being."[54]

The question implied in finitude, therefore, is not only the question of God as the creative and abysmal ground of being, but also "a quest for a courage which is sufficient to conquer the anxiety of finitude."[55] Are we catching here a glimpse of a positive appraisal of finitude? Tillich is referring to a *quest* for courage, not just a question—to an aspiration, not just an impasse. Whatever the deepest core of finite reality is—even though, in thoroughly neo-Kantian fashion, "it cannot be named"—it involves a *quest* for courage. But this quest is ineffective in itself; man's very finitude constitutes his unbridgeable distance from God, and the existential situation of estrangement makes it impossible for man even to accept this finitude and take it into an act of faith. The dialectic between man's positive relationship to God and his estrangement from God is heavily weighted in favor of the latter.

Our task is now to test those parts of Tillich's theological system which we have just summarized by the standard of the triple rhetoric of inclusion, obedience and hope. In doing so, we will see certain

---

[52]*Ibid.*, II, pp. 118ff.
[53]*Ibid.*, III, p. 239.
[54]*Ibid.*, I, p. 273.
[55]*Ibid.*; Tillich uses the word "quest" also in connection with the "New Being": *ibid.*, II, p. 78.

interesting features emerge. We will discover the admirable consistency of Tillich's effort to speak as a Christian to modern man's overriding sense of alienation; we will also encounter the limitations which Tillich's point of departure has caused in his system. These limitations will emerge mainly in three forms, namely, in the questionable quality of the relationship of Jesus Christ as the New Being to man's existential predicament, the reduced significance of the historical life of Jesus, and, finally, in the next to total absence of any emphasis on hope in Tillich's theology.

The New Being set against the human predicament

The paradox of the Christian message, according to Tillich, is "the appearance of the New Being under the conditions of existence, yet judging and conquering them."[56] Man's unshaken reliance upon himself, his self-saving attempts, and his resignation to despair make up his existential situation of estrangement. Characteristically, Tillich adds: "*Against* each of these three attitudes the manifestation of the New Being in Christ is judgment and promise."[57]

Throughout his *Systematic Theology* Tillich is deeply impressed by this againstness.[58] Two sources of this conception are fairly obvious. Tillich betrays a (typically neo-Kantian) agnosticism with regard to the knowability of "essential nature" or "created goodness," as we have already seen. He shares the traditional Protestant emphasis on total depravity, or—in Tillich's terms—on the totality of the conquest of essential nature by the conditions of existence symbolized by the Fall. Finally there seems to be a third, more personal source, namely, a temperamental affinity on Tillich's part, with the type of reality-experience that can be described as "daimonic," resulting in a strong need to present salvation in terms of control.[59]

True, Tillich will say that Jesus Christ is the appearance of

---

[56] *Ibid.*, II, p. 92.

[57] *Ibid.* (italics added): how can one promise against?

[58] Cf., for example, *ibid.*, III, p. 381, where the operative words are "against," "criterion," "struggle," and "victory."

[59] Cf. Rollo May, *Love and Will*, New York, W. W. Norton & Company, 1969, pp. 122–177. For the relationship between Paul Tillich and Rollo May, cf. the latter's *Paulus*, Reminiscences of a Friendship, New York–Evanston–San Francisco–London, Harper & Row, 1973. Tillich's treatment of the demonic (*Systematic Theology*, III, esp. pp. 102–106, 173–182) is far more concerned with control than May's.

essential man, who, "by his very nature, represents God";[60] the agnostic, neo-Kantian approach is never complete. But Tillich prefers to remain as agnostic as possible with regard to what essential manhood involves; its source "cannot be named." The abiding relationship between essential manhood and existential predicament is one of a leap—and it is this leap which is the original fact; the reality from which the leap was made is merely a logical postulate. The existential predicament represents a *total* conquest of essential goodness: "Indeed, there is nothing in man which enables God to accept him."[61]

If the gap between the human situation and divine revelation is so unbridgeable, it is not surprising that the advent of Jesus as the Christ represents the "*New* Being," and that revelation represents a totally supernatural answer to the question implied in human existence—a question which gives absolutely no advance clue to the form or the content of the answer. Tillich's decision to remain agnostic with regard to the deepest core of reality, and to insist on the conditions of existence as the basis of all theological questioning, determines his view of revelation. The latter is totally at odds with the conditions of existence; it directs itself as *against* the human situation in judgment and promise, in total New-ness, in the conquest of the gap between essence and existence.[62]

This conception is open to very serious criticism. However, for the time being we must postpone this, in order to concentrate on the second characteristic of Tillich's theology mentioned above, namely, the reduced significance of the historical life of Jesus. After that, we will be in a better position to state our objections.

Lack of significance of the historical Jesus

Tillich shows a surprising lack of interest in the historical life of Jesus. All that seems to matter for him is that "the event 'Jesus as the Christ' has a factual element,"[63] for if this were denied the foundations of Christianity would crumble. Still, what matters is only the

[60]Paul Tillich, *Systematic Theology*, II, p. 94.
[61]*Ibid.*, II, pp. 44, 179.
[62]*Ibid.*, II, pp. 118–119.
[63]*Ibid.*, II, p. 107.

fact that "in *one* personal life essential manhood has appeared under the conditions of existence without being conquered by them."[64] This is a symptom of a deep-seated ambiguity in Tillich's ontology; it is irresistibly drawn to essential being as the locus of the experience of the ground of being, and thus bypasses the lived concreteness of actual life—the latter is not ultimate, and thus it is not matter for ontological discussion.

This interest, on Tillich's part, in ontology is also evident in his christology: the New Being, in the person of Jesus as the Christ, is the answer to the existential question and manifests essential being, unknowable heretofore by natural means. Yet in order to uphold the reality of this answer, Tillich must claim crucial significance for an historical fact—the life of Jesus. But since historical facts are not ultimate, all that matters is the factuality of the historical Jesus—not his actual words and deeds.

On this tenuous basis, then, Jesus as the Christ is the New Being that appears. This New Being fills—almost by intrusion, and at any rate totally from elsewhere, from beyond the gap—the void left by Tillich's neo-Kantian agnosticism with regard to what is deepest in reality. This New Being, which is Jesus himself, bridges the gap between essence and existence.

How about the actual historical events of Jesus' life? They are not capable of ontological discussion, as we have just seen. Tillich solves this problem by considering the words, deeds, sufferings, and what is called the "inner life" of Jesus *exclusively as expressions* of the New Being.[65] Not a word about Jesus' concrete life—his words, deeds and sufferings viewed *as the ways in which he encountered* his followers and, indeed, everybody around him *with* the mystery that was his. According to Tillich, people do receive the New Being, and they receive it through participation, but he is at pains to point out that the concrete ways in which this participation comes about— Jesus' words, deeds, and sufferings—are nothing in themselves.[66] They are considered purely as *factual*, without any reference to their meaning, and only in this way are they the necessary foundation for

---

[64]*Ibid.*, II, p. 94.
[65]*Ibid.*, II, pp. 121–125.
[66]Cf., for example, *Systematic Theology*, II, p. 116.

Christianity. Tillich's preference for ontology has deprived the concrete historical life of Jesus of all theological significance.

A rhetoric of non-acceptance and judgment

We can now fulfill a promise made a short while ago,[67] namely, the offering of a critique of the sort of positive relation Tillich construes between God's self-revelation and the human predicament.

The first thing we must say is that there is little rhetoric of inclusion in Tillich. The New Being fills a *void*; it places essential goodness—now a nameable actuality in Jesus as the Christ—where previously there was nothing but a gap. This gap had been the result of the *original* fact: the leap from unnameable essential goodness into the all too well known (and unacceptable) conditions of existence. Christ does not revive a long-lost memory; he brings a new goodness.

Hence, the New Being cannot be said, in Tillich's theology, to really *accept* essential manhood—it creates it where formerly there was none. At the *core* of existence—and this is the only thing that really matters, for faith is the state of being *ultimately* concerned— the New Being stands *in total contrast* with the old being; the New Being does not take the old being unto itself; rather, it replaces it.

Tillich's preference for ontology[68] and for the ultimate as the real *locus* of faith and his lack of interest in the life of Jesus cause him to recognize only *two* central symbols of the universal significance of Jesus as the Christ, namely, the cross and the Resurrection in their mutual interdependence.[69] The earthly history of Jesus pales into insignificance in comparison with his death and Resurrection, which really deal with "ultimate concerns" and hence are the only symbols truly capable of revealing Jesus' universal significance.[70]

---

[67] Above, p. 207.

[68] Cf., for instance, *Systematic Theology*, II, pp. 10–12.

[69] *Ibid.*, II, pp. 153–165.

[70] Tillich is here the heir of a long tradition, which has tended to de-emphasize the life of Jesus. P. Smulders (*The Fathers on Christology*, pp. 37–39) sees its first beginnings in Clement of Alexandria's Logos-theology, which views the words and deeds of Jesus primarily in terms of example and education. In this connection it is interesting to note that Oscar Cullmann's treatment of the servant-theme from Isaiah concentrates entirely on Is 52—53 and only makes passing reference to Is 42, so that the chapter-title comes to read "Jesus the *Suffering* Servant of God"—the working and preaching servant is entirely overlooked, in the interest of concentration on the "ultimate" aspects of the life of Jesus. Cf. *The Christology of the New Testament*, pp. 51–82.

And this significance is in the *conquest* of existential estrangement. Jesus' *acceptance* of the human condition in the process of his personal life history is passed over in agnostic silence.

Let us try to sum up our criticism. In his search for God's revelation Tillich drives us out of the concrete concerns of this life under invocation of the thesis that these concerns are theologically irrelevant because they are not ultimate, and, as such, not matter for ontological discussion. Thus he drives us in the direction of the underlying essence of life; what we find there, however, is only a void, for what is conveyed by the symbolic formula "the creative and abysmal ground of being" is inaccessible owing to the existential conditions of estrangement. Once Tillich has us at bay there, with our backs to the wall, he confronts us with Jesus as the Christ, the New Being.[71] His function is then quite consistently characterized as the *judgment* and *conquest* of the structures of evil and the *establishment (ex nihilo?) of a new reality* from which the structures of evil are excluded.

It can be argued, on the basis of a few passages, that Tillich is not too consistent in his rejection of created nature as ground for theological assertions. It can be pointed out, for example, that he mentions "created goodness" and "essential nature," and that he recognizes that existential estrangement is not equivalent to total destruction.[72] But even if these suggestions are to be taken seriously, they never inform Tillich's christology in any consistent fashion; the *total impact* of Tillich's christology is in the direction of non-acceptance of created reality. As a result, Jesus as the Christ is not primarily presented as God's acceptance of, but as his judgment on, the human situation.

There is, of course, New Testament support for Tillich's use of "judgment," "conquest," and "exclusion," but he gives these metaphors a prominence which they do not have in Scripture. In Tillich's synthesis, they are an irritating reminder that in Jesus as the Christ God directs himself *against* the existential situation: "Nothing in man [. . .] enables God to accept him."[73]

---

[71] Bonhoeffer's well-known denunciation of Tillich's procedure in *Letters and Papers from Prison*, pp. 167–170, 182–184.

[72] Cf. *Systematic Theology*, II, p. 167. Cf. also *ibid.*, III, p. 228 for the related thesis that there is an implicit affirmation of truth in all doubt.

[73] *Ibid.*, II, p. 179.

What God can or cannot do is determined here by man's non-acceptance of himself, whereas in the mainstream of the Christian tradition Jesus' acceptance of all human concerns is both the sign and the actualization of God's acceptance. Tillich writes:

> Indeed, there is nothing in man which enables God to accept him. But man must accept just this. He must accept that he is accepted; he must accept acceptance.[74]

But should Tillich not have gone one step further? If man must accept that he is accepted, he must also accept that he is accept*able*. *Ab esse ad posse valet illatio*.[75] To state man's acceptability does not in the least imply that man can now go on to consider his acceptability as his own property and use it as a base of power or self-reliance. That is indeed the essence of sin and the cause of all existential estrangement. Man must *accept* that he is acceptable, that is to say, man's acceptability is something which is originally *given* to him and which remains a gift.[76] The fact that man has, on his part, set himself up as acceptable in his *own* right—which is sin—does not prevent God from remaining faithful to his creation. There *is* something in man which enables God to accept him: man remains, for his very existence, bound to God, who continues to sustain his creation, even when it turns against him. God shows his omnipotence most by showing patience and pity.[77] The true paradox of Christianity is that man in his sinfulness has not succeeded in deterring God from giving himself to him. Judgment, conquest, and exclusion, yes, but through acceptance, suffering and taking upon himself the sin of the world, not through invasion, struggle and againstness.

Tillich's christology, however, does speak about Christ in terms of non-acceptance and condemnation of human concerns. The rhetoric that informs this christology is not one of inclusion and call to obedience. Tillich's negative rhetoric goes back to his axiomatic

---

[74]*Ibid.*

[75]"Inferences from actuality to possibility are legitimate"—an old scholastic adage.

[76]For this "surrender of one's own goodness to God" cf. *ibid.*, III, p. 226. Cf. also above, pp. 164–165.

[77]*Deus qui omnipotentiam tuam parcendo maxime et miserando manifestas*—the Roman Missal of Pius V, Tenth Sunday after Pentecost, Collect.

assumption that the situation of existential estrangement is the fundamental reality. This assumption—a modern version of the traditional Protestant insistence on the corruption of nature—also reflects the life-experience of many modern city-dwellers, with whose existential anxiety Tillich felt such a strong affinity. There is much to commend in Tillich's decision to take this seriously, and much of his importance as a theologian is due to his insistence that modern man's existential anxiety should be theologically interpreted.

But in the final analysis it must be said that Tillich's fundamental assumption, much though it may have been brought to the reality of Jesus as the Christ, has not really been affected by Christ's presidency over it. So the existential question *has* determined the form of the theological answer: it has prevented Tillich from doing justice to the human situation in the name of the christological rhetoric of inclusion. Contrary to Tillich's intentions,[78] God's self-revelation in Christ has been limited by the limitations of the human situation as Tillich sees it.

Courage instead of hope

This lengthy treatment of Tillich's view of the life of Jesus and of the quality of Jesus Christ's relationship to man's existential predicament has given us an opportunity to test his theology by means of the rhetoric of inclusion and the rhetoric of obedience. We are now at last in a position to turn to the third limitation of Tillich's theology mentioned above, namely, the next to total absence of any emphasis on hope. This will also bring us back to the main concern of this chapter, the rhetoric of hope.

A very remarkable feature of Tillich's *Systematic Theology* is that the comprehensive index to its three volumes carries only nine references to hope. What the tradition has called hope is, for Tillich, no more than one of the three elements of faith, and its focus is, not any divine fulfillment of the *creature's* yearning, but the anticipation of "the fulfilling creativity of the divine Spirit"[79]—an expression which, characteristically, has no object: *what* the creativity of the divine Spirit is anticipated to fulfill is not stated. Tillich is again

---

[78]Cf. above, pp. 202–203.
[79]*Systematic Theology*, III, p. 133.

serious about his position: human existence is and remains no more than a question raised by anxiety, not an aspiration to fulfillment. Christian revelation does provide an answer to the existential question, and those who receive it really believe. But although "faith is *in* man,"[80] there is nothing in man that warrants faith. In an analogous fashion, the formula about the anticipation of the fulfilling creativity of the divine Spirit strongly suggests that there is no hope *grounded in the things of this life.*

The function that hope has in more traditional and eschatological theologies is taken over completely by courage, to which Tillich devotes considerable space, including two long passages. Throughout Tillich maintains, with regard to courage, a position that is consistent with, and analogous to, his view of the content of faith as the answer to the question implied in man's existence. A passage like the following is illustrative.

> Faith in the almighty God is the answer to the *quest* for a courage which is sufficient to conquer the anxiety of finitude. Ultimate courage is *based on participation in the ultimate power of being.* When the *invocation* "Almighty God" is seriously pronounced, a victory over the threat of non-being is experienced, and an ultimate, courageous affirmation of existence is expressed. Neither finitude nor anxiety disappears, but they are taken into infinity and courage.[81]

Significantly, it is in the invocation "Almighty God" that the affirmation of existence occurs. Now an invocation is an act—an act of faith in Almighty God. But the problem is: How can an *act* of faith be an *answer* to a *quest*? Are not both act and quest in man?

It seems that we have a glimmer of a more positive relationship between human existence and revelation here. Existence is a quest for courage, and the faith-invocation is the *act* of courage. The act of faith is the realization of an aspiration, for a quest is an aspiration; the quest may be incapable of activating itself, but it remains an aspiration nevertheless. There is a touch of affirmativeness in the notion of "quest"; it betrays that the *dynamics of faith* are grafted on to a dynamic origin.

---

[80]*Ibid.*
[81]*Ibid.*, I, p. 273 (italics added).

Yet here the positive appreciation stops, for Tillich goes on to construct the courage to be as related to the quest for this courage in a manner strictly parallel to his treatment of faith as related to the existential question. At the level of the *content of faith*, as we have seen, Tillich characterizes the positive correlation between man and God by the metaphor of question and answer—a metaphor that suggests two *contrary* movements, and one which we have had occasion to criticize as incomplete. At the level of the *act* of faith Tillich *suggests* that the positive relationship between man and God is a relationship between a quest and a decision—a metaphor that suggests a movement from possibility to actuality. But after this first suggestion, Tillich goes on to explain that the courageous decision to affirm being is made impossible by man's existential predicament: "No act within the context of existential estrangement can overcome existential estrangement."[82] It takes New Being to do this, for in New Being we have the "undistorted manifestation of essential being within and under the conditions of existence."[83] Only by participation in the New Being does this courage become a possibility.

But just as Tillich was not interested, as we saw above, in the ways in which this participation is conveyed,[84] so he seems uninterested in the *basis for participation*; there is no suggestion that participation requires a pre-existing subject capable of participation. It looks as if "quest" was far too positive a word, and that a person only becomes a person in the supernatural act of the courage to be. He used to be caught in the torpor, and even despair, of estrangement, a living question to himself, an impotent quest; now he can live, for he is united to God, he participates in the New Being, he is reconnected with the abysmal ground and power of being, where he finds his identity. Thus the significance of courage lies primarily in *the constituted identity of the believer*, in the actualization of the self.[85] Tillich's entire theology is conditioned by his empathy with

---

[82]*Ibid.*, II, p. 78.

[83]*Ibid.*, II, p. 119.

[84]Above, p. 209.

[85]Cf., for example, *Systematic Theology*, III, pp. 233–235.—Tillich views the suffering of Jesus entirely in terms of *undergoing* the conditions of existential estrangement, not in its *relational* character: the willing and even joyful giving of self, even in the teeth of rejection, which is the essential element in Christian sacrifice (cf. Robert J.

Man's Search for Meaning. [86] Faith comes to mean: *meaning* found in the teeth of meaninglessness, *courage* engaged in in the teeth of anxiety. Tillich's analysis of love is analogous; it hinges on the definition: "ecstatic participation of the finite spirit in the transcendent unity of unambiguous life." Love is a *state* of the believer; Tillich views love primarily as an asset—the ultimate asset—of the person who believes. Courage is an element of this *state* of *agapē.* [87]

It is Tillich's undying merit to have had the courage and the constructive power to cast an entire theological system in the mold of a particular dominant concern, namely, the impasse of modern man in his existential predicament. It is also his strongest limitation, resulting in a painful absence of any theology of creation; and only a theology of creation has room for hope, for it recognizes that there is a ground for fulfillment in the creature itself.

The absence of a theology of hope is thus connected with the absence of a theology of creation in Tillich's system. [88] Tillich cannot place the human condition in any absolute perspective because he does not think that God's self-revelation reveals creation as acceptable and thus as the object of a rhetoric of inclusion. This explains why our discussion had to dwell so long on the absence of the latter rhetoric in Tillich's thought.

Daly, *The Origin of the Christian Doctrine of Sacrifice,* Philadelphia, Fortress Press, 1978). The expression "*experienced* the death of a slave," without so much as a passing reference to Jesus' obedience *for us,* speaks volumes (*Systematic Theology,* II, p. 158). In his discussion of the tragic conflict between Jesus and his enemies Tillich is mainly impressed by the fact that this did not produce estrangement *in Jesus* or split his personal center (*ibid.,* II, p. 133)—his concern is with Jesus' *identity,* not with his love for others. When he discusses sacrifice, Tillich revives the impossible construct of "the sacrifice of himself as Jesus to himself as the Christ" (*ibid.,* II, p. 123)—another sign of Tillich's concern with the constitution of immanent identity. For remarks on this division between divinity and humanity in Christ, cf. Piet Schoonenberg, *The Christ,* pp. 68–69, and P. Smulders, "Dogmengeschichtliche und lehramtliche Entfaltung der Christologie," p. 460, note 38.

[86] Title of Viktor E. Frankl's book (New York, Washington Square Press, 1963). There are many similarities between the theories of Tillich and Frankl, except that the latter's logotherapy takes a far more positive view of the human potential; I suggest that Tillich would be very critical of Frankl's voluntarism.

[87] Cf. *Systematic Theology,* III, pp. 134–135, 274.

[88] Tillich quite consistently holds that "christology is a function of soteriology" (*Systematic Theology,* II, p. 150). The universal significance of Jesus lies in his overcoming existential estrangement, not in fulfilling and surpassing the potentialities of creation.

This also raises the question whether there is a special connection between the rhetoric of hope and the rhetoric of inclusion. In order to probe this question, let us compare Tillich's christology with some thoughts of a theologian who shares two of Tillich's most prominent characteristics, namely his preference for ontological thought and his interest in an analysis of the human situation in a theological perspective: Karl Rahner.

Tillich's christology: confrontation with Karl Rahner

We have already outlined Karl Rahner's attempt to develop the outlines of a "transcendental" christology—a christology based upon a philosophical analysis of the human situation.[89] According to Rahner, man is unavoidably oriented toward an absolute bringer of salvation.[90]

To explain what such a transcendental, *a priori* christology can and cannot achieve, Rahner starts with an explanation of its necessity. A transcendental analysis of the human condition, Rahner argues, serves to meet the present-day *cultural* needs of man. Man has irrevocably entered upon "the historical phase of transcendental anthropology":[91] man can no longer naively accept the Christian faith, but must take stock of what is involved in being human, and determine whether the Christian faith fits humanity's basic aspirations. If this task is neglected, he will end up having no criterion for telling the difference between the true faith-reality conveyed by traditional christology and those interpretations of traditional christology that have lost their power to communicate the meaning of the faith. For Rahner, in other words, transcendental analysis of the human condition is necessary as a *negative norm* to determine what is true christology and what is time-conditioned christological expression. If this distinction is not made, many modern, self-aware people will dismiss the deliverances of traditional christology as naive, mythological involutions of historical events. Rahner's aim is: to enable the believer to differentiate between faith as naive traditionalism and faith as consonant with what is most fundamental in man.

A comparison between Rahner and Tillich on this precise point

---

[89]Above, pp. 57–61.

[90]Karl Rahner—Wilhelm Thüsing, *Christologie—systematisch und exegetisch*, p. 21.

[91]*Ibid.*, p. 20.

yields an interesting crosswise arrangement of intentions and results. Tillich means to claim no standing whatever on behalf of the question involved in human existence when it comes to determining either the form or the content of the theological answer; in the final analysis, however, he shapes his christology entirely in the mold of his fundamental analysis of the human situation, characterized by a rhetoric of non-acceptance. Rahner boldly sets up his transcendental christology as a negative norm to determine what the message of revelation can and cannot mean; in the end, however, he manages to leave the fullness of the Christian faith intact, because he recognizes that the Christian faith precedes and encompasses the existential analysis:

> A transcendental Christology as such cannot highhandedly claim for itself either the task or the capability to state that this absolute bringer of salvation, whom [man's] radical hope for God himself as the absolute future seeks within history, is readily to be found in history, and that he has actually been found in Jesus of Nazareth. *In our day*, however, we would be undiscerning with respect to this factual history, if we were not to meet it with the kind of reflective, articulate hope for salvation that is reflected in a transcendental Christology. Such a Christology invites us to search for, and in searching for it to understand, what we had already found in Jesus of Nazareth in the first place.[92]

In the interest of comparing this with Tillich's position, let us first make a structural observation. Rahner sets up the relationship between what Tillich calls the "question" and the "answer" in a much freer way than Tillich.[93] The "answer" for Rahner encompasses and penetrates all of reality, including man's ability to reflect on his existence, whether this must be attributed to grace or to man's spiritual nature.[94] The correspondence between human reflection and

---

[92]*Ibid.*, p. 24.

[93]Rahner's theological system is far more complex than Tillich's, but complexity tends to give more room for play than systematic simplicity. I find Tillich's system, for all its depth and breadth, very confining, and I think I have observed that *lectores unius Tillich* tend to get locked into a very narrow theological mold. Karl Rahner is not the opposite, but the associate of his brother Hugo, who wrote the delightful *Man at Play*, New York, Herder and Herder, 1967.

[94]On this question, cf., for instance, *ibid.*, p. 21 (11. *Lehrsatz*).

divine self-revelation is not a simple one-to-one relationship between the question and its answer as in Tillich. This structural observation leads to a second, substantive point.

Rahner strongly emphasizes the normative quality of a transcendental christology. Its task is to tell the essential faith-affirmations apart from affirmations that are no longer able to convey faith. Rahner takes the need for human intellectual integrity (*Wahrheitsgewissen*) very seriously. In doing so, he shows that *he is acting on the assurance* extended to him by the christological confession, namely, that *an analysis of man's basic predicament will yield a positive correspondence between man and God.*[95] Thus, for example, he can point out that it is possible to proclaim man's relationship to God by showing

> that man in his very existence already stands encompassed by this hoped-for and given relationship (in virtue of "grace" and "existence"), whether this is explicitly known or not, whether this is freely accepted or rejected, whether the preacher does or does not succeed in making this existing relationship clear.[96]

Rahner finds humanity and its concerns basically oriented to God. Thus he enacts, in his transcendental christology, what we have called the rhetoric of inclusion. The exercise of man's reflective ability vis-à-vis his own existence is warranted by the positive orientation, at the bottom of human existence, to a God who does not abandon. Such a stance cannot ultimately yield the insight that a positive relationship to God is humanly impossible and that man's basic predicament must be said to be unacceptable.

This fundamental acceptance of all things human supports and lends depth to Rahner's exploration of the concrete issues of the human as well as of the Christian life, especially when he writes

---

[95]The idea of humanity's basic orientation to God is the fundamental inspiration of Karl Rahner's theology, from the early works on; cf. *Hearers of the Word* (New York, Herder and Herder, 1969) and *Spirit in the World* (New York, Herder and Herder, 1968). Whether he is discussing the human spirit's being with itself (*das Beisichsein des Geistes*), or man's *potentia oboedientialis*, or even "anonymous Christianity," the idea of the fundamental relatedness of the human person to God is never far to seek.

[96]Karl Rahner—Wilhelm Thüsing, *Christologie—systematisch und exegetisch*, p. 19.

about his preferred field, spiritual theology. In this theology of the lived life Rahner bridges man's orientation toward God and the fulfillment, the hope for which Rahner already identifies as the core of man's basic orientation. Implied in all of Rahner's theology there is a rhetoric of acceptance of all human concerns to the core,[97] which lends depth to a rhetoric of obedience implied in his theology of human and Christian history, and which is oriented, in hope, to the ultimate fulfillment. This amounts to saying that Rahner's theological enterprise is fundamentally christological, in that it operates on the rhythm of acceptance, obedience, and hope. Tillich's conception of the leap from essence into existence as the original fact and his decision to treat the affirmation of created goodness as a purely logical move are fundamentally opposed to christology.

The limitations of conceptuality

Our positive evaluation of Rahner's fundamental theological assumption, however, must not blind us to the limitations of his approach. Heinrich Ott has hit upon a central one in his observation that Rahner reflects on man as the *possible* rather than the *actual* recipient of God's self-communication.[98] In elaborating this critical note we will be able to see more clearly both the affinities and the differences between Paul Tillich and Karl Rahner; this in turn will enable us, in the next chapter, to reach a point where the purpose of the present book can be approached and expressed once again.

Rahner is aware, as we have seen, that the comprehensive christological message cannot be derived from, or cast in the form of, the analysis of the human existential predicament. In fact he maintains that it is part of the task of transcendental christology to show precisely that transcendental reflection can never lead to the establishment of concrete historical facts, including practical life decisions and concrete relationships to concrete persons.[99] The Christian faith involves such a practical life decision and such a concrete

---

[97]A fine example of this is "The Ignatian Mysticism of Joy in the World," in: *Theological Investigations*, Vol. III, Baltimore, Helicon Press, 1967, pp. 277–293.

[98]*Wirklichkeit und Glaube*, 2. Band, *Der persönliche Gott*, Göttingen–Zürich, Vandenhoeck & Ruprecht, 1969, p. 346.

[99]Karl Rahner—Wilhelm Thüsing, *Christologie—systematisch und exegetisch*, p. 20.

relationship, namely, in the Christian's act of faith in Christ. Hence, transcendental theology evolves *within* the setting of the acceptance of the Christian faith, not apart from it. In Rahner's view transcendental necessity and concrete historical contingency are always inextricably bound up in human existence. In this complex, both are unconditionally (*schlechthin*) co-constitutive of human existence; yet the historically contingent can never be reduced to transcendental necessity, and vice versa.[100] The provenance of the thesis and of its wording is clear: it is Lessing's dictum that the "accidental truths of history can never become the proof of necessary truths of reason." The concrete particular is as such never amenable to cogent demonstration: *individuum est ineffable.*[101]

The distinction between transcendental necessity and historical contingency dominates Rahner's thought as it does Tillich's. Rahner holds the two fairly close together. His transcendental analysis of human existence *professes its own limitations*: relationships to concrete persons and practical life decisions fall outside its competence; but they are no less constitutive of human existence and no less reliable for their not being amenable to transcendental reflection.

For Tillich, transcendental necessity and historical contingency are much further apart. The systematic theologian, in his view, is only interested in dogmatically valid judgments, and history is never capable of offering more than probability.[102] History is, in this regard, on a par with legend and mythology:[103] they provide symbols, pointers, probabilities—*not certainty.* Again: Lessings' dictum is in the background, only in much sharper relief.

Both Tillich and Rahner are strongly interested in a conceptual understanding of the Christian faith; both elaborate this interest by means of an ontological style of inquiry, aiming at ontological

---

[100]*Ibid.*, pp. 20–21.

[101]"Individual beings cannot be captured by definition"—an old scholastic adage.

[102]Cf. *Systematic Theology*, II, pp. 99–117. Tillich's view of history has not been affected by the "New Concept of History and the Self" explained by James M. Robinson (*A New Quest of the Historical Jesus*, SCM Press, London, 1959, pp. 66–72). He is aware of the problem of historical interpretation (cf., for example, *Systematic Theology*, III, pp. 362ff.), but solves it entirely in terms of a fact/interpretation (*chronos/kairos*) construct, which leaves out any consideration of such elements as intentions, commitments, personal impact, self-actualization, etc.

[103]*Systematic Theology*, II, p. 108.

insights. Tillich is the more rigid one: his tendency is to *disqualify* all statements and findings that are not dogmatically valid, and to characterize them as symbolic or merely probable. The contingencies of history become insignificant in the light of the overriding importance of ultimate concern expressed in strictly ontological, conceptual terminology. Rahner's conceptualist attitude is much more tolerant of the ambiguities of practical reason and the irreducibility of historical relationships: he *accepts* them and ontologically accounts for their acceptability. Yet, even though Rahner's attitude does not make the mistake of discrediting the particular and the personal, it owes such a large debt to conceptualism that the historical and the personal (and hence, practical-reason judgments and interpersonal relationships) *do not become, as such, matter for reflection.* Rahner's insistence on the need for human intellectual integrity in believing and his reliance on humanity's basic orientation to God cause him to reflect on the revealed preconditions for salvation rather than on its actuality—on man as the potential rather than the actual recipient of God's self-communication.

Thus Tillich and Rahner have a fundamental trait in common, namely, their insistence on exploring the Christian faith in terms of the human reality. To use the metaphor developed in the beginning of this chapter: they speak about the horizon only indirectly, by speaking about the perspective to which the things in this world lend themselves. They concentrate on the human predicament, on human concerns, and discuss the question how this human reality is related to the revelation of God in Christ.

For Tillich the answer to this question is negative: there is nothing in the concrete human situation that suggests in any way an orientation to the divine. For Rahner the answer is positive: the human predicament is open to God. But for *both* the question of the nature of the relationship between the human predicament and the divine fulfillment *as seen from the standpoint of the human predicament* is the core of their respective christologies. In addition, both use a strongly philosophical style of inquiry in their analyses of the human predicament.

This combination—stress on the human predicament and philosophical style of inquiry—leads to christologies that place the emphasis on a conceptual understanding of the Christian faith by means of discernments accessible to modern man. This, however, is by no means the entire task of christology.

Two matters which Tillich and Rahner leave relatively untouched deserve special mention, namely hope and the nature of the Christian fact. We will round this chapter off with a brief discussion of the former, and make the latter the main subject of the next chapter.

The dynamics of hope

It would be hard to disagree with Rahner's emphasis on the modern need for a reflective articulation of man's hope for salvation within the setting of the Christian message handed down, accepted, and believed in. It would be equally hard to disagree with Tillich's contention that the Christian faith must be shown to address modern man's sense of estrangement. Yet we may wonder if those are the chief preoccupations of modern man. The quest for intellectual integrity and personal meaning in life is sometimes best achieved by directing one's energies away from oneself. There is a pressing modern need to live by personal commitments that are non-ideological, non-rational (in the sense of not primarily authorized by reasoning), and not dictated by authority—that is to say, commitments that are admittedly provisional and tentative. There is a cultural need for frankly personal speech, for frankly personal action and for commitments in response to persons, for basic encounter, for the experience of meaning achieved by "trusting the process," and "doing your own thing." There is no doubt that there is a risk of irrationality here or, to call it by its theological name, of sectarianism and fundamentalism; but the risk is precisely the reason why theology must concentrate on this need, not avoid it or ignore it.

Trust, tolerance of provisionality, and other-directedness and dedication to particular commitments are some of the ingredients that go into the making of the attitude just described. Christian faith has every reason to feel an affinity to this attitude, for it is itself an act of total commitment to a particular person—an act, moreover, which justifies trust, makes sense of provisionality and encourages other-directedness on account of the dynamics of hope generated by the total commitment.

As we have seen, it is the presence of Jesus Christ alive in the

Spirit that elicits the Christian act of total commitment. This total commitment results in a surrender that draws a variety of partial human concerns along with itself.[104] In this integration into the act of total surrender, human concerns, humanity itself, and the whole world are revealed as carrying inside themselves, as an essential part of their own make-up, a positive orientation to God. *Reality can be trusted.*

This means that the partiality of concerns, the provisional nature of all human insights and efforts and the continued need for revisions of prior visions is, at bottom, not a cause for despondence but a reason for confidence and hope. This hope is the third dynamic, in addition to inclusion and call to obedience, that animates the Christian life. It does so in a fourfold way.

First, hope is the setting in which the fundamental acceptability of the human person and of all matters pertaining to this life is unveiled: *reality itself* participates in the ultimate perspective. The Tillichian quest is created reality itself, at whatever level of being, in its innate aspiration to fulfillment. "Thou has formed us for Thyself, and our hearts are restless till they find rest in Thee."[105] Here we uncover the coherence between the rhetoric of inclusion and the rhetoric of hope.

Second, hope is the inspiration for historical commitments. It allows us to live in time, amid the countless penultimates that make up the human condition, accepting them, taking them seriously, enjoying them or shouldering the burden of them, in joy and long-suffering and forgiveness, doing justice to them by reliable stewardship, without domination over them or slavery to them. Hope thus becomes the attitude which the Gospel of Luke calls *hypomonē*[106]— the kind of perseverance that at once is fruitful now and holds out for the fullness of life. In this way the concerns of the world are salvaged and redeemed, and so the judgment comes about, the victory is won, the structures of evil are dissolved. Here we discover how obedience, the humble handling of all human concerns, leads from basic acceptability to fulfillment.

---

[104] Above, pp. 198–200.
[105] Augustine, *Confessions*, I, 1.
[106] Lk 8, 15; 21, 19.

There is a third way in which hope animates the Christian life; this third way is not really something in its own right, but an immediate consequence of the historicity of hope. Hope animates relationships. Courage may be contagious and move others to take the leap also; hope inspires a person *to devote himself gratuitously to others* and stay with them. Being for others means service and suffering, for a person who has entrusted himself to God is to that extent no longer appalled at the prospect of self-giving nor threatened by the evil that is to be inflicted upon him. Others elicit his compassion; he is not held back by overconcern with self. When he survives the test of service and suffering, this experience is further ground for hope.[107] There is an essential connection between hope and self-giving, even in its most paradoxical form of undeterred and even joyful self-giving in the teeth of suffering. Thus hope has a quality of self-forgetfulness and other-directedness which courage does not have.

In yet another way hope fosters relationships whereas courage does not. Not only does hope set a person free to be for others, it also enables him to have high hopes for others. I can hope for another person to grow, to be free, to see the light; as I share my unworried self with another person, in confident speech and action, in witness and service, my dedication is predicated on my hope that this will relieve the other person's anxious care and help to let him experience hope, too. Mere courage on my part *can* be a contagious example to another person; he may catch on. But the bridging of the gap, the taking of the leap is left entirely to him. In this way, too, hope is really *in* the shared concerns that pertain to this life whereas courage is not.

Fourth, the dynamics of hope keep all human concerns *responsive*. Hope keeps the Christian from mere optimism; it reminds him of the *absolute* horizon, of the *receding* standard of excellence which is the presence of Christ in the Spirit as the ultimate fulfillment of all things. This fulfillment is already taking shape in the concerns of this life; it remains to be realized in concerns that have not yet been brought into the surrender. Hope is the experience of the assurance that comes toward us out of God's future which is already taking

---

[107]Cf. Rom 5, 1–5.

root here and now. It is trust in the horizon, and only to that extent trust in the perspective in which things are set. True, the person who hopes is also courageous, but he is hardly impressed with his own courage, because the need for courage is not his overriding concern in the first place; he is struck by the encountering presence of Christ in the Spirit; he gains personal identity by being responsive.[108] Thus, the rhetoric of hope in christology clinches the rhetoric of inclusion and the rhetoric of obedience on the strength of the ecstatic encounter with Jesus Christ in the Spirit; in his risen life Christ invites and draws the Christian into the total surrender in and through and beyond all his actual potential concerns.

From our discussion of the christologies of Paul Tillich and Karl Rahner it will be clear that neither is likely to have a full-fledged theology of hope. Paul Tillich's thought positively prevents the development of such a theology; his view of the human predicament does not allow a positive evaluation of creation in relation to its fulfillment. Moreover, history and provisionality do not provide matter for dogmatically valid judgments. In Karl Rahner's theology, there is ample room for a theology of hope; but his christology tends to concentrate on the demonstration of the *consonance* between the historical revelation of God in Christ and the innate and abiding aspirations of human nature as such.[109] Rahner never makes a secret of his own preference for transcendental reflection, although he calls for a theology of the mysteries of the life of Jesus and a theology of history in the first article of the first volume of the *Investigations.*[110] We mentioned the need for emphasis on the historical Jesus and for a christological interpretation of the concreteness of salvation now.[111] It is essential for christology to explore the dynamics of hope if it is to achieve this: we will come back to this at a much later point in this book.[112]

---

[108]Cf., for instance, 2 Cor 3, 1–6; 4, 1.

[109]For an impressive statement of this, cf., for example, "On the Theology of the Incarnation," in: *Theological Investigations*, Vol. IV, Baltimore, Helicon Press, 1966, pp. 105–120.

[110]"The Prospects for Dogmatic Theology," in: *Theological Investigations,* Vol. I, Baltimore, Helicon Press, 1961, pp. 1–18; references pp. 11–12.

[111]Above, pp. 52–53, 62.

[112]Below, p. 471ff.

Outlook: reflection on the Christian fact

A few pages back we mentioned a second task of christology besides the exploration of the dynamics of hope, namely, concentration on "the Christian fact."[113] A few words must be devoted to this in order to introduce the next chapter.

The rhetoric of hope reflects Christ's presidency over all human concerns *insofar as it reflects on the latter* and lays bare the hidden potentiality of all human concerns for the total surrender. In speaking about hope, therefore, we *indirectly* speak about the presence of Christ alive in the Spirit. This indirection is wholesome; we must share some of Marxsen's reluctance to speak too directly about Christ's Resurrection; we must not create the impression that human words or human concerns can easily convey what it means that Jesus is alive. We have expressed this realization by saying that the *act* of speaking, the representative of the *act* of total surrender, alone conveys what is involved in Jesus Christ being the glorified Lord,[114] and that all the discernments are never more than (very substantive) pointers, even those discernments that represent the deepest and most precarious aspirations of the human heart.

Hence, there remains the question whether it is possible *to express directly* what is involved in the Lordship of the risen Christ, rather than merely indirectly. This reflection on the factuality of Christ's presence in the Spirit will be the subject of the next chapter, in which we will consider the Resurrection, not as it relates to the discernments, placing them in a perspective of hope, as we have done in this chapter, but precisely as it addresses, and calls into surrender, the person as a whole.[115]

---

[113]Above, p. 223.

[114]Above, pp. 195, 197–198, 199–200.

[115]Karl Rahner is completely aware of this issue: Karl Rahner—Wilhelm Thüsing, *Christologie—systematisch und exegetisch*, pp. 38–47.

CHAPTER 6

The Origin of Christology

But how shall I . . . make me room there:
Reach me a . . . Fancy, come faster—
Strike you the sight of it? look at it loom there,
Thing that she . . . There then! the Master,
Ipse, the only one, Christ, King, Head:
. . .
Ah! there was a heart right!
There was single eye!

Gerard Manley Hopkins

If Christ is not raised, then our Gospel is null and void, and so is your faith.

The First Letter of Paul to the Corinthians

Timothy, keep safe that which has been entrusted to you. Turn a deaf ear to empty and worldly chatter, and the contradictions of so-called "knowledge," for many who lay claim to it have shot far wide of the faith.

The First Letter of Paul to Timothy

Preliminary: encounter and witness
    The previous chapter ended with a promise. We wondered if it would be possible to express *directly* what is involved in the Lordship

228

of the risen Christ, and we promised to address that issue in the present chapter.[1] We had already stated earlier that the objectivity of the Resurrection is adequately conveyed only by the total surrender.[2] We can expect, therefore, that the direct expression of the Christian fact will have everything to do with *a direct act of surrender.* To lay the groundwork for an exploration into this direct act of response to Jesus Christ alive and present in the Spirit, we must discuss a few aspects of interpersonal communication.

In human-relations training and ordinary life as well, one often hears: "You may be right, but *I don't know where you're coming from.*" Rather new slang, that phrase is a serious request or even demand; it asks the speaker to add a bit of himself to *what* he was trying to communicate. For communication to come off, not only do we need something to communicate, but also actual communication in the sense that partners have a sense of the other person.[3] Without direct and unreflected experience of personal communication the point of the statements is liable to be missed. Interpersonal communication-*with* is the setting of all meaningful and pointed communication-*to.* I—It statements make sense when set in an I—Thou relationship; the latter both is tempered by, and constitutes the ground of effective meaning of, the I—It statements. We have already treated this structure at length in terms of the act of speaking as the setting of discernments.[4] We must now further analyze this, to gain an understanding of what is involved in what we shall call the "direct act" of encounter.

When someone addresses me, however, and I get the point,[5] I actually need to experience *two* sources of meaningfulness or "point." First, I need to experience that, as much as possible, a *real person* is speaking to me. If he or she is parroting, or merely indulging in quotation, or rehearsing compulsive preoccupations, or talking out of mental illness, then the real person stays hidden

---

[1]Above, p. 227.

[2]Above, pp. 195, 197–198, 199–200, 227.

[3]Cf., for example, Samuel A. Culbert, *The Interpersonal Process of Self-Disclosure: It Takes Two To See One,* New York, Renaissance Editions (*Explorations in Applied Behavioral Science,* 3), 1967.

[4]Cf. above, pp. 134–143; also pp. 94–98.

[5]For the following, cf. already above. pp. 135ff.

behind all this verbiage. The statements by themselves, whether true or false, coherent or incoherent, act as a barrier both to me who is addressed and to the person who speaks, ensconced and concealed behind the things he or she says. I may still realize that a real person is speaking to me, but only my care, almost totally unaided by the person's speech, establishes this.

When someone really addresses me, however, I encounter more than that person. There is a *second source* of meaningfulness that I must experience when someone addresses me. I need to know "where the person is coming from" also in the sense of *what prompts him to speak.* It may be an interest we have in common, a spontaneously accepted framework within which the statements the other person makes will have a point. It may be my own self that prompts him to speak; in that case the statements may be straight I—Thou statements, or a whole range of statements that look like I—It statements, but which in fact convey, in some fashion, that it is myself that prompts my partner to speak. It may also be an interest that he has and wants to share; in that case I am dealing with *witness* in the original meaning of that word.[6]

In witnessing, as we have argued,[7] there are three elements involved. First, there is a *cognitive* element; the statements uttered are structured as onlooks—metaphors which clarify a situation on the strength of a similarity between model and reality. There is also a *behavioral* element involved, for the onlook depends for its communicable meaning on obviously-appropriate ways of behaving or thinking in relation to the model used in the onlook; this model, therefore, represents a concern shared by both speaker and listener. A third element in witnessing, we indicated, is *encounter.* This is the element which we will concentrate on in this section.

In the experience of the witness as a real person, we have said, the listener also perceives the witness as having been touched and moved to respond by the reality about which he is making the statement. If the witness-act is to come off successfully, the listener must perceive as realistic the quality of the speaker's response to the

---

[6]This is not to imply that witness among those who already believe is impossible; it is not only possible, but even essential if Christians are to be encouraged to be faithful to their profession of faith. But such witness among believers usually takes the form of admonition, teaching, and encouragement.

[7]Above, pp. 135–138.

reality he is talking about. If the listener does not perceive this, he will have the sense that the speaker is either "talking about nothing" or "not talking to me" or both. The direct experience of the reality of the other person and of the reality of his encounters is the necessary pre-condition for effective communication at the cognitive level.

How does the listener perceive the reality of the speaker's response to things he is talking about and witnessing to? Taken by themselves, the statements are insufficient. We may consider and reflect upon them. This may reveal what they objectively mean and how they are consistent with other statements; but this does not suffice to reveal their *point*. We may verify them in various ways. This may establish the degree of truthfulness or adequacy of the statements, but it will always fail to establish exhaustively what "the real thing" is, and, hence, the *relevance* of making any statements at all about it. Another way to get behind the speaker's statements to what makes him speak is to appeal to a pattern of convergence in the multiplicity of statements. Through his "illative sense," the listener may establish that indeed more is meant than said, but this suggestion of further meaning does not as such convey the reality of what is meant.[8]

Only one source of the listener's perception of the speaker's realism is left, namely, *the speaker himself, personally.* For the listener, *he* is the ultimate guarantor of the *impact*, or the *reality* of what he is witnessing to and making statements about. He does not just meet the listener with the claim that he knows something about something, or that he has suggestions to make, but he presents *himself* as having been moved and touched and having responded— which has changed *him*, not accidentally but personally. His speaking attests to the *direct encounter* that has been his, and in that regard he would have to deny himself, not just part of himself, if he were to deny the reality of what he has encountered.

In every statement someone makes to me, therefore, if I am to experience it as having a point as well as a discernible meaning, two *direct relationships* constitute the pre-conditions of this experience. The first is the direct encounter between me and my partner; this encounter is tempered, no doubt, by the level of significance of the

---

[8]The three possibilities indicated here are associated, respectively, with linguistic analysis, theories of verification, and Newman's theory of knowledge.

statements we exchange, but it remains something in its own right, never reducible to the statements, as we had occasion to argue.[9] The second is the direct encounter between my partner and the reality which he has experienced, to which he is committed, and which he renders present in his person. He conveys this commitment primarily in that he is *speaking* about the reality at all. The *act* of speaking (*parrhēsia!*) conveys the commitment which has been prompted by the reality he has encountered as his abiding response to it.[10] The things he says about it carry the discernments, by which the direct encounter is cognitively structured by means of onlooks I can share and even, at one further remove, by means of terms that I understand.

Direct acts of encounter are the original setting that gives point to all the discernments that mediate the encounter, though they never do so exhaustively. Encounter is the existential *a priori* condition for all thought. With this in mind we must now turn to the theology of Dietrich Bonhoeffer who, unlike Rahner and Tillich, has made the presence of Jesus Christ alive in the Spirit the point of departure of his christological reflections.

BONHOEFFER: CHRISTOLOGY IN ENCOUNTER

Introductory

All of Occidental theology, especially after its break with Oriental orthodoxy, is blind to the Holy Spirit as the lived concreteness of worship, witness, and community. No exception to this characteristic blindness, Bonhoeffer's reflection on the Christian faith is nevertheless remarkable because he bases his entire theology on the factuality of the actual presence of Christ and on the fundamental significance of active interpersonal relationships in the Church as the communion of the Holy Spirit.

The primacy of the actus directus

To appreciate Bonhoeffer's christology, let us go back to his ecclesiology. From *Sanctorum Communio* and *Act and Being*[11] on-

---

[9]Cf. above, pp. 93–98.

[10]Cf. above, pp. 122–125, 126–129.

[11]*Sanctorum Communio,* Eine dogmatische Untersuchung zur Soziologie der

ward Bonhoeffer strove to develop what he called, in the characteristic language of the 1920's in Germany, a sociology of the Church.[12] Only if theology constantly remembers that Christianity is an *event* occurring *among persons,* can it avoid presenting itself as a gnostic system, either in terms of "Being" or "Act." If "Being" becomes the key word in ecclesiology (as in Roman Catholicism), the Church is likely to turn into a system of thought and organization which solidifies, and thus nullifies, God's gracious freedom into a static reality of the ecclesiastical or even purely human kind. If "Act" is the key word, the likely result will be that God's presence is no longer related to the human reality of the Church; thus ensues a "revelational positivism" which pits God's truth against any human truth,[13] and grace becomes a purely vertical, actualistic intervention on the part of God, leaving no room for the recognition of the *humanum* as the true bearer of God's gracious revelation. The defense of God's gracious freedom may never be at the expense of the integrity of the *humanum,* which must have a true theological significance. But the *humanum* may not be allowed to organize itself by ecclesiastical and doctrinal means so that faith in God gets presented as "an idea, a principle, a program, a universally valid proposition or law,"[14] for this would rob God of his gracious freedom.

To overcome this dilemma, Bonhoeffer points to a *reality,* "the fact of Jesus Christ," as the starting-point.[15] He is "a man, a real man

---

Kirche, München, Chr. Kaiser Verlag, [4]1969 (ET *The Communion of Saints*); *Akt und Sein,* München, Chr. Kaiser Verlag, 1964 (ET *Act and Being*).

[12]The word "sociology," in the usage of Max Scheler, Eberhard Grisebach, and others, is the equivalent of what nowadays would be called "theory of social relationships."

[13]Cf. Dietrich Bonhoeffer, *Letters and Papers from Prison,* p. 171. The young Bonhoeffer already saw that Barth's emphasis on God's sovereign freedom over against the *humanum* is predicated on epistemology rather than realism: "The dialectic advocated by the so-called dialectical theology is of a logical, not real, nature, and thus runs the risk of losing sight of the historicity of Jesus." *Gesammelte Schriften,* Eberhard Bethge (ed.), 3. Band, München, Chr. Kaiser Verlag, 1966, p. 47, thesis 9; cf. *No Rusty Swords,* Edwin H. Robertson (ed.), London, Collins, 1970, p. 29; cf. also *Act and Being,* pp. 79–87.

[14]*Ethics,* Eberhard Bethge (ed.), New York, Macmillan Publishing Co., 1955, p. 85.

[15]Cf. *Christ the Center,* pp. 104–106.

like ourselves," and it is as such a real man—not, for instance, as a teacher or legislator—that he matters.[16] Christology starts with a presence that precedes all discussion.

> Jesus is the present Christ as the Crucified and Risen One. That is the first statement of christology. This presence is to be understood in a temporal and spatial sense, *hic et nunc.* That means: it is part of the definition of [Christ's] person. The two are joined in the concept of the Church. Christ is personally present in the Church. That is the second definition of christology. Only because Christ is present can we make him the object of enquiry. This presence is the presupposition for the development of the christological question. Only because proclamation and sacrament take place in the Church can the question of the Christ be raised. Understanding the presence opens the way for the understanding of the person.[17]

This presence may not be reduced to a presence of Christ's influence, or to the abiding availability of a picture or an image of Christ. These latter two are human constructions about a dead Christ.[18] Not historical energy or intuited ideal, but the present Christ is the presupposition of christology; christology is about "the personal structure of being of the whole, historical Jesus Christ."[19]

Christ's personal presence, to be accepted previous to all discussion, will color all of Bonhoeffer's theology. Thus, it will be reflected in the Christian's willingness to act as a neighbor to others:

> We must get into action and obey—we must behave like a neighbour to [our neighbour]. But perhaps this shocks you. Perhaps you still think you ought to think out beforehand and know what you ought to do. To that there is only one answer. You can only know and think about it by doing it.[20]

In the Church, *all* forms of active relatedness among persons are integrated into the communion of the Spirit; the fundamental sociological law of representation remains valid, also in the Church.[21]

---

[16]*Ethics*, pp. 84–85.

[17]*Gesammelte Schriften*, III, p. 178 (cf. *Christ the Center*, p. 43).

[18]Cf. *ibid.*, pp. 179–181 (ET 43–46).

[19]*Christ the Center*, p. 40.

[20]*The Cost of Discipleship*, p. 86.

[21]Cf. *Gesammelte Schriften*, III, p. 47, thesis 7 (*No Rusty Swords*, p. 28).

Even though it is an illusion to believe that true community is the result of human concord or contract,[22] it remains true that Church is made by active personal encounters, and encounter has to be accepted before it becomes matter for reflection.

Because Christ is a person, we also know that the relationship between God and man cannot be thought of in terms of the relationship between entities, but only as a personal relationship. All the "objectifying thought-forms" must come under the critique of the acceptance of "the fact itself,"[23] in order to be finally rejected and eliminated as inadequate. All systems must break down so that "the true system" may become possible,[24] and this true system can only come about in the confrontation with the *reality* of God's *address* to man.[25]

Address and idea—response and reflection

To drive home the importance of the reality of the *present* Christ as the starting point of all christology, Bonhoeffer makes an important distinction. It occurs, significantly, in the first part of *Christ the Center,* entitled *The Present Christ—the 'Pro Me.'* [26] Bonhoeffer's christology starts with Christ as he is present to Christians, inviting them to the total surrender; only in this setting may christological statements be made. He writes:

> Christ as the Logos of God remains distinct and separate from the human Logos. He is the Word in the form of living address to man, *whereas the word of man is word in the form of the idea. Address and idea are the basic structures of the word.* But the two exclude each other. *Human thought is dominated by the form of the word as idea. The idea rests in itself, and is relative to itself;* it extends its validity over space and time. When Christ today is called the Word of God this usually happens with this understanding of the idea in mind. An idea is universally accessible; it is ready-made. Man can appropriate it of his own free will. Christ as idea is timeless truth; the idea of God embodied in Jesus is accessible to any one at any time.

---

[22]Cf. *The Communion of Saints,* p. 137.

[23]Cf. *Christ the Center,* p. 105.

[24]Cf. *Act and Being,* p. 89.

[25]Bonhoeffer's thought here parallels Buber's; cf. above, pp. 112–113.

[26]*Christ the Center,* pp. 43ff.

The word as address stands in contrast to this. Whereas the word as idea can remain by itself, *as address it can only be between two persons. Address gives birth to response and responsibility.* It is not timeless, but takes place in history. It is not in rest, and it is not accessible to everyone at all times. It happens only where address occurs. *The word is entirely the free act of the person who speaks.* In this way it is unique and new every time. The nature of word as address yearns for community. The word as address is also truth; this means that the word seeks for community by placing the partner in the truth. *Truth is not something which rests in itself and for itself, but something that happens between two persons.* Truth happens only in community. Only here does the concept of the word acquire its full meaning.[27]

This is a passage of extraordinary significance. It shows Bonhoeffer's concern to base theology on the *fact* of Jesus Christ as the living presence of God. In this context, he criticizes all attempts to base theology on any philosophical definition of man's relationship to God, based on a reflection on human works, human boundaries or human potentialities. How strongly Bonhoeffer felt about this becomes clear from what he said in his inaugural lecture at the University of Berlin in 1930: "The idea of potentiality has no standing in theology, and hence it has no standing in theological anthropology."[28]

The rejection of reflection as the way of access to God is based on two related positive theses. The first is that faith is a response to the presence of God experienced in address and encounter. The second is that only in such a situation of address does man understand himself; that means that reflection is only reliable in the context of address:

Man understands himself in the active relationship to God, and only God himself posits that active relationship.[29]

The act of faith in direct response to the presence of God and his address is called, by Bonhoeffer, the *actus directus.* Its opposite, the *actus reflexus,* can either be acceptable or unacceptable. It is acceptable if it "copies" the human self-experience in the *actus*

---

[27]*Gesammelte Schriften*, III, p. 185 (cf. *Christ the Center*, pp. 50–51; italics added).

[28]*Ibid.*, p. 78 (*No Rusty Swords*, pp. 59–60); cf. *Act and Being*, pp. 99ff.

[29]*Ibid.*, p. 81 (cf. ET p. 61).

directus of faith; it is unacceptable if it merely reflects on human potentialities in order thence to derive an idea of God. Bonhoeffer writes:

> Given that the idea of potentiality is excluded from theology, we must positively add: it is not in self-reflection, but in his active relationship (*Aktbezug*) to God that man understands himself, *i.e.* only where man really stands before God. Not where he finds potentialities in himself by virtue of which he can stand before God. It is necessary to distinguish here between *actus directus* and *actus reflexus*; only in the *actus directus* is there true self-understanding; in the *actus reflexus* the immediacy is already interrupted, so there can no longer be self-understanding. But theology only occurs in the *actus reflexus*; hence, theology cannot itself *be* true human self-understanding in the same sense in which philosophy claims to be it; theology can only copy (*nachzeichnen*) it. In this copying the all-important task will be: not again to rationalize reality by introducing the category of potentiality.[30]

Bonhoeffer's insistence on accepting the presence of Jesus Christ as God's address to man as the first object of christological reflection is of extraordinary significance for it sets a standard for *all* christological reflections. All "positive christology" is, in Bonhoeffer's thought, firmly measured by the *actus directus* of faith— direct Christian response to that living address which is Christ's ²sence. The believer's response and the presence of Christ are not measured by the standard of reflection, but vice versa. The fact that both the believer's response and the presence of Christ are of an historical and personal nature is not held against them, in the name of the demands of reason. For Bonhoeffer reality-experience in encounter is sovereign; it "places the partner in the truth"[31] and thus demands that he become responsive, and articulate and reflective *in* his response. To use the terminology of this book: Bonhoeffer lays down the ground-rule that reality-experience in encounter is the measure of discernment; thus discernment and reflection are put in their places, and self-centered discernment is unmasked as doing an injustice both to the reality of Christ's presence and to the totality of the discerner's commitment.

---

[30]*Ibid.*, pp. 80–81 (cf. ET p. 61).
[31]Cf. *ibid.*, p. 185 (cf. *Christ the Center*, p. 51).

Bonhoeffer's decision to emphasize the primacy of the *actus directus* will have profound consequences for our understanding of the Resurrection, as we will see in the second half of this chapter.[32] This, in turn, will lead to a restatement of the main thesis of this book, namely, that all christological discernments are only correctly understood if they are set against the background of a worshipful, witnessing act of total surrender to Jesus Christ alive in the Spirit, who accepts, purifies, and places in perspective all human concerns.[33]

There are two points, however, where a word of criticism is in order, namely, where Bonhoeffer completely rejects the idea of potentiality in theology, and where he completely separates idea and address.

First, in the light of what we discussed in the previous chapter we must disagree with Bonhoeffer's complete rejection of potentiality as a possible theological category.[34] As long as the purpose of the reintroduction of potentiality is carefully stated and limited, there is no danger. Karl Rahner's transcendental christology meditates on human potentiality in order to enable modern Christians to believe critically, without having to drop their personal self-awareness. It is possible to engage in an act of reflective self-understanding *within* the context of the acceptance of the Christian message, as Bonhoeffer himself intimates.

Second, we have to reject Bonhoeffer's contention that address and idea exclude each other.[35] As we have argued, the human word has both cognitive and performative functions, in the word and the name respectively. It is true that the Word of God is address, but human language is also address. An analysis of this fact led us, in the second chapter, to the conclusion that there is a possibility for transcendence-experience in the encounter with other persons.[36] We will discuss this further under the next heading in this chapter.

In spite of our disagreement with Bonhoeffer, however, it is important to understand why he posits the mutual exclusiveness of

---

[32]Below, pp. 253ff.
[33]Cf. below, pp. 259ff.
[34]Cf. above, pp. 217–220.
[35]Cf. above, pp. 235–236.
[36]Cf. above, pp. 89–90, 93–98.

word as idea and word as address. There are, it seems, two main reasons. First, Bonhoeffer separates address and idea as the basic structures of the word in order to prevent the living Word, Christ, from being equated with a *merely* cognitive, philosophical *idea*. Such an equation would make the Christian revelation in principle accessible to autonomous reason. Thus Bonhoeffer's eagerness to do justice to Christ as the gratuitous, living Word of address accounts for his thesis that the human word is entirely under the domination of "idea-thinking." Second, Bonhoeffer realizes that man will want to limit the totality of the experience of faith to the capacity of his discernments. He will want to reflect on his own terms. The human concerns, thus isolated, will become the measure of the reality of faith, as it is no longer remembered that these discernments/concerns were first *activated in response to the living Christ.* His presidency must remain the yardstick of the concerns and of the discernments that represent the concerns. Bonhoeffer may be a little too skeptical here, but at least he is not naive. He realizes that theology—involved in the *actus reflexus* as it is—can easily degenerate into autonomous reflection, and from there into a discussion about the meaning of words, and even terms, at the expense of the fullness in the service of which the reflection was first started. He further realizes that when this happens human reflection, words, and terms will start to sit in judgment on the total meaning; this will detract from the fullness of the act of surrender and paralyze the believer. The discernments will assert themselves independently and lose their openness to the total reality.

The pre-condition for the experience of grace

It is Bonhoeffer's view that christology, and indeed all of theology, must first and foremost give an account of itself with reference to the *actus directus* of faith in response to the encountered reality of God in Christ. All idea-thinking needs to be viewed within the context of encounter, and tested with reference to it. We argued this point in the second chapter of this book, on the basis of the recognition that language is primarily an activity occurring among persons in a situation.[37] Bonhoeffer makes the same point, but he makes it as

---

[37]Cf. above, pp. 93–98.

a specifically *theological* one. The human word is the instrument of closed idea-thinking *in actu reflexo*; it has to be redeemed by the Word of God which has that quality of living address which prompts man to be responsive and responsible. This restrictive view, both of the human word and of the *actus reflexus*, must be deemed unnecessary. In fact, how could Bonhoeffer even distinguish between word as idea and word as address if the *functional* difference between the two were not known from ordinary language-use? Given the kind treatment Bonhoeffer accords to the interpersonalist philosophy of Grisebach, there is even reason to suspect that he felt a certain affinity with the latter's analysis of human self-understanding as a function of encounter with others.[38]

It is not fanciful to assume that Bonhoeffer's intellectual sympathies are with an implicit, non-theological thesis, namely, that reality-experience in encounter is the touchstone of discernments, and that reflection is legitimately used only if it respects reality, not if it reduces reality to the size of its own rationalizations.

This assumption is supported by two main features of Bonhoeffer's thought. First, throughout his writings he stresses the overriding importance of the concrete and the particular in the Christian faith. This is not only true in his ascetical writings (where one would expect such an emphasis), but also, and most importantly, in his *Ethics*. In the latter, the experience of transcendence involved in doing what is good is consistently viewed, not in terms of the virtuous execution of a system of generally and eternally valid norms rationally developed, but in terms of *active obedience to reality as it presents itself to responsible human deputyship in the concrete.*[39]

Second, from the outset, Bonhoeffer's sympathies went in the direction of a personalist social philosophy, and away from any kind of idealism or rationalism; his choice of the *present* Christ *pro me* as the point of departure of his christology is in accordance with this early preference. In all of Bonhoeffer's theology, truth is consistently viewed, not in terms of a system of rationally developed necessary affirmations, but in terms of response to the divine address in the

---

[38]Cf. *Gesammelte Schriften*, III, pp. 73, 77–78 (*No Rusty Swords*, pp. 55, 59); cf. also *Act and Being*, pp. 86–88.

[39]Cf. for example, pp. 188–195, 214–235.

person Jesus Christ, who places the believer in the truth in a concrete, particular fashion.

Bonhoeffer consistently *argues* the soundness of these approaches, not by an appeal to personalist philosophy or to an analysis of the speech-event, but by pointing to the fact of Jesus Christ. In him we meet both the reality of God and the reality of the world. He even mediates to the individual Christian his very identity.[40] He is, in person, the mediator of all true human communication and community. Hence Bonhoeffer can even state that, given the fact that revelation does not originate in the self-understanding of the autonomous human I, but in the encounter with Jesus Christ, it must yield its own epistemology.[41] That epistemology, presumably, would be based on the following thesis: *only* in the gratuitous self-revelation of God, to which corresponds the *actus directus* of faith (which itself is totally owed to God's graciousness), is human thought delivered from potentiality-thinking and the word no longer dominated by the idea. This thesis, we have indicated, is unnecessary. The primacy of encounter over reflection can be argued independently of revelation. The demand that reflection and idea-thinking must remain faithful to the encounter-experience is arguable apart from revelation. *Every* encounter-relationship involves an experience of graciousness and spirit in the sense that lived experience is always greater than what we make of it; it is never entirely amenable to integration into our cognitive construct.[42] In addressing humanity in the person Jesus Christ, God is not presenting humanity for the first time with the opportunity to respond to a gratuitous presence. The *natural availability* of the other, and hence *the availability of encounter, is the existential pre-condition of the experience of God's grace and of the Spirit.*

To say this does not in the least imply that God's self-manifestation in Christ is now reduced to a natural given, and hence robbed of its gratuitousness. For one thing, to say that encounter is naturally available does not imply that *God* will actually reveal himself in encounter; a pre-condition is not an actuality. But, more impor-

---

[40]Cf. *Christ the Center*, pp. 61–62.

[41]Cf. *Act and Being*, pp. 15–16.

[42]Cf. above, pp. 90, 92.

tantly, graciousness and spirit are essential aspects of *any* encounter-relationship.[43] In *every* encounter, the other reveals himself as really "other"; this makes us realize that the other's self-revelation is an unowed gift. And to the extent that the "Thou" really affects my "I," my identity is graciously enhanced. Our postulate that encounter is the pre-condition of the experience of God's grace does not rob God of his gracious freedom. Still, human thought *always* tends to declare itself independent of reality. It even tends to conceive of *God* as a reality which—unlike any other reality—*cannot encounter us*, but must be approached by imagination or philosophy. Martin Buber has rightly called this an error. It is a prejudice, to be unmasked as an unwarranted, reductionistic attempt to measure God by the yardstick of human discernments. God *can* encounter us. To say that does not imply that God *actually* encounters us, but merely that encounter with God must not be ruled out, and that, if we are to know God and ourselves, we must wait—without idols—for God to graciously reveal himself, so that we may believe in him *in actu directo*.

Autonomous reflection: a theological evaluation

Why was it necessary to elaborate the point that the availability of the other is the pre-condition of the experience of grace? Why was it necessary to criticize Bonhoeffer on this score? Before we go on, we must answer these questions. We have claimed that Bonhoeffer's emphasis on the presence of Jesus Christ as the starting point of christological reflection was important, and that it would have profound consequences for our understanding of the Resurrection.[44] But in order to accept Bonhoeffer's insistence on the primacy of the divine address in the presence of Jesus Christ, we had to strip his conception of an unnecessary and fundamentalist assumption, namely, that true address is only available when God speaks to man. Encounter and witness, as we saw in the preliminary paragraphs of this chapter, are part of human life; they must be integrated into the new reality brought about by God's address in Christ. But if they must be integrated, they must first be accepted and appreciated, on the strength of the rhetoric of inclusion.

[43]Cf. Martin Buber, *Ich und Du*, pp. 18, 49 (ET *I and Thou*, pp. 62, 89).
[44]Above, pp. 237–238.

A warrant for this corrective interpretation of Bonhoeffer is to be found at the very beginning of Bonhoeffer's career as a theologian. Among the propositions offered by Bonhoeffer on the occasion of his doctoral thesis defense in 1927 there is one which reads:

According to her sociological structure, the Church includes within herself each and every possible type of social relatedness and raises [*überhöht*] them in the "community of the Spirit"; the latter is based on the fundamental sociological law of representation.[45]

The young Bonhoeffer did not take a dim view of the realities of human encounter.

We can now summarize our critique of Bonhoeffer's thesis. We have made three related points. First, reflection on human potentiality is warranted. Second, the human word is also a word of address. Third, the availability of encounter prepares man for the divine address in the person of Jesus Christ.

Acceptance of these three corrections, however, should not make us naively confident. Much reflection presents itself as autonomous. Many human words are dominated by the idea. Openness to encounter is rarely achieved. On these factual issues, Bonhoeffer is a reliable guide with no illusions.

Much theology, and even much ordinary faith-language, fails to stay in touch with the *actus directus* of encounter. This is more than a purely *technical* error, avoidable if people attended to some good personalist philosophy or some decent analysis of language-functions. For Bonhoeffer, *all* attempts to reduce faith to human reflection represent nothing less than

the thinking of the *cor curvum in se*. The I is indeed really present to itself, but that constitutes, not its glory, but its guilt. Thinking caught up in itself is the genuine self-expression of man in quest of himself in the *status corruptionis*.[46]

From a theological point of view, the tendency for *all* language to get stuck in the kind of overhypostatization that ultimately leads

---

[45] *Gesammelte Schriften*, III, p. 47 (cf. *No Rusty Swords*, p. 28).

[46] *Ibid.*, p. 74.—The two Latin expressions mean, respectively, "the heart bent over on itself" and "the state of corruption"; the expression "the I present to itself" is an allusion to the idealist definition of "spirit."—Cf. *No Rusty Swords*, p. 56.

to derealization[47] reflects the tendency of *all* human thought to rationalize reality in terms of what human thought considers "thinkable." This is to say that *all* human thinking reflects the *cor curvum in se.*

Human thought finds it hard to accept that reality always resists total integration into our cognitive construct. We are often ill at ease when we discover that reality always asserts its irreducible strangeness, even in the immediacy of the encounter. We can be disappointed with the realization that all knowledge occurs in models that both give access to, and fail to control completely, the intended reality.

A person *may* indeed remain open to "the other" in a basic attitude of respect, awe, and indeed love. He *may* let himself be placed in the truth, in the light of the gracious self-manifestation of the other. His self-realization, he will then thankfully reflect, is owed to the other, and at the same time it is most intensely his own. In such a case he will also refer all his cognitive discernments about the reality that encounters him to his *total* response, and criticize them in its light. He will not allow the partial discernments that structure *his own* world, or the demand for internal coherence of *his* concepts, determine in advance what the reality he has encountered can or cannot be. He will accept that reality is encountered before it is understood, named before it is worded, taken for granted before it is grasped.

But as a matter of actual fact, rather than accepting the strangeness of the other—whether God, person, or thing—as a gracious invitation, we tend to be threatened by it, to keep it at arm's length, to protect ourselves against it, to sit in judgment on it, to drag it before the tribunal of our ego, to measure it by the standard of our discernments, and to overpower it. In the light of this defensive attitude, the direct act of encounter starts to look like an undesirable thing to do; the available experience of graciousness starts to appear as the enemy of established nature. Reality gets perceived as the foe of the idea: "Human kind cannot bear very much reality."[48]

---

[47]Cf. above, pp. 69–70.

[48]T. S. Eliot, *Murder in the Cathedral,* London, Faber and Faber, Ltd., 1972, p. 75 (*The Complete Poems and Plays,* p. 209). Cf. "Burnt Norton," I, *Collected Poems, 1909–1962,* p. 190 (*The Collected Poems and Plays,* p. 118).

When self-understanding thus develops in opposition to reality and not in encounter with it, it becomes an exercise in arrogance, not obedience; understanding the other becomes a function of domination, not of service. Worried into an attitude of compulsive self-maintenance and self-justification, man does not trust the other to do him justice; instead, he demands that the other justify itself before the tribunal of his sovereign self-awareness. In this way, man refuses to be borne by the other's care; he becomes the prisoner of his own defensiveness; aggressive constructive thought and aggressive constructive action become the instruments of self-justification. *Cor curvum in se.*

Two consequences of the primacy of the actus directus

This factual human reluctance to be open to reality now finds itself confronted by God's address to man.

> If the question about man is to be really asked, then it can only be asked in the situation in which man stands before God. Wherever else it is asked, it is not asked with full seriousness. This means: man gets completely drawn out of himself, he is wholly drawn before God, and it is here that the question about man becomes fully serious, because it no longer includes its own answer; on the contrary, the answer is given to man, completely gratuitously and completely anew, by God, because God has put man in front of him and thus bids him ask the question. This means: man experiences his foundations not through himself, but through God. Truly man is he who is addressed by God. The focus out of which man understands himself lies, therefore, with God.[49]

The *actus directus* of faith consists in the direct experience of God's address, in which is graciously contained, though unthematically, the answer to the question: Who am I? Self-awareness and self-realization, and even selfhood, thus become a free gift, in the encounter with God as he graciously reveals himself.

Bonhoeffer's insistence on the primacy of the *actus directus* has two important implications, one for the nature of theology, the other for the conception of identity. We must briefly explain both.

It is obvious that the thesis of the primacy of the *actus directus* must apply to *faith* itself; to present faith as anything short of an

---

[49] *Gesammelte Schriften*, III, pp. 74–75 (cf. *No Rusty Swords*, pp. 56–57).

actus directus would amount to presenting faith purely as a function of imagination or philosophy. But Bonhoeffer claims that it also applies to *theology*: it is part of theology to measure all its positive statements by the yardstick of their ability to do justice to the *actus directus* of the encounter with God as he graciously manifests himself. Theology must establish the legitimacy of its statements, not primarily by showing that they are consistent with other theological statements or related to secular human reflection, but first and foremost by placing them in the context of the *actus directus* of faith.

The second consequence of the primacy of the *actus directus* is that *authentic identity*, or selfhood, must be understood in relational terms. In the encounter with God man also finds his true identity. True identity is not an achievement—not the result of self-constitution, self-justification, self-reflection or self-actualization; it is a gift resulting from the encounter with God. We will have many occasions to come back to this; we will characterize this type of identity as "responsive identity."

This notion will have its influence on our understanding of the relevance of interpersonal relationships to the question of the Christian's identity. This is in accordance with what we have said about reality-experience in encounter being the touchstone of discernments.[50] If authentic identity-experience is implied in the encounter with God, some form of authentic identity-experience must also be implied in interpersonal encounter; we say, therefore, that *the availability of the other is also the existential pre-condition of the experience of responsive identity.* Bonhoeffer never formulated this thesis, but the question was on his mind; and we claim again that it is consonant with the main themes of Bonhoeffer's thought.

Two issues present themselves for further elaboration at this point. Both of them were among Bonhoeffer's concerns. The first concerns the relationship between encounter with God (as absolutely constitutive of personal identity) and the encounters with other persons. This will raise the issue of representation as a basic issue in christology; we will treat this at a much later point in this book.[51]

The second issue is the further analysis of the fact that faith is

---

[50]Above, p. 240.
[51]Below, pp. 412–417, 423–427.

primarily, and all-embracingly, an *actus directus*. Concretely speaking, this means this must be elaborated in an analysis of the act of faith in terms of the Holy Spirit, and of the experience of Christ's presence-in-the-present. This is the issue we will raise at this point, and, as we will see, it will lead to fundamental conclusions regarding the place of the Resurrection in christology.

"Vergegenwärtigung"—Re-presentation

In August, 1935, Bonhoeffer gave an address to the fraternity of assistant ministers and vicars of the Confessional Church of the Province of Saxony. He spoke on *Vergegenwärtigung neutestamentischer Texte*—"Re-presentation of New Testament Texts"; his talk dealt with the question of the relevance of the Bible to actual life situations.[52]

Omitting any introduction, Bonhoeffer launches immediately into his main contention:

> The question of the re-presentation of the New Testament message is fundamentally capable of a twofold interpretation. People either mean by it that the biblical message must justify itself before [the tribunal of] the present, and thus show itself capable of being re-presented, or they mean that the present must justify itself before [the tribunal of] the biblical message, and that therefore the message must become something in the present.

The context of Bonhoeffer's remarks is clear: it is the demand that Christianity put itself at the service of the Nazi *Volkstum* by becoming "German Christianity." The former of the two options—the Bible must justify itself before the German nation—is being propagated with "ominous and uncanny urgency."[53]

---

[52]It is impossible to render *Vergegenwärtigung* by a word less clumsy than "re-presentation." *No Rusty Swords* (p. 302 and note) opts for "presentation." The meaning is "rendering present," and hence "making something of actual importance or relevance now," "causing something to come to life in the present." The title of Bonhoeffer's address could, therefore, be rendered as "Texts from Scripture Coming to Life." Our problem is complicated by the fact that we will also have to deal with representation in the sense of "deputizing for someone." For this reason the two words "re-presentation" and "representation" are not synonymous in the terminology of this book.

[53]*Gesammelte Schriften*, III, p. 303: "unheimliche Dringlichkeit" (cf. *No Rusty Swords*, p. 303).

For Bonhoeffer, however, the essence of this theological option is much older than the *Putsch* of 1933:

> The question became acute in this form for the first time in the era of the emancipation of autonomous reason, i.e. in Rationalism, and it has determined theology till now, up to and including the German-Christian theology. Rationalism was nothing but the emergence of the long dormant human demand for an autonomous construction of life on the basis of the forces in the world as given, and to that extent the question in hand is indeed a question that is contained in man's very demand for autonomy; that means: if an autonomous man also wants to profess Christianity, he demands that the Christian message justify itself before the tribunal of his autonomy. Should the justification come off, then he calls himself a *Christian*; if it fails to come off, then he calls himself a *pagan*. It makes no difference that the tribunal before which the Christian message has to justify itself is called Reason in the 18th century or Culture in the 19th century or *Volkstum* (i.e. the year 1933, with all its implications) in the 20th century; *the question is exactly the same*: Is Christianity justifiable before us, the way we—thank God!— are? All those who want to lay claim to being called Christians for whatever reasons—whether rational, cultural, or political—have exactly the same urgent need, namely, to justify Christianity before the tribunal of the present; *the assumption is exactly the same*, namely that the Archimedean point, the solid, unquestionable point of departure has already been found (whether in Reason, in Culture, or in *Volkstum*), and that the movable, *questionable*, fluid element is precisely the Christian message; *the method is exactly the same*, namely, to engage in re-presentation in such a way as to run the Christian message through the sieve of one's own knowledge—what does not go through is despised and thrown out; so to trim down and lop off the message as to make it fit the fixed framework; until the eagle can no longer raise itself and soar to his true element, but becomes, his pinions clipped, a peculiar showpiece among the other tame, domesticated animals; just as the farmer who needs a horse for his land leaves the fiery stallion in the marketplace and buys himself a spunkless, tame horse, so domestication has produced a serviceable Christianity; and then it is only a matter of time and common sense to lose interest in this whole construction and turn away from it. *This type of re-presentation* leads straight into paganism.[54]

Bonhoeffer's vivid and passionate language expresses what happens when the discernments and, through them, the concerns they represent become the yardstick of the commitment. Once theology's main preoccupation is with the discernments, it loses its interest in

---

[54]*Ibid.*, pp. 304–305 (ET pp. 303–304).

testing the legitimacy of its statements with reference to the *actus directus* of faith.

> Wherever the issue of re-presentation becomes the *theme of theology* we can be certain that the reality [of the Christian message] is already betrayed and bartered away.[55]

.   If the Christian message is to be a present message of concrete and present relevance, where is this present concreteness to be found? Bonhoeffer answers:

> Not where the present makes its demand before Christ, but where the present stands before the demand of Christ, *is there presence. Reason:* the concept of presence is not determined by determinations of time, but by the Word of Christ as the Word of God. Presence is not a kind of epochal sense, an interpretation of an era, a spirit of the age; no, presence is the Holy Spirit and nothing else. Where God himself is, in his Word, there is presence, there he constitutes presence. The subject of the presence is the Holy Spirit, not us, and that is why the subject of re-presentation is the Holy Spirit himself. *The concretissimum of the Christian message* and exegesis is not a human act of re-presentation, but always God himself, the Holy Spirit.[56]

The concretissimum conveyed in worship and witness

It is important to note that Bonhoeffer places the *concretissimum* of faith, not in the discernments or in the human concerns they represent, let alone in reflection, but in the reality that evokes and informs the *act* of faith. In the terminology of this book: the *concretissimum* of the Christian message is the reality of Christ's presence in the Spirit as he encounters the believer and prompts him to speak. This act of faith is an act of *worshipful* surrender to Christ present in the Spirit. It is the responsive counterpart of this self-revealing presence of Christ. It includes the constitution of the believer's responsive identity: in the act of worshipful response to Christ, the person becomes a Christian. This act of worshipful surrender is conveyed by the *act* of speaking; *what* the believer says does not do justice to the presence which prompts him to speak. The

---

[55] *Ibid.*, p. 305 (ET p. 305).

[56] *Ibid.*, p. 307 (ET p. 306).—Given the subject of his talk, Bonhoeffer seems to restrict the impact of God's present address to man in the Holy Spirit to the Word of Scripture. In his Christology (*Gesammelte Schriften,* III, pp. 184–194—*Christ the Center,* pp. 49–61) he adds the presence of Christ in sacrament and community, while still claiming a special, informing significance for the Word. We will come back to this, and we will add martyrdom to this list: below, pp. 479–486.

rhetoric conveys what the logic only approximates. *In the direct experience of speech* the comprehensive point is made by naming and addressing Christ as he meets the believer and constitutes him in the truth. Later, when the believer considers and reflects on the meaning of the names and titles and words he has used and of the statements he has made, he will realize that they fail to reconstitute the *actus directus*, although they do approximate it. A thousand credal articles and dogmatic pronouncements, even the most vital and culturally relevant ones, do not add up to one act of faith.

Now the Christian believer also *witnesses* to his faith; he cannot help presenting himself to others in his identity as a Christian. How can we account for this process?

The experience of *actual* communication in the present, we argued in the beginning of this chapter,[57] is dependent on the awareness, on the part of the listener, that it is really a "you" that is "talking to me," and that it is that "you" that guarantees, in person, the *reality* of the thing he has encountered. Once this is assured, any I—It statements the other person makes can have present and effective meaning.

"Present and effective meaning," we say. We laid down earlier that discernments in christology are doubly bound.[58] To the extent that they are bound up with the human concerns they represent, they owe their effective *illuminating* force to the familiarity, on the part of both the speaker and the listener, with those concerns. This familiarity, however, does not carry either the speaker or the listener beyond the concerns which they already share. "Present and effective meaning" in the act of Christian witness, therefore, is due to *more* than just the familiarity of the partners with the concerns that constitute the stuff of their discernments; truly present and effective meaning is due to the fact that the speaker represents, in his person and in the act of speaking, the new reality that has touched him, which moves him to speak, which prompts him to worship, and which prompts him to witness to it. Present and effective meaning of biblical texts, therefore, only occurs if these texts are heard and received as the living word of witness to the risen Lord, not if they are used to

---

[57]Above, pp. 228–232.
[58]Above, pp. 141–143.

illustrate present-day concerns.[59] And this does not apply to the word only, but also to the sacraments, to Christian ministry, and indeed to the entire Church: unless they are perceived as acts of witness to the risen Lord, coming forth out of worship, their meaning tends to evaporate. They may still be culturally interesting, but they have lost their soul.

The powerful presence that evokes and must preside over all christological statements is the presence of Christ in the Spirit, conveyed by the total surrender of the speaker. It is the presence of him who says in the Fourth Gospel: "I am the Resurrection." The reality of the risen One, we said in the previous chapter, is adequately conveyed only by the totality of the believer's surrender;[60] far from reducing the reality of the Resurrection to the believer's faith-interpretation, his surrender actually points to the risen One as the *concretissimum* of the Christian message. Hence, though the risen One is re-presented in the act of speaking of the *witnesses*, it is nonetheless *he*, in his presence in the Spirit, who stands behind the witness as the reality that accounts for the urgency and the *parrhēsia* with which he speaks, quite apart from what he says.

All this leads to two conclusions. The first one is that the Resurrection is an eschatological event, and that, as a consequence, the act of Christian faith is essentially future-oriented. We will elaborate this, starting with the next chapter.

Secondly, we must be careful to treat the Resurrection really as the *concretissimum*. To treat it only as one event among many in the story of Jesus is clearly insufficient. The Resurrection must be placed where it belongs, namely at the beginning of all christology, for without the presence, in the Spirit, of the risen Lord there would not be any christology at all.

THE ORIGIN OF CHRISTOLOGY

Retrospect

The thesis just formulated will provide us with the starting point for the entire third part of the present book. Before we proceed to

---

[59]Cf. above, pp. 182–183.
[60]Cf. above, p. 195.

draw some initial conclusions from it, let us briefly summarize the analysis which led up to it.

First, we started our analysis by establishing the fact that the presence of Christ in the Spirit is the all-encompassing situation of all christological statements.[61] We came back to this starting point at the end of our analysis, when we described the presence of Christ in the Spirit as the *concretissimum* to which the Christian responds in the *actus directus* of faith surrender. In christological statements, we said, it is the *act* of speaking which conveys the total surrender.[62] Throughout we reminded ourselves that all particular christological statements must remain "placed";[63] none may be allowed to monopolize or qualify or belie the total surrender.[64]

Second, we found that the Christian's total surrender to Christ present in the Spirit is articulate. This articulation occurs by means of discernments; these discernments are taken up in the act of confident speaking. Discernments are related to significant human concerns. In christological statements, therefore, human concerns are integrated into the surrender.[65] This is done by acceptance and conversion to obedience, in a perspective of hope. The effective illuminating force of the discernments depends on their being connected with familiar common concerns; their present and effective meaning in *christology* is achieved by their becoming the carriers of the total surrender to the present risen Christ.[66]

Third, we wondered if the Resurrection, as the abiding and gracious presence of Christ in the Spirit, could be directly expressed,[67] not just in terms of human concerns accepted, made obedient, and put in perspective. We answered this question in the affirmative: the presence of Christ is directly conveyed by the total surrender on the part of the believer; the believer witnesses, in his very person, to the reality of the present Christ, who has touched

---

[61]Cf. above, pp. 117–122.
[62]Cf. above, pp. 249–250.
[63]Cf. above, p. 141.
[64]Cf. above, p. 128.
[65]Cf. above, pp. 135–143.
[66]Above, pp. 154–183.
[67]Cf. above, p. 227.

him and given him the responsive identity with which he speaks. The act of Christian faith expresses that Christ is risen.[68]

We have answered our question in the affirmative. Still, this should not blind us to the delicacy and the vulnerability of the *actus directus* of faith. The total surrender can only be conveyed, not exhaustively articulated; the witness' personal guarantee for the truth of the act of speaking is never accounted for by a summation of what he says. And yet, if nothing is said, if the witness is silent, if no articulation takes place, then the Resurrection is not conveyed at all. On the one hand it is impossible to reduce the total commitment, the person-as-witness, and the confident act of speaking to the statements made; on the other hand, if there are no discernments, no witness-acts, no statements, then the disclosure will not occur, and the reality of the risen Christ present in the Spirit will not be conveyed.[69]

The Resurrection may not be qualified

From all our analyses one conclusion results: the presence of Jesus Christ in the Spirit is the one reality that may not be qualified. If no discernments must be allowed to monopolize or qualify the total surrender, then the reality which evokes the total surrender may not be qualified *a fortiori*. This leads to the ground-rule of all christology: *No statement made in christology may be allowed to qualify the Resurrection of Jesus Christ*. The *actus directus* of faith is the correlative of the presence of Christ in the Spirit in virtue of his exaltation; if no discernments may be allowed to monopolize or curtail the total commitment involved in the *actus directus*, they may not be allowed to monopolize or curtail the presence of Christ in the Spirit in virtue of his exaltation either.

---

[68]Above, p. 251.

[69]However, for the silent witness of martyrdom and Christian life, cf. below, pp. 479–486.—E. Schillebeeckx, *Jezus*, p. 293, rightly calls the *content* of the Resurrection appearance(s), "as it were, void." This void is filled with the apostolic *kerygma*, which thus *appears* to be the direct result of divine revelation and the direct warrant for the twelve to carry on their authoritative apostolic ministry. What Schillebeeckx calls a void is, in our terminology, the presence of Christ alive in the Spirit, which draws into itself, in the Christian act of total surrender, all human concerns and discernments.

A comparison with Schoonenberg's ground-rule

The formulation of this ground-rule owes a debt to Piet Schoonenberg's style of argument in *The Christ*. It is proper, therefore, to compare our ground-rule with his, and to show how they are related. Schoonenberg is concerned to maintain the integrity of Christ's humanity. It follows that no statements about Christ's divine pre-existence may be allowed to curtail this integrity. Schoonenberg writes:

> What Scripture, tradition and *magisterium* teach us about the divine and pre-existent person of the Son can never be in conflict with what is proclaimed to us with regard to Jesus Christ. Thus it cannot be in conflict with the most primary insights about Christ [. . .], namely, that he is one single person and that he is a human person. *What has been said about the pre-existent divine person can never nullify this one and human person.*[70]

Hence, if "personalness" is claimed on behalf of the pre-existent Word in such a way as to lead to the conclusion that Jesus of Nazareth is not a human person in exactly the same sense as all humans are said to be persons, we must respond with a resounding "No." In this book, we have made the same claim in a different fashion. We argued that no discernment in christology may curtail the total commitment; this total commitment is conveyed by a triple rhetoric of inclusion, obedience, and hope. Curtailing the human personhood of Jesus Christ amounts to a denial of the rhetoric of inclusion.[71] Schoonenberg's argument is correct, but his ground-rule is too limited, for the rhetoric of inclusion is only one phase in a triadic rhetoric. Schoonenberg's rule is only one particular application of the much more comprehensive ground-rule that no discernments may be allowed to monopolize or curtail the total commitment.

The Resurrection and the two types of christology

The last two centuries have seen a complete change in christology. Up to the late eighteenth century dogmatic christology, built

---

[70]P. J. A. M. Schoonenberg, S.J. *Hij is een God van mensen,* 's-Hertogenbosch, L. C. G. Malmberg, 1969, p. 82 (cf. *The Christ*, p. 82).

[71]Cf. above, pp. 156–159, 167–173, 179–181.

around the hypostatic union as the central christological affirmation, was co-extensive with christology *tout court*. Skepticism with regard to the concepts of divine and human nature tended to lessen the acceptability of this doctrine, but it was critical exegesis that created the new situation. In this situation both dogmatic, reflective christology, with its hypostatic-union *a priori*, and historical, critical christology, with its *a posteriori* methods, demand recognition. Mutual integration is not easy, yet it is imperative, as Karl Rahner points out.

> It is necessary to build a bridge to unite present-day exegesis, with its critical methods and findings, to that body of dogmatic teaching on Jesus Christ developed by the Church which must be retained as permanently valid.[72]

Reflective christology and critical, historical christology are both demanded by the human need for understanding. But if the Resurrection is to be characterized as the abiding origin of all christology, both christological recollection and christological reflection owe a primary allegiance to the Resurrection.[73] They must therefore be set in the context of the *actus directus* of worship and witness. A few thoughts on the implications of the thesis about the primacy of the Resurrection for both types of christology must conclude this chapter.

The Resurrection: the setting of recollection

We have already argued that the Resurrection of Jesus Christ must not simply be presented as one *part* of the christological narrative if it is to retain its position of pre-eminence. The *narrative* about Jesus begins with the Baptism of Jesus and runs through his ministry to his execution and burial, and *ends there*. Whatever "happened to Jesus" on "the third day"[74] sums up the meaning of the

---

[72]"The Position of Christology in the Church Between Exegesis and Dogmatics," in: *Theological Investigations*, New York, The Seabury Press, 1974, pp. 185–214; quotation p. 197.

[73]Cf. *ibid.*, pp. 206–214; cf. also Karl Rahner—Wilhelm Thüsing, *Christologie— systematisch und exegetisch*, pp. 40ff.

[74]The expression "on the third day" conveys a decisive turn of events by God's grace—not a chronological fact; cf. Hos 6, 3.

entire life of Jesus; the Resurrection makes the narrative into *christo-logical* narrative. That means: the Resurrection is *the abiding condition for the meaningfulness of any christological recollection.* Safeguarding the objectivity of the Resurrection must, therefore, not be attempted by assigning it a place in the chronological narrative after the death and burial of Jesus, but by pointing out, as we did in the previous chapter,[75] that there is more involved in the Resurrection of Jesus than the faith-interpretation of the believers—which, incidentally, *is* the next event that can be historically established as having followed the burial of Jesus: "He is not here. He is risen." Any attempts to generate an understanding of Jesus Christ by recollection and narrative without first realizing that there would be no *christo-logical* quest for the historical Jesus without his presence in the Spirit now would sin against the ground-rule we have set up.

It is easy to see how—given the modern connotations of the word "God" and the excessively notional character of classical christology[76]—the need for a christology from below should have arisen. Recollection and narrative were going to make up for the loss of credibility which christological dogma had suffered. That quest for the historical Jesus became a failure. The *theological* ground for the failure of the quest is that historical-critical reason (no matter how legitimate its demands, made in the interest of human intellectual integrity) sat in judgment on christology and determined what it could, and could not, responsibly say. In this way the uniqueness of Jesus Christ came to be reinterpreted—Bonhoeffer would say: it was falsely re-presented—in ways that the culture could understand; Jesus became the teacher of the true ethic, the example of the dedicated life, or the warrant for whatever other ideals seemed to be "Christian."

The aims and the methods of the New Quest of the Historical Jesus are *theologically* sounder than the Old Quest's. The New Quest understands that it is at once necessary and sufficient for the Quest to show that the claims made on behalf of Jesus Christ by the *kērygma* are *supported by* the type of person the historical Jesus can be shown to have been and the type of impact he can be shown to

---

[75]Cf. above, pp. 191–199.
[76]Cf. above, pp. 40–50, 53–55.

have had. Thus the uniqueness of Christ no longer depends upon historical proof.[77] The living surrender of the *actus directus* of faith rightly sets the norm for what historical-critical reason can discover in the way of discernments for a "christology from below," and not vice versa. It is true, christology today must be "from below" or not be at all. Christians are concerned about Christ's full humanity; a truly historical, narrative christology will show the full humanity of the Lord. But historical investigation may not lay down the limits of what the christological confession can and cannot say.[78] Otherwise we might well end up seeing yet another face, that of a humanitarian late twentieth-century Christian this time, at the bottom of a deep well. Hence, we must determine how the presence of the risen Christ reflects on historical narrative, and thus in what sense a christology from below is acceptable, and indeed necessary. We will do this at a later point.[79]

The Resurrection: the setting of reflection

Not only historical christology, but also classical, reflective christology must recognize the primacy of the Resurrection. Let us demonstrate the need for this by again studying the *Declaratio* to which we have already had occasion to refer.[80] Its placing of the Resurrection is notable on two scores. First, the Resurrection is connected by means of a merely *temporal* conjunction to Jesus' life, which bore signs of the adorable mystery of his person, and to his obedience unto death. Second, it is connected with the pre-existent Son, as the Logos of creation, by means of a *convenience*-argument. Thus two impressions are created. On the one hand, the Resurrection appears to be just another event in a series of mystery-charged

---

[77]Cf. James M. Robinson, *A New Quest of the Historical Jesus, passim.*—Cf. also Johann Baptist Metz, "A Short Apology of Narrative," in *The Crisis of Religious Language*, Johann Baptist Metz, Jean-Pierre Jossua (eds.), New York, Herder and Herder (*Concilium*, 85), 1973, pp. 84–96.

[78]I have argued that Hans Küng's *On Being a Christian* (Garden City, New York, Doubleday & Company, 1976) suffers from lack of emphasis on worship, which amounts to saying that the Resurrection does not have pride of place. Cf. "Küng's *Christ Sein*: A Review Article," *Andover Newton Quarterly* 16 (1976) 277–281; Dutch: "Hans Küng: Christ sein—een mening," *Vox Theologica* 45 (1975) 242–247.

[79]Below, pp. 347–349, 359–362.

[80]Above, p. 53, where the relevant text is quoted in full.

past events that constitute the life of Jesus. On the other hand, the Resurrection seems to be no more than the final manifestation of a reality that was substantially constituted from eternity, in an *absolute past*, so that the life, death, and Resurrection come to look like a merely enhypostatic terrestrial interlude, a "divine aside," an unsubstantive manifestation of something substantive and essentially complete in itself.

What downplays the Resurrection here is the need for certainty in reflection. Reflective reason tends to work on the basis of *a priori* truths; this may cause a depreciation of history. The *Declaratio* gives us what is usually called a high christology, or a "christology from above." But is that, of itself, a qualification? Theologically speaking it need not be. The demand for fixity, which is such a prominent characteristic of reflective reason, is not more legitimate than critical reason's demand for historical truth. It is obvious why the tradition has had a tendency to favor high christology: when orthodoxy and reliability of confession and consistency of tradition are felt to be very important, then the tools of reflective reason—concepts—and its reliance upon an ideal past—eternal truths—are felt to afford just the right kind of support. But is high christology, to the extent that it is based on this demand for fixity, not a warrant for reflective reason to sit in judgment on the *actus directus* of faith? In a document like the *Declaratio*, the Resurrection of Christ does not play the key role it should play; it is presented on the one hand as a reality whose convenience (if not necessity) is already given with the pre-existence of the eternal Son, and on the other hand as an historical event on a par with the life and the humiliation of Jesus; this must give us pause. There is legitimacy to the demands of reflective reason; but the high christology that results must be "placed," just as the low christology of historical-critical reason must be. How the Resurrection reflects on reflective christology will be the subject of a later discussion.[81]

We conclude that critical reason and reflective reason are to be included, not rejected; but they have to be purified, not allowed to dominate; and thus they will be put in the perspective of the presence of Christ in the Spirit, without forcing the living Christ into their

[81]Below, pp. 402–405, 457–460.

several, potentially reductionist, perspectives. Critical reason can only be preserved from ebionitism and its descendants, and reflective reason can only be rescued from monophysitism and its descendants, by the *actus directus* of faith: worshipful and witnessing surrender to Christ alive in the Spirit will provide the only legitimate placing of christology both high and low.

Summary and outlook

We must reaffirm our main concern in this chapter. The source of all christology, and hence the primary norm to determine the pertinence of all its statements, is the Resurrection of Jesus Christ. The Resurrection must, therefore, be viewed, not as an event subsequent to Jesus' life, passion, and burial, but as the living presence of Jesus Christ in the Spirit, re-presented in and behind the personal commitment of the witnesses. The witnesses' total surrender is their *actus directus* of faith, which alone does justice, responsively, to what is involved in the Resurrection. The witnesses' sayings must be considered, not primarily as discernments that convey their involvement in shared human concerns, but as statements that make their point to the extent that they succeed in re-presenting Jesus Christ alive and present—a point which is made by their very act of speaking. The *kēryssein* rather than the *kērygma*,[82] the word as address rather than the word as idea, do justice to the Resurrection. The person who has encountered Christ alive and who goes on to encounter other persons—he is witness to the Resurrection. Whatever messages are announced and whatever statements are made are always in danger of obscuring the *concretissimum*; though prompted by the presence of Christ alive and present in the Spirit, they do derive their effective *illuminating* force from shared human concerns; thus the impression is created that it is human reason that determines who the living Christ is. To make the same point in our linguistic terms, the direct experience of speech (the correlate of the *actus directus* of encounter with the other), not the consideration of meaning, does justice to the reality I am dealing with.[83] Consider-

---

[82]The Greek words mean, respectively, the act of proclamation and the content of proclamation.

[83]Cf. above, p. 93.

ation of meaning will be true to the encounter only if the meaning of a statement is determined with reference to the point made in the direct experience of speech, and not vice versa.

The demands of human reason appear mainly in two forms, reflective and critical reason; they lead, respectively, to high and low christology.

Reflective reason, in its attempt to gain stability of discourse and understanding, tends to cast its statements into fixed structures, which are presented as normative for understanding. This leads to two consequences. On the one hand, reflective reason tends to identify its constructs with eternal truth, and thus with "God." On the other hand, since it experiences itself as normative for understanding, it tends to uphold the objective validity of its statements in the name of the mind's ability to know the truth, to present them as facts, descriptively.[84] Examples of this tendency in christology are legion: the tendency to derive the nature and the quality of the knowledge of the historical Jesus from the neo-Chalcedonian construct; the tendency to make Christ's *personal* pre-existence into the basic doctrine, to which all other christological statements owe unconditional allegiance; the reduction of the miracles in the life of the historical Jesus to proofs of his divinity; the attack on any critical approach to the so-called nature-miracles as a sign of unbelief in Christ's divinity. The list could be expanded. All these theses represent the domination of reflective reason over faith in the presence of Jesus Christ. They all tend to downplay the significance of the human life of Jesus and the human lives of Christians throughout the ages in the name of high christology and of safeguarding the divinity of Christ. Is not what is upheld here reason's need for fixity in knowing the truth, rather than the primacy of the living Christ's presence?

---

[84]An interesting *démasqué* of Wolffian, rationalist influence on the preliminary drafts for the Second Vatican Council, in M.-D. Chenu, "Vérité évangélique et métaphysique wolffienne à Vatican II," *Revue des Sciences philosophiques et théologiques* 57 (1973) 632–640; the Council corrected this error by a *heilsgeschichtliche* approach without falling into historicism.—Notice also how Tillich presents "Being-itself" as a foundational concept; reflective reason asserts itself as the condition for the possibility of theological understanding: *Systematic Theology*, I, pp. 238–239.

Similarly, critical reason, in its attempt to do justice to the phenomena, tends to cast its statements into descriptive statements of fact, presented as the only legitimate and reliable form of human understanding. This leads, again, to serious consequences. On the one hand, critical reason tends to present its findings as true, and hence it tends to establish them as the norm for what could possibly be meant by the divinity of Jesus. What starts as an attempt at description ends as the setting of a very restrictive norm. Again, the examples of this tendency in christology are numerous, starting with Paul of Samosata's presentation of Jesus as prophet to the various types of christological reductionism (the perfect religious genius, the teacher of the perfect religion, the source of contagious freedom, etc.). All these theories represent the domination of critical reason over faith in the person of Christ as the bearer of a mystery beyond verification. They all tend to downplay the significance of the absolute claims of the christological *kērygma* in the name of low christology and safeguarding the humanity of Christ. Is not what is upheld here merely critical reason's need for particularity in knowing the truth, rather than the person of Christ?[85]

We conclude that what looks like a discussion of the union of God and man in Jesus Christ is very often little more than the spectacle of a fight of reflective against critical reason, of the mind at odds with itself. Theologians will often call for compromises, as in John McIntyre's *The Shape of Christology*, where the relativity of *all* christological constructs is compellingly argued, or in John Knox's *The Humanity and Divinity of Christ*,[86] where christologies are rightly presented as *patterns* of understanding. But compromises, which keep the mind from making war on itself, also leave it restless and filled with doubt. What *will* reconcile reflection and recollection, and hence the person of Christ as apprehended by reflective reason, and the same person as apprehended by critical reason? Not an uneasy truce, a settlement *between* reflection and recollection, but a placing of *both* in the light of the *actus directus* of faith in Christ alive in the Spirit.

---

[85]A brilliant and totally irresponsible presentation of the tyranny of christologies high and low in Malachi Martin, *Jesus Now*, New York, E. P. Dutton & Co., 1973.

[86]Cambridge, Cambridge University Press, 1967.

This brings us to the end of the second part of this book. In the third part we will, in a series of six chapters, develop a christological synthesis that will be characterized by two features.

First, it will be developed out of the *actus directus* of worship. The fact of the Church's worship of Christ was the main *locus* for Athanasius' argument that Jesus Christ is consubstantial with the Father. All of christology should go back to worship as the only adequate human response to the Resurrection.

Second, it will be shown that a christology developed out of worship will lead to the development of the triple rhetoric of hope, obedience, and inclusion in a double way. The person of Jesus himself will emerge as the source of hope, the way of obedience, and the ground for inclusion. But the Church, too, will emerge as the community of hope, as the obedient follower of Christ in patience, and as the divine warrant for openness to all things. Christology will thus not only be about Jesus Christ; it will also turn out to be an expression of the Church's own responsive identity.

Before we will do this, however, we will pause for a short interlude. It is designed to orchestrate the primacy of the *actus directus* in terms of the primacy of the future over the past. This in turn will be expressed in terms of the primacy of witness over document, of hearing over seeing, of faith over knowledge, and of grace over nature.

Interlude

CHAPTER 7

Present, Future, and Past

*Desiderium sinus cordis.**

Augustine of Hippo

The strange Gospel, not the familiar Gospel, will be the present Gospel.

Dietrich Bonhoeffer

Vision alone without acoustic perceptions does not provide understanding.

Clemens Benda

The grace of yesterday appears to have become the nature of today.

Piet Schoonenberg

For we have been saved, though only in hope. Now to see is no longer to hope: why should a man endure and wait for what he already sees? But if we hope for something we do not yet see, then, in waiting for it, we show our endurance.

The Letter of Paul to the Romans

---

*It is yearning that makes the heart deep.

Thought, inextricably bound up with words, is associated in a pre-literate culture not with a world where observation works dispassionately but with the dynamic, the interpersonal. [Modern] objectivity does not get involved in human values as such. This objectivity [. . .] becomes possible when one envisions the world as set off from oneself as essentially neuter. [. . .] Study of such a world is felt to be not a response to the world but an operation upon it.

Walter Ong

Introduction

A compromise is not enough, we said at the close of the sixth chapter,[1] to resolve the dilemma between quasi-Ebionite and quasi-Monophysite christologies. The former reflects the concerns of critical reason, the latter those of reflective reason; both must be placed in the context of the total surrender to Christ alive and present in the Spirit.

From the next chapter on we will argue—often implicitly, though sometimes explicitly—that both low christology and high christology operate on an implicit *common* assumption, namely *that present experience and present hope* must be accounted for and legitimized. This legitimation takes the shape of recollection (in the case of low christology) and reflection (in the case of high christology). In its search for historical particularity, critical reason does justice to the *humanum*; in its search for eternal fixity, reflective reason accounts for the divine. Both are functions of the human need for integrity in believing (*Wahrheitsgewissen*)—not only the latter, as Rahner seems to suggest.[2]

Both recollection and reflection have another thing in common, namely that they are *retrospective*. They seek to account for present experience by looking back. In the process of this retrospective legitimation, christological discernments arise.[3]

---

[1] Above, p. 261.

[2] Cf. above, pp. 217–220.

[3] We argued above (pp. 141–143) that discernments are doubly bound. What we are discovering now is that a discernment's bond with a human concern is retrospective, whereas its bond with the act of worship and witness is prospective, as we will argue in the present chapter.

Discernments, we have argued,[4] must be placed in the setting of the total surrender, which is the Christian's all-encompassing, responsive experience of Christ present in the Spirit. The recollection and reflection that produce critical and reflective christologies build upon this experience, which involves the *actus directus* of faith.[5]

In this chapter, we will begin to argue that the *actus directus* of faith is *a present experience of prospect*, and that any christology, be it of the reflective or of the critical kind, must be placed in an eschatological perspective.

For the time being we will do no more than orchestrate this to some extent. Our thesis is that we experience the present in two ways. The original experience of the present is one which occurs in the light of the future—*sub specie futuri*. The derivative experience of the present is one which occurs in the light of the past—*sub specie praeteriti*. The latter experience is reliable only if it is subordinated to the former. Christological recollection and reflection, therefore, are only reliable if they are subordinated to eschatological christology.

It will be the task of the rest of this book to elaborate the eschatological features of the Resurrection, and the dependence of recollection and reflection on the Resurrection. The present chapter will proceed on a somewhat broader basis. We will argue the primacy of witness over document, hearing over seeing, faith over knowledge and grace over nature. We will do this by suggesting that the former of these pairs involve an experience of the present *sub specie futuri*, whereas the latter involve an experience of the present *sub specie praeteriti*. Thus, it is hoped, the intellectual atmosphere will be set for the third part of this book.

A final caution. The words "intellectual atmosphere" and "orchestrate" are used intentionally. The present chapter is interested in presenting orientations and perspectives rather than rigorous argument. It paints on a wide canvas with a broad brush. It means to suggest dimensions rather than argue points. This means that it appeals to the reader's empathy to a greater extent than has been done in this book so far.

---

[4]Above, pp. 126–129, 137–141.
[5]Cf. above, pp. 254–261.

WITNESS AND DOCUMENT

Bonhoeffer on the experience of the present

In the lecture on the re-presentation of scriptural texts quoted in the previous chapter[6] Bonhoeffer asks what it is that makes the present the present. He answers, relying heavily on etymology:[7]

> Here the *idea of present* (*Gegenwart*) is first brought out to full advantage, also in the language. That which "comes to meet us" (*uns "entgegen" ist*)—that which waits for us (*entgegen wartet*)—bespeaks, obviously, that *present is determined from the outside* and not from the inside; that it is not determinable by us; that it is determined by what comes to us (*auf uns zukommt*) from the outside, by the coming to us (*das Zukommen*), by the future (*die Zukunft*). Present is primarily determined, not by the past, but by the *future*, and this future is Christ, is the Holy Spirit. "Re-presentation" means, therefore, that a person is directed toward this *future*, toward this *outside*—and it is a most fatal confusion of present and past to think that present can be defined as that which rests *in itself* and *bears its criterion within itself.* The criterion of the true present lies outside itself, lies in the future, lies in Scripture and in the Word of Christ which Scripture testifies to. And so it is that realism [in exegesis] will consist in this: an outside reality, the reality which comes to encounter us, the reality of "the future" comes to be heard as present—the strange Gospel, not the familiar Gospel will be the present Gospel. Here's where the scandal starts![8]

The moment of truth, and of the real experience of the present, therefore, is the moment when I am unexpectedly presented with a reality outside me—the presence of Christ in the living Word. When texts from Scripture thus surprise me, true and authentic re-presentation occurs.

Inauthentic re-presentation, by contrast, occurs *when present concerns become the norm for understanding the Scriptures.* This usually happens when it is pointed out that there is an element of

---

[6]Above, pp. 247–249.

[7]Bonhoeffer's etymologizing—a favorite device in German philosophy and theology—has no probative force. The etymological relations between the significant words and terms in the following quotation support the argument; they do not make the point. Hence, though the etymology cannot be reproduced in English, the point can be made.

[8]*Gesammelte Schriften*, III, pp. 307–308 (cf. *No Rusty Swords*, pp. 306–307).

eternity in these writings which is still valid today; thus the *past* becomes the norm for understanding the Scriptures. Bonhoeffer complains:

> In history, it is then said, there is something *eternal*, in contingency there is something necessary, in the individual and the particular there is a universal meaning. This meaning, this element of eternity may be a doctrine, it may be an ethical norm, it may be a universal human feeling, it may be a myth. Re-presentation consists in *discovering* this element of eternity, this meaning, this essence, which is as valid today as it was then.[9]

An interpreter who thus proceeds starts by telling apart, in the text of Scripture, God's Word from human word—a seemingly plausible move. But there is a snake in the grass, for it is implied that human reason can tell what is divine and what is not. What is really happening is that present concerns—reasons, conscience, *Volksempfinden*, contemporary experience, etc.—determine what is eternal and what is not. Bonhoeffer sums up the basis of this false approach.

> The criterion for the Word of God lies outside it, in us—*the norm of re-presentation lies with us, and the Bible is the subject-matter to which this norm is applied.*[10]

Under such assumptions, present and effective meaning is constituted by contemporary concerns and discernments working upon documents from the past.[11] Thus what is really true is *my* or *our*—usually very selective—reading of Scripture; *I* or *we* show that Scripture says something to the present situation. Modern man demonstrates that a document from the past has a bearing on the present, including today's aspirations and plans for the future. Thus Scripture becomes concrete and relevant when the "with it" preacher, moralist, or theologian *applies* it to the present situation. In this way, present concerns have become the norm for understanding

---

[9]*Ibid.*, p. 309 (cf. ET, p. 308).
[10]*Ibid.*, p. 311 (cf. ET, p. 309).
[11]For this point, cf. above, pp. 193, 252.

the Scripture, and a false sense of the present relevance of Scripture has been achieved.

Bonhoeffer is unequivocal in his rejection of this method. He writes:

> Now this thesis must be completely reversed, if our idea of exegesis and re-presentation is to become clear: the norm of the Word of God in Scripture is the Word of God itself, and the givens of our situation, our reason, our conscience, our experience as a people are the subject-matter to which this norm seeks to apply itself. [. . .] This has consequences for the method of re-presentative exegesis: it should not approach Scripture as a book in which universal truths, universal ethical norms or myths can be discovered; rather, sacred Scripture as a whole is, to exegesis, *the witness* of God in Christ, and it will be the concern of exegesis to make the witness-character of the Word audible in every passage. Basically there are no privileged passages, unless the expression is taken to refer merely to the clarity of the witness-character. *Representation does not take place through selection of certain texts, but by making the whole of sacred Scripture audible as the witness of the Word of God.*[12]

The true experience of the present, therefore, occurs when in Scripture I encounter a presence which I do not control, and which addresses me on its own terms and on its own authority—that is to say, when I experience Scripture as *witness*—a testimony in which persons touched by God address themselves to me and, through them, God himself.[13]

Experience of witness as experience of newness

The experience of witness is not limited to the acceptance of Scripture as God's address to me. Whenever I am confronted by a reality that comes unannounced but announcing, I experience, not only the reality that meets me, but also myself as I rise to the encounter. Though I may have anticipated it, in the actual encounter the reality proves to be different from my anticipations; thus I experience, not only the really real, but also the discrepancy between my past self (which provided the material for the anticipation) and

---

[12]*Gesammelte Schriften*, III, pp. 311–312 (cf. *No Rusty Swords*, pp. 309–310).
[13]For our analysis of this, cf. above, pp. 228–232.

my real self as it reveals itself to me in my *present* act of response to the reality that meets me. Reality has a knack for putting my anticipations, and hence my self with my appropriated past, on the spot. The result of the encounter is that I experience, not only a new reality, but also a new, responsive self, actuated by the encounter.[14]

It is in the nature of witness, precisely because I cannot manipulate or calculate it, to do justice to me: it draws forth my true self with an actuality that I could never muster up by myself. Thus witness dissolves my need for self-maintenance and self-justification. To the extent that I am untrue to myself I am unmasked but also restored to myself; to the extent that I am true to myself I need no longer claim my own righteousness.[15] In the presence of witness I become present to myself, and I experience this presence, not as an act of my sovereign self claiming my past, but as a gift which actualizes me by giving me, with my past, to myself, while opening me to the future.

I become my true self even if I reject the witness. Rejecting witness is more than saying it is false; it is refusing to be addressed by the person who bears witness, and hence it is refusing to enter into a new responsive identity. But there's the rub. The irony of such an act of rejection is precisely that I *respond*: the rejection of the witness is drawn forth from me by the address, and thus the act of rejection is an act of my *present* self in a capacity that exceeds my self as establishable with reference to the past. Even the rejection of witness involves an experience of newness.

Any response to witness, therefore, actualizes the self in a response which is not entirely accounted for by the past; this means that the experience of witness is related to the experience of the future. Let us analyze how this occurs.

Experience of witness as experience sub specie futuri
    What makes witness what it is? One decisive characteristic of witness certainly is that it cannot be calculated. Not what I already

---

[14]In applied behavioral science this is expressed in terms of risk-taking and project-orientation. Cf., among many others, Samuel A. Culbert, *It Takes Two To See One.*
    [15]Cf. above, pp. 164–165.

know about myself on the basis of the past as I own and control it, but the word that comes from elsewhere becomes the norm of truth. Witness establishes my identity in a new and actual way, and thus I experience this new identity as coming, not out of the past but out of the future.

When Bonhoeffer insists that Scripture must be received as witness he means the same. Not what I make of Scripture, but what Scripture makes of me constitutes the truth[16]—a truth experienced as actual and present precisely because it meets me out of the unknown, out of the future. The strange Gospel, not the familiar one.

Scripture as witness and living address is only part of the living address constituted by the risen Christ. His presence in the Spirit is the appeal that invites me *now* to total surrender, in and through *and beyond* all my concerns and discernments. My response to the living Christ involves a progressively new responsive identity: I am always invited anew to become who I am not, so that I may be my true self. Thus Christian identity is always experienced *sub specie futuri.* The future is the perspective in which the reality of Christ alive and present in the Spirit is primarily experienced.

Witness and document

What holds true for Scripture also holds true for the tradition; both must be primarily received as appeals to the faith-surrender and to the new responsive identity that the living Lord holds out, as an abiding promise, to those who so respond to him. Both can be so received because the presence of the living Lord called them into being in the first place; if I receive them as appeals I treat them in accordance with their very nature. It is of course possible to mistake them for mere documents from the past (which they obviously *also* are); but only when they are perceived in the context of the appeal coming from Jesus Christ present in the Spirit do they show their true nature, namely, their being witness and appeal to surrender from a future out of which the dead are made to live and things that are not are summoned up as existing.[17] The *actus directus* of faith takes its bearings from the future.

---

[16]Cf. above, pp. 235–247.
[17]Cf. Rom 4, 17.

We must, therefore, distinguish between Scripture and the tradition as documents reflecting the discernments of the past, and as enactments of the freedom in speaking which conveys the *actus directus* of faith. This latter quality causes them to be more than mere documents: they are primarily acts of responsive, worshipful witness to the presence of Christ in the Spirit, who is the presence of the things to come. In this way Scripture and the tradition also appeal to the Christian now to surrender in worship and witness. In this way, too, the Scriptures and the dogmatic tradition are not a closed holy book or a definitive collection of eternal truths, but a *canon*, a touchstone for testing subsequent discernments. What gives them *authority* is primarily the act of speaking which they embody—their responsiveness, in total commitment, to the presence of God. By contrast, the favorite temptation of all ecclesiastical establishments is: to place the authority of the Scriptures and the doctrinal tradition in the past, in the book, in the conciliar pronouncements, *taken by themselves*.

In the Protestant establishment, with its strong cultural admixture of humanist *philologia sacra*, the original meaning of Scripture became normative,[18] but without much explicit reference to the present act of faith in Christ present now. In the Catholic establishment with its strong emphasis on the *magisterium*, characteristically legitimized by means of an appeal to the *past*, to apostolic succession with its guarantee of assistance from the Holy Spirit, the doctrinal deposit of faith came to overshadow the act of faith.[19] Neither Protestants nor Catholics have realized sufficiently that the discernments enshrined in Scripture and in the doctrinal tradition are embedded in the surrender to Christ conveyed by the *parrhēsia* of the apostolic

---

[18]There is a clear connection between the Protestant emphasis upon the Word of Scripture and the humanist discovery of literary and textual method; for Erasmus and many others, theology was identical with "sacred philology," against the philosophical discussions of the scholastics. Still, the Protestant rediscovery of Scripture did not succeed in restoring to its rightful place the ancient *lectio divina*—the reading of Scripture precisely in the light of the *present* experience of the Spirit.

[19]This amounted to an emphasis on the content of faith ("*id quod creditur*") at the expense of the *act* of faith ("*fides qua creditur*"), and to a massively historicist interpretation of the canon of Vincent of Lerins, "*quod semper, quod ubique, quod ab omnibus [creditum est]*": Christians must believe what has been believed "always, everywhere, and by all."

and post-apostolic Church. If, then, we want to understand Scripture and the tradition according to their deepest intentions, we must treat them as *witnesses* placing us in the truth out of the future. Only then will we be able to appreciate them appropriately as documents from the past. Seen in this way, the scholarly discovery that the Scriptures came out of a largely *oral* tradition attains theological significance: they are the products of people bearing witness to the presence of Christ in living speech before they are documents that enshrine their discernments.[20] In this context Rahner's characterization of dogma as rules of *speech* can also gain some relevance.[21] The expression points to the fact that doctrine does indeed lay down the *structures* of theological speaking, but it does not of itself account for the loving urgency with which the believer actually feels the call to speak out.

In this section we have characterized the *actus directus* of faith as an act set in the context of witness and as an act that attains its characteristic quality from its eschatological orientation. Both witness and future orientation are prompted by the living Christ present in the Spirit; the interpretation of Scripture and tradition, and all christological reflection and recollection, must remain mindful of the primacy of witness and of the eschatological perspective if they are to remain true to the *actus directus* of faith.

HEARING AND SEEING—FAITH AND KNOWLEDGE

Cognition and the creation of distance

The dimensions of prospect and retrospect in christology appear not only in the relationship between "witness" and "document" but also in two other, related sets of notions, namely hearing—seeing and faith—knowledge.

---

[20]For related insights, cf. Walter J. Ong's highly original "*Maranatha:* Death and Life in the Text of the Book," *Journal of the American Academy of Religion* 45 (1977) 419–449.—All this has implications for the translation of Scripture. The experts who rendered the perfectly obvious and confident phrase, "For no one of us lives for himself and no one dies for himself" (Rom 14, 7) by the "clear" phrase, "The life and death of each of us has its influence on others" (*Jerusalem Bible, in loco*), made a *theological* mistake, for the *authority* of the passage lies precisely in its tone of voice.

[21]Cf. above, pp. 36–37, and note 10.

We may recall that when we cognitively structure lived experience we make use of the reifying, representative[22] nature of words; words function as semantically constant units of meaning quite apart from situations. Words enable us to create distance between ourselves and the elements that make up situations, to put ourselves at one remove from them, and in that sense to transcend them cognitively. We pointed out that there is already some kind of cognitive transcendence involved in naming; perception, which occurs in *Gestalts*, is already a prelude to cognition proper in that in perception we already place certain units of perception against a background of multiple other things not properly *perceived*. Thus the word as name already enables us to create some distance between us and the situation in which we are involved. If we then proceed to consider words apart from the situations in which they occur it becomes even clearer that words help us create distance: they have a constant meaning apart from any situation.

Is there any relevance to the fact that not until we begin to consider the meaning of words do the cognitive properties of language come into sharp focus? We suggest there is. The reifying, representative nature of words enables us to take some *measured distance* from the *data* presenting themselves to our perceptual and cognitive structuring ability, but it also allows us to take some distance from *our own* spontaneous, egological behavior. The representative nature of words enables us to act as knowers and allows us to structure reality cognitively, as we argued in a previous chapter.[23] We now add that the process by which this is achieved consists in the *implicit creation of distance*. This leads us to our next step, namely, that distance and seeing are related.

---

[22]It may be useful to recall that we may have come to use this term in three different ways by now. "Representative" refers to a *word*'s ability to refer to a reality outside us regardless of situations (above, pp. 87–88). It also means "deputizing for someone" (above, p. 247 and note 52). Thirdly—spelled "re-presentative" (with the cognate noun "re-presentation") and pronounced accordingly—it means "of actual importance now" (above, pp. 247–249).

[23]Cf. above, pp. 87–90.

Cognition, visualization and spatialization[24]

In his analysis of the dimensions of language Verhaar refers to the "cognitive primacy of visual categories." Furthermore, on the assumption that there is a correlation between seeing and spatiality, Verhaar develops his theory to include the thesis of the "cognitive primacy of spatial categories."[25] Let us pursue these suggestions for a while.

Sight, like knowledge, is indeed strongly characterized by *distance*; I cannot see what is too close, yet my eyesight does reach to the horizon. Sight is further characterized by *selectivity*; I have eyes only in the front, I can turn my head, I can choose to close my eyes. I must actively focus in order to see well. When I focus on something, I relegate the rest of what is within my purview to peripheral vision. Thus we can say for vision what we have said for cognitive structuring: both are processes of negotiation. Only so much of our lived experience is amenable to our cognitive construct;[26] only so much of what there is to see is amenable to focus. Both seeing and knowing are characterized by distance and selectivity.

Verhaar further elaborates the affinity between knowing and seeing by means of two illustrations. First, there is a tendency to *visualize sounds* for the purposes of study. Thus, in order to determine which sound-modifications of spoken language are relevant to intelligibility, a laboratory experiment was set up by which a number of different speakers pronounced certain words. The sounds thus obtained were fixated by means of a spectrograph. The common features of the visual renderings of the variously pronounced words were then isolated and the visual pattern thus obtained was translated back into sound; it turned out that a high degree of intelligibility could be achieved even though the sounds had been stripped of many of their sound characteristics in the process of retranslation. What is interesting for our purpose is not so much the result obtained as the assumptions behind the method. It is assumed that visualization is called for when we engage in the reflexive procedure

---

[24]For the following, cf. J. Verhaar, *Some Relations*, pp. 26–43, 75–81, and the literature referred to there.

[25]*Ibid.*, pp. 38, 39.

[26]Cf. above, p. 90.

of analyzing structures and components of speech as it is spoken and heard.[27]

Verhaar alleges a second example to show the affinity between cognition and visualization. Few things are so notoriously difficult to conceptualize as time.[28] To do this we use a spatializing device: the clock.

We may start with the everyday indication of time that we all know: that of the clock. A clock visualizes time. Via a mechanism which, spatially speaking, combines the cyclic with the regular, abstraction is made from any manner in which we might experience time more or less spontaneously, affectively: here, too, we are in the cognitive order. And it is clear that whenever we attempt a determination of time we do so in terms of categories that are primarily spatial. To determine time we have recourse to measurement. In our idiom we cannot help using words with spatial connotation and this seems so perfectly obvious that we hardly stop to realize that indication of time cannot take place unless by spatializing conversion. We call a length of time "long" or "short," a unit of time "small" or "great." We speak of the "far" future, of "long" ago, of the time "before" and "behind" us, of the "course" of time. We "see" what the time is and when, for lack of a clock, a watch or the position of the sun, we have to estimate the time, we try to abstract from any spontaneous experience of time (which, otherwise, may, in this case too, have seemed "long" or "short"), in order to "measure" it "objectively" by estimating the duration of our walk, nap, or whatever we have been doing. Estimating the time is a more or less successful attempt to "measure" it. Likewise, when we "fixate" a certain moment, local "there" spontaneously strikes us as analogous to temporal "then" (in past or future) and "now" is primarily "here" (cf. "*hic et nunc*," "there and then"); it is called "present" in eloquent homonymy. And so we might go on.[29]

Summing up: there is a strong affinity between seeing and knowledge; spontaneously we lean toward visualization and spatialization when intelligibility is called for. The experience of know-

---

[27]J. Verhaar, *Some Relations*, pp. 36–38.

[28]Cf. *ibid.*, p. 40: "There is an *irreflexive* knowledge of time which does not give us the slightest problem so long as reflection is not called for. Here we are made to think of a famous passage of Augustine: 'What, then, is time? When no one asks me I know; but when I am asked to explain what it is, I do not know any longer' (*Confessions*, XI, 14, 17)."

[29]*Ibid.*, p. 39.

ing something is closely related to the experiences of seeing, of being in space, and of distance. This means, as we will see, it appears to us *sub specie praeteriti*.

Cognitive retrospect

We know from everyday experience that we can see something better according as it is less in motion. We can obviously also see something that moves; in fact, sometimes movement is necessary: a relatively small object is visible against a fixed background only when it moves. But when it comes to focusing, not noticing, moving objects are harder to concentrate on than motionless ones, and we see them better if they are at a certain distance—they seem to move less. Thus ordinary seeing already betrays a certain preference for fixity.

This preference becomes a demand when we engage in that particular, specialized form of seeing which is the sustained look. When we want to have a good look, or an ideal view—whether of a painting or of an object of scientific study—*we*, or at least our eyes, may move, but the object must stand still. This implies that sight also has an affinity with the past: the clearer the vision we want to have, the more dependent we are on the object's stabilization before we can have a good look, and on its remaining this way while we look. The greater our preference for fixity in seeing, the greater our inclination to see the present in the perspective of the past.

Also in this respect seeing is analogous to knowing. Knowing, especially knowing with certainty, relates to the present by appealing to the past. We can observe this when something slips our mind and we hear ourselves say: "What *was* that *again*?" The same characteristic turn to the past is found in Aristotle's definition of the concept *ousia*, by which we express our knowledge of what something really is; he uses the *past* tense: *to ti ēn einai*:[30] the fact that something is what it *was*.[31] We know a thing's "nature" (Latin *natura*, from

---

[30]*Metaphysics*, 1017^{b}22. The phrase must be construed as an absolute infinitive with a "philosophic" imperfect, to denote the original essence (the "what was it?"): William Watson Goodwin, *Syntax of the Moods and Tenses of the Greek Verb*, Boston, Ginn and Company, 1893, pp. 13, 312.

[31]Aristotle adds: *hou ho logos horismos*: "of which the word (functions as) the definition"—which shows clearly that he is operating at the level of what we have called consideration of language.

nascor, to be born); the Greek equivalent of nature is *physis* (from Greek *phyō*, to generate, to grow), which, again according to Aristotle, is a being's principle—its beginning, from the Latin *principium*—of motion and rest;[32] when Genesis has set forth what the world is all about, it sums up: "These are the generations (*tôl^edôt*, related to *yālad*, to generate) of the heavens and the earth."[33] Certain knowledge appears to us in terms of substantial, stable fixity in retrospect.

Seeing and knowing as partial

We have already argued a number of times that all discernments in christology are partial.[34] We have also pointed out that they represent familiar shared concerns that have been integrated into the total surrender to Christ.[35] We can now see more of a connection between these two: christological discernments represent the past. They are provisional and must be treated as such. They may not monopolize or qualify the surrender;[36] that means that they may not become more important than the future, out of which new discernments must be continually added to the old.

The connection between knowing and seeing is reflected, in the Christian tradition, by a strong emphasis on the partiality of seeing. From Paul's insistence on the incompleteness of our sight and on the eternity of things invisible, and from the Fourth Gospel's blessing on those who believe without seeing,[37] Christians through the ages have learned to reserve the metaphor of sight for the beatific vision—when at last we will see as we are seen and know as we are known. What seeing is available to the Christian in the present is by the light of faith, by the enlightened eyes of the heart,[38] not by direct intuition.

Faith, prospect, and hearing

The New Testament is far less reserved about the possibilities

---

[32]Cf., for example, *Metaphysics*, 1014^b16, *Physics*, 192^b21ff.: *archē kinēseōs kai staseōs*.

[33]Gen 2, 4.

[34]Cf., for example, above, pp. 189–191, 198–200.

[35]Above, pp. 135–143.

[36]Above, pp. 126–129.

[37]1 Cor 13, 12; 2 Cor 4, 18; Jn 20, 29.

[38]Eph 1, 18; note the reference to hope.

of hearing than about those of seeing. The Word can be heard; there are preachers to address people; faith is from hearing.[39] This emphasis on the living word involves an emphasis on the concrete situation as the setting in which faith occurs; we will come back to this in a discussion of what we will call the "proximity" features of hearing. But the emphasis on the living word also involves an emphasis on the direct experience of speech, and hence on language as activity in a situation rather than as an instrument of cognitive transcendence. It involves an emphasis on rhetoric.[40]

The difference between the Hellenistic tradition and Christianity is most obvious on this point. For Plato, for instance, reliable knowledge is achieved by concentration on the eternal and stable nature (*ousia*) of things, which makes them amenable to rigorous discourse. Situations are but part of the flux of becoming (*genesis*), and the knowledge proportionate to situations can never exceed the status of opinions (*doxa, pistis*); the latter are achieved by means of persuasion and rhetoric—tools in the hands of orators who "cause people to have whatever opinions they (i.e., the orators) want them to have." Those opinions have as much standing as images and shadows (*eikosiai*).[41] Christians, on the other hand, were to use the very words *doxa* and *pistis* to denote what was most certain and reliable: the radiance of God's glory and its reflection in the world, and the faith that gives access to them. But both occur in the flesh and in the context of personal encounter at close quarters, not in an ideal, eternal order of transcendent knowledge. There *is* knowledge and stability and vision involved in Christian faith, but they are firmly subordinated to faith and prospect and hearing. Let us further explore the affinity between the latter three.

Interpersonalness and affectivity

In the direct experience of speech we tend not to advert to the representative nature of words. When I converse with another per-

---

[39]Cf. Rom 10, 14–18.

[40]Cf. above, pp. 93–98, 101–102, 115–116.

[41]Cf. *Timaeus* 29 c: "As reality is to becoming, so is truth to belief." Cf. also *Theaetetus* 201 a 8; *Republic* 510 a 9, 511 e 1; *Gorgias* 453 a. For a commentary on these passages, cf. E. R. Dodds (ed.), *Gorgias*, Oxford, Oxford University Press, 1959, p. 206.

son, what I say or hear strikes me primarily as interpersonal—my utterance and his or hers in response to mine. The point, the interpersonal meaningfulness, is paramount; neither I nor my partner pays attention to the meaning of individual words, and we resent hairsplitting and rationalization, because "you are not talking to *me*." This interpersonal quality even obtains, analogously, in the case of other sounds. When we hear a noise our acoustical attention tends to be drawn to the *source* rather than to the sound itself. In the experience of sound *I* feel "struck" by *something else*; I am experientially united with, rather than separated from, the agent I hear. I experience the other as near. At a symphony concert or a poetry recital, where sounds are aesthetically structured, my acoustical attention does indeed tend to focus on the sound rather than the source, but even there the source is far from irrelevant—the record or the radio is never quite the same as the live performers. When I go to hear a famous author give a scholarly exposition, and the lecture, or the delivery, or both, turn out to be surprisingly bad, I will still have that strange sensation that I have heard the renowned so-and-so, even though, as far as my knowledge of the content of the lecture is concerned, I feel I might as well have read it (visually, silently!) for myself, or, as the case may be, not at all. And we know how an excellent speaker can be a barrier to understanding. The ear is easily lured into the interpersonal dimensions of a situation, to the source of the sounds, at the expense of objectivity and detached knowledge. No matter how profound and interesting the lecture, I may have trouble remembering what was said, because he or she spoke so well.

In conclusion, just as there is a cognitive primacy to visual categories, so there is an *affective, interpersonal primacy to acoustical categories*; this affective and interpersonal quality persists even if my attention is primarily directed to the aesthetic structure or the meaning of what is said or sounded.

Proximity of the other—distraction-experience

The affective, interpersonal primacy of sounds is connected with another feature of hearing, namely, that the limit of my acoustical world is far less remote than my visual horizon. The eye reaches much farther than the ear. Within my visual horizon I can, as a matter of principle, see everything except what is too close; what I hear has to be within earshot, and sounds must be extremely loud to be audible from afar. The ambit of my hearing is relatively small, and sometimes I will have to enhance the sound by moving closer to the source of the sound, even to the point of touching it with my ear. But even without moving close, *what* I hear, I hear as close: the ear is open and sounds penetrate. I see lightning in the distance but the thunderclap strikes me here.

Hearing as such is characterized by *proximity*, and what distance-features it may have are easily outweighed by the fact that we always are personally, "egologically" affected when we hear. This is not only true subjectively—hearing is strongly affective and personal—but also objectively: sounds tend to have emotional overtones to a much greater extent than colors do. When we want to say that a certain color does have a strong emotional impact, we will call it, characteristically, "loud" or "soft"; the acoustical is much closer to the tactile than the visual, and the tactile is the sense of proximity par excellence. The human voice has a special ability to convey proximity-elements—elements that make a situation personal; those elements are part of the total meaning of an utterance, yet cannot be captured by the objective meaning of the statement.[42] In good acoustical fashion, we refer to these conexperiential elements as overtones, just as Ian Ramsey, in his discussion of the way models work, uses a spatial metaphor—"isomorphism"—when he talks about the cognitive function of a model, but an acoustical one—"chime in with and echo the phenomena"—when he conveys how models are in touch with reality.[43]

The affective and interpersonal proximity-character of hearing can be demonstrated in many ways;[44] here we will only treat one telling example, namely the difference between visual and acoustical

---

[42]The difference between the total meaning of an utterance and the objective meaning of the statements can become enormous in the case of a printed text. Not everything that has been attributed to Machiavelli will be found on a more empathetic reading of *The Prince*; when the overtone of pathos of this work is missed, it becomes a collection of crudities.

[43]*Models and Mystery*, p. 12.

[44]For a superb exploration of the history of the sensorium, cf. Walter J. Ong, S.J., *The Presence of the Word*, New York, Simon and Schuster, 1970.—Cf. also Cardinal Newman's motto "*Cor ad cor loquitur*": "Heart speaks to heart," for an expression that associates interiority with an acoustical experience.

distraction experiences. The relevance of the experience of distraction to our present discussion is that distraction is a proximity-experience: I am involved with something I did not intend to be involved with—an unintended element is part of my situation. According to our analysis so far we can anticipate a difference between visual and acoustical distraction. Visual distraction occurs. We can, for example, be distracted from the object we are looking at because something within our peripheral vision is moving. We may want to defend ourselves against such distractions. For better concentration, for instance in study, we tend to subdue the visual environment: there is nothing like a dark room with a single light on the book that I am intently reading. Another cause of visual distraction is an inappropriate background, which can make it difficult and even next to impossible to focus properly on the object we want to focus on. A tasteless frame or garish wallpaper can prevent us from seeing a painting on the wall. Visual distraction occurs when I (gnostically) concentrate on an object; it is always a distraction from *something*—the thing I am focusing on.[45]

Sounds, however, have a much greater power to distract. Our ears lack lids or lenses with which to shut out sounds, to select, and to focus. This undefended openness of the ear is matched by the affective and personal quality of sound and the suggestion of proximity; all the elements combined account for the fact that acoustical distraction is hard to resist—hearing creates almost no distance, so that even faraway sounds can be surprisingly and annoyingly distracting. Whereas visual distraction is almost entirely limited to instances of cognitive or artistic concentration, auditory distraction is almost universal.

The two differ in yet another way. Visual distraction detracts from the *object's* availability to our contemplation and attention,

---

[45]The term "gnostic" and its counterpart "pathic," also used by J. Verhaar, *Some Relations*, are borrowed from Felix Mayer, *Schöpferische Sprache und Rhythmus*, in which visual experience is characterized as distantial (*Augenferne*) and acoustical experience as proximate (*Erlebnisnähe*). J. H. van den Berg, *Het menselijk lichaam*, I, pp. 217–225 (following F. J. J. Buytendijk, *De vrouw*, Utrecht–Brussel, Uitgeverij Het Spectrum, 1951, p. 204) also associates vision with gnostic elements, and, in addition, suggests that a gnostic way of looking is more typical of men than women in our civilization. There is an American translation of Buytendijk's book: *Woman: A Contemporary View*, Glen Rock, N.J., Newman Press, 1968.

whereas in acoustical distraction it is primarily *ourselves* that, we feel, suffer from the intrusion. It is true that the siren of the police car also objectively drowns out the symphony I am listening to on my stereo, but my *primary* response is: Why can't they let *me* listen? This becomes even clearer when what I want to hear is nothing. If the telephone rings when I am meditating, or my neighbors play Beethoven while I try to write an article, or a fighter-bomber crashes through the cool air over a quiet lakeside on a summer evening, then I experience the affective, egological, pathic nature of sound all too well. Whereas visual distraction is always a distraction away from an object of attention, acoustical distraction also occurs when sound intrudes on, and in some cases even rapes, the rich fullness of silence; hence it affects my privacy, myself, rather than an object of attention. When silence itself feels boring, oppressive or anxiety-provoking, *I* need distraction; the characteristic remedy is to turn the radio on, sometimes as loud as possible, and then do something else. I need not listen, but only hear the sound to be assured that I am not alone. Again we see that sounds have the ability to distract or divert me in a quasi-personal fashion away from myself rather than from something I pay attention to. This point leads us to another characteristic of acoustical experience.

Hearing and time-experience—patience

Everyone knows the story about the man in bed in his hotel room getting progressively enraged as he is waiting for the other shoe to drop overhead. The joke illustrates not only the affective, interpersonal quality of acoustical experiences, it also illustrates the connection between hearing and time, a connection analogous to the one between vision and space. What keeps me listening to you is, curiously enough, what you *still* have to say, just as the shoe *not yet* dropped kept the man enraged and *waiting*. Like all sounds, speech moves in time; precisely by being not fixed but fugitive, speech makes the sensory experience of time possible. *Verba volant, scripta manent*[46] is usually said in defense of writing, but the volatile nature of speech has positive characteristics all its own. *I listen as the sound passes* from the unsounded future into the silent past; I listen *as* your

---

[46]"Words fly, writings are permanent."

words strike me in the present and pass, echo-less, into the voiceless past. An echo is so eerie because we expect speech to fly freely, not bounce back to us off spatial obstacles. *If* the word is meant to return to the speaker, it should do so with the fullness of an answer, not with the emptiness of a hollow echo.[47] Few sounds are as disconcerting and ill-recognizable as my own voice played back to me on a tape recorder. Call and response are the appropriate pair, not call and echo. The experience of time enters here again. Unlike an echo, whose lag is predictable, a response is unpredictable: I don't know *what* it will be, nor *when* and even *whether* it will come. But when it does come, it comes out of the *future*, out of the freedom of the other. Time-experience is experience of the future-becoming-actuality-for-me, and hearing is the sensory paradigm of this experience of prospect.

If hearing involves time-experience, it requires tolerance of successiveness. The impatient eye wants to take it all in, but the ear is patient. Everything that is sounded is *being* sounded; listening takes time; reliance on the future is patience in the present. A good listener lets the speaker finish, even though he may already have understood the problem, because he is aware of the personal dimensions of the situation.

Finally, just as there is a cognitive primacy to visual categories, there is a *fiducial* primacy to acoustical categories. Because the as-yet-unspoken keeps me listening, I must trust, wait, and hope. Because I want to speak, I must depend on another's continuing willingness to listen. Speech can convey the invitation to trust as well as trust itself. We may all know that there are more things in heaven and earth than are dreamt of in Horatio's philosophy and that there is more than meets the eye, yet every now and then we need to be assured that we *can* commit and entrust ourselves to that "more." Every child takes his first unsteady steps challenged as well as supported by the encouraging sounds of a human voice that inspires confidence.

There is a strong connection between hearing and faith. We tend to lean toward acoustical and temporal metaphors when trust and faith are called for. Faith-commitment as a *present actuality* is

---

[47]Cf. Is 55, 11!

an experience closely related to the acoustical, the temporal, the proximate, the interpersonal, the affective. It also is an experience *sub specie futuri*; the present certainty of faith is the certainty of assurance and confidence born from the appeal that comes to us out of the future.

We established earlier the primacy of the *actus directus* of faith as the Christian response to the living Lord.[48] We have discovered the affinity between faith, hearing, and the experience of prospect. We must again conclude that the primary act of faith in Christ alive and present in the Spirit will be future-oriented, and affective, interpersonal, and situational. Only in this setting will discernments (for all their partiality) and vision (despite its need for constant revision) remain true.

GRACE AND NATURE

Introductory

> The nature of man is given into his own hands, the culture of yesterday is the nature of today. Can this not also be said of grace? [...] The grace of yesterday seems to have become the nature of today.[49]

Schoonenberg's tentative suggestion, amounting to no more than an aside within the framework of his book *The Christ*, provides us with another opportunity to state the primacy of the *actus directus* of faith and its essential orientation toward the future, namely, by means of a brief discussion of the relationship between nature and grace. The relationship between nature and grace has been the subject of such numerous and extensive theological discussions and controversies that any attempt to do justice to the issue would require far more than the few pages we will devote to it. Our purpose is far more limited. The aim of the next few pages is to state that we experience grace as an encounter with the future and nature as a retrieval of the past.

Our guide will again be Dietrich Bonhoeffer. Let us start with his concern to unite in one conception the Barthian emphasis on the

---

[48]Above, pp. 232–239.
[49]P. Schoonenberg, *Hij is een God van mensen*, p. 30 (cf. *The Christ*, p. 36).

total freedom of grace and the Roman Catholic emphasis on the tradition.

Bonhoeffer: between actualism and naturalism

We have already had occasion to mention Bonhoeffer's early synthesis of "Act" and "Being" in his conception of the Church.[50] In an important passage, in which the word "Revelation" sums up the essence of the Christian faith, he excludes two extremes in order to arrive at his favorite identification of revelation and communion of persons in Christ. He writes:

> The reality of Revelation does not consist in a unique event in the past, in a reality which has no relationship with my old or new existence and which is fundamentally available to me, nor can the reality of Revelation be conceived of as the non-intentional act that is always free and pure, and which in every single case affects an individual existence. Rather, the reality of Revelation is the reality of the communion of persons, constituted and ratified by Christ, in which the individual, in every case, already finds himself in his new existence. In this way three things are safeguarded: 1. The reality of Revelation can be thought of as continuous. 2. It involves the very existence of the person. 3. It is possible to understand the reality of Revelation neither as objectified reality nor as non-objective unreality.[51]

On the one hand Bonhoeffer thus avoids the pure actualism of dialectical theology, in which God's freedom is so heavily emphasized that the fact that God has freely *committed* himself to the covenant is no longer recognized. Against all attempts to lock God up in his sovereignty—his *aseitas*—and to conceive of God's gracious self-revelation as so contingent and individualized as to make it impossible to speak of any real, abiding availability of grace *in* history, Bonhoeffer warns:

> God is free, not from man, but for man. Christ is the Word of God's freedom. God *is* there, i.e. not in eternal non-objectivity, but—let it be said in all provisionality—"haveable," available in his Word in the Church.[52]

---

[50]Above, p. 233.

[51]Dietrich Bonhoeffer, *Akt und Sein*, pp. 92–93 (cf. *Act and Being*, p. 123).

[52]*Ibid.*, p. 68 (cf. ET, pp. 90–91).

Yet on the other hand Bonhoeffer is equally emphatic when it comes to avoiding the opposite error, in which God's Revelation is presented as permanently and immediately available in the form of doctrine, unmediated religious experience, or institution, in which latter case there is the tendency, mainly in Catholicism, to represent "infused grace," administered by the ordained members of the Church, as a thoroughly objective *habitus entitativus*, so that ultimately the *person* need not be *existentially* affected by Revelation.[53]

The present experience of grace

We already know Bonhoeffer's insistence that Christian identity in the present is a response to the presence of Christ outside us. Now he goes on to point out that this experience of Christian identity derives from the future, not the past.

Revelation should only be conceived of in relation to Church, and Church is here regarded as constituted by means of the present proclamation of Christ's death and Resurrection in the community, through the community, for the community. The proclamation must be a present one, because it is only in this proclamation that the Revelation-event touches the community, and, secondly, because it is only in this fashion that Revelation shows itself as essentially contingent, i.e. it comes "from outside"; contingency is always a purely present experience. The past, as the sum of all that has happened, is fundamentally already set in a fixed context, but here the proclamation that "comes to encounter us" (the "future" proclamation) raises the past to the status of present actuality. If contingency is conceived of as an event that comes to meet us from outside, the present is determined by the future; in the framework of a system, in which Reason establishes the connections on the strength of the principle of the "before," the present is determined by the past. The present is determined either by the one or the other, or by both—it is never just there, in and of itself; but the decision is man's. Of Christian Revelation it must be said that the proclamation of cross and Resurrection (determined by eschatology and predestination) and its present effect raises the past to the present, to something—paradoxically speaking—that "comes to meet us out of the future." But from this it follows that the Christian Revelation must not be interpreted as something "that has happened"; this once-for-all event in the past is, for the person living in the Church at any given moment, precisely qualified as future.[54]

---

[53]Cf. *ibid.*, pp. 83ff. (cf. *Act and Being*, pp. 110–111).
[54]*Ibid.*, 89–90 (cf. ET, pp. 119–120). Bonhoeffer uses the same etymological

"Contingency" is one of Bonhoeffer's words for "grace." It refers to whatever cannot be fitted into a rational system, accounted for in terms of cause and effect or necessary inference; whatever must not be domesticated; whatever exceeds the possibilities and powers of the present as determined by the past. The unowed, contingent, gracious self-revelation of God is only experienced *in actu directo*, in the actual experience of unowed newness; even the gracious events of the past, and, most of all, the *ephapax*[55] of the fact of Jesus Christ, strike the believer as coming to meet him out of the *future*, brought home to him by the witness-character of the proclamation. Hence, grace is associated with the experience of the future. This is not only true in the sense that a religious experience, in which actual grace enters into my conscious awareness, strikes me as in no way proportionate to, or owed to, my present self or any of my legitimate expectations; in that sense God always shows himself as greater than I have ever believed him to be: *Deus semper major*.[56] But grace is also associated with the future in the sense that *the actual past events themselves*, and especially the factuality, once for all, of Jesus Christ, have the ability to strike me as something I can never take solid possession of, as something I will never quite know my way around in. The Incarnation is not finished; Jesus is still in agony till the world's end; without hope there is no faith now.

Nature and culture: an open past

What about nature? How is it associated with the experience of the past? Certainly not in the sense that the past adds up to a closed book that can be categorized and experienced as a closed system,

---

devices in this passage as in the passage quoted above, p. 268.—Bonhoeffer adds in a footnote: "On the basis of this idea it would be possible to elaborate a typically Christian philosophy of time, in opposition to the conception of time as counted with reference to motion." The latter half of this phrase is, of course, a reference to the Aristotelian definition of time as *numerus motus secundum prius et posterius*; we will venture a few remarks in the direction indicated by Bonhoeffer below, p. 340 and note 38.

[55]Cf. Rom 6, 10; Heb 7, 27; 9, 12; 10, 10. The Greek word means "once for all."
[56]Cf. Karl Rahner, "Being Open to God as Ever Greater," in: *Theological Investigations*, Vol. VII, New York, Herder and Herder, 1971, pp. 25–46; cf. also J. Moltmann, "Die Zukunft als neues Paradigma der Transzendenz," *Internationale Dialog-Zeitschrift* 1 (1969) 2–13 ("The Future as a New Paradigm of Transcendence").

entirely amenable to human control.[57] If, however, by nature is meant the whole complex of what is given, the whole context that is in principle available to human awareness and activity, the web of what is at humanity's disposal, then the connection with the past is obvious: what is (*natura*) is what has become (*quod natum est*). This is already true, as Teilhard de Chardin has so movingly elaborated,[58] for the development of the most primitive natural givens, through evolutionary processes of interiorization and complexification, into the organization of the biosphere. It becomes even more true when, in the process of hominization, nature reaches a new culmination-point in the noosphere, and thus begins to participate, in humanity, in that essential openness to the infinite that is the characteristic of human "nature." From that point on, natural law ceases to be merely a being's inner orientation toward endless repetition of its own patterned sameness, and starts to *include* mind, language, free choice, and love as interpersonal, and even supernatural, existentials.[59]

"Nature" thus understood, whether infrahuman or human or both, is essentially open and unfinished.[60] Its provisionality is not only due to its own ongoing inner-worldly evolutionary potential, but also, and especially, in that, in its climactic manifestation, humanity, all of nature is marshaled to meet the infinite, and to yearn for the encounter with God beyond all natural possibilities.

Wherever man has accepted the offer of grace in the past by taking the leap of faith into God's future, the results themselves remain open and turn into further challenges to faith. This implies

---

[57]Unless one subscribes to Cajetan's concept of nature; above, p. 66, note 2.

[58]For example, in: *The Divine Milieu*, An Essay on the Interior Life, New York, Harper & Brothers, 1960, and *The Phenomenon of Man*, with an introduction by Sir Julian Huxley, New York, Harper & Row, [2]1965.

[59]The expression "supernatural existential" is Karl Rahner's, and provides him with the basis of his transcendental method; cf. above, pp. 217–220, 226.

[60]One is reminded of Chesterton's whimsical remark that God is strong enough to exult in monotony, and that he says every morning "Do it again" to the sun. And he continues: "It may not be automatic necessity that makes all daisies alike; it may be that God makes every daisy separately, but has never got tired of making them. It may be that He has the eternal appetite of infancy; for we have sinned and grown old, and our Father is younger than we. The repetition in Nature may not be a mere recurrence; it may be a theatrical *encore*" (Gilbert K. Chesterton, *Orthodoxy*, New York/London, John Lane Company/John Lane, The Bodley Head, 1909, pp. 108–109).

that grace received in the past may never turn into a stable, settled establishment; the nature of the Church, for example, may never be separated from her vocation and mission. In fact, in view of the priority of grace over nature, and in view of the primacy of the Church's eschatological orientation, it has rightly been argued that the Church as an establishment is a function of her vocation and mission, and not vice versa.[61] Hence, all ecclesiastical self-righteousness, avaricious banking on the treasuries of past merits, inauthentic confidence in the possession of the truth—all these turn yesterday's grace into today's nature, conceived of as the tyranny of the system: nature as the closed book, the powers that be, the perfect premise with its unavoidable consequences—nature that justifies the knowing skepticism of "human nature being what it is," and the kind of unbelief that the New Testament associates with Pharisaism and self-sufficiency.[62]

Nature as available past

Past grace, past hopes and past process have made the world what it is today. Thus we experience the fixity of our present world—and, in that sense, nature—primarily in the light of the past, *sub specie praeteriti.* This is connected with our experience of the past as knowable—at least as a matter of principle—and better so, the more distant it is. It is then possible, so we say, to be more objective about it; the only thing that may be in the way of our knowledge is lack of evidence, but there are ways to retrieve much of that, too. Modern historical theory may have disposed of historicism and reinstated present interpretation to its rightful place, but there is no denying that history will continue, with the rigor of a true science, to

---

[61]Cf. J. C. Hoekendijk, *The Church Inside Out*, Philadelphia, The Westminster Press, 1965.

[62]Even though yesterday's sin is today's moral impotence, not even the results of failure are foreclosed. The effects of sin do not warrant despair or irresponsibility; rather they are calls to repentance, conversion and responsibility. This has even become an insight in psychotherapy; true healing occurs when a person starts to take responsibility for the disabling experiences inflicted upon him in the past, and ceases to blame his present inadequacies on the past. Cf. Herbert Fingarette, *The Self in Transformation*, Psychoanalysis, Philosophy, and the Life of the Spirit, New York–London, Basic Books, 1963.

try to find the facts as they actually happened, unrepeatable, incorrigible, and, in that sense, the truth.

Thus nature (which in this definition includes culture) presents itself as available to us, as at our disposal, as "what is." The relative stability with which it presents itself is the result of past process "from the beginning." This relative stability, however, is an ambivalent quality. On the one hand it makes I—It talk possible and legitimate, and thus enables us to grasp and manipulate the world we live in with the accumulated knowledge and know-how of the past. But this always leads to the temptation to think of and treat the world as a closed system, with man for its master, or slave, as the case may be. It is imperative to remember that the world we live in is not foreclosed; it remains an invitation to encounter, a call for a personal response beyond the given. Wherever a person fails to heed this call to responsive, responsible stewardship, his I will suffer, as Martin Buber has pointed out, for the I involved in the I—Thou relationship (even if the encounter is with an infra-human reality) is a different I from the I that is involved in the I—It relationship.[63] Even nature itself will suffer if it is restricted to the past; the self-transcendence of the past will be done an injustice if not allowed to continue into the unrealized possibilities of the future. Translated into theological terms, the world will only be a world of faith, and the Church will only be a Church of faith, if they continue to expect everything from God, and if they refuse to look upon the graces of the past merely as the fixed result of a process of accretion that would turn works of God's Spirit into part of the world, and sanctifying grace into part of the Christian's natural equipment. No matter how strong the insistence on the supernatural character of a conventional Church and on the indelibility of the baptismal character may be, this is nothing but naturalism sailing under a merely nominally supernatural flag.

Summary and outlook

The interlude we have just completed has served the purpose of clarifying, in a variety of ways, that the *primary experience of the present*—the experience which allows us to experience the present

---

[63]Cf., for instance, *Ich und Du*, pp. 9–11 (*I and Thou*, pp. 53–55).

vitally—is in the mode of the experience of the *future*. It occurs in the form of encounter with a witness, in the *actus directus* of faith, in the affective experience of the proximity of the other in the act of hearing and speaking, in the experience of the unexpectedness of grace. In all these experiences the person, or the community, find themselves placed in the truth *as a present actuality*.

The secondary experience of the present is one in which we experience the present in the mode of the experience of the *past*. This secondary experience has strongly cognitive, distantial characteristics, and brings into relief the documentary nature of the witness, and the knowledge involved in faith. This experience also has strong visual connotations, and it tends to perceive and rely upon reality as it is, according to its nature.

We have implied that unless the secondary experience of the present is set in the context of, and animated by, the primary one, we run the risk of sclerosis. We pointed out before that when we consider a statement's objective meaning—a move that brings the representative, extra-situational nature of the word into sharp relief—we must do so within the context of the direct experience of speech, or at least be conscious of our debt to it; otherwise the statement's objective meaning will completely dominate the point which the statement was instrumental in making. Analogously, the secondary experience of the present, with its strong reliance on cognitive consonance, objectivity, distance, the given, and the past—must evolve within the context of the primary experience of the present, or at least be conscious of its debt to it; otherwise the past will completely dominate and stifle the experience of the present *sub specie futuri*, offered in the form of witness, spirit, the living word of address, and the actuality of grace.

With this conclusion we are ready for the third part of this book. We will, in six chapters, develop a systematic christology that starts from the *actus directus* of faith. This means that the first object of our attention will be the Resurrection as an eschatological event that calls Christians into an act of total surrender.

PART III

Toward an Open-Ended Synthesis

Let us assume that a young person has the genuine and vital experience of a great love, an experience which transforms his whole being. [. . .] If he is intelligent, and if he has at his disposal an adequately differentiated stock of ideas, he might make the attempt, slowly and gropingly, approaching the subject in a thousand different ways, to state what he knows about his love—to express what he is already aware of in the consciousness that comes with the simple possession of the reality (an awareness at once more simple and more full), in order that he might finally come to "know" (in reflexive propositions). What happens in such a case is not merely the logical development and inference of new propositions out of earlier ones, but the formulation—for the first time—of propositions about a knowledge already possessed, in a never-ending search which approximates its goal only asymptotically.

Karl Rahner

CHAPTER 8

The Presence of the End

Our Gospel came to you not only in words, but also in power and in the Holy Spirit and with full conviction. [. . .] You received the word in much affliction, with joy inspired by the Holy Spirit.

The First Letter of Paul to the Thessalonians

And behold, I am with you always, to the close of the present age.

The Gospel of Matthew

When a person turns to the Lord the veil is removed. Now the Lord is the Spirit, and where the Spirit of the Lord is there is freedom. And with the face unveiled, we all mirror the glory of the Lord and are being transfigured into his likeness, from splendor to splendor—such is the influence of the Lord who is the Spirit.

The Second Letter of Paul to the Corinthians

The full significance of what Peter and the Eleven experienced will only appear in their mission, in what they will do and proclaim, in the practice of their lives. The origin of their Christian faith is the Christian faith's permanent essence itself.

Edward Schillebeeckx

Introductory

Christian faith, as we have seen, is the responsive encounter with Jesus Christ alive and present in the Spirit.[1] Out of this *concretissimum* all christology flows.

Our first task in this chapter will be to show why explicit, thematic reflection on this central Christian experience is a cultural necessity in our day more than ever before. This will lead to conclusions regarding the importance of a rhetorical approach to christology; christologies, we will argue, must be judged according to their performative functions before they are regarded as conceptual systems.

From the previous chapter we recall that the presence of Christ alive in the Spirit is likely to be experienced in a future perspective;[2] today's faith is oriented to the future, even to the absolute future; it is eschatological. Wolfhart Pannenberg's christology takes the eschatological dimension of the Resurrection very seriously; his is also one of the most important recent attempts at synthesizing New Testament christology with the conciliar and doctrinal tradition, a task whose importance we have pointed out. We will, therefore, study the basic structure of Pannenberg's christology and evaluate its success in doing justice to the Christian act of faith.

This treatment will raise again the thesis proposed at the end of the sixth chapter, namely, that both critical and reflective christologies must be placed in the context of the central act of Christian faith in response to the Resurrection.[3] The next chapter will give us an opportunity to start to develop a christology that achieves this.

---

[1]Above, pp. 232–239.
[2]Above, pp. 266–272, 279–286, 288–289.
[3]Above, pp. 254–259.

THE CHRISTOLOGICAL A PRIORI

Critical questions are born

We used to think of the earth as huge and plentiful—nothing to worry about. But the astronauts brought us photographs of a colored globe floating in a sea of black, and there developed the idea of space-ship earth, a particular, relatively small place with fragile structures and limited resources. The new picture forced us to criticize our assumptions, study the environment, and condemn our wastefulness. The earth, for centuries an environment taken for granted, suddenly became the thematic *object* of reflection and criticism.

Similarly, in some periods Christians worry about the Church and in others they just take her for granted. Nowhere in the works of Thomas Aquinas do we find an ecclesiology thematically developed, and it is not as if he could have written one but decided against it. A better explanation is that the medieval Church was like the air one breathed. It pervaded society and culture so thoroughly that no one dreamt of questioning the Church and so no ecclesiology was called for. The Waldensians and Albigensians were not separate new churches, after all, but sectarian movements within Christendom. Obviously there was no need to legitimize the claims and structures of Catholicism in the Middle Ages. Only when the Protestant reformers set up churches of their own, only then did the new cultural picture make the question of ecclesiology both possible and necessary.

We can discern an analogous process in christology. The sensibilities of the ancient Church differed considerably from those of the medieval one, mainly as a result of the conversion of the Germanic tribes and the establishment of some necessary law and order in the *pax et treuga Dei*.[4] The ancient Church had experienced itself as the communion of the motivated minority that viewed themselves as the chosen ones whom God had sanctified; now the Church turned into the popular established Church, most of whose members were ill-

---

[4] "Peace and truce of God"—an allusion to the Church's power, going back to the eleventh century, to order cessation of hostilities among warring feudal chieftains on certain days and during certain seasons.

instructed and semi-pagan, living and believing, in feudal fashion, vicariously, namely, by association with clerical or monastic establishments—the body of religious professionals that guaranteed the faith for the ignorant and wayward multitudes.[5]

Still, the ancient Church and the medieval Church had one feature in common: vigorous worship of Christ and witness to him. When pressed by the culture of the ancient world to account for its faith, the Church had unhesitatingly pointed to the *lex orandi*[6] as the source of all theologically acceptable formulas to express the divinity of Christ in culturally relevant ways. The medieval Church, in its own way, was no less concerned to place Christ at the center of its worship. In fact, it is legitimate to assume that Christian worship and witness was behind most theological discussions long after the waning of the Middle Ages; the complicated controversies of the Reformation and post-Reformation periods, for all the prominence they enjoyed in the churches, never quite eclipsed worship and witness.

Since the mid-eighteenth century, however, the assumption that theological discourse comes out of worship and witness has become less and less justified by the facts—the picture of Kant slipping away and going home just as the academic procession was about to enter the church for the official university service of worship is a telling symbol. Before that time Christendom, for all its fractures, was still a reality; in the modern era, there developed a *real* alternative to the Christian faith. As a result, Christendom vanished and Christianity as one among a number of options remained, in a bewildering variety of churches and movements. This led to a new type of theological discussion, mainly outside the churches, but also to a certain extent inside; this new type of discussion was no longer unequivocally based on worship and witness.

In the modern age, therefore, we can no longer assume that

---

[5]Those appalled at medieval clericalism should read Robert Murray's *Symbols of Church and Kingdom*, which tells the story of the structure of the East Syrian church in the fourth century, where the ecclesiastical elite, the "Covenant," played an even more central role.

[6]"The law of prayer"—a reference to the thesis, first found in the fifth-century treatise known as *De gratia Dei Indiculus* (DS 238–249), that universal official prayer formulas used in the liturgy are a source of orthodox doctrine: "*ut legem credendi lex statuat supplicandi*" (DS 246).

when we talk about Christ or God, we are talking out of worship and witness. Thus it has become necessary to reflect thematically and systematically on what we have called the *a priori* of all christology. The critical question has been posed, demanding recognition and an answer.

Recognizing this fact does not mean lamenting it; in fact, theological discussion also gained much from its severance from worship and witness. The *truth claims* of the Christian revelation have been discussed with more energy and intellectual vigor than ever before. Still, once the *a priori* of all Christian life and speech was no longer shared, the discussion did tend to obscure the demand that Christian theology must primarily rely on a certain way of life, which we sum up in the phrase "worship and witness"—*acts* of commitment *within* which all discernments occur.

Thus the situation since Wolff and Reimarus[7] means that *the christological confession itself* fails to convince, whether it is the traditional "Jesus Christ is God" or the critical "Jesus Christ is the highest, and thus the decisive, manifestation of humanity." In the modern age worship tends to be replaced by an intellectual inquiry into God in the name of the coherence of all reality, or by an emotional sense of religiosity, for rational thought or godly feelings are felt to be the norm for the reality of God. Analogously, witness tends to be replaced by the critical effort to tell the story of Jesus Christ reliably. Both procedures tend to reduce the actuality of religion to imagination or philosophy or history.[8]

But have we not seen recent reaffirmations of Christ's divinity, from the See of Rome, from the General Assemblies of the World Council of Churches, and from other authoritative bodies within Christianity?

There is indeed no doubt that spirited professions of faith have been publicly made by Christians, and with increasing ardor and frequency since the early 1920's, under the influence of ecumenism and the awareness that the Church must address the world. Still,

---

[7]The names of Christian Wolff (1679–1754) and Hermann Samuel Reimarus (1694–1768) are symbolical: the former represents the eighteenth-century's foremost rationalist systematic theologian, the latter its foremost rationalist historical critic. Worship and witness would never be the same again.

[8]Cf. Buber's caution, above, pp. 125–126.

there are several problems with the christological statements that have appeared. First, they are theologically narrow. They tend to sound as if they are very beholden to tradition; they tend to present past formulations as so normative as to exclude practically any new attempts at formulation; they do not convey a sense of newness to a world to which the traditional Christian language sounds too familiar. Second, and of equal importance, they often lack a tone of prayer and personal conviction. The solemn proclamations too often fail to convey a credible commitment to Christ that is also empathetic with the sensibilities of the world to which they are addressed; they often sound as if they are trying to defend or explain something.

But in a world so unaccustomed to credible religious conviction and so skeptical about its possibility, what is at stake is not only a better *conception* of God, but primarily a renewed sense of the *actuality* of God in *history*.[9] Hence our emphasis on the need for a christology that takes the life and death of Jesus Christ and the lives and deaths of Christians seriously,[10] and our insistence on the primacy of the *concretissimum* of the Christian message as the reality that prompts the *actus directus* of faith-surrender.[11] In a world where worship of Christ and witness to him are no longer the spontaneous environment of theology, christology must make the concrete, historical act of faith in the *concretissimum* of the Christian message the primary object of its attention.

Wolfhart Pannenberg has pointed out that the task of christology is not only *explication* of the community's christological confession, but also its *foundation*, based on an understanding of Jesus' past activity and destiny.[12] The point is certainly well taken; the christological confession must be shown to be consistent with Jesus' historical ministry. But the problem is that foundational work, or legitimation—like explication—presupposes that there is something to show the foundation of, something to legitimize. That something is the *actual factuality* of the worship of, and witness to, Jesus Christ alive and present in the Spirit; without this abiding *a priori* of all

---

[9]On this subject, cf. Emmanuel Cardinal Suhard, *Le sens de Dieu*, Paris, Editions A. Lahure, 1948, one of Suhard's Lenten pastorals which are still relevant today.

[10]Cf. above, p. 71.

[11]Above, pp. 232–235.

[12]Wolfhart Pannenberg, *Jesus—God and Man*, Philadelphia, The Westminster Press, 1968, pp. 21–37.

christology, explication and foundation operate in a vacuum. The actuality of Jesus Christ and of the *actus directus* of faith must not be assumed, but systematically reflected upon as part of christology. In the present age, all christological discussions are liable to remain unconvincing if there is a lack of thematic awareness of the context—worship and witness—in which they make their point.

We have argued that the *concretissimum* of the Christian message is a *presence* that prompts an *act*.[13] We have also proposed that reflective and critical christologies—both of them retrospective— must be reconciled by means of their integration into this act.[14] It is understandable that in doing so we will again find that these two types of christology participate in the activity-character of the *actus directus*. They not only say something, they also *do* something. We have already discussed this by pointing out that there is a rhetoric of inclusion and obedience behind christology: human concerns are accepted and converted to the total surrender, in hope, to the living Lord.[15] All christological statements have performative functions, based on the original *actus directus*. We must dwell on this for a moment.

Connecting the christological models—functional christologies

We have just argued that christology must give a systematic account of its *a priori* in our day. In doing so, we were following Bonhoeffer, in his emphasis on the presence of Christ and the *actus directus* of faith.

Our emphasis on the primacy of the exalted Lord is not entirely unprecedented. In the Roman Catholic Church specifically it was the inspiration behind the much suspected kerygmatic-theology movement of the 1920's and 1930's, and the more successful biblico-liturgical movement of the 1950's and early 1960's. Exegesis and liturgical scholarship (and patristics) collaborated in the discovery that the New Testament as a whole had sprung from the experience of the risen Lord, and that he is also the living agent in all sacramental celebrations.[16] In the wake of this realization, catechesis and liturgy started to acquire a vitality scarcely thought possible after the

---

[13]Cf. above, pp. 232ff., 242–251.
[14]Above, pp. 259–262.
[15]Above, pp. 154–183.
[16]There is a parallel movement in Protestantism. Cf. Pannenberg's unfavorable

arid doctrinalism and rubricism of the period before and just after World War II.

The return to the *auditus fidei*[17] was very fruitful in the areas of liturgy and catechesis: better worship, better witness! But it created serious problems in christology.

High christology, represented mainly by the systematicians, had always concentrated on the Incarnation, the point where the hypostatic union arose, not on the Resurrection (except in an apologetic context, to defend its miraculous nature). Low christology, represented mainly by the mostly Protestant and German biblical critics and theologians, tended to concentrate on the historical Jesus and on the historical fact of the rise of the Christian faith, not on the Resurrection as the start of the *present* presence of the risen Lord. Reflective and critical christologies were far apart, but both were equally unprepared for the ringing affirmations of the Resurrection by the kerygmatic theologians and the biblico-liturgical revival. Only recently systematicians like Pannenberg, Schillebeeckx, Kasper, Küng, and O'Collins, and exegetes like Bornkamm, Eduard Schweizer, and Vawter,[18] have begun to integrate critical exegesis, classical christology and kerygmatic, biblico-liturgical christology.

This integration is far from easy. To illustrate the problem in a concrete way, let us briefly discuss a passage from an otherwise interesting study of the encounter with Christ in Ignatius of Loyola's *Spiritual Exercises.* The problem is: How is it possible for the retreatant personally to encounter the living Christ now?

> In the *Exercises* there are not two Christs, the Christ of *then* and the Christ of *now.* There is only one Christ who communicates himself here

---

discussion of the positions taken by Althaus, Kähler, Weber, and Koch, in *Jesus—God and Man,* pp. 25–30. We will come back to this, below, pp. 314–315.

[17]"The hearing of the faith"—the term for the primary faith-experience of hearing the message and believing in it.

[18]Wolfhart Pannenberg, *Grundzüge der Christologie,* Gütersloh, Gütersloher Verlagshaus Gerd Mohn, [2]1966 (ET *Jesus—God and Man*); Edward Schillebeeckx, *Jezus;* Walter Kasper, *Jesus the Christ,* New York–Paramus–Toronto, Paulist Press, 1977; Hans Küng, *On Being a Christian;* Gerald O'Collins, *The Resurrection of Jesus Christ,* Valley Forge, Judson Press, 1973; id., *The Calvary Christ,* Philadelphia, Westminster Press, 1977; id., *What Are They Saying About Jesus?* New York–Ramsey–Toronto, Paulist Press, 1977; id., *What Are They Saying About the Resurrection?* New York–Ramsey–Toronto, Paulist Press, 1978; Günther Bornkamm, *Jesus of Nazareth,* New York, Harper and Bros., 1960; Eduard Schweizer, *Jesus;* Bruce Vawter, *This Man Jesus.*

and now through Scripture. Several statements can be made that might make it easier for a modern exercitant to see this. First, one cannot truly know someone unless one understands something of his past. All of a man's past is part of his present; and that is even more true in Christ. His mysteries continue to exist and to be operative in him in a special way. *Some maintain this is because he is divine, others because he is risen.*[19]

The author affirms that the present Christ addresses the retreatant through Scripture. But how to account for this? The author seems undecided; he appeals to high christology ("because he is divine") and to Resurrection-theology ("because he has risen"), but he cannot connect the two any more than, it seems, other theologians, for the passage ends with a reference to the lack of consensus among them.

Many other examples could be given. Is there a christological significance to the life and death of the historical Jesus, quite apart from the Resurrection? Can the Resurrection be fitted into the same story as the pre-existence?

Such questions have been answered—rightly, we think—by referring to *models*. The countless ways of speaking about Jesus Christ all aim at the inexpressible and are all provisional. Modern theology owes a lot to theorists like Wittgenstein. He saw very well that there is a variety of language-games; they are all relatively autonomous and lead to different insights. The dogmatic reduction of all types of knowledge to one supposedly superior and ultimately normative type of knowledge leads to blindness to the variety of insights which a variety of approaches can achieve. The application of this insight to christology has liberated us from the compulsion of secretly thinking of the hypostatic-union construct, or the Resurrection, or the

[19]Robert L. Schmidt, S.J., "The Christ-Experience and Relationship Fostered in the Spiritual Exercises of St. Ignatius of Loyola," *Studies in the Spirituality of Jesuits,* American Assistancy Seminar on Jesuit Spirituality, St. Louis, St. Louis University, 6 (1974) 217–255; quotation 243. The author alleges Schillebeeckx as an example of a theologian who accounts for the present significance of the life of Christ by recourse to his divinity; he alleges David Stanley as a theologian who attributes it to the Resurrection. For a good discussion of the problems between systematicians and exegetes, cf. Karl Rahner, S.J., "Zur Neuordung der theologischen Studien," *Stimmen der Zeit* 181 (1968) 1–21; Norbert Lohfink, S.J., "Text und Thema," *ibid.* 181 (1968) 120–126; Karl Rahner, S.J., "Die Exegese im Theologiestudium, Eine Antwort an N. Lohfink," *ibid.* 181 (1968) 196–201.

uniqueness of Jesus as historically established—as the case may be—as the "really normative" model.

But it is one thing to recognize a variety of partial approaches to Jesus Christ, quite another to see the connections between the approaches. Once we give free rein to variety, the demand for unity also arises. Some sort of unity must therefore be established, some organic pattern drawn, so that it becomes possible to see how christologies are related to each other, which are more basic and which more derivative, and how, and why.

Let us attempt to elaborate this by going back to an earlier discussion. We have explained that we must advert to the point—the interpersonal situational meaningfulness—of a statement (and of a set of interlocking statements) in order to get a correct idea of the meaning of the statement(s) *as considered*. We have expressed this in various ways: the rhetoric must determine the logic, the direct experience of speech must determine the consideration of meaning, the disclosure must determine the meaning of the metaphor, etc.[20] The same insight has been formulated by saying that the meaning of a word is determined by the company it keeps, or, in Wittgenstein's phrase, that the meaning of a word is determined by its use.

We have already suggested, and we will argue at greater length, that various christologies are very hard to harmonize *at the level of content*. The various christologies are precisely caused by a variety of models, and to the extent that the models are incompatible, the christologies that result will be, too. Thus, for example, it is impossible to harmonize the affirmations that Jesus is the Good Shepherd and that he is the lamb led to the slaughter. In the same way it is hard to harmonize the vocation-theology which animates the Synoptic accounts of Jesus' baptism with the vocation-theology implied in the annunciation pericope in Luke. It has been argued that pre-existence christology and Resurrection-christology are mutually exclusive.

The unity of these various christologies must therefore not be sought in the coherence of their discernments, but in the coherence of their commitment. Since the act of commitment is conveyed by the rhetoric of a statement, we must advert, in the case of each

---

[20]Cf. above, pp. 93–98, 135–143.

christology, to its *function*, to what it attempts to *do*, to the way it purports to *change* people and situations. Many christologies, how-ever—especially the more abstract, conceptual ones—do not explic-itly betray their performative function;[21] still, all have one, even though it may seem at times almost entirely extrinsic to the christol-ogy taken at face value.[22] In this regard, systematic theology must imitate the form-critical approach so successfully applied to the Scriptures: the meaning of a pericope is determined by its *genre*, and the *genre* is a function of rhetorical, performative intentions.[23]

We will therefore have to seek the *coherence of christology*, not by attempting to harmonize various christologies at the level of explicit meaning, but *by seeking to establish the coherence of the performative functions of these various christologies.* We will only be able to do this in the broadest outlines, namely by distinguishing between Resurrection-christology, Incarnation-christology, and as-sumption-christology. Each of these three main types of christology has a particular performative function, and they are coherent in that they proceed from each other: Resurrection-christology generates assumption-christology, assumption-christology generates Incarna-tion-christology. It will take three sets of two chapters to develop this, but we will be able at the beginning of the twelfth chapter to sum up how the three principal types of christology are related at the level of their performative functions.[24]

This chapter and the next will treat the type of christology which is most closely related to the *actus directus* of faith in Jesus Christ alive and present in the Spirit. After two short introductions, in which we will deal with an explicitly eschatological christology

---

[21]On self-involvement and performative language, cf. above, pp. 78–79.

[22]Cf. above, pp. 109–110.

[23]This can be illustrated by an analogy. Recent editions of Denzinger-Schönmetzer carry brief situational introductions above each magisterial text; these introductions are important because they give the student a clue to the text's perfor-mative intentions—to what is *meant*, not only to what is said. Still, a collection like Denzinger tends to draw the student's attention to what was said, and to suppress and tone down those statements in the tradition which *at the level of explicit statement* "contradict" the tradition. In this way the student is deprived of the opportunity to get to know the faith-tradition at a deeper level, namely the level at which Christians express their faith without worrying about the coherence with the explicit tradition.

[24]Cf. below, pp. 465–471. But cf. also below, pp. 397–399.

and with the historical particularity of the Resurrection, we will turn to Wolfhart Pannenberg's christology.

ESCHATOLOGICAL CHRISTOLOGY—WOLFHART PANNENBERG

Introduction: primitive or primary?

In his collection *Twelve New Testament Studies* John A. T. Robinson has an essay entitled "The Most Primitive Christology of All?"[25] Since the *Kyrios*-title is attributed to Jesus only once in the kerygmatic speeches in the first part of the Acts of the Apostles, he concludes that, in the most primitive christology, Jesus was proclaimed as Christ-*designate*. Robinson's view ties in with the clear preponderance of the parousia-expectation in the early communities, summed up by the apostrophe *Maranatha*: "Our Lord, come!"[26] Not until the imminent end of time, in the fulfillment of all things, would Jesus come into his true dignity as the exalted Lord and Messiah.

Now there is no question that the Resurrection of Jesus must have been experienced and viewed primarily as an eschatological event. In his painstaking book *The Formation of the Resurrection Narratives,*[27] Reginald Fuller had argued convincingly that the early Christian community spontaneously grasped at eschatological metaphors to convey the significance of the Resurrection—itself an eschatological metaphor of the first order.

Yet, there are definite disadvantages to referring to eschatological christology as "primitive." The term is so loaded with the prejudices of rationalistic *Fortschrittsglaube*[28] that it has become dangerous. "Primitive" now connotes either regrettable naiveté, lack of intelligence, inability to be sophisticated and absence of culture, or—with good romantic wistfulness, and Robinson seems closer to this—the purity of the beginning, the unadulterated straightforward truth, the unspoiled inspiration, the charismatic insight. If advocacy of *Maranatha* christology is used in the latter way to disqualify or cast doubts upon subsequent christologies, such as the clear profes-

---

[25]London, SCM Press (*Studies in Biblical Theology*, 34), 1962, pp. 139–153.
[26]1 Cor 16, 22; cf. Phil 4, 5; Rev 22, 20; Mt 11, 3.
[27]New York/London, The Macmillan Company/Collier-Macmillan, 1971, esp. pp. 9–49.
[28]"Faith in progress."

sion of Jesus as the Christ now, or the Johannine Logos-protology, or, *a fortiori*, Chalcedon, that is selective reading of the Christian tradition. No single christology is normative, not even the most primitive one, quite apart from the question whether it is possible, on the basis of New Testament evidence, to reconstruct such a clear *historical* development of christology that one type can be described as the most primitive. It is not without good reason that the title of Robinson's article just referred to ends with a question mark.

Still, there is a point to Robinson's article, namely that a thoroughly eschatological christology is the most direct answer to the Resurrection, and since the Resurrection is the abiding source of all christology, eschatological christology must *remain* the ground and context of all other christological statements. We will therefore call the christology that most closely reflects the *actus directus* of faith in the risen Lord a *primary* christology. To call it primitive implies either that it has been rightly superseded, or that it must be reinstated at the expense of other christologies; to call it primary implies that it is an abiding and basic feature of christology.

Hence, the primary christology which reconciles the demands of both critical and reflective reason will be both an eschatological and a Resurrection christology. Its being a Resurrection christology, however, meets with an important difficulty. It is true that the difficulty cannot be satisfactorily answered at this point in our argument. We will not be in a position to do so until the eleventh chapter.[29] But both in view of Pannenberg's treatment of the Resurrection and to signal an important issue, we must at least mention the difficulty here.

The historical particularity of the Resurrection

In chapters five and six we viewed the Resurrection—the reality that calls the Christian faith into being and constitutes its *concretissimum*—exclusively as a present and enduring reality of an "objective" nature: Jesus Christ alive and present in the Spirit.[30] We understood the particularity of the christological *confession* mainly as a striking instance of egological, interpersonal, witnessing speech,

---

[29] Below, pp. 439–446.
[30] Cf. above, esp. pp. 150, 191–198.

in response to the presence of Christ in the Spirit.[31] But what we must also mention is the particularity of this *presence*. Because this presence started at some particular point in the past, the Resurrection of Jesus is an event in the past. The presence of Christ is not timeless and "meta-historical." At a certain moment, and not earlier, it became possible to say: "The Lord is truly risen." The Resurrection happened to Jesus himself, the same person who was dead and buried;[32] it is not just the kerygmatic interpretation, by the faithful, of his death on the cross; if Jesus died on a certain day and was seen on certain days, then the Resurrection is *dateable*. Even those who understand "on the third day" as a theological expression, and who take the widely divergent dating of the appearances in the Gospels and Paul as cues that the single appearances are not historical in the modern sense, even for them the Resurrection is dateable, at least approximately.

But how can the christological *a priori*, of which we have claimed that it is the unobjectifiable, all-encompassing setting in which all christological statements are made, and which is only adequately conveyed by the totality of the surrender, have a beginning in a particular event in the past? And since this particular Resurrection prompts Christians to the total surrender, an even more pressing question arises immediately: How can Christianity credibly make the claim that God manifested himself, in the living Christ, decisively and unsurpassably—*unüberbietbar* ("in a manner not to be outbid") as the Germans put it so graphically—in such a particular way and so late in time?[33] How could God let himself be adored in spirit and truth in such a niggardly fashion? The scandal of particularity is essential to Christianity, and it is a real stumbling block. To solve the problem cheaply, for instance, by a blithe appeal to the world-process, which generates newness by evolutionary quantum leaps in particular places, is unwarranted.[34] How can the univer-

---

[31]Cf. above, pp. 117–120, 195–196, 249–251.

[32]The empty tomb tradition must at the very least be understood to imply an affirmation of the identity of the risen Christ with the historical Jesus. Cf. Hans Küng, *On Being a Christian*, pp. 363–366.

[33]This question is the starting point for Juan Luis Segundo's systematic theology; cf. *The Community Called Church*, Maryknoll, New York, Orbis Books, 1973, pp. 3ff.

[34]This remark is addressed to the vulgarizers of the thought of Teilhard de Chardin; it is not aimed at Teilhard himself.

sal significance of God be reconciled with the Christian claim that his decisive, actual self-manifestation is particular, in appearances of a particular person, with a particular destiny, to particular persons, and hence not equally available to all? How can we account for the *actuality* of *Jesus* Christ alive and present in the Spirit as the key to *all* of reality?

If this is not answered, Christianity must consent to being either one particular form of a *per se* universal religion—the rationalist solution—or a sect—the fideistic solution.

Thus we can see how the question of the historicity of the Resurrection leads to the far more general question of the particularity of Christianity and the universality of its claims. The more general question will have to wait for an answer; the question of the historicity of the Resurrection leads us to the christology of Wolfhart Pannenberg.

Historical prolepsis of the eschaton

Pannenberg treats the Resurrection as the first agenda of christology, immediately after the two introductory chapters, in his book *Jesus—God and Man.* The Resurrection being the original confirmation of Jesus' unity with God, it must be the starting point of christology.[35] Now the Resurrection of Jesus can only be interpreted as an eschatological event, which is obviously also the way the first Christians spontaneously interpreted it; with Jesus' Resurrection the end of the world has begun, Jesus' own pre-Easter activity has been confirmed by God, Jesus is identified as the Son of Man who is to come, Jesus is revealed as the ultimate epiphany of God, and the mission to the Gentiles must begin.[36]

In a striking contrast with these eschatological features of Jesus' Resurrection, Pannenberg treats it primarily *as an historical event.* This is not to deny that all Christian knowledge of the past Jesus-event has an openness to the future. The final divine confirmation of Jesus will be realized in his return in glory; thus the *parousia* will be the final, irresistible glory of God become actual and visible. From this it follows that all we say about the risen Lord will be character-

---

[35]Pp. 53ff..
[36]*Ibid.*, pp. 66–72.

ized by anticipation; it will have, as Pannenberg puts it, proleptic features.

Still, anticipation is less than actuality. How can we explain that Resurrection-talk—originally the symbol of the world's total fulfillment—now has only proleptic significance? The reason is that the Christian community has come to terms, ever since its second and third generations, with the fact that the Resurrection of Jesus did not prove to be the immediate prelude to the general resurrection and God's final judgment and self-revelation, as the apocalyptic tradition understood these. Thus the Resurrection of Jesus and the eschatological glory of God in the world got dissociated. In the interim, Christians look upon the Resurrection—backed up by the pre-Easter history of Jesus—as a separate past event, yet proleptically connected with the last things.[37]

Historical event

How does Pannenberg deal with the Resurrection as a past event? He first rejects all attempts to reduce the Resurrection to a kerygmatic interpretation of the death of Jesus (Barth, Bultmann);[38] the earliest sources appeal to factual, unforeseen appearances to legitimize its *kerygma*. To account for the Resurrection in terms of psychogenic phenomena is equally unwarranted, and for the same reason.[39] There remains only one possibility, and Pannenberg sets it forth as follows:

> The Resurrection of Jesus, it is suggested, must be called a historical event in the following sense. The origin of primitive Christianity is traced back to appearances of the risen Jesus, also according to Paul, quite apart from other traditions. It becomes intelligible only—in the face of all attempts to analyse the total tradition critically—when considered in the light of the eschatological hope for a resurrection from the dead. But in that case what we are talking about is a historical event, even if we have no further knowledge of it. Then we must affirm as historical an event which can only be expressed in the language of eschatological expectation.[40]

---

[37]*Ibid.*, pp. 106–108.
[38]Cf. *ibid.*, p. 111.
[39]*Ibid.*, pp. 95–97.
[40]*Grundzüge der Christologie*, p. 95 (cp. *Jesus—God and Man*, p. 98).

Thus the historicity of the Resurrection is maintained after the *elimination* of alternative possibilities. *Positively*, it is tied to the language of eschatology as the only way to convey the event, even though this language is symbolic and has no relevance to history.

Pannenberg orchestrates his emphasis on the historicity of the Resurrection in a variety of ways. He points out that science cannot pre-judge the possibility of the Resurrection from the dead; it is the competence of the historian, not the scientist, to determine whether something so unusual as the Resurrection has occurred or not. If science cannot prejudge the issue, neither can theology. Often the theological claim is made that the risen Christ belongs to the new aeon, and is therefore not perceivable as one among many worldly objects; he can, therefore, only be experienced by vision and referred to symbolically; the Resurrection is real, but not historical. Pannenberg counters with the observation that faith does not determine what actually happens, but history does; and as a matter of fact Jesus did show himself as the risen Lord at a certain time, in certain events and to certain people, and we have historical evidence for that, namely, in the testimony of the eye-witnesses, which admits of no other reasonable explanation, and in the tradition about the empty tomb.[41] Purely historically speaking we must call the Resurrection of Jesus highly probable, and that means, as always in historical investigations, it has to be presupposed until contrary evidence appears.[42]

Thus Pannenberg insists, on the one hand, on the historicity of the Resurrection; on the other hand he admits that it can only be expressed in the language of eschatological expectation, and that historically speaking it must be called very probable. This raises a question. What is gained by emphasizing the historicity of the Resurrection *itself?* There is no doubt that the appearances to the eye-witnesses must be called historical, but the Resurrection is not identical with the appearances. Though it is true that the risen Lord must be held responsible for the historical events known as the appearances, this does not imply that the Lord's Resurrection is an historical event in the same sense as the appearances. The twin

---

[41]*Jesus—God and Man*, pp. 98–106.
[42]*Ibid.*, p. 105.

historical events of Jesus' burial and his appearances lead to the historical *postulate* that the Resurrection must have happened in between, in time, and hence, as an historical event. But why this *emphasis* on the Resurrection's historicity? One suspects an agenda behind this.

Lack of present christological actuality

There is indeed a very definite background to Pannenberg's emphasis on the Resurrection as an historical event backed up by the events of Jesus' life and death. That background is his refusal to allow for any direct awareness of the risen Lord in the Church *now*. This causes Pannenberg to seek the basis of the Christian faith entirely in the past, while its orientation remains entirely toward the future: an attractive arrangement, but one which must be seriously qualified to be acceptable. He writes:

> If we are to speak about Jesus as the foundation of our profession, as the ground of our faith in him, then this can only refer to the Jesus of the past. True, this ground of our faith is borne out and proved true— as it must be—in connection with our present experience of reality, but it lies itself completely in what happened then. Certainly, the believer knows very well that Jesus not only lived then, but that he is also the One presently alive as the risen and exalted One. But this kind of knowledge about the living, present Lord cannot be attained through immediate present experience in personal association with the exalted One.[43]

This last phrase contains a cue. The Christian knows that Christ is alive; how does he know it? Not from direct experience in encounter with the Lord; *ergo*, he knows it from the past. This interpretation is entirely in keeping with Pannenberg's conception of the task of christology, which is to base the present confession and faith that Jesus is the Son of God on the historical Jesus, the crucified and risen One.[44]

But the immediate context of the quotation also provides a cue to its interpretation. It is a complete rejection of the kerygmatic theologians' emphasis on the presence of the living Lord to the

---

[43]*Grundzüge der Christologie*, p. 21 (cf. *Jesus —God and Man*, p. 27).
[44]*Jesus—God and Man*, pp. 21–32, esp. p. 28; cf. above, pp. 302–303.

Church as the abiding source of her faith. For Pannenberg, such a theology smacks of fideism; claims to a present awareness of the living Lord cannot convince us that we are dealing with the person of Jesus, and not only with our own self-deception. Pannenberg even mentions the enthusiasm of the Corinthians in this context, as a warning against such delusions.[45]

In Pannenberg's view, the direct *experience* of Christ is only a matter of promise to be realized in the last days; our faith *now* is primarily concerned with what Jesus *was*, and based, not on the experienced presence of the living Lord, but only on the testimony to the appearances of the risen Jesus. Our awareness of him *now* is in the nature of *knowledge* guaranteed by the past. Thus present Christian faith is based on eschatological promise supported by past testimony; it must be lived out in an—experientially speaking— empty present.

But did Pannenberg not say that the believer knows very well that Jesus is now alive? Yes, but the question is what the quality of this knowledge is. And the answer to that is that it has no truly ecclesial dimension; nowhere in Pannenberg's book is there a hint that present worship and witness—and the knowledge involved in them—are the ways in which the Christian experiences the actual presence of the living Lord. Thus the actuality of the risen Lord in the present is pared down to mere assurance inherited from the eye-witnesses and to patterns for present action and thought. What is left over is recollection and promise; the presence of the Spirit goes unnoticed. This is all the more surprising because Pannenberg does mention the "fundamental Christian conviction that the same Spirit of God, through whom Jesus is raised, already dwells in the Christians";[46] still, this has not caused him to question the lack of actuality of Christ alive and present *now* in his own christology. Pannenberg is right in making the Resurrection the starting point of his christology; he is wrong in missing its abiding significance beyond mere knowledge.

The New Testament is very much aware of the actuality of the living Lord and his presence, in the Spirit, to his Church. This can be

---

[45]*Ibid.*, pp. 25–28. Cf. also pp. 108–114.
[46]*Ibid.*, p. 67.

illustrated in various ways. We will make two points.

First, for all their significance, the appearances are not absolutized in the New Testament. It is true that the eye-witnesses appeal to them, but the appearances also leave room for doubt, in the sense that it is possible to doubt not only whether they happened, as Thomas did, but also whether the appearance itself was believable, as we read in Matthew: "When they saw him they worshiped him; but some doubted."[47] It is legitimate, therefore, to point to the appearances as the *principal source* of the credibility of the *kerygma*; but they are not the object of faith. They have an element of relativity in them like all historical events; they move in the ambiguity of history as symbols of, and invitations to, the kind of faith-surrender which alone does justice to the reality of the risen Lord. Now this is precisely the point which the pericopes relating the appearances have in common with the strictly kerygmatic passages in the New Testament; they mean to state and orchestrate the reality of *the risen One himself*.[48] The faith of Easter has for its object neither the empty tomb—the story of which Pannenberg very consistently considers a basically factual account rather than a supportive legend—nor the appearances, but the *living Jesus himself*. The appearances, like the story of the empty tomb, leave room for doubt; the certainty of the presence of the living One exceeds the certainty warranted by the appearances. Pannenberg overestimates the credibility of the appearances, and underestimates the mystery and the power of the Resurrection.

The New Testament's awareness of the actuality of the living Lord and his presence, in the Spirit, to his Church can be demonstrated in a second way. The New Testament knows of other legitimations of the reality of the risen Lord besides the appearances. There is the Thessalonians' welcome extended to the *kerygma* and their joy in the Holy Spirit in the teeth of suffering; there are the signs and miracles mentioned in the so-called inauthentic Mark-ending, and, most impressively, the conviction that the believers will do what Jesus did *and even greater things*.[49] For Pannenberg to put so

---

[47]Mt 28, 17.
[48]Cf. Hans Küng, *On Being a Christian*, p. 347.
[49]1 Thess 1, 6; Mk 16, 17–20; Jn 14, 12.

much emphasis on the appearances that they seem to be the only warrant for the Resurrection amounts to ignoring these and other texts, in which the presence of Christ is a matter of present experience, not mere knowledge going back to the eye-witnesses of the appearances. To postulate that those who come to believe without being the privileged eye-witnesses of the appearances do so only on the strength of the testimony of the eye-witnesses amounts to attributing only a *mediated knowledge* of the living Lord to them.[50] But this in turn amounts to construing a *complete discontinuity* between the faith of the eye-witnesses of the appearances and those who come to believe.[51] This runs counter to the early tradition, which was aware of the *continuity* of the Easter faith, no matter how privileged the witnesses of the appearances. The eschatological congratulations addressed to those who have believed without seeing[52] make the point forcibly: there is more the matter in the Christian community than knowledge that Jesus is alive.

At first blush, then, Pannenberg's proposal to look at the Resurrection as an historical event is attractive: it places God's absolute future squarely in the stream of human history. But on closer inspection the price is too high: Christians through the centuries must pay for the privilege of the witnesses. Present Christian faith is reduced to faith in past events as attested to by these witnesses. Encounter with the present Christ is reduced to a mere knowledge that he is now alive. The hope for the *eschaton* is entirely based on a past event. The truth of the Christian faith can indeed be borne out *in connection with* present experience of reality; but there is no way

---

[50]Cf. on this subject, Felix Malmberg, S.J., "Die mittelbar-unmittelbare Verbindung mit Gott im Dogmenglauben," in: *Gott in Welt*, Festgabe für Karl Rahner, Freiburg–Basel–Wien, Herder, 1964, pp. 92–102.

[51]Pannenberg's isolation of the appearances takes the form of a strong stress on the limited, closed period during which the appearances took place: *Jesus—God and Man*, p. 110; he neglects the fact that it is mainly Lk–Acts that is interested in periodization, and that the concern behind this is theological, not chronological.—Our position makes it possible to take a less exclusive view of the original appearances and to attribute an analogous significance to the "revelations and visions" of the Lord in the time of the Church, say, from 2 Cor 12, 1ff. on down through the ages. This analogy can be made even more compelling by showing that such visions have analogous effects on their recipients.

[52]Cf. Jn 20, 29; 1 Pet 1, 8.

the Christians can enjoy any christological actuality *in* their present experience of reality.

Calling, conversion, and mission of the witnesses

In his treatment of the Resurrection, Pannenberg focuses on God's historical endorsement of the life of Jesus, by raising him from the dead.[53] Pannenberg, as we have seen, enumerates the principal features of the significance of this event in the framework of apocalyptic expectation: the onset of the world's end, the identification of Jesus as the coming Son of Man, the definitive self-revelation of God in Jesus, and the transition to the mission to the Gentiles. There is an obvious implication here, too obvious perhaps to mention, namely, that the Resurrection—or rather, the risen One—must have had this significance *for those who were given the appearances.* Yet Pannenberg consistently underplays this aspect of encounter in his treatment of the appearances; eager as he is to establish the *theological* meaning of the Resurrection, he overlooks the essential element of *personal* meaning. After refuting all views of the Resurrection as a psychogenic construction or a faith-interpretation on the disciples' part and after insisting that the Resurrection was a genuine *occurrence*, he should have drawn out the consequences at the *personal* level: *those persons were changed.*

Pannenberg raises this question with regard to Paul, but solves it in a very incomplete fashion.[54] Paul did not receive his message ready-made in the appearance of the risen One; rather his preaching is the explication of the very meaning of the Resurrection itself, become visible in the appearance. It is rather doubtful whether it is legitimate thus to make Paul's autobiographical account in Galatians normative for our understanding of all the other appearances. But the main problem is Pannenberg's rendering of the relationship between the Lord's appearance to Paul and Paul's preaching ministry. The appearances, Pannenberg explains, were not brute but significant facts in the sense that they carried their specific meaning with them, so that no extrinsic interpretation was needed. Ordinary

---

[53]Above, p. 311.

[54]*Jesus—God and Man*, pp. 72–73.—Schillebeeckx (*Jezus*, pp. 295–310) has a good analysis of Paul's vision of the risen One, in which he stresses that Acts moves from a conversion-vision to a paschal mission-vision and that Paul's vision need not have been visual (cf. esp. pp. 302, 309–310).

experience provides a parallel; some events come at us with such irresistible meaning that we cannot doubt their interpretation; others are so enigmatic and confusing that they keep us in suspense about their meaning. The appearances of the risen One—given the context of Jewish apocalyptic—were of the former kind, the crucifixion of the latter; hence the great unanimity about the significance of the Resurrection, and the divergence of interpretations of the cross in the theology of the early community.

This construct is not so much wrong as limited; it suffers from intellectualism. Occurrences are first and foremost encounters: *persons* are changed by realities that meet them. The explication or cognitive structuring is always secondary, at one remove from the interpersonal experience. In real life no such simple, direct connection between occurrence and interpretation prevails. Something that meets a person "with irresistible meaning" can be accepted and correctly interpreted; it may *also* be kept at arm's length precisely because of the power of its significance; its "irresistible meaning" is so strong that the person will go to any lengths in order to distort it, and even to rationalize it away. This is exactly what has happened with the Resurrection ever since the chief priests' bribe to the soldiers, and with the presence of the Spirit in the witnesses ever since the allusion to deep draughts on the first Pentecost.[55] Conversely, enigmatic events are sometimes the occasion for a slow, tortuous and haphazard process of interpretation that takes a long time to settle down, as Pannenberg suggests for the crucifixion. But enigmatic events may *also* provoke precipitate interpretation: the very void of puzzlement demands that it be filled with meaning— which can easily consist in a defensive projection of the fears and prejudices of the person who experiences the event. Pannenberg's solution labors under a lack of awareness of the possibilities inherent in a personal world.

We must view the appearances primarily as *encounters*, in which the person of Jesus Christ alive changed the people to whom he appeared. This means, for example, that Paul's Gospel is the *personal living-out* of his encounter with Christ, not primarily the explication of the appearance that befell him.

Only in this fashion is it possible to account for Paul's extraordi-

---

[55] Cf. Mt 28, 11–15; Acts 2, 13.

nary identification with his kerygmatic mission, as an apostle, even to the point of identifying with Christ—though never substituting himself for him.[56] The author of Acts was also conscious of the *personal* consequences of faith in the living Lord. The kerygma of Stephen before the Council is depicted as the *martyrion* of a *person* who resembles his Lord in his life and passion, with the exception that, where Jesus referred himself to the Father, Stephen refers himself to the Lord Jesus now fully identified as the Son of Man.[57] Hence the fullness of grace and power, the miracles and signs among the people, the adversaries not holding their own, the alleged blasphemy against the Law and against God, the accusation by false witnesses before the Council regarding the temple and the Law, Stephen's "face" (= presence, *panim!*) like a "messenger" (= the One Sent, *mal'ak!*), the appeal to the Son of Man before the Council, the martyrdom outside the city, the commendation of his spirit to the Lord Jesus, the prayer for forgiveness for his tormentors.[58] Similarly, in Acts, the early community and its leaders first trace the steps of Jesus in his earthly ministry, and only then go decisively beyond the limits set by Jesus to his own mission.

Thus the appearances are revelations in the affective, interpersonal, rhetorical, action-and-future-oriented sense. They are *encounters in which the witnesses find themselves called, converted, and sent.*[59] What is enacted in the appearances is a *process* of inclusion, conversion to obedience, and the opening of a perspective that draws the witnesses into action and speech: their *lives* become the expression of their meeting with Jesus Christ alive and present.

Foundation and legitimation are insufficient

Earlier in this chapter we referred to Pannenberg's conception of foundation as the task of christology. Pannenberg shares this concern with foundation with the entire new quest of the historical Jesus. A short excursus on this point will enable us again to see the importance of the position we took at the beginning of this chapter,

---

[56]Cf., for example, 1 Cor 9, 1; 2 Cor 2, 1–17.
[57]Acts 6, 7—7, 60.
[58]Acts 6, 8. 10–13. 15; 7, 55–60.
[59]On calling and mission, cf. Hans Küng, *On Being a Christian*, pp. 376–381; on conversion, cf. Edward Schillebeeckx, *Jezus*, pp. 310–314.

namely, that thematic reflection on the *concretissimum* of the Christian message is the primary task of christology today.

The principal result of the old quest of the historical Jesus was a seemingly insuperable separation of the Christ of faith from the Jesus of history. This created the theological impasse conveyed by the familiar thesis: "The Announcer of the Kingdom became the One Announced," or in Loisy's ironical phrase: "Jesus announced the Kingdom, and we got the Church." The new quest of the historical Jesus, with its more refined historical tools and its better conception of history, has managed to establish a badly needed continuity between the life of Jesus and the kerygma of the Church. Yet the question must be asked: Is the continuity established by the new quest, theologically speaking, enough? Is it enough to demonstrate that the historical Jesus was the kind of person, with the kind of impact, about whom the primitive community was liable to make the kind of statements it did? No doubt, legitimation of the kerygma by recourse to the historical Jesus is important, and indeed indispensable, for two reasons. The essential continuity between the historical Jesus and the Christ of faith must be shown, and the picture of the historical Jesus must keep present faith in Christ in check if it is not to become the kind of uncontrolled enthusiasm Pannenberg is right in rejecting.

But it must be remembered that it is the *present* faith in Christ alive that demands this legitimation by recourse to the historical Jesus. Still, this does not mean that the historical Jesus has thereby become the only object of the Christian faith, as Pannenberg states.[60] People have indeed a need to legitimize what they live on; but that does not mean that they live on legitimizing.[61] Christology must show how the present profession of faith in Christ is justified by the life, death, and Resurrection of Jesus, but if it stops there the task is left unfinished. We may then be certain that the kerygma is historically responsible since it is backed up by the life and death and Resurrection of Jesus as the prolepsis of the eschatological hope held out to us; but we will have lost the actuality of the risen One present to us now.

This is why we have maintained that christology must account,

[60]Cf. above, pp. 314–315.
[61]Cf. Frans J. van Beeck, "Küng's *Christ Sein*: A Review Article," p. 281.

not only for the *legitimacy* of the *kērygma*, but also for its *present and effective significance*. This is only possible if we go beyond the content of the *kērygma* and pay attention to the rhetoric, the act of speaking, the *kēryssein* that carries it.[62] This act of speech expresses the witnesses' responsive self-surrender, as we have already seen.[63]

In the beginning of this section we raised the question of the historical particularity of the Resurrection.[64] We are now in a position to give an answer to the question.

To call the Resurrection itself an historical event is an unnecessary historical postulate predicated on Jesus' death and burial and on his appearances, which *are* historical events. What is directly *historical* about the Resurrection as the beginning of *the actual presence, in the Spirit, of the living Lord to his Church* is: *the lives of the witnesses expressed in their confident testimony.* For them, to live is from now on Christ.

We deny any suggestion that Jesus is thereby somehow absorbed into the witnesses; they are witnesses to him, not substitutes for him. But the rise of their personal testimony is historically verifiable; its continuation in response to the abiding presence of the Lord is historically verifiable, too. Christians still witness to Jesus alive and "together sing hymns to Christ as to God,"[65] as they have done since the appearances. The latter are indeed a very privileged, prototypical beginning startling in its particularity; but the ensuing generations—"those also who through *their* [the witnesses'] words will put their faith in *me*"[66]—do not believe just vicariously. They do not merely believe the witnesses' *kērygma that* Jesus lives, they also believe in Jesus alive. The particularity of the witnesses' faith in the living Christ who has appeared to them is carried on in the particularity of all those Christians through the centuries who realize that their faith *now* is a very particular *calling*. This calling has made them new people, "in Christ"—people for whom the shape of the things to come has already become a living reality.

---

[62]Cf. above, p. 259.
[63]Cf. above, p. 195.
[64]Above, pp. 309–311.
[65]Cf. above, p. 138 and note 61.
[66]Jn 17, 20.

Retrospect and outlook

Pannenberg's construction of a consistently eschatological christology is an important event in the history of christology. It has
definitely put an end to that tradition in christology which tended to
accord to Resurrection and eschatology a merely corollary treatment.

Our criticism has been twofold. First, Pannenberg's christological construct leaves too little room for the essential Christian conviction about the *actuality* of Jesus Christ alive and present in the Spirit
now. The purview of christology must be broadened to include a
thematic reflection on the present Christ, as Bonhoeffer did. We will
argue that this will lead to the *primary* christology which also
conveys an *experience of prospect*.[67]

Consequently, we criticized Pannenberg's definition of christology. Positively, the definition marks a definite advance over traditional speculative christology, which tended to take the development
of the christological confession, both in the New Testament and in
the tradition of the Church, for granted as normative, and to treat
the problems raised by the historians about the earthly Jesus as
relatively unimportant. Pannenberg is right when he views foundational christology as essential, for it provides us with the historical
reality of Jesus, which is indispensable if the kerygma is to be
legitimized, and if the history of the Christian confession is to be
critically evaluated by means of the standard of the historical Jesus.
Our negative criticism is that Pannenberg's definition of christology
is too narrow: it limits christology to the tasks of explication of the
Christian confession and its foundation. It leaves out a reflection on
the christological *a priori*: the actuality of Jesus Christ alive and
present in the Spirit. This reflection, we have claimed, is necessary if
foundation—critical christology—and explication—reflective christology—are to make sense. Pannenberg's lack of attention to the
christological *a priori*, amounting to an unwarrantable restriction of
the actuality of the Lord to a mere *knowledge that* Jesus is the living
Lord, flaws his definition of christology.

In the first section of this chapter we also raised the issue of the
coherence of the various types of christologies at the level of their

---

[67]Cf. above, pp. 292–293.

performative functions.[68] Pannenberg, along with most other christo-logical authors, does not raise this issue. He takes the profession of faith in Christ for granted as material for explication; he takes the documents of the New Testament for granted as material for founda-tion. But the tradition of the profession of Christian faith in Jesus' unity with God is more than a series of noetic statements which christology must explicate, and the recounting of the life, death and Resurrection of Jesus is more than a series of recollections which christology must allege as the basis of the Christian faith. The total point of the recounting of the life, death and Resurrection, as we shall see, is praise and thanksgiving; this performative function determines the quality of the recollection. The total point of the Christian profession of Jesus' unity with God, as we shall see, is the living out of the *imitatio Christi*—the compassionate welcome ex-tended to all creation to enter into communion with God. But these performative functions are only realized if christology starts with a consideration of the *actus directus* of faith, not when it rushes into legitimation by explication and foundation.

Thus we can see how failure to reflect on the *concretissimum* of the Christian message has led, not only to too narrow a definition of christology, but also to failure to appreciate the performative func-tions of christological profession of faith and recollection. The *auditus fidei* has been restricted by too much eagerness to achieve the *intellectus fidei*. The shape of the intellectual question has blinded the questioner to the fact that there is more here than matter for a correct answer to his question. In the next chapter, therefore, we will have to see to it that the primary Christian response to Jesus Christ alive and present in the Spirit is heard correctly, namely as an act of worship and witness. From there on, the more retrospective christologies are likely to be heard correctly, too.

---

[68]Above, pp. 303–308.

CHAPTER 9

The Way to the Father

"Come!" say the Spirit and the bride. He who gives this testimony
speaks: "Yes, I am coming soon!" Amen. Come, Lord Jesus!

The Revelation of John

You know about Jesus of Nazareth, how God anointed him with the
Holy Spirit and with power. He went about doing good and healing all
who were oppressed by the devil, for God was with him. And we can
bear witness to all that he did in the Jewish countryside and in
Jerusalem. He was put to death by hanging on a gibbet, but God raised
him to life on the third day, and allowed him to appear, not to the
whole people, but to witnesses whom God had chosen in advance—to
us, who ate and drank with him after he rose from the dead. He
commanded us to proclaim him to the people, and affirm that he is the
one who has been designated by God as judge of the living and the
dead.

The Acts of the Apostles

All the promises of God find their Yes in him. That is why we utter the
Amen through him, to the glory of God. [. . .] We are not, like so
many, peddlers of God's word; but as people of sincerity, as commis-
sioned by God, in the sight of God we speak in Christ.

The Second Letter of Paul to the Corinthians

You are children of God—God has sent the Spirit of his Son into our hearts crying, "Abba! Dear Father!"

The Letter of Paul to the Galatians

Retrospect

The Resurrection is not an historical event, yet its impact—from the appearances on—is one. This impact is not just a momentary revelation, on the basis of which the Church henceforth knows that Jesus is alive; it is also an abiding actuality, startling in its particularity. The proper name of a particular individual—which is what the title Christ became very early—identifies a community. This community is a *present* event, constituted by a present Jesus Christ alive in the Spirit.

In the previous chapter we argued that today's cultural situation, where God-talk tends to be a matter of philosophy or imagination rather than a matter of worship and witness, demands that the christological *a priori* be thematized and reflected upon as such, as a *given*.[1] We also argued that Pannenberg's construct, in spite of his effort to place the Resurrection in its proper central position in christology, failed to appreciate adequately the christological a priori for what it is: the present worship of, and witness to, Jesus Christ present and alive in the Spirit.[2] Legitimation of the Christian faith is indeed called for, both to demonstrate the inner consistency of the Christian faith and to show its coherence with the rightful demands of critical reason and human reflection. But it will have to come out of the Christian fact, as a structural feature of the *given*; otherwise autonomous discernment will end up sitting in judgment on the Christian fact.

In this chapter, therefore, we must begin to analyze the structure of the Christian fact. We will do so, after a short preliminary section on the primary Christian self-expression, by describing the relationship between the Church's worship and witness—as expressive of her life—and the life of Jesus Christ. This will lead us to consider the form which Christian worship typically takes. The next

---

[1] Above, pp. 299–303.
[2] Cf. above, pp. 314–318, 321–322.

chapter will then concentrate on the Christian witness and the christology that it embodies, to lay the groundwork for an analysis of its legitimations.

Preliminary: Christian self-expression

If Christians believe in Jesus Christ alive and present, what are we to expect when they express their faith? In view of what we surveyed in the Interlude,[3] their primary self-expression as believers will be future-oriented; it will bear the marks of witness—it will be acoustical in tone, it will derive its effectiveness from being spoken and heard rather than from being seen and read and known; it will involve the experience of time. Christians' original self-expression will also be strongly egological; it will express their existential self-awareness—that unifying awareness which underlies and suffuses all their concerns, which latter are conveyed by discernments. Now this peculiar Christian self-awareness is activated by their gracious encounter with Jesus Christ alive and present; the identity conveyed in the self-expression will therefore be a *responsive* identity. Christians' self-expression, therefore, will convey their self-awareness as called, converted, and sent. With *their* being called, all their concerns are invited to be included; with *their* being converted, all their concerns are summoned to be obedient; and with *their* being sent, all their concerns are challenged to hopeful surrender.[4]

Furthermore, just as a lover spontaneously turns his autobiography into a testimony to his beloved, the Christian self-expression will be a witnessing story about Christ. Because the point is neither the beloved's nor Jesus' biography, the story will be pre-critical; historical accuracy is not the point. The point is that the narrator of the story identifies himself under invocation, in the name of the person who, by encountering him, has called forth the identity he now enjoys and wants to express and share. Hence, the story told will be a *significant story*, not a critical narrative account. Here if anywhere it

---

[3]Above, pp. 265–293.
[4]Cf. Hans Küng, *On Being a Christian*, p. 553: "In a word: for both the individual human being and the community Jesus Christ in person, with word, deed and fate, is invitation ('you may'), appeal ('you should'), challenge ('you can')." Cf. also Hans Küng, *20 Thesen zum Christsein*, München, R. Piper & Co. Verlag, 1975, p. 8, thesis 17, and, of course, above, pp. 154–182, 189–202.

is the *tone* of the narrative that determines its point; only when heard as the language of love will Christian self-expression be correctly understood.

Let us phrase this with the help of the terminology we have used. Spontaneous Christian self-expression achieves its point in the direct experience of speech rather than in the consideration of language. It must be heard as address to be understood; an analytic, cognitive approach to it may cause the point to evaporate.

The original Christian self-expression must be heard as address; this means that it must be heard as witness.[5] Now it is characteristic of witness for the speaker to present himself personally as the guarantor of the reality he is witnessing to. In this way the listener experiences not only the direct encounter that occurs between himself and the witness, but also, *in* the person of the witness, the direct encounter between the witness and the reality he is witnessing to.[6] If we apply this to Christian self-expression we must say that it has the shape of witness backed up by worship. The Church's spontaneous self-expression is in the nature of personal address, and the Church's identity, which animates the address, is the responsive identity shaped by the presence of Christ alive in the Spirit which has prompted the Church's worshipful act of total surrender.

This connection between worship and witness in the Church's spontaneous self-expression is of great importance, for if the two are separated, what results is neither worship nor witness. If the Christian self-expression is uttered *only* to praise God it gets isolated from the world and turns into an act of tribal religiosity—an inauthentic, defensive gesture of self-affirmation directed against outsiders and against all questions, and thus an instance of "historical atavism"[7] unfortunately popular in certain brands of evangelism ancient and modern. If, on the other hand, it is uttered merely as witness, it turns into proselytizing—no loving surrender to others, but a summons to others to surrender themselves; witness becomes party propaganda. Thus the Church's witness is not compelling unless she is *over*heard to worship Jesus Christ as she speaks to the world; the Church's

[5]Cf. above, pp. 235–238.
[6]Cf. above, pp. 228–232.
[7]Cf. Karl Rahner, "The Development of Dogma," p. 67.

worship is vacuous if she drops her witness and loses her confidence before the world. Worship and witness will be the ways in which the Church must imitate Christ in his total surrender to the Father and his total self-giving to others. Only then will Christian self-expression be understood to convey *the Christian life itself*, if it is heard as the language of worship and witness. When considered as a series of statements, Christian self-expression may *look* as if it is merely a story *about* Jesus Christ; in the direct experience of speech, the Spirit of the risen Lord is heard.

This chapter will study three aspects of the Christian self-expression. First, we will concentrate on the fact that the Church expresses her identity under invocation of Jesus; this will lead to a consideration of the imitation of Christ in an eschatological perspective. Second, we will discover another feature of the close connection between Christian self-expression and the story of the life of Jesus, namely, that the latter is the warrant for the Church's involvement in history. Third, we will describe praise and thanksgiving to the Father as the source of all christological speech as well as the prime act of the Church's imitation of Christ.

INVOCATION AND IMITATION

Introduction: the need for original Christian confession

There is a cultural need for a thematic reflection on the christological *a priori*, as we said before.[8] What we did not say at the time is that this cultural need is also a theological necessity in the Church. Since the Church is not a closed language-community anymore, the traditional patterns of understanding are no longer effectual. The emphasis here is on the *patterns of understanding* into which the original Christian confession has been cast in the interest of *defining* the Church's identity, in the course of the great christological debates from the late third to the late seventh centuries.[9] For a considerable time, both the original Christian confession and also its *doctrinal shape*, the outcome of past debates, were experienced as effectual. But, owing to many sociohistorical factors, religious in-

---

[8]Cf. above, pp. 299–303.
[9]Cf. above, pp. 35–38.

struction gained more prominence than liturgical initiation and preaching, and so doctrine, not profession of faith, became the *primary* form in which the Christian confession was available to members of the Church.[10] But orthodoxy, along with orthopraxy, tends to identify people with the Church in an extrinsic rather than a personal and expressive way. Knowing the catechism and observing the church order appear to be much firmer identifications than they really are; when detached from the original Christian confession they turn into routine, and in the long run routine without conviction will not last. Moreover, the doctrinal and practical shapes of Christianity are themselves rather easily invaded and eroded by shifts in the culture at large, for they are themselves the product of culture. Doctrine and ecclesiastical practice reflect past encounters between faith and culture, and are therefore derivative rather than original. Thus there are personal as well as ecclesial reasons why emphasis on the original Christian self-expression is always indicated.

Still, in our own day there are special reasons for emphasizing the original Christian confession. We said at the outset of this book that the Church has become an open language-community. This situation demands concentration on the original Christian confession. Precisely because Church doctrine (and practice) are being invaded by new cultural sensibilities, Christians must have deeper resources than orthodoxy and orthopraxy to fall back on. Hence our emphasis on Christian identity in our introductory chapter.[11]

But if Christian identity is to be sought, it can in the first instance only be found in response to the living Lord. Christian identity is responsive identity, and its original expression is the worshipful confession of Christ's Lordship. This means that Christian identity must not be sought primarily in the development of new theologies in close touch with the present-day cultural concerns. We live in such a pluriform world that it is not advisable to engage in the "remaking of Christian doctrine"[12] by latching on to one or a few live

---

[10]It is interesting to note that "profession of faith" (*professio fidei*) originally meant the Christian's live witness to his faith, and only later became the technical term for statements of orthodox doctrine.

[11]Cf. above, pp. 16–18, 22–28.

[12]Cf. the titles of two books by Maurice Wiles, *The Making of Christian Doctrine*, A Study in the Principles of Early Doctrinal Development, Cambridge–London–New

cultural concerns. What is relevant to some may be irrelevant to and even exclude others. Theologies new or old do not always lead to Christian identity; the original Christian confession is a much better point of departure for the development of particular theologies that are relevant to cultural concerns. What the ecumenical movement has come to realize more and more over the last fifty years must become the program for the wider ecumenism that welcomes the whole world into its force-field: less emphasis on doctrinal consensus and more on worship and witness; concentration on Christian identity while allowing and encouraging divergence and pluriformity where it belongs, namely, in the area of the varieties of the Church's past or present relationships to the world—the main origin of doctrinal specialization and differentiation.

We conclude that there is a theological need, in the churches, to concentrate on Christian identity as expressed in the original profession of faith in response to Jesus Christ alive and present in the Spirit. Let us now turn to the shape of this original profession.

Totus Christus: the way

The Christian self-expression is the story of the Church's life in Christ. No wonder that Christians will express their responsive identification with Christ by pointing to a reality where the fullness of their faith attitude and the fullness of Christ coincide. That point is the *eschaton*. Our experience of faith appears to us *sub specie futuri*; our certainty is the certainty of assurance and confidence born from the appeal that comes to us out of the future as a never-ending prospect in process of patient actualization. The Christian self-expression, therefore, takes the form of a response to the absolute future.[13]

In the earliest Christian tradition, we find christologies which put the fulfillment of *Jesus himself* squarely in the *eschaton*. Since faith is future-oriented, we ought not to be surprised at expressions,

---

York–Melbourne, Cambridge University Press, 1967, and *The Remaking of Christian Doctrine*, The Hulsean Lectures 1973, London, SCM Press, 1974, except that Wiles seeks to define essential Christian doctrine by means of its reduction to a coherent and economical minimum, and not by taking the Church's worship and witness as the norm of all doctrine.

[13]Cf. Hans Küng, *On Being a Christian*, pp. 223–226, for a good discussion of the need for eschatology, not just futurology.

in Acts, which present Jesus as Christ-designate,[14] and at the famous passage in the first Letter to the Corinthians, where the Resurrection of Christ and his present kingship are presented as provisional, pending the *parousia* and Christ's final act of worship to the Father.[15] This apparent denial of Christ's *present* glory becomes un-understandable if we remember that the encounter with the risen Lord in the Spirit leads Christians to find their *own* identities in Jesus Christ; how, then, could *he* be completely fulfilled *apart from the complete fulfillment* of all the promises held out to those who believe—apart from God being all in all? If we identify, in faith, Jesus as the "absolute bringer of salvation" and leave it at that, this amounts to ignoring that there is a remainder of salvation outstanding, that God's promises are *not* completely fulfilled, that he whose very being is for us men and for our salvation is not fully himself until *all* of us find ourselves in glory, through him, with him, and in him, in the Father's house.[16] If in the actual experience of faith we experience the appeal of the absolute future, then we will not be able to view Jesus Christ as completely risen and instated as Son of God in power until the end of the world. To proclaim the glory of Christ may not separate us from him, and thus Jesus will be in agony till the world's end, as Pascal wrote; and he added that we must not sleep in the meantime.[17] But sleep in false assurance we will, in a safe but inauthentic possession of faith in the fulfillment of Jesus, once and for all, if we do not keep our sense of provisionality alive, also in christology. Christ's own hope is not fully realized, and so neither are his sufferings[18] nor, as a consequence, his instatement as Son of God in power.

A christology that really reflects the Christian's identification with the living Christ will not be reluctant to speak from the point of view of the fulfillment of history looking back, from the future, at what is still unfulfilled in history: how much humanity remains to be included; how many powers remain to be redeemed and how many

---

[14]Discussed by J. A. T. Robinson, "The Most Primitive Christology of All?"
[15]1 Cor 15, 20–28.
[16]Cf. Karl Rahner–Wilhelm Thüsing, *Christologie—systematisch und exegetisch*, pp. 104ff., and above, pp. 60–61.
[17]Blaise Pascal, *Pensées*, 553, p. 191.
[18]Cf. Col 1, 24.

burdens and sins remain to be borne in patient obedience; how many hopes remain yet to be brought to fulfillment. God the Father is the future of both Jesus Christ and the Church, because he went to the Father to prepare a place for us; he himself remains unfulfilled as long as he has not received us to himself, as long as where he is we are not yet also.[19]

If original Christian profession of faith is called for in our day, this thoroughgoingly eschatological christology has features that are very attractive. It is a witnessing christology; it is one which places the divinity of Christ in an eschatological perspective; and it is a christology which is identical with an ecclesiology. Let us briefly clarify these points.

First of all, a thoroughly eschatological christology sounds egological; speaking so affirmatively about the final fulfillment of Christ and of all things in him can only be done by Christians who put themselves on the line; it has the ring of witness and confidence. In this christology there is no danger that Christ might get isolated from the Church and isolated from the Father—two serious risks run by the hypostatic-union tradition, as we will argue in the next chapter; this means that there is no danger for such an isolated Christ to turn into an idol for the kind of believer who wants to affirm Christ's divinity while keeping his own personal faith-surrender somehow out of the discussion.

Second, this type of christology avoids the ambiguities which are connected with the uncritical attribution of "divinity" to Christ; it reserves the word "God" for the end of the discussion[20]—but "God" refers not to an idea but to an actuality: "God all in all."

Third, it avoids presenting Jesus Christ as unique in such a fashion as to raise suspicions of exclusivity. Instead, the uniqueness of Jesus Christ is presented precisely as his ability to do justice, inclusively and in an ultimate perspective, to all things. The rhetoric of inclusion is manifest in this type of original Christian self-expression. But the rhetoric of obedience is not less in evidence. The Pauline text speaks of "all things subject to him": the defeat of the powers that be and the final victory over death. It also speaks of the

---

[19]Cf. Jn 14, 2–3.
[20]Cf. Rahner's words, above, pp. 39–40, and 1 Cor 15, 28.

final actuality of God in terms of Christ's *own* subjection.[21] Thus the Church now lives in obedience in anticipation of the world's final obeisance, in Christ, to the Father.

In this eschatological christology we have an instance of the Church's self-expression in the closest possible identification with Christ. It reflects inclusion and obedience as the themes of the Church's life in the world in anticipation of the *eschaton*, and it expresses how these themes find their origin in the person of Christ himself yearning for the *eschaton* at the head of the Church. The Church expresses her own present identity with reference to Christ, and expresses her faith in him by having him share, in his very glory, in her own present struggle. Christology and ecclesiology coincide in an eschatological perspective.

Not every self-expression of the Church is such a confident statement of her own eschatological identification with the living Lord. More often than not the difference between the risen Lord and the present predicament of the Church is part of the affirmation. This does not mean that Church and Christ are separated; it does mean that the Church expresses her identity by means of a definite gesture of outreach in response to the presence of the living Lord. This leads us to the subject of invocation.

"In the Name of Jesus"

The apocalyptic genre, as Pannenberg points out, provided the early Christian community with a number of immediate recognitions now that Jesus was risen: the onset of the world's end, Jesus as the coming Son of Man, and the decisive self-revelation of God in Jesus.[22] How did the Church act on these recognitions?

First, the apocalyptic genre, which provided the Church with the aspirations and the metaphors to recognize and interpret the Resurrection, also provided the Church's earliest generations with some disillusionment in due course. They had to learn that the *parousia* was being indefinitely postponed. Was it from this delay that the community also learned that the risen Lord Jesus presided over their discernments?[23] Jesus Christ did not behave according to

---

[21]1 Cor 15, 27–28.
[22]*Jesus—God and Man*, pp. 66ff.
[23]Cf. above, pp. 146–153.

their expectations, shaped by apocalypticism; these expectations, therefore, were severely tested. But they survived. The delay of the *parousia* modified apocalyptic expectation—it did not abolish it. The former anticipation of an imminent *parousia* gave way to a spirituality of watchfulness and prayer in an attitude of faith that was still future-oriented but less definite in its anticipations.

The *survival* of apocalyptic expectation proves that the Resurrection did confirm and fulfill the aspirations of apocalypticism. The community's *modification* of the eschatological expectation is only intelligible if it is assumed that from the outset faith in the risen Lord was an indisputable faith in his absolute presidency over any aspirations, including those of apocalypticism. The risen Lord had become the name of the *eschaton*; apocalyptic hopes—those boldest of expectations—had been included, purified, and made absolute from the outset, even though it took years of patient perseverance in the confession of Christ's Lordship—that ever-recurring theme of the Letter to the Hebrews[24]—to realize the full implications of the Lord's presidency over the concerns expressed in the apocalyptic genre. Once again, what occurred was not so much the identification of Jesus as the eschatological Son of Man ("known" from apocalyptic expectation), as the actualization and refocusing of eschatological expectation and its metaphors in the encounter with the risen Lord. Jesus becomes the name not only of the *eschaton*, but also of continuing eschatological expectation.

Second, not only does the risen Lord, from his position of presidency, modify the Christian eschatology so that it comes to mean "eschatology in course of realization"; he also personalizes the *eschaton* to a degree unknown in apocalyptic expectation. The attention is irresistibly drawn to "this man Jesus."[25] Nowhere does the individuality of Jesus get blurred by the brilliance and the comprehensiveness of the eschatological fulfillment. The Resurrection, in other words, far from making Jesus an eschatological cipher for the fulfillment of "all things," emphasizes and asserts the individuality of the historical Jesus, who went about doing good and was crucified under Pontius Pilate. This in turn means that, when Christians

---

[24]Cf. Heb 3, 1; 4, 14; 10, 23.
[25]Cf. Acts 2, 32.

express their faith, they do so, indeed, prospectively, with reference to the glorified Jesus who is the judge of history; but they also do it retrospectively, with reference to the life of Jesus. This man Jesus becomes, not only the forerunner of life and of salvation, but also the forerunner and perfecter of faith.[26]

The Church's present life of faith, as she yearns for the fulfillment of which the risen Jesus is the first-fruits and the gift of the Spirit the anticipation, is summed up in the expression "in the Name of (the Lord) Jesus (Christ)." The phrase is a Semitism; it can best be rendered by "under invocation of the Lord Jesus Christ." It occurs in a variety of contexts in the New Testament: baptism, prayer, healing, preaching, suffering, persecution, miracles, forgiveness of sins, community meeting, petition, the risks of the apostolic life, anointing of the sick; it even occurs in the context of "everything you do."[27] Christians worshipfully refer themselves for their identity to Jesus of Nazareth present and alive, in the Spirit, as Lord, and all their undertakings are taken up into that basic act of worshipful surrender.

Why this emphasis on invocation? Because the Church's living speech, in response to the present Christ and inspired by the Spirit, bridges the gap that separates the Church from her Lord. In actual fact the Church is only in progress *toward* the *eschaton*—but at least her worshipful invocation of the Lord is the responsive actualization of the *eschaton* in her midst. The actual incorporation of Christians and indeed of the world has proved to be a slow process, but the confession of Christ's Lordship allows the Church to enjoy the ultimate in response to the present Christ.

Thus primary christology is born. The Church invokes Jesus Christ alive; in that living word of invocation the presence of the living Lord is heard and the Church expresses her own responsive identity. Worship and witness are the responsive actualization of Christ's presence.

This invocation takes two shapes. First, there are the names of Jesus; Christians address the living Christ with a variety of titles to

---

[26]Cf. Acts 3, 15; 5, 31; Heb 2, 10; 12, 2.
[27]Cf. Col 3, 17; 1 Pet 4, 14 registers the expression in the context of cursing.

orchestrate his glory and their own surrender to him.[28] Second, there is the story of Jesus' life, from his Baptism on. That the titles are prompted by the presence of Christ in the Spirit is obvious. That the story of Jesus' life is prompted by his presence in the Spirit is less obvious, but nonetheless true; the impetus for the recital of the life of Jesus comes from the future; it is the product of recollection stirred by the eschatological fulfillment.

This has consequences for the theology of the Word. Any affirmation of the primacy of the Word will have to draw its inspiration from the pneumatological tradition: the *living* speech of the Church is only accounted for if heard as the community's Spirited "Amen" to the presence of Christ in the Spirit.[29] The Church's living speech primarily bespeaks the prompter of that speech, and only secondarily is it the Church's own word. The Church must, therefore, live in awe of her own self-expression, and she must let herself be called into her identity and guided by the Word which she hears herself speak. This living Word expresses her very selfhood but it also challenges her to be her responsive self. The invocation of the Name of Jesus becomes both the expression of, and the call to, faith as the Christian's way to God.[30]

The invocation of the Name of Jesus expresses both the Church's unity with the living Christ and her separation from him. He has come into his glory; we are still on the way. The names of Jesus born from radicalizing transformation and from naming by

---

[28]Cf. above, pp. 137–143, 146–150.

[29]The Church endorses the presence of the living Christ by uttering her "Amen." This is connected with the view of Jesus Christ as the confirmation ("Amen" and "Yes") of God's promises, so much so that "Amen" is one of the titles of Jesus (Rev 3, 14). Joachim Jeremias (*The Prayers of Jesus*, London, SCM Press [*Studies in Biblical Theology*, Second Series, 6], 1967, pp. 112–115) shows that "Amen" at the beginning of a sentence is original Jesus-usage, conveying his response to the Father. A modern treatment of prayer that takes its inspiration from all this is Alan Ecclestone, *Yes to God*, London, Darton, Longman & Todd, 1975.

[30]This should also determine the theology of the sacraments. Sacraments are indeed self-actualizations of the Church, but only in response to the living Lord, who is therefore the primary agent, operating through the living word; Aquinas still attributes priority to the word in all sacraments, by calling it *forma sacramenti* (for example, *S. Th.*, III, q. 60, a. 6). The institution of the sacraments by Christ must also be primarily interpreted with reference to the living Lord now as the prime agent and motivator of the sacraments; a similar emphasis in 1 Cor 11, 23 where Paul traces the tradition about the Lord's Supper, not to the historical Jesus, but to "the Lord."

way of excellence as well as the key and headship images convey this unity in separation.[31] But this unity in separation is not static; it is a dynamism; it involves a program. The encounter with the living Lord, the *concretissimum* of the Christian message conveyed by the Christian invocation of Jesus, draws the Church into the *eschaton*. The living word of faith is a call to move into the future.

Drawn to the eschaton

In response to Christ, *the self-designations of the Church*—those expressions of her responsive identity—*take shape out of the future*, in reverse, so to speak. In two previous chapters we discussed the rhetoric of christology as one of inclusion, obedience and hope. Now we must say that in the Church's actual experience the order is reversed: hope, obedience and inclusion, as we have already suggested in our treatment of eschatological christology. The original christological confession is drawn out of the Church by the call of the future; its inspiration, its motoric force comes out of the Resurrection. The first chapter of the First Letter of Peter is a *locus classicus* for this dynamic. It starts with the "living hope through the Resurrection of Jesus Christ from the dead," moves on to the themes of suffering by trials and testing of faith (with an allusion to the sufferings of Christ) and of the call to sobriety and holiness (with another reminder of Christ's sufferings), and finally points to the predestination of Christ "before the foundation of the world," thus providing the ground for what we have called the rhetoric of inclusion.[32]

It is important to take this dynamic quite seriously. Nowhere in the New Testament do we find the abiding significance of Jesus and his cause, and hence the Church's sense of identity, traced back to the past, to abiding results of his works, to people who were once healed by him and are still alive, or to the inspiring memory of his person impelling his former followers to continue the good work.[33]

---

[31]Cf. above, pp. 150–152.

[32]1 Pet 1, 3–21.

[33]There is no indication in the New Testament that the Eleven traced their apostolic vocation back to their fellowship with the historical Jesus, except in 2 Pet 1, 16–19, which is a secondary text, and 1 Jn 1, 1–5, where the point is different. Peter's kerygmatic speeches in Acts (2, 14–37; 3, 12–26; 4, 8–12; 10, 34–43) never mention his

This fact has some relevance to modern apologetics. Teachers who want to open the eyes of modern people to the reality of the Resurrection, while (rightly) avoiding a cheap miraculism, must think twice before they attempt to suggest its credibility by extrapolating from some supposed abiding effects of Jesus' work or person on his associates, after a short period of shock. This would place the Resurrection in the same category with the survival of a beloved deceased person in his children, in his achievements, and in the fond memories of his associates. The Bible does not know such a construction. The New Testament is quite explicit in stating that—as far as the associates of Jesus were concerned—he and his mission were finished and the hopes he had raised were dashed, with a criminal's death to clinch the failure. The Resurrection is an absolute vindication by God—not by any person—of what was by human standards a total failure; what is more, it is God's vindication not only of a just man unjustly killed (an Old Testament commonplace understandably activated to convey the significance of the Resurrection)[34]—but of an equivalently impious man executed under the Law. *That* was what the first community had to cope with. Paul will only manage to make sense of this by using an *oxymoron*: Jesus was made into a curse under the Law; he was even made into sin—he who knew no sin himself.[35]

The Christian community *will* cherish the memory of Jesus as the just and holy man and his good works and undeserved sufferings, but this recollection is not the basis of its faith in the risen One; the

---

discipleship; only in one place is there a reference to "our" having been witnesses to all the things Jesus did in Judaea and Jerusalem, but from the context this refers clearly to Peter *and* his audience. When the "eating and drinking with him" is mentioned it refers to the time "after he rose from the dead." When Matthias is chosen by lot to complete the Twelve, he is found qualified because he is one of the men "who accompanied us during all the time that the Lord Jesus went in and out among us" (1, 21); this does refer to the earthly ministry of Jesus but makes no mention of any close following, on Matthias' part, of the historical Jesus; he is chosen to bear witness, with the others, to the *Resurrection*. Summing up: there is no claim on the part of the disciples that their present witness is directly continuous with their following of the earthly Jesus. The apostolic vocation derives from the Resurrection, and includes, purifies, and puts in perspective the apostles' frail discipleship around the earthly Jesus.

[34]Esp. Is 52, 7—53, 12; Wis 2, 10—3, 9.
[35]Gal 3, 10–14; 2 Cor 5, 21.

past did simply not warrant such a conclusion.[36] Rather, it is the Church's faith in the risen One that becomes the basis of the recollection; the *concretissimum* of the Christian message addresses the community from the future and thus revives the past.

This leads to two conclusions. First, since the Church is not just a continuation of the task or cause of Jesus owing to the abiding impact of his personality, the *imitatio Christi* is more than following the good example given by Jesus in the past. It would be a Pelagian, moralistic distortion of Christianity to point to Jesus' life as one on which God's blessing was manifest in the Resurrection, so that by following Jesus one might well count on similar divine recompense.

Second, *along with the life he lived in the flesh*, Jesus is placed, for the faithful, in the *eschaton*,[37] into which he leads the Church and whence he empowers her, his body marked by his life, summed up by the wounds. In the Christian experience of time,[38] the way of Jesus lies primarily in the future, at the head of the column of the faithful; he has already "entered the sanctuary" as the Letter to the Hebrews does not tire of saying.[39] The Church still has to go her way which is the way of Christ; thus the life of Christ, in the experience of the Church, is in the future. The *imitatio Christi* is not living while looking backward, but forward,

> with eyes fixed on Jesus, the forerunner and perfecter of the faith, who, for all the joy that was set before him, endured the cross, despising the shame, and is seated at the right hand of the throne of God.[40]

The true meaning of the life of Jesus, therefore, strikes the Church only in the light of the risen One, out of the future, as a call to discipleship. This is why the Gospels address the Church primar-

---

[36]Seen as an act of the historical Jesus the founding of the Church was a failure.

[37]Cf. above, pp. 288–289, for Bonhoeffer's insistence that Christ meets us out of the future.

[38]Since the Resurrection has made the *eschaton* into a totally reliable reality, Christian time-experience is no longer bound by the merciless irreversibility of time, according to which the present can only be reliably determined by the past. Cf. for this Donald MacKinnon's "Remarques sur l'Irréversibilité du Temps," in: *Archivio di Filosofia*, Roma, Istituto di studi filosofici, 1975, pp. 39–47.

[39]Heb 6, 20; 9, 12. 24.

[40]Heb 12, 2.

ily as witness, as Bonhoeffer well saw.[41] Precisely because he is the *eschatos* he becomes the forerunner, the *archēgos*, of the Church's *exodos* into the land of promise.

Way toward judgment

We have already mentioned some of the sets of related metaphors which the early Christian tradition came to use to orchestrate the *imitatio Christi*: body/head, flock/shepherd, community of faith/high priest, etc. On account of the preponderance of apocalyptic sensibilities activated by the Resurrection, however, one metaphor certainly occupies a key position: Jesus Christ is the Judge to come, for with his Resurrection the *eschaton* and God's judgment have become an actuality. The Fourth Gospel and Paul elaborate this association of Jesus with God's judgment most consistently. The former does so by casting the message consistently in an apocalyptic frame of reference, with "glory" and "judgment" for some of the main metaphors. Paul elaborates the theme mainly in the Letter to the Romans. He shows that by failing to acknowledge God in his manifestations in the Law and in the world both Jews and Gentiles are completely dependent for their salvation on God doing merciful justice to them.[42] The Resurrection has placed Jesus, whom the powers that be—in retrospect, of course—failed to recognize as the Lord of glory, as Paul writes elsewhere,[43] in the position of being the personal norm for what it means to believe. Thus faith has become an act, not of human power of wisdom or discernment, but of obedience—obedient faith, after the pattern of Abraham, to God's justice manifest in Jesus Christ, in the power of the Spirit.

Does this mean that general human religiosity and the Law have been definitively rejected? Far from it. In fact, the whole creation, caught in futility against its deepest intentions, still groans for the freedom-in-glory of the children of God; true, in the light of God's judgment, the creation is manifested as enslaved and subjugated to transience, but hope, not slavery, is the last word.[44] From

---

[41]Cf. above, pp. 268–270.
[42]Rom 1, 18—3, 20.
[43]1 Cor 2, 8.
[44]Cf. Rom 8, 19–23.

this perspective of hope activated by the Resurrection, Paul states that all of creation can count on having its deepest concerns done justice to. From the same perspective the Law, too, finds itself truly established, for the election that lies at its root finds itself fulfilled in Jesus Christ.[45] Elsewhere, Paul even puts forward his own life as a devotee of the Law as a case in point; in his coming to know "Jesus Christ my Lord" and "the power of his Resurrection" he has realized that he was set apart before he was born. He has found his deepest identity in his coming to the knowledge of Christ, and in his being found in him; so he strains forward toward what lies ahead. His former seeking for religious self-affirmation on the basis of the prestige of the Law becomes, in the light of the Resurrection, "a loss" and "refuse"; righteousness religiously achieved by self-justification and self-discipline in the name of the Law does not last.[46] The risen Christ present in the Spirit is the source of the life of faith and its judge.

Summary: Imitatio Christi

The inspiration for the Church's imitation of Christ, we argued, comes out of the future whence the risen Christ draws the Church into the total surrender. We have just added that the judgment of the Church's discipleship is also in the future. We can now, by way of retrospect, sum up the characteristics of the *imitatio Christi* as it is shaped by the Church's responsive invocation of the living Christ.

First, the Church's way of life is set in the context of her responsive surrender to the present Christ in an eschatological perspective. This means: it is set in the context of worship and hope. Paul's instructions on the Christian life in the Letter to the Romans are an eloquent demonstration of this: they are wedged in between an opening exhortation to spiritual worship to God and a concluding promise of abundant hope.[47] The whole range of life, from the ordinary duties involved in being part of the Christian and secular communities to the Christian's response to persecution, is shaped by worship and hope.[48]

---

[45] Cf. Rom 3, 31; Gal 3.

[46] Gal 1; Phil 3.

[47] Rom 12, 1—15, 13.

[48] E. Schillebeeckx, *Jezus*, pp. 334–339, points out that the creed of the community behind Q lacked an explicit Resurrection-kerygma, but did acknowledge the activity

Second, this orientation toward the future makes the *imitatio Christi* more far-reaching and realistic than the mere following of the example of Jesus in the past.[49] It reaches farther, because the Church herself can discern, in virtue of the Spirit, the way of Christ in any concrete circumstances of place and time in which she finds herself.[50] It is also more realistic: the historical Jesus' recounted actions are not necessarily the best guide to Christian decision-making in the present; *imitatio Christi* is not repetition of particular precedents, but living in the Spirit of the risen Lord in a world whose ever-shifting realities must always be welcomed, converted, and put in perspective anew with the mind of Jesus Christ.

Does this mean that the historical, documentary aspect of the *imitatio Christi* is completely superseded? Can the historical Jesus be dropped completely as a source of *imitatio*? Obviously not. He remains the prototype, the touchstone, the warrant, the canon; the Church on her way will have to model herself after him. But the light in which the historical Jesus' actions are understood comes from the future.

Third, the orientation toward the future will prevent the Church from worrying unduly about whether her decisions are right in the sense of being in accordance with the historical Jesus. She knows that judgment rests ultimately, not with herself as she tests her behavior against the New Testament, but with the Father judging the world in the risen Christ, who is to come to do justice to the living and the dead. The Church's surrender to God's judgment in Christ strengthens her continued invocation of the Name of Jesus. Never will the Church live up to him in such a way as to *be* completely his presence in this world. She will always, in her worship, have to appeal to his merciful presence and to profess her reliance on his advocacy with the Father on her behalf.

---

of the heavenly Lord in the Christian prophets' kerygma, and expected Jesus' parousia in an active attitude of religious-ethical concern. Thus the eschatological expectation of the Q-community becomes its warrant for the *imitatio Christi*.

[49]I have argued that Küng's *On Being a Christian* tends to present the imitation of Christ too much as the following of past example; this is connected by Küng's relative neglect of worship. Cf. Frans J. van Beeck, "Küng's *Christ Sein*: A Review Article," pp. 279–281.

[50]Cf. Paul's assurance ("I, not the Lord"; "I have the Spirit of God") in 1 Cor 7, 12. 40; the point of the promise of the Counselor in Jn 14, 16 is analogous.

By invoking Jesus Christ alive and present in the Spirit, the Church expresses her own responsive identity. This invocation also sets a program for the Church: it draws her into the *imitatio Christi*. In the Name of Jesus the Church is on her way to God's judgment.

A few pages ago we stated that the invocation of Jesus Christ occurs in two principal forms, namely titles by which Christians bring themselves and their concerns into the total surrender, and the story of Jesus. These two are connected; we will argue this point and describe its significance in the twelfth chapter of this book.[51] For the time being we must concentrate on the type of invocation represented by the story of the life of Jesus.

The life of Jesus and the life of the Church

The Church tells the story of the life of Jesus as a worshipful and witnessing expression of her own responsive identity as she goes on her own way to meet the *eschaton*. The story of Jesus is the Church's autobiographical testimony to Christ; if the Church is on her way to the *eschaton*, it is not surprising that she should give an account of her own faith by means of a story in which Jesus is pictured as going to his death and Resurrection. Even the shortest kerygmatic formulas, which reflect the original apostolic proclamation,[52] are characterized by this transition from the world into the *eschaton*. Thus we read in the beginning of the Letter to the Romans:

> [. . .] the Gospel of God [. . .] concerning his Son, who was descended from David according to the flesh and designated Son of God in power in virtue of the Holy Spirit by his Resurrection from the dead, Jesus Christ our Lord.[53]

Besides short formulas such as the one just quoted, the apostolic *kērygma* is also found in somewhat more ample form, in which we can already recognize, in outline, the Synoptic Gospels. In the Acts of the Apostles there are several good examples; one of them reads:

---

[51]Below, p. 510.
[52]The classic account of this is still C. H. Dodd, *The Apostolic Preaching and Its Developments*, New York–Evanston, Harper & Row, 1964.
[53]Rom 1, 1–4.

You know what happened in all of Judea, beginning from Galilee after the baptism that John preached: Jesus from Nazareth: how God anointed him with the Holy Spirit and power; how he went about doing good and healing all those who were oppressed by the devil, for God was with him; and we are witnesses to all that he did both in the country of the Jews and in Jerusalem. They put him to death by hanging him on a tree. He is the man whom God raised on the third day and whom he made manifest, not to all the people, but to witnesses elected by God in advance—to us, who ate and drank with him after he rose from the dead.[54]

This short summary of Jesus' life clearly has a triple agenda. The first one is to state that the telling of the story is a testimonial invocation warranted by the Resurrection. The second one is that the life of Jesus was a climactic journey, marked by goodness to others and struggle with the powers that be, and ending in final rejection followed by divine vindication. Third, the implication for the Church is that the story of Jesus provides her with a programmatic parallel to her own life; the story becomes a charter for the Church's imitation of Christ.

In the Synoptic Gospels this agenda reappears in many places, except that the explicit reference to the Resurrection as the warrant for the telling of the story is usually absent; it is assumed rather than stated.[55] This is doubtlessly due to the fact that the early communities did not have to be reminded that the presence of the risen Lord was the context in which the recollection of the life of Jesus occurred. The other two items, however, are very frequently visible: the parallelism between the Church's present life and Jesus', and the eschatological orientation of Jesus' own life.

It would be easy to give many examples of this. There are, for example, the accounts of Jesus' baptism,[56] with their emphasis on acknowledgment of human sinfulness in response to John's apocalyptic preaching and their pointers to divine sonship, presence of the Spirit, and mission to service. The relevance of this to the Church's

---

[54]Acts 10, 36–41. Cf. also Acts 13, 23–25. 27–31.

[55]But cf. Mk 1, 35: "In the morning, a great while before day, he rose and went out to a lonely place, and there he prayed." Is it fanciful to see here a cryptic pointer to the Resurrection—Jesus going to the Father alone at the break of day?

[56]Mk 1, 9–11 parr.

interpretation of Christian baptism is obvious: acknowledgment and rejection of sin, acceptance of the Spirit, and commitment to holiness and service. But the Baptism pericopes also stress the climactic nature of Jesus' life: he sets out on his road—in the midst of temptations—to the cross; his Baptism is Jesus' act of commitment to his eschatological journey.

Similar analyses could be made for the temptation pericopes and for the passages in Luke's Gospel where Jesus is invited to preach in the synagogue and where he sets his face against Jerusalem.[57] They all have a clear ecclesiastical relevance and they present Jesus' life as a climactic journey. A very good example, too, is afforded by the series of pericopes in the beginning of the Gospel of Mark, an ancient literary subunit starting with Jesus' "proclamation of the good news of God" and ending with the plot to destroy him.[58] The whole series is a summary of all the elements of Jesus' ministry: he calls the disciples, teaches with authority, drives out unclean spirits, heals the sick, and associates with the unclean; he forgives sins and associates with sinners, which leads to confrontation with the Pharisees and, through them, with the claims of the Law, culminating in the conflict about the healings on the sabbath. But it is not the ministry, but the person of Jesus that is the focal point of the story: he announces God's present kingship with unprecedented authority; he is tempted and obeyed by evil spirits; he goes out alone to pray; in his encounters he shows pity; he perceives "in his spirit" what others are thinking; he has power to forgive sins, and so his mission is not to righteous people but to sinners. He refers to his being "the bridegroom" who is to be "taken away"; he calls himself the Lord of the sabbath; finally, he faces accusation and realizes, with anger *and* sympathy for his accusers, that he is marked out for destruction.

Again, on the one hand the account of the life of Jesus in all these pericopes is clearly suffused by the Church's need to tell the story of Jesus in the light of her present faith-experience. On the other hand, the story is also told as the climactic life-story of the risen One: his life and his ministry led to the death out of which God raised him, so that the Church now enjoys the gift of the Spirit in his Name.

---

[57]Mt 4, 1–11 par.; Lk 4, 1–12; Lk 9, 51ff.
[58]Mk 1, 14—3, 6.

Thus the presence of Jesus Christ alive in the Spirit prompts the Church's expressive account of her identity; the Church expresses her identity responsively, by witness, in the Name of Jesus who calls her into the future; invoking Jesus means telling the story of his going to the Father; telling that story means finding the paradigm for the Church's own way, through history, to the Father.

In the next chapters we will have to come back to the story of Jesus and its significance for the Church. In the present chapter we have one point of discussion outstanding, namely, the connection between the telling of the life of Jesus and worship.

A Sacrifice of Praise and Thanksgiving

Homologia as unity of worship and witness

The Christian self-expression, we said in the introduction to this chapter, is a witnessing story about Christ. This witness, we went on to say, is backed up by worship.[59] If, then, the Church's self-expression takes the form of a recounting of the life of Jesus, we can expect that the recounting of the story of Jesus also occurs as an act of worship.

Why is it important to establish this? Because our later under-standing of the life of Jesus will be determined by the performative function we attribute to the original telling of the story of Jesus' life. Wolfhart Pannenberg's christology is an example of this. Because of his lack of awareness of the significance of Christ's presence now, he reads the life of Jesus primarily as recollective material for the foundation of christology.[60] We have argued that the original Christian self-expression occurred as a response to the living Christ and it took the form of a recounting of the life of Jesus. The story of the life of Jesus, therefore, will have features that are not done justice to if it is primarily considered as a series of recollections.

Ever since Charles Harold Dodd's important study of the apostolic preaching, it has become customary to refer to the original christological confession as the *kērygma*—the message. The term and the interpretation of the New Testament it promoted have

---

[59]Above, pp. 328–329.
[60]Cf. above, pp. 314–315, 323–324.

doubtlessly succeeded in focusing the attention of theologians on the original message of the Gospel and on the centrality of the Resurrection which provoked the message. Yet there is reason to wonder whether the term has not obscured a very fundamental aspect of New Testament christology. What we have been accustomed, since Dodd, to call the *kerygma* (a term that derives more authority from Evangelical Word-theology than from the New Testament) is in fact not just the apostolic preaching—the Spirited call to conversion and obedience of faith in Christ alive—but first and foremost it is the Christian *homologia*, the narrative recital, in praise of God, through Jesus Christ, on the strength of the Spirit, of the great things God has done among us.

Unfortunately, modern English Christian idiom has no one word to express what Christian Greek conveyed by *homologein* and Christian Latin by *confiteri*, reflecting the Hebrew *hōdāh* (the related nouns are *homologia, confessio, tōdāh*). All these words meant three things *in one*: worship, witness, and self-expression—the third often in the sense of confession of sins. These three have had a tendency to drift apart, with consequences for all three of them. Worship apart from witness tends to become self-centered and dissociated from the world. Witness apart from worship tends to become mere preaching and teaching. The third ingredient, self-expression, is also dissociated: in witnessless worship the self is very much involved, but without expression; in worshipless witness there is much expression, but the question is always: Does the witness believe his own message? We must, therefore, realize that for the New Testament self-expression, praise and thanksgiving to God and telling the story of salvation as a message for others are basically one.

The Old Testament provided the New with the model for this. For the Jew, worshiping God means praising him and thanking him by recalling and enumerating in detail, for all to hear, the concrete events in his life that have come to him as blessings; he remembers them in thanksgiving but he also reminds God of them in petition for further evidence of his faithful love. Blessings received, however, are also a summons to responsibility; having received them, the Jew must now act as the guardian and the teacher of whatever is good and noble in the world.

The New Testament communities' response to the Resurrection

was analogous. They recall the life, death and Resurrection of Jesus (*anamnēsis*), both to praise and thank God (*eulogia, eucharistia*) and to pray for the coming of the kingdom.[61] With these words of eucharistic recollection, which also express their own responsive identity as Christians (*homologia*), they address themselves to the world as witnesses and messengers *(martyrion, kērygma),* and to each other in teaching, exhortation and admonition: the sacrifice of praise and thanksgiving becomes the call to obedience of faith and imitation of Christ.

In this light it is not surprising that David Stanley should have discovered worship behind numerous passages in Paul's letters,[62] and that such writings as the First Letter of Peter and Revelation suggest liturgies as the background for exhortation. Yet, in many of these and other New Testament passages the life of Jesus is hinted at rather than told in full. It is not until the second century that the Christian liturgy will begin to orchestrate its worship by means of (sometimes lengthy) renderings of the way of Jesus.[63] But there is one basic principle behind all of this, namely, that the invocation of Jesus Christ is both worship of the Father and witness to evoke faith in others.

Now that we have discussed the connection between witness and worship in the telling of the life of Jesus, we must further concentrate on the nature of the latter. We will do so by two points. First, we will discuss its primary attitudinal characteristic— *parrhēsia;* second, we will discuss its primary shape—*eucharistia*—as the original and typically Christian form of worship. We will then end this chapter with a conclusion about the relationship between worship and doctrine.

Parrhēsia as the experience of Jesus' unity with the Father
The Church's *act of speaking* in telling the story of Jesus' life at once expresses her own identity "in the Name of Jesus" and respon-

---

[61]For a discussion of *anamnēsis* as an act of remembering as well as reminding, cf. Joachim Jeremias, *The Eucharistic Words of Jesus,* New York, Charles Scribner's Sons, 1966, pp. 237–255.

[62]Cf. his book *Boasting in the Lord.*

[63]For examples cf. Cyprian Vagaggini, *Theological Dimensions of the Liturgy,* pp. 224–225, 164–168, etc.

sively actualizes his presence in the Spirit. This confident act of speaking, we have argued, conveys more than the things said, just as the proclamation of the message *(kēryssein)* conveys more than the content of the message *(kērygma)*. Now we must say the same for the Church's act of worship: it is primarily an act of boldness and confidence *(parrhēsia)*. In thus telling the story of Jesus in response to his presence in the Spirit the Church makes two related claims. First, the living Christ is the ultimate and complete actualization of the glory of the Father. Second, the telling of the story of Jesus is the ultimate glorification of the Father—worship wholly and totally adequate to God.

The Church, in other words, takes up the Jewish tradition of praising God by telling the story of Abraham, Isaac and Jacob, the story of the Exodus, the story of "Gideon, Barak, Samson, Jephthah, David and Samuel and the prophets" and all the other worthies of the repressed post-exilic nation alluded to in the Letter to the Hebrews.[64] But she claims that all these persons, even though they were well attested on account of their faith, did not live to see the fulfillment of the promises.[65] Now the promises are fulfilled in Jesus, and hence the telling of his story carries the tradition of praising God one decisive step further: the Church's story of Jesus is the act of faith that succeeds in reaching the living God. And since the story of Jesus expresses the Church's own identity in response to Jesus, the Church herself has unobstructed access to the throne of God.[66] The temple veil is torn, the true sanctuary is open, the heavens are no longer impregnable. Through Jesus the Church is called "to offer a sacrifice of praise to God, that is, the tribute of lips that acknowledge his Name," and she herself has become "a holy priesthood, to offer spiritual sacrifices to God through Jesus Christ." It is owing to the Church's being God's own people that she is enabled "to declare the wonderful deeds of him who called you."[67]

---

[64]Cf. Heb 11, 4–38.

[65]Cf. Heb 11, 39.

[66]The mere frequency of the word *thronos* (throne) in Revelation (meaning the throne of God and of the Lamb) has a cumulative effect: it conveys the incredible confidence in worship underlying the book, whose main performative emphases are consolation and encouragement in times of trial.

[67]Heb 13, 15; 1 Pet 2, 5; cf. Rev 1, 6.

It is obviously impossible here to make an inventory of the images and allusions that the New Testament uses to convey the Church's certainty of having direct access to the living God through Jesus Christ alive and present in the Spirit.[68] All sorts of expressions from the Old Testament are mustered up to convey this one certainty: in Christ, the Church has confident access to God himself, and as a result the Gospel message is the revelation of God's innermost secret. No room for inadequacy here: Paul boasts of his God-given sufficiency through Christ toward God, and so his ministry is guaranteed by the life-giving Spirit himself.[69] It may be that the words spoken and the metaphors used are not entirely compelling and that they leave a gap to be bridged; the Church does not experience the gap as a void,[70] but as the fullness of God's presence, through Jesus Christ, in the Holy Spirit.

It is from this experience of *parrhēsia* in response to the risen Christ that the essential Christian doctrine of the divinity of Christ will eventually be developed. God is no longer just experienced in a variety of complementary ways, as of old, nor is he known any longer just by the names of a "cloud of witnesses"; he is now experienced in the glory of Christ and known by the name of "the reliable witness"[71]—his very Son, present and alive in the Spirit, very God from very God.

It is an understatement to say that the Church's identification of Jesus Christ as divine while keeping him separate from the Father was an extraordinary gesture. Christians must have felt that the use of the *Kyrios*-title and the gradual obsolescence of such provisional titles as "the prophet" and "the just man" flew in the face of Jewish monotheism. But the first Christians were aware, with a confidence that knew no bounds, that, in the *homologia* of Jesus' life and Lordship, they themselves became part of a new reality, an unprece-

---

[68]Cf., for example, Heb 1-2; Mk 12, 35-37 parr.; 2 Cor 2, 14-4, 6.

[69]2 Cor. 3, 4-6.

[70]I wonder if the problems I have with Maurice Wiles' *The Making of Christian Doctrine* and *The Remaking of Christian Doctrine* go back to this. If the gap between faith-surrender and faith-expression is experienced as empty, there will be a tendency to stress "economy" in doctrine (cf. *The Remaking of Christian Doctrine*, p. 17); if the gap is experienced as full, there will be a corresponding urgency to do justice to this fullness by bold and maximally expressive doctrine.

[71]Cf. Heb 1, 1; 12, 1; Rev 1, 5.

dented glorification of God. Only this confidence will account for the freedom with which the early community addresses, in the Spirit, their "dear Father" and associates Jesus with him in an unqualified manner. No matter how unprecedented the historical Jesus' usage of "Abba" may have been, in and of itself it does not account for its acceptance by the Church; only in the vindication of Jesus' person in the Resurrection will the community also take over his bold usage and start to address God as "dear Father."[72] Thus the Church endorses the unity of Jesus and the Father; thus she recognizes herself, in the Spirit, as sons and daughters in the Son. As a result, the Church will have to settle for the accusations of insanity and blasphemy which Jesus suffered;[73] that she did so points to the power of conviction and confidence with which she identified Jesus' person as the presence of the actuality of God.

Eucharistia as thankfulness for the presence of God

Homologia is the unity of worship and witness; its main characteristic is *parrhēsia*. In the confident telling of the story of Jesus in response to his presence in the Spirit, the Church is certain that her worship does justice to God. In her own confession the Church begins to know Jesus himself as the person who does total justice to God.

In all this, we argued, the Church is aware of being involved in an unprecedented glorification of God. We must briefly examine what it is that makes the Church's sacrifice of praise and thanksgiving—of which we said that it was a continuation of the Old Testament tradition—so unprecedented.

In his study "Daily Prayer in the Life of Jesus and the Primitive Church" Joachim Jeremias writes:

A new way of praying is born. Jesus talks to his Father as naturally, as intimately and with the same sense of security as a child talks to his father. It is a characteristic token of this new mode of prayer that it is

---

[72]Cf. Joachim Jeremias, *The Prayers of Jesus*, pp. 11–65.—Jesus' use of the Father-metaphor is in itself neither unprecedented nor normative; what is both unprecedented and normative is the *tone of familiarity* of the Aramaic *Abba.* This observation is of some relevance to feminist concerns.
[73]Cf. Mk 3, 21–22.

dominated by thanksgiving. The only personal prayer of Jesus of some length from the time before the passion is a thanksgiving in spite of failure (Matt. 11.25 par. Luke 10.21). An echo of this predominance of thanksgiving is preserved in John 11.41, where Jesus gives thanks *before* being heard. There is a profound reason for this predominance of thanksgiving in Jesus' prayer. [. . .] Thanksgiving is one of the foremost characteristics of the new age. So when Jesus gives thanks he is not just following custom. There is more to it than that; he is actualizing God's reign here and now.[74]

Is Jeremias right in considering thanksgiving the typically Christian form of the praise of God? When he gives thanks to the Father, is Jesus not following Jewish tradition? What, then, is the novel element? It is *the reason why* he gives thanks: here are people— "children" he calls them—who have recognized the *actual presence* of the living God in the person of Jesus. No longer is God known merely indirectly, in the blessings of life; he is now known directly, in the Son. The new thanksgiving is the living response to the actuality of God, and thus it is also the responsive actualization of the kingdom.

In the passage from Matthew it is still only Jesus who utters the *eucharistia on behalf of* the "children" who have come to faith—a faith that will prove as brittle as it is now buoyant—in the Father's self-revelation in his own person. For the time being it is only Jesus—the "kingdom in person"[75]—who thus thanks the Father. The self-offering of the Church in thanksgiving for the adoption to sonship—warranted by the historical thanksgiving of Jesus—will only come when Jesus is raised to the glory of God the Father, and thus when the actuality of God impinges on the scattered and disenchanted ex-followers. That actuality of God born out of the life and suffering of Jesus revealed "with the dynamic power of the Holy Spirit, and carrying complete conviction," will be none other than Jesus Christ alive and present, "Christ the power of God and the wisdom of God."[76] By invoking him the Church will associate herself with him and thus enter into his eternal act of *eucharistia* to the Father; and as she sings his praise she will become a witness to the

---

[74]*The Prayers of Jesus*, p. 78.
[75]Origen's word *autobasileia*; cf. above, p. 193.
[76]1 Thess 1, 4; 1 Cor 1, 24.

Father's glory. The story of Jesus, self-expression of the Church and the actualization of his presence, is a eucharistic story; and as she tells this story, invokes Jesus' Name, and turns to him in the Spirit, the Church knows that she also does justice—boldness beyond words!—to the living God. Thus the Church thanks God for being enabled to praise him as he deserves to be praised.[77] And in this responsive praise, the living God himself is actually present in the world.

The fact that all christology starts with worship has profound consequences for the development of christology. We will elaborate the principal one, namely, that doctrine is only rightly understood in the context of worship.

"Disciplina arcani"

"I am speaking to the faithful. If I say anything which the catechumens do not understand, let them stop balking and hurry to the fold. For there is no need to give away the mysteries," said Augustine in a sermon.[78] With these words he provided an instance of the growing custom of the ancient Church not to communicate the central teachings—really the worship of the Church—to anyone until Baptism. The handing-over (*traditio*) of the Lord's Prayer, the Eucharistic Prayer, the other sacraments, and the Creed—whose doxological form betrays its original function—became part of an initiation process. Only within the setting of the worshiping community was the fullness of the mystery revealed to those who had rejected idolatry and believed in the one true God and in his Son Jesus Christ.[79]

---

[77]Cf. *Deus, de cuius munere venit ut tibi a fidelibus tuis digne et laudabiliter serviatur* in the Old Roman Missal, Twelfth Sunday after Pentecost.

[78]*Enarr. in CIX Ps.*, 17, *PL* 37, col. 1450, quoted by P. Batiffol, art. *"Arcane,"* in *Dict. Théol. Cath.*—Cf. also Tertullian's *omnibus mysteriis silentii fides debeatur*: "In all mysteries the very fact that they are mysteries requires the pledge of silence" (*Apol.* VII, 6). In drawing the Christian mysteries so close to the Samothracian and Eleusinian mysteries Tertullian put the Church wide open to Izaak Casaubon's charge, 1400 years later, that the *disciplina arcani* was nothing but a pagan invasion of Christianity.—Dietrich Bonhoeffer revived the issue in order to preserve genuine worship; cf. Eberhard Bethge, *Dietrich Bonhoeffer*, New York–Hagerstown–San Francisco–London, Harper & Row, [2]1977, pp. 784–786.

[79]Cf. 1 Thess 1, 9–10.

The term *disciplina arcani* was produced in the sixteenth century and utilized by seventeenth-century controversialists to account for the absence, in the early authors and even in Scripture, of certain mandatory doctrines and practices of the Catholic Church. The phrase conveys very aptly the care with which the early Church, demonstrably from Cyril of Jerusalem until after Augustine, went about her catechetical task. The fear of persecution cannot have been more than a secondary motive for the practice, for early apologists like Justin wrote about the Christian mysteries with great freedom, and the discipline was made stricter rather than looser as the persecutions ceased. A better explanation for the practice is the probability that Christians might be suspected of such heinous idolatry as tritheism or theophagy[80] if the Trinity or the Eucharist were communicated out of context. This explanation is strengthened by the fact that the discipline disappeared as Christianity became more and more the popular and established religion, so that misunderstanding on the part of outsiders ceased to be a live possibility.

The *disciplina arcani* conveys that the ancient Church was aware of the possibility that doctrine outside the context of worship might be misunderstood by unbelievers. Evidence for this awareness is also found elsewhere, for example, in the stated reluctance of Church Fathers like Ephrem the Syrian and Hilary of Tours to get involved in doctrinal speculation and definition.[81] Their reluctance may have been excessive, but it does indicate their conviction that *worship is the only safe context of doctrine.* And indeed, such central Christian doctrines as the Trinity, the incarnation, and the Eucharist—"we have no [pagan] altar," Minucius Felix assures his pagan readers[82]—might repel outsiders by their ostensible crudeness. But more importantly, the intellectual discussion of these doctrines might imply that they were intellectually cogent—a suggestion which might also block the road to faith. The *intellectus fidei* must never precede the *auditus fidei.*

Doctrine comes out of worship; doctrine by itself *may* lead to

---

[80]The words mean "the worship of three gods" and "god-eating."

[81]For Hilary, cf. Maurice Wiles, *The Making of Christian Doctrine*, pp. 32–33; for Ephrem, cf. Robert Murray, *Symbols of Church and Kingdom*, pp. 89–90.

[82]*Octavius* X, 2; XXXII, 1.

worship, but then again it may not. Whatever the original status of the *disciplina arcani* may have been, it reminds us that the core of the Christian faith-experience is the Church's worshipful act of surrender in the Name of Jesus Christ. This eucharistic surrender, itself beyond observation, justification and cogent argument, nevertheless inspires all Christian witness and, further down the road, all Christian recollection and reflection.

This leads to an important conclusion. In this entire chapter we have characterized the Church's responsive self-expression in worship and witness as an act, a dynamism, a movement to the *eschaton*. This dynamic self-expression also draws the Church into the dynamism of the imitation of Christ, whose own life, recounted by way of worship and witness, is the warrant for the Church's going to the Father. The Church's worship, her witness, and her life, are thus a dynamic response prompted by the dynamic presence of the Father in Jesus Christ alive and present to the Church in the Spirit.

Worship is the only safe setting of doctrine, we said. Whatever doctrines may be derived from this *actus directus* of worship, witness and imitation of Christ in response to the dynamic presence of God in Christ, *they may never belie this responsive dynamism.* It is in the nature of doctrine to be propositional and in that sense fixed. But doctrines are only instrumental in comparison with the *actus directus* of faith; the properties of the instrument must not be transferred to the reality in the service of which the instrument is used. Christian thought will have to make sure that it does not affirm the divinity of Christ as if it were a static reality of an objective nature; wherever this happens, Christian doctrine has lost touch with the act of worship and witness in response to the *concretissimum* of the Christian message.

Retrospect and outlook

The past two chapters have dealt with the original Christian fact, which, we argued, must be thematically reflected on in our day for cultural as well as ecclesiastical reasons. This original Christian fact, we discovered, is the Church's self-expression in response to the presence, in the Spirit, of Jesus Christ alive. This original fact is also future-oriented: the *actus directus* of worship and witness draws the Church into the *eschaton* with a confidence and a hope that can only come from the Father who has given the Church, in Jesus Christ, the assurance of eschatological fulfillment. Thus these chapters have dealt with two themes we discussed earlier in this book: the rhetoric of hope and the primary experience of the present, which is an experience *sub specie futuri.*

Now we are ready to study the present *actus directus* of faith in a more retrospective way. In the process, we will also discover how christological recollection (or critical christology) and christological reflection (or reflective christology) are related to, and reconciled in, the act of total surrender to the risen One.

CHAPTER 10

God With Us

Power is a form of Ate. The victims of power, and any power has its victims, are themselves infected. They have then to pass it on, to use power on others. This is evil, and the crude image of the all-powerful God is a sacrilege. Good is not exactly powerless. For to be powerless, to be a complete victim, may be another source of power. But Good is non-powerful. And it is in the good that Ate is finally quenched, when it encounters a pure being who only suffers and does not attempt to pass the suffering on.

Iris Murdoch

There are two kinds of solitude, depending on what the solitary person turns away from. If this be solitude: to free oneself from the kind of intercourse with reality that consists in experiencing and using it—then we must say: this kind of solitude is always necessary if a person is ever to achieve any act of relationship at all, not just the highest. If this be solitude: absence of relationship—then we must say that he who is abandoned by those to whom he uttered the true *Thou* is taken up by God, not he who himself abandoned them. Only he who craves to use things can be the captive of anything; he who lives on the strength of present encounter can only be united with them. But he who is thus united, he is the person who is ready for God. For only he brings a human actuality with him into the encounter with the actuality of God.

Martin Buber

If we are faithless, he remains faithful.

The Second Letter of Paul to Timothy

Retrospect and outlook

The risen Lord, present to the Church in the life he lives for God, calls the Church to the Father in confident, thankful self-surrender, in a boundless hope of which he himself is the pledge. The Church responds by expressing her identity, in the Spirit, under invocation of Jesus, by telling the story of his life.[1] This story is significant narrative, and thus it is only natural that the question should arise: What does the story mean? The Church is called to account for her faith. When this happens, it is not enough to point out that God is being praised by the story, or that people are being called to believe; worship may be the original performative function of the story of Jesus, and those who believe may be unable to resist the urge to testify to their faith; the question about the meaning of the story *as such* remains, and it requires an answer.

Thus far in the third part of this book we have made no attempt to answer this question. We first treated the *actus directus* of worship and witness in response to the *concretissimum* of the Christian message: the presence of Christ alive in the Spirit.[2] We did so because both the theological assumptions of the modern age and the diaspora-situation of the Church today require a systematic reflection on this *a priori* of all christology.[3] But from now on our task will be of the legitimizing kind: by means of critical analysis, reflection and theologizing in the strict sense of the word, we must try to give an account of the Christian faith. In the course of these endeavors we will naturally encounter the great christological doctrines which the tradition has bequeathed us as the authoritative statements of Christian faith.

Now, no matter how authoritative these doctrines are, they have one thing in common with non-authoritative theological statements, namely, that they come out of reflection. And the *actus reflexus*, Bonhoeffer reminds us, is at one remove from the immediacy of that Christian self-understanding which the *actus directus* of faith enjoys.[4] In the next four chapters, therefore, we will be in constant danger of

---

[1] Above, pp. 327–328.
[2] Cf. above, pp. 249–251.
[3] Cf. above, pp. 299–303, 329–331; also pp. 16–18.
[4] Cf. above, pp. 235–237.

succumbing to the temptation of treating Christian doctrine and theology as somehow autonomous—a temptation which can only be avoided if we keep on asking the question how Church doctrine and our theological discussions are related to the risen Christ—that is, how they are related to hope and worship.

In the previous chapter we pointed out that the rhetoric of obedience and the rhetoric of inclusion flow out of the rhetoric of hope.[5] Earlier, we stated that Resurrection-christology generates assumption-christology, which in turn generates Incarnation-christology.[6] In the present chapter we will begin the development of assumption-christology, which will be characterized by the rhetoric of obedience. This assumption-christology takes the story of Jesus' life for its point of departure; we will, therefore, start with a theological analysis of the life of Jesus. When this is done, however, we will encounter a difficulty: the tradition of classical christology poses serious obstacles to an assumptionist interpretation of the life of Jesus. A discussion of these obstacles will, therefore, form the second part of this chapter. Finally, the most important systematic attempt in recent theology to deal with these obstacles is Piet Schoonenberg's *The Christ*; a critical discussion of this book will therefore form the third part of this chapter.

MAN FOR OTHERS—MAN FOR GOD

Jesus' own history

In the previous chapter we pointed out that the story of Jesus was told in such a way as to provide a paradigm for the Church's own way to the Father.[7] This was not to imply that the story-form of the Christian confession was purely the result of a need, on the part of the Church, to find a paradigm and a warrant for her own historical existence. *Jesus' own life* justified the narrative form of the christological confession; nowhere in the Gospels does Jesus turn into an impersonal wandering stranger onto whom the Church projects a personal life-story. The mere fact that realistic narrative[8]

---

[5]Above, p. 338.
[6]Above, p. 307.
[7]Above, pp. 344–347.
[8]It is the great merit of Hans W. Frei (*The Identity of Jesus Christ*, The Hermeneutical Bases of Dogmatic Theology, Philadelphia, Fortress Press, 1975, esp.

became the form of the christological confession is sufficient: "this man Jesus" led a personal life. This life could be truly rendered by a story, in which personal intentions and actions on the one hand and surroundings on the other are involved in a constant interplay to show us who Jesus really is. To know who Jesus is we do not necessarily need descriptive, factual answers to strictly historical questions, nor do we need direct biographical information about the personality, inner motivation, or even the ethical quality of Jesus. To realize who "this Jesus" is, all we need is a story, a realistic narrative, for it is characteristic of realistic narrative to present the identity of a subject by means of a fusion of intention and circumstance. As Hans Frei explains:

> We are, in fact, thrown back on the story simply as a story, regardless of whether or not it is well documented. But, then, do we actually have testimony to Jesus' obedience in his story? Here the answer is a decisive "yes." The testimony we have is not of a detailed sort. It does *not* light up the motives, the decision-making process, the internal ambiguities, or the personality of the story's chief protagonist. Nor is there, precisely at those points in the story where claim is laid to a knowledge of Jesus' intentions, any evidence whatever that there were others present or that he had shared his thoughts with them. In other words, at those few points at which the story gives an inside glimpse of Jesus' intentions, they are *not* provided in the same way a biographer or historian provides inferential or indirect clues from the witness' testimony or other external data. The insight we are allowed is far more sparse and restrained than that, and yet also more intimate. It is like that of the novelist who tells us from the inside, as it were, of his subject's intentions and the bond by which they lead into action. This is what the Gospel story does at one or two crucial points; but it does so in exceedingly spare terms that do not search out the personality, inner motivation, or even the ethical quality of Jesus. The glimpse we are provided within the story of Jesus' intentions is just sufficient to indicate the passage of intention into enactment. And what is given to

pp. xiii-xvii) to have restored "realistic narrative" to its rightful place in biblical hermeneutics. The traditional preponderance of the non-narrative approach to the New Testament comes from the prominence of German literary theory; Frei suggests that there is a connection between the non-narrative approach to the New Testament and the lack of realism in German literary history (Hans W. Frei, *The Eclipse of Biblical Narrative*, A Study in Eighteenth Century Hermeneutics, New Haven–London, Yale University Press, 1974, esp. pp. 202–232). English exegesis never succumbed to the debilitating faith-history dilemma to the same extent as the Germans did; but then, the English novel dates back to the late seventeenth century, whereas German fiction is a late nineteenth-century product.

us is neither intention alone nor action alone, neither inner purpose alone nor external circumstance alone. Rather, *he becomes who he is in the coincidence of his enacted intention with the train of circumstances in which the story comes to a head.*[9]

Jesus' individualization

The identity of Jesus, so manifest in the Resurrection, is never unequivocally presented in the course of the Gospel story.[10] There are intermittent flashes of explicit revelation such as the calming of the sea and the transfiguration, but these are usually followed by wonderment and exhortation to silence rather than by certainty and vocal proclamation. There are stylistic devices like the alternation between "Jesus" and "the Lord." There is the ambivalence of expressions like "the Son of Man." There are the short anecdotes (dubbed "paradigms" by Dibelius) which are—ambivalently—narratives about particular incidents as well as short exemplary summaries of the whole meaning of the Gospel.[11] These and other literary devices keep the listener in suspense between "We know it is the Lord" and "Who do we say that he is?"

Yet there is more in the Synoptic story than these permanent subtle irritants; there is also a *developing relationship* between the individuality of Jesus and the response of his surroundings; this to and fro keeps the question about the identity of Jesus alive throughout the Gospel story. We will refer to this process as Jesus' individualization.

From the outset, of course, Jesus identifies with the kingdom of God; in fact, in the beginning of his ministry the identity of Jesus lies almost entirely in his consistent pointing to God's kingship. But then the interplay starts. In the very act of pointing away from himself Jesus places himself, as an individual, squarely at the heart of his hearers' concerns. Some follow him; some reject him; most people are undecided. They are fascinated by the tone of his teaching; it is "free and authoritative." They are amazed and even stupefied at his style. The question arises: "Where does he have it from?" They

---

[9]*The Identity of Jesus Christ*, pp. 103–104 (italics added).

[10]This is especially true in Q and Mark, with their non-triumphalist christologies; cf., for instance, Edward Schillebeeckx, *Jezus*, pp. 334–345.

[11]Cf. Amos Wilder, *Early Christian Rhetoric*, pp. 68–78.

cannot help but respond to *him*; yet *he*, this Jesus who refers only to the kingdom, who is he? Thus the issue of Jesus' individuality is raised in the context of the way in which he addresses himself, with his message, to others.

The same dynamic can be seen in the ministry of Jesus as a wonder-worker. The signs are spectacular; yet Jesus repeatedly exhorts demons and witnesses alike not to spread the knowledge. More disturbingly, he reproaches people for their lack of faith, manifested in their searching for signs; he confronts them with the charge that they are looking for gifts rather than for God, the giver. Jesus' signs and wonders are taken for the powerful acts of a prophetic miracle-worker establishing his leadership; Jesus rejects this interpretation as false, so that the issue of his identity remains in suspense. Thus we get the poignant situation in which Jesus and those around him begin to act at cross-purposes.

On the one hand there is Jesus, "knowing what is in man."[12] He has an inner, sympathetic awareness of the predicament of the people: he identifies their concerns with unfailing precision; he heals them by the power of the Spirit. But on the other hand, the beneficiaries of his sympathetic power are short-sighted and selfish; they become the obstacles to his ministry to them. Thus Jesus himself comes to be identified as the one who understands and identifies with others and brings about the signs of the kingdom, and at the same time as the one who is misunderstood and misidentified by the very sharers in the kingdom's blessings. Jesus contributes to the confusion by his refusal to point to anything but the kingdom and the necessity of faith. Whenever the crowds accept the teaching and the blessings, they also discover that they are given more than they bargain for, and resistance eventually wins out over gratitude. Jesus becomes the lonely sympathizer whose gifts of power are mistaken in the very act of acceptance. His identity is established with reference to his personal identification with the human condition[13] and with the power

---

[12]Jn 2, 25. For other references to Jesus' awareness of others' thoughts and feelings cf. Jn 1, 42. 47; 4, 29; 16, 30; Mt 9, 4; 12, 25; Mk 2, 8; Lk 6, 8; 9, 47. Heb 4, 15 places Jesus' sympathy with our weaknesses in the context of his common humanity with us, including temptation.

[13]Cf. Amos Wilder's point about Jesus not being a charismatic personality, but a person addressing himself to his fellows in self-identification: *Early Christian Rhetoric*, p. 27.

of the kingdom, but also increasingly with reference to the loneliness inflicted upon him by his surroundings, down to the flight, eventually, of the last disciple. Thus the story of Jesus among his contemporaries makes its point by means of a double dynamic.

First, Jesus unfailingly identifies, in the name of the kingdom, with the human condition around him; those around him who recognize the power of his humanity experience "faith"[14] and the wonders worked by it. In recognizing Jesus, they are restored to themselves to the glory of God.

Second, a sense of giddiness overtakes Jesus' followers; they are walking on water and yet cannot believe it is happening; they grasp for comfort; they want to own what can be theirs only gratuitously; afraid to have their identity revealed as a gift, they want the props of identity so as to be sure of themselves; they lose their souls by wanting to hang on to them; they forget the giver, and, in vain, attempt to secure the gifts; the life-giving recognition of Jesus fades in the harsh light of the need for firmer, less breathtaking assurances. They join, at least passively, with the forces that have failed to recognize Jesus from the beginning.

But at this point something important happens. The isolation of Jesus is not the last word; it becomes the source of a new dynamic interplay, in which Jesus and those around him are individualized in a new way. In the very act of failing to recognize Jesus, those around him are revealed as people who would live by self-established assurance rather than by faith. They prefer ego to self-in-encounter; they would rather define themselves by their skins than entrust themselves to this strange neighbor; they would rather be the serfs of those who give them the means to save their skins than be the friends of one so selfless, one who calls to such unworried freedom. Provoked by Jesus' continuing appeal to them, they isolate him and make him the butt of their worry turned aggression. But when they take their fearful selves out on him, he does not defend himself or run away. Thus he comes to stand in front of them as the revealing

---

[14]"Faith" is always used absolutely in Jesus' speech; the lone exception is Mk 11, 22.

[15]Jn 19, 5.

mirror of their own wounded nature: "Here, this is man."[15] In this way, Jesus' very isolation also brings about Jesus' individuality: he becomes the picture of man's inhumanity. In the end, as Jesus surrenders to the Father, he also brings humankind, death-bound from self-inflicted wounds, into the encounter with God.

This dynamic interplay between Jesus and his surroundings, which leads to an increasing individualization of Jesus in the course of the Gospel narratives, must remain the basis for the theological interpretation of the Gospels. To postulate, for example, that Jesus was the same from the beginning of his ministry (and, indeed, his life) to the end, and that it was only his surroundings that were changing is not supported by the New Testament. Not that the New Testament gives us direct access to Jesus' consciousness, so that we have direct evidence of a personal, psychological development on Jesus' part. The development of Jesus is indirectly conveyed, namely, by the narrative shape of the New Testament's account of Jesus' present significance as the risen One. No theological statements may lead to such a christology as would render the narrative shape of the christological confession meaningless, for instance, by presenting Jesus as personally unaffected by his surroundings.

So far in this section we have concentrated on two points. First, there is a dynamic interplay between Jesus and his surroundings. Second, this interplay brings about Jesus' individualization in the Gospel narrative by means of Jesus' identification with the kingdom and the human condition, and by means of his isolation by those who reject him. We must now analyze this story more thoroughly. This analysis will allow us to establish two points: the individuality of Jesus, and the redefinition of humanity in the person of Jesus.

Personal relatedness to others, personal surrender to the Father

As Jesus' ministry comes to a climax, we have said, Jesus stands out as an individual in ever sharper relief. As we indicated, this individualization is not only due to the contribution that Jesus brings to the interplay between himself and his surroundings; it is also, and more dramatically, brought about by his isolation by his surroundings. Those around him make him what he is as much as he does himself.

This does not mean that Jesus is depersonalized. Nowhere in the Gospel story does the figure of Jesus become purely symbolic.[16] He does not get rarefied into an Everyman, a metaphor for man, a supreme impersonal exemplification of the human condition, a tragic mirror of mankind. The Gospels do not present Jesus as neuter or passive, for Jesus becomes, in one and the same process, a picture of human inhumanity as well as an individual *choosing* his destiny, including his death. Neither are there any hints of other kinds of depersonalization. Jesus is not depicted in a stance of masochistic *apatheia*[17] that opens itself to untold affliction at the cost of the extinction of personalness and free choice. He does not adopt the stance of heroic[18] *apatheia*: the defiant, impassive clinging to the rightness of one's cause—the attitude that dares tormentors to inflict more suffering.

Jesus' active individuality increases as the forces of rejection bear down upon him; their effect on him is not one of diminishment of individuality. This is because he is presented as a willing sufferer. He becomes more identified with the human condition by accepting human inhumanity. He does not try to beat his opponents. He does not attempt to drive a wedge between them, so that by association with a few trusty followers over against a hostile majority he might save himself by saving the cause. He is abandoned or rejected by all; but as he accepts their worst, he does not turn into a passive victim; on the contrary, he reveals to them what they are doing. He predicts his disciples' flight. He predicts his betrayal; he addresses Judas as "friend." He reminds his captors of his daily availability, in broad daylight, for arrest. His repeated "You have said so" confronts the high priest and Pilate with their own words. His glance after the betrayal causes Simon to realize what he has done. He faces with a "Why?" the attendant who strikes him. He confronts the wailing

---

[16]Cf. Hans Frei, *The Identity of Jesus Christ*, pp. 29–33.

[17]Originally a Stoic concept denoting a person's transcendence over passion, suffering, and change.

[18]The word "hero" does not occur in the New Testament, nor in Kittel's dictionary, nor even in Lampe's *Patristic Greek Lexicon*. The Christian idiom refers to martyrs, not heroes; this will not change till the end of the fourth century. Evidence for this change, and for Augustine's reluctance to accept it, is found in his *The City of God*, X, 21 (*The Modern Library*, New York, Random House, 1950, p. 326).

women with a pointer to their own destiny. Finally, in his very prayer for forgiveness, he reminds his enemies of the enormity of the sin involved in his execution. All these elements in the story are repeated pointers to Jesus' individuality as he suffers rejection; in fact, in the accepting of his rejection, Jesus becomes more rather than less of an individual, for as more human inhumanity is inflicted on him, his confrontation with those he encounters becomes more personal, too. Jesus' individuality is never submerged by his undergoing isolation, rejection, and execution; rather, it stands out in sharper relief.

This leads us to the second point of this section, namely, the redefinition of humanity in the person of Jesus. We have already stated that the isolation forced upon Jesus becomes the source of a new dynamic by which Jesus is individualized in the very act of accepting his rejection. He is individualized as the one who willingly accepts the inhuman condition of humanity. This growing identification of Jesus with humanity never loses its characteristic interpersonalness. In fact, the ministry of confrontation reaches its pinnacle on the cross, where the outcast Jesus is both totally identified with the human condition—the epitome of humanity—and totally individualized. There Jesus surrenders himself to the Father and takes humanity's inhumanity upon himself in a final prayer for forgiveness.

The incorporation of humanity into the crucified Jesus is not in the nature of an abstraction; Jesus does not confront his opponents with an idea of humanity that they have rejected. He presents them with himself as he willingly accepts their rejection. Thus the incorporation of humanity into the crucified Jesus is a matter of *sustained relationships.* The rejected one does not reject. The rejectors, in rejecting Jesus, reject the one who does not reject them; they also reject themselves, for Jesus has received the imprint of their inhumanity into his own person. Yet precisely because Jesus does not cease to relate to them, they cannot help but respond: their very rejection of Jesus becomes an implicit testimony to the defectiveness of their own humanity and to the fullness of his.

What is this full humanity? Jesus does not limit himself to loving those who love him or to saluting his recognized brethren; he insists on loving one's enemies, turning the other cheek, not resisting one who is evil, giving one's cloak to the thief of one's coat[19]—in short, on not being defeated by evil but defeating evil with good.[20] In Jesus, humanity is redefined. Being human no longer consists in conformity to a generic nature, or in the obedience to, and the enforcement of, an ideal of humanity; all definitions of humanity, no matter how well-intentioned, lead to discrimination, exclusion, rejection, and even death; there will always be human beings who do not conform to whatever definition of humanity prevails. If Jesus does not define humanity, neither does he adopt the beautifully detached, meditative attitude vis-à-vis the glory and the folly of human kind exemplified by the third *stasimon* in Sophocles' *Antigone*;[21] such a stance, for all its empathy with man's tragic predicament, is both impotent and merciless.

The man on the cross does more than teach a new ideal of humanity; he embodies it.[22] He does more than rest in an attitude of pained contemplation of humanity's grandeur and misery; he reaches out and takes on the human inhumanity. By keeping himself related to humanity in search of its own justification and destruction, the individual man, Jesus of Nazareth, takes on humanity, including its sin, and redeems it and brings it to the Father in his own person.

Both Jesus' individuality and his significance for all humanity are clinched in the Resurrection. Only "this man Jesus," abandoned and rejected by all, and nobody else is affirmed and confirmed and placed in glory by the Father. He is the one and only person who kept faith with the Father's kingdom. But though it is only this one person who is glorified, his glory does not exclude humanity at large. In fact, in Jesus all of humankind is raised in glory precisely because he kept himself related to it as he absorbed and outsuffered their

---

[19]Cf. Mt 5, 44–48. Cf. Lk 6, 36 for the parallel to Mt 5, 48: God's perfection lies in his being *oiktirmōn*—compassionate.

[20]Cf. Rom 12, 21.

[21]Sophocles, *Three Tragedies, Antigone, Oedipus the King, Electra*, trans. into English verse by H. D. F. Kitto, London–Oxford–New York, Oxford University Press, 1962, pp. 21–23; the contrast with the second *stasimon* (pp. 13–14) is obvious.

[22]Cf. Hans Küng, *On Being a Christian*, pp. 258–262 for an excellent emphasis on the concrete, practical (the German original uses the word *faktisch*) universalism of Jesus' teaching. The same is, of course, the point of the parable of the Good Samaritan (Lk 10, 25–37), where Jesus does not give an answer to the question "Who is my neighbor?" but points out that the real question is "Whom shall I be a neighbor to?"

total rejection of him. The Resurrection, therefore, not only affirms the centrality of Jesus, it also proclaims his redemptive significance to *all* of humanity.[23] The particular events of Jesus' rejection and death, taken by themselves, did not warrant this proclamation; the disciples knew that Jesus was dead and their hopes were dashed. Only the *parrhēsia* inspired by the risen One accounts for the proclamation of Jesus' significance for all humanity.[24] But this *parrhēsia* did not forge the proclamation of Jesus' universal acceptance of humanity out of nothing. The dying Jesus was indeed rejected by particular people at a particular time for particular reasons; from a purely historical point of view it is impossible to attribute universal significance to events that were so particular. But Jesus' total surrender to the Father in death and his abiding *sympatheia* with those who rejected and abandoned him go a long way to justify the later proclamation of Jesus as the new Adam. Thus Jesus comes to stand up in God's glory in the Resurrection, and all of humankind stands there with him, drawn into a life beyond every definition, every boundary. The risen Jesus becomes God's own invitation, extended to all the world, to come to him and be made anew.

The main emphases of our analysis so far have been on the individuality of Jesus and on the redefinition of humanity in his

---

[23]C. F. D. Moule accounts for the paradox of the individuality of Jesus and his being the corporate person of the Church, and indeed of all mankind, by pointing to the experience of the Holy Spirit. "According to the predominant usage in the Pauline epistles, Christians are in Christ but the Holy Spirit is in Christians. And the Holy Spirit in Christians enables them to utter the cry of intimacy and obedience, 'Abba, your will be done!' which the individual, Jesus of Nazareth, uttered in his lifetime" ("The Manhood of Jesus in the New Testament," in: S. W. Sykes, J. P. Clayton [eds.], *Christ, Faith and History*, Cambridge, Cambridge University Press, 1972, pp. 95–110; quotation p. 110). We consider the rejected, dying Jesus on the cross already a corporate person in the sense that he represents humankind in virtue of *his* relationships—in the Holy Spirit—to it; in the Resurrection the Holy Spirit then goes on to call on the Church to respond and to continue the taking-on of humanity on the strength of the presence of the risen Jesus. Our view corresponds with Schillebeeckx' contention that the decision vis-à-vis Jesus took place at least partly in his lifetime, and not just after his death, in the Resurrection experience: "After all, he died, not on a deathbed, but by execution" (*Jezus*, p. 242).

[24]Jesus' significance for all of humanity takes the shape of an historical process; according to Schillebeeckx its starting point is the regathering of the disciples at the historic initiative of Peter. Cf. *Jezus*, pp. 315–319, and p. 577, note 119.

person in virtue of his abiding relatedness to those who eventually abandoned and rejected him. Both raise questions. What supports Jesus? What supports his personal, living redefinition of humanity? These are urgent questions, but they must not be answered too quickly. Before we begin to develop an answer, therefore, let us allow the same questions to arise in two different ways. We will do so by pondering the infancy narratives, and by analyzing Jesus' relationships with others in terms of graciousness and mediation.

The assumption of humanity in the infancy narratives

There is no doubt that the infancy narratives in the Gospels according to Matthew and Luke have the function of characterizing Jesus by accounting for his origin. In the Matthean narrative, Jesus unites and sums up, in his person, the faith and the struggles and the sins of Israel and its mission; in the Lucan account, Jesus appears as the epitome of the faith of Israel in the perspective of the salvation of the whole world. Thus Jesus appears as the product of Israel rather than as an individual; Hans Frei is doubtlessly right when he remarks that the identity of Jesus in the infancy narratives is virtually submerged by his identification with the destinies of the chosen people and (to some extent) all of humanity.[25] Initially, therefore, Jesus is presented as "a product of the process."[26] This includes not only genetic and psychological determinations, but also the whole complex of historical blessings and woes that went into the making of the situation the infant Jesus finds himself heir to; the Child[27] certainly assumes humanity into his very person in the sense of being produced by it.

But there is another side to the infancy stories: they are legendary renderings of the typical traits of Jesus' ministry as well as accounts of Jesus' origin. It is not surprising, therefore, that we find Jesus also presented as already *encountering* and taking on his people, and, indeed, in the magi and the Roman census, the whole

---

[25] *The Identity of Jesus Christ*, pp. 128–130.

[26] Expression taken from John A. T. Robinson, *The Human Face of God*, pp. 42ff.; Robinson takes too narrow a view of what went into the making of the person of Jesus.

[27] Mt uses this word no less than six times: 2, 8. 9. 11. 13. 14. 20, thus stressing the individuality of Jesus even in the infancy narrative.

world. He engages the world around him in a kind of infancy ministry, in which he is already significantly absorbing the impact of the human condition. Jesus' identification with the fate of Israel and the world, pointed out by Frei, is as much due to his *encounter* with his surroundings as with his being the product of the process. This is already clear in Matthew. The infant king impinges upon Herod, all of Jerusalem, and all the high priests and scribes of the people; thus he challenges them to respond to the message that the eschatological, universalist visions of Psalm 72 and Isaiah 60 are fulfilled. Israel's establishment responds by rejecting the Child and, in the Child, its own identity; a new journey into Egypt and a new exodus are necessary.

In the Lucan infancy narrative, however, the parallel between the infancy of Jesus and his ministry is much clearer. Jesus is not so much the product of the process as the one who comes to encounter Israel. Jesus' identification with humanity is achieved by means of a narrative which recounts the process by which Jesus comes to be "the one set apart" as the touchstone for the "deliberations of many."[28] The past history of Israel's faith is represented, in Luke, not so much by Jesus as by Mary, the faithful daughter of Zion and the new Sarah, for whom nothing is impossible with God.[29]

The narrative starts with John the Baptizer; his conception becomes the pledge for the virginal conception of Jesus by the power of the Spirit, just as his preaching was to be the pledge for the inauguration of the kingdom at Jesus' baptism, under the wings of the Spirit. Then there is the vocation of the shepherds at his birth and the prediction, at Mary's purification, of his rejection in Jerusalem, the future place of the decision, on the part of many, for or against Jesus; the parallels with Jesus' later ministry to the lost sheep of the house of Israel and with his meeting his crisis in Jerusalem are obvious. The narrative finally reaches its climax in Jesus' lonely disappearance in Jerusalem at Easter, and his reappearance, after three days, when he opens the Scriptures to the teachers of the

---

[28]Lk 2, 34; "deliberations" renders Gk. *dialogismoi*, a favorite word in Lk to denote persons' deepest response to Jesus and his awareness of it: 5, 22; 6, 8; 9, 47; 24, 38; 11, 17 has *dianoēmata*, a NT *hapax*.

[29]Lk 1, 37 coll. Gen 18, 14.

people. At that point, speaking for the first time in the whole narrative, and with Johannine overtones,[30] Jesus *identifies himself* as "being in the things of my Father" by divine appointment. The parallel with the climactic death and Resurrection pericopes in the adult ministry of Jesus is clear.[31]

In the final scenes of the Lucan infancy narrative Jesus finds himself identified in two ways. As we have just pointed out, he is identified as the one among many who is in touch with God. But he is also identified by isolation. This is emphasized by the repeated references to the amazement and incomprehension of those around him and even of his parents, especially his mother, who is cast, as the narrative progresses, not only in the role of "daughter Zion" and of the willing believer, but also as the prototype of Israel faced with the urgency of the faith-decision,[32] as the uncomprehending witness, and as the Church treasuring Jesus' ministry.

In the final analysis, therefore, the Lucan infancy narrative is not only about the identity of Jesus vis-à-vis the Father, in the Holy Spirit, but also about his identity vis-à-vis the human condition out of which he arises. The significance of Jesus lies in this: while gathering up humankind in his person, he proceeds to take on those around him in a decision of ultimate import; out of this encounter he emerges both as the individual he is *and* as the epitome of humanity in relation to God.

So again the question arises: What supports this individual child in his identification with the destinies of chosen and wayward Israel and, indeed, of the whole of humankind?

Assumption of humanity by graciousness and mediation

In this chapter we have taken up the life of Jesus, and we have argued that the story of Jesus presents us with a person whose final individuality is worked out in an ongoing pattern of relationships to

---

[30]Cf. the expression "Did you not know . . ." (Lk 2, 49), a ubiquitous theme in Jn, where Jesus is presented as knowing without needing instruction.

[31]The parallel with the Resurrection is strengthened by the expression "I must be" (*dei*—2, 49), which parallels the post-Resurrection retrospect found, for example, in Lk 24, 26.

[32]Cf. Lk 2, 35. The sword is the word of God; cf., for example, Is 11, 4; 49, 2; Hos 6, 5; Heb 4, 12; Eph 6, 17; Rev 1, 16.

humankind. We must now ponder the quality of these relationships.

We have already stated that the unity with humankind which Jesus inaugurates in his ministry and maintains even in the face of death is not a unity of a philosophical kind, based on a static concept of a generic nature to be respected in each individual. Jesus' unity with others is not a unity which derives its cogency from a static conceptual norm. No such norm is upheld in Jesus' ministry; he neither reminds his hearers of the dignity of their humanity, which they must live up to, nor does he place himself under an obligation to do justice to his fellow-humans in the name of humanity. Rather, the style of Jesus' relationships with those around him—and again, these relationships enter into Jesus' individuality in a decisive manner—is one of freely undertaken engagement that meets all, including the imperfect, the moral failures, the marginal, the possessed, the outcasts, the self-righteous, the women, the foreigners—all those to whom full humanity was (and is) denied either as a matter of fact or as a matter of right. Those who were considered, or considered themselves, as somehow entitled to being taken notice of, were scandalized. Still Jesus did not exclude them; he related to them, too. But the fact that he related to them as well as to those unworthy of notice was a sign that Jesus did not relate to them on the strength of their own accepted qualifications. His relationships with all those around him were acts of free personal confrontation and engagement. Jesus related gratuitously to all; his notice could not be demanded as a matter of right.

What we see here, enacted and lived out, is the fulfillment of one of the deepest and most paradoxical desires implicit in human existence. On the one hand we experience the refusal or failure to relate to even *one* human being, be he or she ever so repulsive, as a failure to do justice to the demands of humanity; such behavior fails to meet the standards of humanity. On the other hand, when somebody *actually* reaches out to *any* other human being, we experience this as a blessing, as something whose cogency cannot quite be argued by an appeal to humanity; it is essentially unowed and gracious; it exceeds the strict standards of humanity. We tend to experience "ordinary human decency" as something gracious, and formally correct and legally adequate treatment as a slight. Human beings are born for more than mere justice done to them in the name of a generic nature; such justice, in the concrete, always amounts to inhumanity. The "supernatural existential" is built into the human condition, and it comes to life in every encounter with the particular, in which man's innate openness to the infinite is actuated by the graciousness that must actuate every encounter.[33]

In the relationships of Jesus this graciousness is lived out to its fulfillment, even in the fact of rejection and execution. The assumption of humanity into the person of Jesus is the act of a person who freely *chooses* to relate himself to all of humankind. "When I shall be lifted up from the earth, I will draw all to myself."[34]

The union of humanity in the person of Jesus is a union that might be called, with a term that has a suspect ring in the history of christology, a *henōsis kat'eudokian,*[35] a union according to God's gracious will; Jesus' full humanity is actualized in the active relationships to humanity sought by Jesus in his ministry *and* in his rejection. In virtue of that union, all of humanity finds itself graciously and freely drawn into the total surrender to God. This free and gracious surrender of humanity to the Father is anticipated in the life and death of Jesus, as in his very person he enacts both the total surrender to God and the concrete unity of all humanity beyond the borderlines of any definition. This means that Jesus becomes the mediator, for the medium in which all of humanity finds itself unified and united with God is the human person Jesus Christ as such.[36] As Paul van Buren well saw, it is in the remarkable and

---

[33]Karl Rahner has elaborated the question behind this paragraph in "Nature and Grace," in: *Theological Investigations,* Vol. IV, Baltimore, Helicon Press, 1966, pp. 165–188.

[34]Jn 12, 32.

[35]The expression is connected with Paul of Samosata's view of Jesus as the greatest of the prophets and with Theodore of Mopsuestia's christology, if, that is, it is viewed as heretical.

[36]Cf. *S. Th.,* III, p. 26, a. 2. Calvin argues that Christ's mediatorship must be attributed to his entire person as such, in virtue of the hypostatic union of the two natures; cf. *Institutes of the Christian Religion,* 2 vols., Grand Rapids, Wm. B. Eerdmans Publishing Company, 1972, Vol. I, pp. 400–408, 415–424 (= Book II, chaps. 12, 14). The problem with this theory is twofold. First, Christ cannot be said to *mediate* between God and man if mediation is attributed to the divine *persona* as such. Second, Christ's mediating function *among* people is excluded from the notion of mediation. Calvin's position becomes understandable if it is remembered that he treats

gracious *freedom* of this man Jesus that his unique significance can be seen.[37] This freedom is not just an admirable moral quality of the individual Jesus; it is the human person of Jesus himself as he opens himself to all that is human, including man's inhumanity, and thus mediates to all of humanity access to the Father. The fullness of humanity, we argued earlier, was attributed to Jesus in the service of relational concerns.[38] We can now add to this that it points to the process of free and gracious mediation between the Father and humankind which is enacted in the life of Jesus.[39]

And so the question comes up again. What is it that animates this man to stand so long-sufferingly firm in his kindly determination to welcome all that is human into his person and thus graciously create in his person the medium where all that is human is reconciled and opened to a life beyond all borderlines and definitions, including the bounds of death?

THE LEGACY OF CLASSICAL CHRISTOLOGY: A CRITIQUE

Introduction: classical christology and the life of Jesus

The question just formulated has been answered by classical christology by means of the first *homoousion*: Jesus is consubstantial with the Father in godhead. That is the secret of his identity, of his life and of his death, of his significance for all humanity. Thomas Aquinas wrote the mystery into the office of Corpus Christi:

---

the question in the abstract: whether Christ is mediator *according to his humanity alone*. The Thomist tradition places Christ's mediatorship in his *concrete* humanity as such: *secundum quod homo.* This concrete human Jesus Christ is full of grace and glory; he shares God's truth and his gifts with his fellow human beings, and he is their vicarious sacrifice and intercessor. Cf. also Joseph N. Tylenda, "Christ the Mediator: Calvin vs. Stancaro," *Calvin Theological Journal* 8 (1973) 5–16, and *id.*, "The Controversy on Christ the Mediator: Calvin's Second Reply to Stancaro," *ibid.*, 131–145.

[37] *The Secular Meaning of the Gospel*, pp. 133–134, 152–154.

[38] Above, p. 158.

[39] From the preceding paragraphs it is clear that I agree with the suggestion made by C. F. D. Moule, where he says that the problem of the continuity/discontinuity between Jesus and the rest of us is to be resolved "in terms of will and of personal relationship, and of perfection of response on the part of Jesus to particular circumstances" ("The Manhood of Jesus in the New Testament," p. 110).

Verbum supernum prodiens,
Nec Patris linquens dexteram,
Ad opus suum exiens
Venit ad vitae vesperam.

Se nascens dedit socium,
Convescens in edulium,
Se moriens in pretium,
Se regnans dat in praemium.[40]

The heavenly Word supports the life of Jesus; in the person of Jesus, God's eternal Son became visible, went forth to do his work and met his death. He gave himself as a fellow human being at birth, as food at the Last Supper, as ransom in his death, as reward in his glory.

The age in which we live has serious problems with the straightforward and unequivocal pointer to the divine Word as the true subject of the life of Jesus. We must stop here and explore the dimensions of the problems presented by classical christology. It would be irresponsible to disregard them. Classical christology arose out of a sensibility characterized by a very explicit and often worshipful search for God by means of a love of wisdom. There was no doubt about the divine reality, but it was felt to be "above"; if there was any solidity, any ground for strong affirmations, *in* this world, it was to be found in contemplation; the human mind was the only faint but real glimmer of an eternal harmony, amid the flux of cheapness and change down here. The eternal stability and reliability of God could not be found *in* the humdrum flux of passion, compassion, suffering, and change, but only before it, after it, above it, and maybe under it.

In this spiritual context the great Church Fathers struggled to express the Christian mystery. They looked, in Jesus, for the stable reality by which he could *afford* to be part of, tolerate, and maybe even welcome, the fickle human condition and the sin of the world. To think of God as having a deep affinity with this changing and suffering world because of a very deep affinity with change and

---

[40]"The Word on high going forth/nor leaving the Father's right hand/going out to do his work/has reached the eve of life./ He gave himself at birth as a companion/ at table as food/in death as ransom/in regal glory as reward."

suffering itself was out of the question; God's impassibility was axiomatic. From Ignatius of Antioch to the end of the patristic period we find the truth of the passion anchored in the deeper truth of impassibility: *apathēs menōn epaschen*—he suffered while remaining impassible. Stoicism? Certainly—but a stoicism that found a ready echo in a world in which human life was nasty, brutish, and short, a world yearning for a stability which it was convinced was only available beyond itself.

A culture that lives in this way will be either utterly relieved or totally incredulous at the *homoousion*. If it is accepted that the immutable and the immortal united itself with the mutable and the mortal, then there is ultimate and absolute salvation. The Church, therefore, focused on the fact that God was once, uniquely, revealed in the flesh; there was no point in insisting on an intrinsic value of Jesus' human life as such.[41] As a result doctrine tended to focus on the most dramatic manifestations of the paradox of Jesus Christ: the Incarnation, as the joining of the unjoinables, and the final catastrophe, Jesus' death and Resurrection, where the bargain of the *admirabile commercium*[42] was definitively clinched and the glory of the Son became most prominent. The *life* of Jesus was seen as significant, not in itself, but mainly in its revelatory character: God manifesting himself in Jesus Christ as he powerfully moves among people.

The assumptions behind, and the mood of, classical christology are very much at odds with the concerns of what is called, with convenient vagueness, the "modern world." We can mention four points. First, we live in a post-Enlightenment world; in this world, assertions about God are not made with great confidence, and to rely on God is not experienced as a necessity. Second, the modern experience of the world has increasingly—despite continuing setbacks and discouragements—become aware of its deep reliability; the world is not capricious. This reliability of the world has two faces. On the one hand, it challenges human ingenuity to investigate the world in order to

---

[41]For this point, cf. Piet Smulders' comments on Alexandrian Word-christology: *The Fathers on Christology*, pp. 32ff. Cf. also, above, our remarks on Tillich, p. 210 and note 70.

[42]"Wonderful bargain"—an expression used by the Latin Fathers to express the soteriological exchange principle: God becomes man so that man may become God.

discover its solidity and its pliancy to human manipulation. On the other hand it tends to foster the feeling that everything is pre-determined, and that man is but a function of natural determina-tions. This had generated a yearning for a God who is not so strongly characterized by stability, who is atmospheric rather than thing-like, personal rather than unmoved, ready to be experienced rather than impassible and impassive. Modern man tends to be agnostic vis-à-vis a very determinate God. Third, not abstract knowledge but partici-pation at close quarters has become the norm for actuality. A Christ who reveals the Father in a life that is mainly interpreted—at a distance—as a lofty drama and a truly divine lesson, and whose death and Resurrection are mainly aimed at assuring mankind of its *ultimate* destiny, such a Christ has little credibility nowadays. Mod-ern man desires to understand Jesus' ministry as a life, not only *for*, but also *with* others. Fourth, the ancient world may impress us by the wealth of its knowledge and the depth of its insight; it also amazes us by the poverty of its know-how and its inability to change the world. For the Fathers, God's revelation in Jesus may have been abundant proof of God's love; for us revelation remains a faraway show if it has no practical impact. If Jesus did not credibly move among people as one of them and touch them in their *penultimate* concerns, his ultimate significance will be incredible.

The modern answer to the christological question, therefore, must emphasize, on the one hand, the mystery of God, and, on the other, the theological significance of Jesus' human life, of his growth and suffering, of his mutual relationships with others.

As it is, however, classical christology has often served to take the "bite" out of the life of Jesus. Hans Frei has shown, in a commanding monograph,[43] how the late seventeenth century began to be unable to read the story of Jesus as a unity of history and figural meaning, which led to the disintegration of christology into two separate elements, namely, religious significance unsupported by history on the one hand and historical fact with ethical significance but not adding up to religious significance on the other. Frei's analysis is certainly accurate, but it must be said that, in locating the

---

[43] *The Eclipse of Biblical Narrative.*

start of the problem in the seventeenth century, he underestimates the influence of classical christology.

The traditional emphasis on the divine person of the Word as the true subject of Jesus' human life had made a realistic reading of the human life of Jesus questionable long before the seventeenth century. No wonder that history came to be summoned as a witness for the prosecution when christological dogma was impeached.

This chapter started with an interpretation of the life of Jesus leading up to the christological question: What supports the person of Jesus and his relationships?[44] We went on to point out that classical christology had answered this question by confessing Christ's consubstantiality with the Father; but we also pointed out that this affirmation has tended to lessen the credibility of the life of Jesus as a truly human life.[45] But if the life of Jesus cannot be made humanly credible, the confession of Jesus' Lordship is bound to have little significance for our all-too-human lives.

Does this mean that classical christology must be rejected? Far from it. What is needed is a critique, not a rejection. In this part of the present chapter we must, therefore, state the ways in which classical christology contributed to the lack of theological significance of the life of Jesus. In this way we will clear the ground for a theological interpretation of Jesus' earthly life in the following chapter.

We will divide our treatment into two parts. First, we will show how the affirmation of Christ's consubstantiality with the Father has tended to separate Jesus from his brothers and sisters. Second, we will show how the affirmation of Christ's consubstantiality with us had tended to have the same effect. We will then close this part of the chapter with some cautionary remarks about the use of the proclamation of Jesus' uniqueness.

Jesus isolated from humanity by the first homoousion

The christological tradition has left us with an ambivalent heritage in its authoritative answer to our question. This ambivalence is due, among other things, to certain very restrictive terminological

---

[44]Above, pp. 370, 372, 375.
[45]Cf. also above, pp. 52–53.

agreements. Thus, the assumption of human nature into the *person* of the *Logos* was called a hypostatic union *(henōsis kath'hypostasian)*. This was to rule out a merely gracious, or attitudinal, or moral union *(henōsis kat'eudokian, kata schesin)*, which was considered, in the final analysis, to be no more than a variation of adoptionism: it made Jesus into a mere man *(psilos anthrōpos)*, although one supremely obedient to God, because he was graced by the inhabitation of the *Logos*. Gracious union with God was the characteristic, not of Jesus but of the faithful; they became "gods by grace" *(theoi kata charin)* in virtue of their union, by faith and the gift of the Spirit, with Jesus Christ, who is "God by nature" *(theos kata physin)*.

In this set of assumptions, a very misleading equation occurred, namely, that the expression "by grace" *(kata charin)* is to be read as "only in a secondary sense":[46] the faithful were primarily—that is to say, by nature—human; only secondarily are they gods—"by grace." Thus the equation of "gracious" with "secondary" is contingent on the prior assumption that "nature" equals "primary," and that "nature" has nothing to do with "grace." However, this *logical* separation of "nature" and "grace" gives us no access to the *inner quality* of what we designate by means of "nature"; to say that Jesus Christ is *theos kata physin* mainly reflects *our understanding* of Jesus' unity with the Father as "being the same thing with" the Father. To determine the inner quality of his divine nature, we must go beyond the concept of "nature."[47] We must remember that it is God's very

---

[46]For an example of this misunderstanding cf. Maurice Wiles, *The Making of Christian Doctrine*, pp. 107ff. In my view, Wiles' analysis disastrously locks both God and the world up in their several *physeis*, so that the patristic exchange principle is no longer understandable "with full seriousness"—which is exactly what Wiles attributes (wrongly) to the Fathers.

[47]Cf. D. M. MacKinnon, " 'Substance' in Christology—A Cross-Bench View," in: S. W. Sykes, J. P. Clayton (eds.), *Christ, Faith, and History*, Cambridge, Cambridge University Press, 1972, pp. 279–300. For example: "If we learn anything from the *homoousion*, it concerns less the manner of Christ's relation to the Father than the way in which that relation is to be understood; it is a second-order rather than a first-order christological proposition. That is to say, it is more something we say about what we say concerning Christ, than something we actually say concerning him that begins to lift the veil from the face of God whom he discloses, with whom he is one. For that we must use the language of *kenōsis*, but use it in closest relation to a reconstructed doctrine of the trinity" (p. 297).

nature to be gracious; hence, for the human nature to be united with the divine nature is the pinnacle of graciousness, not its exclusion. We must also remember that the concrete shape of Jesus' divine nature is his union with the Father in total and unconditional surrender. Finally, we must remember that it is in the nature of God to be communicative;[48] hence, Jesus' total surrender to the Father, far from claiming his person to the exclusion of all else, opens his person to encounter with all.

"Divine nature," therefore, may not be attributed to Jesus in the interest of separating him from humanity. Yet this is how the phrases "hypostatic union" and "divine nature" have often been used. As if it were not enough for Jesus of Nazareth to be a particular individual, with all the limitations which individuality entails, his divinity has been invoked to remove him further from his fellow human beings. A *cordon sanitaire* is drawn around *Christus medicus*, and the Father is made responsible for what, in actual fact, human beings did (almost!) achieve at Calvary: the separation of Jesus from his fellows.[49]

The second homoousion to be concretized

Just as the notions of "divine nature" and "consubstantiality with the Father" give us little access to the inner quality of Jesus' unity with the Father, so the notion of "consubstantiality with us" gives us little access to the inner quality of Jesus' true humanity, namely, his being totally available, as a human being, for relationships with others. "Consubstantiality with us" does not refer merely

---

[48]Cf. *S. Th.*, III, q. 1, a. 1, in c.

[49]This separation of Jesus from the rest of humanity in the interest of affirming his uniqueness (understood as meaning what the tradition has called his divine nature) is, interestingly enough, also found in some modern, seemingly purely technical principles of New Testament interpretation. To test Synoptic materials in such a way as to identify the *ipsissima vox* or the historical Jesus in his unique individuality may be a good way to legitimize the kerygma; it is unwarrantable to *limit* the significance of the New Testament's deliverances about Jesus Christ to these *ipsissima dicta et facta.* Jesus' "ordinary" dealings with reality are also part of his significance, and the Church's faith-testimony is not just a "veil" which conceals "the face of the Son of Man," as, for example, Joachim Jeremias seems to think. In the interest of the affirmation of his uniqueness, Jesus has had all too many exceptional things attributed to him, including absolutely unique teachings, and even absolutely novel literary forms! If this were true, how would people have known what he was talking about?

to the true humanity of the *individual* Jesus Christ, to his member-ship, *as an individual*, in the generic human nature. If that were meant, the concrete individual man Jesus Christ would still be presented as utterly and irreducibly exceptional; he would be the only individual hypostatically united with the divine nature in the *persona* of the Word. Such a conception would, as we have seen, force Jesus Christ into an isolation that contradicts his very being "for us human beings and for our salvation" (except, perhaps, in a purely exemplary or substitutionary sense). Rather "consub-stantiality with us" is the conceptual tool to state that Jesus is "the same thing with us" *in* his active stance of free self-giving to others in a total, gratuitous, and sympathetic identification with the concrete human condition.[50]

It follows that the confession of Jesus' consubstantiality with the Father and the confession of his consubstantiality with us may not be separated from each other. Both are meant to relate Jesus to us, the former by pointing to Jesus as the origin and the fulfillment of the Christian life of grace, the latter by pointing to the concrete relation-ships with his fellow human beings. Both are meant, in other words, to give theological significance to Jesus' human life. As soon as the double *homoousion* is interpreted as the attribution of two separate, inert natures to Jesus, serious misunderstandings occur, and Jesus is separated from humanity. Let us end this section with a short sketch of this danger.

When we define the uniqueness of Jesus Christ *only* in terms of his consubstantiality with the Father in the divine nature, we run a double risk. First, the Incarnation could come to be conceived of in tritheistic terms. If we let the concept of consubstantiality obscure Jesus' active relation of utter receptivity vis-à-vis the Father, the impression is created that one of three divine *personae*—*personae* united only in an (abstract!)[51] divine *physis* or *ousia*—is incarnate in a

---

[50]From this it follows that the anti-Apollinarian emphasis on the reasonable soul in Christ remains more important than the very formal maxim of Gregory Nazianzen ("What the Word has not assumed has not been saved"—*Ep.* 101, *ad Cledonium*) seems to indicate. Jesus is not just consubstantial with us inasmuch as he takes his corporeal nature from the common material stock of humanity and world, but also inasmuch as, in virtue of his reasonable soul, he relates as a person, body and soul, to other persons.

[51]I modestly agree with Donald MacKinnon's modest doubts about the rightness of J. N. D. Kelly's contention that "the substance of the *homoousion* is the form (or

particular man, and that, as a matter of principle, any one of the three *personae* could have been incarnate.[52] This amounts to speaking of the divine *personae* far too uncritically as co-equal *individuals*, with serious consequences for christology; the pre-existent *persona* of the *Logos*, in the Incarnation, undercuts the human personhood of Jesus Christ, so that his life loses credibility as a human life. Speculation along the lines of the *Quicumque vult*,[53] with its enormous emphasis on consubstantiality, has not always been able to avoid these pitfalls.

The second risk then follows from the first. If we merely speak of the Incarnation of a *persona* consubstantial with the Father in godhead, without exploring the inner quality of this consubstantiality, we also tend to lose sight of the fact that the *concrete* relationship of Jesus to his fellow human beings enters into the definition of his *concrete* consubstantiality with the Father. "His 'being there for others' is the experience of transcendence," as Bonhoeffer put it so compellingly.[54]

For this reason the proclamation of Jesus' consubstantiality with the Father must include the proclamation of his mediatorship in his humanity; the impression must be avoided at all costs that the consubstantiality with the Father alienates Jesus from his brothers and sisters. Only in this way will there be a possibility of constructing a theology of the *life* of Jesus.

What we have said so far about a correct understanding of the double *homoousion* is only a first statement. A far more fundamental reinterpretation of the Christian doctrine of the divinity of Jesus must follow; we will do so in the next chapter. For the time being, let

---

essence) which in the *Categories* Aristotle characterizes as secondary substance" (" 'Substance' in Christology—A Cross-Bench View," p. 291). The unity of God cannot be in the nature of a generic, and hence abstract, *ousia* or *physis*; that would make God's unity secondary in respect to the *personae*. The unity of God must be concrete and intrinsic; but then it is obvious that *ousia* and *physis*, with their abstractive and circumscriptive overtones, are almost totally inadequate conceptual tools, whose main use is heuristic: they enable us to speak coherently and are tools of discovery. The *inner* quality of God's concrete *physis* or *ousia* can then be clarified by means of the *perichōrēsis* (*circumincessio*) of the persons, both in the immanent and in the economic Trinity.

[52] For this thesis, logically defensible but theologically inappropriate, cf., for example, *S. Th.*, III, q. 3, a. 5.

[53] DS 75–76.

[54] *Letters and Papers from Prison*, p. 202.

us draw one conclusion from the thesis that Jesus' consubstantiality with the Father does not alienate him from his brothers and sisters; the conclusion is: that the proclamation of Jesus' uniqueness must not alienate any of his brothers and sisters either. After that, in a new section, we will study Schoonenberg's proposal for a christology designed to promote a realistic and credible interpretation of the human life of Jesus.

The proclamation of Jesus' uniqueness not against anyone

If our understanding of Jesus' consubstantiality with the Father must not be allowed to alienate Jesus from his brothers and sisters, *neither must its proclamation.* The first and basic means to achieve this is thanksgiving. A Christian's witness to the *homoousion*, to Christ's uniqueness, and to his sole mediatorship must convey his thankful, worshipful *awareness of his own gracious inclusion* into Christ's total surrender to the Father. Only in this way can a credible case be made for the thesis that Christ's uniqueness is not proclaimed *against* anybody. The proclamation of Christ remains a witnessing act on the part of the Church as Christ's own continued presence; and since Christ's uniqueness is shown in his being the Man for (not against) others, the Church can hardly appeal to Christ to justify christological warfare to "confound" other claims.

Such aggressive defenses of Christ's uniqueness are little more than expressions of the type of christianity that has forsaken the *imitatio Christi* in order to set itself up as a power, a cause at odds with other causes. Most declarations of the "Jesus-and-not-the-Buddha" type are neither about Jesus nor about the Buddha, but are feeble-faithed Christians' attempts at defending themselves. The same applies to much intra-church discussion of the uniqueness of Jesus Christ; many strong affirmations of Christ's divinity are feeble believers' attempts at safeguarding, not doctrine, but themselves, against understandable doubts and legitimate questions. Such defensive affirmations lack the sympathy and compassion of Christ. True *magisterium*, whether of the official or of the unofficial variety, must as a rule be patient and hospitable, in imitation of Christ, the Man for Others. The christological confession is meant to draw people to Christ; it is not meant to sound like the monotonous, never-ending clang of a hammer of heretics forged, once and for all, at Nicaea in 325 A.D.

NOTES ON SCHOONENBERG'S PROPOSAL

Introductory

One of the most constructive efforts in recent years to reflect on the uniqueness of Jesus has been Schoonenberg's *The Christ.* We have already had occasion to express our agreement with Schoonenberg's concern with personalness, and with his decision to use the term "person" in a way that is closer to natural language.[55]

It is time now to address ourselves to Schoonenberg's proposal in a somewhat more critical vein. The focus of our treatment, however, will remain the same, namely, an understanding of Jesus' personhood in the light of his human life; in this regard, Schoonenberg's concerns and our own are identical. We will, therefore, start by exploring the basic affinity of the present book with the concerns represented by Schoonenberg's *The Christ.* After that we will express our reservations on two points. We will argue that Schoonenberg's proposal labors under a lack of awareness of the Resurrection-dimension of christological statements, and that it shares the tradition's narrowness in concentrating too much on the individual Jesus. We will conclude our chapter with a retrospect-and-outlook and with a note on the order of our treatment of the christological question; these will prepare the ground for the next chapter.

The human reality of Jesus

If there is anything in Schoonenberg's christology that receives the fullest possible emphasis, it is the true humanity of Jesus Christ. The groundwork for this affirmation is laid in the introductory chapter of *The Christ:* "God or Man" is a false dilemma.[56] Affirming the fullness of Christ's humanity, therefore, does not in the least abridge the fullness of his divinity. In fact, an understanding of the life of Jesus as a human life in exactly the same sense as ours, with the exception of sin, is required by the New Testament as well as Chalcedon.

Now in order to achieve this understanding of Jesus' life, it is essential to understand Jesus as a fully human *person;* only the

---

[55] Above, pp. 167–173, 254.
[56] Pp. 13–49.

knowledge and the decisions of a truly human subject can be called fully human.[57] This means that the pre-existent person of the *Logos* must not be affirmed in such a way as to deny the full personhood of the man Jesus Christ; a divine person subsisting in an anhypostatic human nature does not lead a credible human life. The *Logos* must, therefore, be presented as anhypostatic in the sense that no claims of fully constituted personhood must be made in behalf of the *Logos*. Schoonenberg finds support in the tradition for his construct. First, the persons of the Trinity, though referred to as *hypostaseis* and *personae*, have never been considered persons in the sense of subjects with personal self-consciousness and freedom; in the Incarnation, therefore, the second "person" of the Trinity *becomes* personal in the human person Jesus, who *does* have individual self-consciousness and freedom. Second, this emphasis on divine becoming not only has good pre-Origenist credentials in Justin and Hippolytus, but it is also considered compatible with God's immutability by such authors as Karl Rahner and Felix Malmberg.[58]

If the affirmation of Jesus Christ as the pre-existent divine person of the *Logos* Incarnate in an anhypostatic human nature is rejected, what are the characteristics of the resulting christology? Schoonenberg gives four answers to this question. First, this is a christology without duality understood as a duality of competition between the humanity and the divinity of Christ. Second, it is a christology of God's total presence in the man Jesus Christ. Third, it is a christology of Jesus' transcendence in his very humanity as the locus of God's self-revelation. Fourth, it is a christology that views Christ as the absolute, eschatological culmination of humanity, by God's salvific action.[59]

Thus the way is paved for an understanding of Jesus Christ as the Son of God, *transcendent precisely in his humanity*, and an explanation is provided for the extraordinary clarity and immediacy of his relationship with the Father, as well as for his love of humanity. Thus we also come to understand Jesus' freedom, in which love of God and love of humanity meet.[60]

---

[57] Cf. *ibid.*, esp. pp. 66–74.
[58] *Ibid.*, pp. 54–58, 78–89.
[59] *Ibid.*, pp. 91–98.
[60] *Ibid.*, pp. 98–105.

Once this groundwork is laid, Schoonenberg goes on to describe the life of Jesus as truly historical, guided by true human knowledge, and shaped by true human decisions—an earthly life that led up to a heavenly completion in the Resurrection.[61] The fully human person of Jesus Christ—this man who is God's Son—accounts for a life that is both credible as a fully human life and credible as God's decisive act of salvation among us.

To achieve this considerable gain—for the restoration of credibility to Jesus' human life is a true gain—Schoonenberg sacrifices the understanding of the pre-existent *Logos* as hypostatic. In this way the Chalcedonian pattern, with its emphasis on human *anhypostasia* and divine pre-existence, is complemented and corrected without in any way confessing Christ "as less divine than the Church has confessed him, especially in Chalcedon."[62]

It is precisely on this point that Schoonenberg has met with considerable opposition, some fair, some unfair. It is obvious that Schoonenberg intends to affirm the full divinity of Jesus Christ, less "mythically" and less "religiously" perhaps and more humanly, but his full divinity nevertheless.[63] The fair opposition has entered into a discussion with Schoonenberg; as a result, he has significantly expanded his christological discussion to include even the possibility, excluded in *The Christ*, of saying that the man Jesus is enhypostatic in the *Logos*.[64]

This, however, is not the place to treat Schoonenberg's christological development since *The Christ*. We will simply take Schoonenberg's book as our text and suggest points of criticism.

Lack of awareness of the Resurrection

In an article he wrote by way of reply to one of his critics, Schoonenberg protests against the objection that he downplays the doctrine of Christ's pre-existence; he claims that he only wants to

---

[61]*Ibid.*, pp. 105–175.

[62]*Ibid.*, p. 65.

[63]Cf. *ibid.*

[64]Cf., for example, Klaus Reinhardt, "Die menschliche Transzendenz Jesu Christi—Zu Schoonenbergs Versuch einer nicht-chalkedonischen Christologie," *Trierer Theologische Zeitschrift* (formerly *Pastor Bonus*) 80 (1971) 273–289, and Schoonenberg's reply, "Ich glaube an Gott," *ibid.* 81 (1972) 65–83.

discuss the "how" of Christ's pre-existence.[65] The objection as well as the reaction are typical. At the strictly theological level, Schoonenberg obviously does not downplay; he reconceptualizes. The *Logos* is no longer hypostatic, but enhypostatic; the *human* person Jesus Christ is the Son of God; God reveals himself uniquely in a human *person*. Schoonenberg insists that the de-hypostatization of the *Logos* is no denial of divinity, and that God and man are not competitors, so that emphasis on Jesus' human personhood is no denial of his divinity either. But the *impression* is created that something is lost.

What lies at the basis of the reservations about Schoonenberg's proposal, even after all his explanations? We suggest: Schoonenberg does not account for the *affirmativeness* with which the tradition has spoken about the *Logos* and Jesus as the co-eternal Son of God. When he states that *Logos* of itself does not imply personalness, and that the *Logos* in the Old Testament is a power and a kind of divine presence rather than a person,[66] Schoonenberg is only restating the obvious. But it sounds as if he is diminishing and paring down the Christian confession; it sounds as if, in stressing the non-personalness of the *Logos* apart from the Incarnation, he is also denying the full divinity of Jesus Christ, for that which makes him God is non-hypostatic and, hence, not a fit subject for predication. Schoonenberg underrates the impact which his proposal has on a tradition used to speaking about the pre-existent *Logos* and about the eternal Son only in the most affirmative terms. There is clearly more than logic involved here; Schoonenberg's *tone* arouses suspicion.

The complexity of the discussion is compounded by the fact that the tradition, on the other hand, has been largely unaware of the consequences of the shape of its christological affirmativeness.[67] The strong affirmation of Christ's divinity took a particular shape; the *Logos*, or the eternal Son, came to be presented as a pre-existent hypostatic reality in its own right, incarnate in the historical Jesus—

---

[65]Cf. "Ich glaube an Gott," p. 79: "Damit will ich nicht die Präexistenz 'herunterspielen,' sondern nur ihre Art und Weise befragen."

[66]*Ibid.*, pp. 78, 81–82.

[67]Schoonenberg implicitly makes this point in the discussion of "patterns" that opens his critique of Chalcedonian christology; cf. *The Christ*, pp. 51ff.

at the expense of his full human personhood. Schoonenberg's rejection of this latter construct is fully justified; but while justified, his proposal is bound to meet with resistance, given the tradition's unawareness.

We suggest that what is behind the problem is a lack of awareness, on the part of *both* Schoonenberg and the tradition, of the *source* and the *significance* of the tradition's affirmativeness. The source of all christological affirmativeness is the *Resurrection*;[68] the significance of all christological statements is in their conveying the act of *total surrender, in worship and witness.* Both Schoonenberg and the tradition have speculated about christological titles like "Logos Incarnate" and "God's only-begotten Son" without sufficiently appreciating the original significance of the statements in which these titles occur.

"Jesus is the *Logos* Incarnate" is not an identifying statement, in which either a known and pre-conceived divine *hypostasis* or a non-hypostatic power are declared to be personally identical with "this man Jesus." Rather, it is what we have termed a radicalizing transformation[69] in response to the risen One; "this man Jesus" is made to preside, in person, over the whole treasury of aspirations and discernments conceived over centuries to express God's creative involvement with the world, and man's attunement to God's presence by the gifts of prophecy and wisdom. In the same way, "Jesus is the only-begotten Son of God" is not an identifying statement, by which a known divine *hypostasis* and "this man Jesus" are declared to be identical. Rather, it is a name by way of excellence,[70] by which "this man Jesus" is made to preside, in person, over the whole treasury of Old Testament discernments about Israel's filial response to God's love and mercy. If we call Jesus the *summum* of all the self-manifestations of God as well as the *summum* of all human responses to God, or if we call him the eschatological revelation of God as well as the eschatological revelation of man, what we are

---

[68]The connection between Resurrection and pre-existence is still preserved in expressions like the following, found in Clement of Alexandria's *Protreptikos* (IX, 84): "Awake, sleeper, rise from the dead, and Christ will shine upon you: the Sun of the Resurrection, he who was born before the dawn, whose beams give life."

[69]Cf. above, pp. 150–151.

[70]Cf. above, p. 151.

doing is repeating or restating affirmations originally made in the act of Christian response to the risen One. Hence our fundamental ground rule: Nothing may be said about Jesus that would amount to a qualification of the Resurrection.[71]

Traditional christology has had a tendency to do just that by mistaking the affirmativeness of christological statements for affirmations of a hypostatic, pre-existent person who becomes incarnate. Thus the life and death of Jesus come to be viewed as somehow extraneous to this divine person as such, and the Resurrection tends to be viewed as a kind of happy homecoming of the pre-existent *Logos*. Traditional christology has insufficiently realized that the hypostatization of the *Logos* and the eternal Son is primarily an act of *parrhēsia* inspired by the risen One,[72] not an affirmation which serves as the fundamental premise for a definitive christology. We will come back to this in the next chapters.

What about Schoonenberg? In de-hypostatizing the *Logos* and the eternal Son he has given evidence of the same lack of awareness of the significance of the Resurrection in prompting christological statements. It is indeed permissible to anhypostatize the *Logos*. In fact, as we have argued, it is not only terminologically feasible, but also a good application of the rhetoric of inclusion.[73] It is also a good theological move in that it is consonant with the tradition of not viewing the *Logos* as a person with an individual freedom and consciousness;[74] it prevents us from thinking of the Incarnation as the insertion of a hypostatic entity, of a pre-conceivable, pre-subsisting "somebody" to be reckoned with, into the world. But the result of Schoonenberg's proposal is that the tradition's strong affirmativeness about the divinity of Christ has been diminished. Even though it is linguistically and theologically warrantable to refer to the *Logos* as non-hypostatic, the fact of the matter is that strong affirmations about non-hypostatic realities are hard to make; they will always sound hesitant. And this hesitancy does not reflect the *parrhēsia* traditionally associated with the Christian response to the risen One.

---

[71]Above, pp. 253ff.
[72]Cf. above, pp. 349–352.
[73]Above, pp. 169–173.
[74]Above, p. 386.

It is important to see where exactly this hesitancy occurs in Schoonenberg's christology. It does *not* occur in his christological discussions of the life, death, and glorification of Jesus, which abound with numerous affirmations of the fullness of Jesus' divinity; again, there is no reason to suspect Schoonenberg of heresy. It *does* occur, however, in the *terminology* of Schoonenberg's proposal for a new speculative construct. To call the *Logos* anhypostatic is a negative move, whereas a strongly affirmative terminology is needed to convey the confidence of the Christian confession, and to state what the anhypostatic *Logos* represents in positive terms. Christians proclaim that "Jesus is Lord" in a confident act of worship and witness—"to the glory of God the Father." But when Christians claim access to the living God in their confession of Jesus' Lordship, they also claim that it is the very identity of Jesus, whom they confess, to be to the glory of God the Father. This insight could have led to a far more positive rendering of what the *anhypostasia* of the *Logos* really means. Instead, Schoonenberg remains tentative:

> Our concept could now be called the theory of the enhypostasia of the Word. Or in other words: of the presence of God's Word, or of God through his Word, in Jesus Christ, and indeed in such a way that this Word enters him wholly, that it becomes in him a historical person, that it becomes flesh.[75]

Instead of turning the de-hypostatizing of the *Logos* into a confident assertion of the essential relationship of Jesus Christ to the Father, this passage is hesitant. "The presence of God's Word" is proposed as an alternative to "[the presence] of God through his Word"; the Word, though anhypostatic, serves as the subject of three clauses;[76] the passage is exploratory rather than affirmative.

We have argued that lack of awareness of the Resurrection as the source of all christology has led to lack of affirmativeness in Schoonenberg's christology; we have also argued that the tradition criticized by Schoonenberg labors under the same lack of awareness

---

[75] *The Christ*, p. 89.

[76] From a linguistic point of view this is no problem, for words, and especially terms, reify and hypostatize; cf. above, pp. 87–88. The problem is the *theological* ambivalence of the whole passage.

of the Resurrection. The difference is that whereas the tradition's unawareness led to the postulate of the pre-existent person of the *Logos* pre-empting the personhood of the man Jesus, Schoonenberg's reinterpretation *seems* to reduce the *Logos* to—almost—a quality of the human person Jesus.

There is another area where Schoonenberg is an heir to the tradition he rejects, namely, in his concentration on the individual Jesus. We must elaborate this somewhat.

The individual Jesus as the point of departure

We have already indicated that the tradition has had a tendency to concentrate on the individual person Jesus Christ without sufficiently emphasizing his essential relatedness, both in his divinity and his humanity, to the Father and to the rest of humanity.[77] In traditional christology, this concentration on the individual Jesus Christ took the shape of a strong emphasis on the Incarnation of the pre-existent Word in the man Jesus Christ; the life, death, and Resurrection of Jesus were developed out of this conception of his unique person.

In Schoonenberg's christology this concentration on the individual person Jesus Christ remains. The treatment of Jesus' relationship with the Father and of his love of mankind *follows* the explanation of the theory of the *enhypostasia* of the Word, spelled out in the treatment of Jesus' human transcendence; the earthly and glorified life of Christ as a man is discussed in such a way as to be an application and confirmation of the theory about the ontological constitution of Christ's person.

Since, however, Schoonenberg no longer bases his christology upon the person of Christ viewed as the pre-existent *person* of the Word Incarnate, his concentration on the person of Jesus takes on a very questionable form, namely, the almost axiomatic thesis that the obvious fact that Jesus Christ is one person, and a completely human person at that, is the point of departure of christology.[78] It is this thesis which leads to Schoonenberg's ground-rule that nothing may

---

[77]Above, pp. 379-384; cf. also above, pp. 157-159.
[78]Also noticed by Klaus Reinhardt, "In What Way Is Jesus Christ Unique?" *International Catholic Review: Communio* 1 (1973) 343-364, esp. p. 362.

be said about the pre-existent Word that would detract from the one and human person Jesus Christ.[79]

Now there is every reason to question the assumption that the common-sense statement that Jesus is a human person can act as the point of departure of christology. Even if we agree that we must not think of the *Logos* or the eternal Son in terms of a pre-existent person, this does not commit us to the view that the clear fact of Jesus' human individuality is to be taken as the basis for christological statements. The point of departure of christology is the Resurrection. If we deny, with Schoonenberg, that pre-existence is the fundamental thesis, we must also deny, against Schoonenberg, that the human person Jesus is.[80] There are several reasons for this.

First of all, as we have stated, there is a concern behind Schoonenberg's apparently common-sense point of departure, namely a concern with human personalness. This concern makes it imperative to insist that Christ be called a human person.[81] But it is equally true that this concern may not be allowed to dictate the terms on which we can use *Logos*-talk.[82] Even if we agree that we must not think of the *Logos* or the eternal Son as a pre-existent person, this does not mean that the fact of Jesus' human individuality is henceforth to be taken as normative for all christological statements. The rhetoric of inclusion calls for the attribution of human personhood to Jesus; but the rhetoric of obedience calls for a conversion of our concerns with human personhood.[83] *Logos*-talk, as the expression of the Church's response to the risen Lord, should convey Christ's presidency over our concern with human personalness, not vice versa.

Second, the New Testament does not know of common-sense affirmations of Jesus' human individuality. Affirmations about "this man Jesus" are always set in a context of confident, worshipful, witnessing response to the risen One. Affirmative *Logos*-talk about the historical Jesus comes from a reflection on the risen One; it is the

---

[79] *The Christ*, p. 82. Cf. above, p. 254.

[80] I have argued the same thesis with regard to Hans Küng's *Christ Sein*; cf. "Küng's *Christ Sein*: A Review Article," p. 280. Cf. also above, pp. 254–259.

[81] Above, pp. 171–173.

[82] This is an application of the ground-rule we formulated on p. 128.

[83] Cf. above, pp. 174–179.

hypostatization of the presidency of Jesus Christ over human concerns, or, in other words, it is the hypostatization of that which prompts and warrants the total surrender. And since the glorification of Jesus is the manifestation as well as the vindication of Jesus' own total surrender to the Father, we must say that *Logos*-talk is the hypostatization of *Jesus' own total surrender* to the Father.[84] Just as we said that the response to the risen Lord is "object-language and more,"[85] so we must now say that in Christian language "this man Jesus" is always "this man Jesus and more." In the former expression, "more" indicates, not an additional element over and above the object, but the object's relatedness to a disclosed reality of a higher order. Analogously, in the latter expression, "more" (the *Logos*) points, not to a separate additional entity, but to this man Jesus' total relatedness to the Father.

This opens a perspective. Would it be possible to follow Schoonenberg in speaking about the *Logos* in anhypostatic terms, but at the same time to turn his tone of irresolution into a tone of affirmativeness, by speaking about the *Logos* entirely in terms of the man Jesus' relational identity with the Father? If it should thus prove to be possible to dispose of that traditional tendency to ignore the inner quality of Jesus' consubstantiality with the Father, we may also be in a position to show more clearly that this consubstantiality does not separate Jesus from humanity. In other words, it may enable us to stop overconcentrating on the individual Jesus. Thus we may be able to speak about his identity in consistently relational terms, by showing that Jesus, in his very person, is absolutely irreducible to his own concrete individuality—to borrow an expression used by Vladimir Lossky.[86] This in turn may enable us to do

---

[84]Cf. above, pp. 347–354.

[85]For this expression, cf. above, pp. 153, 200.

[86]Cf. *In the Image and Likeness of God*, [Crestwood, New York], St. Vladimir's Seminary Press, 1974, chapter 6, "The Theological Notion of the Human Person," pp. 111–123 (it is important to check the English translation off against the original French *A l'image et à la ressemblance de Dieu*, Paris, Aubier Montaigne, 1967). Lossky stresses that the Fathers did not work with a precise definition of the human person, although they developed a very precise definition of the divine *hypostaseis* (pp. 111–112). He then goes on to use the relationship between the divine *hypostasis* and the human nature in Christ as a model for the development of a concept of human personhood. The *hypostasis*, though one element of man's composite nature, does not

justice to the narrative shape of the christological confession, which, as we have shown, answers the question about Jesus' identity in terms of the developing pattern of his relationships.[87]

Restrospect and outlook

Our concern in the beginning of this chapter was to read the story of Jesus, not primarily as an act of worship and witness, but as the account of an individual life story, in which Jesus' individualization was a function of his taking on humankind and vice versa. We found ourselves repeatedly asking the question: What is it that enables this man to stand so long-sufferingly firm in his kingly determination to do full justice to humanity—and thus to enact, in his person, a humanism in surrender to God beyond the bounds of any definition?[88]

---

have any definable property or attributes foreign to the *physis*; it is not a separate entity. Hence, " 'person' signifies man's irreducibility to his nature. Note that we say 'irreducibility' and not 'something irreducible' or 'something which makes man irreducible to his nature,' precisely because there can be no question here of 'something distinct,' of something 'of a different nature,' but [only] of *someone* who distinguishes himself from his own nature, of *someone* who goes beyond his nature while still containing it, who makes it exist as human nature by this overstepping, and who yet does not exist himself outside the nature which he 'enhypostatizes' and which he constantly exceeds" (p. 120). In the usage proposed by Schoonenberg, "person" renders what Lossky calls "*physis*," understood as concrete individuality in a generic nature; this changes the terminology, but not the idea. What we need to investigate is the human Jesus' absolute irreducibility to his own human person—which is exactly what the tradition has called the human nature's *anhypostasia*.

[87]Above, pp. 360–370.—Since *The Christ* Schoonenberg has both refined his proposal and expanded it in the direction of trinitarian theology, with the result that the concept of relationship has become more prominent in his christology. Cf. "From a Two-Nature Christology to a Christology of Presence," in: Joseph Papin (ed.), *Theological Folia of Villanova University*, Speculative Studies, Vol. II, Villanova, The Villanova University Press, 1975, pp. 219–243; "Trinität—Der vollendete Bund," *Orientierung* 37 (1972) 115–117; "Trinity—The Consummated Covenant, Theses on the Doctrine of the Trinitarian God," *Studies in Religion/Sciences religieuses* 5 (1975) 111–116; "Process or History in God?" *Louvain Studies* 4 (1973) 303–319 (cf. "Process or history in God?" *Theology Digest* 23 [1975] 38–44, with an original postscript); "Gott als Person und Gott als das unpersönlich Göttliche—Bhakti und Jñāna," in: Gerhard Oberhammer (ed.), *Transzendenzerfahrung, Vollzugshorizont des Heils*, Das Problem in indischer und christlicher Tradition (*Publications of the De Nobili Research Library*, Vol. V), Wien, 1978, pp. 207–234. Cf. also Steven Pujdak's summary of his Louvain dissertation: "Schoonenberg's Christology in Context," *Louvain Studies* 6 (1977) 338–353.

[88]Cf. above, pp. 369, 373, 374.

We then went on to state that classical christology had answered that question by pointing to the *Logos* Incarnate; but we argued that, for reasons mainly attributable to cultural shifts, it had failed to account for the decisive significance which Jesus' human life and sufferings *in and of themselves* have in the New Testament, not only for the salvation of the world, but also *for Jesus' very identity*.[89] The great tradition of classical christology has blind spots, and the most notable ones, we said, are the following. First, Jesus' divinity is mainly understood conceptually, by means of the consubstantiality concept, without enough attention to the inner quality of this consubstantiality, which is Jesus' being related to the Father. Second, Jesus' humanity is mainly understood conceptually, as an attribute of his individual person; as a result the web of human relationships that contributes decisively to his individuality is kept out of the definition of Jesus' person. Third, as a result of both, Jesus is isolated from the rest of humanity.

We went on to analyze Schoonenberg's proposal for a christology that does justice to the full humanity of Jesus' human life. In the final analysis, however, we concluded that Schoonenberg's speculative construct had found no satisfactory alternative to the tradition's affirmativeness about the divinity of Christ, owing to a lack of awareness—a lack shared by the tradition—of the significance of the Resurrection in the making of christological statements. We also argued that Schoonenberg's emphasis was still characterized by the tradition's overconcentration on the individual Jesus.

----

[89]This is an oft-neglected point. Many christological tracts endorse the distinction between *actiones deiviriles*—"theandric," god-manly acts—which *were* relevant to our salvation (miracles, healings, teaching, enduring, etc.), and acts with no such significance (undergoing, eating, sleeping, walking, etc.). This distinction, which applies the old scholastic distinction between *actus humani* and *actus hominis* to Christ, is crypto-Monophysite and perhaps even crypto-Pelagian: it restricts the relevance of the Incarnation to the so-called "higher" functions of the person Jesus Christ, but at the expense of their full humanity (special divine powers, abiding beatific vision, etc.), and places the salvific efficacy of Jesus' life in conscious and intentional acts, and not in his very humanity. In this construct the human nature becomes purely instrumental, as a merely indispensable means to reveal the Father, just as a film-screen is purely instrumental with regard to the pictures projected, and has no relevance of its own. Note that Aquinas, while holding the view that Christ's humanity is instrumental, does not attribute salvific significance to Christ's powerful actions only, but to all the things he did *or suffered* in his humanity (*S. Th.*, III, q. 48, a. 6, *i.c.* and *ad* 1; q. 56, a. 1, *ad* 3). Cf. also D. Bonhoeffer, *Christ the Center*, pp. 92, 99.

Schoonenberg's critique of the Chalcedonian pattern and our own discussions in this chapter have set the agenda for the next chapter. We will have to develop a theology of Jesus Christ's person that is consistently relational, so that the inner quality of both Jesus' relationship with the Father and his significance to all of humanity may become clearer, and thus also the meaning of the double *homoousion*. In doing so, however, we must be careful to speak in such a way that the Resurrection and the life of Jesus are not lost sight of. This last remark leads us to the final observation of this chapter.

A note on the sequence of our treatment

In the previous chapter we stated that the order in which the triple rhetoric of christology is actually experienced is: hope—obedience—inclusion.[90] We treated the rhetoric of hope in the previous two chapters, where we treated the Resurrection. In the beginning of this chapter we started our discussion of the life of Jesus—a move which must have raised the expectation that the present chapter and the next would be devoted to the rhetoric of obedience. Instead, we arc involving ourselves in a discussion of what the tradition refers to as the hypostatic union. A few remarks to explain this decision are appropriate at this point.

The principal effect of the risen One on those who came to believe was, as we have argued, that he brought them to surrender and thus prompted them to speak with *parrhēsia*—confidence inspired by hope. This speaking was both worship to the glory of the Father and the witnessing self-expression of the Church; the latter also involved the commitment, on the part of the Church, to live out the *imitatio Christi*.[91] Now *what* was spoken was a narrative, a story. This story not only recounted what Jesus did; it also conveyed who he is. We discussed this in the first part of the present chapter.

It was at this precise point that the problem arose. The doctrinal tradition of the Christian Church had little, if any, room for a theologically significant *story*; the first *homoousion* seemed to have taken the bite out of Jesus' relationships with his fellows; the glory of

---

[90]Above, p. 338.
[91]Above, pp. 327–329, 342–344, 347–349.

the only-begotten One seemed to have prevented the Church from having a realistic conception of Jesus' developing individuality and of the patient assumption of human concerns into his own person, viewed as person-in-surrender to the Father. For this reason, we decided to offer a critique of the tradition first, and thus to make room for a theologically significant rendering of the life of Jesus. This theological significance would have to consist, not only in an interpretation of Jesus' life that would show its theological relevance *for us*, but also (and here the tradition was especially defective) in its relevance to *Jesus' own identity*. Schoonenberg's proposal went a long way toward reasserting the full humanity of Jesus Christ, but it still shared some of the non-relational thought-forms of the tradition. Now, as we will argue, it is precisely this lack of relational understanding of Jesus' life that precludes an understanding of its significance in terms of obedience, mercy, and compassion.

In offering this critique of the tradition, we necessarily involved ourselves, ahead of schedule, in a treatment of the rhetoric of inclusion. Why?

The strong point of the Chalcedonian tradition is precisely that it expresses conceptually the *universal* salvific significance of Jesus, by speaking of his humanity in the most comprehensive terms possible, namely in terms of its *nature*. As Bonhoeffer wrote:

> The advantage of the concept of *ousia* as opposed to a dynamic understanding of the situation (Paul of Samosata) lies in the fact that this concept affords a fundamentally universalist conception of salvation. This makes it possible to speak of the reality of salvation in a way different from the situation where everything is made to depend on the dynamic act of the human will, and where Nature undergoes a process of divinisation.[92]

The strong point of the tradition is its fundamental ability to do justice to what we have called the rhetoric of inclusion; in presenting the divine *Logos* as assuming humankind *as such*, nothing that is human is left outside God's saving mercy. The idea, in fact, is capable of an even greater expansion: if we conceive of the pre-existent *Logos* as *Verbum Incarnandum*[93] the whole world is founda-

---

[92]*Gesammelte Schriften*, III, p. 230 (cf. *Christ the Center*, p. 105).
[93]"The Word to be incarnated"; cf. P. Schoonenberg, *The Christ*, p. 86.

tionally drawn into God's salvific purpose, and a fundamental affinity between the whole of creation and the person of Jesus becomes establishable—in accordance with the cosmic hymn in the Letter to the Colossians and the prologue to the Fourth Gospel.[94] Thus, the rhetoric of inclusion comes to strike roots in protology, in an impressive meditation on the depth and the riches of the Christ-event, whose mystery, by God's gracious decree, reaches back into God's eternity. To trade this in for an easy adoptionist christology, in which everything depends on Jesus' obedience to God's will as a precondition for the transformation of human nature, would amount to a terrible loss of depth, as Bonhoeffer rightly points out.

Yet there is no doubt that *Logos*-protology has mistakenly been used, both to take the bite out of the Resurrection and to diminish the credibility of Jesus' human life. The former error must be countered by the observation that *Logos*-talk draws its confidence from, and is warranted by, the Resurrection, and must, therefore, refrain from qualifying the Resurrection in any way. The latter must be countered, not only by insisting that Jesus is a fully human person, but also by pointing to the relational style of Jesus' human personhood, as we will attempt to do in the next chapter.

This is, therefore, our task: to reinterpret the *Logos*-protology in such a way as to show the fundamental affinity between the *Logos* and the human life of Jesus—a life credible as truly and fully human, a life theologically relevant *in itself*, and not just a purely instrumental expedient used by God to reveal his glory. Once this task is accomplished, we will be in a better position to explore the implications of the humiliation of Jesus, in an exploration of the rhetoric of obedience—a task to be accomplished in the twelfth and thirteenth chapters.

---

[94]Col 1, 12–20; Jn 1, 1–18.

CHAPTER 11

The Lamb Slain
from the Beginning

Jesus' Lordship is the endorsement of his Servanthood. He has the power over history as the Servant, he is the Lamb slain that opens the scroll. Jesus' resurrection means, not re-animation, but instatement as Lord; but this Lordship must be stripped of all lordliness in the recognition of the Spirit of service that comes to us from him. But that implies that God himself, too, unlords himself in Jesus. He turns out to be greater than our notions of lordship would make him; he is just as much a servant God. [. . .] God's Lordship is so much in what he bestows on us, that we may call him a God of service, of self-emptying. He is the highest "I," but not an "I" that places itself at the center of everything, but one that says "Thou" to all.

Piet Schoonenberg

Jesus Christ is not God in any divine nature, *ousia*, substance, essence—hence, not in any way that would be open to observation and description—but in faith. That divine essence does not exist. If Jesus Christ is to be described as God, there must be no talk about his divine essence, no talk about his omniscience, but about this weak man among sinners, about his crib and about his cross. If we treat Jesus' divinity, we must speak precisely of his weakness.

Dietrich Bonhoeffer

Preliminary

Both at the end of Chapters Six and Nine and in the beginning of the previous chapter we reminded ourselves of the duty to keep in mind that reflective and critical christologies must keep in touch with the Resurrection—that is to say, they must betray a fundamental allegiance to worship and witness.[1] In the course of the previous chapter, after interpreting the life of Jesus in terms of his relationships[2] (and thus seemingly broaching the questions connected with critical christology) we decided first to treat the question of Jesus' identity, traditionally cast in the form of reflection on the *Logos* Incarnate. The reason for this decision was that classical, reflective christology had to be critically evaluated, in order to make room for a realistic understanding of the life of Jesus.[3] As a result, by the end of the previous chapter, we found ourselves faced with a double task: we must develop a theology of Jesus' identity in such a way that the Resurrection remains central and that the life of Jesus retains its credibility as a truly human life.

In this chapter we propose to do this in four main sections. We will first discuss what it means to be related; this is in accordance with our stated intention to treat the double *homoousion* in a consistently relational fashion. This section will be followed by two sections dealing, respectively, with Jesus' relationship with the Father and with his relationship with humanity and, indeed, with the whole world. Finally, in a fourth section, we will discuss the possibilities of a reaffirmation of the *Logos* in christology.

Before we broach this large agenda, however, we must point to an important aspect of our task, namely, the *attitudinal* dimensions of our discussion. To speak about Jesus' deepest identity requires (and evokes!), we will argue, an attitude of prayer and patience in the theologian. Traditional christology, with its emphasis on the pre-existent *Logos* as the point of departure of christology, has not only been deficient at the level of *content*, by downplaying the Resurrection and by diminishing the credibility of Jesus' human life; it has also sinned by prayerlessness and impatience. These attitudinal er-

---

[1]Above, pp. 251–262, 397–399, 401.

[2]Above, pp. 360–375.

[3]Above, pp. 375–384.

rors on the part of the tradition may not be overlooked in a book especially devoted to the performative functions of christology.[4]

Our interest in attitudinal questions, however, is not just a matter of a short introduction to this chapter. The reader will notice that the tone of our exposition will change in this chapter (and the next). Precisely because so much harm has been done by harsh affirmations of Christ's divinity, it is appropriate to attempt to approach this mystery in a more tentative, exploratory manner without, however, sacrificing precision and rigorous argument. This involves certain risks, but they are worth taking.

On prayerlessness and impatience

In the course of our analysis of Schoonenberg's christology we stated that underlying the identification of Jesus as the Father's consubstantial Son, the eternal *Logos* Incarnate, was the issue of worship.[5] Affirmations of Jesus as the *Logos* Incarnate derive from the *parrhēsia* involved in the Spirited response to the risen One, to the glory of God the Father. But the Resurrection does encourage reflection and retrospect. Thus Christians come to see the mystery of the *Logos* in Jesus' unique missionary consciousness, in his unique relationship with the Father, and in the graciousness and the faithfulness with which he lived among us; finally, in a daring protological retrospect, they confess his coming from the Father.[6] In this way, Christian speaking about the eternal *Logos* is born. In the

---

[4]Cf. what was said above, pp. 306–307.

[5]Above, pp. 388–389; cf. also above, pp. 299–303, 329–331, for the reasons why emphasis on worship is important.

[6]The Synoptic "I have come" (*ēlthon*; *elēlytha* only in Lk 5, 32) reflects historical Jesus-usage, and thus Jesus' own missionary self-awareness, without necessarily being an historical Jesus-word in every instance. The expression occurs in Mt 10, 34 par. Lk 12, 51; Mk 2, 17 parr. Mt 9, 13 and Lk 5, 32; Mk 10, 45 par. Mt. 20, 28; Lk 12, 49 and 19, 10; Mt 5, 17; Mt 11, 18–19 par. Lk 7, 33–34. Jesus' "coming" is also a mission (*apestalēn*—"I was sent"): Mt 15, 24; cf. also the references to "him who sent me" in Mt 10, 40; Lk 10, 16; cf. Mk 9, 37 par. Lk 9, 48. Whereas the usage in the Synoptics clearly reflects Jesus' self-awareness and the community's understanding of it, in the Fourth Gospel it is used in the interest of explicit christological confession and explanation. *Elthon* is expanded by means of the formulas "into the world" and "from the Father," and the metaphor of "sending" and "mission," derived from Jewish emissary-law, is used to justify the claims Jesus makes on his own behalf as the duly constituted emissary of the Father.

final analysis, however, neither the assurance with which statements about the *Logos* Incarnate are made nor the statements themselves may ever become simply the products of autonomous reason asserting *itself* in the act of asserting its statements. In Christian doctrine, all assertiveness on the part of reason exists by the *grace* of the confession, to the glory of the Father, of Jesus' Lordship. It is a serious theological error for reason to mistake Jesus' consubstantiality with the Father for something which can be affirmed without essential reference to the Resurrection, and hence without essential reference to the human life and sufferings of Jesus. The Church's confident affirmation of the Son's consubstantiality with the Father involves a claim to the kind of familiarity with the Father that only worship in Spirit and truth can give. And this worship must be at once conscious of its sufficiency *and* of its total dependence on God's gracious self-revelation in the *risen* Christ. Hence, speaking about the *Logos* must remain, at heart, an act of intellectual worship called forth by the revelation of God's graciousness and truth.

Confident *Logos*-talk about Jesus Christ is the hypostatized, substantialized shape of the *parrhēsia* evoked by the Resurrection; it owes its existence to, and derives its continued relevance from, the worshipful surrender. The *shape* of *Logos*-talk may be determined by the conceptualizing, hypostatizing, terminologizing habits of human reason; its appropriate *use* is intellectual worship. This is not always sufficiently realized.[7] In fact, *the way in which* the pre-existent *Logos* and our knowledge of his subsistence, from eternity, in the mystery of God is asserted is often far too reminiscent of the way in which human reason asserts truths on the strength of its own ability to know. The eternal *Logos* is presented in such a factual way, and our knowledge of it is presented as so perfectly certain an idea, that the connection with the Ressurection and the act of worship evoked by the risen One is virtually lost.[8] *Logos*-talk then becomes an exercise of the power of autonomous reason; we have argued that the neo-

---

[7]This will have consequences for the practice of Christian apologetics; for some suggestions on this subject, cf. below, pp. 486–501.

[8]The *Declaratio* of the Congregation for the Doctrine of the Faith discussed above (pp. 52–53, 257–258) is a good example of the kind of affirmativeness rejected here. Cf. especially p. 238 (*Origins*, p. 667).

Chalcedonian tradition has been unprayerfully unaware of this problem, and that Schoonenberg's efforts are not sufficiently critical of this unawareness.

The kind of *Logos*-talk which we have just described leads to a second attitudinal problem: it often betrays the characteristic intolerance and impatience of the idea. This raises the suspicion that the inability of traditional christology to accommodate the life and especially the passion of Jesus goes back to a deeper problem. Human reason tends to be impatient with a God who does not let himself be captured by an idea or an ideology, a God who does not conform to man's devotion to power-tools, least of all to man's supposedly most powerful tool: the idea.

The impatience at the root of the strongly ideational affirmation of the *Logos* tends to be intolerant of the narrative shape of the Gospels. Hans Frei writes:

> It is not going too far to say that the story is the meaning or, alternatively, that the meaning emerges from the story form, rather than being merely illustrated by it, as would be the case in allegory and, in a different way, in myth. A great theme in literature of the novelistic type, like a pattern in a historical sequence, cannot be paraphrased by a general statement. To do so would approach reducing it to meaninglessness. In each case the theme has meaning only to the extent that it is instantiated and hence narrated; and this meaning through instantiation is not *illustrated* (as though it were an intellectually pre-subsisting or preconceived archetype or ideal essence) but *constituted* through the mutual, specific determination of agents, speech, social context, and circumstances that form the indispensable narrative web.[9]

We have said before that there is significance to the fact that the original christological confession takes a narrative shape: it reflects, not only the life of Jesus, but also the Church's commitment to the *imitatio Christi*.[10] If, then, the affirmation of the pre-existent *Logos* downplays the significance of the life of Jesus, we must conclude that it will also have consequences for the Church's own commitment. Emphasis on the eternal *Logos* as the true identity of Jesus is often used to evade the real questions involved in the process of Jesus'

---

[9] *The Eclipse of Biblical Narrative*, p. 280.
[10] Above, pp. 344–347.

human life; often, the same emphasis is also used, impatiently, to silence legitimate christological questions and answers arising from human life now.[11] In both cases, the affirmation of the pre-existent *Logos*, no matter how orthodox it sounds, is illegitimate.

An important conclusion follows from this. If we are to reaffirm the *Logos* in christology, we will have to do so in terms that convey that *the Logos has a positive affinity with the realities of human life and suffering, and not merely an impassive tolerance of them.* In the words of the Apocalypse, we will have to speak of the Lamb slain from the foundation of the world.[12] This means that our reaffirmation of the *Logos* will have to heed Donald MacKinnon's advice that the consubstantiality of the person of Christ with the Father must be determined in terms of *kenōsis.* In MacKinnon's own passionate words.

> [. . .] if Jesus is to reveal that 'He is the revealer', thus disclosing that his significance is not in himself, and that where he is concerned, the most important fact is this, that he is the identifiable historical individual through whom God has addressed the world, we may claim that this is only possible through the realization in his historical individuality, of a total receptivity. [. . .] At the heart of that ministry we find realized a final, a haunting receptivity. Yet that receptivity never rots away into a passive acceptance.[13]

The determination of Christ's consubstantiality with the Father in terms of receptivity and *kenōsis,* we may expect, will also have consequences for the style of christology. Intolerant, gnostic idea-thinking downplayed the life of Jesus in the name of the pre-conceived *Logos*; patient, pathic process-thinking will have to cherish the life of Jesus and thus discover a *Logos* that is anything but impassible—a *Logos* whose revelation *in the flesh* is taken with utter seriousness as saying something about the *Logos* itself.

As a first move toward such a reaffirmation, we will explore the dimensions of being-related. We will first consider being-related as a

---

[11]This will be somewhat elaborated in the next chapter; below, pp. 507–518.

[12]Rev 13, 8 (read according to its natural syntactical structure).

[13]"The Relation of the Doctrines of the Incarnation and the Trinity," in: Richard W. A. McKinney (ed.), *Creation, Christ, and Culture,* Studies in Honour of T. F. Torrance, Edinburgh, T. & T. Clark, 1976, pp. 92–107; quotation pp. 96, 98.

mode of being that is a perfection of the person, and then discuss inclusiveness, transcendence-experience, representation, and receptivity as the four main dimensions of this mode of being. This will provide us with the conceptual framework for the following, more strictly theological sections of this chapter.

ON BEING RELATED

Introduction: the contribution of humanistic psychology

We have already mentioned that concern with personalness and personal relationships is part and parcel of present-day sensibility.[14] It is not surprising, therefore, that our intention to speak about Jesus' identity in relational terms can look for encouragement in modern psychology, especially among the practitioners of what has been called "third force" or "humanistic" psychology. A few suggestions from the writings of two of the best-known authors in this field may, therefore, serve as an introduction.

From everyday experience we know that a person can meet others with less worry or inhibition or aggression according as he experiences himself as more secure. Far from constituting a threat to his identity, others will be able to enter into his world relatively freely; the less defensiveness on my part, the more others feel permitted and even encouraged to be themselves more fully around me, and, especially, more truthfully. In this way, a secure person has presence, but not of the forceful kind; he seems hardly to endeavor to be himself. Mature persons use little power, either to protect themselves, or to establish themselves as factors to be reckoned with in the lives of others. No forceful presence on their part causes others to modify, or even distort, their behavior, their self-perception, or their self-acceptance.

Abraham Maslow[15] has connected these and other phenomena with "self-actualization": the realization of personal values, not out of a need or a felt deficiency, but on the basis of their "being-value" in and of themselves—on the strength of the person's own basic

---

[14]Above, pp. 99–101, 171–172.
[15]In *Toward a Psychology of Being* and *Religions, Values, and Peak Experiences.*

"need" to actualize himself. It is indeed true that secure persons enjoy their selves in such a way that they seem largely unaffected and undeterred by their own and others' deficiencies. They are familiar with their own limitations as well as strengths. They can face, endure, and even understand empathetically—with the objectivity of love—suffering, immaturity, antagonism and willful irresponsibility on the part of others, even if they should be directed against themselves. In such a case, we say, the person has deeper resources to fall back upon; we may attribute to him or her a marvelous knowledge of human nature; and we may find ourselves wondering sometimes when such a person will finally be driven to the end of resourcefulness and tolerance.

Maslow has coined the formula "self-actualization" to describe the phenomenon and to provide it with a theoretical basis. The term is slightly misleading, in that it suggests that the person is essentially a closed circuit; Maslow is at pains to point out that the self-actualizing person is also the person who best relates with reality outside himself in positive, altruistic ways.[16]

In Carl Rogers' writings[17] this relational aspect of human maturity is at the center of attention. Persons are entitled to and need and are capable of "unconditional positive regard"—the only attitude which uncovers the fact that the person's basic leanings and urges, so often suspected of being disruptive and chaotic, are essentially good and constructive. At the basis of both Maslow's and Rogers' theories lies the conviction that there is a quality of "being" to a person, something positive which underlies all specialized structures and all partial behaviors, a quality in virtue of which a person demands to be himself freely and originally *and* to exist with other things and persons, not as with competitors but as with partners in being and letting be.[18]

---

[16]Cf. esp. *Toward a Psychology of Being*, pp. 74–79, 92–94; *Religions, Values, and Peak Experiences*, pp. 60ff.

[17]Esp. *On Becoming a Person*.

[18]The points just made do not imply that Maslow and Rogers are above all theological criticism. Thus, for instance, questions can be raised about Maslow's idea that B-behavior is "self-justifying"; and there is every reason to wonder if Rogers' "*unconditional* positive regard" is a human possibility.

Martin Buber's fundamental thesis: the modus of being-related

What we are touching on here is, of course, what Martin Buber has approximated by distinguishing between "I—It" and "I—Thou." The *I* that thinks and lives in terms of "I—It" is a qualitatively different *I* from the *I* that thinks and lives in terms of "I—Thou."[19] The former lives by definition and hence by exclusion; the objectifying nature of our conceptual understanding is consequently taken for the norm of reality, too. The latter lives in the *modus* of being-related, and, hence, in his very life makes a difference between encounter with reality, which unites, and his understanding-by-categories, which divides.

This *modus* of being-related determines the inner quality of what it means to be a person. It affects the person in his relations to other things and persons as well as in his relation to himself. The person who lives in the *modus* of being-related will not be in the world as a self-maintained, self-justifying, closed-off area of anxious physical, psychic, and spiritual sovereignty with territorial rights, warding off any invasion of privacy; not a *cor curvum in se*, whose dealings with the "outside world" are at best borderline negotiations animated by a "human-nature-being-what-it-is" approach. No, a person living in the *modus* of being-related refuses to reduce, or be reduced, to "human-nature-being-what-it-is." Such a person recognizes in the other the demand issued to himself to be more than a source of output or a receptacle for input. He feels called upon by the other to be more than "just there" as a useful asset, or as a factor to be reckoned with, let alone "just there" as an obstacle. He is even aware that there is more to life than the most constructive relationships: helping, befriending, teaching. Underlying and embedding and suffusing everything objectifiable, he feels the demanding call for pure relationship: presence calls for presence. The person who thus lives in the *modus* of being-related experiences his own identity, not as property, but as gift. Out of this experience of himself as gift he

---

[19]Cf. *Ich und Du*, pp. 9–12 (*I and Thou*, pp. 53–56). That Buber treats the question of being-related at a much profounder level than Carl Rogers is shown in the "Dialogue Between Martin Buber and Carl R. Rogers," published as the Appendix to Martin Buber, *The Knowledge of Man*, London, George Allen and Unwin, Ltd., 1965, pp. 166–184.

will proceed to give himself to others, even if they defend themselves against him.

So far, we have only sketched what it means to be related, and the sketch has been negative rather than positive. Being-related means not to live on the strength of "I—It." We must now try to determine some positive characteristics.

The modus of being-related as perfection of the person

The first characteristic is that being-related is not rooted in some inner core of the person (*Personkern*), which would then have to penetrate the respective outer layers of its spiritual, psychic, and physical envelope in order to deal with the world. The concrete individual person along with his powers of freedom and consciousness is neither the prison nor the *organon* of a jinnee—the "inner core of the person." Being-related, in other words, is not the specific activity of the innermost part of a person; it is an *entire* person's *modus* of being in such a way that the person is a self in the act or the attitude of encounter.[20] A person's authentic identity is nothing but that very person in the act or in the attitude of being-related; a person's false identity is nothing but that very person in the act or in the attitude of inability or refusal to encounter. This latter attitude is that of the *cor curvum in se*: the person becomes his own prisoner. That this is ultimately a perversion of personhood lies in the façt that the other *is* available, as an invitation to encounter. Keeping this perspective of encounter in mind, we must say that it is of the perfection of the person to exist as an invitation to gracious encounter.[21]

Let us sum this up in a provisional fashion. Being-related is a *modus* of being, and hence affects the very quality of being a person. In refusing to be related a person hardens into an ego-fortress that does an injustice to self as well as to others. However, no matter how necessary relationships are, being actually related is irreducible ei-

---

[20]"Attitude" here refers to a habitual predisposition and readiness to engage in "acts" of encounter.

[21]For this paragraph, cf. above, pp. 239–247. One of the classic psychiatric treatments of the defensive person remains Anna Freud, *The Ego and the Mechanisms of Defense* (*The Writings of Anna Freud*, Vol. II), revised ed., New York, International Universities Press, Inc., ⁴1973, no matter how much its underlying theory remains tied to the classical Freudian denial of personhood as a spiritually interpretable identity.

ther to the powers or to the strict demands of being a human person, and hence it is always gracious.[22]

Being-related, inclusiveness, and transcendence

The second point concerns the fact that at the level of encounter there is no question of "room." Being-related, in and of itself, is not concerned with the limitations which are the obvious lot of every person.[23] It is true, the person who lives in the *modus* of being-related does not thereby gain an infinite capacity for *effective* or *actual* encounter with others in the sense of undergoing or wielding substantive influence: he remains tied to the limitations of his individuality. But he is not worried about his finitude. He does not attempt, frantically, to have an impact on the maximum number of people; he evinces none of that frantic trophy-hunt for the maximum number of interesting people and experiences. Both are attempts to deny finitude, and, thus, loud affirmations of it. At the level of *actio* and *passio*[24] I have only so much of myself to go around when it comes to giving, and only so much capacity for influence when it comes to receiving. At the level of "I—It," persons and things tend to crowd each other out; they share in the condition of contiguity proper to things: the room something or somebody occupies cannot be occupied by anything or anybody else.

Where a person's being-related to others is concerned, however, things are different. To the extent that I cherish the presence (even the past presence!) of others who have, by being with me, encouraged me to be myself, I become *more*, not less, capable of being present to others. The more I relate, the more I experience myself as a gift; that means, relationships make me a self-giving person. I will not treat myself as property subject to quantitative laws. My true identity is actuated in encounter, and *every* other—whatever may be my *func-*

---

[22]Cf. "The You encounters me by grace—it cannot be found by seeking": *I and Thou*, p. 62 (*Ich und Du*, p. 18).

[23]Readers familiar with Thomist thought will recognize in this sentence two transpositions of familiar maxims. The first is that relationship, or *esse ad*, in and of itself does not imply accidentality or finitude. The second is that the human person, in virtue of the soul, enjoys an affinity with all that is: *anima est quodammodo omnia*.

[24]*Actio* and *passio* are here understood in the sense of the Aristotelian categories; they refer to accidental (and usually mutual) changes produced and/or undergone by the (inter)actions of finite substances.

tional relationship to him—is important as a matter of principle, simply by being there; nobody is "too much." Even when I am "finished" when it comes to either giving or receiving good or evil things, I can still present myself, "finished" as I am, to others: with empty hands and unable to give, or at the end of my tolerance and unable to take any more grief. Even when I realize that I cannot reach the other person, inhibited as he is, with my gifts, I can still present myself, excluded as I am, to the other: with my hands full and yet prevented from giving, or at the end of my endurance and yet without hope for any comfort. This means that I can always give *myself.* If I do, I become the invitational representative of the other's true, relational identity, even in total ineffectualness. Generosity and receptivity meet in such a stance; in fact they are identical.

Considerations like these, of course, raise the question whether we are still speaking realistically. Who is he who will indeed remain faithful to the other down to his own bitter end? Who is he who will not eventually draw the line somewhere and resort to some form of self-assertion? Who is he who will keep fully alive the awareness of his indebtedness, for his gifts, and indeed for his identity, to those in back of him? In fact, *are* there people in back of me who can be held responsible for my whole *self*? And who is he who can give to others in such a way as to really, unconditionally give *himself* in the things he gives?

Before we answer any of these questions affirmatively, hesitation is in order. Both the finitude of the gifts we give and receive, and the self-assertion so frequently involved in the act of giving and receiving must make us wary of facile talk about "total self-giving" and "total indebtedness." In actual fact, is anyone, be he ever so generous, really fully responsible for anyone else's relational identity? Granted my real indebtedness, for my relational identity, to others, is my indebtedness ever *total*—am I anyone's creature? And granted my real responsibility for others' relational identity, is my responsibility total—am I anyone's maker? Thus it becomes clear that all *actual* acts of mutual presence and actual encounters are limited. These limitations derive from the finitude of persons' actual availability and from their anxious moves toward self-preservation.

Still, underneath all these limitations, being-related as such is not subject to quantitative laws; no other must be excluded. This means that the presence of the other as such is an offer of the experience of transcendence in every encounter.[25]

This leads us to our third point: representation as an essential feature of being-related. Alas, a drier, more technical jargon must serve as the vehicle of our thought for a moment; the thesis we want to formulate is so important that it requires the utmost accuracy in arguing.

Being-related as representation

We have already, in a previous chapter, pointed out that there is a connection between encounter and witness.[26] We must now expand that discussion.

The person (A) living in the *modus* of being-related becomes a witness in a double way. First, he witnesses to those persons (and things) (B) who, by encountering and touching him, have affirmed him and set him free to transcend himself and meet others (C), even if the latter refuse to be called into the relationship. In fact, since this very refusal to be called into an active relationship is also a gesture, it is an implicit acknowledgement of their (C) being-related; thus, the person (A) who encounters an unwilling or unable other person becomes a witness, not only to those (B) who have set him free, but also to *the refusing person's own orientation* (C) toward being-related. By extending himself he (A) takes the part of the other's (C) relational self, and to that extent he takes on responsibility for the other's (C) true identity; he becomes the other's representative.

In order to clarify our point by means of a contrast, let us ask ourselves a negative question. How does failure to relate occur? Our contention is that it occurs in three principal ways.

The first way is: the person (A) is disabled because those (B) in back of him have not really acted in accordance with the demands of relationship, but have influenced him (A) in such a way as to expand the area of *their own* sphere of influence at the expense of his

---

[25]Cf. Emmanuel Levinas, "Liberté et commandement," *Revue de Métaphysique et de Morale* 58 (1963) 264–272. Cf. also above, pp. 94–98. Notice the strict analogy between the *act* of speech and the *things said* on the one hand, and between the *encounter-relationship* and the *concrete mutual effects* of an act of encounter on the other hand.

[26]Above, pp. 228–232.

(A) integrity—hence his (A) diminished ability to relate to others (C) in his turn. The second way is: those (B) in back of the person (A) *have* acted in accordance with the demands of relationship, by giving themselves in giving their gifts and not by giving out of an overt or covert need for self-establishment; but the receiver (A) takes what was *meant* as a gift and turns it into an ego-asset, thus missing the point of the gift as well as the givers (B); when he (A) proceeds to relate to others (C) he (A) will do so in the interest of self-establishment: the being-related stops.

In neither case is the person (A) a witness to those in back of him (B). In the former case they (B) diminished his (A) identity, and hence his ability to give of himself; in the latter case he (A) turns in on himself in spite of the self-giving of others (B), and thus, in his defensiveness, refuses to acknowledge that his identity is the fruit of their (B) self-giving.

This can also be expressed in terms of representation: in neither case does the person (A) really *represent* those in back of him. In the former case his (A) true identity—his relational identity—has been impaired; consequently he becomes, not a personal witness to those (B) who have touched him, but a pawn of those who have manipulated him; to others (C) he (A) is a substitute (a replacement) of them (B). In the latter case he himself (A) diminishes, or blocks, his own true, relational identity; consequently, instead of personally—in his *own* relationships with others (C)—testifying to those (B) in back of him, he sets himself (A) up as unrelated to them (B), and in that sense replaces them (B).

The third way is: the person (A), encouraged by those (B) in back of him, really reaches out to another person (C), but the latter interprets his (A) gesture not as an encounter, but as an interference. The person (A) cannot tolerate the rebuff; rather than staying with the refusing person (C) as the representative of his (C) true relational identity, he (A) withdraws.

Something extremely important follows from this. *Representation is based on being-related as such*, quite apart from any demonstrable, identifiable, particular, substantive effects upon a person. To put it more bluntly: representation is independent of behavioral transactions. This qualification is very important. It is based on the recognition that particular effects upon another person *may* also be due to force and invasion, which diminish rather than enhance the other's relational identity, and hence his capacity for further relationships. Parents, teachers, employers, men and women in the helping professions, and so many other significant others who prize personalness in encounter know the risks involved in the fact that others substantially depend on them for certain substantive goods. Influencing others and giving to others and letting oneself be influenced and receiving *may* indeed be acts of being-related, but they may also be acts of self-maintenance and self-justification—attempts to maintain or expand the area of one's defensive autonomy—that is to say: one's inauthentic identity.

A few pages ago, before we discussed the three forms of failure, we mentioned another possible case. We can now allege this as a confirmation of our thesis that representation is constituted by being-related as such, quite apart from the give-and-take of *actio* and *passio*. We stated that a person who encounters an unwilling or unable other person becomes a witness to the refusing person's own orientation toward being-related.[27] Purely by extending himself to the other person he becomes the latter's representative, in that he takes his part and takes on the responsibility for the other person's relational identity. But since the other person refuses to endorse his own being-related, the person who encounters him also becomes a witness against him. This againstness is not of the kind that takes action against a person. It is merely the presential act of a person who offers himself to the other for encounter. To the extent that the former opens himself to the latter, to that extent he invites him to be his responsive self. But the other refuses, and in doing so rejects his own real self, represented by the person who encounters him. In such a situation, the unwilling partner is likely to strike out at the representative of his true, relational identity. If he does this, he will take his own defensive, non-relational self out on the person who meets him. Then it becomes the hard and thankless task of the person who encounters him to remain faithful to the encounter, by *willingly* taking upon himself, not only the other's true identity, but also the burden of the other's non-relational self. That means vicarious suffering, which will last as long as the suffering person remains

---

[27]Above, 411, 412.

faithful to the other's relational identity and stays with him, without, however, letting his receptivity "rot away into a passive acceptance," to use Donald MacKinnon's graphic expression.[28] *Passio* merely passively undergone stultifies, and makes of the sufferer a mere butt for the other's self-defensive aggression; moreover, such a passivity often cloaks an inner desire to strike back.[29] By contrast, suffering animated by the receptivity proper to encounter makes the sufferer the representative, both of the attacker's true, relational identity, and of the attacker's defensive, non-relational self—that is to say, of his entire person.[30]

Being-related is a mode of existence of the person, we have argued. It involves the entire person, and is in itself unlimited in

---

[28]Cf. the quotation, above, p. 405.

[29]Paul H. Schlüngel, writing about suffering as an attribute of God ("Der leidende Vater," *Orientierung* 41 [1977] 49–50) expresses this very well. He writes: "Not every kind of suffering is of this [divine] quality, but only such suffering as grows out of self-involvement in what is good and out of concern with the other person—suffering that remains sincerely concerned about the good of the cause and of the other person, even if one is rejected. If a person suffers injustice, and if he would like to cause his enemy as much grief in return, if only it were in his power to do so—such a person does not represent the suffering of God" (50).

[30]Readers familiar with Dorothee Sölle's *Christ the Representative* (Philadelphia, Fortress Press, 1967) will have recognized my indebtedness to that stimulating essay. There are, however, two main differences between the present treatment of representation and Sölle's. The *first* is that I treat *two* kinds of substitution (or replacement). One is active: the "representative" threatens to replace the person he represents. This is the case elaborated by Sölle; in the present treatment it is referred to as the second possible case. The other one is passive: a person is manipulated into being a substitute or replacement of his "benefactors," but has the illusion that he represents them. Sölle does not consider this possibility, mentioned in the text as the first possible case. The *second* difference between my treatment of representation and Sölle's is that I consider relationship the constitutive element. Much as the concrete shape of representation is determined by the give-and-take inherent in human finitude, in which the person finds himself to be neither completely unique nor completely replaceable (as Sölle beautifully elaborates), representation is not reducible to this; its inner quality is encounter and witness. As a consequence, I am not so sure about provisionality—so strongly advocated by Sölle—as an essential element in representation. It is true, provisionality mellows the harshness of the total uniqueness/total replaceability dilemma, but the question remains: What is the sustaining and animating force underneath the stance of provisionality? In my view this force is the faithfulness by which a person keeps himself related to another person.—All this has obvious consequences for christology. Thus, for instance, I am of the opinion that Sölle underplays the importance of Jesus' witness to the Father in the act of representing him, and that the abiding nature of Jesus' vicarious function is left in doubt.

scope, which accounts for the transcendence-experience involved in encounter. In encounter, the person becomes the representative of those who have encountered him as well as those he encounters, quite apart from demonstrable effects; it was this insight which led us to the insight that encounter may mean vicarious suffering. This opens the way to a consideration of the fourth and deepest characteristic of being-related: receptivity, or sympathy.

Being-related as sympathetic

We have already alluded several times to a feature of being-related which deserves special attention, namely, its sympathetic nature. We did so by pointing to the mature person's ability to empathize, and to the fact that the person who relates becomes the representative of the other's true, relational identity. We must now expand this somewhat in order to appreciate the point; we will do so by briefly characterizing the style of knowing and the style of acting of the person who lives in the stance of being-related.

Living in encounter causes a person to know in such a way that objectifying, defining knowledge—the type of knowledge that puts a construction on reality—does not take pride of place. Rather, such a person's active, constructive knowledge is set in the context of his awareness of his familiarity and affinity with what he encounters. Hence, such a person will not test the other's mettle without letting his own mettle be tested, too. He will not mold or shape the other without being molded and shaped by the other. His knowledge is not primarily a matter of mastery, but of kinship and affinity. The knowledge involved in encounter does not become autonomous, let alone domineering; it does not create undue distance from reality, let alone lose its respect for it. The knower's intent is to do justice to reality, not to show his own mastery over it; he is more interested in the thing known than in the power or the structure of his own knowledge.

The sympathetic nature of being-related will show itself also in the style of action of a person who lives in this stance. We have characterized encounter as sympathetic, but this does not in the least mean that it is passive. The person who lives in the attitude of encounter is not a pushover, for he confronts; nor is he (which would be worse) a sly manipulator of others. The sympathetic nature of encounter, in other words, is a matter of receptivity, not of passive acceptance. And if there is compliance, it is a matter of fiber, not of spinelessness.

Because of this sympathetic stance, activity-in-encounter is not of the kind that attacks and subdues an object in order to force the object to suit the agent's style and purposes. Rather, a person in the stance of being-related understands, and has an empathetic feeling for, the possibilities that lie hidden in the other, even if the other is apathetic or aggressive; when he acts, he gets the best out of the other. His own success is not the norm for successful action; the other's growth is. Because of this attitude of receptiveness, such a person can act without domineering. That means that he can also suffer without being devastated, as we pointed out a few paragraphs ago. The sympathy of being-related provides deep anchorage to all *actio* and *passio*. Cut loose from this mooring, *actio* tends to become domination, in the style of the Roman paterfamilias' *ius utendi et abutendi*—the right to make and to mar; *passio* without sympathy becomes the completely passive undergoing of the onslaught of the powers that be. But if sympathy is at the root of a person's life with others, his actions are characterized by care and responsible stewardship, and the suffering he undergoes by compassion for the person who inflicts it.[31]

---

[31]Since encounter and sympathy do not as such imply finitude and imperfection, it is possible to use the themes developed in this section as stepping-stones for God-talk. In such a framework of thought, for example, the concept of creation would be analyzed, not on the analogy of "making something," but rather on the analogy of "calling forth": God calls the world into existence, and the world responds by being present to God. To mention another application (and one which has received increased attention of late): it is possible to ascribe suffering (*pathos*, not *pathē*, passions) to God. On this subject, cf. Jürgen Moltmann, *The Crucified God*, pp. 267–278. Also J. K. Mozley, *The Impassibility of God*, Cambridge, Cambridge University Press, 1926; Abraham J. Heschel, *The Prophets*, 2 vols., New York, Harper & Row, 1969, 1975, esp. Vol. II, pp. 87–103; Jung Young Lee, *God Suffers for Us*, A Systematic Inquiry into a Concept of Divine Impassibility, The Hague, Martinus Nijhoff, 1974; also Robert T. Sears, "Trinitarian Love as Ground of the Church," *Theological Studies* 37 (1976) 652–679.

JESUS AND HIS FATHER

Outlook

It is time to return to the christological question. As we formulated it in the previous chapter: What is it that animates this man Jesus to stand so long-sufferingly firm in his kindly determination to welcome all that is human into his person and thus to create in his person the medium where all that is human is reconciled and opened to a life beyond all borderlines and definitions, including the bounds of death?[32] We promised to answer the question in continuity with the tradition, by pointing to the *Logos* as the answer; but we also promised to do so in such a way that Jesus would not be separated from his brothers and sisters, that the *Logos* would have a positive, inner affinity with the human life of Jesus, and that the *Logos* would be conceived in strictly relational terms.

In this section we will attempt to accomplish this task; the ideas developed in the previous section will provide us with some conceptual tools. After an introductory section on Jesus' total surrender to the Father we will start our analyses. First, we will deny that Jesus' divinity is in some divine *Personkern*. Then we will characterize his relation to the Father as inclusive of all his human relationships, and thus as the source of his double role as the representative of God and the representative of humanity. We will then point to two characteristics of Jesus' relationship to the Father, namely its actuality and its graciousness. Then, after a brief summary, we will describe Jesus' union with the Father as attitudinal, and hence as a mode of being *(modus essendi)*. This will lead to the thesis that Jesus' real humanity must be unequivocally affirmed. Finally, we will argue that Jesus' divinity is identical with his attitude of total receptivity.

Total surrender and the Resurrection

Jesus, we said, does not cease to relate to those around him, even when they abandon and reject him. Thus, the man on the cross embodies a new definition of humanity. Thus he also redeems it and brings it to the Father in his own person.[33]

---

[32]Above, p. 375; cf. also above, pp. 370, 372.
[33]Above, pp. 367–369.

What are we to make of a person who goes to the bitter end of a slave's execution, and yet keeps himself related to those at whose hands he is done away with? A man who does not claim righteousness, not even in death? A man, therefore, who does not set himself up as saved by association with an enduring cause which those over against him reject? A man who does not endorse their exclusion or abandonment of himself by excluding or abandoning them?

His person is not his last line of defense, for there is no last line of defense, no deepest resource to be tapped into for the purpose of self-maintenance, no inner core where a sense of individuality provides ultimate, sovereign self-assurance. On the cross, Jesus does not appeal to his conscience to claim victory.[34] He does not even claim any felt presence of God for an ultimate support.

The God with whom Jesus lives does not let himself be invoked as Jesus' personal savior; such an invocation would amount to Jesus' setting himself up as saved *over against* those who reject him. This is the deepest meaning of Jesus' abandonment by God: God is not on his side at the expense of others. It is precisely this absence of any self-justifying appeal to God that conveys Jesus' total surrender to him. Thus Jesus becomes Man for Others to the end, the representative of all of humanity, and the faithful witness to, and representative of, a God who is Father to each person at the expense of none.

Jesus refused, even when pressed to death, to look upon being equal with God as a matter of snatching or claiming.[35] With the

---

[34]This absence of the claim to victory in conscience is an essential difference between the Christian interpretation of suffering and the Jewish one. Cf. Emmanuel Levinas, "Aimer la Thora plus que Dieu," in: *Difficile Liberté*, Essais sur le Judaisme, Paris, A. Michel, 1963, pp. 171–176. Levinas' article is a commentary on what he assumes is a truly Jewish story circulating anonymously in Yiddish, and translated into French by Arnold Mandel for the Jewish-French periodical *La Terre Retrouvée* (March 15, 1955). It is, in fact, an original story by Zvi Kolitz written in English: "Yossel Rakover's Appeal to God," in: Albert H. Friedlander (ed.), *Out of the Whirlwind*, A Reader in Holocaust Literature, New York, Union of American Hebrew Congregations, 1968, pp. 390–399. Barry Walfish made the identification for me, from a letter by Kolitz in the Israeli periodical *Sh'demot*, Winter (No. 45) issue of the year 5732 (1972).—Both Kolitz' story and Levinas' commentary are profound challenges directed at Christians by the Jewish tradition, summoning them to speak of the meaning of suffering and the love of God in continuity with the tradition Jesus himself came out of.

[35]Cf. Phil 2, 6, with *harpagmos* read as *nomen actionis*, not as *nomen objecti*—the act of snatching, not the object snatched—following C. F. D. Moule. R. W. Hoover's

deepest reverence for the mystery we must say—and we can say it only with the boldness that comes from the Resurrection—that, had Jesus claimed God for himself in his extremity, he would have made God equal to himself. In one and the same gesture he would have reduced himself to his own person, excluded all others in a final act of self-justification, and cut God down to his own size in a final act of private "religion"; and in doing so he would have made his god into a force comparable with, and opposed to, the forces that killed him. That ultimate gesture of snatching would have been as good as more than twelve legions of angels in the garden or a successful descent from the cross—only the Scriptures would not have been fulfilled.[36]

We can say these things only on the strength of the Resurrection, for the perfection of Jesus' historical surrender to his Father withdraws itself, not only from observation, but also from human credibility. It takes the *parrhēsia* in response to the risen One to affirm Jesus' surrender to the Father as total; but once made in the light of the Resurrection the affirmation *does* do justice to the

---

interpretation, though, may be more accurate; he translates: "He did not regard being equal with God as something to take advantage of," or ". . . as something to be used for his own advantage." Moule and Hoover, however, have this in common—that they assert the selflessness of Jesus. I agree with Jerome Murphy-O'Connor, against Moule and a host of others, that the idea of pre-existence is not pre-supposed in the text; cf. "Christological Anthropology in Phil. II, 6–11," *Revue Biblique* 83 (1976) 25–50.

[36]Cf. Mt 26, 53–54; 27, 42.—What has been said here must also be applied to the question of the self-consciousness of Jesus. Rahner's treatment of this much-disputed question ("Dogmatic Reflections on the Knowledge and Self-Consciousness of Christ," in *Theological Investigations,* Vol. V, Baltimore, Helicon Press, 1966, pp. 193–215) rightly views Jesus' awareness of God as non-thematic and non-objectified. Such an awareness of God is obviously unusable as an asset to be used against enemies, precisely because it involves a *total,* all-encompassing awareness of God's presence on Jesus' part. Rahner's explanation also accounts for Jesus' sense of abandonment by God on the cross; it must be viewed as the absence of any specific, conscious, "religious" awareness of God, on the basis of which Jesus might have justified for himself his own surrender to God. This absence of conscious religiosity is the prime analogue of what the mystics of all times have stammered to express: the union of the human will with the divine will beyond any reliance on known resources. Cf. John of the Cross' *Y en el monte nada* ("And on the summit there is nothing") and *Vivo sin vivir en mí* ("Not living in myself I live"); cf. Gerald Brenan, *St. John of the Cross—His Life and Poetry,* with a translation of his poetry by Lynda Nicholson, London, Cambridge University Press, 1975, pp. 45, 133ff., 170–171, and the plate opp. p. 49.

historical facts, inconclusive though they are when viewed merely objectively: Jesus commends himself, in his life as in his death, totally to God, who is his total security. In this selfless abandon to his Father he becomes Man for Others. The identity which humans tend to seek in self-maintenance and self-justification—those sources of definition and division—is "superessentially"[37] realized by God, to whom Jesus abandons himself in worship, obedience, and trust.

In the Resurrection, the Father does abundant justice to this man Jesus in the Holy Spirit. This means that the gift of the Spirit in which Jesus had had immediate access to the Father in his lifetime, and in virtue of which he had related himself to his brothers and sisters, is now actually offered to all men and women. The historical process, inaugurated by Jesus, of the assumption of humanity into the total surrender to God the Father can now continue in the mission of the Church. It is not surprising, therefore, that the first letter of Peter pictures Jesus, after his death, as the first evangelizer, whose mission, in the Spirit, is to those not directly accessible to the Church: he preaches to the cosmic spirits in the place of custody.[38] Humanity present and future will be the Church's charge: she must preach the Gospel to all nations, call them to discipleship, and baptize them[39]—thus drawing the whole world into the total surrender to the Father inaugurated by Jesus.

Jesus' divinity not an inner core of his person

This man Jesus, now risen, this human person with his particular life story and his particular destiny, is the consubstantial Son of God. He is this in virtue of his being-related to God. This being-related is a *modus* of being a person, and in the case of Jesus we affirm that it consists in the total receptivity of this human person to the Father, without the slightest trace of that distrust of God that is involved in self-maintenance, self-justification, and self-affirmation. That means: the "I" of Jesus is that "I," that moral, responsive identity, which is constituted by God's address to him and by the

---

[37]For this term, derived from the fourteenth-century mystic John Ruysbroeck, cf. Evelyn Underhill, *Mystics of the Church*, Cambridge, James Clarke & Co., 1975, pp. 148–151.

[38]1 Pet 3, 18–20; note the baptismal context.

[39]Cf. Mt 28, 19–20.

perfection of his response to God, to such an extent that there is, in Jesus, no defensive recourse to personal identity. Jesus really lets God be *God*, and thus he is true God from true God.

It is important again to emphasize here that we are not talking about some divine *Personkern*. John A. T. Robinson has rightly insisted that this would amount to drawing a *cordon sanitaire* around some irreducible core in Jesus, which would be outside the process of human reality and interaction—a core where Jesus' divinity could then be located.[40] Rather, the whole human person of Jesus, at all levels and without remainder, along with his entire life-history, stands in an attitude of abiding, selfless abandon to the Father.

One particular form of the *Personkern*-approach must be mentioned here for criticism. If the inner core of Jesus' person is conceived of as the seat of his divinity, it is also placed beyond the flux of change. But then, in view of this divine *Personkern*, all of Christ's gracious actions and his endurance tend to be viewed as no more than par for the course. The divinity of Jesus becomes an isolated, inner-core entity that pushes his human behavior into pre-determined patterns; the life-story of Jesus becomes the running-off of a pre-conceived, pre-subsistent divine program—and thus, humanly speaking, irrelevant.

To avoid this error, we are proposing a reversal for which we are deeply and unmistakably indebted to Schoonenberg. This reversal also amounts to a reversal in appreciation, in the service of doing justice to the full humanity of Jesus. What the tradition refers to as "enhypostatic human nature" we call "the human person of Jesus Christ in its concrete individual nature"; what the tradition refers to as "the *hypostasis* (or person) of the *Logos*" we call "Jesus' absolute irreducibility to his concrete individual nature in virtue of his total surrender to the Father."[41] This surrender-in-relationship denotes

---

[40] Cf. *The Human Face of God*, pp. 47–56.—For this reason the explanation of the relationship between divinity and humanity in Christ by means of the body-soul analogy, used by Alexandrians and Antiochenes alike, retains its usefulness. The soul animates the body, not from some inner, purely spiritual stronghold, but as the body's *own* spiritual power. The analogy continued to be of interest even after the condemnation of Apollinarianism. Cf. Frances M. Young, "A Reconsideration of Alexandrian Christology," *Journal of Ecclesiastical History* 22 (1971) 103–114.

[41] For these expressions, taken from Vladimir Lossky, cf. above, p. 394 and note 86.

the inner quality of what the tradition has termed Christ's consubstantiality with the Father. The mystery of Jesus is not a reality contained in an inner core of his person, but his relationship to the Father, which makes the complete person of Jesus a mystery. What the tradition referred to as Jesus' consubstantiality with the Father is, in the lived life of Jesus, his abiding relationship of total abandon to the Father.

Robinson's rejection of the *cordon-sanitaire* construct—the image comes to mind of an inner space devoid of humanity at the center of Jesus, where the divine *hypostasis* is enthroned—is quite legitimate; Robinson's rejection of *anhypostasia*, though repeated *ad nauseam*, must be endorsed, if only for the concept's *de facto* inability to do justice to a crying human concern with personalness;[42] both rejections are in agreement with two of the Chalcedonian adverbs, namely, "without division, without separation" *(adiairetōs, achōristōs).*[43]

Still, the truth conveyed by the traditional concepts of *anhypostasia* and *enhypostasia* must be conveyed. In our proposal this is done by saying that Jesus Christ is absolutely irreducible to his own person in virtue of a *modus essendi*, which consists in his being totally related to God as his Father.

Jesus' relation to God as inclusive—representation

Jesus' relationship to God must not be placed in a *Personkern*. Instead, it must be seen as a qualifier, a *modus* of his entire person: his *modus* of being a person is one of absolute relatedness to the Father.

This *modus* becomes clear in two ways. Proximately, it is the unifying principle of Jesus' concrete, effective ministry to the lost sheep of the house of Israel and to a few marginal outsiders. But this concrete ministry carries a perspective with it. Sometimes, people dimly surmise this, for example, when they wonder about the source of his wisdom and power; and sometimes they have to be reminded of it, for example, when they are told to seek the bread that lasts. That perspective, evoked by Jesus' concrete ministry, is no less than the

---

[42]Cf. above, pp. 167–181.
[43]DS 302.

actual presence of the living God, and Jesus lives and speaks in that concrete perspective.

Being thus related to the living God, Jesus is God's representative. He absolutely refuses to appropriate for himself any glory which is God's alone, any goodness which is God's alone, any position of leadership in any venture that would fall short of being God's kingdom, any reputation as a wonderworker apart from faith. That Jesus is God's representative in person is shown by the fact that he means in no way to replace God.

This, however, does not subdue Jesus himself. His being-related to the Father makes him personally free and lends him a personal authority that amazes those around him. While living in total dependence on, total familiarity with, and total orientation to God, the man Jesus Christ is himself in a way no self-affirmation could ever hope to produce. This selfhood, however, is not an isolated selfhood, for Jesus' relationship to God precisely enables him to relate to others boundlessly. He is really there, present to others, in an availability for encounter which, while it animates the humblest gesture of outreach, knows no bounds.[44]

Total abandon to God and total freedom: so God becomes concrete in the actual encounter with Jesus. As Jesus' total surrender opens him to the Father, so that he is totally irreducible to his own person, so it opens him totally to others, so that they are offered the opportunity for total receptivity toward God in the encounter with Jesus. Jesus becomes the representative of others; in meeting them, he becomes the witness to *their* relational identity vis-à-vis the Father.

His surrender to the Father enables Jesus to relate to others boundlessly, we said. It also accounts for the inclusiveness with which Jesus becomes the witness to others' relational identity. He becomes the witness to their faith; wherever he sees living faith he

---

[44]This last clause paraphrases a sentence from the literary epitaph for Ignatius Loyola found in the (in)famous *Imago primi saeculi Societatis Jesu* (1640) and used by Hölderlin as the epigraph for his *Hyperion: Non coerceri maximo, contineri tamen minimo divinum est* ("Not to be limited by the greatest, yet to be contained by the smallest—that is divine"). Cf. Hugo Rahner's essay "Die Grabschrift des Loyola," in: *Ignatius von Loyola als Mensch und Theologe*, Freiburg–Basel–Wien, 1964, pp. 422–440.

congratulates the believer[45] and praises the Father. But Jesus' openness to others is not limited to faith; his concern is not only with ultimate reality; he is not acosmistic.

Jesus sees a positive resemblance between people ("evil though you are") giving gifts to each other and his Father giving himself in the Spirit; they are indeed "good gifts,"[46] not to be despised because they are not ultimate. The sphere of the penultimate, the provisional, and the finite is not of a *purely* allegorical significance. True, faith is enough, and in his life of poverty and homelessness Jesus is a living witness to the all-sufficient care of the living God. But he enjoys particular gifts like food and wine, unlike the Baptist. He accepts invitations from important people; he even invites himself to Zacchaeus' table; he accepts the care of pious women of distinction.[47] All these particular good gifts are set in the perspective of the good Father. This is not only true for Jesus, but also for those who offer their gifts to them, for gifts given to a poor man do more for the giver than for the receiver: they free him from the worry which is the price of self-affirmation, and thus open him up to unconditional abandon.

Jesus not only receives particular gifts, he also gives them. He does so as a teacher, a master, an example, a prophet, a healer, a friend. Where his gifts are accepted they evoke, in the receiver, the confession of sin and the turn to faith; there is more to the gifts than meets the eye. Where his gifts are mistaken, by being appropriated as property, as with the nine lepers, Jesus' concern is not his own disappointment, but the want of glory given to God and the people's blindness to the life that lasts, and so he calls on them to go further than they do.[48] When his gifts are rejected he still remains faithful to the encounter that undergirds the offer of the gifts: it becomes clear to the refuser that the gift was tied to an unconditional offer of self. The fact that Jesus was accused of complicity with the prince of devils betrays the far-reaching perspective opened by Jesus' gifts and

---

[45]The expression "Blessed are you" has been called an "eschatological congratulation." It occurs in Mt. 16, 17; 5, 11; Lk 6, 20. 21. 22; cf. also Mt 11, 6; 24, 46; 5, 3–10; 13, 16 par. Lk 10, 23; Lk 11, 28; 12, 37–38; 14, 15.

[46]Cf. Mt 7, 9–11 par. Lk 11, 11–13.

[47]Mk 14, 3–9 parr.; Lk 7, 36ff.; 19, 1–10; 10, 39; 8, 2–3; 23, 49. 55–56; 24, 10.

[48]Cf. Lk 17, 17–18; Jn 6, 26–27.

by the refusal to accept them, just as the deeply puzzled question about the origin of Jesus' wisdom and power betrays the realization of the far-reaching nature of Jesus' teaching and healing, and the depth of their impact on those around him.[49] But there is never any doubt that it is in *this particular man in his particular dealings with these particular people* that the ultimate call from the Father takes shape. Jesus' active stance of total relatedness to the Father is the source, the setting as well as the explanation of his significance of his person and also all his particular relationships.[50] Thus Jesus is the total representative of God, and the reliable witness to him. Thus he is also the witness to, and the representative of, his brothers and sisters in their true and deepest identity: their relationship to the living God. Alas, he is more than human beings bargain for. In the end, faith becomes too much to take for them; they want substantive goods, including even religion, to bolster their self-affirmation; they want the goods, and themselves, and Jesus, without that dizzying reliance on an incalculable Father; such a reliance would result in the breakdown of too many human certainties. Such faith in God is too much to ask. But Jesus, thus reduced to impotence—the end of all *actio!*—still stands before them as the living representative of their true identity-in-relation, and he comes eventually to hang before them as the dying bearer—the end of all *passio!*—of the burden of their estrangement from God.[51]

In Jesus, God himself becomes the witness to man's true identity. If Jesus' life was not his own independent achievement, neither are his suffering and death. In Jesus—"the Christ of the Father compassionate"[52]—the Father loses his only Son, whose likeness

---

[49]Cf. Mk 3, 22–30 parr.; 6, 2–3 parr.

[50]This is a reformulation of what the patristic tradition referred to as the priority of the penetration of the divine nature into the human nature (i.e., the deification of the human nature) in the otherwise mutual *perichōrēsis* of the two natures in the one *hypostasis*. Cf. H. A. Wolfson, *The Philosophy of the Church Fathers*, Cambridge, Mass., Harvard University Press, ²1964, pp. 418–428, esp. 423–424.

[51]It will be realized that this discussion of Jesus as the representative must be read against the background of our previous discussion of being related, above, esp. pp. 410–412, 414–416.

[52]Gerard Manley Hopkins, "The Wreck of the Deutschland," st. 33, in: *Poems*, W. H. Gardner, N. H. MacKenzie (eds.), London–Oxford–New York, Oxford University Press, ⁴1970, p. 62.

with sinful flesh is now complete, at the very hands of those whose hardness he yearns to soften. The Father will vindicate Jesus because of his total abandon down to the final test—a test that failed to drive him into complicity with his sinful brothers and sisters. But in vindicating Jesus, the Father does not raise him against or at the expense of any of his brothers and sisters; had Jesus not been faithful to them beyond all limits?[53] In Jesus, therefore, the Father draws the sinful flesh to himself and transforms it, in his compassion, into the body of glory—an invitation to all who believe to "christen *their* wild-worst Best"[54] also.

Jesus' relationship with God as actual and gracious

In previous passages dealing with encounter and relationships we have pointed to the gracious nature of every actual encounter. Every encounter-relationship is greater than what we can make of it. It is of the perfection of the person to exist as an invitation to gracious encounter. True identity, the result of relationship, is not a property but a gift from God.[55]

Hence, if we define the mystery of Jesus in terms of his being-related to the Father, we must also say that his divinity is a matter of actuality and grace. This will create an obvious problem, since the tradition has always spoken about the mystery of Jesus in terms of the eternally subsistent *Logos*, and reserved actual grace for the Christians; we will come back to this problem in the course of this section. For the time being, let us follow our insights and discuss Jesus' relationship to God in terms of actuality and graciousness.

Jesus' relationship to God is not an exemplification or an elaboration of a known principle or the actualization of a definable essence. Whatever Jesus' consubstantiality with the Father may

---

[53]The Fourth Gospel, with its strong stress on the relationship between the Father and Jesus, speaks of the resulting relationship between Jesus and humanity and the world in terms of omniscience (2, 24; 16, 30), comprehensive stewardship on behalf of the Father (3, 35; 6, 37. 39; 10, 29 [reading *meizon*, neuter]; 13, 3), universal judgment (5, 22), power (17, 2).

[54]Gerard Manley Hopkins, "The Wreck of the Deutschland," st. 24, in: *Poems*, p. 59.

[55]Cf. above, pp. 241, 245–246, 409.

mean, we may not reduce it to something substantial and permanent; that would deprive it of its striking originality.[56] Jesus' relationship to God is not simply a matter of his being particularly religious by the norms of the culture he was part of; while he may have appeared as the fulfillment of Israel's faith to some, he certainly was also looked upon as a blasphemer. Even Jesus' prophecy, healing, and authoritative teaching—things well known to Jews from Israel's history—struck those around Jesus as so original as to provoke, in some, astonished questions about the origin of his *exousia*; for others, they amounted to madness, for yet others to blasphemy.[57] No shared religious attitudes, assumptions, or ideas account for the quality of Jesus' faith, for Jesus' faith actualizes the common religion beyond its established, quasi-absolute limits.

But if Jesus' religious attitude is unprecedented, he does not account for it by alleging a *new* conception of God or a new, authoritative religious principle. Jesus does indeed criticize established religion, but his critique does not appeal to a new authority or tribunal; Jesus does not even appeal to himself or his own religious experience to legitimize his faith. Jesus appeals only to God—the God in whom all those around him believe, and yet the God whom they hardly credit with being the living God. Jesus, *in* his personal witness to the living God, becomes the guarantor of the actuality of God beyond any known precedent or principle.[58] And God's actuality is that he is "dear Father."[59]

Such a self-presentation, in the encounter with others, in the Name of the living God is essentially gratuitous, and Jesus implies as much when he reminds his hearers of their privilege: they see with their own eyes and hear with their own ears what the kings and the prophets—Israel's model authorities when it comes to faith—did not live to see and hear.[60]

Let us sum this up. The mystery of Jesus is not a principle, an essence, an inner core, a heightened version of something already

---

[56]Cf. above, p. 356.
[57]Cf. Mk 3, 21–22. For *exousia*, cf. above, p. 124 and note 35.
[58]On witness and personal warrant, cf. above, pp. 228–232.
[59]On "Father," cf. above, p. 352 and note 72.
[60]Cf. Lk 10, 23–24 par. Mt 13, 16–17.

known, or a new idea; it is his own life in the actual presence of the living God. Jesus' irreducibility to his own individual nature, therefore, is not a lazy, static fact, establishable once for all and to be conceptualized as a *hypostasis* (except, as we will argue later, on very stringent conditions).[61] No, it consists in a living relationship of actual encounter—a process of encounter with the Father in the Holy Spirit, which situates Jesus' relational identity, and hence all his concrete relationships as well.

Hans Küng has rightly pointed to the concrete, factual, and hence gratuitous nature of the universalism involved in Jesus' mission,[62] in spite of the consciously-accepted limitations of his ministry, just as we have characterized Jesus' encounters as gracious. Now we must equally stress the *source* of this, namely, the concrete, factual, and hence gratuitous nature of his relationship with God. No arguments for faith in God; the living God is the argument for faith, and hence, for Jesus, the comprehensive motive for his own active availability to all. In virtue of God's actuality for him he is Man for Others in actuality. Now this living availability for encounter, quite apart from its success or failure, is the constitutive element of Jesus' being the witness to, and the representative of, people's true, relational identity. As a matter of historical fact, Jesus did, at first, enjoy successful interaction with those around him; at that point, however, the depth of encounter, the attitude of total openness behind his ministry of teaching, healing, and prophecy, is as yet not laid bare in its stark reality. Not until Jesus has willingly accepted the burden of human self-disfigurement does the actuality of Jesus' surrender to the Father and his relatedness to all his brothers and sisters begin to show its true nature; in his death, he is totally Man for God on behalf of all, and the bearer of humanity's whole burden of estrangement from God.[63]

We have already pointed to the gracious nature of Jesus' relationships to others. We can now expand this somewhat. In Jesus' encounter with others, he offers himself to them, and with himself the actual presence of God his Father. This means that the others are

---

[61]Below, pp. 458–463.
[62]*On Being a Christian*, pp. 258–260.
[63]Cf. again above, pp. 414–415.

offered a new, gracious relational identity in relation to God the Father.

But now we must be consistent. We have argued that, if Jesus becomes the representative of the actuality of God to others, his own relationship to God must be characterized by actuality. Analogously, if Jesus extends himself to others, not on account of the demands of a norm, but entirely graciously,[64] then we must characterize his motivating relationship to God as totally gracious. Jesus' irreducibility to his own person consists in the living God's totally gracious presence "in the Holy Spirit" to Jesus, and in Jesus' unconditional and gracious responsiveness to God, "in the Holy Spirit."

Let us sum up what we have said so far in this section. The human person Jesus Christ is decisively determined by his total surrender to his Father. This surrender is not limited to an identifiable core of his person; rather, it is a mode of being related to God as his Father, which includes his entire person. It accounts not only for the actual, effective relationships which he engages in, but also, and far more profoundly, for the active stance of relatedness with which Jesus presents himself to all. This *modus* of being-related to the Father, moreover, is actual and gracious. It is not identifiable as the supreme actuation of an independently recognizable human potential.

Jesus' relationship to his Father is the source of his identity—an identity totally irreducible to the concrete individual Jesus as he can be named and categorized. It is, moreover, an identity in the truest possible sense, for it is entirely relational and an unconditional gift; it accounts for Jesus' unconditional self-giving to others. For no matter how much Jesus' being-related to his Father is irreducible to his concrete individuality, it does account for the extraordinary presentiality of that same human individual to others. Thus Jesus is the person who lives in a free relationship to God which makes him totally irreducible to his own person,[65] and in virtue of which he addresses others with a relational identity which is his own because it is the Father's.[66]

---

[64]Cf. above, pp. 372–375.

[65]In the terminology of Chalcedon: "unconfused, unchanged."

[66]In the same terminology: "without division, without separation."

Attitudinal union with the Father

We must elaborate this, though with the care and reverence the subject matter demands and with the caution counseled by the tradition. We have argued that the union of all humanity in the person of Christ is a gracious union, a union *kat'eudokian*, an actualization of humanity beyond all definition, according to God's gracious will. We have also argued that this gracious assumption of all humanity in virtue of Jesus' total availability for gracious encounter can only be rooted in Jesus' relationship to the Father understood as a relationship of total graciousness. The divinity of Jesus, expressed by the first *homoousion*, is not a pre-conceived program run off in his human life, but an absolute relationship to the Father; how could that relationship be anything but supremely gratuitous and free? To say otherwise would make Jesus an impassive slave of his Father in a divine nature that is in reality a prison. This would be even more blasphemous than to think of his life as the running-off of a pre-set divine program with no real regard for those among whom Jesus moved. Hence, we must affirm Jesus' total relatedness to his Father as a relationship of total grace; it is in a totally free surrender to a totally gratuitous call that Jesus lives his human life out of, with and toward the living God.

We make these affirmations, not only because they are consistent with our own treatment of the christological question, but also to do justice to the concerns behind two expressions which the tradition has always viewed with suspicion. The expressions are *henōsis kat'eudokian* (union by good pleasure) and *henōsis schetikē* (attitudinal or moral union), used to express the relationship between the concrete human individual Jesus Christ and the *hypostasis* of the *Logos*. The expressions are Antiochene, and reflect the Antioch school's traditional efforts to do justice to the humanity of Jesus; they were denounced as heretical by the school of Alexandria, whose emphasis on the single divine personalness of Jesus Christ made the expression *henōsis kath'hypostasian* normative: in Jesus Christ, the human and the divine natures are hypostatically united in the one person of the *Logos*. Hence, the human nature in Christ must be viewed as anhypostatic and as enhypostatic in the *Logos*.

The christology of the school of Alexandria is characterized by the *Logos-sarx* (World-flesh) pattern; Antioch tended to work with a *Logos-anthrōpos* (Word-man) scheme, in order to emphasize the true humanity of Jesus. This emphasis, so prominent in the school of Antioch, and especially in its greatest thinker Theodore of Mopsuestia, appeared to be laid to rest for good after Theodore's unjustified condemnation at the Second Council of Constantinople in 553 A.D.[67] Still, the idea surfaced again in the Franciscan school and in the modalism proposed by Durandus de Sancto Porciano in the high Middle Ages, in Francis Suarez' christological constructs in the late sixteenth century, and in the *Assumptus-Homo* christology of Déodat de Basly about fifty years ago.[68] All these christologies have this in common with our proposal, that they mean to do justice to the relative autonomy of Jesus' humanity, either by taking Jesus' attitudinal fidelity to God throughout his life seriously, or by emphasizing his true, concrete humanity.

However, there is also a difference between these christologies and our present proposal. In all the christologies just mentioned, the union (conceived as a *modus realis essendi* or as a *relatio substantialis*) is *between Jesus' concrete humanity and the Logos*; we propose to consider the *Logos* as that *modus* of Jesus' concrete humanity in virtue of which he is irreducible to his own nature, and totally related to the Father in the Holy Spirit. In other words, we identify the *modus essendi* of the man Jesus as the *Logos*; the *Logos* is Jesus' being-related to the Father.[69]

There is a reason why the medieval and Renaissance modalists set up their christologies with the *Logos* and the humanity as the terms of the union. The Nicaean affirmation of the *Logos* as *homoousios* and as a proper subject for predication, and the later

[67]DS 425. On Theodore, cf. Aloys Grillmeier, *Christ in Christian Tradition*, ²1975, pp. 421–439, and the literature mentioned there.

[68]Cf. Philipp Kaiser, *Die gott-menschliche Einigung*, pp. 11–39, 80–93, 94–156, 224–232.

[69]In this regard we are aligning ourselves with such different modern approaches as those undertaken by W. Pannenberg (*Jesus—God and Man*, esp. pp. 115ff., 158ff., 283ff.), E. Schillebeeckx (*Jezus*, pp. 210ff., 531ff.), and W.Kasper (*Jesus the Christ*, pp. 163ff.). All these approaches have this in common: that they insist on predicating the first *homoousion* about Jesus on the basis of *his relationship with the Father*, whether this relationship is characterized as "revelation," "personal communion," "eschatological-prophetic mission," or however else.

conciliar decisions to cast christology in terms of two natures hypo-statically united in the one *hypostasis* of the Word made it impossible to think of the *Logos* as anything but substantial. In the last section of this chapter we will investigate the conditions on which such hypostatizing of the *Logos* can be done. For the time being, however, we must further explore the consequences of our proposal.

Unequivocal affirmation of Jesus' real humanity

If we define the *Logos* as the human person Jesus' total irreduc-ibility to his own concrete individual nature, what is unequivocally implied is that Jesus is a concrete, individual human person about whom concrete statements can be made, and, above all, about whom a true narrative makes sense. With this, we are aligning ourselves with a concern which animates most modern christologies: the affir-mation of the true humanity of Jesus Christ. Modern christology has more and more come to understand that the truth of any doctrinal christological deliverances is dependent on the realism with which the historical Jesus can be said to have had a true life story—quite apart from the question of the degree of historical accuracy with which this story can be told.

Let us mention some examples. Studies like E. Schweizer's *Jesus* or H. Küng's *On Being a Christian* speak about Jesus in terms of a true life story with a true impact on the world; in that context, however, they have insisted that even the historical Jesus somehow eluded all categorizations. For all the realism of the narrative about Jesus, we must present the secret of his life in negative terms: he "fits no formula"; he is neither priest nor theologian, nor is he hand in glove with the rulers; he is neither a social revolutionary nor a religious elitist.[70]

Treatments like these are truly notable when compared to christologies of the hypostatic-union variety; they dare to concretize Jesus' relationship to the world he lives in and to present him as a human person with a remarkable mission from God working itself out in terms of a truly individual destiny. Still, authors like Schweizer and Küng rely heavily on the post-Resurrection, Christian interpretations of Jesus' life and person while telling the story of

---

[70]Cf. *Jesus*, pp. 13ff.; *On Being a Christian*, pp. 178ff., 187ff., 195ff., 206ff.

Jesus' life; it is in the light of the Lordship of Jesus that the mystery of his life becomes more apparent: he "fits no formula." This reliance on post-Resurrection interpretation, whether explicit or implicit, is thoroughly legitimate; the Gospels themselves do that very thing.

Schillebeeckx's recent proposal for a christology of the human Jesus is far bolder. He proposes to treat Jesus' identity in terms of the *contemporary* identification of the *historical* Jesus as the eschatological prophet. Schillebeeckx's treatment has raised considerable doubts about the significance he attributes to the Resurrection; a case can be made that his stance on that score is ambiguous. However, there is no doubt about the legitimacy of his efforts to give a *theological* account of the historical Jesus apart from the Resurrection, and he makes a convincing case for the thesis that the impact of the *historical* Jesus activated in his contemporaries the metaphors connected with eschatological expectation, concretized in the anticipated appearance of "the prophet." Also, there is much to be said for the thesis that this pre-Resurrection identification of Jesus as the eschatological prophet represents the link between the uninterpreted facts of Jesus' life and the various types of embryonic post-Resurrection christological creeds that the early communities developed.[71]

To appreciate Schillebeeckx's proposal, it is necessary to forget for a moment the fact that the title "prophet" became the password of the adoptionist heresy in the third century; the centrality of this primary identification of Jesus demands attention. Christology must recover its ability frankly to speak of Jesus as a human person living in a singular relationship with God, a relationship that accounts for his unique moral identity in his encounter with others. Thus, Schillebeeckx's proposal for a christology of Jesus the eschatological prophet can be alleged as a support for our proposal for a christology which views the *Logos* as the human Jesus' *modus* of being absolutely related to the Father. This can be argued as follows.

A prophet is a human person with a human identity and a human destiny of his own, but he is shaped by the divine call in such a way that he almost does not recognize himself, so amazed is he at the way the living God's call affects him. When he starts to speak, therefore, the prophet will address his audience with a new respon-

---

[71]*Jezus*, pp. 329–358.

sive identity, namely, his identity as shaped by his encounter with the living God.[72]

It is important to note the word "identity" in the previous sentence; the prophet's relationship to God has true *ontological* status. The prophet's mission is based on personal encounter with God, resulting in a new mode of being-related, a new moral identity with which he encounters others, thus causing for them a crisis-situation on account of the demand-characteristics of his personal witness to the divine will. In this way, the divine inspiration enhances the identity of the prophet; it does not destroy or replace it. The prophet's personal responsibility, too, is enhanced in that he receives the vocation to become, for others, the personal guarantor of the actuality of the living God.[73]

Now to call Jesus the ultimate prophet—and the Letter to the Hebrews, with its high christology conveyed by the titles "Son" and "Word," certainly also places Jesus in the perspective of the prophetic tradition, as its fulfillment[74]—amounts to saying that in Jesus

---

[72]Cf. the vocations of Moses (Ex 3, 1ff.), Samuel (1 Sam 3, 2ff.), Amos (Amos 3, 8; 7, 14f.), Isaiah (Is 6), Jeremiah (Jer 1; 20, 7ff.: seduction!), Ezekiel (Ez 3, 14; God's heavy hand). The prophet often expresses his message in his behavior (cf. Jer 28, 10; 51, 63ff.; Zech 11, 15ff.; Ez 3, 24—5, 4; Hos 1—3), for the message does not leave the messenger alone; it is not an idea that he teaches, but a new responsive identity he lives out.

[73]If the nature of the prophetic office is not viewed as an ontological relationship to the living God resulting in a new moral identity with which the prophet encounters others, but as a form of *theopneustia* (divine inspiration), it becomes impossible to retain the title "prophet" in orthodox christology. In *theopneustia*, the prophet's mind (*nous*)—and, with it, his own responsibility and moral identity—are *replaced* by an *indwelling* divine agency, which causes the *exodos* of the human spirit, and thus can be said to "possess" the person (*katokōchē*). This is a Hellenistic reconceptualization of prophecy, undertaken to legitimize the Scriptures before the tribunal of neo-Platonism; cf. Sidney G. Sowers, *The Hermeneutics of Philo and Hebrews*, Richmond, Virginia, John Knox Press, 1965, pp. 34–40. Whenever this Hellenistic construct is applied to Christ, the result is heresy. If the *Logos* is made to inhabit the man Jesus, we get, either a Nestorian duplicity of *hypostaseis* (although one of them is reduced to a purely passive instrumentality), or an Apollinarian half-humanity without *nous*, or an adoptionist take-over of the man Jesus by means of a permanent replacement of his *nous* by the *Logos*. But *theopneustia* is not the only way, nor even the best, to think about prophecy!

[74]Heb 1, 1 is the introductory formula for the entire first part of the letter, 1, 1—4, 13. Cf., for example, Heb 3, 5–6, where Moses, that prophet's prophet, is pictured as the faithful witness in his capacity as the live-in (*en oikōi*) family *servant*, whereas Jesus is faithful in his position *over* (*epi*) the family, as a *son*.

we have a human person who meets the world with the gracious relational identity that comes from God, and that therefore Jesus, *in his humanity*, must be said to be totally irreducible *to* his humanity. This irreducibility is the result of his being-related to the living God.

The consequence of this move is clear: it enables us to speak of the historical Jesus unequivocally as a human person, and as a real participant in the ordinary concerns of human life. Our words about him are about "this man Jesus," even though *what makes us speak about him the way we do* has everything to do with his style, with the *modus* of his being himself. For what makes us speak about "this man Jesus" the way we do is not "this man Jesus" falsely abstracted from his being-related to those around him and, even more radically, to God, but precisely "this man Jesus" *in his relational identity*, in virtue of which he confronts others with the call to free surrender, thus challenging them to find their true relational identity with respect to God and each other. Hence, the critical element in Jesus is not his individual person, but the relational stance that accounts for his prophetical identity.

In virtue of his relatedness Jesus mediates both the call of the living God to humanity to live in wisdom and obedience, and humanity's surrender to the care of the living God in its own pursuit of God's good pleasure. That is to say, Jesus is the actualization of *Logos* to the point of total identification: in Jesus, God's word is accomplishing God's purpose and returning to God bearing full fruit.[75] No wonder that, in a daring overstatement, the Christian *parrhēsia* could come to reverse the terms. The non-hypostatic *modus* of being-related, being the critical element in Jesus, gets hypostatized; the hypostatic individual person gets adjectivized. Jesus is no longer the man who lived with God, but the divine *Logos* who became man. But that is a story for the next sections of this chapter. First, we must further explore how the affirmation of Jesus' fully human individuality entails the affirmation of the *Logos* in terms of total receptivity.

Logos as total receptivity; grace as divine nature

We have already said that Jesus' total surrender to God as his Father involves him in a relational stance; in virtue of this stance

[75]Cf. Is 55, 11.

Jesus is, *in* his individual humanity, completely irreducible *to* his individual humanity. This relational stance, moreover, is characterized by inclusiveness, actuality, and graciousness. This means that the relationship, which suffuses and determines the person of Jesus in every respect and leaves no corner or level or moment of his existence untouched, is also the relationship that is beyond any accepted human potential. Jesus encounters the world with a relational identity that completely exceeds the powers of his own nature. This means, as we have argued, not only that the union of all of humanity in the person of Jesus is gracious and gratuitous, but also that the enabling relationship with God, in virtue of which Jesus actualizes God's good pleasure for the world, is totally gracious and gratuitous. It is in his total response to God's free graciousness that Jesus is the beloved Son, in whom God is well pleased. That means that we must affirm that the man Jesus could—and would!—bow down in holy awe before the mystery of God,[76] whose living presence cannot be demanded, but only waited for; a God whose very being withdraws itself from all efforts to make him amenable to worldly categories; whose presence is what counts, not his nature.[77] And thus we must also say that this mortal man's total reliance on, and receptivity to, a living God who is irreducible to any establishable nature completely determines the "I" with which he addresses himself to the world. In Jesus, we meet the living God because we meet a human person totally determined by the ineffable intimacy with which God communicates himself to him beyond any establishable measure, and with which he casts himself upon this God without reservation—and all this in the Holy Spirit, the "We" in which Jesus and the Father give themselves to each other as "I" and "Thou."

Jesus' being-receptive, his irreducibility to his own individual nature is unowed to—and thus of a different order from—his person, while yet informing his person completely. Jesus' relational identity—though in itself not of a substantial nature, but an utterly

---

[76]For an impressive explanation of the reasons why this affirmation is demanded by Chalcedonian orthodoxy, cf. Karl Rahner, "The Position of Christology Between Exegesis and Dogmatics," pp. 198–199.

[77]God's irreducibility to any conception or idea is, of course, part and parcel of Israel's tradition. Cf., for example, Henry Renckens, *The Religion of Israel*, New York, Sheed and Ward, 1966, pp. 97ff., esp. 128–139. Also G. von Rad, *Old Testament Theology*, Vol. I, Harper & Row, New York–Evanston, 1962, pp. 179–187.

gracious *modus*—totally determines his human individuality. In Jesus, the supposedly self-reliant solidity of human individuality finds itself utterly confirmed and established and upheld by a seemingly unsubstantial relatedness in total trust and surrender to God. This man Jesus comes into his own on the strength of his surrender to God, whom no one has ever seen.[78]

In this active and totally gracious receptivity toward the Father Jesus is himself as the *Logos*: God's living address to humanity. This constitutes the inner quality of what the tradition, in a bold gesture of hypostatization, has called: divine nature.

We will try, in the fourth and last section of this chapter, to give a critical, yet positive account of this move; for the time being, let us restate the results of our efforts so far. Whatever "divine nature" will prove to contribute to our reverent understanding of Jesus' mystery, it is imperative for us to remember that *Logos* means: *this man Jesus, in* his grace-filled stance of total and actual surrender-in-receptivity to God as his dear Father. This also means that whatever "divine nature" will prove to mean, it will have to mean that God is actively gracious and freely self-giving.[79] The revelation of this is Jesus, a human person so completely responsive to, and so freely dependent on, the Father, that in this person, *precisely in virtue of his relatedness*, the *Logos* becomes concrete and hypostatic,[80] and the living God becomes present to the world as the compassionate Father.

---

[78]Augustine and Leo the Great expressed the reality we are trying to express here by saying that the humanity of Christ has no independent existence apart from its being assumed into the person of the *Logos*, so that it must be said to be created in the act of being assumed: *ipsa assumptione creatur.* Cf. Felix Malmberg, *Ein Leib—ein Geist*, pp. 315–333; *id., Ueber den Gottmenschen*, pp. 27–70.

[79]Cf. Schillebeeckx' observation: "That absolute generosity which the Trinity simply *is* remains the universally dominant background of the mystery of saving worship in Christ":*Christ the Sacrament of the Encounter with God*, New York, Sheed and Ward, 1963, p. 39.

[80]Cf. *S. Th.*, III, q. 2, a. 10: "In quo [Christo] humana natura assumpta est ad hoc quod sit persona Filii Dei"—"In whom [Christ] human nature was assumed in order that it might be the person of the Son of God." For the reading *persona* (instead of *personae* in the *Leonina*), cf. E. Schillebeeckx, *ibid.*, p. 14, note 10.

JESUS' UNIVERSAL SIGNIFICANCE

Retrospect and introduction

In the previous chapter we stated that the confession of Jesus' consubstantiality with the Father—the first *homoousion*—has tended to isolate him from the rest of humanity. We also argued that it is necessary to explore what we called the "inner quality" of the reality designated by the concept of consubstantiality.[81] In the section just completed of this chapter we have proposed a christological construct aimed both at conveying this inner quality—the *Logos* as the man Jesus' being-related to the Father—and at showing that, far from separating Jesus from humanity, it unites him with it. At the same time, we have emphasized Jesus' human individuality far more strongly than the tradition of classical christology has ever been capable of doing. We did so by analyzing Jesus' life story as well as his relationship with the Father in terms of relationships rather than natures.

Unity with humanity and pronounced individuality: this raises again an issue raised already in the course of our eighth chapter, when we put in relief the particularity of Jesus and the universality of the claims made by Christians in his behalf.[82] It also brings back to mind our discussions, in the fourth chapter, about the rhetoric of inclusion and the point of the use of the concept of "human nature" in christology.[83] The time has come to bring these and other elements together in one coherent picture, and thus to bring our discussion of the particular Jesus' universal significance to a conclusion.

We will do so by first briefly summarizing the tradition and by stating (or restating) its strengths and weaknesses. After that we will investigate in what way the individual Jesus with his individual characteristics is of universal significance, and what consequences this has for the Christian interpretation of all things particular. We will then ponder the ways in which the notions of human nature and divine immanence are affected by Jesus' relationship to the Father and by his universal significance. The next point of discussion will be

---

[81]Above, pp. 380–381.
[82]Above, pp. 309–311.
[83]Above, pp. 154–159.

the manner in which the *Logos* is the condition for a realistic understanding of the life of Jesus. Finally, we will go back to the question raised at the end of the sixth chapter, and state how critical and reflective christologies are reconciled in the *actus directus* of faith prompted by the risen One. Having thus treated, in the second and third sections of this chapter, the divinity of Jesus and his humanity, we will be in a position, in the fourth section, to draw our conclusions regarding the furthest-reaching perspective opened by Jesus Christ, namely, the relationship between the *Logos* and the world.

The fullness of humanity again

We have already explained that the attribution of the fullness of humanity to Christ is evoked by the Resurrection, and that its point is relational.[84] We have also heard Dietrich Bonhoeffer emphasize the importance of this doctrine for the essential Christian affirmation of Jesus' universal significance.[85] The great tradition's strength lay precisely in the fusion of christological and soteriological motifs; the *Logos'* assumption of human nature as such was affirmed with the salvation of all of humanity in mind: "What is not assumed is not healed, but what is united with God is also saved."[86] The term "human nature" was thus originally intended to create room, in the concrete, individual person Jesus Christ, for the entire process of assumption and union with God held out to humanity and indeed to the world, down to the end of the ages.[87]

When this connection between Christ and humanity is lost sight of—and this has regrettably happened in the tradition[88]—the affirmation of Jesus' full humanity is taken to refer purely to the individual Jesus Christ. This leads to two possible sets of conclusions. Either the attribution, to Jesus Christ, of "human nature" is taken for a tautology or even a truism, to affirm the obvious fact that Jesus is human; in this case the agenda behind the attribution is usually the denial of any universal significance of Jesus beyond his being a

---

[84] *Ibid.*
[85] Above, p. 398.
[86] Gregory Nazianzen, *Ep.* 101, *Ad Cledonium.*
[87] Cf. Felix Malmberg, *Ein Leib—ein Geist*, pp. 269–273.
[88] Cf. above, p. 158, and esp. note 45.

teacher, an example, or a prophet of historic significance. Or the attribution of human nature as such, "without the individual characteristics," tends to purchase Jesus' universal significance at the expense of the concreteness and individuality of his humanity—that is, at the expense of his concrete relationships with others—in other words, at the expense of the realism of the Gospel *story*.[89] This second possibility, which we have discussed a number of times already, leads to two undesirable consequences. First, it makes Jesus' humanity anhypostatic, with all the unfortunate associations that this impersonalness carries; there is no need to develop this point again. Second, the attribution of an anhypostatic human nature to a Jesus whose personalness resides entirely in the divine person of the *Logos* tends to lead to a purely *instrumental* interpretation of Jesus' humanity, as the *organon* of his divine person. This interpretation, it must be granted, has excellent credentials in the patristic and scholastic tradition. If, however, the metaphor is pushed too far—and if it is perceived as derived from mechanics rather than music!—salvation tends to be viewed as the "work" of salvation, as the producing, by means of an instrumental humanity, of salvific *effects*, by a divine person whose identity remains outside the network of saving relationships. Further down the line, grace comes to be considered as an accidental effect of this divine person (and, through him, of the Trinity) on humanity and the world as a whole. But in this construct, humanity and the world are not really assumed and drawn into the divine life through the mediation of the man Jesus Christ; rather, they are extrinsically repaired and restored by a God who remains personally outside the ongoing process of salvation.[90]

---

[89]Cf., for example, above, pp. 52–53, 375–379, 399, 404–405.

[90]In the context of the issues raised in this paragraph it is interesting to recall that particular variety of monophysitism associated with Julian of Halicarnassus, who taught that Christ's humanity was discarded after the completion of the work of redemption, when the tool became expendable.—For instances of the use of *organon* in christology, cf. G. W. H. Lampe, *A Patristic Greek Lexicon*, Oxford, Clarendon Press, 1961, *s.v. organon*, 6; notice the not infrequent use of *organon* in musical, not mechanical, metaphors.—Karl Rahner has rightly insisted that grace must be understood in terms of formal, not efficient, causality; God's saving activity must be viewed, not as the production of effects, but as the assumption of the world into the divine life. Cf. "Some Implications of the Scholastic Concept of Uncreated Grace," in: *Theological Investigations*, Vol. I, Baltimore, Helicon Press, 1961, pp. 297–346, esp. p. 326; cf.

We must draw an important conclusion from this. Although the affirmation of Christ's full humanity—the second *homoousion*—is a powerful statement of his universal significance, it gives us no access to the way in which the *particular individual man Jesus of Nazareth concretely lived out* this universal significance. To gain insight into this, we must raise the question of the inner quality of Jesus' consubstantiality with us in human nature. Just as we argued that the inner quality of the first *homoousion* must be explored, so we argued that Jesus' consubstantiality with us must be concretized in terms of free self-giving in a total, gratuitous, and sympathetic identification, on Jesus' part, with the concrete human condition.[91] Let us elaborate this somewhat.

Particularity as a window on the transcendent

In the course of the second chapter we observed that the experience of transcendence is not only available to us in our acts of cognitive transcendence, but also in the experience of encounter with the other as such.[92] Scholastic philosophy expresses this in a rather more formal way by saying that in finite beings essence and existence are not identical. According to its essence, each finite being may or may not exist: *potest esse et non esse.* This means that each concrete finite being, in virtue of its very existence, raises the most far-reaching question, namely the question of the source of its existence; this is because its actual existence is not adequately accounted for by an appeal to the universal concept that denotes its essence. Hence, when I meet the other—whether thing, plant, animal, or person—I experience an actuality out there that demands that justice be done to it beyond the grasp of my cognitive construct.[93] Its very presence, its actuality, its sheer givenness refers me to the God on whom it continuously depends and in whose being it participates; thus it invites me to let my own identity be renewed in the encounter. In

---

also Felix Malmberg, *Ueber den Gottmenschen*, pp. 69–70.—Aquinas (*S. Th.*, III, q. 62, a. 5, *in corp.*) sees Christ's humanity as the *instrumentum coniunctum*, thus making an extremely close connection between divinity and humanity; still, from the context it appears that Thomas is speaking in terms of efficient causality.

[91]Above, pp. 381–382.
[92]Above, pp. 97–98.
[93]Cf. above, pp. 90–92; cf. also pp. 244–245.

this way every particular being has a universal significance in virtue of its very actuality; in the act of representing God it invites all who encounter it to see it in a universal, all-encompassing perspective.

All this is decisively and qualitatively enhanced in the case of human persons. Every human individual is original in the same sense in which every concrete individual infra-human being is original in virtue of its very actuality; but in addition the human person can be *aware* of his own givenness; in virtue of what the tradition has called the spiritual soul, every human person finds himself placed in the conscious perspective of infinity.[94] A human person is therefore called to realize, and live out of, an absolute dependence on the living God; in virtue of the possibility of that realization, every human person also has a conscious affinity with all that exists, especially human persons, whose presence constitutes an unconditional demand for personal encounter.[95]Thus all human persons have a potentially universal significance, not only in virtue of the actuality of their existence, but also, and especially, because they are called consciously to relate to the God on whom they depend for their existence, to represent him, and thus to relate to whatever exists with an openness without limits. This ability to consciously experience their own givenness and the givenness of others in an absolute perspective also accounts for the yearning for the absolute at the heart of every person.

However, the perspective remains a perspective and eludes every attempt at objectifying it, and the yearning remains a yearning, never to be fulfilled. This causes human persons to balk at the perspective and the yearning. Rather than interpret the givenness of their own existence as a gift, they experience it as a danger and a threat; rather than take the givenness of the others as an invitation for ever renewed openness, they restrict their purview and call this limited purview humanity. Rather than rely on the openness to the infinite as a lifeline, and thence gain the capacity for limitless

---

[94]For a fine reconceptualization of the "spiritual soul" in terms of relationship to God, cf. Piet Smulders, S.J., *The Design of Teilhard de Chardin*, An Essay in Theological Reflection, Westminster, Md., The Newman Press, 1967, pp. 60–77.

[95]Cf. above, p. 409. Cf. also Emmanuel Levinas, "Liberté et commandement."

encounter, they engage in self-maintenance and self-justification, and thus they come to forfeit their own presence to others, their own openness to encounter. And thus they trade in their potential for universal significance for its impossibility: no longer *cor ad cor loquitur*, but *cor curvum in se*.[96]

In Jesus of Nazareth, we have said, we encounter a total, unconditional, and actual reliance on the living God in an attitude of surrender characterized by an unprecedented familiarity. The human person Jesus is all-encompassingly determined by the *modus* of being-related to God; he is absolutely irreducible to his own individual nature.[97] Jesus does not tentatively grope for God as he experiences his givenness; he relates his entire self to the living God with an unprecedented sense of actuality and an affirmativeness that decisively surpasses the tentativeness of human faith in God. His givenness as a human person is in no sense a question to Jesus; he lives in the luminous awareness of his being God's personal gift to himself.

If Jesus' total, actual receptivity in relationship to God makes him a gift to himself, he also presents himself to others as a totally gratuitous gift. He is available for encounter without reservation or restriction, regardless of success, down to death—his final gesture of sympathetic identification, in patience and hospitality, with humanity, beyond the bounds of any definition.[98] This stance of total and unconditional availability for encounter with human persons is the basis, in the historical person Jesus of Nazareth, for the attribution, in the light of the Resurrection, of the fullness of human nature to him.

Let us sum up this discussion before we explore the implications of Jesus' universal significance. It is on a double score that the individual man Jesus of Nazareth, now alive as the risen One, is of universal significance. He is so *proximately*, in virtue of the very fact of his actual existence as a human individual. No individual is ever entirely reducible to a universal nature, and, in addition, human persons, in virtue of their spiritual nature, are gifted with that

---

[96]For these two expressions, cf. above, pp. 243, note 46, and 282, note 44.
[97]Cf. above, pp. 394–395, 423–430.
[98]Cf. above, pp. 164–165, 174–177, 365–369, 429–430.

openness to the absolute which Karl Rahner has rightly identified by means of the traditional concept of *potentia oboedientialis*, in virtue of which a human person also enjoys an openness to all that is.[99]

But the decisive and *ultimate* ground for Jesus' universal significance is the *modus* of being-related in which he lives out his human individuality. The latter is entirely shaped and informed by his actual being-related, in total surrender and receptivity, to God as his Father. Of the man Jesus we can say: *ipsa assumptione creatur*—his creaturely reality is entirely embedded in, and suffused by, his being-related to God.[100] As a human person, Jesus is total gift; by actualizing beyond all human power human nature's native potential for total surrender and receptivity in relationship to God, he also actualizes human nature's native yet unheard-of potential for total self-giving and total openness to others.[101]

The Christian tradition has drawn many conclusions from the experience of Jesus' self-giving in virtue of his total openness to the living God. We must point out some of them. The first, to be touched on briefly, concerns the Christian appreciation of all things particular that make up our world. The second, to be elaborated more fully, concerns the Christian understanding of human nature and of the relationship between God and the world.

Particularity as blessing

The Christian experience of this one particular man, Jesus Christ, as the living God's special gift to humanity has radically affected the way Christians have interpreted the things and persons that surround them and make up the world. Once "God" has become "the Father of our Lord Jesus Christ," it is impossible to be anything less than affirmative about the nature of the world of which Jesus Christ is a part. Christians through the centuries have taken particular things and particular persons as gifts and godsends, have thanked God for them, and have prayed for them with a concreteness that has always been an embarrassment and a source of irrita-

[99]Cf. above, pp. 218–220, and note 95.
[100]Cf. above, pp. 437–438, and note 78.
[101]Cf. Karl Rahner, "On the Theology of the Incarnation," p. 110: "The incarnation of God is therefore the unique, *supreme*, case of the total actualization of human reality, which consists of the fact that man *is* in so far as he gives up himself."

tion to the "pure" deist. God is more than a distant creator, a hidden enabler, or an anonymous providence; things and people are not to be taken for granted; God's graciousness can be found in the actuality of every person and every thing. No matter how much superstition and even magic may, at times, lurk under this religious concern with particularities, the Christian tradition, having once been granted access to the Father through, with and in one particular person, cannot get itself to adopt the view that the world is related to God only in some general fashion, to be explored with the help of philosophical concepts.[102] Nature has been revealed as embedded in grace, and so Christians will insist that we are to seek the kingdom of the living God first, and all the rest will be thrown in for good measure. Given the gift which is Christ, Christians will trust that God will "give them all things with him."[103] The contingency with which people and things meet us is not a matter of chance, but of divine care.[104] Each concrete particular being is indeed beyond the mind's cognitive power: *individuum est ineffabile*;[105] only this is not a sign of the limitations of human understanding, which always fails to capture concrete reality in its cognitive construct; rather, it is a pointer to God's graciousness. Even the humblest and most normal of things bespeak the Father, not just a First Cause.

---

[102]I have argued that something very close to this thesis lies at the basis of Hopkins' "The Wreck of the Deutschland": "Hopkins: Cor Ad Cor," *The Month*, Second New Series 8 (1975) 340–345.

[103]Rom 8, 32.

[104]A responsible case could be made that Aquinas' five ways (despite his insistence that he takes his arguments from Aristotle) are a natural-reason version of the dynamics of christology. The first three *viae* make the case for God's existence on the basis of efficient causality; the *quarta via* alleges formal causality; finally, the fifth way invokes final causality. The rhythm thus becomes: creation, concurrence, and providence. There is a striking parallelism between these three and what we have called inclusion, obedience, and hope. The risen Lord is the eschatological ground for hope, just as he is the model for the life with God in the present, and the Word through which all things were made. Now the persuasiveness and the cogency of an argument are very much dependent on the tacit convictions of the milieu in which it is used. Hence, it is understandable that Thomas' arguments lost their probative force according as the culture's dominant mood became one of reason rather than faith.

[105]"An individual being cannot as such be captured by a definition"—an old scholastic adage.

The depth of human nature discovered in Jesus

We have already stated that, in the person of Jesus, human nature's potential for total surrender and receptivity in relation to God is actualized, and that this openness to God involves an unconditional openness to all of humanity. Jesus, therefore, is the revelation of human nature's dormant possibility to exist as the person of the Word of God.[106]

It is in the light of Jesus that this deepest characteristic of what it means to be human offers itself for meditation and reflection. The definition of human nature in terms of openness to the transcendent and the world (the definition we so confidently used a few pages back) is ultimately set against the background of the Christian confession of Jesus as Lord; it is a discovery matured in patient meditation on the mystery of humanity revealed in him, not an arrogant self-assertion of the human spirit setting itself up as the sovereign standard of humanity's native potential; thus it embodies an insight that leads to knowledge respectful and full of awe, not knowledge domineering and overbearing.

The *Logos*, understood as this man Jesus' *modus* of being absolutely related to God, is the total and absolute and unowed actualization of humanity's deepest potential. Something extremely important follows from this, namely, that we must think of the *Logos* in terms of *affinity* with the depth of human nature, *not in terms of contrariety.* In the man Jesus, we see humanity re-created by total relatedness to God; this re-creation is the gracious fulfillment of what transcendental reflection identifies as humanity's deepest essence; as a result, we must not think of the *Logos* in terms of a reality that fills a vacuum. To put it bluntly, in Jesus the human thirst for God is not allayed, but rendered absolute; there is no fullness in Jesus but the fullness of God; there is no identity in Jesus but his responsive identity vis-à-vis his Father. In Jesus, the "weakness" of the human condition, the yearning for God as human nature's essential foible, is carried through to the end. The human reliance on God is not *replaced* by the *Logos*, but *fulfilled.*

In this way, God's weakness does indeed become stronger than human strength,[107] for the latter, taken by itself, is nothing but the

---

[106]Cf. above, pp. 436–438, and note 80.
[107]Cf. 1 Cor 1, 25.

inauthentic strength that comes from self-maintenance and self-justification —the kind of strength that becomes domination. From the point of view of human potential Jesus is the ultimate fulfillment and revelation of humanity's deepest and *real* strength. He becomes the place where utter and total human receptivity is identical with the deepest human originality and resourcefulness. In Jesus, God from God and Light from Light, the debilitating debate about strength and weakness, about "which of them was to be taken to be the greatest,"[108] is graciously undercut.

Two insights follow from this. The first is connected with the notion of "human nature." The second is related to the question raised at the end of the sixth chapter, namely, how critical and reflective christologies can be constructively reconciled, without recourse to the kind of compromise that would do an injustice to both.

Human nature as a project in freedom—divine immanence

If "this man Jesus" has a truly universal significance, then two important conclusions follow. The first concerns our understanding of human nature; the second deals with our understanding of divine immanence.

We have, in the course of this book, discussed a great number of misunderstandings caused by the concept of "human nature without the individual characteristics" as used in christology; there is no need to repeat them here. There is one, however, which we have not mentioned yet. The proclamation that humanity as such has been saved and healed in the person of Jesus Christ has often led to a serious misinterpretation of objective atonement, namely, the presentation of the "work of salvation" as essentially finished and now only waiting to be "applied." If "human nature" is used in this definitive and totalitarian way, it may be (and has been) used to claim and seize, as if by eminent domain, all of humanity for Christianity, in the name of Christ the all-encompassing Savior. And since concepts, those tools of thought, are often alleged to justify action, there is reason to wonder if the historical practice of discrimination against non-Christians (especially Jews)[109] and their forced or bought conver-

---

[108]Cf. Lk 22, 24.

[109]The plight of the Jews deserves special mention here. Not only have many of them suffered from this totalitarian misinterpretation of the significance of Jesus, but

sions to Christianity have not in some way been connected with this idea. Therefore, however we are to understand the inclusion of all human concerns in the person of Christ, its affirmation may not jeopardize the freedom of humanity's participation in the process of its own inclusion in Christ.

Let us, therefore, go back to "this man Jesus," in his particularity, encountering others. We characterized the basic attitude of presence-in-encounter as an attitude of inclusiveness (a person is called to encounter an *a priori* unlimited number of others), graciousness (encounter comes out of freedom and appeals to freedom), and sympathetic representation (the encounter appeals to the other's true, relational identity).[110] In Jesus, we went on to claim, particular encounters were undergirded by an absolute availability for encounter, which was but the actualization of his absolute irreducibility to his own person, in virtue of his total surrender to the Father.[111]

Thus Jesus' universal significance is based upon the *modus* of his being an individual: Jesus lived in the attitude of unconditional acceptance of himself as God's gift to himself, and thus he lived in an attitude of unconditional self-giving to others. In this way, Jesus uncovers the essence of what it means to be human, namely, openness to God. This openness to God demands that it be lived out in a life of encounter without exclusion, a life of graciousness and of sympathetic representation. Hence, the concept of "human nature" as used in christology does not refer to a definitively known quantity, whether it be established by sovereign human reason as the measure of all things, or by an authoritarian, dogmatic definition allegedly based on Christian revelation. Rather, "human nature" in christology refers to an unfolding and emerging reality—a developing pattern of freely undertaken relationships transcending every barrier

---

also the *terminology* in which Jesus' universal significance was couched was so alien to the mainstream of Jewish thought that even the correct interpretation was virtually inaccessible to them. That Schillebeeckx' *Jezus* is partly intended as a christology accessible to Jews has been well noticed by Robert Schreiter, "Christology in the Jewish-Christian Encounter: An Essay-Review of Edward Schillebeeckx's *Jezus, Het Verhaal van een Levende*," *Journal of the American Academy of Religion* 44 (1976) 693–703. Cf. also Thomas A. Idinopulos and Ray Bowen Ward, "Is Christology Inherently Anti-Semitic? A Critical Review of Rosemary Ruether's *Faith and Fratricide*," *ibid.*, 45 (1977) 193–214.

[110]Above, pp. 410–417.

[111]Above, pp. 419–420, 423–427.

and animated by compassion, based on a fundamental openness to all that is, and leading to the fulfillment where God will be all in all in actuality.[112]

Human nature is not a once-for-all reality, not a prison, but a divine project in responsible freedom. It is not a closed system; it is a resource, not a *fait accompli*; it is from the outset open to the infinite, and consciously and responsibly so. This means that humankind is innately called to ongoing change and self-manipulation—modifications that enter into the very definition of human nature.[113] And all this is based on the recognition of a radical receptivity as the most basic trait of human nature, a trait graciously and superabundantly actualized in Jesus Christ as the *Logos*.[114]

And thus we come to our second point, namely, our understanding of divine immanence. If it is true that "human nature" and "*Logos*," humbly and worshipfully understood as receptivity and total receptivity to God, are the key to the discovery of what it means to be human in this world, then we are also in a position to state the conditions upon which the characterization of God as immanent—a question raised many pages ago[115]—is legitimate. If God is to be discovered in this world, he is to be discovered in everything and everybody, and specifically in the *openness* to God which constitutes the very being of persons and things. Thus God is to be discovered as the God who has reserved for himself, as the

---

[112]Cf. David Jenkins, *The Glory of Man*, pp. 91–92.

[113]The fact that human nature is essentially reformable makes any facile natural-law ethic impossible. For an application of this thesis, cf. Karl Rahner, "The Problem of Genetic Manipulation," in: *Theological Investigations*, Vol. IX, New York, Herder and Herder, 1972, pp. 225–252.

[114]This is the basis for Karl Rahner's notion of anonymous Christianity—a way to express the existential pre-condition for salvation. Hans Küng has blamed Rahner for watering down the Christian confession to a general human orientation, and for unacceptably annexing all non-Christians to Christianity, by means of this notion; cf. *On Being a Christian*, pp. 97–98, 126. It is quite clear that Küng misunderstands Rahner, and that his own theology presupposes the very notion he opposes; see the debate in *Orientierung*: Heinz Robert Schlette, "Rahner, Küng und die anonymen Christen," *Orientierung* 39 (1975) 174–176; Hans Küng, "Anonyme Christen—wozu?" *ibid.*, 39 (1975) 214–216; L. Bruno Puntel, "Hans Küng, die Logik, und die theologische Redlichkeit," *ibid.*, 40 (1976) 3–6. Küng's not-so-hidden agenda is his contention that the Church has de facto *changed* her ancient doctrine: "No salvation outside the Church."

[115]Above, pp. 55–57.

creatures' guest, an inner chamber, a positive emptiness at the heart of them all, in virtue of which all created beings are mellowed, from the inside, so that their natures need not turn into prisons or fortresses. Only a truly transcendent God can be so close to the heart of creatures as to keep them open to his very transcendence and to each other. And as for the road to the discovery of this meekly immanent God, we are to remember that this is only achieved in an attitude that is consonant with the reality to be found. Only the receptive will find God in the creature's receptiveness; only the patient will find God as he bears and goes along with the creature's history; only the hospitable will taste the creature's innermost hospitality to the *dulcis hospes animae*.[116] A lazy and cheap proclamation of God's immanence, aimed at asserting one's intellectual superiority by means of statements of the "God-is-nothing-but-simply-this" variety, misses both the road to the immanent God and his mystery, and thus also the mystery of creation itself.

Logos, human nature, and the life of Jesus[117]

But now another very important insight is available to us. Far from being in the way of lived concreteness, far from being a hindrance to encounter, the *Logos* actually demands them. If rightly understood, the *Logos*, defined as Jesus' absolute being-related to the Father in total receptivity, *requires the living-out of this relationship in a concrete life-story with others. Logos* is not the denial of Jesus' human personalness and of his individual destiny in his dealings with others, but their divine affirmation. The *Logos* is the absolute enhancement, in the root, of Jesus' very nature as a human individual: his openness to God and his orientation to others in encounter. Far from being a hard foreign body, far from displacing, as if by intrusion, the essential openness of human nature in Jesus, the *Logos* is precisely the divine warrant for Jesus' human openness, for his life of service and for his abiding faithfulness to others down to the bitter end.

---

[116]"The sweet guest of the soul"—a phrase from the Pentecost sequence *Veni, Sancte Spiritus*.

[117]For the next few paragraphs, cf. the introductory comments to this chapter, above, pp. 403–406.

Thus the majestic, tradition-hallowed *Logos*—human nature construct in christology does not, in the final analysis, obscure either the total relatedness of Jesus to his Father or the reality of his individuality in his encounter with others. If rightly understood, the *Logos*—human nature construct precisely states the essence of the Gospel, namely, that Jesus Christ is not a lord but the servant. By placing him squarely in a stance of absolute being-related to the Father, attention is concentrated on the receptiveness and the servanthood of Jesus as the shape and the inner quality of his divinity; by predicating "human nature without the individual characteristics" of him, attention is focused on the inner quality of his humanity, namely, the openness with which he enters, without reservation, into relationships with others, thus actualizing beyond every measure the basic orientation of every human life, no matter how encrusted with anxious self-maintenance. If the *Logos*—human nature construct is interpreted as referring to a divine person, impassible and sovereign in his own right, coming into the world and changing it by means of an impersonal, purely instrumental humanity not really capable of an individual life story, what we get is the picture of an omnipotent *deus ex machina*, unrelated to the world he comes to redeem and to the people whose likeness he bears except in the most general way, through a human nature without individual characteristics. Such a construct may look like a powerful conception. In reality it is humanly unattractive, for it does an injustice to the *humanum* by making the life of Jesus theologically irrelevant. But what is even worse is that it presents God in a way that is alien to the Christian tradition, which has always insisted that God's omnipotence is embedded in his compassion.

Critical and reflective christologies reconciled

Now we have finally reached the point at which we can round off a question raised at the end of the sixth chapter, namely, the need for reconciliation between critical and reflective christologies.[118] At that point we already stated that both must be seen in the perspective of the Resurrection: the risen Lord prompts the *actus directus* of faith. Now since the act of faith is a future-oriented experience that

---

[118]Above, pp. 254–262.

finds its expression in the sacrifice of praise and thanksgiving, it is clear that the reconciliation must take the latter for its point of departure.

Now the story of Jesus (which is the warrant for the Church's own history[119]) is the result of eucharistic recollection. It is told in response to the living Lord's gracious presence and remembered in thankfulness.[120] The total fulfillment, in the Holy Spirit, of the risen One illuminates and vindicates the long-suffering way of Jesus; accordingly, the Church's account of the life of Jesus is suffused with a hope and an assurance that is not warranted by the facts as established by historical investigation. The life of Jesus thus becomes a lesson in patience and hospitality, as we will elaborate in the next chapter. Because the narrative account of the life of Jesus comes out of worship and hope, it becomes an account of the life of Jesus in obedience to the Father and as Man for Others; the material for critical christology is a lesson in obedience.

The history of Jesus' obedience to the Father and his self-giving to others moves the Church to patient and hospitable *imitatio Christi*. But in patience and hospitality—that is to say, in receptivity—the Church also acquires the attitude necessary to ponder and contemplate the mystery of the depth of Jesus' life. In his life he comes to be seen as the *Logos* in person—a man existing in total surrender to the Father and thus bringing the openness of human nature to fruition beyond the ken of all known human resources. To call Jesus the *Logos* in person and the New Man becomes an act of contemplation—the fruit of patient living and pondering—of the endless possibilities of human nature endorsed and enlarged beyond all definition by a unique relationship to the living God. Jesus becomes the divine warrant and charge for the Church's inclusion of all human concerns, beyond all known limits.

In the beginning of the eighth chapter we argued that the coherence between the various types of christology must be achieved by establishing the coherence of the performative functions of these various christologies.[121] In the few paragraphs that follow, therefore,

---

[119]Above, pp. 344–347.
[120]Above, pp. 347–349.
[121]Above, pp. 303–307.

the emphasis on the attitudinal components of critical and reflective christologies, far from being incidental to the argument, is essential to it. Critical christology must be set in a context of obedience, and reflective christology in a context of inclusion, if they are to be reconciled in the perspective of the hope warranted by the presence of the risen Lord. We will elaborate this at greater length in the next chapter,[122] but it is already important at this point to put the performative aspects of christology in relief.

The devil of critical christology is its tendency to fasten, myopically, on certain facts of the past, and thus to offer a reductionist version of Christianity. It must be exorcised by hope and thanksgiving, which bring out the true significance of those facts. The devil of reflective christology is its tendency to control the freedom of life by means of the compelling and domineering idea, and thus to offer an ideological and totalitarian version of Christianity. It must be exorcised by patience and hospitality, as two discoveries are made, namely, first, that *Logos* and *humana natura* refer to the conditions for the possibility of a realistic life of Jesus and not to its denial, and, second, that, since Jesus' life is to be characterized as one of encounter, he is "the Christ of the Father compassionate"[123]—God is revealed, in Jesus Christ, as the God who shows his omnipotence most by relenting and being merciful.

Now that we have argued that the *Logos* is not in the way of a realistic understanding of the human life of Jesus, we are in a better position to explore the consequences of Jesus' life for the life of the Church; the next chapter will be devoted to this. Yet before we do so, we must, for the sake of intellectual integrity, recall that the great tradition, from Nicaea onward, has *not* spoken of the *Logos* as we have proposed. We have called the *Logos* the man Jesus' irreducibility to his own concrete individuality, in virtue of his being absolutely related to God. The great tradition has consistently referred to the Logos, not as a *modus essendi*, but as a divine *hypostasis*. We must try to state the conditions for the legitimacy of the tradition's usage in the light of our own discussions.

---

[122]Below, pp. 465–470.

[123]Gerard Manley Hopkins, "The Wreck of the Deutschland," st. 33, in: *Poems*, p. 62.

Toward A Reaffirmation of the Logos

The linguistic case

The first point to be made is that there is no linguistic reason why the *Logos* could not be referred to as *hypostasis* or *persona*. There are two main arguments in favor of this thesis.

First, *hypostasis* and *persona*, when considered as *terms*, are subject to definitions that govern their stable meaning and to habits of discourse that govern their appropriate use. It is true, we have argued that it is *advisable*, both linguistically and theologically, to discontinue the use of the term "person" for the *Logos*, in the interest of the unequivocal affirmation of Jesus' human personalness;[124] but this does not *exclude* the possibility of using the term "person" as the tradition has used it.

There is, however, a second, more basic reason why we can refer to the *Logos* as *hypostasis* and even *persona*. Language itself hypostatizes (and often personifies); words are representative.[125] This is the reason why, in the case of the hypostatization of non-"things," we must be so careful not to let the hypostatizing features of language contaminate our perception of the reality we mean to refer to. This caution is doubly important when we refer, in words, to God. And the highest degree of watchfulness is called for when we refer to God in *terms*, because there we run the additional risk of losing sight of the instrumental properties of terminology; if we do, very undesirable connotations may come in through the back door, undetected on account of the denotative stability of the term.[126] The Greek patristic tradition has always been keenly aware of this; it has always pointed out that no inferences about the nature of the Trinity are warranted on the basis of the meaning of the word *hypostasis*. The Latin tradition could have learned much from this; its use of *persona* would have been far more cautious.

Is hypostasis purely heuristic, or transcendental, or referential?

Once it is agreed that we have a linguistic warrant for the use of

---

[124]Above, pp. 167–181.
[125]Cf. above, pp. 87–88, 66–71.
[126]Cf. above, pp. 79–80, 85–87.

hypostasis or *persona* to refer to the Logos, three possibilities are open.

The first possibility is to look upon *hypostasis* as a purely heuristic device.[127] This yields formulas like the following: "*Hypostasis* refers to that of which there are three in the Trinity and one in Jesus Christ." There is a positive *theological* gain in this option, in that the term *hypostasis* becomes an instance of apophatic language; it denotes a reality without claiming any objectifiable knowledge about it—a thoroughly responsible attitude when God is spoken about. The disadvantages are that the term becomes a purely nominal, instrumental counter which has lost, by definition, all connection with natural language, and that the inner quality of the reality thus nominally referred to remains entirely to be stated and understood. It is hard to imagine that the christological tradition has ever used either *hypostasis* or *persona* in this way. For all its emphasis on the need for the *via negationis*, it has always understood *hypostasis* and *persona* to be more than nominal counters. Some analogy was understood to prevail; this applies both to the affinities between *hypostasis* and *persona* in natural language and their meanings as theological terms, and to the analogies between their meanings with reference to human persons and those with reference to the Trinity.[128]

The second possibility is to look upon *hypostasis* and *persona* as transcendental utterances—in the Kantian sense of the term. In this case, the *Logos* is referred to hypostatically because there is a real experience *on the part of the person(s) referring to the Logos*; this experience compels them to speak very affirmatively, without, however, implying that the nature of the reality they have experienced is hypostatic. We used this interpretation when we argued that affirmative *Logos*-talk is the hypostatization of the *parrhēsia* in worship

---

[127]Cf. Bernard Lonergan, "The Dehellenization of Dogma," p. 25, and "The Origins of Christian Realism," p. 259.

[128]I suggest that a case can be made to look at *hypostasis* and suchlike as classifying numeratives. Unlike numerals, which are purely nominal counters, classifying numeratives have a residual referential meaning, which links them up with natural language. They usually mediate between numerals and nouns. Examples in English are: "ten *head* of cattle," "three *pair* of bellows," "five *dozen* eggs," "a *set* of teeth," "a *brace* of partridges," "a *pride* of lions," etc.

and witness called forth by the risen Lord.[129] This kind of *Logos*-talk
is analogous to expressive utterances, in that they tell the listener
more about the speaker than about the nature of the reality the
speaker has been touched by. The speaker lends it hypostatic status,
so that the question remains whether the hypostatization is merely
due to his sense of reality, or to the structure of the reality that has
touched him.

The third possibility is that there is a reality out there, for which
the term *hypostasis* or *persona* can be realistically used, no matter
how analogically and with how much stretching of meaning. We
have already suggested that the Christians' affirmative stance on
Jesus as the *Logos* is also the hypostatization of *Jesus' own total
surrender* to the Father. What is happening here?

Jesus' being-related to the Father, we argued, is inclusive and
total, actual, and gracious. This means that Jesus' *modus essendi*, his
being-related to the Father, his relational identity, which is the
pinnacle of grace and which reveals the divine nature *as grace*, is the
decisive factor in his person, not his creaturely reality. The *modus* of
being-related embeds and enhances and totally carries Jesus' individual human person. And what is more, this *modus* of being-related is
now, after the Resurrection, the living Lord's abiding response, on
behalf of the whole world, to the Father's eschatological self-com-
mitment to his creation.

At this point the Christian faith engages in a dizzying act of
surrender, reflected in Christian speech. Human personalness used to
be experienced as solid and hypostatic; now it is called "earthen
vessels," an "outer man wasting away," "visible and transient," an
"earthly tent-house."[130] And what seems to every person a risky
enterprise, namely, total relatedness to the living God and unconditional reliance on him, becomes solid and hypostatic: Jesus is called
the *Logos Incarnate*. In so doing, the Christian tradition clinches the
age-old Jewish tradition of awe at God's fidelity to his creation—a
fidelity hypostatized in the figures of pre-existent and eschatological
mediators, in the *Torah*, and in the personification of divine wis-

---

[129]Cf. above, pp. 349–352, 389–391, 394, 402–403.
[130]Cf. 2 Cor 4, 7. 16. 18; 5, 1—all occurring in a letter that has confidence and
freedom of speech for some of its principal themes.

dom.[131] Israel's experience of God had always been an experience of saving graciousness and reliability, and, only in that context, also an experience of creation.[132]

Thus *relational identity becomes more important than human individuality; grace becomes more important than nature; salvation becomes more important than creation.* And the reason for this shift is that absolute relational identity and fullness of grace have proved, in Jesus, to be the permanent and reliable and all-encompassing and sustaining milieu for human individuality and nature—as permanent and reliable as the living God. Thus, finally, the *Logos* becomes the divine pre-condition for created nature: all things were made in the Word, and nothing was made without the Word.[133]

To speak in this way, *starting* from the *Logos* and moving toward Creation and Incarnation, is the distinctively Christian way to convey "Jesus' origin in God's very being, i.e., the origin of his love for all creatures, his unique union with God as well as his true humanity."[134] In this way there is cancelled out every inkling of an understanding of salvation in terms of human self-perfection, or, for that matter, in terms of a mythological intervention of a sovereign but in the final analysis uninvolved God. The Christians' ability to speak in terms of what has, unfortunately, been termed "descent-christology"[135] is the test of their conviction that the God in whom they believe is the God revealed and warranted by the life and death of the risen Lord—the Father of all mercies and the God of all comfort.[136]

The need for rules for a hypostatic understanding of the Logos

To call the *Logos* hypostatic, therefore, is not only a heuristic move or an expression of Christian *parrhēsia;* it is also the

---

[131]Cf. Martin Hengel, *The Son of God*, The Origin of Christology and the History of Jewish-Hellenistic Religion, Philadelphia, Fortress Press, 1976, pp. 48ff., 66ff..

[132]Cf. Henry Renckens, *The Religion of Israel*, p. 20.

[133]Cf. Jn 1, 3.

[134]Martin Hengel, *The Son of God*, p. 93, corrected after the German *Der Sohn Gottes*, Die Entstehung der Christologie und die jüdisch-hellenistische Religionsgeschichte, Tübingen, J. C. B. Mohr (Paul Siebeck), 1975, p. 143.

[135]Cf. *ibid.*, p. 92.

[136]2 Cor 1, 3.

recognition of the primacy of Jesus' being-related over his human individuality, and thus also the recognition of the primacy of grace and of its sustaining reliability.

Now *Logos* and *hypostasis* and *persona* are largely used, in christology, as *terms*, and the rules for the appropriate use of terms tend to be implicit, and thus easily forgotten. In addition the use of *hypostasis* and *persona* for a reality that is relational and gracious involves an enormous enlargement of sense,[137] especially if it is remembered that these terms have strong and lasting roots in Aristotelian *nature*-philosophy. Both realizations must make us cautious. It is necessary to lay down some rules for the correct understanding and the appropriate use of the terminology "the *hypostasis* (or *persona*) of the *Logos*."

We have already pointed out that the *attitude* in speaking about the *Logos* must be one of awe; the tone of voice of autonomous reason is out of place when speaking about the *Logos*. We connected this with the fact that the act of speaking about the *Logos* ultimately derives from the Resurrection; nothing, therefore, may be said of the *Logos* that would qualify the Resurrection.[138]

Now we can take the next step. The story of Jesus, we have argued, told by way of worship and witness, must be realistically understood if it is not to degenerate into myth or moral fable.[139] It follows that nothing may be said about the *Logos* that would rob the narrative of the life of Jesus of its realism and thus of its theological significance. This leads us to our first rule.

The Logos as openness to the world
    The first rule: It is unwarrantable to use *Logos* in such a way as

---

[137]Cf. Donald MacKinnon (" 'Substance' in Christology—A Cross-Bench View," p. 289): "One can only dodge the use of these notions [of substance, *homoousios*, etc.] if one supposes that the doctrine of Christ's person is something that excuses rather than compels full intellectual effort in the attempt to grasp its implications. But if it is a mistake to suppose that the use of these notions can be avoided, it is also a mistake to forget that their employment must include the enlargement of their sense by reason of the totally novel use to which they are bent. [. . .] The notion is now being used in ways to which the habitual routes of its employment offer no exact guidance."

[138]Above, pp. 402–404, 253.

[139]Above, pp. 404–405.

to imply that the divine Son, or the divine Word, is autonomous and set over against created nature.

It is indeed necessary, for the purpose of stability of theological discourse, and in order to maintain the absolute freedom of God's self-communication to his creation, to keep "divine nature" and "human nature" distinct and unconfused. But this does not commit us to the thesis that they are mutually exclusive;[140] if this position is taken, then the conclusion is bound to follow that the *Logos*, in becoming Incarnate, must *displace* something in the human nature of Jesus Christ—which would amount to a warrant for some form of monophysitism. The divinity of the *Logos*—his consubstantiality with the Father—consists precisely in openness and receptivity; the *Logos* is, of himself, *kenōma* receiving the *plērōma* of God. The *Logos* is, in other words, the absolute response to the Father's absolute gift of himself.[141] But this means that the *Logos* Incarnate is the divine "open space," the room made by the Father in creation for the reception of his self-gift, as well as the divine possibility for creation to return, in thankful, responsive surrender, to God. The Incarnation of the *Logos* is not to be viewed as a divine expedient to produce salutary and powerful effects in the wayward world by means of the victory over evil by one of the persons of the omnipotent Trinity. Rather, the Incarnation of the *Logos* means that humanity and the world are called and cared for and coaxed and drawn, disarmed through and with and in the beloved Son, into total surrender to the Father, in the living dynamism of communion which is the Holy Spirit. The answer to the question: "Is Jesus God?" therefore is: "Yes, for us and all the world, with the Father, in the unity of the Holy Spirit." Any other answer runs the risk of making the *Logos* into an intrusive god, omnipotent in his own right, and impassive because incapable of participation in the life of humanity.[142]

---

[140]Cf. the discussion early in this book: above, pp. 51–55.

[141]For the Son as response to the Father, cf. P. Smulders, "Dogmengeschichtliche und lehramtliche Entfaltung der Christologie," pp. 410–411, esp. notes 66 and 75 (on Irenaeus), and p. 420, esp. note 59 (on Origen). For the thesis that consubstantiality can be conceived in terms of willing *coniunctio* (*synapheia*) in knowledge and love, cf. p. 421 (on Origen).

[142]According to Mary Daly, the *Logos is* intrusive, and completely identified with the male Jesus to boot. The question may be asked if her rendition of classical

Hence, however affirmatively and hypostatically we think and speak about the *Logos*, we must think and speak in such a way as to attribute to the *Logos* an attitude of fundamental sympathy with the world. A mystic like John of the Cross saw this with uncommon clarity and expressed it very well in the first of his incomparable *romances* on the creation, where the Father presents the pre-existent Son with creation for his bride.

> A bride, one who will love you,
> my Son, I want to give you;
> for your worth she will merit
> to share our company
> and eat bread at our table,
> the same bread that I eat;
> thus she will know the blessings
> I have in such a Son,
> and with me call herself happy
> with your grace and beauty.[143]

Thus the *Logos* welcomes the creation into his spaciousness; in the encounter with Jesus, the world has found an answer to the frantic question:

> where, where was a, where was a place?[144]

In Jesus the world finds itself at home, in its deepest identity, with God. He is the open place, the *locus communis*, the tabernacle of God among people, the tent of the meeting.

The Logos as the Lamb

The second rule: It may not be implied that the *Logos'* omnipotence has anything to do with impassibility, impassiveness, or over-

---

christology is correct or even fair. Still, I venture to suggest that, had the tradition emphasized the *pathos* of the *Logos* and the *passio* of Jesus a bit more, Mary Daly might have recognized in Jesus an ally, not an enemy of "those who live precariously on the boundary of patriarchal space—the primordial aliens: women." Cf. *Beyond God the Father, passim*, but esp. pp. 69ff..

[143]The third section of the *Romance sobre el Evangelio 'In Principio erat Verbum'*; cf. Gerald Brenan, *St. John of the Cross—His Life and Poetry*, p. 191, or any standard edition.

[144]Gerard Manley Hopkins, "The Wreck of the Deutschland," st. 3, in: *Poems*, p. 52.

powering; sympathy, meekness and gentleness must be recognized as the characteristics of the *Logos.*

Is it fanciful to assume that Nicaea's definition of the first *homoousion* was affected by the fact that this was the Church's first official piece of dogmatic teaching as a politically recognized power in alliance with the emperor? Did status and stoicism perhaps conspire to place the "blame" for suffering on the Incarnation (that is to say, on Christ's humanity), while placing God outside the reach of passion? Might the Nicaean formula owe something to Christian complicity with the human idealization of power, and thus reflect something rather more human than the glory of the risen One— whose glory is identical with long-suffering faithfulness to the Father?[145] If the *Logos* is too readily called glorious and powerful, we might well lose sight of what the pre-Nicaean *Letter to Diognetus* still saw very well; it balances its account of the Son's power by a moving emphasis on God's clemency, clinched by the phrase: "Force is not an attribute of God."[146] If this had been remembered, Thomasius' idea of the "depotentiated *Logos*" would never have struck anyone as an enlightening formula, since *kenōsis* (or rather *kenōma)* enters into the definition of the *Logos* to start with. The *kenōsis* brought about by Jesus Christ is a *kenōsis* of *humanity.* The *Logos* becomes Incarnate in a rough-and-tumble world full of violent people, disarms them by meekness and long-suffering, and thus leads the world into the arms of a clement God. *Pathos* and compassion and receptiveness and defenselessness are at the heart of God; they look like forced impotence only to those who view life primarily as an exercise in self-maintenance, at the expense of others if need be.

This understanding of the nature of God *and* of human nature is profoundly conveyed in Gertrud von le Fort's magnificent novella *The Song at the Scaffold.*[147] It is precisely the fearful and powerless

---

[145]P. Smulders suggests that it was the anti-Arian legacy of the Antiochene school that prevented Theodore of Mopsuestia from affirming as far-reaching an involvement of the Son of God in the human reality as he might have affirmed, given his strong emphasis on the assumption of the human nature into the divine ("Dogmengeschichtliche und lehramtliche Entfaltung der Christologie," pp. 437–438, esp. note 79, and pp. 441–449, esp. 445).

[146]VII, 1–6. Cf. also Irenaeus, *Adv. Haer.*, V, 1, 1, in Harvey's edition.

[147]*Die Letzte am Schafott*, München, Ehrenwirth, 1959. There is a tolerable English translation: *The Song at the Scaffold*, Olga Marx (trans.), New York, Henry

Blanche de la Force who eventually comes to sing the praise of God, by completing, from among the crowd surrounding the scaffold, the *Veni Creator*[148] intoned and left unfinished by her former Carmelite community as they are being guillotined, one by one. The *Deo Patri sit gloria* welling up out of utter weakness! How is this possible? The answer is that there is something deeper and more fundamental than courage, namely, fear;[149] and it is precisely in her fear that Soeur Blanche de Jésus au jardin de l'Agonie had been united with Jesus. The heroical Sister Marie de l'Incarnation had indeed seen the novice's fear, but in her preoccupation with the courage required by the threat of martyrdom she had completely failed to see the mystery of weakness; ironically, she will be the only member of the community to be deprived of martyrdom—she whose entire spirituality had been focused on it. Only Madame Lidoine, the staunch prioress, who had taken over the spiritual direction of the young and nervous novice, came around, slowly and almost reluctantly, to catch a glimpse of the mystery:

> O my God, can it be, then, that Thou, who dost enhance natural human virtues beyond the reach of nature, dost also deign to exalt one of our natural imperfections in the same manner? Is Thy mercy so great that Thou dost follow a poor soul, one unable to overcome her weakness, down into this her very weakness, in order there to unite her with Thy love? [. . .] Was it Thy will, O my Lord Jesus, to choose the frightened nature of this poor child, so that she might, as it were, abide with Thee in Thy agony, while others readied themselves jubilantly to die Thy death? Was this the worship that was still lacking to Thee, and was I about to rob Thee of it?[150]

Need we still be surprised that the Book of Revelation presents us, in the context of a world full of violence, in which God gives the Beast the power to wage war against the saints and defeat them, with the picture of the pre-existent Son as the Lamb slain from the beginning of the world?[151]

Holt and Co., 1933.—The novella was worked into an opera scenario by Georges Bernanos, music by Francis Poulenc: *Les Dialogues des Carmélites*.

[148]"Come, Creator Spirit"—the opening words of the ninth-century hymn attributed to Rabanus Maurus. The last stanza starts with the words *Deo Patri sit gloria*—"Glory to God the Father."

[149]*Die Letzte am Schafott*, p. 33.

[150]*Ibid.*, p. 69 (cf. ET, pp. 58–59).

[151]Rev 13, 7–8.

CHAPTER 12

Doing the Compassionate Father's Will

After the Resurrection, it seems to me, Jesus Christ lets only his wounds be touched: *Noli me tangere.** We are to unite ourselves only to his sufferings.

Blaise Pascal

We hear our hearts grate on themselves: it kills
To bruise them dearer. Yet the rebellious wills
Of us we do bid God bend to him even so.

And where is he who more and more distills
Delicious kindness?—He is patient. Patience fills
His crisp combs, and that comes those ways we know.

Gerard Manley Hopkins

The gift of perseverance, [Augustine] had said, was the greatest of God's gifts to the individual. For it bestowed on frail human beings the same unshakeable stability as the human nature in Christ had enjoyed: by this gift, a man was joined forever to the Divine, could be confident that the *'hand of God'* would be stretched above him to shield him, unfailingly, against the world. 'Human nature could not have been raised higher.' But the elect received this gift so that they, also, could tread the hard way of Christ. It was for this that they needed 'a liberty

---

*Do not touch me (Jn. 20, 17, Vulgate).

. . . protected and made firm by the gift of perseverance, that this world should be overcome, the world, that is, in all its deep loves, in all its terrors, in all its countless ways of going wrong.'

Peter Brown

Brethren, warn the fractious, encourage the nervous, stand by the weak, have patience with all.

The First Letter of Paul to the Thessalonians

Preliminary

In the past four chapters we have dealt with two of the three dynamisms of christology, namely, the rhetoric of hope and the rhetoric of inclusion. We are now faced with the task of exploring the rhetoric of obedience.

Before we do so, however, it seems appropriate to honor a promise made long ago,[1] namely, to survey our findings so far, in order to show, in a small compass, the inner coherence of the christological system we are building in this third part of the book. This will enable us to see more clearly what still remains to be treated in this chapter and the next.

After our survey we will proceed to treat the rhetoric of obedience under five headings. First, we will briefly explore the place of patience, especially in the New Testament. After that, we will see how the Church's vocation to patience has its consequences for the Christian understanding of martyrdom, apologetics, and ethics. Finally, we will bring up the subject of patience as a feature of christology itself; this last theme will in turn prove to be the introduction to the thirteenth and last chapter.

THE STRUCTURE OF CHRISTOLOGY:
A SURVEY

Retrospect

When we started the third part of this book we stated, among many other things, that it is important to seek for the coherence of

---

[1]Above, p. 307.

christology, not primarily by attempting to harmonize various christologies at the level of explicit meaning, but by seeking to establish the coherence of the performative functions of these various christologies.[2] In carrying out this program we have now made almost all of the necessary moves. Let us review them at this point, and thus also discover what remains to be done.

We started by identifying the Church's confident and hopeful *actus directus* of worshipful surrender to the Father in the Spirit as the point of departure and thus as the basic performative function of all christological deliverances; the Church's *parrhēsia* in response to the presence of the living Lord is the all-encompassing setting of all subsequent christological utterances.[3] This *actus directus* of faith is an experience of prospect; the risen Lord appears to the Church in the future.[4] Hence, the rhetoric of hope is the basic and foundational dynamic of christology, and all christological discernments ultimately find their places in the perspective of hope.[5]

We proceeded to show how the story of Jesus is the concrete shape of the Church's act of worship.[6] The fact that the story's performative function is worship rescues it from being perceived purely as a recounting of facts. Far from being a bare commemoration, the story is eucharistic *anamnēsis*—the sacrifice of praise and thanksgiving in which the Church also identifies herself under invocation of the Name of Jesus. The story carries commitment, and thus it is the primary Christian self-expression, or witness, to the world.[7]

We also pointed out that the story of Jesus, especially when its eschatological orientation is fully appreciated, also constitutes the warrant for the Church's own historical way. Thus the *imitatio Christi* must be understood, not primarily as the following of a past example, but as the Church's way, in the light of the risen One, into the future, on the way to judgment.[8]

After this we made the first decisive step. The story of Jesus, we

---

[2]Above, pp. 306–307.
[3]Above, pp. 349–354.
[4]Above, pp. 334–341.
[5]Above, pp. 189–192.
[6]Above, pp. 347–349.
[7]Above, pp. 344–347, 327–329.
[8]Above, pp. 338–344.

said, must also stand on its own, in the sense that it must also be considered apart from its primary performative function in the *actus directus* of worship and witness. We must subtract, so to speak, from the Church's eucharistic story the eschatological orientation, the rhetoric of hope, the tone of worship and witness. What remains after the subtraction, however, is again not a bare recounting of events, but the story of Jesus' individualization by inter-personalness—a process in which we saw all of humanity being graciously assumed into the direct encounter with God, in the person of Jesus.[9] Thus we discovered a number of things.

First, we discovered the assumptionist structure of primary christology. Humanity's being drawn into the person of Jesus Christ is based on Jesus' own life-story viewed as a life of total surrender to the living God as his Father; thus he becomes the universal representative-in-encounter of all of humankind.[10] Second, we discovered that the story of Jesus is a true story—a story, that is, capable of being told in true, realistic narrative.[11] And the theme of the story is Jesus' compassionate, patient, long-suffering, welcoming encounter with all.[12] Third, we discovered a second, implied performative function of the telling of Jesus' story, namely, the Church's *hypomonē*—her steadfast anticipation of the *eschaton*, in obedient perseverance.[13] Just as the act of confident worship and witness is the performative counterpart of the recognition of Jesus' as the risen Lord, so the life of obedient perseverance is the performative counterpart of the recognition of Jesus' obedience—his surrender to the Father result-ing in his doing the Father's will. The vision of the risen Lord has evoked the story of his obedience unto death; the rhetoric of hope has thus engendered the rhetoric of obedience. We have already treated the first two of the points just mentioned. What we have not elaborated is the third point: the style of the Church's way through history in imitation of Christ; this will therefore have to be the subject of this and the following chapters. The rhetoric of obedience must be shown to be the second setting of all christological discern-ments.

---

[9] Above, pp. 360–375.
[10] Above, pp. 423–427.
[11] Above, pp. 359–362.
[12] Cf. above, pp. 406-417.
[13] Cf. above, pp. 342–344.

But let us first complete our survey of the structure of christology. In pondering the process of Jesus' individualization by interrelationships, we came upon a fundamental, abiding dimension of the historical Jesus, namely, his irreducibility to his own individual nature.[14] We came to understand Jesus' life with God as a life of a person totally and inclusively related to the Father, in a living surrender, in the Holy Spirit, in a total receptivity that was also the secret of his universal significance. What we found in Jesus, in other words, was an abiding and total openness as the pre-condition for the historical life he led.[15]

Now just as we argued that the story of Jesus has to stand on its own, in the sense that it must be considered apart from its performative function in the *actus directus* of hopeful worship and witness, so we discovered that the affirmation of Jesus' total relatedness could stand on its own. We made, so to speak, another subtraction—of Jesus' historical life and destiny this time. What was left over was Jesus' abiding relational identity, his eternal union with the Father. However, just as Jesus' life story, after the first subtraction, did not become a bare recounting of events but a thankful recollection of Jesus' life and obedience, so the affirmation of the *Logos*, after the second subtraction, did not become a bare positing of an eternally fixed, immovable divine *hypostasis* to be incarnated, but an awed meditation on God's eternal, personal commitment to compassion with humankind and the whole universe. The *anamnēsis* of the obedient servant evoked the vision of the eternal Son—the Lamb slain from the beginning; the rhetoric of obedience engendered the rhetoric of inclusion—the final setting of all discernments about the person of Jesus Christ.[16]

The importance of the attitudinal, performative components

In the previous chapter we already stated that the attitudinal components of christology—worship, witness, and hope, obedience, patience and hospitality, and inclusion and intellectual worship—are by no means incidental to the christological statements themselves,

---

[14]Above, pp. 394, 422.
[15]Above, pp. 418–439.
[16]Above, pp. 439–463.

but essential to them.[17] In making this claim we were restating claims made especially in the second and third chapters, and which we can now best sum up by repeating that statements are not only cognitive but also behavioral and hence situational, not only objectifying but also intersubjective, not only logical but also rhetorical, and that statements are correctly used and understood only if used and understood in the context of the concerns they are meant to serve.[18] In christology, this context is threefold. The first and all-encompassing one is confident and hopeful worship and witness, which is the pre-condition for an appropriate understanding of christologies both critical and reflective. The second context then becomes the Church's commitment to Jesus' patient and hospitable obedience, learned in the school of eucharistic narrative; a christology of the life of Jesus, no matter how critical, must recognize the theme of obedience if it is to understand the life of Jesus. The final context is the attitude of all-inclusive intellectual worship born out of the practice of Jesus' patience and hospitality; a christology of the pre-existent *Logos*, no matter how profound and metaphysical, must recognize the theme of compassionate openness to the whole universe if it is to understand the person of Jesus in his deepest identity.

It is impossible to overemphasize this indebtedness of christology to attitudes, commitments, and contexts in a culture like ours today—one which has concealed its partialities under a cover of objectivity for over two hundred years.[19] Christianity has over the past two or three centuries come up against thought-systems which claim total logical consistency, total impartiality, total independence of stances and attitudes, and hence supreme authority to judge. Rather than admit defeat, Christian theology has all too often let

---

[17]Above, pp. 401–402, 453–454.

[18]Above, pp. 93–98, 111–114, 129–135.

[19]The idea that an attitude of prayer is the setting of philosophical reflection is part and parcel of the classical Platonist tradition, found, for example, in Plotinus. The Judaeo-Christian tradition integrated this into its conception of the sacrifice of praise and thanksgiving. The combination produced such masterpieces of recollective and reflective prayer as Augustine's *Confessions*; cf. Peter Brown, *Augustine of Hippo*, Berkeley–Los Angeles–London, University of California Press, ²1975, pp. 165–167, esp. note 8 on p. 166. The combination also allowed Christian thinkers to be very rational in their way of expressing themselves; the assumption was always that

itself be put on the defensive and given in to the temptation to present itself as a theological ideology of universal significance, either uncritically hand-in-glove with the prevailing culture or diametrically opposed to it. It is the contention of this book that this is a fundamental mistake, for the universalism of Christianity is basically factual, not theoretical; invitational, not prescriptive; rhetorical, not logical. Christianity does indeed propound universalist doctrinal statements, but they are based on a commitment to confident worship and witness, on hope that breeds endurance, and on patience that teaches awe. If Christian doctrine is cut loose from these attitudes, it gets decontextualized and turns into ideology. There may be many antinomies and contrasts between Christian doctrine and the tenets of rationalism in all its forms, but the basic antinomy lies not in the statements made, but in the attitude behind the statements and the uses to which they are put. Hope full of worship, obedience to the will of the Father, and universal inclusiveness form the context of all christological statements. Any other context and any other set of performative intentions will both lead the Church—no matter how orthodox—away from the *imitatio Christi*, and prevent those who hear the Church's teaching from understanding it.

We argued a long time ago that christology should do more justice to the life of the historical Jesus and to the concreteness of salvation in the "matters pertaining to this life."[20] We have already shown how the question of the interpretation of Jesus' life is raised by the narrative shape of the hopeful sacrifice of praise and thanksgiving.[21] We must now demonstrate how the dynamics of Christian

---

thought arose in the context of prayerful meditation. The modern divorce between prayer and philosophical reflection is well illustrated by Heidegger's claim that an "abstract God" is "a God to whom man can neither pray nor offer sacrifice. Before the *causa sui* man cannot fall on his knees in awe, nor can he sing and dance before this God." This position overlooks a possible alternative, namely, that the very act of saying "*causa sui*" is an act of intellectual worship and an expression of awe. Depending on the speaker's (or writer's) attitude and tone of voice, expressions like "pre-existent *Logos*" may be acts of "reason illumined by faith" or acts of intellectual arrogance; in the latter case, worshipful *sens de Dieu* is replaced by the self-affirmation of autonomous reason, and thus *Logos*-talk becomes idolatrous. Cf. Hans Küng, *On Being a Christian*, p. 309.

[20]Above, pp. 52–53, 62.
[21]Cf. the promise made above, p. 226, note 112.

hope must generate the attitude which should most characterize the Church's concrete, day-to-day existence in obedience to the call to the *imitatio Christi:* patience.

PATIENCE, THE FRUIT OF HOPE

The Church's responsive identity again

Primary christology, we have argued, is the Church's self-expression in worship and witness to the risen Lord. Thus the identity which the Church conveys in her self-expression is a responsive identity. It is the moral identity which the Church and all her members gain, not as property, but as gift, in virtue of the gracious encounter with Christ in the Spirit; hence, the Church's identity in turn brings to expression and actuality the presence of the One who prompts the Church to live under invocation of his Name, which will henceforth identify the members of the Church as Christians. In this way the Church lives while telling the story of Jesus Christ alive in the Spirit, of his ministry and long-suffering obedience—his story which stamps and marks her.

The consequence of this is that the living Word of faith, and the sacraments in which the living Word of faith takes shape, have a primacy over everything else in the Church. The Church's vocal and active praise to the Father in response to the presence of Christ alive is unsurpassably valid, as is its eucharistic expression: the story of the life and death and Resurrection of Jesus. This indefeasible validity comes from the Resurrection; the faith-surrender prompted by the living Lord produces, as its first-fruits, lips acknowledging his Name.[22]

What this means is that the Church—viewed here as the concrete Christian community on her way—may quite possibly not live up to her own Word of praise and thanksgiving; she may fail to actualize her own deepest identity. After all, the partial concerns which are the stuff of the Church's historical existence resist quick integration into the total surrender; there is no end to the human concerns to be drawn into the worshipful surrender and into the

---

[22]Cf. Heb 13, 13.

imitatio Christi; and, moreover, there is the dullness of sin, a factor which will always prevent the surrender from being complete.[23] Thus the Church must always live in surprise and awe at the Word which she hears herself utter and the offering which she sees herself bring, and this on two grounds. First, the Word and the offering are prompted by the living Lord; they are not the Church's independent achievement. They do convey the Church's deepest identity, but that identity is responsive, not self-established. Second, there is always a gap between the Church's deepest identity and the way she lives it out. On both counts we must conclude that the living Word and the living sacraments may never be considered the Church's own assets. The Church as a concrete community lives by overstatement, and thus she has reason for humility, not pride, for sympathy with the world, not judgment on the world.[24] We must elaborate this somewhat.

The Church's identity not set against the world

To say that the Church never quite lives up to her own living Word of faith and to her sacraments amounts to saying that the historical Church never quite lives up to the Resurrection.[25]

The Resurrection prompts the Church to live in surrender to the Lord and so to speak up and follow Christ; only in the light of the risen One do the life and death of Jesus become the paradigm of, and the warrant for, the historical Church. But the Resurrection of Jesus never becomes the Church's property; it remains a call to surrender, conversion, and hope. The Church's identity consists precisely in her being called and her being responsive; never must the Church make her identity the object of self-empowered assertions or claims. The Church's life—including her living speech—in the Name of Jesus to the praise of God is Christian to the extent that it is in the nature of an abiding response to a graciously abiding presence; it turns into sectarian tribalism and ideology as soon as it is presented

---

[23]Cf. above, pp. 189–191.

[24]For the sequence Word–Sacrament–Community as the *loci* of Christ's presence, cf. Dietrich Bonhoeffer, *Christ the Center*, pp. 49–61 (GS, pp. 184–194), where the references to the possibility of scandal are also found.

[25]Cf. above, p. 343.

as a demonstrably superior way of life based on an independently defensible thesis. When that happens, the reliance on the living God in the Spirit is traded in for religious prestige at odds with the world, ready to oppose the weak and the strong alike, and always on the verge of becoming the accomplice of the latter. When the Church tries to beat the world, she has already joined it. Christian witness has been known to sour into impatient and unthankful dogmatism, triumphalist posturing, or formularized mumbo-jumbo; hope has turned into vapid overstatement, desperate stubbornness, or dull assurance, whenever the Church has treated Christ alive as an ecclesiastical asset.

When the living Lord is thus ecclesiasticized the Church also loses touch with her mission. We argued that the assumption of humanity into the person of Jesus Christ was precisely clinched by the fact that Jesus did not justify himself over against others by *claiming* God for his Savior.[26] Analogously, *the Church must not claim the risen Lord for her Savior to establish her identity over against the world.* Christians must not use the risen Lord as an ego-booster. What we have said here is nothing but a transposition of what Paul wrote about Christ Jesus' frame of mind: just as his equality with God was not a matter of snatching, to seek his own advantage, and his relationships with others not a matter of judging or commanding but of servanthood,[27] so the Church's (and the individual Christian's) identity may not consist in appropriating the glory of the risen One as their own. When that happens the Church and the Christians become the judges and arbiters of humanity, and

---

[26]Above, pp. 419–420.

[27]Above, p. 419, and note 35.—Philippians 2, 4–11 must be read in the context of the whole passage 2, 1–18. Paul is recommending an attitude of love and concord to the Philippians *among themselves,* to be achieved by unselfishness, the avoidance of vainglory, and the practice of humbly treating others as better than oneself *on the part of individuals.* The desire for, and the execution of, these hard virtues can only come from God, in whom all should place their trust. Paul understands why the Philippians should be nervous about their salvation, now that he, Paul, is away; so he refers them to God's graciousness (*hyper tēs eudokias*). Jesus is their perfect example, both of trust in God and of subjection to others: no act of snatching (*harpagmos*) in regard to God, self-emptying and subjection unto death with regard to others.—This implies, of course, that I read the *kenōsis* of Jesus as a characteristic of his relationships *to other human beings*; Phil 2, 7 is not a valid source for the development of kenotic christology.

thus they discontinue the assumption of all of humanity into Christ. This raises a problem. Does this mean that the Church must adopt an attitude of passivity?

Neither active nor passive self-justification

Nowhere in the New Testament is the Church's *parrhēsia* toward the Father and the certainty of her hope in the Name of the risen One construed as a claim to prestige. Yet nowhere in the New Testament does this refusal to lay claim to prestige rot away into spineless, passive submission to the powers that be, or to the naive illusion that the world and the powers that be are basically all right; the New Testament knows no passive self-justification, either by submission to a bad world or by deference to a good world. But if passive self-justification is rejected, so are all kinds of combative self-assertion, self-maintenance, and self-justification, whether based on enthusiasm, as in Corinth, or on legalism, as in Galatia. They are rejected as a return to the elements of this world, which will not stand up in the consuming fire of God's presence.[28] Thus, both the harmlessness of doves and the shrewdness of serpents are commended;[29] both the combative—those who want to beat the world —and the passive—those who join it by default—lack the patience in which harmlessness and shrewdness meet. The overbearing can be bribed and the passive can be bought; the patient are not for sale, for they derive their identity from Christ crucified and risen.

Patience in the New Testament

Hence, what the Church is commanded to cherish on her way is not the glory of the Lord as a claim to fame, but the Cross of Christ as the epitome of the will of the Father compassionate. The Church's way is the way of patience, empathy with the lowly, absence of conceit, hospitality, ordinariness, modesty, forgiveness, joyful suffering, and—to sum it up in the language of Paul's First Letter to the Corinthians—*agapē*. *Agapē* consists in ordinary, humdrum things: avoidance of unkindness, jealousy, bragging, arrogance, rudeness,

---

[28]Cf. Gal 4, 9; 1 Cor 3, 13.
[29]Cf. Mt 10, 16.

stubborness, irritability, resentment, and glee.[30] To take another example, Paul's characterization of the Christian way of life in the Letter to the Romans, wedged in between appeals to surrender to God in spiritual worship and hope, is one long plea for modesty, sober judgment, tolerance, unselfconscious use of one's gifts, love, joy, patience, prayer, forgiveness, empathy, goodness shown to enemies, civil obedience, hospitality extended to worrisome brethren without contentiousness, and long-suffering.[31] The First Letter of Peter is full of exhortations to patience and unselfishness, in the name of the living hope into which Christians have been born through the Resurrection of Jesus Christ[32]—*the* cause for thankful praise to God. The high christology of the Letter to the Hebrews, both in its catechesis about the eternal Son and in its emphasis on the immediacy of the Church's access to the throne of God's graciousness through Christ, does not tire of stressing the need for patient perseverance in the confession of faith;[33] the whole letter closes with an exhortation to the community to stand in awe at its own mysterious relationship with God, whence is derived the need for care for brotherly love, hospitality, concern for prisoners and outcasts, marriage discipline, wariness of greed, faithfulness, patient non-conformity, and obedience.[34]

Only people who have left their ego-needs and their identity up to God and who trust him to do justice to them in Jesus Christ can be so disconcertingly human. Only persons who experience their identity as unowed—because they experience it as graciously given to them in their encounter with the risen Christ in hope—can meet others with the kind of unworried security that leads to unselfconscious self-giving.

They can afford to be carefree and liberal with themselves; they neither give gifts out of self-importance, nor do they derive self-importance from giving. They can also receive others' gifts; the goodness of others does not threaten their self-esteem, nor are they dependent on others' goodness to be assured of their own impor-

---

[30]Cf. 1 Cor 13, 4–6.
[31]Cf. Rom 12, 1—15, 13.
[32]Cf. 1 Pet 1, 3.
[33]Cf., for example, Heb 2, 1; 3, 6. 12–14; 4, 1–2. 11; 6, 18; 10, 19–25. 35–39.
[34]Cf. Heb 12, 18—13, 17.

tance. They can afford to be honest about their own failings; they have no desperate need to be perfect in their own or others' eyes, and thus the free confession of their sins is praise to God. They can face, and even welcome, the failings of others without glossing them over or condoning them; not only do they recognize themselves as partners in failure, but also, more importantly, in virtue of their hidden lives, with Christ, in God, they can afford to welcome all that is human, whether righteous or unrighteous, into their lives.[35]

A patience so relaxed and so hospitable requires self-discipline. This self-discipline is not self-oriented or self-centered; it is not a form of self-improvement based on a negative self-judgment; it is not born out of contempt of one's own human foibles. These latter forms of self-discipline are nothing but ethical forms of self-justification; they usually lead to self-righteousness and often to disciplinarian authoritarianism. Christian self-discipline distrusts everything that is too final, definite, harsh, clear-cut, loud, authoritative, busy, ambitious, and overstated—in short, everything that smacks of violence. Its inspiration is the call to be of service to others—to encounter them, whoever they are, in meekness, kindness, and compassion.[36]

The Letter of James is in many ways the most compelling characterization in the New Testament of the disciplined life animated by total reliance on God and bent on doing justice to others for their sakes. For James, the faith of our Lord Jesus Christ, the Lord of glory, involves the rejection of all partiality—the establishing of oneself by association with some to the exclusion of others *(prosōpolēmpsia).*[37] Hence the condemnation of anger, discrimination of the poor, self-styled faith, jealousy and ambition, violence, judgmental attitudes, injustice, arrogance, and overstatement by swear-

---

[35]The frequent (and depressing) emphasis on the Christian's own sinfulness as a motive for forgiving others is theologically inadequate. Christians *are* called to forgiveness, but not because they have a chip on their shoulder themselves; the real reason is that they have been forgiven themselves. Thus the call to forgiveness is a call to *saving forgiveness*; the Christian is *empowered* to forgive in virtue of his sharing in Christ's *holiness*. And the manifestation of this holiness in the life of Jesus was, not his distance from sinners, but his active identification with them as Savior.

[36]Cf. above, pp. 416–417.

[37]Jas 2, 1.—The word is used of God in Rom 2, 11; Eph 6, 9; Col 3, 25. In Acts 10, 34 Peter's recognition of God's impartiality becomes the motive for his own.

ing.[38] When James commends "works," they are the works, not of power, but of meekness and patience: endurance of trial, care for the needy, peace-making, care for the sick in the name of the risen Lord, bringing sinners back from the errors of their ways[39]—all of them works of care and mercy. In this light, the fact that references to Jesus the Lord are scarce and very subdued in the Letter of James[40] becomes profoundly significant: there is not a hint of triumphalism in this deeply realistic appreciation of the demands of a truly human and meek and merciful faith. In this context James' skepticism with regard to the tongue also becomes relevant to the interpretation of the letter. The tongue though small is violent; it can produce words that sound like words of faith but are not, because they are devoid of mercy.[41]

The Church's assertiveness

Meekness, patience, hospitality—these are the attitudes that are born from the Church's responsive identity. Yet this does not in the least imply that the Christian confession of faith must lack affirmativeness and assertiveness, or that the Church's mission must be hesitant. Confession and mission emerge out of a responsive *identity*, which is conveyed by the story of Jesus. The presence of the risen Lord must keep the Church watchful, and this watchfulness must take the shape of a resolute involvement with the world, in a stance of appreciative and realistic deputyship. But this stance requires patience. The Church can confess Jesus as Lord with more vigor and move about in the world with greater assurance according as she lives her own life more patiently, that is, with a healthy sense of the provisional, animated by the assurance of God's merciful judgment in Christ to come.[42] Neither her own judgment nor the judgment of others are her final tribunal, so she need not be nervous about conforming to the prevailing powers. Thus the Church is

---

[38]Cf. Jas 1,19; 2, 2ff., 18ff.; 3, 14ff.; 4, 2ff., 11f, 13ff.; 5, 12ff.

[39]Cf. Jas 1, 12ff.; 2, 14ff.; 3, 17–18; 5, 14. 16. 19–20.—Significantly, James (2, 26) compares faith to the body and works to the spirit, not the other way round, as the mainstream tradition will have it.

[40]Only Jas 1, 1; 2, 1; 5, 7–9. 14(?).

[41]Jas 6, 6–10; 2, 15–17; cf. 1, 19–20. 26.

[42]Cf. above, p. 343.

called to be free to endure and sympathize, not to dominate.[43]

Does this have consequences for established churches, which have—often deservedly, as a result of past services to the culture—become part of the intellectual, cultural, sociopolitical and economic power structure? Obviously. First, no church must be afraid of de facto power or too apologetic about it, nor certainly with false and unhealthy modesty deny its own clout. Second, no church must have qualms about admitting that its powers are descended from poverty and long-suffering. And there's the rub, for the rich and the powerful have never been especially fond of being reminded of their poorer and less cultured ancestors. Still, when a church's memory starts to fail in this regard, it is unlikely to acknowledge as present relatives all those strangers who are physically or spiritually hungry, thirsty, foreign, ill-dressed, unhealthy, or held in custody by the police—let alone if they attempt to take your coat, hit you in the face, or force you out of your house for a mile's walk.[44] Hence, third, a powerful church's compassionate identification with those who live in the margin of the establishment is the test of the seriousness of its commitment to the imitation of Christ in patience and hospitality.

Retrospect and outlook

Our discussions of patience and assertiveness lead to conclusions regarding a number of aspects and activities of the Church in her relationship with the world. We will touch on three of them briefly in the next three sections, and discuss a fourth rather more fully in the last section of this chapter and in the next chapter. The

---

[43]Endurance tends to be few people's spontaneous choice; hence, the Church has been known to pray that God, in his mercy, might *force* us into it: *et ad te nostras etiam rebelles compelle propitius voluntates* (Roman Missal of 1570, Fourth Sunday after Pentecost, *secreta*; cf. Gerard Manley Hopkins: "yet the rebellious wills / Of us we do bid God bend to him even so"—*Poems*, n. 68, p. 102). This is also the source of the tradition that holds, against the gnostic optimism of all times, that the fear of God, though merely an accessory motive in comparison with love, must not be spurned. At times the Church has even been known to interpret natural and political disasters as a divine *disciplina* inflicted upon a humanity refractory to divine mercy (cf. Peter Brown, *Augustine of Hippo*, pp. 233–243). Still, from there *il n'y a qu'un pas* to Père Paneloux' sermon in Albert Camus' *The Plague*, where the God of mercy has been completely obscured by a God of vengeance, preached by an authoritarian, know-it-all church.

[44]Cf. Mt 25, 35–36; 5, 39–41.

former three are martyrdom, apologetics, and ethics. The fourth is christology itself, viewed, not primarily as an internally coherent system of doctrinal and theological statements, but as an ongoing activity of the Church.

We will make a number of claims on behalf of these four activities. These claims will vary as the subjects vary, but all of them are based on three fundamental theses of a christological nature; these theses also sum up much of our discussions so far in this chapter. Let us then state these theses by way of retrospect as well as outlook.

First, the Church's activities must derive their assertiveness from the responsive act of worship and witness in the encounter with the living Lord. Second, this responsive act is an act of eschatological hope, and not an act which in and of itself enjoys, or is dependent upon, worldly acceptance. Hence, patience and compassion must shape the Church's activities in her encounter with the world. In this way, the Church's true familiarity with God, in the assurance that comes from hope, will manifest itself in understanding. Third—and here the christological theme is most prominent—patience and compassionate understanding will insure that the continuing assumption of all of humanity into Christ's continuing surrender to the Father is truly inclusive, and that the call to obedience implied in the assumption of all human concerns does not take the shape of a forced submission to an ecclesiastical yoke. This must be so because the true shape of the Church is that of the obedient servant, bent on doing justice to those realities that have not yet been assumed, and calling them, too, to the obedience of faith in the hope of the Resurrection.

MARTYRDOM:
AFFINITY WITH THE SUFFERING WORLD

Martyrdom and homologia

The sacrifice of praise and thanksgiving, which is the Christian's total surrender to the Father in Christ, is actualized not only in Word and sacrament, those verbal acts of worship and witness to the present Christ, but also in the active life of obedience, in patience and hospitality. The imitation of Christ, therefore, will be in the nature of a life of witness to the obedient Christ, the original model of what it means to witness.[45] Wherever this witness meets with the violence of the powers that be, the sacrifice of praise and thanksgiving may take the shape of the eloquent silence of martyrdom. In Word and sacrament the witness is vocal; in the martyr's confession, the witness is gestural. Nowhere in the great Christian tradition do we find this so well expressed as in the letter to the Romans written by Ignatius of Antioch on his way to his martyrdom in Rome, in the early years of the second century. He explains to the Christians in Rome why he does not want them to secure his release from the authorities. In his going to God without the benefit of human support, he writes, he will be the "word of God"; if he is released, he will be "a mere voice again." Where he is going he will attain his true self: "I will be a man," and so he asks: "Allow me to be an imitator of the suffering of my God."[46]

The essence of martyrdom, therefore, is the living-out, in suffering, of the *homologia*—the sacrifice of praise and thanksgiving to the Father in the Spirit in response to the living Lord; it shares this trinitarian nature with Baptism, as its fulfillment.[47] If the praise of God is the martyr's primary focus, it follows that the martyr is neither a hero nor a fanatic, and his confession is not a defiant statement of a counter-cause in the teeth of the powers that be. It is a witnessing encounter with the powers that be, in the confident knowledge that human tribunals are not the last word.

Some brief reflections on this basic thesis are in order. They will concentrate on the significance of the concrete issue that occasions the martyrdom, on the stance of weakness involved in martyrdom, on the martyr's affinity with the world's suffering, and on the love of one's enemies. At the end we will draw some conclusions and illustrate them by means of two examples.

The concrete issue

In every martyrdom there is a concrete issue, alleged as the cause for the martyr's death. Very few, if any, Christians have been

---

[45]Cf. 1 Tim 6, 13.

[46]*To the Romans* II, 1; VI, 2–3 (Lightfoot).

[47]Cf. W. Seibel, art. "Bekenntnis," in *Handbuch theologischer Grundbegriffe*, I. Band, München, Kösel, 1962, p. 157.

martyred merely out of hatred for the faith. This holds true even for the martyrs in the early persecutions, which can to a large extent be explained in terms of the social process known as scapegoating. In order to appease the restive majority, some group had to be blamed for a common calamity that might become a threat to the established powers. The charges brought were usually trumped up, but there *were* real reasons for the persecution; though the persecutions were not ordinarily aimed at the Christians and their faith as such, their non-conformity and their doubtful loyalty to the all-important state were real and concrete issues, vague as they were. In many later cases of martyrdom, however, there are far more concrete issues that occasion the martyrdom. Now the question arises how these concrete issues are relevant to martyrdom as a confessional act.

The first observation must be that there is always an element of inconclusiveness, and even futility, in martyrdom. The concrete issue is always arguable. There is always room for maneuvering, for compromise, and even for mental reservation—in short, for a weighing of the issue in terms of loss and gain in order to avoid discomfort or death while maintaining one's basic integrity as a Christian. Consequently, it is always possible for others to arrive at the judgment that so-and-so's martyrdom was avoidable, and even that it was really only a matter of dubious identification with a cause wrongly, or at least unnecessarily, espoused for non-compelling reasons of belief. And as a matter of fact, it has very seldom been impossible for Christians to buy life and a fair measure of religious freedom in return for some accommodation on concrete issues. In fact, accommodation of some sort is even a touchstone of true martyrdom. Christians making a public nuisance of themselves by openly courting martyrdom had to be warned by Clement of Alexandria to calm down. And to cite a very different case, Christians violently pushed out of positions of great power or wealth obstinately held on to and defended in the name of the faith may have been unjustly treated; they are not martyrs.

Hence, though martyrdom in the concrete is always involved with an issue, its essence is not: the suffering of death for an issue. The essence of martyrdom is the *homologia*, the confessional story of Jesus' life and execution and Resurrection, which has never much actual credibility before the tribunal of humanity defining and defending its establishments. Martyrdom, therefore, is not primarily characterized by the strength of the martyr's defense of an issue, but by his weakness in basing his case upon a *homologia* that enjoys such limited credibility. At bottom, the Christian *homologia* is a proclamation made in weakness, not triumph. This weakness has three aspects.

Confident confession born out of weakness

The first is that Christians faced with the threat of suffering never quite live up to the *homologia*; they feel inadequate in the very act of testifying. The *parrhēsia* and the courage to witness, after all, come from the encounter with the risen One, not from self-assurance. In the encounter with the aggressive self-assurance of the powers that be, how tempting it must be to let oneself be drawn into a self-justifying attitude of self-assurance in the very act of Christian *homologia*! And yet, such a heroic attitude would cut the heart out of Christian witness, which consists of boasting in the Lord, not in one's own cause. We must conclude that the very act of *homologia* is an experience of weakness to those who are called to the martyr's witness. Small wonder, then, that we find, in a variety of New Testament traditions, Jesus exhorting his followers not to worry about what to say when confronted with the princes of this world.[48] Such worry would only lead to attempts to respond to the powers on *their* terms. The true witness will speak out of the Spirit of God in response to Christ crucified and come to life.

Affinity with all losing causes

Second, because the focus of martyrdom is in the *homologia* and not in the concrete issue as such, the martyr's posture involves more than his identification with the particular lost cause that is the issue immediately at stake. The martyr is rooted in a weakness so profound as to undercut all issues. He finds his roots in an attitude of receptiveness and vulnerability that has nothing in common with the competition for ascendancy that results wherever parties are opposed to each other on the basis of competing causes. The martyr is neither

---

[48]Mk 13, 11; Mt 10, 19–20; Lk 12, 11–12; 21, 14–15; Jn 14, 26.

a partisan nor a fanatic. He freely represents all losing causes,[49] all oppressed concerns, and all the people and things caught in the middle. In this way, the *homologia*—that total, Spirited surrender to the Father under the invocation of Jesus—becomes a freely undertaken act of solidarity with all the suffering in the world, as well as a freely undertaken profession of divinely inspired hope on behalf of all of wounded humanity.[50]

Love of one's violent neighbor

Third, precisely because the concrete ground for martyrdom, no matter how important, is not the determining factor, the martyr is *not identified as the opponent* of his persecutors, who, with their cause, *are his* opponents. On the strength of his *homologia*, the martyr is enabled to open himself and to let the error and the terror of the powers that be become a personal issue with himself. What keeps the martyr in touch with his persecutors is not the issue on which he and they differ, and on which a compromise is always possible, but the persecutors' very enmity. On the surface, we have the spectacle of the opposition between the martyr's relative loyalty to the lost cause and his enemies' identification with the victorious cause; deep down, the martyr is concerned with those who use their presumed right by way of might. And so we come to the supreme irony of martyrdom: in his witness, the martyr puts himself on the line, not only on behalf of the world's suffering, but also on behalf of the world's oppressors, those violent victims of their own fears of losing their lives. The Christian tradition has called this loving one's enemy. Loving one's enemy is suffering for him at his own hands.

Conclusion: the presence of Christ in martyrdom

We must conclude that the *homologia*—that essential trait of martyrdom—places the martyr in a stance of *pathos* on a double

---

[49]The word "freely" in this sentence is essential, given the labyrinthine possibilities for inauthentic martyrdom (inverted impotence, passive aggression, aggression by means of verbal identification with sufferers, etc.), to which Rollo May's *Power and Innocence*, A Search for the Sources of Violence, Delta Book, New York, Dell Publishing Co., 1976, provides a reliable and detailed map.

[50]Cf. Eberhard Bethge, *Bonhoeffer: Exile and Martyr*, edited and with an essay by John W. de Gruchy, London, Collins, 1975, pp. 161ff..

score. First, the *homologia* clinches his *responsive* identity; his identity as a martyr is an identity in receptiveness; it is not an identity that arises from self-affirmation. Second, the martyr becomes in his own person the representative of all the suffering and all the lost love in the world. The martyr does not claim the risen Christ as a taunt to his persecutors or as an analgesic to deny or dull his own or the world's grief, or as a personal asset that secures his own individual salvation to the exclusion of others. The martyr suffers. He does so because the risen Christ gives him hope, calls him to suffering out of sympathy with all, and provides him with the ground for the inclusion of all.

In this way, the martyr becomes the paradigm of yet another presence of Christ, besides his presence in the Word, the sacraments, and the Church. Christ is present, in a most hidden manner, in the willing surrender of self, in love and *sympatheia*, for the sake of others, especially the weak and the suffering. Christ's presence in the Word, sacrament, and Church can be (and has been) mistaken for gloriously powerful presence in virtue of the Spirit. The Church, with her *cultus publicus*, is often tempted to forget that the glory is the risen Lord's and not her own apart from him. She is often tempted to forget that Word and sacrament—and indeed she herself—are divinely warranted overstatements directly responsive to the risen Lord. It is in the martyr—and in every good Christian as he imitates the Lord in the patient business of everyday life with all comers—that the true shape of the *body*, the true shape of the Church as the physical basis of spiritual worship appears.[51] The risen life of Jesus can only be reflected in mortal persons if they obediently agree to be the unceremonial bearers of his death.[52]

Two illustrations: Dietrich Bonhoeffer and Edmund Campion

The case of Dietrich Bonhoeffer provides us with a most poignant demonstration of real *martyrion* as well as with its tragic misinterpretation. Bonhoeffer first helped the Church to ground its

---

[51] For a moving account of "The Pattern of Christ's Presence," cf. Hans Frei, *The Identity of Jesus Christ*, pp. 154–165.
[52] Cf. 2 Cor 4, 11.

resistance to Nazi *Gleichschaltung*[53] firmly on the Confession—the *homologia*. Once so constituted, however, the Confessing Church, humiliated by the powers, turned out to be incapable of attributing theological relevance to the suffering that occurred outside its own limits.[54] The Confessing Church never quite succeeded in positively accepting and theologically interpreting her role of subjection as a share in Christ's passion on behalf of the world; she failed to see that she suffered together with so many others, the Jews above all. She tended to concentrate on her own martyrdom, as an established Church unjustly attacked, and she did not realize that the Confession of Christ's Lordship is meant to *unite* the Church with humankind, not to alienate her from it. Bonhoeffer decided in the end to create some distance between himself and the Church he had himself helped to ground on the *homologia*. As a result, many Christians in the post-war Confessing Church have refused to recognize him as a martyr; he was not ecclesiastical enough, and too much involved with the crudity and the ambiguity of the human predicament.[55]

Eberhard Bethge has attempted to defend Bonhoeffer as a true martyr by suggesting that he is not a classical martyr, of the kind characterized by saintliness, but a modern martyr, characterized by association with human guilt.[56] It may be so. Still, a different inter-

---

[53]The official Nazi policy, whereby dissent was proscribed as contrary to the concerted national effort needed to achieve the aims of national socialism; all organizations were affected by it, including schools, artistic associations and institutions, and the churches.

[54]Cf. Eberhard Bethge, *Dietrich Bonhoeffer*, New York–Hagerstown–San Francisco–London, Harper & Row, 1970, pp. 696–702.

[55]Cf. Eberhard Bethge, *Bonhoeffer: Exile and Martyr*, pp. 159–166.

[56]Cf. "Turning Points in Bonhoeffer's Life and Thought," in: Peter Vorkink (ed.), *Bonhoeffer in a World Come of Age*, Fortress Press, Philadelphia, 1968, pp. 73–102, reference p. 100. Bethge quotes one of Bonhoeffer's sermons before the Nazi takeover (*Gesammelte Schriften*, Eberhard Bethge [ed.], 4. Band, München, Chr. Kaiser Verlag, ²1965, p. 71; cf. *Bonhoeffer: Exile and Martyr*, p. 155) to support his contention. I venture to suggest that Bethge misinterprets Bonhoeffer here; the sermon identifies the "human guilt" with the conservatism of the church as a whole— hence, a church ill-prepared for the challenges that are appearing on the horizon, and which may require martyrdom. Incidentally, the "classical martyr" was never considered "saintly"; the fact that the martyr's *confessio* was traditionally considered to involve the remission of his sins is proof of this. Cf. W. Seibel, "Bekenntnis," p. 157.

pretation is also possible. Could it be that what Bethge calls a "classical" martyr is characterized, not so much by saintliness as by ecclesiastical claims to saintliness? That the classical martyr is in reality a true martyr, but one who is now idealized and featured as an ecclesiastical champion by an established church boasting its past struggles and its heroes? And could the "modern" martyr, exemplified by Bonhoeffer, really be the true martyr of *all* times—the witness to Christ and the compassionate lover of Christ's suffering brothers and sisters—and thus not only a glory of the Church but also a challenge to her? Canonization is not the Church's idealization of one of her own, but her recognition of one of Christ's own—one of those who invite her to continue on the hard road of the imitation of Christ.

To take another example, the Roman Catholic recognition accorded to a martyr like Edmund Campion has all too often been too triumphalistic. Campion's renunciation of readily available secular advancement, his typically sixteenth-century gallantry, and his delight in controversy about very partisan theological issues have often been wrongly placed at the heart of his martyrdom. In this way, other more important features came to be neglected: his very personal surrender to Christ, his compassion for the humble and the ignorant who were being manipulated, his respect for and empathy with the opposing party, his complete submission to God's judgment, and his hope for eventual reconciliation.[57] These latter features make Campion into a martyr; ironically, they are also basic ingredients of ecumenical dialogue. No church may flaunt martyrs like Campion; that would amount to turning a patient witness to the risen Lord into an intolerant banner-waver for a polemical cause.

APOLOGETICS:
CRITICAL SYMPATHY WITH THE DOMINANT CONCERNS

Introductory

In martyrdom, the assumption of all of humanity takes on the

---

[57]For the life of Edmund Campion, a Jesuit executed at Tyburn in 1581, cf. Evelyn Waugh, *Edmund Campion*, New York, Doubleday, 1956.—The characterizations enumerated in this paragraph may be readily identified in Campion's famous so-called "Brag"; cf. the appendix to Waugh's book, pp. 191–196.

shape of the Christian witness encountering and absorbing the violence of the powers that be, in an act of solidarity with the suffering world. In the martyr, Christian patience and hospitality combine, in imitation of Christ and on the strength of the Spirit, to produce the highest act of obedience to the Father compassionate, who gives sunshine to the good and the evil, and rainfall to the just and the unjust.

Now it must be said that the powers that be are usually not violent, and not even hostile. They mostly take the shape of forces producing or supporting a relatively stable cultural establishment, concretized in a variety of institutions, and legitimized by a more or less coherent system of assumptions, tastes, convictions, priorities, and concerns, some explicit, some implicit. It is in the midst of such a world, and indeed permeated by it, that the Church must take shape, again, in patience and hospitality.

This raises the issue of the Church's relationship to the powers that be in a different fashion. How must the Church concretize her readiness to make a defense to all who ask her to account for her hope?[58] And how is she to do this in such a way as to be understood? Thus the question of apologetics is raised as part of the Church's vocation to imitate Christ in this world.

We will be able to make only a few absurdly brief remarks on this subject. The history of apologetics is so varied, and its structures, methods, and aims have become so complex, especially since the mid-eighteenth century, that a much fuller analysis than the one here given is required.[59] But, then, we wish to make only one point, though a fundamental one, namely, that apologetics is part of the *imitatio Christi*, and that this has consequences for its practice.

The older traditions: apologetics in a confessional setting

The written defense of the Christian faith appears in two main forms, namely, attempts at correction and refutation of particular misconceptions opposed to the Christian faith, and full-scale demonstrations of its credibility as a whole. The former is the more ancient

---

[58]Cf. 1 Pet 3, 15.

[59]A good survey is Avery Dulles, *A History of Apologetics*, New York/Philadelphia/London, Corpus/Westminster/Hutchinson, 1971.

genre. *Apologiae* to correct popular or sophisticated misrepresenta-
tions of particular Christian beliefs and practices are as old as
Christianity itself, as are defenses of the Christian faith achieved by
exposing certain specific errors of others. This genre, represented by
the classical Christian apologists, but also by the numerous early
medieval *apologiae* addressing themselves to the errors of the Jews
and the "Saracens," remained, of necessity, somewhat patchy, given
the need to concentrate on specific practical goals (for instance,
obtaining religious toleration for Christians) and on specific errors.

Although the ancient Church did produce a few attempts, by
authors like Lactantius and Eusebius of Caesarea, to demonstrate the
credibility of the Christian faith as a whole, comprehensive apologetics with no particular axes to grind were not successfully attempted
till the Middle Ages. The masterpiece in this second genre is without
doubt Aquinas' *Summa contra Gentiles*; its apologetic function—a
few dutiful references to "Mahumetus" and the credulity of his followers aside[60]—is no longer the defense of Christian beliefs against
real live enemies, but the explanation of the harmony between "the
truth achieved by demonstration" and "the faith of the Christian
religion."[61]

The bitter controversies of the Reformation and Counter-Refor-
mation, with their extremely doctrinaire aftermaths, forced a return
to more particular, issue-oriented apologetics, within divided Christendom this time. But a real change was in the making, and it gained
in prominence during the late seventeenth and early eighteenth
centuries. The result was the rise of a totally new genre of apologetics. To understand this shift, let us go back for a moment and ponder
the common characteristic of the two genres of apologetics just
discussed.

For the ancient apologists, and even for Boethius, apologetics
had always been firmly confessional. Established pagan thought still
controlled the philosophical scene. It was impossible for Christianity

---

[60]Cf. *ScG*, I, 6, *Hi vero.*—For a suggestive sketch of medieval Christendom's
relationships with the world of Islam, cf. R. W. Southern, *The Making of the Middle
Ages*, London, Hutchinson, 1967, pp. 30–67, esp. 37–42, 64–67. For a survey of tracts
against the Saracens, cf. Avery Dulles, *A History of Apologetics*, pp. 72–76, 81–82, 94–
98, 106–109.

[61]Cf. *ScG*, I, 2, *Simul autem.*

to claim superiority over paganism on the sole ground of a superiority claimed on the basis of rational argument. Christianity's self-defense had to be frankly confessional. It could not disguise its partiality.

Aquinas was the first to depart from this. But even in his apologetics the exercise of the powers of natural reason remained firmly set in the context of the Christian faith. A quick reading of the opening chapters of the *Summa contra Gentiles* will show this without a doubt.

After pointing out that it is the task of the wise person to pursue the truth, which is the intellect's very own good as well as both the origin and the end of the universe, Thomas goes on to speak about this intellectual enterprise in unequivocally religious terms.

> Therefore we derive from the divine goodness the confidence it takes to exercise the task of the wise person, even though it exceeds our own ability, and we propose, for our limited part, to expound the truth professed by the Catholic faith, while removing errors opposed to it.[62]

Thomas goes on to point out that it is difficult to refute the errors of individual opponents, for two reasons. First, unlike the ancient *doctores*, we do not have the advantage of immediate familiarity with the "blasphemous utterances of those in error," so that we cannot refute them by an analysis of their own words. Second, arguments from Scripture do not carry any weight with some of the opponents, like the Mohammedans and the pagans. And Thomas concludes:

> Hence, it is necessary to have recourse to natural reason, to which nobody can refuse his assent. However, [the disadvantage is that natural reason] does not measure up to matters of faith.[63]

After this candid admission it comes as no surprise that the entire fourth book of the *Summa contra Gentiles* is devoted to matters which God, "out of his superabundant goodness," has "revealed about himself" in order that "man might know God more firmly."

---

[62]*Ibid.*, *Assumpta igitur.*
[63]*Ibid.*, *Contra singulorum.*

These are the matters that "surpass the human intellect."[64]

The *Summa contra Gentiles* represents the start of a tradition of apologetics, in which the exercise of natural reason was *at once* firmly set in the context of revelation and well distinguished from it. It was to continue till the early part of the eighteenth century, when Bishop Joseph Butler wrote his *Analogy of Religion*. For all its differences with the ancient *apologiae*, the tradition just explored had this in common with them, that the Christian confession remained the setting of all the arguments, including those based on natural reason.

The cultural shift to objectivity

The shift which we have come to associate with the late seventeenth and eighteenth centuries led to a reversal of this relationship.[65] The period witnessed the disestablishment of Christianity as the intellectual milieu governing the presuppositions of thought. Increasingly, the normative conception of truth became universalist and conceptual, and the normative conception of the expression of truth become definitionist and propositionist. Thus, the deliverances of the faith were summoned before the tribunal of reason and challenged to answer for themselves on (allegedly) purely rational, logical terms.[66]

At the same time, pure reason's estranged relative,[67] historical objectivity, was producing a different conception of history. The search for historical factuality became paramount, and hence designations like "B.C." and "A.D." became purely chronological devices without any interpretative status—replaceable, as a matter of principle, by other, perhaps more significant historical reference-points, let us say the year 1789. Time became (allegedly) a purely neutral continuum. As the normative conception of history became more and more objectivist, the Christian story was, with increasing insistence, summoned before the tribunal of historical criticism, and

---

[64]*Ibid.*, IV, 1, *Quia igitur.*

[65]For a good brief account of the shift, cf. David E. Jenkins, *Guide to the Debate About God*, pp. 21–55, with this reservation, that the importance of Immanuel Kant is insufficiently stressed.

[66]Cf. the long quotation from Bonhoeffer, above, pp. 248.

[67]Cf. Lessing's *dictum:* "Accidental truths of history can never become the proof of necessary truths of reason." Cf. also above, pp. 53–54, 221.

it did not take long before it was exposed as a tale of good moral example at best, and as an historical hoax at worst.

Rationalism and historicism in apologetics

We can now say, with the advantage of hindsight, that at this point the theological defense of the Christian faith made the capital mistake of endorsing the stance adopted by the new intellectual powers. On the one hand, a massively historicist apologetic came to be elaborated to counter the historicism of the culture. Quite apart from the theological distortions this process led to, the move was the beginning of a losing battle, since the arguments for the faith had to be fetched farther and farther away, as the opponents' attacks on the facts at the basis of Christianity became more sophisticated, though also very often more immoderate and even downright hostile.[68] On the other hand, an overly rationalist apologetic came to be elaborated, based on the thesis that the human mind has the innate capacity to know the truth, including the essential truths at the basis of all religion. Among the latter, the following held pride of place: God's existence and his main attributes, the creation, the natural moral law, the divine origin of the Mosaic and Christian revelations, the historical existence of Jesus Christ, and the truth of the Christian religion as attested by prophecies and miracles, knowable as supernatural occurrences. By this emphasizing the mind's ability to know—to be justified much later by means of a mistaken appeal to Aquinas' theory about the *praeambula fidei*—it was thought that the battle against the proponents of the total autonomy of reason could be brought to a victorious conclusion.[69] Needless to say, the effort

---

[68]For a pointed analysis of the dimensions of the historicist problem, followed by an eloquent plea for confessional apologetics, cf. Avery Dulles, *Apologetics and the Biblical Christ*, Westminster, Newman Press, 1963.

[69]For a statement of this tradition, cf. the encyclical *Humani Generis, Acta Apostolicae Sedis* 42 (1950) 561–578, esp. 571–573 (DS 3892–3894; there is an English translation: [Pius XII], *The Encyclical "Humani Generis,"* with a Commentary, A. C. Cotter [ed.], Weston 93, Mass., Weston College Press, 1951; reference pp. 28–34).— For Aquinas' *Summa contra Gentiles* and the questions it raises, cf. Avery Dulles, *A History of Apologetics*, pp. 87–94, and esp. the most important footnote on the *praeambula fidei* ("the preliminaries to the faith") on p. 93. Cf. also M.-D. Chenu, "Vérité évangélique et métaphysique wolffienne à Vatican II."—Cf. also, interestingly, the sequence of the *Index systematicus* in Denzinger-Schönmetzer, which now merely serves the purpose of classification, but which still reflects the structure of the

foundered, because of the underlying endorsement of the rationalist stance. The Wolffian contention that the credibility of the Christian faith was an independently defensible thesis led to the thesis that Christianity was but one of many concretizations of general natural religion. The claim to revelation was easily dismissed; revelation had come to be understood as involving a small number of revealed additions to a solid body of essential natural-reason truths; such an extrinsicist revelation could be dispensed with.

One of the results of the historicist and rationalist stance in apologetics in the Catholic Church was an inordinate emphasis on the authority of the *magisterium* as the only way to hold together the thesis of the mind's adequacy to know the credibility of the faith on the one hand, and the thesis of the necessity of a revelation that transcends natural reason on the other. This invocation of authority to hold together rationalism and fideism, autonomy and heteronomy, pitted the Church's hierarchy against the secular culture in a deadly battle for the loyalty of the faithful. Accusations of priestcraft and obscurantism were countered by accusations of laicism and intellectual pride, thus allowing the common assumption of both parties to go undetected. This assumption was that objective fact historically established and necessary truth propositionally defined establish incontrovertible premises in matters of faith. Never did it seem to occur to either party that personalist and valuational[70] concerns were the necessary substructure of their respective theses. Thus Christians feared that, should they give up their historicist and rationalist power-apologetics, the only alternative would be a spineless compliance with the demands of the culture. They feared that it would lead to an historicist reduction of the faith to an ethic exemplified in Jesus, or to an idealist reduction of the faith to a mythical version of natural religion. The two dangers were real enough, but what the Christian world realized insufficiently was that there was an alternative to both the apologetics of power and the apologetics of submission. That alternative is a confessional apologetics firmly grounded in the Spirited *homologia* prompted by the Resurrection, and thus an

---

theological system of argument of most late nineteenth- and early twentieth-century Roman Catholic theological manuals. The *Index* reminds one of a fortress now turned into a harmless, and even interesting museum.

[70]Avery Dulles, *Apologetics and the Biblical Christ*, pp. 40–43.

apologetics that is carefree and unworried, in advance, about its own power to convince, persuade, or compel the powers that be.

Persuasiveness not based on power

Christianity must not base its credibility on the assumption that it can be argued with a power and cogency to match the (real or alleged) power and cogency of a culture's tenets. This applies in a very special way to the Resurrection. Given its crucial relevance to the Christian confession, any massively historical interpretation of the Resurrection as an objectively recognizable miracle proving the truth of the Christian faith beyond the shadow of a doubt is unacceptable. It is the religious, redemptive significance of the Resurrection that must provide the basis for Christian apologetics, not the other way around.[71]

This leads to a problem. Apologetics is about defense and persuasion. If the Resurrection of Christ is the source of the Christian confession, and if it can only be accepted by faith, how, then, can a system of apologetics be constructed that is at once unabashedly confessional—because totally dependent on the Resurrection—and truly persuasive to secular persons and secular establishments?

It could be argued that the faith of the witnesses to the Resurrection, especially shown in their willingness to put up with accusations of blasphemy and folly,[72] and even with death, is the clinching argument of apologetics. It is true, the joyous endurance of such accusations and the perseverance of Christian martyrs have, as a matter of fact, been known to lead to conversions. Still, from the point of view of apologetics, it is hard to distinguish between a martyr and a deluded fanatic; it is the task of the defense of the Christian faith to present the *convictions* of people considered blasphemers and fools as credible and persuasive. Christian martyrdom is a defense of the Christian faith only in a confessional sense; it carries no persuasiveness readily understandable to the powers that be.

We must, therefore, attempt a different approach. On the one hand, the confessional nature of the Christian faith forbids the

---

[71]Cf. *ibid.*, pp. 56–59.
[72]In view of Mk 3, 21–22.

establishment of power-apologetics; on the other hand, the need for persuasiveness demands that Christianity give an account of itself in terms that are understandable to the prevailing culture.

Patient understanding

The solution of our problem must be that Christian apologetics must not let itself be impressed by the *dominance* of the prevailing concerns *as such*, either by being cowed into self-defense, or by being pulled into an alliance. If the Church had to rely on worldly power for her assurance and maintenance, she would naturally have to take such a defensive or collusionary interest in powerful ideas and causes and concerns. But since the risen Christ is the source of the Church's assurance, Christian apologetics can afford to take an interest in the prevailing cultural concerns, not because they are powerful, but because they are *concerns*.[73] This interest will take the shape of an empathetic, appreciative stance with respect to all ideas and concerns and establishments that present themselves with claims to authority dominance, and even finality. In this way, the hope generated by the Resurrection will inspire the Church to develop a style of apologetics primarily characterized by open-mindedness, suspense of judgment, and an attitude of sympathy with the concerns of the culture. There are three aspects to this.

First, Christian apologetics must demonstrate—sometimes directly, but very often merely indirectly—a compassionate understanding of *the human process by which* certain concerns and ideas maintain, or attain, dominance. The cultural powers that be are always somewhat unsettled; they are always anxious; for all their ostensible assurance, they know they have feet of clay. Just as overstatements often mask a person's lack of knowledge and his subliminal need for assurance, so the cultural powers that be often assert themselves as the final tribunal of taste, truth, value, and action, because they are afraid of their own limitations. This applies, not only to countercultural trends and novel discoveries, which always arouse so much excitement and exhibit so much nervousness, and whose claims to finality are often so raucously made; it also applies to settled establishments, which are always aware of their

---

[73]For a clarification of this term, cf. above, p. 122, and note 31.

own incompleteness, and of the restlessness ever at work to unsettle them. The rash affirmations and the overbearing posture of all powers that be, whether they are established or novel, are always due to an underlying fear of embarrassing questions and the threat of a takeover. In this way, the powers that be are witnesses to humanity's craving for assurance. They offer stability, but never without the threat of disturbance; in fact, the very fact that they present themselves with such aplomb and self-assurance drives home the realization that they will not last.

A truly Christian apologetics will realize the pathos underlying all establishments, and fundamentally refuse to become a party to claims to power and finality. Absolved from the need for self-affirmation, Christian apologetics can afford to take a compassionate interest in the people that have become the willing or reluctant subjects of self-appointed powers and authorities. This, therefore, *is* a reason why apologetics must take an interest in dominant concerns: they shape people and their societies, and in doing so they inevitably both build up and abridge humanity. It must be a central concern of apologetics to show that the Church's main interest is not in what happens to be the going concern, but in the roots of its dominance, and especially in its influence on people.

A second aspect of Christian apologetics is closely connected with this. Precisely because the Church need not be a party to the scuffle for ascendancy, she can direct her attention to a true understanding of the concerns that shape humanity. Understood in this way (and not as a strategic expedient to attain influence), Christian humanism is nothing but an exercise of the essential Christian mission, not to conquer, but to understand and love the world, in patience and appreciative hospitality. The history of Christianity shows many examples of true understanding extended to the culture, especially in the area of the humanities and the arts; the profound understanding of human nature which Christianity has shown itself capable of has been a most persuasive apologia for the Christian confession. The Church's record of understanding the concerns that animate the natural and social sciences is far less impressive;[74] all too

---

[74] Cf. David Jenkins' words, above, pp. 190–191. This should also be applied to communism; Christianity tends to focus far too much on the atheism of dialectical materialism, and not enough on the concerns represented by it.

often these have met with a Christian establishment trying to discredit them. In the case of the natural sciences and history, such efforts have become quite quixotic. Scientism and historicism are both abandoned; science and history are far more modest now than they were even forty years ago; a valuational attitude to facts is no longer taken to be a mark of ignorance or religious prejudice.[75] The way of patient understanding and suspense of judgment is no longer at odds with the best of human wisdom.

The same cannot be said for much of modern social science and psychology—both of them often so adept at playing the trump-card of "professional expertise," and so eager to regard the social and psychological construction of reality as final. Still, Christianity should not engage in a crusade against these trends. What, then, should be done? This leads to the third point to be made about Christian apologetics.

Patient, empathetic, and hospitable understanding makes heavy demands, not only on the Christian practicing apologetics, but also on the powers that be. The Christian may find himself tempted to become defensive when faced with intolerance, rash judgment, and prejudice; instead, he will have to become patient and hospitable, even to somewhat raucous guests. But this does not in the least imply that he will have to become harmless and gullible. The patient person who wants to understand is a demanding, and even an infuriating, questioner. In its determination to understand, sound Christian apologetics presents the powers that be with a formidable test—a test made more, not less, demanding by the patient and gentle style of inquiry. The failure of the power-apologetics of the past was to a large extent due to the fact that Christians were giving answers long before they could afford to stop asking questions.

Only an open mind—and a mind not afraid of its own open-

---

[75]The lack of modesty in Francis Crick's *Of Molecules and Men* (Seattle and London, University of Washington Press, 1966), pp. 84–99, now strikes one as somewhat comical and old-fashioned. By way of comparison, cf. the appreciative words by Sir Julian Huxley (one of Crick's predecessors in the John Danz Lectures, and a person whose pedigree of scientific atheism is rather impressive) in his introduction to Pierre Teilhard de Chardin, *The Phenomenon of Man*, pp. 11–28, esp. 26–28. On Crick's modesty, cf. the opening sentences of the book by Crick's fellow Nobel Prize winner James D. Watson, *The Double Helix*, New York, New American Library (1969).

ness—can be so patient in its approach to reality. The cultural powers that be are so insistent on absolute ideas because they are so anxiously dependent on intellectual self-assertion that they feel they have to foreclose the discussion. Christian apologetics need not operate that way. Its experience of the mind's power to know is the experience of reason enlightened by the kindly light of faith— industrious, sober, and godly.[76] It need not base itself on the mind's power to know understood as the possession of "unshakable meta-physical principles," "principles of themselves known to the human mind," "principles and concepts drawn from true knowledge of created things."[77] The mind's power to know can be quietly affirmed and demonstrated in the patient practice of understanding, precisely because the Christian's security and identity does not depend on it. Neither need Christian apologetics base itself on facts, if, that is, "facts" means events whose divine origin can be unequivocally proven by an incontrovertible demonstration of their supernatural character. The true power of Christian apologetics lies in its empa-thetic attitude to the concerns of the culture—an attitude inspired by the assurance that comes from the risen One, and warranted by the Christian conviction that all concerns can be integrated into the sacrifice of praise and thanksgiving. In this way, apologetics will share in the *imitatio Christi*, bid farewell to triumphalism, and defend the faith by sympathetic and questioning confrontation with the cultural establishment.

The test: hospitality to countervailing tendencies

What entitles dominant concerns to a sympathetic Christian hearing, we argued, is the fact that they are concerns, not that they are dominant. At least, the only reason why apologetics must take an interest in dominant concerns is the uncritical subjection proffered to

---

[76]Cf. DS 3016, taken from the dogmatic constitution *Dei Filius* of the First Vatican Council; cf. Tit 2, 12.—The fundamental openness of reason discovered in the light of faith is the basis of much of modern apologetics; cf., for example, art. "Immanenzapologetik," in: *Lexicon für Theologie und Kirche*, 1960, and Avery Dulles, *A History of Apologetics*, pp. 202–221. For a contemporary (and somewhat one-sided) restatement of this type of "threshold apologetics" (*apologétique du seuil*) by means of the "immanence method" (*méthode d'immanence*), cf. Gregory Baum, *Man Becoming*, esp. pp. 1–60.

[77]Cf. *Humani Generis*, DS 3892, 3893, 3883.

them by so many; the unaware must find an ally, so the alarum may have to be raised! This all implies that the true test of the seriousness of Christian apologetics is its ability to do justice, not only to the dominant concerns of the culture, but also to its countervailing tendencies. If apologetics were to reckon only with the intellectual and cultural powers that be, with their uncanny establishmentarian tendency to present themselves as the obvious and only thinkable, objective truth—might is right!—might it not be said that apologetics is only interested in power after all?

Hence, just as the martyr has the world's sufferers as his special constituency, so apologetics must find its special allies in all those concerns not covered by the protection of the establishment; concerns whose representatives cannot rely on any sense of obvious appropriateness; concerns frankly based on partial commitments; concerns represented by people who realize that odd attitudes have an essential role to play when it comes to establishing the truth.[78] Christianity owes it to its very nature as "the Way"[79] to take a dim view of all claims to finality, timelessness, ultimacy, and self-evidence whenever truths or interests or priorities are declared. Citizenship in the holy city and membership in God's household, far from making the Christian into an establishmentarian, are meant as an encouragement to persevere in the insecure position of aliens and exiles.[80] This imposes a special burden on the defense of the Christian faith: Christians are especially called to extend hospitality to those concerns (and to their representatives) which share the Christian community's own position of insecurity.

Might it not be said that the Church could have unmasked the rationalist claims a bit more quickly, if she herself had been less interested in defending the eternal validity of her own tenets? Seen in an historical perspective (and Christianity, of its very nature, must view things in that perspective!) claims to timeless truth and ultimate

---

[78]To give an example, Leslie Dewart (*The Future of Belief*, New York, Herder and Herder, 1966, pp. 52–76) has well shown that Christianity, as a "relative theism," has a natural affinity with "relative atheism"; the Christian discussion with atheism, therefore, need not be an exercise in pitting one dogmatism against another; it can be a dialogue between two *commitments* that share a common assumption, namely, that relational issues lie at the basis of their opposing faiths.

[79]Acts 9, 2; 19, 9. 23; 22, 4; 24, 14. 22; cf. 18, 25–26.

[80]Cf. Eph 2, 19; Heb 11, 13–16; 1 Pet 2, 11.

meaning have themselves turned out to be nothing but a transitory historical phenomenon—part of that phase of history (let us say, from about 1700 to 1914) when the basic significance of partial concerns and commitments for the discovery and formulation of truth went unrecognized. Unhistorical thinking, it is now clear, is part of history.

The Church does indeed have claims to timelessness and ultimacy to make, but they are a matter of eschatological assurance, not of self-constituted certainty. And, as we have argued, the test of the Church's assurance of timeless and ultimate truth is her ability to be empathetically involved with the innumerable partial concerns of this world, treating all things with the understanding they deserve, and refusing to be dominated by anything. Nowhere is this attitude of empathetic understanding better conveyed and more fruitfully practiced than in encounters with the particular, the provisional, the partial. For "things counter, original, spare, strange"[81] resist quick integration into comprehensive systems and categories. What more powerful *and* vulnerable critics of monolithic ideologies than particular things and particular persons?[82]

Hence, thought-systems and voluntary action-groups with strong partial commitments—mostly expressed by telling, often irritating discernments and metaphors—ought to evoke the Christian's empathetic response, or at least his sincere interest: movements to protect the environment; to stress the human side of the enterprise; to accord a fair share to women and other minorities; to raise the critical consciousness of the consumer; to criticize monopolies (one might think of the medico-technological establishment, the big private or state-run broadcasting systems, etc.); to do justice to the marginal, especially the elderly and the unborn, the not-quite-dead and the not-quite-alive; to change the global food-distribution system in order to give the hungry a fair share; to lift the faceless out of degradation by a pedagogy of the oppressed; to keep on denouncing the fallacy of an arms-race to insure a lasting peace; and a host of others, too many to mention.

To call such movements prejudiced is at once to state the

---

[81]Gerard Manley Hopkins, "Pied Beauty," *Poems*, pp. 69–70; quotation p. 70.
[82]Cf. Frans Jozef van Beeck, "Hopkins: Cor ad Cor."

obvious and to distort them. They are prejudiced inasmuch as they embody a partial concern, and one that is unrecognized by the establishment to boot; no wonder that such a concern strikes one as sectarian, crazy, and prejudiced. In addition, the very partiality of these concerns opens them wide to the kind of benign neglect that consists in pointing out that there are other, more important, "more universal" matters to attend to. Thus the invocation of the more universal good becomes the means to silence outcries as well as the tranquilizer of the establishment, always so defensive, so easily made nervous by the particular, and oh so enamored of painting the large canvas with a broad brush and calling it the common good. Only a truly compassionate attitude will prevent the Church from thus discriminating against minorities and their powerless concerns.

We should stress that Christianity should feel an affinity with the above-mentioned groups and movements simply because they are committed to particular concerns. The mere fact of the commitment justifies the Christian's interest and participation; *how* the commitments are presented or what degree of relative importance is attributed to them is entirely secondary. Very often commitment-groups will show a tendency to get even with the established order by presenting their central commitment as a counter-ideology. What started as a true concern may become a doctrinaire ideology, and what started as a commitment-group may become an authoritarian sect, whose tenets are completely at odds, not only with the culture, but also with Christian faith and doctrine. In such a situation it is very tempting for the Church to forget that she herself is originally a commitment-group, too, and that she, too, lives out of a very particular commitment. When the Church becomes forgetful in this way, she will start to compete with such ideological commitment-groups at the ideological level, pitting cause against cause and tenet against tenet. When this happens, Christian doctrine once again becomes an ideology associated with an intolerant cause—the kind of cause that will push itself by hook or by crook, forever denouncing the errors of others and mistaking denunciation for teaching.

Christian apologetics has a different vocation. It must regain its ability, so magnificently demonstrated by Aquinas, to speak the language of secular reason inspired, not by the urge to display power, but by an appreciative and questioning empathy with the world. This empathy, in turn, is derived from the assurance that comes from the risen Christ. It may not always be possible or advisable in our own day to witness to that assurance aloud;[83] the empathy itself can be practiced. But, then again, in our day, in a world that has witnessed the devastating havoc wreaked by the alliance between dispassionate science and absolute creeds, quite a few people may again be prepared to listen to the overt profession of the Christian commitment, partial and particular though it is.

ETHICS:
SYMPATHY WITH THE NATURE OF THINGS

Introductory

In the previous section we were already moving away from an exclusive concern with apologetics; in fact, we touched on a number of questions that are roundly ethical. We are, therefore, prepared for a brief discussion of patience as the basis of Christian ethics.

We have argued that those who respond to the risen Lord in worship and hope will be obedient to the Father's will in the *imitatio Christi*; they will be ready to suffer and to be compassionate. By suffering and compassion they will be open to every person and every concern, and find God in everything; patience and a single eye will discover the ground of each being. Thus they will do justice, in patience and hospitality, in the assurance that every concern and every person, once welcomed into the Church, can be converted to the living Christ, be disarmed by him, discover that self-assertiveness can be dropped, and that the turn to obedience is not a defeat. The sole moving force of this entire process of assumption is the living Lord, drawing his chosen into a carefree devotion to the world, for which the only sufficient argument is the witnessing confession: "The love of Christ leaves us no rest."[84]

If, therefore, we are to understand the specific difference of Christian ethics, we must be careful not to launch immediately into the question whether there are specifically Christian values opposed to, or at least distinct from, natural or rational morality. Such

---

[83]Cf. Karl Rahner's words, above, pp. 39–40.
[84]2 Cor 5, 14.

specifically Christian values may or may not turn out to exist; what is certain is that there is a specifically Christian motivation, resulting in a specifically Christian attitude, in ethical matters. The brief remarks about to be made here are meant only to discuss this foundational point.

Christian ethics, like all of Christian life, must be christological, and Christian ethics must give evidence of this in its very structure; it clearly will not do to limit the Christian part of Christian ethics to the theological virtues and to the thesis that grace is absolutely necessary to do anything good. Hence, Christian ethics must show that it is called forth by the Resurrection. It must show how it consists in the imitation of Christ. It must show how the *imitatio Christi* causes Christians to do justice to the very nature of reality.

The Christian motivation and attitude

What is the specifically Christian motivation for ethical action? The answer to this question must be that it is the *homologia*—the confessional sacrifice of praise and thanksgiving to the Father, for the sake of the living Lord who has overcome sin and death, and whose gift of the Spirit is the forgiveness of all sins. Christian ethics, therefore, does not have the restoration of a good world for its ultimate objective; it *starts* with the forgiveness of sins. The passionate desire for the knowledge of good and evil is not the root of Christian ethics, neither is any alleged human ability to judge what is right and what is wrong, and why, and under what circumstances. Irresponsible though this may seem at first, the basic Christian ethical vocation does not consist in getting involved in the struggle to determine what a just world looks like, and then to help build it; Christian ethics starts with the Christian casting all his worries, including those about his own righteousness, upon the Lord,[85] and entrusting himself to his merciful judgment.

This leads to the first characteristic of the Christian ethical attitude—the characteristic that must most reflect the reality of Christ's Resurrection. The Christian is called to a moral life out of *freedom*; he is not primarily concerned with his duties, and in that sense with himself. His first ethical priority is not to determine

---

[85]Cf. 1 Pet 5, 7.

whether his own moral choices are correct, nor how others judge his own moral choices,[86] nor whether others' moral choices in his own regard and in regard to other persons and things are correct. Rather, the Christian who has cast his ethical worries on the Lord can afford to take the part of others, persons as well as things, and care whether justice is done to them the way he himself would like to be done justice to.[87] Seen in this perspective, it is not surprising that Christianity should always have felt a strong affinity to natural-law ethics; Christian moral thinking is predicated on the selfless conviction that reality out-there, not the agent's own interest in righteousness, is the norm for morality.[88]

The second characteristic of the Christian ethical attitude is its quality of *sympathy*—the characteristic that must most reflect the *imitatio Christi*. We have argued that freedom is the inspiration behind Christian natural-law ethics; far from being incidental to Christian ethics, freedom is its foundation. It is out of this freedom that the Christian is called to be objective; but the objectivity which Christian ethics calls for is the objectivity of love—appreciative, empathetic openness to reality. This requires an attitude of receptiveness, a pathic stance, a caring relatedness to the world.

This leads to the third characteristic, in which the *realism* of Christian ethics becomes most prominent. Christian moral judgment, we just argued, is informed by persons and things outside the moral agent. Not what the agent can do, or is prepared to do, with or for or to other things and persons, but what other things and persons require is the norm for Christian morality.[89] It is not Christian, therefore, to bend other things and persons to uses contrary to their nature, not even for the noblest of motives; it is Christian to sympathize with other persons and things and to take their part when they

---

[86]Cf. 1 Cor 4, 3–4.

[87]The golden rule of Mt 7, 12, par. Lk 6, 31, where it is set in the context of the love of enemies.

[88]The connection between a being's inner reality, its operations, its finalities, and its instrumentality in relation to God is a fundamental feature of Aquinas' thought. Cf., for example, *S. Th.* I, q. 29, a. 1, ad 4; I–II, q. 1, a. 2, *in corp.*; q. 6, a. 1, ad 3; *ScG* III, 2; 3.

[89]Cf., for example, Rom 15, 1–3; 1 Cor 8, 7–12; 10, 25–29.

are mistreated, even if these other things and persons are not blameless themselves.

All this can be summed up in the evangelical injunction not to judge.[90] The primary use of conscience in Christian ethics is not in the service of the moral agent's own satisfaction, whether this should consist in determining his own righteousness or in determining the righteousness of others. The primary use of conscience is in putting it at the service of other things and persons, by determining whether they are treated as they by nature deserve to be treated. There remains, of course, a Christian obligation to examine, and even to judge, oneself; and in the Church there is a duty to judge also.[91] Still, what elicits these particular judgments is not a fascination with what is right and wrong, but the good of others. Fundamentally, the Christian has been freed from the concern with his own conscience as a way to determine where he, and others, stand with God. This freedom allows him to be compassionate and to ask the question whether others, persons as well as things, have been done justice to. Bonhoeffer summed this up in the thesis that deputyship and correspondence with reality form the essential shape of the Christian obligation; the Christian is called to be the guarantor of the other person's (or thing's) very reality, in virtue of Christ's universal deputyship.[92]

Natural-law ethics, situationism, and judgment

If natural-law ethics is not set in the context of freedom and compassion, it tends to become an exercise of human reason's autonomous powers of construction. The result is invariably a natural-law ethics which is more interested in prescribing, judging, and condemning (that is, in including and excluding) than in sympathy and understanding (that is, in reconciliation). Even if such an ethics succeeds in avoiding downright fanaticism, it can hardly ever avoid being impatient and authoritarian. While extolling human freedom, its presentation of the natural law is usually so objective, and its identification of moral goodness with obedience to objective de-

---

[90] Mt 7, 1.
[91] For examples, cf. 1 Cor 5, 1–5; 6, 1–6; Mt 18, 15–18.
[92] Cf. *Ethics*, pp. 224–235.

mands so complete, that human freedom becomes something hardly more than the physical possibility to make choices in matters in which there is, morally speaking, very little choice. In order to be human and practical, therefore, such an "immobilist" system of prescriptive ethics must develop ways to tolerate, and even to justify, deviant behavior. It is at this point that norms like the principle of double effect arise, in order to make room for discretionary judgment where the objective norms are insufficient to deal with the complexity of the situation. Other examples of ways to deal with deviance are cases in which a moral agent pleads extenuating circumstances in virtue of his own diminished awareness, consent, or freedom, and cases in which competent authority issues dispensations from the rigor of the norm, or even condones objectively unethical behavior in the interest of the common good. In this way, a system of objective natural-law ethics generates a system of subjective appeals to justify departure from the norm.

This creates a very ambiguous situation. Subjective authority, either on the part of the moral agent who appeals to his conscience, or on the part of authorities appealing to their authority, is given a decisive role, pitted against the otherwise unquestionable validity of the objective system. No wonder, then, that the very immobility of the objectivist natural-law ethics, which requires that great authority be accorded to subjective judgment to make the system humane and practical, has produced a system of pure situationism, in which love becomes the sole moral norm, and personal decision, not natural law, determines what is moral and what is not.

Legalism and *anomia*, uptightness and permissiveness, tend to perceive each other as each other's opponents. Legalists perceive themselves as responsible agents in a world whose very structure calls for order. Situationists perceive themselves as responsible agents in a world whose continuous flux calls for personal integrity. Both legalists and situationists have appealed to Christianity for obvious reasons, and Christian ethicists themselves have espoused both approaches. After all, both the idea of the God-given law and the idea of love have excellent credentials in Christian thought. The problem is hard to solve, but since legalism and situationism are dependent upon each other to be practical, we may surmise that they are based on a common assumption. Hence, we must detect this assumption and subject it to a Christian critique.

In both systems the chief concern is with reliable, authoritative norms. Both approaches are chiefly interested in authoritatively stating obligations, making judgments, and seeking justifications for moral decisions. The principal *use* of these statements, judgments, and justifications is to enable a person *to judge himself and his behavior* and *to judge others and their behavior*. The factual use to which both types of ethics are put, therefore, is authoritative justification and condemnation of self and others. It makes little difference whether a person is a conservative living by an objectivist natural-law ethic and looking upon situationist ethics as dangerous and irresponsible, self-serving subjectivism, or a liberal living by an existentialist decision ethic and looking upon natural-law ethics as dangerous and self-serving Pharisaism that shirks personal decision. Both assume the primacy of judgment in ethics, and both lead to self-righteousness.

Obligation, freedom, and compassion in Christian ethics

Now it is at this point that Christian ethics must become the critic of authoritative natural-law ethics as well as authoritative situationism. Christian ethics is not primarily interested in prescription to, and judgment of, self and others, but in sympathetic understanding. This means, on the one hand, that *the structure of reality*, or natural law, must never turn into an immobile, tyrannical demand to which the good person must defer in the interest of his moral standing. The Christian, called "to judge angels," does not become a slave to objectivity; he views reality as a never quite fathomable, never-ending call to caring and responsible deputyship; this involves a growing awareness of the complexity of life and its potentialities, and thus also a growing awareness of the imperfection of one's own moral sense in dealing with reality as a truly free person. On the other hand, the Christian does not become the tyrannical master of reality either; the *individual conscience* must never become the sovereign, final source of ethical authority; the Christian is never satisfied that he has done complete justice. In this way, the Christian is free enough to be able to entertain the realization of his own sinfulness *and* free enough to venture decisions without having to claim that he is right. Dietrich Bonhoeffer has summed this up in an admirable phrase. He writes:

> The obligation assumes the form of deputyship and of correspondence with reality; freedom displays itself in the self-examination of life and of action and in the venture of a concrete decision.[93]

Not devotion to law and authority, but freedom and compassion are the basic ingredients of Christian ethics. In this respect, Christian ethics is only following him who did not come as God's judgment on the world, but as God's agent of the world's salvation, and who threatened others with judgment only to the extent that they themselves judged others.[94] For God's perfection is manifested, not in judgment, but in compassion; not judgment of sin, but the welcome extended to the sinner is the heart of Christian ethics.

From this, a final consequence follows. Norms, decisions, discussions, judgments, and guidelines, whether of the legalist or the situationist kind, tend to divorce their practitioners from the actual encounter with the self-righteous and the sinners in the real situations of everyday life; wherever this happens we can be sure that Christian ethics has lost touch with Christ. For the identification of freedom and compassion as the basic attitudes of Christian ethics makes sense only to the extent that they inform the practice of the Christian life. A church that preaches morality and advocates moral decisions without involving itself in this most distinctive *and* disturbing aspect of the imitation of Christ is involving itself in *gnosis* at the expense of *agapē*.

PATIENT CHRISTOLOGY

Retrospect and outlook

In the previous three sections we explored ways in which patience and hospitality are basic ingredients of the Christian's dealing with the world in the *imitatio Christo*. We discussed the "pathic"

---

[93]*Ibid.*, p. 224.

[94]Cf. Jn 3, 17 (*ho theos* is the subject of *krinēi*; *sōthēi*, which stands in parallelism with *krinēi*, must be read as a divine passive); Mt 7, 1–2.

nature of the Christian witness as applied, respectively, to martyrdom, to the defense of the Christian faith, and to Christian ethics.

It is time now to turn to christology itself, and to ask ourselves the question of how the imitation of Christ applies to it—how it, too, must be marked by patience and hospitality. It is a long time since we first mentioned patience as a characteristic of the practice of christology.[95] We are now at last in a position to discuss the ways in which it must do its share in the patient process of the assumption of all of humanity into the person of Christ.

Christology: imitatio Christi in response to the risen Lord

The practice of christology is one of the activities of the Church; it is not autonomous; it must confront the demands made by the Church's identity.

In the first place, christology must give evidence of an abiding responsiveness to, and dependence upon, the risen One. This realization has already informed many of our discussions. Thus we formulated the ground-rule that no discernment or insight in christology may be allowed to qualify the Resurrection.[96] We based this rule on the recognition that only the Christian's total surrender in the *actus directus* of faith, conveyed by the *act* of speaking in the Holy Spirit, does justice to the Resurrection. Since this act of speaking is the setting of all christological discernments, the Resurrection of Christ turns out to be the *a priori* condition for the possibility of all christology, never to be robbed of its pride of place by subsequent discernments.[97] By observing this ground-rule, therefore, christology must, in its own way, pay tribute to the risen Lord.[98]

But christology must also show its dependence on the *imitatio Christi*; in this way, too, it must show that it does not dodge the

---

[95]Above, p. 104.

[96]Above, p. 253.

[97]Above, pp. 195–196, 249–251.

[98]Hans Frei explicitly recognizes the worship dimension of theology: "By and large, then, reflection about the presence of Christ is, for the believer, a pleasurable exercise in arranging or, as I should prefer to say, ordering his thinking about his faith and—in a certain sense—a praise of God by the use of the analytical capacities" (*The Identity of Jesus Christ*, p. 5). The reviewer—I seem to recall he was British—who called this fideism was out of touch with the first calling of all Christian activity.

scandal of the Incarnation.[99] Let us elaborate this by developing our ground-rule somewhat.

We must start by recalling two points made before. First, the identity of Jesus Christ as manifested by the Father in the Resurrection entails the assumption of all of humanity into Christ's person. Second, this assumption is the work, not of power, but of patience.[100] Now given the abiding presidency of the risen Lord over the Church, the Christian witness to the Resurrection is a permanent feature of the Church's life, including her theological activity. Christology itself does not take place in a christological vacuum; it is continuously based on an abiding act of surrender by which Christians testify to the power of the living Lord.[101] Now in this very act of surrender and witness the Church continues the assumption of all of humanity into the Body of Christ, beyond the limits of any definition. It follows that the abiding presence of the risen One demands that this process continue; but this means that, if christology is to be true to the risen Lord, *no discernment in christology may be in a position to preclude the integration of any new human concern into the christological confession.* The truth of the claim that the Resurrection holds pride of place in christology must be tested by asking the question whether the established discernments in christology are patient of, and even positively hospitable to, new christological discernments. Now discernments, we recall, are representatives of human concerns;[102] established christological discernments, therefore, are the memorials of the Church's thoughtful compassion extended to human concerns in the past. Now it would seem that these established concerns, having once experienced compassion, must be compassionate in their turn; if established christology is hospitable to new discernments, it is merely true to its own tradition. But beyond that, hospitable christology is a sign that the Church is true to her calling by being hospitable to new human concerns— concerns that must also be assumed into the humanity of Christ if the Church is to do justice to the *totus Christus* as well as to all of humanity.

---

[99]Cf. above, p. 61.
[100]Above, p. 467, and the references given there.
[101]Cf. our critique of Pannenberg, above, pp. 314–318.
[102]Cf. above, pp. 135–143.

The story of the life of Jesus and the christological titles

We are now in a position to argue a point made long ago. We stated that there is a connection between the two forms which the invocation of Jesus Christ takes on, namely, titles by which Christians bring themselves and their concerns into the total surrender, and the story of Jesus.[103]

The story of Jesus, we argued, is the shape of the sacrifice of praise and thanksgiving, in which the Church, expressing her responsive identity, offers herself to the Father under invocation of the Name of Jesus. Hence, the story of Jesus conveys the act of surrender evoked by the risen Lord. We also argued that in telling the story of Jesus the Church also commits herself to the *imitatio Christi*, to follow him on her way to the *eschaton*. As the Church follows the Lord, she brings herself, along with the concerns of her members, into the encounter with the living Lord. The *record of this ongoing encounter* is the names and titles of Jesus and the discernments contained in them—the memorials of the process of assumption into the Body of Christ, and of the Church's compassionate hospitality to humanity in the footsteps of her Master. This is entirely in accordance, as we have already pointed out, with the narrative shape of the sacrifice of praise and thanksgiving, which is the story of Jesus' own patient and hospitable taking-on of the human condition. The significance of the names and titles of Jesus, therefore, lies in their being the verification of the Church's commitment to the consequences of her worship. They show to what extent the Church has succeeded in not only saying "Lord, Lord," but also doing the will of the Father, who does not want anything he entrusted to Jesus to get lost.[104]

A tradition of impatience

Now it must be frankly admitted that the tradition of classical christology—unlike the tradition of painting, poetry, sculpture, popular devotion, and much non-Catholic theology in the past two centuries—has been scandalously out of touch with the patience and hospitality demanded of it by the Resurrection. Normative christol-

---

[103]Above, p. 344; cf. pp. 336–337.
[104]Cf. Mt 7, 21; Jn 6, 37–39.

ogy got frozen, and has ever since contented itself with (some) refinement and (much) repetition. It is true that its very intractability and intransigence have had an impact; discontent with the great tradition, for example, has caused the raising of quite a number of important modern christological problems, especially since the mid-eighteenth century. Still, the classical tradition itself has been hardly capable of making room for, let alone welcoming, any significant new answers, ever since the sixth or seventh century. What had started with the Church extending a welcome to Hellenistic power of thought slowly turned into the spectacle of the Church proposing as normative a more and more intolerant christological establishment. Potentially significant christological developments found themselves relegated, first to the realm of devotionality, later to the outer darkness of heterodoxy. Overconcerned with self-maintenance, normative christology lost touch with the Resurrection in two ways; not only did it consistently underplay the importance of the Resurrection in the christological system, it also failed to give evidence of its own reliance on the Resurrection by giving evidence of an awareness of its own provisionality. Under cover of a defense of the divinity of Jesus, the Eternal Word Incarnate, traditional christology often engaged in aggressive self-defense; in insisting on the glory of Jesus, it often involved itself in self-glorification. No wonder, then, that it has become possible, on the part of some of the disenchanted, to speak of "christolatry," and that Christianity has been depicted as an inevitably aggressive and even murderous religion, because it is neurotically committed to the defense of the divinity of a man who did not consider equality with God a matter of snatching, and who died like a lamb, without so much as opening his mouth.[105] Normative christology may sometimes have legitimately functioned as a challenge, to elicit responses from different cultures; more often, alas, it has looked disturbingly similar to an examiner who expects from his students, not insight, let alone originality, but only a correct recital of the words he has in his mind.

No wonder (again) that a christology so impatient (and, it must be added, so jaded; from Leontius on, how little has been left of the passionate struggle for meaning of the third, fourth, and fifth centur-

---

[105]Cf. for example, Mary Daly, *Beyond God the Father*, esp. pp. 69ff..

ies!) had little room, not only for the Resurrection, but also for the earthly life of Jesus, and hence for the systematic connection between worship and ethics. It is rightly said that the quest of the historical Jesus turned out to show mainly the languid face of a nineteenth-century liberal Protestant. It is also rightly said that the failure of the quest provided the first half of the twentieth century with little more than a blank silhouette on which it could project its own socio-political concerns, its own existential resolve, or (worst of all) its own notions about "love." But is all this not largely due to the fact that traditional christology, in regard to both content and style, had long ceased to take an interest in human features? A good case can indeed be made that christology had long betrayed its allegiance to the Resurrection and to the life of Jesus alike. It had traded in the assurance that comes from hope for the impenetrability that comes from complicity with a prestigious thought-system.[106] It had come so to canonize its own notionalist *apatheia* (under invocation of *apatheia* as a divine attribute?[107]) that it could piously, without getting involved in conflict, leave a world caught in misery and violence to its own ethical devices; hence the failure of christology in the first half of this century to recognize theologically the face of the human Jesus when it was there to be seen, and to participate in his passion as it was taking place—in the world's untold sufferings. Seen in this way, does the lack of renewal in christology not bear witness to the official Church's reluctance to relate itself to suffering humanity? Have the Church's teaching offices not for too long shrunk back from involvement in the human struggle for meaning, and preferred the denunciation of the errors of the ideologies produced by the struggle? If Christians had felt freer to take part in the intellectual

---

[106]Cf. Jürgen Moltmann's touching references to Whitehead and Zinzendorf in *The Crucified God*, pp. 250–251, where not only the philosophical concept of God is accused of distorting Christianity, but also the imperial and the moralistic. Cf. also John Coventry's sharp disagreement with the underlying theories of Bernard Lonergan's *The Way to Nicaea*, The Dialectical Development of Trinitarian Theology, Philadelphia, The Westminster Press, 1976; the book implies, wrongly according to Coventry, "that only judgment abiding by the canons of this form of critical realism is true judgment, and therefore orthodox theology"; this is connected with a very partial notion of dogma, namely, that of an intellectual control language, drawn from a particular philosophy of nature, to regulate the profusion of symbolic religious languages. See "Doctrine as Verbal Process," *The Tablet* 231 (1977) 57.

[107]Cf. above, p. 377.

and moral struggles in order to absorb and outsuffer the impact of the confusion of our times, the results would have been as noticeable in christology as they are in the poetry of T. S. Eliot and the painting of Georges Rouault. Wherever Christians trust the assurance held out to them by the risen Lord, they will take on human concerns and lead them, laboriously, in the *imitatio Christi*, into the Father's open arms; the clarifications that come out of this process will show themselves in new christological discernments. Is it necessary to suggest, in the light of this insight, that the courageous attempts of liberal Protestant theology—not to mention the so-called modernists—deserve a more sympathetic treatment at the hands of the doctrinal establishments?[108]

When the Resurrection ceases to be the source and the point of departure of christology, hope ceases to inform it; and when hope ceases to inform christology, the need for present power replaces the memory of the passion, and through such forgetfulness of the way of Jesus the poor and the passionate are forgotten, too. A high christology easily becomes a high and mighty christology, one that functions as the family ideology of a church that wages war, colludes or negotiates with the intellectual powers that be, or ensconces itself in the fortress of past deliverances. Such a christology has lost the way, and the cries of the poor and the suffering and the searching go unheeded.

Defenses of doctrinal impatience

Several attempts have been made to argue why the immobility and the intolerance of classical christology is a positive good. The principal justification is that neo-Chalcedonian christology represents the definitive end-product of a long process of gradual clarification, sanctioned by the authority of the *magisterium*.[109] This reasoning is in reality nothing but an authority-argument, not to be despised on that account, but still open to further questioning.

Of the many substantive defenses of the immobility of classical

---

[108] For a fine example of this, cf. Hamish Swanston's empathetic treatment of Benjamin Jowett, in: *Ideas of Order*, Assen, The Netherlands, Van Gorcum & Comp. B. V., 1974, pp. 133–199.

[109] Cf. the text of the Roman *declaratio*, in note 20 on p. 27 above.

christology we will mention only two, in order to comment on them in the light of our central contention, namely, that christology must show evidence of its being a participation in the *imitatio Christi*, in patience and hospitality.

First, it is often argued that the history of the ecumenical councils must be viewed as a progressive series of doctrinal steps. Nicaea and Constantinople I settled the Trinity, Ephesus, Chalcedon and Constantinople II and III the Incarnation, Nicaea II, the Lateran Councils and Trent the atonement and the sacraments, and, finally, Vatican I and II the Church in its relation to the world. The argument is clear: the immobility of christology must be placed in the context of a wide-ranging overall development. The problem with this solution is not just its narrowly Roman Catholic focus, and its total disregard of the ecumenical situation,[110] also in regard to Eastern orthodoxy. It also ignores the considerable variety of the tradition which the Roman Catholic Church recognizes as her own, and it overlooks the considerable losses which that very tradition has suffered at the hands of her own development. The main problem, however, is that the theory harbors a potentially disastrous implication for the future.

If the history of the Church is read in terms of the development of the classical sequence of the dogmatic tracts, as our theory does, the impression is created that *all* further developments will have to take place *within the purview of the angle firmly and irrevocably set by the initial phases of this wedge-shaped history of doctrinal development.* As long as Christianity *de facto* moved within the developmental angle of Hellenistic and Occidental civilization, this expectation had some plausibility to it, although the so-called "young churches" (and *a fortiori* Judaism[111]) have legitimate cause for complaint about the way in which the "planting" of the Church has been made dependent on the enforcement of Occidental ways. Still, whatever may be said about the past, it is clear that for the future, the

---

[110]Analogous forms of immobilism occur outside the Roman Catholic Church. Cf., for example, the Orthodox view that the first six councils are absolutely normative, and the traditional Protestant canonization of the *sola Scriptura* principle. Ironically, the Lutheran acceptance of the so-called *adiaphora*—"indifferent" things, neither against Scripture nor demanded by it—has led to conservatism: the *adiaphora* don't matter—so don't touch them!

[111]Cf. Robert Schreiter, "Christology in the Jewish-Christian Encounter."

authoritarian, paternalist requirement that new doctrine should be related to the existing doctrinal deposit *by linear development* is not only totally unrealistic, but also unchristian. Rather, the existing tradition of doctrine will have to show that it is capable of becoming a compassionate neighbor to other traditions of thought and sensibility. The question of the Chinese rites may not be allowed to recur. It is not enough for established doctrine to assure others that it can produce, or make room for, doctrinal development that will take them into account and integrate them in the long run; established doctrine itself must develop by going *laterally, out of its way*, to the side of the road, so that its own angle, its own purview, its own capacity for development gets broadened. Such a widening of the tradition's angle of vision *from Nicaea on* will doubtlessly cause some rearrangement of traditional doctrine, but such a rearrangement is consistent with the realization that even the most established and authoritative doctrine remains provisional.[112]

A second justification of the intolerance of doctrine consists in claiming that *propositional* statements of orthodox doctrine (especially those employing concepts derived from the *philosophia perennis* and alleged to be universally applicable and intelligible) must in virtue of their very nature be "hard" and unyielding, and in that sense definitively and universally true. The immobility of doctrine, in this theory, therefore, is given with its definitionary character. What this would mean is that doctrinal truths, which are the memorials of the Church's past hospitality, would of necessity have to betray their origin and harden into purely objective givens; in the propositions as such there would be no room for Christian attitudes.

This conception must be rejected because it places the essential Christian attitudes of thankfulness, humility, patience, and hospitality outside the profession of faith. In this framework of assumptions, the experience of grace would be restricted to the Christian's subjectivity, and show itself only in the modesty with which he professes his faith, in his personal friendliness to unbelievers, and in his willingness to put up with misunderstanding; in the sphere of objec-

---

[112]Or, to put the same thing in terms that recall Rom 11, 17–24, the wild olive-shoot that was once compassionately grafted on to the old, rich olive-tree must not forget that the tree supports it, and not it the tree; God may still cut it off if it becomes too preoccupied with its own excellence.

tivity, however, he would have to be intolerant. The result of this construction is what might be called "fideistic orthodoxy"[113] (or traditionalism), by which is meant a faith which keeps the believer as a person, and the Church as a community, entirely under self-imposed tutelage, incapable of relating present life experience to present faith, and certainly incapable of relating to the questioning of others in an empathetic and compassionate way, and with the sincere desire to understand.

Patience as a remedy against liberalism

It may seem that the present treatment glorifies patience and pliancy to such a degree as to relativize established doctrine to an unwarrantable extent. This, however, is only so in appearance, for lack of patience and hospitality in matters doctrinal, as we in the Roman Catholic Church have learned in the last twenty-five years, also has an opposite effect. Impatient, intolerant, inhospitable doctrine generates impatient, gullible faithful, easily misled by indiscreet devotions (the incidence of private revelations among integralists is high!) or by new, superficial, quasi-theological ideas. Disenchanted Christians brought up on intolerant doctrine are fair game for the hawkers of fads; people brought up on crypto-Monophysitism are easy targets for Arianism. People are born for the glow of passion, and if given nothing but cold doctrinal comfort, they will take their bearings from any straw fire and thus get lost. Doctrinal impassiveness and immobilism breed superficial doctrinal liberalism. The proud Roman assurance *pensiamo in secoli*[114] is certainly wrong, for it leaves the poor and the searching, who have less than one century to live, to their own devices, while allowing the Church to stand benignly by, without participating in the world's struggle. But it is not completely wrong, for there are few things more vulgar than instant christology knocked together to suit every fad that strikes the fancy of the disenchanted.[115] Such a process has nothing to do with the assumption of humankind into the Body of Christ, or with the integration of human concerns into christology. Who wants to be the

---

[113]Cf. above, p. 73.

[114]"We think in terms of centuries."

[115]For examples, cf. the caricatures in Malachi Martin, *Jesus Now*, pp. 41–100.

Church's guest on the cheap? If Jesus withstood the temptation to make religion out of non-involvement and religious withdrawal, he certainly also withstood the temptation to attract others by catering to the demand for quick gratification.

The truly patient are not only tolerant and flexible, they are also steady and sober-minded; they can wait. They have not sold their souls to the past for safety's sake; they will not throw their lives away for popularity's sake. The Church is called to live in the memory of Christ's passion; from it she must derive, not only the humility and openness that will keep her from haughty uninvolvement, but also the fortitude that will keep her from courting popular favor.

In this way, too, the Church must show her affinity with the poor and the struggling in this world. For the poor are shrewd. They do not believe in quick solutions; they have been fobbed off with those a few times too often. If she is to do justice to the poor, the Church must get ready for the long haul. Both the sovereign church and the pop church aim at quick conversions; the patient Church must abide with the poor in patience. Both the poor and the patient are poor consumers; they buy neither the latest products nor the latest assurances of the powers and authorities. They do not go out of their way as soon as they hear that the christ is in the desert or in such and such a house.[116]

The shrewdness of the poor and the patient, and their refusal to be lured into compliance and complicity is a source of deep embarrassment to the powers that be. To the extent that the Church has the courage to live, with the poor, in the memory of Christ's passion, that memory will really turn out to be a "subversive memory" in the present.[117] The "rulers of this age" still do not understand the folly of

---

[116]Cf. Mt 24, 26.—In this context it is useful to recall the Pastoral Epistles, with their caveats against new and "relevant" teachers, and their emphasis on *pistoi logoi*—"reliable things to say": 1 Tim 1, 15; 3, 1; 4, 9; 2 Tim 2, 11; Tit 1, 9; 3, 8. Rev 21, 5; 22, 6 shows that the expression can (and should) be read in an eschatological perspective, and not just in the context of a defense of traditional doctrine.—On the connection between patience and poverty, cf. Alfred C. Kammer, " 'Burn-Out'—Contemporary Dilemma for the Jesuit Social Activist," *Studies in the Spirituality of Jesuits*, American Assistancy Seminar on Jesuit Spirituality, St. Louis, St. Louis University, 10 (1978) 1–42.

[117]Cf. the inspiring article by Johannes B. Metz, "The Future *Ex Memoria Passionis*," in: Ewert H. Cousins (ed.), *Hope and the Future of Man*, Philadelphia, Fortress Press, 1972, pp. 117–131.—Cf. also Adrian Hastings: "To proclaim the

the Cross; if they did, they would not go on crucifying the Lord of glory.[118] But in truth the violent *are* tripped up by the patient.

Retrospect and outlook

In this final section we have argued that christology must not seek to be exempted from the *imitatio Christi*—the way of patience and hospitality, to which the Church is called in virtue of her hope generated by the risen Christ. Christology must do its share of the assumption of humankind into the Body of Christ. It must do so by being open and hospitable to the concerns of the world without selling out to them. The record of classical christology in this regard, we have argued, is not splendid; but hospitality and openness *have* been practiced outside the classical tradition. In fact, our next and final chapter will suggest that this is exactly what happened when Jean Eudes came to look upon the heart of Jesus and Mary as the burning furnace of love, and when Friedrich Schleiermacher pointed to Christ as the mediator of the awareness of God.

Gospel cannot be done with political naivety, unless indeed it be with the political naivety of the poor" (*The Faces of God*, London, Geo. Chapman, 1975, p. 131).
[118]Cf. 1 Cor 2, 8.

CHAPTER 13

Two Birds Come to
the Mustard Tree

The wounded surgeon plies the steel
That questions the distempered part;
Beneath the bleeding hands we feel
The sharp compassion of the healer's art
Resolving the enigma of the fever chart.

T. S. Eliot

The quality of a religious system depends perhaps less on its specific doctrine, than on the choice of the problems that it regards as important, the areas of human experience to which it directs attention.

Peter Brown

Jesus, Mary's most sacred Heart, be forever your heart's heart.

Jean Eudes

But what did He see around Him that was not finite and in need of mediation, and where was aught that could mediate but Himself? "No man knoweth the Father but the Son, and he to whom the Son shall reveal Him." This consciousness of the singularity of His knowledge of God, of the original way in which this knowledge was in Him, and of the power thereof to communicate itself and awake religion, was at once the conciousness of His office as mediator and of His divinity.

Friedrich Schleiermacher

519

> What can we compare the kingdom of God with, or what image can we find for it? When mustard seed is sown on the ground, it is the smallest of all the seeds on the ground. But once sown it grows and becomes bigger than all the kitchen herbs, and it produces branches so big that the birds can nest in its shade.

The Gospel of Mark

Introduction: understanding alternative christologies

Toward the end of the previous chapter we brought a serious charge. We stated that the tradition of classical christology has been scandalously out of touch with the patience and hospitality demanded of it by the Resurrection. But we also alluded to some positive developments; we mentioned the rich tradition of painting, poetry, sculpture, popular devotion, and non-Catholic theology.[1] It is true, the latter developments often became immoderate in various ways, in the direction of crudity or sentimentality and even heresy; but who will blame these christological flowers for being somewhat too luxuriant in their well-shielded corners, given the fact that the alternative was the unfriendly climate of public, normative, diphysitic christology?

This book, we stated long ago, considers christological statements primarily as expressions of dialogue among persons in dialectical response both to the living Lord and to the concerns of their cultures;[2] it is also a plea in favor of a more integrated style of thought in closer touch with natural-language use.[3] In the light of this position, we have been forced to characterize the great tradition as insensitive to the need for *ongoing* dialogue between faith and culture. In the same light, we must pay attention to the christological thinking that occurred outside the ever narrowing swath cut by the great tradition—to the wild flowers neglected and even condemned by the great tradition after it had ceased to be in dialogue with the world. In this way we will have an opportunity to learn, not only from the undeniable depth of classical christology, but also from the

---

[1] Above, p. 510.
[2] Above, p. 102.
[3] Cf. above, pp. 84, 87.

breadth of Christian sensibility. And it is mainly the latter which has continued, unlike the normative christological tradition, to speak the language of faith with the language of the world, and to use the sensibilities of the culture to speak to the culture with the confidence and freedom of the Gospel.[4]

In thus positively appreciating alternative christologies we are merely doing something wholly consistent with the deepest inspiration of classical christology, if, that is, the latter is properly understood. Far from being an intrusive god, we argued in the eleventh chapter, the *Logos* Incarnate is precisely God's own invitation, extended to all of creation, to return to him in thankful surrender.[5] Those affirming the divinity of Christ, therefore, have a theological duty to welcome all human concerns, and to integrate them into the Christian confession. To achieve this, we argued in the twelfth chapter, the Church is called to patient and hospitable encounter with all the concerns that either nervously clamor or patiently wait for recognition and understanding.[6] In obedience to the *imitatio Christi*, the Church must welcome all these concerns, trusting that, in the encounter, they will drop their defenses, stop being worried about their autonomy, be converted from self-assurance, and become the stuff of obedience. In this way the Church will turn out to be the follower of the long-suffering Jesus also in this regard, that she will do justice to all concerns by compassionately questioning and assaying and testing them. This involves, not acts of forensic judgment, but gestures of acceptance so total and so searching that all concerns find themselves enlightened and laid bare by the kindly light of a judgment that brings with it, as part of itself, the ability to accept correction gladly. Thus all concerns are healed and humbled and purified and converted to obedience in the very act of the Church's acceptance.[7]

We have argued that the tradition of classical christology has been intolerant of new christological developments. By dint of repetition of the neo-Chalcedonian formula, new developments have been

---

[4]Cf. above, p. 38.
[5]Above, p. 460.
[6]Above, pp. 471–479, 494–501.
[7]Cf. above, pp. 163–165.—The expression "laid bare" is a rendering of *gymna kai tetrachēlismena* of Heb 4, 13.

kept outside the pale of mainstream orthodoxy. Still, the fact that new developments did occur proves that the Church continued somehow *behaviorally* to follow Christ in patience and hospitality, even though *vocally* she tried to prohibit, or at least discourage, new christological formulas. We have indicated that this has led to some unfortunate results; normative christology has suffered from isolation and sclerosis, and devotionalities and new christologies have shown tendencies toward immoderation. But there is also a very important positive gain, namely, the existence of legitimate christological statements which yet are in no way lineal descendants of Chalcedon. This can only be taken as a confirmation of the thesis defended in the previous chapter, namely, that non-linear developments in doctrine are possible.[8] This, of course, raises the question of the connections between these non-linear developments and established doctrine, and thus it raises the question of the criteria for sound doctrinal development. We will treat this issue at the end of this chapter, where we will argue that doctrinal developments must be judged by behavioral and rhetorical standards rather than by the standard of thematic or conceptual coherence with the tradition.[9]

Before we bring up this subject, however, we will choose, out of the many christological developments of the past millennium, two christologies not usually associated with the great tradition. They have this in common, that they represent cultural concerns that have come to nest permanently in the growing tree of the kingdom, undeterred by neo-Chalcedonian orthodoxy. They are the Roman Catholic Sacred Heart devotion and the Protestant christology of the great Friedrich Schleiermacher. It is obvious that our treatment will have to be essayistic and suggestive rather than complete and compelling. This will be especially true with regard to the latter topic; the former, of its nature, will demand a somewhat more circumstantial account. This lack of rigor as this book comes to a close is not without purpose. An impressionistic closing chapter is appropriate in a book written to argue the need for free speech in christology. It puts a needed emphasis on the essential open-endedness of all chris-

---

[8] Above, pp. 514–515.

[9] Cf. below, pp. 566–575.—About "thematic or conceptual coherence with the tradition," cf. Buber's statement about "linkage in an intellectual system" and Verhaar's concept of "internal reference," above, p. 126 and note 39.

tology. It may even serve as an encouragement to Christians to testify freely, so that all comers may hear them speaking in their own languages about the marvels wrought by God.[10]

BURNING FURNACE OF LOVE OR BLOOD-PUMPING MUSCLE?[11]

Introduction: a negative Roman decision[12]

In the course of the year 1726, Prospero Lorenzo Lambertini, one of the outstanding canon lawyers in the papal curia, and a man who was eventually, in 1740, to become Pope Benedict XIV, wrote an opinion on the advisability of the institution of a liturgical feast in honor of the Sacred Heart of Jesus. It was the third time that the request was being considered; earlier attempts in 1686 and 1696 had met with negative answers. The reasons alleged for the refusal in 1696 had been numerous and compelling: the novelty of the devotion; the division of Christ into parts; the crudely material nature of a devotion directed to one isolated part of Christ's body; the dangerous turns popular piety might take when encouraged to address prayers to only one portion of Christ, such as the heart; the opposition of prestigious persons (a reference to the growing antagonism, among the ruling classes, to the Jesuits?); the absence of supernatural interventions; and finally, the risk of encouraging further requests for feasts of the eyes, the hands, and the tongue of Jesus.

The petitioner of 1726, however, seemed undeterred by these arguments. Joseph-François de Galliffet, of the Society of Jesus, had written a learned treatise, to be translated and reprinted many times

---

[10]Cf. Acts 2, 11.

[11]The entire section under this heading owes a profound debt to J. H. van den Berg's two-volume *Het menselijk lichaam*, not only as regards the objective data, but also in the area of method and interpretative style. There are some discrepancies between van den Berg's interpretations and those given here, but they are negligible in comparison with the large area of agreement.

[12]For the refusal of 1726, cf. Benvenuto Matteucci, "Il sinodo di Pistoia e il culto del SS. Cuore di Gesù," in: A. Bea, H. Rahner, H. Rondet, F. Schwendimann, *Cor Jesu*, Commentationes in litteras encyclicas Pii Pp. XII "Haurietis Aquas," 2 vols., Roma, Casa editrice Herder, 1959, Vol. 2, pp. 235–261, esp. pp. 240–241; A. Hamon, *Histoire de la Dévotion au Sacré Coeur*, 5 vols., Paris, Gabriel Beauchesne, ⁵1923, 1925, 1927, 1931, 1940 (henceforth *Histoire*); Vol. IV, pp. 5–60, esp. 44–45; J. H. van den Berg, *Het menselijk lichaam*, Vol. II, pp. 128–129.

during the next few decades, entitled *The Cult of the Most Sacred Heart of Our God and Lord Jesus Christ.*[13] In it, he set forth theological as well as practical, pastoral reasons for the feast; all the difficulties against its introduction seemed to be disposed of. Unfortunately, however, the zealous Father had considerably weakened his position by adding a physiological argument that had for some time been a matter of controversy: he had argued, with a rich display of scientific knowledge, that the human heart was the seat and organ of love.

Lambertini saw the weak spot. He wrote that physicians and philosophers had indeed long thought so, and some of them thought so even now; hence, Père de Galliffet was welcome to his opinion. But it was a mistake to base the case on such a disputable and disputed opinion, since many philosophers and even more physicians were already teaching that the soul's instrument for the affective life is the brain; the heart is merely the organ where these feelings are manifested. If the Congregation of Rites were to grant Father de Galliffet's request, it would seem to favor a rather improbable thesis, which, moreover, would be outside the Congregation's competence.

The petition was declined. It was not till 1765 that the Congregation revoked its decision of 1726 and allowed a liturgical celebration of the feast of the Sacred Heart to be introduced in Poland; soon afterward, the feast was being introduced all over Europe. The pressure of popular devotion supported and even encouraged by local bishops had prevailed over the repeated prohibition.[14]

The incident just related is not particularly memorable; it is only one event in a whole history, which spans almost two hundred and fifty years, starting in the year 1523 with Lanspergius' book *The Quiver of Divine Love*,[15] and ending, at least provisionally, with the permission given to the Polish bishops to celebrate the feast of the Sacred Heart liturgically. Lanspergius' book picked up an old devotion in a new fashion; the theme went through some transformations; suddenly, around 1640, it gained a new shape and a new, explosive

---

[13]*De Cultu sacrosancti Cordis Dei ac Domini nostri Jesu Christi*, Romae, 1726; on Père de Galliffet, cf. A. Hamon, *Histoire*, Vol. IV, pp. 5–31.

[14]*Ibid.*, pp. 195–223.

[15]*Pharetra divini amoris.*

popularity; it went on, in the next one hundred and fifty years, to establish itself so firmly in Roman Catholic sensibility that it became part of the liturgical calendar, in spite of three refusals by Rome; its influence continued into the twentieth century, which saw the publication, in 1956, of Pope Pius XII's encyclical *Haurietis Aquas*.[16]

From a different point of view, however, the incident of 1726 is extremely memorable, for it is part of two histories, not just one. It is, in fact, the meeting-point of two seemingly unrelated series of events, both of which had started around two centuries before, and both of which had peaked between 1625 and 1650. The first series is the history of the development of the Sacred Heart devotion; the other series is the history of the development of the anatomical investigation of the human body. The two peak events are the publication, in 1628, of William Harvey's little treatise on the movement of the heart and the circulation of the blood,[17] and the start, in the years between 1629 and 1643, of a completely new form of the devotion to the Sacred Heart of Jesus. We must briefly review and characterize both developments.

From Galen through Vesalius to Harvey

The year 1543 saw the publication of the first truly modern anatomical atlas. Its author was the youthful Andries van Wesel or Wessels, better known as Andreas Vesalius, born in Brussels on New Year's Eve, 1514. The book, *De Humani Corporis Fabrica*, which was to be reprinted in 1555, was not his first publication; in the year 1538, at the age of 24, and within months of his doctoral defense at Padua, he had published his famous *Tabulae Anatomicae Sex*—a set of six anatomical plates made of woodcuts; they became so popular among medical students that only two or three copies have survived complete.[18]

In the preface to this earlier work Vesalius makes an extraordinary claim. In these plates, he writes, there is not a single line drawn that is not based on his actual anatomical demonstrations at Padua;

---

[16]*Acta Apostolicae Sedis* 48 (1956) 309–353; cf. DS 3922–3926.

[17]*Exercitatio anatomica de motu cordis et sanguinis in animalibus.*

[18]Cf. J. B. deC. M. Saunders and Charles D. O'Malley, *The Illustrations from the Works of Andreas Vesalius of Brussels* (henceforth *Illustrations*).

his students will vouch for that, as will his learned teachers in Paris and his ditto colleagues at Louvain.[19] This emphasis on *visual demonstration* is at once typical of Vesalius' approach and yet very puzzling.

Vesalius is obviously an observer who wants to look, and who wants others to look as he does, so that they may see what he has observed and be impressed. The plates are drawn so as to have maximum visual impact; they combine two of the principal elements of the emerging baroque style—dramatic effect and visual clarity.[20] But why, then, a breast-bone consisting of seven parts instead of only three on plate 4? Why a bladder-shaped uterus with two *cornua* or "horns" on plate 1? Why a five-lobed liver on plates 1 and 2, with— enigmatically—a two-lobed liver (a correct one!) in the upper right-hand corner on plate 1?[21] The answer is simple. Long, authoritative tradition still prevented Vesalius, along with his entire profession since Mundinus had started the art of human anatomy in the late thirteenth century, from doing what in the mid-sixteenth century was slowly becoming a new and startling human ability: to observe, to tell apart, to describe, to simplify, to define, and to manipulate on the basis of what one could *see*, not on the basis of what one had been authoritatively *told*.[22] In the three features just mentioned Vesalius is still following Galen, the second-century physician from Rome and the author of the authoritative medical text for more than a millennium, *Peri chreias mōriōn*—"On the functions of the parts of the body." Galen never dissected a human body, and thus routinely attributed to the human anatomy features he had noticed in his

---

[19]Cf. *Illustrations*, p. 234; J. H. van den Berg, *Het menselijk lichaam*, Vol. I, pp. 173–174, esp. note 8.

[20]This is especially noticeable in plates 4–6 of the *Tabulae sex* and plates 21–28, 32–37 of the *Fabrica*, which owe a large debt to the Dance of Death theme in late fifteenth- and early sixteenth-century painting, represented, among others, by Memlinc. Plate 1 of the *Fabrica* pictures Vesalius showing, in a dramatic pose, the anatomy of the arm of a (huge) corpse. The title-pages of the *Fabrica* of 1543 and of its reprint of 1555 also stress visual features and drama; notice, for instance, the skeleton with the flail (1555: the scythe) looming over the corpse, and the combination of eager looking and dramatic interaction among the onlookers in this precursor of Rembrandt's Anatomical Lessons. Cf. *Illustrations*, pp. 2, 42–46, 84–101, 108–119, 242–252. Cf. also J. H. van den Berg, *Het menselijk lichaam*, Vol. I, pp. 176–180.

[21]Cf. *Illustrations*, pp. 237, 239, 243.

[22]Cf. above, p. 66 and note 2.

dissections of animals; but more importantly, Galen's anatomy was primarily a *physiology*, and in particular, a physiology based on reflection upon vital bodily *experience* at least as much as on observation of anatomical structures.

Vesalius, therefore, had to cope with a climate created by the Galenic tradition. J. H. van den Berg characterizes this climate as follows:

> Actually, we can say that the entire period between Galen and Harvey is characterized by scant interest in precisely these matters [i.e., the anatomy and the functioning of the human body]. Or rather, there was interest, but it was an interest of the kind that strikes us as peculiar, as "uninterested." That is to say, people thought about the body and what occurs in it, but they did not examine it. They reflected on the body, they meditated on its contents as if it were a theological proposition; but they did not open the body. Not the scalpel but the pen was the tool of the anatomist, who, therefore, we would think, did not deserve the name of "anatomist."[23]

As he spent more time in the *theatrum autopsiae* Vesalius saw more and more, and was less and less afraid to break with tradition. In his masterpiece of 1543 the style has become detailed and maximally visualizing, resulting in a dramatic impact far stronger than that achieved by the *Tabulae sex*. The closer observation has also yielded anatomical results: the liver now has definitively two lobes, the *cornua uteri* are identified as occurring in cows and dogs, not humans, and the text about the breast-bone explains the problem of the number of its parts.[24] But most importantly of all, *the heart*, left unopened and respectfully identified as the place "where the vital forces are kindled and the arteries originate" in 1538,[25] is opened and has its inside made maximally visible in 1543.[26] And remarkably, it is precisely here, inside the opened heart, that Vesalius most notably fails to *see*; faced with the open heart, he stops short of trusting his otherwise so observant eyes.

---

[23]*Het menselijk lichaam*, Vol. I, p. 40.

[24]Cf. *Illustrations*, pp. 166–169, 170–171, 68–69. Problems that remain are the coccyx, the scalenus anterior, and the optic chiasm, pp. 66–67, 100–103, 196–197; cf. J. H. van den Berg, *Het menselijk lichaam*, Vol. I, pp. 171–172.

[25]*Cor Vitalis Facultatis Fomes et Arte[riorum] Prin[cipium]: Illustrations*, p. 241.

[26]*Ibid.*, pp. 180–183.

To appreciate this, we must go back to Galen, and in particular to Galen's physiological theory. J. H. van den Berg admirably characterizes the Galenic convictions about the heart as follows:

> Blood is produced in the body's largest organ, the liver. From the intestine to the liver there runs a vessel which transports the nutrients out of which the liver prepares the blood. In its freshly prepared, pristine shape, however, the blood is not yet ready for its function. Essential elements remain to be added, such as *air*, and *heat*, and last but not least, *life*, spirit, *spiritus.* The physicians of the century immediately preceding Harvey put much emphasis on this last ingredient. It is in the heart that all these essential ingredients are added to the blood. In the heart all things meet: blood (or rather, the lifeless fluid that is about to become blood) from the liver, air from the lungs, heat from the heart itself, and *spiritus* or life, also from the lungs, transported along with the air and largely identical with it. But—and here I am again drawing on the publications of the century preceding the appearance of Harvey's treatise—the heart itself is also the origin of something like spirit and life; what I mean is that there is a connection between this spirit or life and the second ingredient added to the blood by the heart—heat.
>
> To sum up: the inanimate, dead, raw blood, prepared by the liver out of dead nutrients made fluid, gets provided, in the heart, with air, heat, spirit, and life—indispensable ingredients derived from the air inhaled and from the heart itself, this center of life and heat, of spirit and vitality.
>
> The fresh, mobile, light, *living* blood now leaves the heart by way of the aorta. [. . .] The heart gives it an impulse; the blood "understands" the impulse; it dances, as it were, to the tune of the heartbeat. In this way the blood reaches the organs in waves, penetrates them, withdraws again from them, plays with them.
>
> [. . .]
>
> Respiration has three simultaneous purposes. Air is inhaled and flows into the body. By way of a few (air) vessels this delicate matter reaches the heart, where it mingles with the crude, as yet unspiritualized blood. But air is also characterized, in comparison with the body, by coolness. Respiration cools the body; this is its second function. And the heart especially needs cooling—this furnace where fluids, air, and spirit are forged together. The heart, for that matter, is hot "by nature"—so hot, in fact, that its heat warms the whole body, even though the weather is cold outside, let us say, when it freezes. Even then the heart has heat enough and to spare. It has too much heat even; were the heart not cooled, it would consume itself. And so the air tempers the heat of this all too fiery organ.
>
> Finally, there is the third function. With the exhalation, "smoke

and soot" are evacuated—the exhausts produced by this burning melt-ing-pot, in the process of manufacturing the fluid of life. No one can survive in the vapors that exhalation produces. Air breathed out causes death; we get asphyxiated by the poison produced by the synthesis that gives us life—the synthesis of matter, air, spirit, and heat.[27]

We can now go back to Vesalius, as, with scalpel and probe, but especially with the trained eye, he penetrates into the heart. He looks at the interventricular wall and examines it thoroughly. *There are no openings.* We must praise the Maker of all things for causing the blood to ooze through a visibly closed interventricular septum.[28] What is the significance of this sudden encouragement to prayer?

In the Galenic conception, there are two main ebb and flood systems. One is venal; it has its center in the liver, which first charges the fluid drawn from the intestine with "natural spirit" and then sends it, as venal blood, through the *vena cava* and its tributaries, to the organs, for their nutrition.[29] The other system—the principal one—is arterial; it has its center in the heart, which charges venal blood with "vital spirit," as we have seen. The question is now: How precisely does the heart acquire the venal blood? Galen answers that the *vena cava* runs through the right atrium of the heart; from there, venal blood goes to the right auricle, and from there to the right ventricle. And it is here that the blood "sweats" through the interventricular septum, and thus reaches the left ventricle of the heart, which is properly arterial. This "sweating" takes place through *meatus visum fugientes*, as Vesalius calls them—"pores invisible to the human eye." So when he examined the inside of the heart Vesalius ceased to trust his eyes; instead, he relied on what he had been told. It prompted a religious exhortation.[30]

But Vesalius kept looking. He must have become increasingly ill

---

[27]*Het menselijk lichaam*, Vol. I, pp. 34–36. The author admits that the character-ization just quoted is composite; it includes elements based on later developments and refinements of Galenic medical knowledge. The picture is also simplified; van den Berg concentrates on the heart, which causes him to bypass mention of the semi-independent ebb and flood system that originates in the liver.

[28]Cf. above, p. 41.

[29]Cf. *Illustrations*, p. 238.

[30]J. H. van den Berg, *Het menselijk lichaam*, Vol. I, pp. 41, 172; cf. *Illustrations*, p. 182.

at ease with his leap of faith, as he reached the conclusion that in all probability there were no openings at all. In the second edition of the *Fabrica* he writes:

> It is true, these grooves [*foveae*, superficial grooves in the septum, which had lent credibility to the conviction that there were pores] are obvious, but none of them run all the way through the septum, from the right ventricle to the left ventricle. And I cannot find even the tiniest pores through the septum, even though the anatomy professors have a lot to say about them, given their firm conviction that the left ventricle receives blood from the right ventricle. It all amounts to this [. . .]: I have the worst doubts about the workings of the heart in this regard.[31]

The praise of God has given way to the admission of an *impasse*. Fracastorius, the physician-in-residence of the Council of Trent, sums up the middle and late sixteenth-century's feeling about the heart by exclaiming that "the movement of the heart can only be comprehended by God";[32] one wonders how much of this fervor is due to faith, and how much to frustration. In any case, those who believe without seeing seem not so aware of being blessed anymore.

From now on the combined pressure of eager observation and impatient ignorance about the heart becomes irresistible. The focus of interest is entirely the heart. In Galen's theory, reflected in Vesalius' order of treatment, the heart had been part of the life-giving system that fills the noble human breast; it had been the principal part, more important than its intake and exhaust accessories, but still, it had been a *part*. Now, with Vesalius, the heart becomes more central; significantly, the lungs are represented in the *Fabrica* by two clumsy drawings, as against nine detailed drawings of the heart in various positions and stages of dissection.[33] The workings of the (now relatively isolated) heart are more and more becoming the anatomist's challenge.

The results come soon. In the early and middle fifties, the

---

[31]Quoted by J. H. van den Berg, *Het menselijk lichaam*, Vol. I, p. 42, note 13; cf. *Illustrations*, p. 182.

[32]Quoted by J. H. van den Berg, *Het menselijk lichaam*, Vol. I, pp. 44–45, esp. note 14.

[33]Cf. *Illustrations*, pp. 182–183.

Spaniard Michael Servet, burnt at the stake along with his books (one charred copy remains, retrieved from the execution), and the Italian Realdo Colombo are teaching that the blood *circulates* from the right ventricle through the lungs to the left auricle. And in 1603 Fabrizio publishes a book that shows that valves inside all veins prevent the blood from going in two directions; the ebb and flood theory becomes untenable. In 1616 William Harvey, in London, is teaching that the blood circulates; in 1628 his treatise, *Exercitatio Anatomica de Motu Cordis et Sanguinis in Animalibus*, is published in Frankfurt on the Main, to this day a center of the international publishing trade.[34]

Three arguments clinch the thesis, proposed by the *Exercitatio*, that the blood circulates. The first one is based on the impossibility of the Galenic construction that with each heartbeat blood leaves the heart, *never to return*. If this were true, and if the underlying assumption, namely that blood is highly refined food, were also true, then the heart would every day have to move a quantity of blood equivalent to many times a person's body-weight, and the person himself would, as a consequence, have to take in enormous quantities of food to keep the blood-supply going.[35] Secondly, Harvey points out another impossibility in the Galenic system; it is, significantly, of an explicitly *mechanical* nature. Between the left auricle and the left ventricle there is a set of valves which, as we now know, prevent the blood from flowing back into the pulmonary vein when the heart contracts. In the Galenic theory, these valves at once *prevent* air from being pushed out of the heart when it contracts *and permit* the passage of blood saturated with "soot" to be exhausted by exhalation. "Good God,' Harvey exclaims, "how can the mitral valves keep the air from flowing back, and not the blood?"[36] Finally, Harvey's

---

[34]Cf. J. H. van den Berg, *Het menselijk lichaam*, Vol. I, pp. 33–34, 42–44.

[35]*Ibid.*, pp. 45–49. Van den Berg rightly stresses the significance of the glaring inaccuracies in Harvey's computations of the quantity of blood moved daily by the heart. They show that dispassionate arithmetic was not (yet) felt to be applicable to the living human body. More than a century before Harvey, Leonardo da Vinci had had the same insight as Harvey without ever calculating anything; he had merely contented himself with the observation that the quantity of blood moved daily by the heart amounts to "a lot of weight"—*v'à gran peso*. Harvey does calculate, but seems as yet unable to face the result of his multiplications.

[36]*Ibid.*, pp. 50–53.

third argument is the absence of pores in the interventricular wall—a problem presented as important but not central, and for a good reason. After all, Harvey himself had to postulate invisible channels in all organs permitting the blood to return to the heart by way of the venal system; the capillary systems were invisible for the time being; they were to remain so until the years 1661 and 1668 respectively, when Malpighi and van Leeuwenhoek first saw them through their microscopes. Harvey was dead by then.[37]

We are ready to sum up this history. We will do so in three points. The first will take the form of a descriptive analysis of the title-page of an anatomical atlas published about a century after Vesalius' *Fabrica*. The second will be a short reflection on the difference between observation and meditation. The third point will bring us back, as promised, to Prospero Lorenzo Lambertini's problem in 1726.

Nathanael Highmore, or Highmorus, published his anatomy in 1651. The book carries a highly significant title-page. As in the Galenic system, only even more so, the heart occupies the central place in Highmore's view of the human body, but *the difference in metaphor is striking*. J. H. van den Berg offers the following eloquent description of the title-page:

> At the top, in the middle, we see the goddess of anatomy, seated in her temple, over which the words *Sacrum Anatomiae* [Temple of Anatomy] are inscribed. She is "Pallas of the skulls"—thus identified in the course of Highmore's own description a few pages further on— armed with her royal orb and scepter, a skull and a thigh-bone. To her right, in the *Theatrum Autopsiae*, the noble art of anatomy is practiced. To her left, a doting old man indulges in abominable contemplation; on the low roof of his dwelling [marked *contemplationis musaeum*] there are inscribed the words *monon theōreō*—"all I do is contemplate." He has no access to the goddess of anatomy, for the temple-veil is drawn across the way on his side. The anatomist to the right does have access; he can be seen kneeling [toward the goddess], with the temple-veil drawn to the side. Reverently he proffers to the goddess an organ (the heart?) just taken from the opened body. Underneath this significant triptych we see the two fathers of medicine, Hippocrates and Galen, each off to one side, pulling aside a drapery made of human skin. Behind the drapery—that means, under our skin—the truth about

---

[37]*Ibid.*, pp. 49–50. Harvey died in 1657.

human life is uncovered. A pump—a pump, complete with piston, rod, and handle, kept moving by a hand whose owner, alas, must remain concealed by a cloud overhead[38]—yes, a pump lifts water into an overflowing crater, from which it irrigates the earth, the stuff of life. The flow returns to the place of origin. Irrigation turns out to be circulation. In the left bottom corner there is a little fellow operating a sluice; he lets the undesirable elements (the urine) drain away. In the lower left-hand corner of the page the faculty of *sight* is revealed; the eye is a *camera obscura* which reproduces the world upside down [. . .]. Finally, in the lower right-hand corner, we see Highmorus himself, Nathanael Highmore, born at Fordinbridge, deceased in 1685; he is the author of the work introduced by this plate; its title is, as the inscription on the skin-drapery tells us, *Corporis Humani Disquisitio Anatomica in qua Sanguinis Circulationem . . . prosequutus est*—a title whose wording indicates the extent to which the circulation of the blood—that is, the idea that the heart is a pump—has come to control the attention.[39]

Our second concluding observation concerns the stress on visualization and the dramatic style of presentation—the two characteristics of the entire development we have surveyed. There is no doubt that both have much to do with the nervous excitement inherent in discovery, and also with the fact that the new learning had to *overcome* a whole way of experiencing resistant to the new findings as well as to the methods employed to arrive at them. Meditation and tradition on the one hand, and detached observation and dramatic novelty on the other—they are hard to keep together; the seventeenth-century dissociation of sensibility so well described by T. S. Eliot[40] has strong roots in sixteenth-century processes, one of which we have just described. For between 1540 and 1630 the human heart was the focus of much concern; the result was a deep and lasting shift of sensibility, which can be illustrated by an interesting fact. People of all times, but especially the lunatics, the lovers, and

---

[38]Is there any relevance to the fact that Adam Smith, about a century later, will entrust the basic mechanics of the economic processes to an *invisible* hand?

[39]*Ibid.*, pp. 55–56. The full translation of the title runs: "Lectures on the Anatomy of the Human Body, Containing an Account of the Circulation of the Blood in Every Part of the Body, Provided with Many New Plates and a Succinct Explanation of Medical Riddles, by Nathanael Highmore, Doctor of Arts and Medicine, Formerly of Trinity, Oxford."

[40]T. S. Eliot, "The Metaphysical Poets"; cf. also above, pp. 53–55.

the poets, have always known that the heart beats and throbs and palpitates, that it can be felt moving just below the left nipple, that it can be felt pounding in one's throat, that it can be heard beating, "like a soft drum,"[41] in one's ears, especially when lying down on a pillow. Yet, when William Harvey wrote, in his *Exercitatio*, that the heartbeat can be heard (and when hĕ compared the phenomenon with the esophageal noises of a drinking horse!) he was widely ridiculed—who had ever heard of such a preposterous claim, that the heart can be *heard* beating! The conclusion must be that the early seventeenth-century was witnessing *a new way of hearing*—a way so novel that it was hard to associate it with the traditional way. The heart had always been audible in a vague, unthematized, "diffuse" way; next to this audibility, and opposed to it, a new audibility arose, namely that of the mechanical heart, the heart viewed as a separate organ, the heart viewed as a pump.[42] The two ways of perceiving are hard to entertain together; meditation and observation look like enemies for the time being. They fought; the fight was hard; it took decades for Harvey's discovery to be universally accepted; eventually it was.

And so, finally, we come back to Lambertini. His problem was that he was caught between the meditations of Père de Galliffet and his tribe on the one hand, and the observations of "many philosophers and even more physicians" on the other. He opted for the latter.

From Lanspergius to Jean Eudes and Margaret Mary Alacoque

In his comprehensive five-volume history of the Sacred Heart devotion, Père Auguste Hamon devotes an entire volume, the second, to "the dawn of the devotion."[43] Toward the end of this volume, a special chapter is devoted to the "Cologne movement," and especially to Johann Gerecht, or Johannes Justus, better known as Lanspergius the Carthusian, after his birthplace Landsberg in Ba-

---

[41]Henry King (1592–1669), Bishop of Chichester, "The Exequy," line 111; for this magnificent poem, cf. Helen Gardner (ed.), *The Metaphysical Poets*, Harmondsworth, Penguin Books, 1957, pp. 108–111.

[42]Cf. J. H. van den Berg, *Het menselijk lichaam*, Vol. II, pp. 29–44; the term "diffuse audibility" is van den Berg's.

[43]*Histoire*, Vol. II, *L'Aube de la Dévotion*.

varia, and after the Cologne Charterhouse he entered at the age of twenty in 1509, and where he spent most of the rest of his life.[44] Hamon judges that "at the beginning of the sixteenth century, Lanspergius brings together, in his soul and in his writings, the scattered features of the Carthusian devotion to the Sacred Heart, and becomes its most illustrious worshiper and apostle before the seventeenth century."[45] Hamon is right. Lanspergius is an important figure; in fact, he represents a watershed. Not only does he sum up the past, he also points the way to the future.

In what way does Lanspergius represent the past? Hamon observes that the centuries before the seventeenth had not witnessed the firm establishment of the Sacred Heart devotion, despite the fact that its representatives had been, not only numerous, but also notable.[46] It had started, hesitantly, when, in the late eleventh and early twelfth centuries in France, Christians slowly turned away from the symbolisms of the tradition, in order to address themselves very explicitly to the *humanity* of Christ. The crucifix starts to exhibit romantic, emotional features, instead of being primarily hieratic. In Chartres, *Notre Dame de la belle verrière* softens the formal rigidity of the Byzantine tradition from which it emerges. Anselm meditates on the life and especially the passion of Jesus, in order to fathom the inner mystery of the atonement. In the glow of the courtly romanticism which so touchingly suffuses the early Cistercian movement, Bernard of Clairvaux writes that "the secret of the heart [of Jesus] can be seen through the open wounds of the body."[47]

The next four hundred years will continue to show many scattered instances of meditations on, and devotions to, the Heart of Jesus and the open wound of the side, *viewed together* as one reality and interpreted in the context of Jesus' passion as the manifestation of divine love. In this way the Middle Ages reinterpret, in a humanizing fashion, a *locus classicus* of patristic theology, which

---

[44]*Ibid.*, pp. 265–318—a fine survey of the enormous influence that the Cologne Charterhouse had on the spirituality of the sixteenth century.

[45]*Ibid.*, p. 278.

[46]*Ibid.*, pp. 347–353; cf. also Vol. III, p. 5.

[47]For a fine account of this movement, cf. R. W. Southern, *The Making of the Middle Ages*, pp. 209–244.—A. Hamon, *Histoire*, Vol. II, pp. 85–89; the quotation from Bernard is on p. 98, note 1: *Patet arcanum cordis per foramina corporis.*

held that the Church was born from the breach in the wall of the sanctuary—the opened side and the transfixed Heart of Christ on the cross—in the water of Baptism and the blood of the Eucharist. This tender association between the passion, the wounds, and the Heart of Jesus reaches mystical dimensions in the life of Gertrude, the thirteenth-century Benedictine nun of the abbey of Helfta, near Eisleben in Saxony.[48] It remains a theme with Franciscans, Dominicans, Carthusians, and others up to the beginning of the sixteenth century,[49] when Lanspergius writes his works, among which *The Quiver of Divine Love* is the most important.

Hamon briefly characterizes Lanspergius' Sacred Heart devotion as follows:

> It is in the wound of the side that Lanspergius finds the Heart; his devotion to the Sacred Heart is a form of his devotion to the five Wounds. He understands and lives it better than anyone before him, but he does not separate it from his veneration for the Passion. He kisses and adores the hands and the feet, while at the same time kissing and adoring the side.[50]

Thus Lanspergius represents the medieval devotion to the Sacred Heart, in which the Heart of Jesus was venerated together with the wounds in the context of the passion, which latter two were the primary ingredients of the devotion.

In another, rather different respect, however, Lanspergius looks forward. J. H. van den Berg draws attention to the fact that *visualization* plays a large part in Lanspergius' approach to the devotion;[51] he might have added that the visualization was meant to stir the practitioner of the devotion to some rather *dramatic actions.* Hamon writes:

> To aid the devotion, Lanspergius proposes [. . .] that one should keep before one's eyes a picture of the Heart, the five Wounds, or the Crucifix; it should be put in a place where one often comes by, so that the sight of it may cause one to elicit numerous acts of love. Should one

---

[48]A. Hamon, *Histoire*, Vol. II, pp. 109–152.

[49]*Ibid.*, pp. 153–263.

[50]*Ibid.*, pp. 280–281.

[51]*Het menselijk lichaam*, Vol. II, pp. 78–80.

feel moved by inner devotion, one might even kiss this picture of the Heart of Jesus, and firmly pretend that one is pressing one's lips to the divine Heart; thus one may wish that one's heart, one's spirit, one's entire being be plunged and absorbed in it forever."

What we have here is the first important witness to the pictorial representation of the Sacred Heart of Jesus for devotional purposes. Lanspergius' biographer, quoted by Hamon, gives a description of a picture of the Sacred Heart and the wounds, which was drawn for the Cologne Charterhouse in 1535, and which may very well represent the kind of picture Lanspergius was thinking of.

> The heart, radiant and pierced by the lance, is affixed to the upright beam of the cross. The radiant hands and feet are set around it, below the cross-beam, in the form of a quadrangle; they are marked by the glorious stigmata. The crown of thorns hangs on the cross-beam in the middle; the three nails are placed at the top, with the sponge on the right and the column [of the scourging] on the left.[53]

Lanspergius' visualization of the Sacred Heart does not occur in a vacuum. In fact, it is only one particular, though early, example of the pictorial and literary tradition of *emblematic art*. The flowering-period of this art-form lasts from around 1530 till around 1640—roughly, the period between Vesalius and Harvey, the period during which the structure of the human heart was known, while its workings still remained a mystery. The emblematic tradition, which inspired many significant artists and scholars, has a few important characteristics.[54] First, it was mainly *secular* and arose out of the humanist movement; the editors of a recent massive collection of emblems could make the decision to exclude sacred emblems without giving a seriously distorted picture of the genre.[55] Second, the em-

---

[52]*Histoire*, Vol. II, p. 282; for the Latin text of Lanspergius' recommendation, cf. *ibid.*, p. 330.

[53]*Ibid.*, p. 331. For the antecedents and subsequent developments of this picture, cp. *ibid.*, p. 319ff..

[54]For a very full and learned account, cf. Mario Praz, *Studies in Seventeenth-Century Imagery*, (Sussidi eruditi, 16), Roma, Edizioni di storia e letteratura, [2]1964. This volume also contains a very full bibliography, pp. 233–576.

[55]Arthur Henkel und Albrecht Schöne (eds.), *Emblemata*, Handbuch zur Sinnbildkunst des XVI. und XVII. Jahrhunderts, Stuttgart, J. B. Metschlersche

blematic art was extremely *intellectual, analytical,* and *moralistic*; the pictures, visually striking though they are, represent some kind of intricate anatomy of life; the explanatory and exhortatory texts that accompany the pictures are by no means superfluous; careful consideration and analysis are necessary before the meaning of an emblem and its applicability to human life become clear.

In view of the obvious parallels between the emblematic art and the style of Vesalius' anatomical atlas, it is not surprising that the heart should be one of the most frequently occurring parts of the body in the emblem-books. The area of its emblematic and allegorical significance is mostly that of passions, virtues, vices, and aspirations, although there are occasional references to religious meanings, such as the idea that only God can judge the heart or fathom its mystery.[56]

Thus the *context* of Lanspergius' advice to use the picture of the Sacred Heart of Jesus is the emblematic tradition. But this context suggests that Lanspergius' primary focus is not so much the worship of the Heart of Jesus as the spiritual progress of the *human* heart; it looks as if the picture of Jesus' Heart primarily serves to stimulate the pious person's own meditations and heartfelt devotions. This suspicion is confirmed by the emblem that opens Pierre Regnart's *The Practice of the Crucified Heart* of around 1525, which bears a clear resemblance to the picture recommended at the Cologne Charterhouse in 1535.[57] Regnart's emblem, according to Hamon, consists of

a heart, with the cross above it and with thorns around it; inside it, we can distinguish the point of the lance and the three nails. The lance is named *Cherité*; the nails *Obédience, Povreté, Charité* (?). The heart contains an escutcheon with the two monograms of Jesus and Mary, and a scroll with the word *Patience*; it is adorned with the flowers of *Pénitence, Fidélité, Bénignité, Joie.* This heart, affixed to the cross by means of the lance of charity and the three nails—the three vows of poverty, chastity, and obedience—is most certainly the heart of the

---

Verlagsbuchhandlung, 1967.—The Scolar Press of Menston, Yorks., England, has published a series of English emblem books; general editor is John Horden.

[56]Cf. *Ibid.*, Index, coll. 1973–1974, which mentions 53 emblems featuring the human heart. By way of comparison, there are only 48 emblems featuring hands in the collection.

[57]*L'Exercice du Coeur crucifié*; cf. A. Hamon, *Histoire*, Vol. II, p. 335.

believer, where, through patience and the virtues of the vows, and with
the help of Jesus and Mary, faithfulness and benevolence, penitence
and joy flourish.[58]

Much as Lanspergius may have summed up the tradition, the
trend toward visualization and ascetical focus on the heart of the
devout person himself, both of which he helps to inaugurate, also
marks the end of the pictorial representation of the Sacred Heart of
Jesus. The emblematic tradition is primarily interested in the human
heart of the Christian, which starts to occur with an increasing and
nervous frequency. The first book of religious emblems, Georgette de
Montenay's *Emblemes ou Devises Chrestiennes*, published in 1571,
modeled after Andreas Alciatus' purely humanist *Emblemata* of
1531, contains no less than twelve Christian hearts.[59] At about the
same time, Luther is closing his letters with a wax seal picturing a
heart surmounted by a cross and set in the middle of an open flower.
Calvin is using the emblem of an outstretched hand bearing a
burning heart as his own personal coat of arms. In 1584, an alternative seal of the Society of Jesus suddenly appears—no one knows
how or why. The official one had consisted of the Jesus monogram
IHS surmounted by the cross, with three nails, pointing downward
and arranged in a semi-circle, underneath. The new seal has the three
nails stuck in a heart, and the heart will stay there, despite repeated
protests, till the eighteenth century. The Jesus-monogram may suggest, at first sight, that the heart underneath is the Heart of Jesus,
but Hamon concludes, after a careful examination of the evidence,
that it is the heart of the Jesuit or the Christian.[60]

The emphasis on the human heart at the end of the sixteenth
century can also be demonstrated from a well-known English poem,
namely, Robert Southwell's *The Burning Babe*. The Infant Jesus is
pictured as a Christian transposition of the humanist figure of *Eros*
or *Amor*—a conceit which was to become extremely popular, under

---

[58]*Ibid.*, pp. 335–336. *Cherité* is a misprint for *Charité*, and *Charité* is one for
Chasteté, as Hamon's commentary makes clear.

[59]Cf. M. Praz, *Studies in Seventeenth-Century Imagery*, pp. 431–432, 44–46, 248–
252, 25ff.; also, J. H. van den Berg, *Het menselijk lichaam*, Vol. II, pp. 84–85.

[60]J. H. van den Berg, *Het menselijk lichaam*, Vol. II, pp. 85–87; A. Hamon,
Histoire, Vol. II, pp. 336–341.

the influence of Bérulle, in the first half of the seventeenth century in France.[61] The theme of divine love, of which the Babe is the embodiment, is orchestrated, in Southwell's poem, by means of a consistently allegorical interpretation of Galenic physiological processes; remarkably, the Babe's heart is not mentioned. The hearts that *are* mentioned are Southwell's own and all human hearts (or their equivalent, "mens defiled soules").

As I in hoarie Winters night stoode shivering in the snow,
Surpris'd I was with sodaine heate, which made my hart to glow;
And lifting up a fearefull eye, to view what fire was neare,
A pretty Babe all burning bright did in the ayre appeare;
Who scorched with excessive heate, such floods of teares did shed,
As though his floods should quench his flames, which with his teares
    were bred:
Alas (quoth he) but newly borne, in fiery heates I frie,
Yet none approach to warme their harts or feele my fire, but I;
My faultlesse breast the furnace is, the fuell wounding thornes:
Love is the fire, and sighs the smoake, the ashes shames and scornes;
The fewell Justice layeth on, and Mercie blowes the coales,
The mettall in this furnace wrought, are mens defiled soules:
For which, as now on fire I am to worke them to their good,
So will I melt into a bath, to wash them in my blood.
With this he vanisht out of sight, and swiftly shrunk away,
And straight I called unto minde, that it was Christmasse day.[62]

But let us return to the emblem-books, for we have a surprise awaiting us. Suddenly, in the ten years between 1620 and 1630, there is a veritable explosion of heart-emblems with religious significance; and without exception, the hearts pictured are believers' hearts, not that of Jesus. J. H. van den Berg mentions eight collections;[63] we will mention only four of them—the most famous and the most frequently translated. All of them are entirely aimed at providing the reader (or rather, the user) with emblematic food for thought and ingenious explanatory texts to help him train his heart in responding to divine love.

---

[61] Cf. M. Praz, *Studies in Seventeenth-Century Imagery*, pp. 83–168; for the reference to Bérulle, cf. p. 144.

[62] Text from Helen Gardner (ed.), *The Metaphysical Poets*, p. 37.

[63] J. H. van den Berg, *Het menselijk lichaam*, Vol. II, pp. 87–96.

There is Antoine Sucquet's *Via Vitae Aeternae*—"The Way of Eternal Life"—with its elaborate, extremely analytical plates for the purpose of meditation, eighteen of which contain hearts, some small, some huge.[64] Then there is Herman Hugo's much-translated *Pia Desideria*—"Pious Desires"—which pictures, in its emblems, a whole series of encounters between *Anima*—the Christian soul—and the Child Jesus—clearly a transposition of pagan *Amor.* The heart occurs only twice in this collection; the first time it is found on the title-page, appropriately equipped with wings and flames to convey the ideas of desire and love; the second time it occurs in the body of the book, when *Anima*, on her knees, holds her heart in her right hand (with the left she spurns a dressing-table with a variety of cosmetic perquisites), and lifts it up to Jesus holding in front of him the two tables of the law, each with a heart on it (thus making the absence of a picture of his own heart truly notable here).[65] An equally famous collection is *Cor Jesu Amanti Sacrum*—"The Heart a Temple for the Loving Jesus"—with eighteen plates by the famous Antoon Wierix, used many times to illustrate works by other authors.[66] J. H. van den Berg describes the progress of this immensely popular and oft-copied series of emblems as follows:

> In the first picture the Infant Jesus protects the heart against the guiles of World, Flesh, and Devil. Next, we see the heart opened, and the *amor divinus* is seen with a broom, cleaning out the heart, which is filled with an ample supply of vermin. This done, the labors of the holy Cupid can properly start. Thus he adorns the inside of the heart with attractive, visual, emblematic representations of the last things, and, in his capacity as the Son of David, he plays the harp while seated inside the heart. Finally, the Infant Jesus rewards the heart thus chastened, adorned, and glorified with decorations made of palm-leaves and flowers.[67]

Finally, there is the work of Benedict van Haeften, the *Schola Cordis*—"The School of the Heart"—of 1629. In this fat little book

---

[64]Cf. M. Praz, *Studies in Seventeenth-Century Imagery*, pp. 506–507.

[65]Cf. *ibid.*, pp. 376–379, 143–147. The second plate alluded to in the text occurs as plate XXI in *Liber II.*

[66]Cf. *ibid.*, pp. 535–536, 152–154.

[67]J. H. van den Berg, *Het menselijk lichaam*, Vol. II, p. 91.

of over seven hundred pages, which contains fifty-six copperplates by the well-known engraver Boëtius à Bolswert, *Amor* and *Anima* get company, namely *Anima*'s own heart—a conceit clearly derived from the emblem-books of Georgette de Montenay and the German Daniel Cramer. *Amor* subjects *Anima*'s heart to a series of rather drastic ascetical treatments, all of them administered in the sight or with the active collaboration of *Anima*; the purpose of the treatments—stretching the heart on a cross, flattening it under a printing-press, etc.—is to train the heart in the school of love, so that it may become more like the heart of Jesus, which, however, is never pictured. The preface of van Haeften's book explains that it is the function of the heart to be the source of heat and vitality; it is the place where the fire of life produces words by way of sparks and sighs by way of exhaust-fumes; it is also the place where the soul's spiritual heart, the repository of the divine fire, cooperates with the vital forces; thus the human heart is the center and the source of *all* life, light, heat, fervor, and movement.[68] We are in 1629 when this collection is published, one year after Harvey's *Exercitatio.*

We must pause at this point, for this is a watershed. The next fifty years will witness a dramatic reversal. The tables will be turned. The emblematic genre will die as an original art-form around the year 1640; the production of translations, reprints, and imitations will go on for some time to come, but the inspiration and the elegance and the eloquence will be gone. Along with the emblematic genre, the interest in the human heart will decline. The mood of the culture will become more austere, rational, and even classical— "Augustan." These will also be the years during which Harvey's discovery will gradually win acceptance. Is there a connection? It seems likely.

At any rate, while this process will be taking place, the Heart of Jesus, hardly ever pictured in the sixteenth and early seventeenth century, will gain an unprecedented prominence. In 1643, Jean Eudes will leave the Oratory, the community where he had been imbued with the spirituality of Bérulle and Condren, and start a new

---

[68]Cf. M. Praz, *Studies in Seventeenth-Century Imagery,* pp. 361–362, 151–152. For Cramer, cf. pp. 310–311. Cf. also J. H. van den Berg, *Het menselijk lichaam,* Vol. II, pp. 93–96.

community, which he will call the Congregation of Jesus and Mary; he will look upon the Heart of Jesus, together with the Heart of Mary, as "the founder and the superior, the source and the goal, the heart and the life" of his congregation.[69] And thirty years later, in December of 1673 and January of 1674, Marguerite-Marie Alacoque, the nun of Paray-le-Monial, will receive her mission to become the disciple of the Sacred Heart of Jesus. She will have her heart plunged in the furnace—"like a small atom, vanishing in that burning furnace"—and receive it back all aglow. She will *see* the Heart of Jesus

> enthroned in flames, brighter than the sun and transparent as crystal, with that adorable wound, and [. . .] with a crown of thorns around it, which signified the wounds inflicted on it by our sins, and surmounted by a cross, which meant that, from the first moment of the Incarnation, that is to say, as soon as this Sacred Heart was formed, the cross was planted in it, and it was filled, from the first moments, with all the bitterness which was to be caused by the humiliations, the poverty, the sorrow, and the contempt which the sacred humanity was to suffer during his entire life and in his sacred passion.[70]

And a few years later, in June of 1675, she will see Jesus "uncover his divine Heart" to her with the words:

> This is the heart which has loved people so much that it has not stopped short of exhausting and consuming itself in order to testify to them its love.[71]

Equipped with the hindsight that comes with the passage of time and the study of history, all the important historians of the Sacred Heart devotion have agreed that, since the proper object of the Sacred Heart devotion is the physical Heart of Jesus as the symbol of his love for humanity,[72] Saint Margaret Mary is the first

---

[69]Cf. A. Hamon, *Histoire*, Vol. III, pp. 191–195, 178.

[70]*Ibid.*, Vol. I, pp. 141, 148; cf. Vol. III, p. 271.

[71]*Ibid.*, Vol. I, p. 173.

[72]Cf. *ibid.*, Vol. II, pp. xv–xxxiii.—Cf., for example, J. V. Bainvel, *Devotion to the Sacred Heart*, The Doctrine and Its History, New York–Cincinnati–Chicago, Benziger Brothers, 1924, pp. 68–72; Louis Verheylezoon, *Devotion to the Sacred Heart*, London–Glasgow, Sands & Co., 1955, pp. 1–10.—Recent attempts to revive

true representative of the devotion. And it is true that in the years between 1673 and 1675 we have the first firm synthesis of three elements never before so closely united.

First, there is, unmistakably, the visual concentration on the physical Heart of Jesus as a separate organ, the summing-up of almost a century and a half of nervous concern with that mysterious center of the human anatomy. Second, the spiritualization of Galenic physiology has moved beyond the instruction and exhortation of the human heart, and into the purely *theological* contemplation of the one Heart which could continue to be called, without reservation, a burning furnace of love, and which finds itself now depicted after a long period of invisibility. Finally, there is the move from soteriology to christology, from the Passion and the wounds to the Heart of Jesus, symbol of his person, and the center, not only of his un-requited love for humanity, but also of his attitude of love, gratitude, and abandon to the Father, as Margaret Mary points out in her writings.[73]

One question remains. What happened between Benedict van Haeften's *Schola Cordis* of 1629 and the visions of Margaret Mary Alacoque of 1673–1675? To find the answer to this question we must briefly look at the life of Jean Eudes. His devotion to the Sacred Heart is characterized, by Hamon, as beautiful, powerful, and ar-dent, but also as lacking in precision.[74] The reason for this is that Jean Eudes marks the transition.

Formed by the tradition of Bérulle and Condren in the Oratory, which he enters in Paris at the age of twenty-two in 1623, Jean Eudes

---

the Sacred Heart devotion have argued that the Sacred Heart symbolically represents the *person* of Christ; cf., for example, Karl Rahner, " 'Behold This Heart!': Prelimi-naries to a Theology of Devotion to the Sacred Heart," in: *Theological Investigations*, Vol. III, Baltimore/London, Helicon Press/Darton, Longman & Todd, 1967, pp. 321–330; also, *id.*, "Some Theses for a Theology of Devotion to the Sacred Heart," *ibid.*, pp. 331–352. It would appear that these and similar efforts involve a real transposition; a dying concern is replaced with a contemporary one, namely, the concern with personalness (cf. above, pp. 171f). Incidentally, when Hamon appeals to Aquinas to argue that the Sacred Heart devotion addresses itself to the person of Christ (*Histoire*, Vol. II, pp. xxx-xxxi), he is arguing philosophically that the devotion is not addressed to one isolated portion of Christ; he has no modern concern with personalness in mind.

[73]Cf. A. Hamon, *Histoire*, Vol. III, pp. 288–290.

[74]*Ibid.*, pp. 177, 203–209.

becomes a successful preacher of popular missions in his native Normandy and in Brittany. From the sermons, devotional writings are born, chief among which is *The Life and the Kingdom of Jesus* of 1637.[75] Jean Eudes' preaching and writing come out of pastoral dedication that goes beyond the ordinary; when there had been an outbreak of the plague in 1626, he had spent almost six months helping the victims both spiritually and corporally. His style, both in the written word and in action, is more simple, direct, and fervent than that of his admired teacher, the aristocratic and sophisticated Bérulle, who feels completely at home in the circles where the governmental affairs of Church as well as State are decided. Thus, when Jean Eudes speaks of the Sacred Heart, he does so in imitation of Bérulle, but with greater warmth and enthusiasm. Père Hamon quotes a typical passage:

O my dear Jesus, [. . .] stamp into my heart and the hearts of all people [your] affections and dispositions [. . .]. O King of all hearts, here I am. I offer and sacrifice to you all those poor human hearts which you have created to love you, and who no longer care to draw any other breath but your love [. . .]. Ah! how blessed are those hearts who will do nothing for all eternity except worship, praise, and love the most adorable and most lovable heart of Jesus.

And Hamon comments, also in the light of other writings:

The affections, the feelings, the Heart of Jesus are also the affections, the feelings, the heart of Mary; the affections, the feelings, the heart of Père Eudes and of all the righteous. When we say to Jesus: I love you with all my heart, "we must understand this of the Heart of Jesus, of that of the blessed Virgin, and of all the choirs of angels and saints in heaven and on earth, who all together form but one heart with the most Holy Heart of Jesus and of Mary in virtue of the union which prevails among all hearts [. . .]."[76]

Summing up, to Jean Eudes, the expression "the Heart of Jesus" refers primarily to the love of Jesus as it affects the Blessed Virgin

---

[75] *La Vie et le Royaume de Jésus, ibid.*, p. 188. Cf. the entire chapter on Eudes' earlier life, pp. 177–209. Cf. also J. H. van den Berg, *Het menselijk lichaam*, Vol. II, pp. 68–75.

[76] A. Hamon, *Histoire*, Vol. III, p. 190.

Mary first of all, but then also all the saints and angels and all people. In this way, Eudes stands midway between the *Schola Cordis* and Margaret Mary—at least till around 1640.

For, as Jean Eudes' life moves on, he becomes more and more affirmative about the heart of Jesus and Mary, especially after his encounter, between 1641 and 1643, with the troubled, saintly mystic of Coutances, Marie des Vallées.[77] Under her influence his life is taking, in his own words, a new direction. He founds the Congregation of Jesus and Mary, entirely devoted to the Sacred Heart (singular!) of Jesus and Mary. He becomes more and more explicit about the presence of the Heart of Jesus in the heart of Mary and in the hearts of all Christians, and about the need for its presence in all human hearts. In 1643 the feast of the heart of Mary is celebrated liturgically for the first time, an incident that provokes many discussions among ecclesiastical authorities. From 1672 on, the feast of the Heart of Jesus, now distinct from the feast of Mary's heart, is solemnly celebrated in Eudes' religious family.[78]

In 1673, Jean Eudes' portrait is painted. We see a pensive, shy, relatively young-looking septuagenarian, his arms crossed in front of himself; in his left hand he holds a crucifix; in his right hand he holds a heart, a visible human heart, surmounted by a cross surrounded by flames, and with the Latin inscription "Heart of Jesus and Mary, Furnace of Love" on the side facing us.[79]

Thus, while Harvey's discovery, born out of visual observation, that the heart is a pump was slowly gaining acceptance in the years after 1628, the focus of the visualizing devotion to the heart was slowly shifting away from the human heart and its affections, until, by way of the heart of Mary, it reached the Heart of Jesus and settled there. Around 1675, both developments are complete. Prospero Lambertini, in 1726, will still be puzzled by the connection; popular devotion, with its instinctive ability to appreciate symbols, will not. It will proceed to worship the Sacred Heart of Jesus with a fervor

---

[77]Cf. *ibid.*, pp. 193–194; J. H. van den Berg, *Het menselijk lichaam*, Vol. II, pp. 65–68.

[78]Cf. A. Hamon, *Histoire*, Vol. III, pp. 195, 231.

[79]Reproduction in J. H. van den Berg, *Het menselijk lichaam*, Vol. II, opp. p. 64; the Latin text reads *Cor Jesu et Mariae Fornax Amoris.*

that will not significantly abate till sometime in the twentieth century. But that story must be told some other time.

The heart accepted, purified, and put in perspective
We must now, by way of conclusion, briefly look at the theological implications of the process we have reviewed. Starting in the second quarter of the sixteenth century, the human heart became the focus of cultural concern in a double way. It became an anatomical and physiological problem; as a result, it became questionable as the center of human life experience, thus leaving a serious vacuum. In connection with this, the heart's significance as a—we would now say—symbolic way of dealing with human affective and religious interiority became dubious.

The living Church opened herself to this nervous preoccupation with such precious and precarious concerns as life and love. In the course of a long process of clarification, the impasse was integrated into the Christian life. The integration, however, was also a purification. The isolated heart was accepted, but it acquired a symbolic significance which it had never quite so clearly had before; the Sacred Heart of Jesus served as a reminder—lost on Lambertini—that there was more to the human heart than its being part of a mechanically conceived anatomy. The concern with human affective interiority was accepted, too; but it was gradually brought within the theological ambit of the Sacred Heart, and thus stripped of its overriding concern with rational, natural morality. Finally, the heart became a new way to worship—a liturgically telling symbol of the mystery of the person of Christ.

Our analysis leads to a thesis, namely, that in the Sacred Heart devotion we have an instance of a christology forged out of a human concern accepted, converted to obedience, and placed in the perspective of worshipful surrender in hope. That is to say that in the Sacred Heart devotion we also have a memorial of the Church's patient hospitality to the culture, and thus of the Church's obedience to the will of the Father compassionate, in imitation of Christ.[80]

---

[80]The preceding account is far from complete. To do justice to the place of the heart in the sixteenth and seventeenth centuries, the picture of the Sacred Heart would have to be complemented by analyses of the practice of *la garde du coeur* and of

EXEMPLAR AND MEDIATOR

The subjectivity of feeling

Friedrich Schleiermacher's theological inspiration, which is also the core of his christology, is unthinkable outside the context of romanticism and its basic inspiration. The romantic inspiration, in turn, cannot be appreciated for the venture in originality it really is, if the sensibility that immediately preceded it is not taken into account. Hence, a brief characterization of the mood just before the dawn of romanticism must open even the incongruously brief treatment of Schleiermacher's christology that is to follow.

As early as May 1736, Bishop Joseph Butler noted that—"I know not how"—many "people of discernment" had come to consider Christianity as "fictitious," and hence "not so much as a subject of inquiry."[81] Butler shows he was a witness of the development of the idea that religion is not concerned with matters that are the province of knowledge. In the terminology of the mid-twentieth century, he saw the growth of the view that religious utterances are unverifiable, and hence incapable of being either true or false. As a result, the theology of the eighteenth century found itself in a continuous process of retreat to safer and more defensible positions. It was a brave struggle, made all the braver by the fact that many people, smelling defeat, had already made a virtue out of necessity and taken refuge in the sanctuary of the heart—pietism was popular. Thus it had become the hard and thankless task of doctrinal Christianity to stand its ground in the no man's land between the claims staked out by reason and its companion, natural religion, on the one hand, and those staked out by feeling and its associate, pietism, on the other.

In the earlier stages of the development, the domain of ethics still remained open—a circumstance that allowed theologians to claim it as a basis for religion. Kant's association of religion with

---

Pascal's *logique du coeur*, to mention only the two themes treated by van den Berg (*Het menselijk lichaam*, Vol. II, pp. 97–104). On the other hand, to understand the anatomizing tendencies of the period, studies of phenomena like *concettismo* in poetry would be necessary to complete the picture.

[81]In the "Advertisement" to the first edition of the *Analogy of Religion* of May 1736, as quoted by David Jenkins, *Guide to the Debate About God*, pp. 21–22.

practical reason reflects a widespread movement in the eighteenth and nineteenth centuries to ground the *proprium* of religion outside the province claimed by objective knowledge while avoiding its exclusive association with purely subjective feeling.[82]

Still, as not only knowledge but also morality was increasingly brought within the ambit of pure rationality, it is not surprising that religion resigned itself more and more to being associated with feeling. Lessing tells the story of the little community on one of the Bermuda islands, whose only connection with the Church consists in a pair of antique wooden book-covers that once held together the pages of an old edition of Luther's *Catechismus*. The pages have been worn away by dint of use over the 150 years since the time when the group's ancestors suffered shipwreck and were cast ashore. Are these people Christians? Of course, Lessing exclaims. "Of what interest to a Christian are the opinions of theologians, as long as he feels blessed in his faith?"[83] It would be hard to find a better expression of the pietistic stance, and a stronger endorsement of the thesis that the credibility of the faith rests on inner experience. Large sections of Christianity—including many sophisticated circles—thus got identified with a cultural movement which regarded the non-objective nature of feelings (and, with feelings, of aesthetic and religious experience) as axiomatic.

For that had become a basic assumption of the late eighteenth century—that feeling was entirely immanent and subjective, and in no way related to objectivity. This was not just a matter of theory. The immanence and subjectivity of feeling, or at least its utter disproportionateness to external causes and events, were a matter of actual experience among the milieus that counted.[84] J. H. van den

---

[82]J. Bots, *Tussen Descartes en Darwin*, Geloof en Natuurwetenschap in de achttiende eeuw in Nederland, Assen, Van Gorcum & Comp. N. V., 1972, has shown that the religious experience of the early physico-theologians was still a genuine sense of transcendence, evoked by their scientific discoveries. But as the century wore on, the theologians' reactions to the wonders of nature increasingly became purely moralistic.

[83]Related by J. H. van den Berg, *Psychologie en geloof*, Een kroniek en een standpunt, Nijkerk, Uitgeverij G. F. Callenbach N. V., ³1965, pp. 16–17. The story occurs in Lessing's *Axiomata*, in: *Sämmtliche Werke*, (ed. Gosche), Vol. VII, pp. 395ff.; Lessing's comment is on p. 407.

[84]Cf. above, pp. 44–47, 83–85.

Berg reviews a large and varied number of incidents, taken from the history of eighteenth-century sensibility, and comes to an interesting conclusion.[85] In the eighteenth century, he states, the questioning approach to nature and morality becomes so analytical and dispassionate that the connection between feeling and objectivity gets lost. As a result, feeling, detached from the external world, is not regulated and moderated by reality any longer; it becomes deregulated and immoderate. And choosing one pregnant example from a host of telling incidents, van den Berg sums up: "Rousseau could sob *profusely*, because there was *nothing* he was sobbing *about*."[86]

The theoreticians of the period endorse the experience. Johann Georg Sulzer writes in 1763:

> What Descartes has said, [namely,] that the pain is not in the needle that causes it, is true of all objects that arouse a certain feeling [*Empfindung*] in the soul. We feel [*empfindet man*] not the object, but ourselves.[87]

In 1777 we hear from Johannes Nikolaus Tetens that feeling is "something about which I know only this, that it is a change within myself." Kant writes in 1790 that feeling is "related exclusively to the subject" and that it "must always remain purely subjective." Fichte, in 1795, defines feeling as "the most original interplay [*Wechselwirkung*] between the I [*Ich*] and itself." And even Hegel will sound a faint echo of this tradition, when, in 1817, he imaginatively defines feeling as *das dumpfe Weben des Geistes*—"the deep-sounding surging of the Spirit."[88] However, by that time such a profound shift in sensibility has taken place that Hegel's

---

[85] *Het menselijk lichaam*, Vol. II, pp. 165–205.

[86] *Ibid.*, p. 200.

[87] Quoted by J. H. van den Berg, *Het menselijk lichaam*, Vol. II, p. 182, in the context of a long discussion of Sulzer, *ibid.*, pp. 179–188. Cf. also *Psychologie en geloof*, p. 17, and Hans Frei, *The Eclipse of Biblical Narrative*, pp. 139ff.—The statement Sulzer attributes to Descartes is not found in any of the latter's known works.

[88] All these quotations—together with a few others—are found in J. H. van den Berg, *Het menselijk lichaam*, Vol. II, pp. 188–189. Cf. *Psychologie en geloof*, pp. 16–18, 24–25, 26.—In both publications, van den Berg fails to distinguish between sentimentalism/rationalism and romanticism. The latter contains elements of depth and objectivity which the former never had.

definition has come to mean something really different. Hence, Hegel's definition can only be correctly understood if placed in its proper context—romanticism.

The romantic discovery: the objectivity of innermost awareness
Few English writers convey the essence of the romantic inspiration as well as William Wordsworth. Though not a man with overriding theoretical interests like his friend Coleridge, he was nevertheless deeply interested in, and aware of, the intellectual implications of the romantic movement. For this reason Wordsworth is a reliable guide, both to the central experience of romanticism and to the nature of the intellectual venture it gave rise to. To characterize, therefore, the central discovery of romanticism and its intellectual aspirations, let us look at three texts by Wordsworth. This will lay the groundwork for a brief characterization of the central inspiration of Schleiermacher's christology and, indeed, of his entire theological enterprise.

Few poems match and orchestrate Hegel's description of feeling as *das dumpfe Weben des Geistes* better than one of Wordsworth's best-known sonnets.

> It is a beauteous evening, calm and free,
> The holy time is quiet as a Nun
> Breathless with adoration; the broad sun
> Is sinking down in its tranquillity;
> The gentleness of heaven broods o'er the Sea:
> Listen! the mighty Being is awake,
> And doth with his eternal motion make
> A sound like thunder—everlastingly.
> Dear Child! dear Girl! that walkest with me here,
> If thou appear untouched by solemn thought,
> Thy nature is not therefore less divine:
> Thou liest in Abraham's bosom all the year;
> And worshipp'st at the Temple's inner shrine,
> God being with thee when we know it not.[89]

The child—Wordsworth's little daughter—actualizes, in her very thoughtlessness, what the poet realizes is at the innermost core

---

[89] *The Poetical Works of William Wordsworth*, Vol. III (E. de Selincourt and Helen Darbishire, eds.), Oxford, Clarendon Press, 1946, p. 17.

of every person: the experienced affinity with the Infinite. Just as the surging of the sea is the symbol of the divine presence ("*his*—not: its—eternal motion"!) which animates the universe, so the wash and the dash of the waves of inner feeling are the sign that the native instinct of each person is in tune with the Infinite. Feeling, therefore, is ultimately *not* purely subjective; rather, it is the experienced impact of the Infinite on the person's deepest interiority. As such, feeling is essentially religious; but what is more, feeling, being the repercussion of Reality at its highest, is essentially *objective*: no faculty in the person does more justice to Reality than that innermost awareness which permanently underlies, and often belies, all our "solemn," self-important thought.[90] The dawn of creation and the inner nature of a child—they are one, in the original Emmanuel-experience: "God being with thee." When Wordsworth says, in the famous preface to the second edition of the *Lyrical Ballads*, that the poet "considers man and nature as essentially adapted to each other,"[91] he is making a *religious* statement, for underneath the adaptedness between man and nature lies an even deeper connection: to be deeply in touch with nature is to be even more deeply in touch with the Infinite.

This is why, in adulthood, we are to remain attentive to, and thankful for

> those first affections,
> Those shadowy recollections,
> Which, be they what they may,
> Are yet the fountain light of all our day,
> Are yet a master light of all our seeing;
> Uphold us, cherish, and have power to make
> Our noisy years seem moments in the being
> Of the eternal Silence: truths that wake,
> To perish never;
> Which neither listlessness, nor mad endeavour,

---

[90]This idea is the wider cultural context of the interpretation of Schleiermacher's theology as a "return to the objective." Cf. Claude Welch, *Protestant Thought in the Nineteenth Century*, Vol. I, 1799–1870, New Haven and London, Yale University Press, 1972, p. 60, n. 2.

[91]*The Poetical Works of William Wordsworth*, Vol. II (E. de Selincourt, ed.), Oxford, Clarendon Press, 1944, pp. 384–404, quotation p. 396.

Nor Man nor Boy,
Nor all that is at enmity with joy,
Can utterly abolish or destroy!
Hence in a season of calm weather
Though inland far we be,
Our Souls have sight of that immortal sea
Which brought us hither,
Can in a moment travel thither,
And see the Children sport upon the shore,
And hear the mighty waters rolling evermore.[92]

This abiding availability of the access, both to the innermost, original self and to the all-encompassing Infinite, leads to a criticism of life, and especially of the life of the mind. In the third book of *The Prelude* Wordsworth relates to us his experiences as a student in Cambridge, suffering from the humiliations of the classroom routine and the weariness of regular study. To be revived, he tells us, he would go away into the countryside in order to contemplate "earth and heaven."

I called on both to teach me what they might;
Or, turning the mind in upon herself,
Pored, watched, expected, listened, spread my thoughts
And spread them with a wider creeping; felt
Incumbencies more awful, visitings
Of the Upholder of the tranquil soul,
That tolerates the indignities of Time,
And, from the centre of Eternity
All finite motions overruling, lives
In glory immutable. But peace! enough
Here to record that I was mounting now
To such community with highest truth—
A track pursuing, not untrod before,
From strict analogies by thought supplied
Or consciousness not to be subdued.
To every natural form, rocks, fruit, or flower,
Even the loose stones that cover the high-way,
I gave a moral life: I saw them feel,

---

[92]From: *Ode (Intimations of Immortality from Recollections of Early Childhood)*, in: *The Poetical Works of William Wordsworth*, Vol. IV, (E. de Selincourt and Helen Darbishire, eds.), Oxford, Clarendon Press, 1947, pp. 279–285, quotation lines 149–168, pp. 283–284.

> Or linked them to some feeling: the great mass
> Lay bedded in a quickening soul, and all
> That I beheld respired with inward meaning.[93]

Thus the romantic experience sets a new agenda for thought. True thinking must go beyond the mere understanding (*Verstand*) which Kant, along with the rationalists, had wrongly taken for reason (*Vernunft*). Thought must reach for the spiritual insights of true reason (*Vernunft*), which scans *and penetrates* the entire universe and beyond, by means of an all-encompassing dialectic of immanence and transcendence that does justice to the very texture of all that is. Coleridge was to try this, but his achievements were to remain somewhat spotty.[94] Hegel was to achieve it, and thus he became the commanding figure in the movement to translate the romantic inspiration into a sublimely integrated intellectual system.

Of this movement, Friedrich Schleiermacher was a part, too.

Religion and the person of Christ

The young Schleiermacher, tutored and encouraged by the great romantic seeker and theorist Friedrich Schlegel, wrote his *Speeches* in a mood of enthusiastic discovery. It is true that there is also an element of calculation in the way he makes his case. Throughout the *Speeches*, the young Schleiermacher shows that he is completely aware of all the points which his audience, the cultured despisers of religion, will or will not grant him, and why. The author is obviously a skilled apologist. Still, the style of argument is too vivid and the arguments themselves too passionate to be the mere products of apologetics; not dexterity in argument but firm convictions and sure insights prompt the author to write as he does. At bottom, Schleiermacher's convictions and insights are independent of the despisers' opinions.[95] The *Speeches* echo a world much larger than the eigh-

---

[93] *The Prelude, or, The Growth of a Poet's Mind*, (E. de Selincourt, ed.), London, Geoffrey Cumberlege, Oxford University Press, 1926, lines 115–135, pp. 75, 77.

[94] On Coleridge's insistence that reason must be understood more deeply than either rationalism or emotionalism had done, cf. Claude Welch, *Protestant Thought in the Nineteenth Century*, Vol. I, pp. 113–121.

[95] David Jenkins' rendition of Schleiermacher's fundamental insight in the *Speeches* places too much emphasis on his apologetical intentions, and too little on his constructive power. Cf. *Guide to the Debate About God*, pp. 25–55.

teenth-century debate about God and religion had been prepared to recognize. The young Schleiermacher's first theological writing may have started as a venture in apologetics; its inspiration is deeper and its scope much wider. Thus, when he writes,

> Wherefore, my friends, belief must be something different from a mixture of opinions about God and the world, and of precepts for one life or [even] for two. Piety cannot be an instinct craving for a mess of metaphysical and ethical crumbs—[96]

he deliberately uses condescending terms to refer, not only to religion (as his audience understands it!), but also to natural science and metaphysics, and to practical philosophy and ethics. It is obvious from the tone of the passage that this young romantic is convinced that there is something radically more profound about life than the subject-object relations involved in knowledge and action. Hence, he wants to *undercut* the superficiality of rationalism and pragmatism, not merely to correct it. When, therefore, he directs his audience's attention to feeling and religion, he is not staying at the same level as his audience. His concern is not with feeling as if it were a regrettably neglected third faculty of the human person, on a par with knowing and acting, or with religion as if it were a regrettably neglected third part of human life, comparable to philosophy and ethics. He is concerned, not with an oversight on the part of the despisers of religion, but with the *basic integrity of human life.* That is why he urges his readers to "descend into the inmost sanctuary of life"—the self—in order there to discover "the original relation of intuition and feeling" that provides all subject-object activity with fundamental meaningfulness.[97] Hence, what is most basic about Schleiermacher's inspiration is not the emphasis on feeling as such, but the stress on experiential *Selbstbewusstsein*—the person's basic self-awareness, the person's identity-experience. This central experience of the self is both luminous and affective; it is the experienced

---

[96]*On Religion*, p. 31.—The addition of "[even]" reflects Schleiermacher's intentions, as appears from the original text in the first German edition: "oder gar für zwei." Cf. *Ueber die Religion—Reden an die Gebildeten unter ihren Verächtern,* in: *Schleiermachers Werke,* O. Braun and Joh. Bauer (eds.), Vol. IV, Leipzig, Felix Meiner, pp. 207–399, quotation p. 236.

[97]*On Religion*, p. 41.

unity of intuition and feeling. In the final analysis, Schleiermacher's insistence on feeling in the *Speeches* serves to point to the inalienable nature of the self-consciousness-experience that underlies all knowledge and all action. It is not meant to separate immediate self-awareness, feeling, and religion from all other human pursuits.[98]

This luminous and affective self-awareness is, at its deepest level, an immediate, affective awareness of utter dependence, and an immediate, intuitive understanding of one's being-related to God. In the more mature, reflective and theoretical style of *The Christian Faith*, Schleiermacher came to express this fundamental insight of his younger years as follows.

> Now this is just what is principally meant by the formula which says that to feel oneself utterly dependent and to be conscious of oneself as being in relation with God are one and the same thing; and the reason is that utter dependence is the fundamental relation which must include all others in itself. The second expression also includes the God-consciousness in the self-consciousness in such a way that [. . .] the two cannot be separated from each other. The feeling of utter dependence becomes a clear self-consciousness only as this idea comes simultaneously into being. In this sense it can indeed be said that God is given to us in feeling in an original way; and if we speak of an original revelation of God to man or in man, the meaning will always be just this, that, along with the utter dependence which characterizes not only man but all finite beings, there is given to man also the immediate self-consciousness of it, which becomes the consciousness of God.[99]

In this way Schleiermacher places at the basis of his theology the central experience of romanticism: the experienced unity of intuition and affection given in the immediate experience of self-identity and utter dependence, and all this as the pre-condition for meaningful life in the human community and in the world. The deepest self is not

---

[98]On this subject, cf. Richard R. Niebuhr's elegant and balanced account in *Schleiermacher on Christ and Religion*, London, SCM Press, 1964, pp. 116–134. The chapters in Claude Welch, *Protestant Thought in the Nineteenth Century*, Vol. I, pp. 59–85, and James C. Livingstone, *Modern Christian Thought*, From the Enlightenment to Vatican II, New York/London, The Macmillan Company/Collier-Macmillan Limited, 1971, pp. 96–114, are largely dependent on this important monograph.

[99]*The Christian Faith* (trans. H. R. Macintosh and J. S. Stewart), Edinburgh, T. & T. Clark, 1928, § 4, pp. 17–18, corrected after *Der christliche Glaube*, (Martin Redeker, ed.), 2 vols., Berlin, Walter de Gruyter & Co., ⁷1960, Vol. I, p. 30.

neutral, nor is it a merely formal postulate of objective knowledge and practical action. It is a positively experienced source of life. It is the fundamental condition for the possibility of all realism in knowledge and action. It is the inner sanctuary, and the source of our assurance that religion relates our deepest and truest self to the most high and most reliable God.

There is an opinion, as widespread as it is mistaken, that Schleiermacher developed his idea of Jesus Christ directly out of his analysis of human self-awareness. Were this so, then Schleiermacher's Jesus would indeed be no more than *homo religiosus* writ large. As a matter of fact, however, Schleiermacher's Christ is characterized by particularity and historicity, and it is precisely in this capacity that he is presented as the origin of faith. Richard R. Niebuhr has quite rightly written that Schleiermacher "was able to give cogent grounds for believing that it is unreasonable to attempt to derive the figure of Christ from the religious imagination," and that, according to him, "Christ completes the creation of faith; faith does not create Christ."[100] We will come back to this important insight later, in a more appropriate context. However, given the widespread misinterpretation of Schleiermacher's christology, it was necessary to make the point right here at the outset of our treatment.

Once it has been recognized, however, that Schleiermacher did not develop his christology out of his idea of fundamental human self-consciousness, no perceptive reader can miss the enormous indebtedness of his picture of Christ to the romantic idea of man. The following text from the *Speeches* illustrates well the balance of indebtedness to, and freedom from, romantic prejudice in Schleiermacher's picture of Christ, besides giving another telling example of his disdain for superficial attempts to reduce religion to rationalist ideals.

> When, in the mutilated delineations of His life I contemplate the sacred image of Him who has been the author of the noblest that there has yet been in religion, what I admire is not the purity of His moral teaching, which but expressed what all men who have come to the consciousness of their spiritual nature have in common with Him, and which acquires no greater value, either from the fact that He enunciated it, or from the

---

[100]*Schleiermacher on Christ and Religion*, pp. 218, 225.

fact that He first enunciated it. Nor do I admire the individuality of His character, the close union of high power with touching gentleness, for every sublimely simple soul cannot but display, in special situations, some traces of great character. All those things are merely human. But the truly divine element is the glorious clarity to which the great idea He came to exhibit attained in His soul. This idea was, that all that is finite requires a higher mediation to be connected with the Deity [. . .].[101].

For all the stress on the exceptional, and indeed unique, nature of Christ's fundamental inspiration, and on its irreducibility to mere teaching and human character, the *structure* of Christ's inner identity is indubitably romantic: it is in the nature of an "idea" in Christ's "soul." The former denotes, of course, much more than a mere concept or a piece of knowledge; "idea," in the language of early romanticism, stands for the inner ideal that informs and structures a reality as its normative essence; in this case, Jesus *is* the mediator in virtue of his idea. The latter, "soul," refers, in good romantic fashion, to Jesus' innermost self-awareness. At the very heart of Jesus' self-awareness, the young Schleiermacher says, is his unclouded sense of identity as the mediator between God and all finite beings.

No wonder that his sense of the total originality of Jesus' self-awareness drives Schleiermacher directly to the *origin* of Jesus' self-awareness. For him—and for the entire period that expressed its religious identity in *Stille Nacht* and *Minuit Chrétiens*—Christmas becomes the vantage-point from which to reflect on the Christian mystery. In 1805, Schleiermacher writes his poetic dialogue *Die Weihnachtsfeier*, which places the Christ *child* at the center of the Christian experience. As the new-born Savior, Christ is the model and the source of the peaceful, spiritual joy which is the prerogative of all those who have been reborn as children by the experience of this most holy night, this feast of piety and melody.[102] It is hard to conceive a more romantic (and a more touchingly German!) meditation on the Incarnation.

---

[101]*On Religion*, p. 246, corrected after *Ueber die Religion*, pp. 392–393.

[102]Cf. Richard R. Niebuhr, *Schleiermacher on Christ and Religion*, pp. 37–43. Cf. also Emanuel Hirsch, *Schleiermachers Christusglaube* [Gütersloh], Gütersloher Verlagshaus Gerd Mohn, 1968, pp. 7–52.

Schleiermacher's appeal to childhood and youth as having special theological significance is not limited to *Die Weihnachtsfeier*. It is also found, in the second edition of the *Speeches* of 1806, in the touching reference to that prototype of the young romantic, the poet Novalis, who had died in 1801 at the age of twenty-nine.[103] It occurs again in the crucial § 93 of *The Christian Faith*, where "a happy childlike nature" is used as an approximation of Jesus' innocence—an innocence due to the singular power and serenity of his God-consciousness, and to the perfect identity of his person, without the least trace of opposition.[104] This amounts to the rejection of the characterization of Jesus as merely exemplary (*vorbildlich*); he must be appreciated in his *Urbildlichkeit*—his original, prototypical, ideal exemplarity.[105] Again, in typical romantic fashion, the perfection of humanity in Christ is conceived in terms of origin. And so Schleiermacher can move to the key idea of his christology, which consists in viewing Christ in terms of the origin of the human race—as the second Adam.

[The beginning of Jesus' life] had to be free, in advance, from every influence of earlier generations which disseminated sin and disturbed the inner God-consciousness, and it can only be correctly understood as an original act of human nature, i.e., as an act of human nature as unaffected by sin. Now the beginning of his life was also a new implanting of the God-consciousness, and in such a way as to exhaust the capacity of human nature; hence the content [*Gehalt*—"substance"] of his life and the manner of its origin are so closely related that they mutually condition and explain one another. That new implanting came to be through the beginning of his life, and therefore this beginning must have been elevated above all detrimental influence coming from his immediate surroundings; and because it was such an original and sin-free act of [human] nature, this act could result in [human] nature being filled to capacity with God-consciousness. The conclusion is that this mutual relationship is most perfectly elucidated by regarding the beginning of the life of Jesus as the completed creation of human nature. The appearance of the first man is at the same time the establishment of the physical life of the human race; the appearance of the second Adam establishes for this same nature the new spiritual life, which develops and communicates itself by spiritual fecundation.

---

[103]*On Religion*, p. 41.
[104]Pp. 377–385, quotation p. 383.
[105]*Ibid.*, p. 378.

And just as in the case of the former its originality (which is the quality of human nature at its first appearance) is identical with the act of its emergence, due to God's creative activity, so the two are also identical in the case of the Redeemer: his spiritual originality, free from all detrimental influence due to natural descent, and that [singular] creative presence of God in him, which parallels [the creativity of the first beginning]. The imparting of the Spirit to human nature which took place in the first Adam was insufficient, because the Spirit remained sunk in sensuousness, and only showed itself in its entirety now and then, by way of a presentiment of something better yet to come; the work of creation has only been completed through the second, equally original imparting [of the Spirit] to the second Adam; still, both components [*Momente*] go back to *one* undivided eternal divine decree, and so, from a higher viewpoint, they form only one consistent essential reality [*Naturzusammenhang*], even though as such it is outside our [natural] reach.[106]

Again, Schleiermacher does not tire of stressing that his picture of Christ is not the product of the religious imagination, for—as a modern commentator has phrased it—"the religious self-consciousness vitiated by sin could not of itself produce the impression of a sinless redeemer."[107] But, nevertheless, the features of the second Adam are obvious. They are the features, supernaturally enhanced and reshaped to divine perfection, of the first Adam—as he was perceived in the virgin light of the dawn of romanticism, the unspoilt child of God, celebrated in the uncomplicated lyricism of the recitativos and arias of Haydn's *The Creation*.

Christianity and religion

The structure of Schleiermacher's christology, we have argued, owes much to romanticism. The identity of Christ is explored by means of such notions as God-consciousness, inner awareness and affectivity, childhood and originality—all of them essential ingredients, as we saw, of the romantic discovery. What is remarkable, though, is that Schleiermacher's Christ never turns into a mere projection of the ideal of human religiosity—*homo religiosus* writ

---

[106]*Ibid.*, § 94, pp. 388–389, corrected after *Der christliche Glaube*, Vol. II, pp. 47–48.

[107]Richard R. Niebuhr, *Schleiermacher on Christ and Religion*, pp. 216–217.

large. This is so important that it requires some elaboration, as we promised a few pages ago.[108]

The first point we must make is that the temptation to accept human religiosity as the highest, because most general, form of all religion was formidable, and that Schleiermacher resisted it. The entire eighteenth century had dragged all particular religions, with their claims to special revelations, before the tribunal of natural religion as establishable by reason. Much of the aesthetic atmosphere of the romantic movement was decidedly pantheistic, and the intellectual development of a man like Hegel shows how attractive it was to make the essential discovery of romanticism—the subject's spiritual identity-experience, given in the inner experience of the original unity of affect and intuition, as *the* cue to the nature of all reality—into the ultimate in theology.

Schleiermacher does not shrink from the full acceptance of the religious experience of romanticism. He writes, without the slightest sign of confessional nervousness:

> The contemplation of the pious is the immediate consciousness of the universal existence of all finite things, in and through the Infinite, and of all temporal things in and through the Eternal. Religion is to seek this and find it in all that lives and moves, in all growth and change, in all doing and suffering. It is to have life and to know life in immediate feeling, only as such an existence in the Infinite and Eternal. Where this is found religion is satisfied, where it hides itself there is for her unrest and anguish, extremity and death. Wherefore it is a life in the infinite nature of the Whole, in the One and in the All, in God, having and possessing all things in God, and God in all.[109]

Still, for all his acceptance of the romantic intuition, Schleiermacher neither draws the conclusion that Christianity is one particular form of a *per se* universal religion, nor does he reduce Christ to a particularly striking example [*Vorbild*] of human religiosity.

This leads us to our second point. In Schleiermacher's view, the determinative datum in matters of religion is not religion, but *the religions.* The fifth of the *Speeches* is the statement of principle in this

[108]Above, p. 557.
[109]*On Religion*, p. 36.

matter. With uncommon theological shrewdness, and also with what must be a strong personal interest in particular persons and particular events, Schleiermacher writes:

> The different existing manifestations of religion you call positive religions. Under this name they have long been the object of a quite preeminent hate. Despite your repugnance to religion generally, you have always borne more easily with what for distinction is called natural religion. You have almost spoken of it with esteem.
>
> I do not hesitate to say that from the heart I entirely deny this superiority. For all who have religion at all and profess to love it, it would be the vilest inconsequence to admit it. They would thereby fall into the openest self-contradiction. For my own part, if I only succeeded in recommending to you this natural religion, I would consider that I had lost my pains.
>
> For you, indeed, to whom religion generally is offensive, I have always considered this preference natural. The so-called natural religion is usually so much refined away, and has such metaphysical and moral graces, that little of the peculiar character of religion appears. It understands so well to live in reserve, to restrain and to accommodate itself that it can be put up with anywhere. Every positive religion, on the contrary, has certain strong traits and a very marked physiognomy, so that its every movement, even to the careless glance, proclaims what it really is.[110]

And with true evangelistic fervor he perorates:

> Go back then, if you are in earnest about beholding religion in its definiteness, from this enlightened natural religion to those despised positive religions. There everything appears active, strong and secure, every single intuition has its definite content and its own relation to the rest, and every feeling has its proper sphere and its peculiar reference.[111]

Piety, therefore, is not a fundamental reality necessarily overlaid, and even distorted, by particular accretionary religious forms, and in need of continual restoration by means of a reduction of all particular religious forms to a more basic, universal, and valid natural religion. On the contrary, piety exists in a variety of concrete forms, some higher than others, and in any case all different from

---

[110]*Ibid.*, p. 214.
[111]*Ibid.*, p. 234.

each other; the Christian faith is the loftiest of all. We must say, therefore, that the Christian identity is the result of the dynamic process of religious self-consciousness forming and reforming itself under the influence of the Spirit of Christianity.[112] In fact, the Christian self-consciousness actualizes, to the full, the *identity* of the Christian particularity, which is the Holy Spirit, and the ultimate depth of the human subject, which is its affinity with the infinite. Emanuel Hirsch has summed this up in a compelling fashion.

> The Christian religion is, in virtue of the Spirit that has appeared in Christ as the Redeemer, more than a self-contained and self-moving form of pious God-consciousness. The Spirit that appears in [the Christian religion] is not just the Holy Spirit, who lifts up to eternity and infinity the hearts and senses of the people he touches with divine closeness. It is also and at the same time the human Spirit, the reasonable [*vernünftiger*] shaper of the world, aware, by divine warrant, that it bears the responsibility for the shaping of world history, that it is the world's creative Reason. The religious community which possesses in Christ its Redeemer and Quickener has a pious self-awareness [of its own], which constitutes the subject-matter for dogmatic reflection. This self-awareness, however, is fundamentally identical with Reason, which penetrates all of reality, and which forms the underlying principle of the philosophical ethic that enlightens world history. Because the Redeemer is the Spirit of the world [*Erdgeist*], his wondrous appearance on earth coincides with the emergence of the higher human self-consciousness—the power which had tried to find the way to itself, in the first epoch of world history, in childlike unawareness and in dreamlike ways.[113]

Thus Schleiermacher elaborates the relationship between the romantic ideal of human religiosity and the Christian faith in such a way as to do justice to the claims to universalism associated with the former as well as to the claims to historical particularity and theological superiority associated with the latter. In the process of the elaboration, however, both are put in their places. The romantic ideal finds itself reminded that its universalism amounts to nothing if it presents itself as the only true religion; religiosity comes to fruition only in the concreteness of the particular religions. The Christian

---

[112]Cf. Richard R. Niebuhr, *Schleiermacher on Christ and Religion*, p. 231.
[113]*Schleiermachers Christusglaube*, p. 43.

faith is reminded that it must recognize itself as one among many religions, and the highest and noblest at that; but far from being a reason to despise other religions, Christianity's very position of eminence enables and obliges it to understand and appreciate all human religiosity.

This positive appreciation of human religiosity in all its forms is one of the more characteristic and engaging features of Schleiermacher's theological universalism. We cannot but wonder where he found the inspiration to endorse the religious universalism of the romantic movement, by basing it, not on the sovereignty of natural religiosity, but on the universal attractiveness of all religious forms— an attractiveness established by the Christian faith itself, in the experience of its own particular form of God-consciousness.

This leads us to our third, more properly christological point. The romantic emphasis on the human religious *a priori* could easily have led, in Schleiermacher's theology, to a purely exemplarist version of the atonement: Christ exemplifies the perfection of the God-consciousness available, as a matter of principle, to every person. Instead, Schleiermacher considers the Christian faith's dependence on Christ the Redeemer axiomatic,[114] and he elaborates this in two principal ways. The first, as we have indicated, is the thesis that Christ is not just example (*Vorbild*), but also, and principally, the original, prototypical, ideal *exemplar* (*Urbild*)—the ideal pinnacle of God-consciousness actualized in a particular person.[115] The second is the characterization of Christ as *mediator*. The universal human religious *a priori* is formless and impotent until it is quickened; it stands in need of mediation. Only Christ's God-consciousness is unmediated and totally original. In virtue of this unmediated originality Christ's God-consciousness is also universally mediating; it has the "power to communicate itself and awake religion."[116]

Thus the notion of Jesus' mediatorship involves the notion of Jesus' *mission*. There is little emphasis on this in Schleiermacher's

---

[114]Cf. propositions §§ 11 and 14 in *The Christian Faith*, pp. 52, 68. Cf. *Der christliche Glaube*, Vol. II, p. 505, nn. 11 and 14, and p. 504, nn. 18, 19, 21, for a comparison between the 1821 and 1830 editions.

[115]Above, p. 559.

[116]*On Religion*, p. 247 (cf. above, p. 519).

christology, and the reasons for this limitation are clear. The first is his typically romantic emphasis on the contemplative nature of religion,[117] which is hard to reconcile with the idea of mission. The second reason lies in his concept of Christian doctrine, which he defines as the elaboration of the specifically Christian form of God-consciousness.[118] Doctrine, therefore, reflects Christianity's self-awareness rather than Christ's. Such a conception of doctrine obviously does not favor a strong stress on the personal story of Christ. But in view of this, it is all the more striking, in the *Speeches*, that the mediatorship of Christ is described in terms of *Christ's own concern* with the finitude and the need for mediation around him.[119] And it is most striking to find Christ's mediatorship described, not as his own exclusive prerogative, but as a charge that is passed on to his followers.

> Yet He never maintained He was the only mediator, the only one in whom His idea actualized itself. All who attach themselves to Him and form His Church should also be mediators with Him and through Him.[120]

There is little doubt that Schleiermacher's predilection for particularity in religion[121] is fundamentally connected with the position of pre-eminence and originality which the historical, particular, biblical Christ occupies in his rendition of the Christian faith. And it even looks as if Schleiermacher's curious, rather unromantic insistence on the mediatorship-by-participation of all Christians reflects the missionary consciousness of Christ, devoutly recognized by a man deeply identified with a culture which otherwise took a dim view of the religious significance of action.

The romantic inspiration accepted, purified, and put in perspective
    It has been fashionable in many quarters in the past half-century to dwell upon the limitations and dangers of Schleiermacher's theol-

---

[117]Cf., for example, *On Religion*, p. 36.
[118]Cf. for example, *The Christian Faith*, § 15, pp. 76–78.
[119]Cf. again *On Religion*, p. 247 (above, p. 519).
[120]*Ibid.*, p. 248.
[121]For a fine discussion of this, cf. Hans Frei, *The Eclipse of Biblical Narrative*, pp. 282–324.

ogy, often without the knowledge required to arrive at a balanced judgment.[122] This is not the place to state the very real limitations of Schleiermacher's system, let alone to condemn them. The purpose of our brief analysis was much more modest. It was to argue that in Schleiermacher's theology we have another example of the Christian faith's power of empathy and understanding, and of its ability to integrate human concerns without being dominated by them.

Emanuel Hirsch is probably the victim of some traditional German Protestant chauvinism when he writes:

> Schleiermacher is the originator of the neo-Protestant sensibility; this he is on account of the certainty of his conviction that a divorce between Christian faith and human rationality [*Vernünftigkeit*] can be avoided only on the basis of evangelical liberty [*auf dem Boden evangelischer Freiheit*].[123]

Still, partisan ecclesiastical discussion aside, Hirsch is certainly right in emphasizing that the critical openness exhibited by Schleiermacher in his confrontation with the most precious and precarious insight of his day is the result of freedom—the confident freedom that goes back to Christ and shows itself in hospitable *sympatheia* with humanity's struggle for meaning.

DEVELOPMENT OF DOCTRINE
AND IMITATION OF CHRIST

The deeper norms of doctrinal development

It is time to wind up this chapter, and indeed this book, in a final retrospect and outlook. This will consist in a brief exploration of some implications of the fundamental ideas of this book for the question of doctrinal development.

In the twelfth chapter we argued a thesis which we have attempted to illustrate in the present chapter. The thesis was that non-linear developments in christology were possible and desirable.[124]

---

[122]It is good to bear in mind Karl Barth's opinion that Schleiermacher "does intelligently, instructively and generously what the useless folk of more recent times do stupidly, unskillfully, inconsistently and fearfully": Eberhard Busch, *Karl Barth*, p. 151.

[123]*Schleiermachers Christusglaube*, pp. 8–9.

[124]Above, pp. 514–515.

The basic reason for this thesis, we stated, is that no discernment in christology may be in a position to preclude the integration of any new human concerns into the christological confession.[125] This ongoing integration is of the essence of christology, if we recall that it is the record, at the level of doctrine, of the ongoing process of assumption of humanity into the Body of Christ—the process whose dynamics have been the subject of chapters twelve and thirteen.

We have now explored two concerns which as a matter of historical fact were integrated into the christological confession. The integration was not achieved without problems. A first set of problems were connected with the actual process of integration itself. The human heart and the romantic discovery were not won over without challenge and counter-challenge. The process of integration involved a painstaking process of "conversion" of the meaning of the human heart and the romantic ideal—away from autonomy and in the direction of loyalty to the presidency of Christ by means of what we have called the rhetoric of obedience.[126] The enrichment of Christian sensibility that resulted from the rise of the Sacred Heart devotion and the christology of Schleiermacher was not bought cheaply.

However, this proved not to be the end of the struggle. For the human heart and the *homo religiosus*, once accepted into the christological confession and converted to obedience, still turned out to be strangers to the existing doctrinal establishment. Where did they fit, and how?

In the case of the Sacred Heart devotion, this situation is well illustrated by the nervous efforts made by the encyclical *Haurietis Aquas* to legitimate the devotion by recourse to authoritative doctrine already established. The encyclical concedes that the Bible does not expressly refer to the Sacred Heart,[127] and that the Fathers of the Church never treated the devotion in a direct way.[128] The only biblical warrant for the devotion is inferential: the heart of Jesus "must doubtlessly have been struck by the thrust of the lance."[129]

---

[125]Above, p. 509.—For the subject of this concluding section, cf. also above, pp. 262, 303–307.

[126]Cf. above, pp. 162–165.

[127]*Acta Apostolicae Sedis* 48 (1956) 317.

[128]*Ibid.*, 327.

[129]*Ibid.*, 334.

The warrant from tradition is vague: the transfixed heart of the Redeemer "has always been part of the devotion of the faithful."[130] But happily, the theological warrant is solid, and it is roundly christological. It is the hypostatic union, in virtue of which the humanity of Jesus, and his physical heart as the symbol of his love in particular, are worthy of true adoration. The gap between the Sacred Heart and the doctrinal establishment has been bridged, though only barely, for the encyclical only argues the Sacred Heart devotion's *a posteriori compatibility* with the central christological affirmation. What is not established is linear continuity—the Sacred Heart devotion is not presented as the result of doctrinal development *in christology*. It is a doctrinal development, but the question is: What is its real warrant, besides its compatibility with christological dogma?

In the case of Schleiermacher's christology the same problem appears, only in much sharper relief. The doctrinal establishment reacted much more nervously to the new christology, and to its author's trenchant comments on the liabilities of the tradition. Schleiermacher did not reject the central affirmation implied in the traditional construct:

> [. . .] it is undeniable that the intention [in the traditional affirmations] is the same as in the propositions so far laid down [in *The Christian Faith*], namely, to describe Christ in such a way (*frater, consubstantialis nobis*) that in the new corporate life a vital fellowship between us and Him shall be possible, and, at the same time, that the existence of God in Him shall be expressed in the clearest possible way; from which it follows at once that the most unconditional veneration and brotherly comradeship are united in our relation to Him. With this we are in complete agreement.[131]

However, once this has been said, Schleiermacher starts to apply his thesis that the ecclesiastical formulas regarding the person of Christ must be subjected to a sustained critique. This must be done in the light of the "immediate Christian self-consciousness." This self-consciousness may never be allowed to get overlaid with useless determinations, which are merely the result of specious ques-

---

[130]*Ibid.*, 338.
[131]*The Christian Faith*, § 96, p. 391, corrected after *Der christliche Glaube*, Vol. II, p. 50.

tions or past polemics. Moreover, doctrine must be continuously pruned of elaborations which have become obsolete or irrelevant with the passage of time.[132] Schleiermacher illustrates what he means in a lengthy and sometimes drastic critique of the christological tradition, especially as practiced by the Schoolmen.[133]

Schleiermacher clearly recognizes that his own christology cannot be harmonized with two-nature christology *at the level of expression*. Unlike the Sacred Heart devotion—to limit ourselves to the present context of discussion—Schleiermacher's christology cannot be legitimized by recourse to the hypostatic union. At the same time Schleiermacher claims that his construct is consonant with the fundamental Christian self-consciousness. Its compatibility with the tradition, therefore, can be established *at the level of intention*—the intention to express the immediate Christian self-consciousness.

We must pause here for a moment. To Christians less at ease with pietism than the Moravian-educated[134] Schleiermacher, his stance may look like one of excessive skepsis with regard to doctrine. Still, he deserves a careful hearing. Let us begin by remarking that the term "immediate Christian self-consciousness" is far too romantic and idealist an expression to characterize the Christian's, or rather the Church's, fundamental stance of faith. This is why in this book we have preferred to characterize this fundamental faith-stance in rather more dialogical terms, by referring to the Church's (or the Christian's) faith-*response* to Christ—the response in which the responsive Christian identity takes shape. But of this response to Christ we have said that it surpasses knowledge, and that—as the basic Christian commitment to Christ—it is the setting of all christological discernments.[135] The basic Christian response to Christ, therefore, is the ultimate tribunal where the acceptability of christological discernments is established. Schleiermacher's emphasis on the preeminence of the immediate Christian self-consciousness is theologically correct.

---

[132]*Ibid.*, § 95, pp. 389–390.

[133]*Ibid.*, § 96–97, pp. 391–413.

[134]Cf. Schleiermacher's own words, later in life: "I may say that after all I have passed through I have become a Moravian again, only of a higher order." Quoted by James C. Livingstone, *Modern Christian Thought*, p. 97.

[135]Cf. above, pp. 113–115, 126–129.

But does this position not commit us to fideism after all? Can the basic Christian response to Christ really serve as a norm by which to judge christological statements? What is the standing of the more traditional norms, such as conformity with Scripture, conformity with the doctrinal tradition, and obedience to the Church's authentic magisterial authority?

It is important at this point to identify the problem under discussion with some precision. What is *not* at issue here is the question whether the fundamental Christian response to Christ (Schleiermacher's "immediate Christian self-consciousness") is ever available apart from articulations that are theologically true and meaningful. To say it is would amount to radical fideism. This kind of fideism has been rejected throughout in this book (and even Schleiermacher nowhere endorses it). We have argued that the Christian faith-commitment, lived out in a world full of human concerns, engenders true discernments and is thus essentially articulate.[136] But to say that the Christian faith-commitment is essentially articulate does not amount to saying that it is *reducible* to its articulations and discernments. All discernments are *partial* in *what* they *say*, though they *convey* the *total* surrender in *the act of speaking*.[137]

So the problem at stake here is not radical fideism. What is at stake is the question of the norms by which new discernments and articulations are to be judged. In other words, the question is the legitimation of doctrinal development.

Once the Christian tradition had recognized the problem posed by the factual rise of new doctrines, it developed a series of theories designed to explain and legitimize both the fact of doctrinal development and its products, the new doctrines. Owen Chadwick's study *From Bossuet to Newman*[138] provides an authoritative account of this history of increasing subtlety and breadth of vision in dealing with a complex problem, culminating in Newman's *Essay on Development*. Newman was the first to argue with conviction that doctrinal devel-

---

[136]Cf. above, pp. 125, 135–143.

[137]Cf., for example, above, pp. 95–96, 191, 199–200, 252.

[138]*From Bossuet to Newman*, The Idea of Doctrinal Development, Cambridge, Cambridge University Press, 1957.

opment, in most cases, is not simply a matter of developing further propositions, whose legitimacy could be easily established by reference to the language of Scripture and the authoritative tradition. Development, he argued, is a true integration of new elements into an existing and growing body of beliefs. In this way, development is a two-way process. Doctrines and beliefs originally foreign to the Christian faith are assimilated, and the Christian faith itself grows as the original "idea" generates further truths.[139] In Newman's view, the judgment on the acceptability of new developments occurs mainly in retrospect, and even then not through the establishment of strict logical sequence, but by the perception of "a vague but general intellectual coherence," by the perception of "a harmony or congruity or 'naturalness' in the way in which ideas have developed."[140]

Newman's theory, for all its power, has two limitations that are especially noticeable today. The first is that the idea of development creates the impression of continuity and coherence, whereas in fact the process is far more haphazard and discontinuous, not to mention the fact that it includes loss of tradition as well as gain. Secondly, the theory does not include a statement of norms to evaluate the process of development of new doctrine *as it is taking place.*

The first limitation is taken quite seriously in recent discussions of doctrinal development, and this is understandable.[141] We live in such a complex world that we tend to be far less sure that it will always be possible to establish even the most general and vague coherence between new developments and the tradition. The pace of modern life, the speed with which scholarship is producing data, and the globalization of our awareness, which is now confronted with the bewildering variety of cultures and interests, demand a theory of doctrinal development even more basic and broad than Newman's. It is not surprising, therefore, that there has been a tendency, of late, to drop the word "development" and instead to refer to "successive structurings," resulting from the confluence of "structured data"

---

[139]This idea is analogous to what we have referred to as the "double binding" of discernments; cf. above, pp. 137–143, esp. 141–142.

[140]Owen Chadwick, *From Bossuet to Newman*, p. 157.

[141]A fine survey of the state of the discussion by Paul Misner, "A Note on the Critique of Dogmas," *Theological Studies* 34 (1973) 690–700.

and "structuring cultural elements."[142] In this way the modern awareness of the variety and unpredictability of human experience has called into question the traditional norms used to establish the legitimacy of new theological ventures, namely, consistency with the authoritative discernments given in Scripture and tradition.

This makes it even more necessary to concentrate on the second limitation of Newman's theory—his failure to give norms for the actual process of doctrinal development. Where are such norms to be found? We will not find them in the doctrinal establishment, since the norm of clear consistency with the tradition is no longer expected to apply in every case. What we need is more fundamental norms. Such norms, however, cannot be directly read off from the "fundamental Christian faith-commitment" (Schleiermacher's "immediate Christian self-consciousness") *as such*, since that is not separately available, apart from past discernments and articulations. The only alternative left to us is *the dynamics of the theological process by which discernments arise*—the process of growth by which the Church assimilates ideas and beliefs foreign to her and uses them to develop new doctrine. The norms to determine the legitimacy of new doctrine are, therefore, *behavioral*: it is the Christian commitment in action, the Christian faith as it operates upon human concerns, the Church as she lives in the world.

What we are proposing here is that conformity with the tradition fundamentally means conformity with the *laws of the process* which informs the tradition. New doctrinal constructs, therefore, *may* show no affinity with the authoritative doctrinal establishment at the level of expression while at the same time being deeply in line with the tradition, because they are the upshot of a process that is entirely traditional. What are the elements of this process?

Let us limit ourselves for the moment to christology, although a good case could probably be made for the wider applicability of what is to follow. We have argued that all discernments in christology are placed in a rhetorical setting, whose dynamics are inclusion, obedience, and hope. If, then, we are to judge a new christological construct, we must ask three questions. The first is concerned with inclusion: Does the new construct integrate an important human concern, thus far left unmet by Christian thought? The second

---

[142]*Ibid.*, 692ff.

question concerns obedience: Does the new construct, in using this human concern to speak about Christ, also show a deeper and purer understanding of the concern? The third question is concerned with hope: Does the new construct convey a sense of freedom, give a glimpse of an ultimate perspective, and encourage people to worship and witness? An affirmative answer to the last question is especially important, for christologies that do not find their origin in the Resurrection are likely to be closed ideologies, incapable of patience and hospitality when they in turn are invited to show understanding and power of integration. To put this briefly: new christologies are reliable if they come out of confident worship, if they bear joyful witness, and if they involve a critical identification with precious and precarious human concerns. Such christologies are part of the Christian tradition, even if the explicit analogies with the tradition should be hard to establish.

Christology and imitatio Christi

There is a final reason why Christian theology, and christology in particular, should be the fruit of the triple rhetoric of inclusion, obedience and hope, namely, that the triple rhetoric sums up the person of Christ himself. A theology that grows out of critical sympathy with the world and turns humanity into the stuff of worship and witness is re-enacting, in an intellectual fashion, God's love of the whole world in the person of the *Logos* Incarnate, the way of Jesus Christ in obedience to the Father's will, and the hope that comes from the presence of Christ alive. Good christology, in the final analysis, is a fruit of the Spirit, borne in lives that proclaim Christ as the Way, to the everlasting glory of God the Father.

This is not said in order to bring this book to an edifying conclusion, but to stress that all christology, and indeed all Christian doctrine, whether traditional or new, has deep roots. There has never been an intellectual short-cut to good theology, and there is none now. Inclusion, obedience, and hope are the sources of all good christology, and the fundamental norms by which to judge new christological discernments; they are not recipes for quick doctrinal concoctions. Karl Rahner said, in a recent interview:

> Theoretical discussions about the right language in theology are about as helpful as recipes for stirring lyrical poetry. What you should do is

focus on the thing itself and try to express *it* in such a way as to grasp it and be grasped by it.[143]

Words will come to those Churches and those Christians that are united with Jesus Christ, and united with him in his love for the world. No new knowledge without participation in the experience.

ENVOI

Few works of literature make this point more compellingly than the fifteenth-century Spanish *romance*, or ballad, known as *El Conde Arnaldos*.[144] On the morning of the feast of Saint John, Count Arnaldos rides out to hunt, hawk on gauntlet. He looks up and there, on the smooth sea, he sees a galleon sailing land ward. Its sails are made of silk, its mast is cedarwood, and the sailor at the helm sings a song so entrancing that the sea and the wind are calmed, the fish of the deep are called to the surface, and the birds alight on the rigging. Count Arnaldos, struck by the sight and the music, speaks up. In his words we can hear the yearning of all humanity for words of knowledge to control experience:

> 'For the sake of God, our maker!
> (Count Arnaldos' cry was strong)—
> 'Old man, let me be partaker
> In the secret of thy song!

> *'Por Dios te ruego, marinero.*
> *digasme ora ese cantar.'*

The answer comes. What it says is that only those will know who join in the venture—in its risks and in its rewards:

---

[143] *Herder-Korrespondenz* 31 (1977) 606–614, quotation 611a.

[144] Spanish text in *Cancionero de Romances* (Anvers, 1550), Antonio Rodríguez-Moñino (ed.), Madrid, Editorial Castalia, 1967, p. 255, spelling modernized. The translation is from *Ancient Spanish Ballads*, J. G. Lockhart (trans.), London, John Murray, 1841, pp. v[2–4], and reflects the mood of the late eighteenth- and early nineteenth-century appreciation of the medieval ballad genre. The Spanish text is far more terse: "By God I ask you, mariner, now tell me that song."—"I tell that song only to him who comes with me."

'Count Arnaldos! Count Arnaldos!
   Hearts I read, and thoughts I know;—
Wouldst thou learn the ocean secret,
   In our galley thou must go.'

   'Yo no digo esta canción,
   sino a quien conmigo va.'

BIBLIOGRAPHY

Thomas J. J. Altizer, *The Gospel of Christian Atheism*, Philadelphia, The Westminster Press, 1966

Ancient Spanish Ballads, trans. J. G. Lockhart, London, John Murray, 1841

J. A. Appleyard, "How Does a Sacrament 'Cause by Signifying'?" *Science et Esprit* 23 (1971) 167–200

Augustine, *The City of God* (*The Modern Library*), New York, Random House, 1950

D. M. Baillie, *God Was in Christ*, New York, Charles Scribner's Sons, ²[1955]

J. V. Bainvel, *Devotion to the Sacred Heart*, The Doctrine and Its History, New York–Cincinnati–Chicago, Benziger Brothers, 1924

James Barr, *Biblical Words for Time*, London, SCM Press, 1962

———"Hypostatization of Linguistic Phenomena," *Journal of Semitic Studies* 7 (1962) 85–94

———*The Semantics of Biblical Language*, London, Oxford University Press, 1961

Karl Barth, *Credo*, New York, Charles Scribner's Sons, 1962

Gregory Baum, *Man Becoming*, New York, Herder and Herder, 1970

Warren G. Bennis, Kenneth D. Benne, Robert Chin (eds.), *The Planning of Change*, New York, Holt, Rinehart and Winston, ²1969

W. J. Berger, "Die Seele verkauft und zurückgewonnen?" *Orientierung* 40 (1976) 241–245

Eberhard Bethge, *Bonhoeffer: Exile and Martyr*, edited and with an essay by John W. de Gruchy, London, Collins, 1975

———*Dietrich Bonhoeffer*, New York–Hagerstown–San Francisco–London, Harper & Row, 1970

———"Turning Points in Bonhoeffer's Life and Thought," in: Peter Vorkink (ed.), *Bonhoeffer in a World Come of Age*, Philadelphia, Fortress Press, 1968, pp. 73–102

Dietrich Bonhoeffer, *Act and Being*, London, Collins, 1962

———*Akt und Sein*, München, Chr. Kaiser Verlag, 1964

———*Christ the Center*, New York, Harper & Row, 1966 (German original: "Christologie," in: *Gesammelte Schriften*, III. Bd., pp. 166–242)

———*The Communion of Saints*, A Dogmatic Inquiry into the Sociology of the Church, New York and Evanston, Harper & Row, 1963

——————*The Cost of Discipleship*, New York, The Macmillan Company, ²1959
——————*Ethics* (Eberhard Bethge, ed.), New York, Macmillan Publishing Co., 1955
——————*Gesammelte Schriften* (Eberhard Bethge, ed.), III. Bd., München, Chr. Kaiser Verlag, 1966; IV. Bd., ²1965
——————*Letters and Papers from Prison*, New York, The Macmillan Company, ²1967
——————*No Rusty Swords* (Edwin H. Robertson, ed.), London, Collins, 1970
——————*Sanctorum Communio*, Eine dogmatische Untersuchung zur Soziologie der Kirche, München, Chr. Kaiser Verlag, ⁴1969
J. Bots, *Tussen Descartes en Darwin*, Geloof en Natuurwetenschap in de achttiende eeuw in Nederland, Assen, Van Gorcum & Comp. N. V., 1972
Leland P. Bradford, Jack R. Gibb, Kenneth D. Benne (eds.), *T-Group Theory and Laboratory Method*, New York–London–Sydney, John Wiley & Sons, 1964
Herbert Braun, "The Meaning of New Testament Christology," in: Robert W. Funk (ed.), *God and Christ: Existence and Provi[de]nce* (*Journal for Theology and the Church*, 5), New York, Harper & Row, 1968, pp. 89–127

Gerald Brenan, *St. John of the Cross—His Life and Poetry*, with a translation of his poetry by Lynda Nicholson, London, Cambridge University Press, 1975

Peter Brown, *Augustine of Hippo*, Berkeley–Los Angeles–London, University of California Press, ²1975

Raymond E. Brown, *Jesus God and Man*, Milwaukee, Bruce, 1967

Walter Brueggemann, "The Triumphalist Tendency in Exegetical History," *Journal of the American Academy of Religion* 38 (1970) 367–380

Martin Buber, *Eclipse of God*, New York, Harper & Row, ²1957
——————*I and Thou* (Walter Kaufmann, trans.), New York, Charles Scribner's Sons, 1970
——————*Ich und Du*, Köln, Verlag Jakob Hegner, ²1966
——————*The Knowledge of Man*, London, George Allen and Unwin, 1965
Kenneth Burke, *The Rhetoric of Religion*, Studies in Logology, Berkeley and Los Angeles, University of California Press, 1970
Eberhard Busch, *Karl Barth*, Philadelphia, Fortress Press, 1976
F. J. J. Buytendijk, *Algemene theorie der menselijke houding en beweging*, Utrecht–Antwerpen, Uitgeverij Het Spectrum, ⁷1974
——————*De Vrouw*, Utrecht–Brussel, Uitgeverij Het Spectrum, 1951
——————*Woman: A Contemporary View*, Glen Rock, N.J., Newman Press, 1968
John Calvin, *Institutes of the Christian Religion*, 2 vols., Grand Rapids, Wm. B. Eerdmans Publishing Company, 1972
James I. Campbell, *The Language of Religion*, New York/London, The Bruce Publishing Company/Collier Macmillan Ltd., 1971
Albert Camus, *The Plague* (*The Modern Library*), New York, Random House, Inc., 1948

Cancionero de Romances (Anvers, 1550), Antonio Rodríguez-Moñino, ed., Madrid, Editorial Castalia, 1967

Dorwin Cartwright, Alvin Zander (eds.), *Group Dynamics*, New York, Harper & Row, ³1968

Owen Chadwick, *From Bossuet to Newman*, The Idea of Doctrinal Development, Cambridge, Cambridge University Press, 1957

M.-D. Chenu, "Vérité évangélique et métaphysique wolffienne à Vatican II," *Revue des Sciences philosophiques et théologiques* 57 (1973) 632–640

Gilbert K. Chesterton, *Orthodoxy*, New York/London, John Lane Company/John Lane, The Bodley Head, 1909

Ewert Cousins, "Models and the Future of Theology," *Continuum* 7 (1969) 78–92

John Coventry, "Doctrine as Verbal Process," *The Tablet* 231 (1977) 57

Francis Crick, *Of Molecules and Men*, Seattle and London, University of Washington Press, 1966

Frederick Crowe, "Development of Doctrine: Aid or Barrier to Christian Unity?" in: *Proceedings of the Twenty-First Annual Convention of the Catholic Theological Society of America*, Yonkers, N.Y., St. Joseph's Seminary, 1967, pp. 1–20

Samuel A. Culbert, *The Interpersonal Process of Self-Disclosure: It Takes Two To See One (Explorations in Applied Behavioral Science*, 3) New York, Renaissance Editions, 1967

Oscar Cullmann, *Die Christologie des Neuen Testaments*, Tübingen, J. C. B. Mohr (Paul Siebeck), ⁴1966

——*The Christology of the New Testament*, Philadelphia, The Westminster Press, 1963

Mary Daly, *Beyond God the Father*, Toward a Philosophy of Women's Liberation, Boston, Beacon Press, 1973

Robert J. Daly, *The Origins of the Christian Doctrine of Sacrifice*, Philadelphia, Fortress Press, 1978

"Declaratio ad Fidem Tuendam in Mysteria Incarnationis et Sanctissimae Trinitatis a Quibusdam Recentibus Erroribus," *Acta Apostolicae Sedis* 64 (1972) 237–241 (ET in: *Origins* 1 [1972] 666–668)

Henri de Lubac, *The Mystery of the Supernatural*, New York, Herder and Herder, 1967

H. Denzinger and A. Schönmetzer, *Enchiridion Symbolorum Definitionum et Declarationum de Rebus Fidei et Morum*, Barcinone–Friburgi Brisgoviae-Romae-Neo-Eboraci, Herder, ³²1963

Leslie Dewart, *The Future of Belief*, New York, Herder and Herder, 1966

C. H. Dodd, *The Apostolic Preaching and Its Developments*, New York–Evanston, Harper & Row, 1964

Avery Dulles, *Apologetics and the Biblical Christ*, Westminster, Newman Press, 1963

——*A History of Apologetics*, New York/Philadelphia/London, Corpus/Westminster/Hutchinson, 1971

——*The Resilient Church*, The Necessity and Limits of Adaptation,

Garden City, N.Y., Doubleday & Company, 1977

Louis Dupré, *The Other Dimension*, Garden City, N.Y., Doubleday, 1972

Gerhard Ebeling, *Introduction to a Theological Theory of Language*, Philadelphia, Fortress Press, 1973

Alan Ecclestone, *Yes to God*, London, Darton, Longman & Todd, 1975

Gerard Egan, *Encounter: Group Processes for Interpersonal Growth*, Belmont, Brooks/Cole Publishing Company, 1970

Mircea Eliade, *Images and Symbols*, New York, Sheed and Ward, ²1969

————*Myth and Reality*, New York, Harper and Row, ²1968

T. S. Eliot, *Collected Poems, 1909–1962*, London, Faber and Faber, 1963

————*The Collected Poems and Plays*, New York, Harcourt, Brace and Company [n.d.]

————"Hamlet and His Problems," in: *Selected Essays*, New York, Harcourt, Brace & World, ³1950, pp. 121–126

————"The Metaphysical Poets," *Ibid.*, pp. 241–250

————*Murder in the Cathedral*, London, Faber and Faber, 1972

Donald D. Evans, *The Logic of Self-Involvement*, New York, Herder and Herder, 1963

Thomas Fawcett, *The Symbolic Language of Religion*, Minneapolis, Augsburg Publishing House, 1971

Herbert Fingarette, *The Self in Transformation*, Psychoanalysis, Philosophy, and the Life of the Spirit, New York–London, Basic Books, 1963

Helmut Fischer (ed.), *Sprachwissen für Theologen*, Hamburg, Furche-Verlag, 1974

Antony Flew, R. M. Hare, Basil Mitchell, "Theology and Falsification—(i) From the University Discussion," in: Antony Flew, Alasdair MacIntyre (eds.), *New Essays in Philosophical Theology*, New York, The Macmillan Company, ²1964, pp. 96–108

Han Fortmann, *Heel de mens*, Bilthoven, Uitgeverij Ambo, 1972

Viktor E. Frankl, *Man's Search for Meaning*, An Introduction to Logotherapy, New York, Washington Square Press, 1963

Hans Frei, *The Eclipse of Biblical Narrative*, A Study in Eighteenth and Nineteenth Century Hermeneutics, New Haven–London, Yale University Press, 1974

————*The Identity of Jesus Christ*, The Hermeneutical Bases of Dogmatic Theology, Philadelphia, Fortress Press, 1975

Anna Freud, *The Ego and the Mechanisms of Defense* (*The Writings of Anna Freud*, Vol. II), revised ed., New York, International Universities Press, Inc., ⁴1973

Reginald H. Fuller, *The Formation of the Resurrection Narratives*, New York/London, The Macmillan Company/Collier-Macmillan, 1971

J. Galot, *La personne du Christ*, Gembloux–Paris, Duculot-Lethellieux, 1969

————*Vers une nouvelle christologie*, Gembloux–Paris, Duculot-Lethellieux, 1971

Helen Gardner (ed.), *The Metaphysical Poets*, Harmondsworth, Penguin Books, 1957

Langdon Gilkey, *Naming the Whirlwind*, Indianapolis–New York, The Bobbs-Merrill Company, 1969

William Watson Goodwin, *Syntax of the Moods and Tenses of the Greek Verb*, Boston, Ginn and Company, 1893

Aloys Grillmeier, *Christ in Christian Tradition*, New York, Sheed and Ward, ¹1965

————*Christ in Christian Tradition*, Atlanta, John Knox Press, ²1975

————"Die altkirchliche Christologie und die moderne Hermeneutik," in: Joseph Pfammatter–Franz Furger (eds.), *Theologische Berichte I, Zürich–Einsiedeln–Köln, Benziger Verlag, pp. 69–169*

Georges Gusdorf, *Speaking* ["*La Parole*"] (Paul T. Brockelman, trans. and intro.) [Chicago], Northwestern University Press, 1965

Ferdinand Hahn, *The Titles of Jesus in Christology*, New York–Cleveland, The World Publishing Company, 1969

A. Hamon, *Histoire de la Dévotion au Sacré Coeur*, 5 vols., Paris, Gabriel Beauchesne, ⁵1923, 1925, 1927, 1931, 1940

Ray L. Hart, *Unfinished Man and the Imagination*, New York, Herder and Herder, 1968

Adrian Hastings, *The Faces of God*, London, Geo. Chapman, 1975

Martin Hengel, *Der Sohn Gottes*, Die Entstehung der Christologie und die jüdisch-hellenistische Religionsgeschichte, Tübingen, J. C. B. Mohr (Paul Siebeck), 1975

————*The Son of God*, The Origin of Christology and the History of Jewish-Hellenistic Religion, Philadelphia, Fortress Press, 1976

Arthur Henkel and Albrecht Schöne (eds.), *Emblemata*, Handbuch zur Sinnbildkunst des XVI. und XVII. Jahrhunderts, Stuttgart, J. B. Metschlersche Verlagsbuchhandlung, 1967

Abraham J. Heschel, *The Prophets*, 2 vols, New York, Harper & Row, 1969, 1975

Emanuel Hirsch, *Schleiermachers Christusglaube*, [Gütersloh], Gütersloher Verlagshaus Gerd Mohn, 1968

Peter C. Hodgson, *Jesus—Word and Presence*, An Essay in Christology, Philadelphia, Fortress Press, 1971

J. C. Hoekendijk, *The Church Inside Out*, Philadelphia, The Westminster Press, 1965

Gerard Manley Hopkins, *Poems* (W. H. Gardner, N. H. MacKenzie, eds.), London–Oxford–New York, Oxford University Press, ⁴1970

A. Hulsbosch, "Jezus Christus, gekend als mens, beleden als Zoon Gods," *Tijdschrift voor theologie* 6 (1966) 250–273

A. Hulsbosch, E. Schillebeeckx, P. Schoonenberg, "Gods heilspresentie in de mens Jezus Christus," *Tijdschrift voor theologie* 6 (1966) 249–306

Thomas Idinopulos and Ray Bowen Ward, "Is Christology Inherently Anti-Semitic?—A Critical Review of Rosemary Ruether's *Faith and Fratricide*," *Journal of the American Academy of Religion* 45 (1977) 193–214

David E. Jenkins, *The Glory of Man*, The Bampton Lectures for 1966, New York, Charles Scribner's Sons, 1967

————*Guide to the Debate About God*, London, Lutterworth Press, 1968
Joachim Jeremias, *The Eucharistic Words of Jesus*, New York, Charles Scribner's Sons, 1966
————*The Parables of Jesus*, New York, Charles Scribner's Sons, ²1963
————*The Prayers of Jesus* (*Studies in Biblical Theology*, Second Series, 6), London, SCM Press, 1967
John of the Cross, *see* Gerald Brenan
Pope John [XXIII], "Opening Speech to the Council," in: Walter Abbott (ed.), *The Documents of Vatican II*, [London/New York], Geoffrey Chapman/The America Press, 1966, pp. 710–719
Carl Gustav Jung, *Psychology and Religion*, New Haven, Yale University Press, [1960]
Philipp Kaiser, *Die gott-menschliche Einigung in Christus als Problem der spekulativen Theologie seit der Scholastik* (*Münchener theologische Studien*, II. Systematische Abteilung, Bd. 36), München, Max Hueber Verlag, 1968
Alfred C. Kammer, " 'Burn-Out'—Contemporary Dilemma for the Jesuit Social Activist," *Studies in the Spirituality of Jesuits*, American Assistancy Seminar on Jesuit Spirituality, St. Louis, St. Louis University, 10 (1978) 1–42
Ernest Käsemann, *Jesus Means Freedom*, Philadelphia, Fortress Press, 1972
Walter Kasper, *Jesus der Christus*, Mainz, Matthias-Grünewald-Verlag, 1974
————*Jesus the Christ*, New York–Paramus–Toronto, Paulist Press, 1977
Patricia A. Kendall (ed.), *Women and the Priesthood: A Selected and Annotated Bibliography*, [Philadelphia], The Episcopal Diocese of Pennsylvania, 1966
John Knox, *The Humanity and Divinity of Christ*, A Study of Pattern in Christology, Cambridge, Cambridge University Press, 1967
[Zvi Kolitz], "Yossel, fils de Yossel Rakover de Tarnopol, parle à Dieu" (Arnold Mandel, trans.), *La Terre Retrouvée*, 15 mars 1955
————"Yossel Rakover's Appeal to God," in: Albert H. Friedlander (ed.), *Out of the Whirlwind*, A Reader in Holocaust Literature, New York, Union of American Hebrew Congregations, 1968, pp. 390–399
Hans Küng, "Anonyme Christen—wozu?" *Orientierung* 39 (1975) 214–216
————*The Church*, New York, Sheed & Ward, 1967
————*Menschwerdung Gottes*, Eine Einführung in Hegels theologisches Denken als Prolegomena zu einer künftigen Christologie, Freiburg–Basel–Wien, Herder, 1970
————*On Being a Christian*, Garden City, N.Y., Doubleday & Company, 1976
————*20 Thesen zum Christsein*, München, R. Piper & Co., Verlag, 1975 (ET "On Being a Christian: Twenty Theses," in: *Signposts for the Future*, Garden City, N.Y., Doubleday & Company, Inc., 1978, pp. 2–40)
G. W. H. Lampe, *A Patristic Greek Lexicon*, Oxford, Clarendon Press, 1961

F. R. Leavis, *The Great Tradition*, Garden City, N.Y., Doubleday & Company, 1954

Jung Young Lee, *God Suffers for Us*, A Systematic Inquiry into a Concept of Divine Passibility, The Hague, Martinus Nijhoff, 1974

Emmanuel Levinas, "Aimer la Thora plus que Dieu," in: *Difficile Liberté*, Essais sur le Judaïsme, Paris, A. Michel, 1963, pp. 171–176

——*Het menselijk gelaat* (Ad Peperzak, trans. and ed.), Utrecht, Ambo, 1969

——"Liberté et Commandement," *Revue de Métaphysique et de Morale* 58 (1953) 264–272

——*Totality and Infinity; An Essay on Exteriority*, Pittsburgh, Duquesne University Press, 1969

James C. Livingstone, *Modern Christian Thought*, From the Enlightenment to Vatican II, New York/London, The Macmillan Company/Collier-Macmillan Limited, 1971

Norbert Lohfink, "Text und Thema," *Stimmen der Zeit* 181 (1968) 120–126

Bernard J. F. Lonergan, "The Dehellenization of Dogma," in: *A Second Collection* (William F. J. Ryan and Bernard J. Tyrrell, eds.), Philadelphia, Westminster Press, 1974, pp. 11–32

——"The Origins of Christian Realism," *Ibid.*, pp. 239–261

——*De Verbo Incarnato*, Romae, Pontificia Universitas Gregoriana, 1964

——*The Way to Nicaea*, The Dialectical Development of Trinitarian Theology, Philadelphia, The Westminster Press, 1976

Vladimir Lossky, *A l'image et à la ressemblance de Dieu*, Paris, Aubier Montaigne, 1967

——*In the Image and Likeness of God*, [Crestwood, New York], St. Vladimir's Seminary Press, 1974

Joseph Luft, *Group Processes*, An Introduction to Group Dynamics, Palo Alto, National Press Books, ²1970

W. Luijpen, *"De erwtensoep is klaar!"* Bilthoven, Ambo, 1970

Douglas McGregor, *The Human Side of the Enterprise*, New York–Toronto–London, McGraw-Hill Book Company, 1960

John McIntyre, *The Shape of Christology*, Philadelphia, The Westminster Press, 1966

Donald MacKinnon, "The Relation of the Doctrines of the Incarnation and the Trinity," in: Richard W. A. McKinney (ed.), *Creation, Christ, and Culture*, Studies in Honour of T. F. Torrance, Edinburgh, T. & T. Clark, 1976, pp. 92–107

——"Remarques sur l'Irréversibilité du Temps," in: *Archivio di Filosofia*, Roma, Istituto di studi filosofici, 1975, pp. 39–47

——" 'Substance' in Christology—A Cross-Bench View," in: S. W. Sykes and J. P. Clayton (eds.), *Christ, Faith, and History*, Cambridge, Cambridge University Press, 1972, pp. 279–300

John Macquarrie, *God-Talk*, London, SCM Press, 1967

Felix Malmberg, "Die mittelbar-unmittelbare Verbindung mit God im

Dogmenglauben," in: *Gott in Welt*, Festgabe für Karl Rahner, Freiburg–Basel–Wien, Herder, 1964, pp. 92–102

———*Ein Leib—ein Geist*, Freiburg–Basel–Wien, Herder, 1960

———*Ueber den Gottmenschen* (*Quaestiones Disputatae*, 9), Basel–Freiburg–Wien, Herder, 1960

Malachi Martin, *Jesus Now*, New York, E. P. Dutton & Co., 1973

Willi Marxsen, *The Resurrection of Jesus of Nazareth*, Philadelphia, Fortress Press, 1970

E. L. Mascall, *Existence and Analogy*, London, Longmans, Green & Co., 1949

Abraham H. Maslow, *Religions, Values, and Peak-Experiences*, Columbus, Ohio State University Press, 1964

———*Toward a Psychology of Being*, New York, Van Nostrand Reinhold Company, ²1968

Benvenuto Matteucci, "Il sinodo di Pistoia e il culto del SS. Cuore di Gesu," in: A. Bea, H. Rahner, H. Rondet, F. Schwendimann (eds.), *Cor Jesu*, Commentationes in litteras encyclicas Pii Pp. XII "Haurietis Aquas," 2 vols., Roma, Casa editrice Herder, 1959, Vol. 2, pp. 235–261

Rollo May, *Love and Will*, New York, W. W. Norton & Company, 1969

———*Paulus*, Reminiscences of a Friendship, New York–Evanston–San Francisco–London, Harper & Row, 1973

———*Power and Innocence*, A Search for the Sources of Violence, Delta Book, New York, Dell Publishing Co., 1976

Felix Mayer, *Schöpferische Sprache und Rhythmus* (Erich Simenauer, ed., with a postscript), Berlin, Walter De Gruyter & Co., 1959

Johannes B. Metz, "The Future *Ex Memoria Passionis*," in: Ewert H. Cousins (ed.), *Hope and the Future of Man*, Philadelphia, Fortress Press, 1972, pp. 117–131

———"A Short Apology of Narrative," in: Johann Baptist Metz and Jean-Pierre Jossua (eds.), *The Crisis of Religious Language* (*Concilium*, 85), New York, Herder and Herder, 1973, pp. 84–96

Cyril R. Mill (ed.), *Selections from Human Relations Training News*, Washington, D.C., NTL Institute for Applied Behavioral Science, 1969

Paul Misner, "A Note on the Critique of Dogmas," *Theological Studies* 34 (1973) 690–700

Jürgen Moltmann, *The Crucified God*, New York, Harper & Row, 1974

———"Die Zukunft als neues Paradigma der Transzendenz," *Internationale Dialog-Zeitschrift*[1] (1969) 2–13.

C. F. D. Moule, "The Manhood of Jesus in the New Testament," in: S. W. Sykes and J. P. Clayton (eds.), *Christ, Faith, and History*, Cambridge, Cambridge University Press, 1972, pp. 95–110

J. K. Mozley, *The Impassibility of God*, Cambridge, Cambridge University Press, 1926

Heribert Mühlen, "Das unbegrenzte Du—Auf dem Wege zu einer Personologie," in: *Wahrheit und Verkündigung*, Festschrift für M. Schmaus, München–Paderborn–Wien, 1967, pp. 1259–1285

———*Die abendländische Seinsfrage als der Tod Gottes und der Aufgang einer neuen Gotteserfahrung*, Paderborn, Ferdinand Schöning, 1968
———"Die epochale Notwendigkeit eines pneumatologischen Ansatzes der Gotteslehre," *Wort und Wahrheit* 4 (1973) 275–287
Jerome Murphy-O'Connor, "Christological Anthropology in Phil. II, 6–11," *Revue Biblique* 83 (1976) 25–50
Robert Murray, *Symbols of Church and Kingdom*, [London], Cambridge University Press, 1975
John Henry Newman, *An Essay in Aid of a Grammar of Assent*, Westminster, Md., Christian Classics, 1973
———*Fifteen Sermons (Oxford University Sermons)*, London–New York–Bombay, Longmans, Green & Co., 1906
Richard R. Niebuhr, *Schleiermacher on Christ and Religion*, London, SCM Press Ltd., 1964
Robert North, *In Search of the Human Jesus*, New York–Cleveland, Corpus Books, 1970
Gerald O'Collins, *The Calvary Christ*, Philadelphia, Westminster Press, 1977
———*The Resurrection of Jesus Christ*, Valley Forge, Judson Press, 1973
———*What Are They Saying About Jesus?*, New York–Ramsey–Toronto, Paulist Press, 1977
———*What Are They Saying About the Resurrection?*, New York–Ramsey–Toronto, Paulist Press, 1978
Walter J. Ong, *The Barbarian Within*, New York, The Macmillan Company, 1962
———"*Maranatha*: Death and Life in the Text of the Book," *Journal of the American Academy of Religion* 45 (1977) 419–449
———*The Presence of the Word*, New York, Simon and Schuster, 1970
———*Rhetoric, Romance, and Technology*, Ithaca–London, Cornell University Press, 1971
Heinrich Ott, *Wirklichkeit und Glaube*, 2. Band, *Der persönliche Gott*, Göttingen–Zürich, Vandenhoeck & Ruprecht, 1969
Wolfhart Pannenberg, "Analogy and Doxology," in: *Basic Questions in Theology*, Vol. I, Philadelphia, Fortress Press, 1970, pp. 212–238
———*Grundzüge der Christologie*, Gütersloh, Gütersloher Verlagshaus Gerd Mohn, ²1966
———*Jesus—God and Man*, Philadelphia, The Westminster Press, 1968
Blaise Pascal, *Pensées* (Léon Brunschvicg, ed.), Paris, Editions de Cluny, 1934
[Pope Paul VI], Encyclical *Mysterium Fidei, Acta Apostolicae Sedis* 57 (1965) 753ff.
[Pope Pius XII], Encyclical *Haurietis Aquas, Acta Apostolicae Sedis* 48 (1956) 309–353
———Encyclical *Humani Generis, Acta Apostolicae Sedis* 42 (1950) 561–578
———*The Encyclical "Humani Generis,"* with a Commentary (A. C. Cotter, trans. and ed.), Weston 93, Mass., Weston College Press, 1951

Plato, Gorgias (E. R. Dodds, ed.), Oxford, Oxford University Press, 1959

Mario Praz, *Studies in Seventeenth-Century Imagery* (*Sussidi eruditi*, 16), Roma, Edizioni di storia e letteratura, ²1964

G. L. Prestige, *God in Patristic Thought*, London–Toronto, Heinemann, 1936

Steven Pujdak, "Schoonenberg's Christology in Context," *Louvain Studies* 6 (1977) 338–353

L. Bruno Puntel, "Hans Küng, die Logik, und die theologische Redlichkeit," *Orientierung* 40 (1976) 3–6

Hugo Rahner, *Ignatius von Loyola als Mensch und Theologe*, Freiburg–Basel–Wien, Herder, 1964

————*Man at Play*, New York, Herder and Herder, 1967

Karl Rahner, " 'Behold this Heart!': Preliminaries to a Theology of Devotion to the Sacred Heart," in: *Theological Investigations*, Vol. III, Baltimore/London, Helicon Press/Darton, Longman & Todd, 1967, pp. 321–330

————"Being Open to God as Ever Greater," in: *Theological Investigations*, Vol. VII, New York, Herder and Herder, 1971, pp. 25–46

————"The Development of Dogma," in: *Theological Investigations*, Vol. I, Baltimore, Helicon Press, 1961, pp. 39–77

————"Dogmatic Reflections on the Knowledge and Self-consciousness of Christ," in: *Theological Investigations*, Vol. V, Baltimore, Helicon Press, 1966, pp. 193–215

————"The Eternal Significance of the Humanity of Jesus for Our Relationship with God," in: *Theological Investigations*, Vol. III, pp. 35–46

————"Die Exegese im Theologiestudium, Eine Antwort an N. Lohfink," *Stimmen der Zeit* 181 (1968) 196–201

————*Grundkurs des Glaubens*, Einführung in den Begriff des Christentums, Freiburg–Basel–Wien, Herder, 1976 [ET *Foundations of Christian Faith*, An Introduction to the Idea of Christianity, New York, The Seabury Press, 1978]

————*Hearers of the Word*, New York, Herder and Herder, 1969

————"The Ignatian Mysticism of Joy in the World," in: *Theological Investigations*, Vol. III, pp. 277–293

————[Interview mit Karl Rahner], *Herder-Korrespondenz* 31 (1977) 606–614

————"Kirchliche und ausserkirchliche Religiosität," *Stimmen der Zeit* 191 (1973) 3–13

————"Nature and Grace," in: *Theological Investigations*, Vol. IV, Baltimore, Helicon Press, 1966, pp. 165–188

————"Zur Neuordnung der theologischen Studien," *Stimmen der Zeit* 181 (1968) 1–21

————"On the Theology of the Incarnation," in: *Theological Investigations*, Vol. IV, pp. 105–120

————"The Position of Christology in the Church Between Exegesis and Dogmatics," in: *Theological Investigations*, Vol. XI, New York, The Seabury Press, 1974, pp. 185–214

————"The Problem of Genetic Manipulation," in: *Theological Investigations*, Vol. IX, New York, Herder and Herder, 1972, pp. 225–252

————"The Prospect for Christianity," in: *Free Speech in the Church*, New York, Sheed and Ward, 1959, pp. 51–112

————"The Prospects for Dogmatic Theology," in: *Theological Investigations*, Vol. I, pp. 1–18

————"Some Implications of the Scholastic Concept of Uncreated Grace," in: *Theological Investigations*, Vol. I, pp. 297–346

————"Some Theses for a Theology of Devotion to the Sacred Heart," in: *Theological Investigations*, Vol. III, pp. 331–352

————*Spirit in the World*, New York, Herder and Herder, 1968

————"Theos in the New Testament," in: *Theological Investigations*, Vol. I, pp. 79–148

————"What Is a Dogmatic Statement?" in: *Theological Investigations*, Vol. V, pp. 42–66

————"What Is Heresy?" in: *Theological Investigations*, Vol. V, pp. 468–512

Karl Rahner and Wilhelm Thüsing, *Christologie—systematisch und exegetisch* (*Quaestiones Disputatae*, 55), Freiburg–Basel–Wien, Herder, 1972

Ian T. Ramsey, *Models and Mystery*, London, Oxford University Press, 1964

————*Religious Language*, London, SCM Press, [2][1967]

Joseph Ratzinger and Hans Maier, *Demokratie in der Kirche—Möglichkeiten, Grenzen, Gefahren*, Limburg, Lahn-Verlag, 1970

[H. S. Reimarus], *Reimarus: Fragments* (Charles H. Talbert, ed.), Philadelphia, Fortress Press, 1970

Klaus Reinhardt, "Die menschliche Transzendenz Jesu Christi—Zu Schoonenbergs Versuch einer nicht-chalkedonischen Christologie," *Trierer Theologische Zeitschrift* (formerly *Pastor Bonus*) 80 (1971) 273–289

————"In What Way is Jesus Christ Unique?" *International Catholic Review: Communio* 1 (1974) 343–364

Henry Renckens, *The Religion of Israel*, New York, Sheed and Ward, 1966

James M. Robinson, *A New Quest of the Historical Jesus*, London, SCM Press, 1959

John A. T. Robinson, *Honest to God*, London, SCM Press, 1963

————*The Human Face of God*, Philadelphia, The Westminster Press, 1973

————"The Most Primitive Christology of All?" in: *Twelve New Testament Studies* (*Studies in Biblical Theology*, 34), London, SCM Press, 1962, pp. 139–153

Carl R. Rogers, *Client-Centered Therapy*, Its Current Practice, Implications, and Theory, Boston, Houghton-Mifflin Company, 1951

————*On Becoming a Person*, Boston, Houghton-Mifflin Company, 1961

François Roustang, "Le troisième homme," *Christus* 13 (1966) 561–567

Leopold Sabourin, *The Names and Titles of Jesus*, New York, The Macmillan Company, 1967

J. B. deC. M. Saunders and Charles D. O'Malley, *The Illustrations from the*

Works of Andreas Vesalius of Brussels, New York, Dover Publications, 1973

E. Schillebeeckx, *Christ the Sacrament of the Encounter with God*, New York, Sheed and Ward, 1963

———"Persoonlijke openbaringsgestalte van de Vader," *Tijdschrift voor theologie* 6 (1966) 274–288

———*Jezus, het verhaal van een levende*, Bloemendaal, H. Nelissen, ²1974

Friedrich Schleiermacher, *The Christian Faith* (trans. H. R. Mackintosh and J. S. Stewart), Edinburgh, T. & T. Clark, 1928

———*Der christliche Glaube* (Martin Redeker, ed.), 2 vols., Berlin, Walter De Gruyter & Co., ⁷1960

———*On Religion, Speeches to Its Cultured Despisers*, New York, Harper & Row, 1958

———*Ueber die Religion—Reden an die Gebildeten unter ihren Verächtern*, in: *Schleiermachers Werke*, O. Braun and Joh. Bauer (eds.), Vol. IV, Leipzig, Felix Meiner, 1911, pp. 207–399

Heinz Robert Schlette, "Rahner, Küng und die anonymen Christen," *Orientierung* 39 (1975) 174–176

Paul H. Schlüngel, "Der leidende Vater," *Orientierung* 41 (1977) 49–50

Robert L. Schmidt, "The Christ-Experience and Relationship Fostered in the Spiritual Exercises of St. Ignatius Loyola," *Studies in the Spirituality of Jesuits*, American Assistancy Seminar on Jesuit Spirituality, St. Louis, St. Louis University, 6 (1974) 217–255

Piet Schoonenberg, *The Christ*, New York, Herder and Herder, 1971

———"Christus zonder tweeheid?" *Tijdschrift voor theologie* 6 (1966) 289–306

———"Gott als Person und Gott als das unpersönlich Göttliche—Bhakti und Jñāna," in: Gerhard Oberhammer (ed.), *Transzendenzerfahrung, Vollzugshorizont des Heils*, Das Problem in indischer und christlicher Tradition (*Publications of the De Nobili Research Library*, Vol. V), Wien, 1978, pp. 207–234

———*Hij is een God van mensen*, 's-Hertogenbosch, L. C. G. Malmberg, 1969

———"Ich glaube an Gott," *Trierer Theologische Zeitschrift* (formerly *Pastor Bonus*) 81 (1972) 65–83

———*Man and Sin*, Notre Dame, University of Notre Dame Press, 1965

———"Process or History in God?" *Louvain Studies* 4 (1973) 303–319 (cf. "Process or history in God?" *Theology Digest* 23 (1975) 38–44, with an original postscript)

———"Spirit Christology and Logos Christology," *Bijdragen* 38 (1977) 350–375

———"Trinität—Der vollendete Bund," *Orientierung* 37 (1972) 115–117

———"Trinity—The Consummated Covenant, Theses on the Doctrine of the Trinitarian God," *Studies in Religion/Sciences religieuses* 5 (1975) 111–116

———"From a Two-Nature Christology to a Christology of Presence," in: Joseph Papin (ed.), *Theological Folia of Villanova University*, Speculative

Studies, Vol. II, Villanova, The Villanova University Press, 1975, pp. 219–243

Robert Schreiter, "Christology in the Jewish-Christian Encounter: An Essay-Review of Edward Schillebeeckx' *Jezus, Het Verhaal van een Levende*," *Journal of the American Academy of Religion* 44 (1976) 693–703

William C. Schutz, *The Interpersonal Underworld*, Palo Alto, Science & Behavior Books, ²1966

Eduard Schweizer, *Jesus*, Richmond, John Knox Press, 1971

Robert T. Sears, "Trinitarian Love as Ground of the Church," *Theological Studies* 37 (1976) 652–679

Juan Luis Segundo, *The Community Called Church*, Maryknoll, Orbis Books, 1973

W. Seibel, art. "Bekenntnis," in: *Handbuch theologischer Grundbegriffe*, Bd. I, München, Kösel, 1962, pp. 156–160

Herbert A. Shepard, "Changing Interpersonal and Intergroup Relationships in Organizations," in: James G. March (ed.), *Handbook of Organizations*, Chicago, Rand McNally & Company, 1965, pp. 1115–1143

Clovis R. Shepherd, *Small Groups*, Some Sociological Perspectives, San Francisco, Chandler Publishing Company, 1964

Philip E. Slater, *Microcosm*, New York–London–Sydney, John Wiley & Sons, 1966

Piet Smulders, *The Design of Teilhard de Chardin*, An Essay in Theological Reflection, Westminster, Md., The Newman Press, 1967

———"Dogmengeschichtliche und lehramtliche Entfaltung der Christologie," in: Johannes Feiner and Magnus Löhrer (eds.), *Mysterium Salutis*, Band III/1, *Das Christusereignis*, Einsiedeln–Zürich–Köln, Benziger Verlag, 1970, pp. 389–476

———*The Fathers on Christology*, De Pere, Wisc., St. Norbert Abbey Press, 1968

Dorothee Sölle, *Christ the Representative*, An Essay in Theology after the "Death of God," Philadelphia, Fortress Press, 1967

Sophocles, *Three Tragedies, Antigone, Oedipus the King, Electra*, translated into English verse by H. D. F. Kitto, London–Oxford–New York, Oxford University Press, 1962

R. W. Southern, *The Making of the Middle Ages*, London, Hutchinson & Co., 1967

Sidney G. Sowers, *The Hermeneutics of Philo and Hebrews*, Richmond, Va., John Knox Press, 1965

Aelred Squire, *Asking the Fathers*, London, SPCK, 1973

David M. Stanley, *Boasting in the Lord*, New York, Paulist Press, 1973

Emmanuel Cardinal Suhard, *Le sens de Dieu*, Paris, Editions A. Lahure, 1948

Harry Stack Sullivan, *Conceptions of Modern Psychiatry*, Washington, D.C., The William Alanson Psychiatric Foundation, ³1947

Hamish F. G. Swanson, *Ideas of Order*, Assen, The Netherlands, Van Gorcum & Comp. B. V., 1974

Vincent Taylor, *The Names of Jesus*, New York, St. Martin's Press, 1953

Pierre Teilhard de Chardin, *The Phenomenon of Man*, with an Introduction by Sir Julian Huxley, New York, Harper & Row, ²1965

――――*The Divine Milieu*, An Essay on the Interior Life, New York, Harper & Brothers, 1960

Paul Tillich, *The Courage To Be*, London and Glasgow, Collins, ²1962

――――*The Shaking of the Foundations*, Harmondsworth, Penguin Books, ²1962

――――*Systematic Theology*, Vols. I–III, Chicago, University of Chicago Press, 1967

Joseph N. Tylenda, "Christ the Mediator: Calvin vs. Stancaro," *Calvin Theological Journal* 8 (1973) 5–16

――――"The Controversy on Christ the Mediator: Calvin's Second Reply to Stancaro," *Calvin Theological Journal* 8 (1973) 131–145

Evelyn Underhill, *Mystics of the Church*, Cambridge, James Clarke & Co., 1975

Cyprian Vagaggini, *Theological Dimensions of the Liturgy*, Collegeville, The Liturgical Press, 1976

Frans Jozef van Beeck, "Hans Küng: Christ sein—een mening," *Vox Theologica* 45 (1975) 242–247

――――"Hopkins: Cor ad Cor," *The Month*, Second New Series 8 (1975) 340–345

――――"Küng's *Christ Sein*: A Review Article," *Andover Newton Quarterly* 16 (1976) 277–281

――――*Priesthood: Ordained and/or Real?* Kansas City, The Propers, 1975

――――"Sacraments, Church Order, and Secular Responsibility," *Theological Studies* 30 (1969) 613–634

――――"Thesen zur Ordination von Frauen," *Orientierung* 39 (1975) 153–154

Paul M. van Buren, *The Edges of Language*, New York, The Macmillan Company, 1972

――――*The Secular Meaning of the Gospel*, New York/London, The Macmillan Company/Collier-Macmillan, ²1968

W. H. van de Pol, *The End of Conventional Christianity*, New York, Newman Press, 1968

J. H. van den Berg, *Het menselijk lichaam*, 2 vols., Nijkerk, Callenbach, 1965

――――*Leven in meervoud*, Nijkerk, G. F. Callenbach, ⁵1967

――――*Metabletica van de materie*, Vol. I, Meetkundige beschouwingen, Nijkerk, G. F. Callenbach N.V., 1969

――――*Psychologie en geloof*, Een kroniek en een standpunt, Nijkerk, Uitgeverij G. F. Callenbach N.V., ³1965

Bruce Vawter, *This Man Jesus*, Garden City, Doubleday & Company, 1973

J. Verhaar, "Language and Theological Method," *Continuum* 7 (1969) 3–29 [Dutch original in *Bijdragen* 30 (1969) 39–65]

——*Some Relations Between Perception, Speech and Thought*, Assen, Van Gorcum, 1963

Louis Verheylezoon, *Devotion to the Sacred Heart*, London–Glasgow, Sands & Co., 1955

Andreas Vesalius, *see* Saunders

Gertrud von le Fort, *Die Letzte am Schafott*, München, Ehrenwirth, 1959

——*The Song at the Scaffold* (Olga Marx, trans.), New York, Henry Holt & Co., 1933

Gerhard von Rad, *Old Testament Theology*, Vol. I, Harper & Row, New York–Evanston, 1962

James D. Watson, *The Double Helix*, New York, New American Library, [1969]

Evelyn Waugh, *Edmund Campion*, New York, Doubleday, 1956

Claude Welch, *Protestant Thought in the Nineteenth Century*, Vol. I, 1799–1870, New Haven and London, Yale University Press, 1972

Amos Wilder, *Early Christian Rhetoric*, New York, Harper & Row, 1964

Maurice Wiles, *The Making of Christian Doctrine*, A Study in the Principles of Early Doctrinal Development, Cambridge–London–New York–Melbourne, Cambridge University Press, 1967

——*The Remaking of Christian Doctrine*, The Hulsean Lectures of 1973, London, SCM Press, 1974

H. A. Wolfson, *The Philosophy of the Church Fathers*, Cambridge, Mass., Harvard University Press, [2]1964

William Wordsworth, *The Prelude, or, The Growth of a Poet's Mind* (Ernest de Selincourt, ed.), London, Geoffrey Cumberlege, Oxford University Press, 1926

——*The Poetical Works of William Wordsworth*, Vol. II (E. de Selincourt, ed.), Oxford, Clarendon Press, 1944; Vol. III (E. de Selincourt and Helen Darbishire, eds.), 1946; Vol. IV, 1947.

"Women in the Ministerial Priesthood," *Origins* 6 (1977) 519–531

B. Xiberta, *Enchiridion de Verbo Incarnato*, Matriti, Consejo Superior de Investigaciones Cientificas, 1957

Frances M. Young, "A Reconsideration of Alexandrian Christology," *Journal of Ecclesiastical History* 22 (1971) 103–114

NOTES TO THE EPIGRAPHS

Page 11: *The Unicorn*, chapter 12.

Page 13: *Hymns on Faith*, 20, CSCO 154, 74–76 (trans. Robert Murray)—Eph 2, 14–22

Page 30: Quoted by Eberhard Busch, *Karl Barth*, p. 114—"Burnt Norton," V, *Collected Poems, 1909–1962*, p. 194 (*The Complete Poems and Plays*, pp. 121–122)— Jn 1, 18.

Page 64: "Truth is not the secret of a few," *A Coney Island of the Mind*—No. 69, *Poems*, p. 103—*Omne enim dictum ex causa est, et dicti ratio ex sensu erit intelligenda dicendi* (reference mislaid)—Reference irretrievably lost.

Page 105: *De Incarnatione Verbi Dei*, Liber III, Caput 24, titulus et I.

Page 107: *Hymnus 7*, 24—*Early Christian Rhetoric*, p. 28—Trans. R. McL. Wilson, London, 1962, pp. 128–129—Quoted by Aelred Squire, *Asking the Fathers*, p. 118—1 Cor 14, 15.

Pages 144-145: Ed. W. Wright, p. 117, 2—*Hymns on Faith*, 5, 6–7, CSCO 154, 18–19 (trans. Robert Murray)—*De Perfectione*, PG 25½ C-25¾ A—Jn 6, 37–40.

Page 184: "The Love Song of J. Alfred Prufrock," *Collected Poems, 1909–1962*, pp. 14, 16 (*The Complete Poems and Plays*, pp. 4, 6)—Col 1, 27—*Asking the Fathers*, p. 15.

Page 228: "The Wreck of the Deutschland," stanza 28–29, *Poems*, p. 60–1 Cor 15, 14—1 Tim 6, 20–21

Pages 265-266: *Tract. in Joh.*, 40, 10 (quoted by Peter Brown, *Augustine of Hippo*, p. 156)—*Gesammelte Schriften*, III, p. 308—Quoted by Amos Wilder, *Early Christian Rhetoric*, p. 19—*The Christ*, p. 36 (corrected)—Rom 8, 24–25—*The Presence of the Word*, pp. 224, 223.

Page 295: "The Development of Dogma," *Theological Investigations*, I, pp. 63–64 (slightly corrected).

Pages 297-298: 1 Thess 1, 5–6—Mt 28, 20—2 Cor 3, 16–18—*Jezus*, p. 288.

Pages 325-326: Rev. 22, 17. 20—Acts 10, 36–42—2 Cor 1, 20; 2, 17—Gal 4, 6.

Page 358: *The Unicorn*, chapter 12—*Ich und Du*, p. 123 (*I and Thou*, p. 152)—2 Tim 2, 13.

Page 400: *The Christ*, p. 181 (corrected)—*Christ the Center*, p. 108 (corrected).

Pages 464-465: *Pensées*, 554 (Brunschvicg)—*Poems*, No. 68, p. 102—*Augustine of Hippo*, p. 407—1 Thess 5, 14

Pages 519-520: "East Coker," IV, *Collected Poems, 1909–1962*, p. 201 (*The Complete Poems and Plays*, p. 127)—*Augustine of Hippo*, p. 393—Qutoed by A. Hamon, *Histoire de la Dévotion au Sacré-Coeur*, III, p. 213—*On Religion*, p. 247—Mk 4, 30–32.

INDEX OF BIBLICAL REFERENCES

594   INDEX

INDEX OF PROPER NAMES

SUBJECT INDEX

Acceptance, *see:* rhetoric of inclusion.

Act of speech, *see:* speech, act of —.

Actus directus, 232–235, 236–238, 239–242, 245–247, 249, 252, 253, 258–259, 261–262, 267, 274, 286, 289, 293, 302–303, 307, 309, 356–357, 359, 466, 508.

Actus reflexus, 236–237, 239, 240, 359.

Address, *see:* word as address.

Anhypostasia, 51, 133, 159, 168, 172, 177–181, 386–387, 390–391, 395*n*, 423.

Apocalyptic, 334–335.

Apologetics, 50, 56*n*, 486–507, 554*n*.

Auditus fidei, 304, 324, 355.

Being-related, 229–232, 234–235, 406–417.

Canon law, 14.

Christ, Body of —, 16; central position of —, 120ff.; earthly life of —, 52–53, 210*n*, 260, *see also:* Jesus, historical —; —'s fullness of humanity, 56, 156ff., 167, 173, 374–375, 385, 433ff., 440–443; — as judge, 341–342, *see also:* judgment; presence of —, 22, 120ff.,

193, 223, 232–237, 249–251, 252–253, 272–273, 304, 310, 315–318, 322; presidency of —, 139–140, 148, 149*n*, 151, 152–153, 155*n*, 164–165, 193, 199, 213, 239, 335, 393; response to —, 112–115, 126–127, 142, 197, 237, *see also:* commitment: risen —, 150, 191ff., 197*n*, 250–251, 302ff., 316–317, 338ff.; *see also:* Jesus; *Christus, totus* —; Resurrection.

Christian(s), life and death of —, 71, 103, 139-140, 173, 182, 260, 302; — self-expression, 327–329, 331, 334.

Christological, — *a priori,* 299, 302–303, 310, 323, 359; — formula(s), 51–52; — models, 305–308, *see also:* models; — narrative, *see:* story.

Christology, — as activity, 108, 508ff.; assumption(ist) —, 307, 360, 467; classical —, 102–103, 257–259, 375–384, 439, 510–512, 513ff., 518, 520–521; critical — (Bonhoeffer), 128*n*; critical (historical) —, 254–257, 258, 261, 266–267, 303–304, 452–454; — as cognition, 108; eschatological —, 266–267, 308–324, 331–334; — from above (descent, high—)

609